*Property of
Suzette
Starr*

# Praise for *Learning Exchange Server 2003*

"This is the book every Exchange administrator and consultant should read from cover to cover. Bill Boswell offers an original approach to a complex topic using deep technical insight and a warm style."

Jeffery Hicks, M.C.S.E., M.C.T
President and Principal Consultant
JDH Information Technology Solutions

"*Learning Exchange Server 2003* is an insightful book practical advice for the novice and expert alike. It will a place on your reference shelf."

"Bill Boswell enlightens readers with a bal the underlying mechanics and the 'how-to's' of Exchang 2003 Administration. This book will appeal to both new and seasoned Exchange administrators."

William Lefkovics
Senior Messaging and Systems Analyst, eEye Digital Security

"An insightful journey into the heart and soul of Exchange 2003 technology. Excellent reading for technology professionals."

David Chun
Chief Technology Officer, SunGard

"An excellent read. *Learning Exchange Server 2003* covers a lot of information—from the basics to advanced topics—and Bill explains some difficult concepts very well."

Neil Hobson, Exchange Server MVP
Lead Messaging Consultant, Silversands

"Bill Boswell's *Learning Exchange Server 2003* covers security the right way by integrating it directly into the relevant Exchange topics. Exchange administrators who follow Bill's prescriptive advice will find their implementations adhere to good security practices, even if they're not specifically focusing on security."

Christopher Budd
Security Program Manager, Microsoft

# Learning Exchange Server 2003

# Microsoft Windows Server System Series

Books in the **Microsoft Windows Server System Series** are written and reviewed by the world's leading technical authorities on Microsoft Windows technologies, including principal members of Microsoft's Windows and Server Development Teams. The goal of the series is to provide reliable information that enables administrators, developers, and IT professionals to architect, build, deploy, and manage solutions using the Microsoft Windows Server System. The contents and code of each book are tested against, and comply with, commercially available code. This series should be an invaluable resource for any IT professional or student working in today's Windows environment.

## TITLES IN THE SERIES

Paul Bertucci, *Microsoft SQL Server High Availability,* 0-672-32625-6 (Sams)

Peter Blackburn and William R. Vaughn, *Hitchhiker's Guide to SQL Server 2000 Reporting Services,* 0-321-26828-8 (Addison-Wesley)

William Boswell, *Learning Exchange Server 2003,* 0-321-22874-X (Addison-Wesley)

Bill English, Olga Londer, Shawn Shell, Todd Bleeker, and Stephen Cawood, *Microsoft Content Management Server 2002: A Complete Guide,* 0-321-19444-6 (Addison-Wesley)

Don Jones, *Managing Windows® with VBScript and WMI,* 0-321-21334-3 (Addison-Wesley)

Sakari Kouti and Mika Seitsonen, *Inside Active Directory, Second Edition: A System Administrator's Guide,* 0-321-22848-0 (Addison-Wesley)

Shyam Pather, *Microsoft SQL Server 2000 Notification Services,* 0-672-32664-7 (Sams)

**For more information please go to www.awprofessional.com/msserverseries**

# Learning Exchange Server 2003

*William Boswell*

✦Addison-Wesley

**Boston** • **San Francisco** • **New York** • **Toronto** • **Montreal**
**London** • **Munich** • **Paris** • **Madrid**
**Capetown** • **Sydney** • **Tokyo** • **Singapore** • **Mexico City**

Library of Congress Cataloging-in-Publication Data

032122874X
Text printed on recycled paper
1 2 3 4 5 6 7 8 9 10    0605040302
First printing, September 2004

Publisher: *John Wait*
Editor: *Karen Gettman*
Editorial Assistant: *Elizabeth Zdunich*
Marketing Manager: *Curt Johnson*
Marketing Specialist: *Heather Mullane*

Publicity: *Joan Murray*
Managing Editor: *Gina Kanouse*
Full Service Production: *Specialized Composition, Inc.*
Manufacturing Buyer: *Dan Uhrig*
Cover Design: *Chuti Prasertsith*

*This book is dedicated to Christine, who always listened with utmost concentration when I insisted on reading some of the process descriptions in this book aloud to her. She even managed to smile as if she really thought I did a good job. You're the best, sweetheart. Thanks.*

# Contents

## About the Author

Bill Boswell, MCSE, is an independent consultant and trainer, and the author of two previous books, *Inside Windows Server 2003* and *Inside Windows 2000*. His firm, Bill Boswell Consulting, Inc., is based in Phoenix, Arizona. Bill is a contributing editor for *REDMOND* magazine (formerly *MCP* magazine) and a sought-after speaker at TechMentor and other conferences. Contact Bill at `bill@bill-boswellconsulting.com` and visit `www.billboswellconsulting.com` for up-to-date information about Windows servers and Exchange.

# Preface

Thanks for taking a moment to browse this book. It is intended to guide a system administrator with at least a year of experience with Windows servers, Active Directory, and networking through the deployment of an enterprise messaging system based on Exchange Server 2003. It does not assume that you have any prior experience with Exchange or any other messaging server.

It also does not make any assumptions about the size of your organization. You might be the sole administrator for a small firm or a service technician working for a Value Added Reseller (VAR), or a member of an Exchange team in a large company. The challenges are the same, really. The only difference is the scale of the project and the resources you have at your disposal. Administrators in smaller firms often have to fend for themselves, which adds to the difficulty of dealing with Exchange issues if you're new to messaging. If you belong to an Exchange team, you can draw on the experience of your colleagues, but this book will help you get up to speed as quickly as possible so you can contribute your fair share and avoid making mistakes.

If you're flipping through pages in a bookstore, or browsing content online, you'll notice that this book takes a slightly different approach to learning Exchange than other references. In addition to the standard how-to guides and feature descriptions, you'll find detailed process analysis and discussions about underlying concepts and dependencies. That's because Exchange is rich with complex ties to other Windows services and a variety of network components. My hope is that you'll come to see Exchange as an organic part of an overall communications infrastructure rather than just an e-mail server in a rack.

The chapters are arranged to get you up and running quickly and they expose layers of detail as you progress. Each topic contains elements to help you design and configure a particular set of features, streamline your daily operations, diagnose problems, safeguard data, and evaluate third-party applications and tools. The topic elements include

- **Protocols and processes** used by Exchange, Active Directory, and the Windows operating system to fulfill critical messaging functions.
- **Design specifications and constraints** you'll need to observe when performing a task.
- **Security practices** that help you prevent system compromise.
- **Precautions and prerequisites** to ensure reliable operations.
- **Procedures** that describe, step-by-step, how to perform each critical task and assess the results.

- **Monitoring and management** suggestions to help you ensure ongoing system functionality.
- **Troubleshooting hints** to help guide you through isolating and correcting problems.

The topics are structured so that you can choose to skip over low-level details, jump right to the step-by-step procedures, and then flip back if you have questions.

As you work your way through the book, I urge you to perform the procedures and tests in each topic. They're designed for use both in lab testing as well as for production deployment. Chapter 1 describes how to use virtual machines to build a lab with all the servers and clients you need to test the major features of Exchange.

The most important thing to do is to have fun. An e-mail administrator provides a vital service that nearly everyone appreciates, even if they complain to you on a regular basis. If you keep the e-mail servers stable, deliver features that help your users do their jobs efficiently, and avoid losing messages from (or to) bosses and clients, you'll be everybody's best friend. Good luck.

# Acknowledgments

I would not have been able to write this book without help from many extraordinary people who lent their time, talent, and expertise to the project. I want to take this opportunity to introduce them and to thank them individually and collectively.

The project team at Addison-Wesley did a phenomenal job. Sondra Scott originally championed the book and convinced me that readers wanted a fresh approach. Elizabeth Zdunich took over from Sondra and shepherded the book through final production. Take a minute, if you would, and read through the names of the production staff listed in the first pages of the book. These are people who love technical books and who work under crushing deadlines to make sure that their titles contribute innovative and technically sound ideas to the marketplace. I'm unbelievably lucky to have the chance to work with them.

Thanks to a ground-breaking program put together by Susan Bradley at Microsoft, I was able to draw upon the expertise of some of the best and the brightest in the Exchange product development team, product support team, field consulting team, and documentation team. Teresa Appelgate, User Education Specialist and author/contributor for many Exchange white papers, fielded my piles of questions and spent lots of time helping to find the right person with the right answer. I got a great deal of information from Per Farny, National Practices Consultant in the Microsoft Consulting Services Enterprise Messaging team; Tejas Patel, an Exchange server specialist in the Messaging Support group; Christopher Budd, CISSP and author of Microsoft's *Exchange Server 2003 Message Security Guide*; and Brad Clark, a program manager for Exchange. You can gripe all you want about Microsoft as a corporate entity, but these folks are superstars and I'm grateful for their help.

I was also fortunate to have an incredible group of tech reviewers. Barrie Sosinsky and David Chun reviewed the manuscript from the point of view of experienced system administrators who want to learn about Exchange from the ground up. Not only did I benefit from their fresh perspective, they also did a great job of ferreting out glitches in my descriptions that might stymie a newcomer. Barrie was especially generous with his time and became an ardent spokesman for harried administrators everywhere. Neil Hobson and William Lefkovics, consultants who have earned Microsoft's prestigious Most Valuable Professional (MVP) status in recognition of their expertise and willingness to support the Exchange community, did me the honor of giving the manuscript a careful read. They shared their wealth of knowledge about Exchange design and operation, troubleshooting tools, and third-party products. They also demonstrated a truly scary mastery of the Microsoft KnowledgeBase articles on Exchange. Their feedback is present on nearly every page of the book. I invite you to read their contributions in the MS Exchange blog, hellomate.typepad.com/exchange.

# CHAPTER 1

# Installing an Exchange 2003 Server

You might be an e-mail administrator in a vast corporation, barely casting a shadow on the wall as you pass from the building entry to your cubicle. Or you might be the sole administrator of a modest network where all the users know you by name and bring you chocolate snacks when they want new software on their computers. Or you might be a student who hopes to find gainful employment and a measure of personal satisfaction running one of the most critical pieces of information technology in an organization, the e-mail system.

Whatever your role, I'm assuming that you opened this book and started reading here instead of some later chapter because you want the whole story of Exchange, from the beginning, without commercial interruptions. And so you shall. But this isn't a work of fiction where you can follow the action and hope for a dramatic twist. You need to follow along with the examples and experiments. To encourage you to take an active part, I'm about to reveal the ending of the story right here on the first page of the book.

The story ends with a reliable, high-speed messaging system that has servers located in sufficient critical locations so that all your users, from any location—Windows desktops in Guam, kiosk machines in a Starbucks, laptops in hotel rooms from Tangiers to Truth or Consequences, New Mexico—can send their thoughts, hopes, aspirations, and accomplishments to each other through your messaging system with absolute confidence that their e-mails will arrive intact at the intended destination.

And you're the hero who is going to make it all happen. Ready to get started?

# Preparations

Before you start installing Exchange, you need a fairly extensive infrastructure. You need Active Directory domain controllers and Global Catalog servers to hold account information, distribution lists, and configuration parameters for the Exchange servers in your organization. You need a solid set of security policies to ensure that e-mail information can't be used in some nefarious way by unauthorized individuals. And you need an enterprise-wide set of Domain Name System (DNS) servers that your Exchange server can query to find all the services required for proper operation.

The details for installing and configuring those servers fall outside the scope of this book, but without a good working knowledge of their operation, many of the design, configuration, and security requirements of Exchange 2003 won't make sense to you. Frankly, very few issues initially classified as an "Exchange problem" actually involve a failure of Exchange itself. Most problems involve the infrastructure used by Exchange. For that reason, you might want to refer to Appendix A, "Building a Stable Exchange 2003 Deployment Infrastructure," which takes a detailed look at these topics:

- DNS design and operation
- Authentication and authorization mechanisms
- Active Directory design and operation

This information will help you avoid nearly all problems commonly encountered by Exchange administrators. If plowing through mountains of concentrated reference material seems like a dreary way to start your Exchange experience, take heart. You're going to begin your deployment in a lab, so you can recover from any mistakes quickly.

# Major Exchange System Components

Every information delivery system has boundaries that determine who gets a particular service and who doesn't. In the corporate mailroom example, the company phone book defines the boundaries of the delivery system. If correspondence arrives for an addressee not listed in the phone book, the mailroom clerks hold the letter for a while and then send it back to the sender with a terse, Elvis Presley scribble: *Return to sender, address unknown, no such number, no such zone.*

Exchange 2003 draws a boundary around an Active Directory forest and calls it an *organization*. (An Exchange organization bears no relation to an Organizational Unit in Active Directory.) Although it's possible to connect different organizations into a single messaging infrastructure using tools like Microsoft Identity Integration Server (MIIS), in many cases, the organization defines the line between "our mail" and "their mail." Figure 1.1 shows the basic components of an Exchange organization.

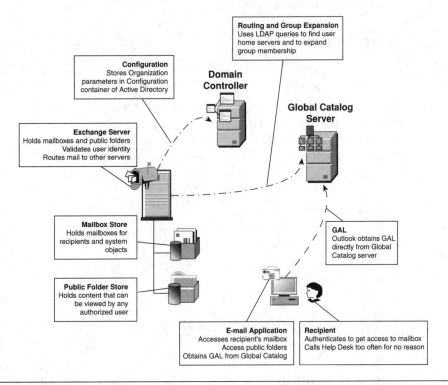

**Figure 1.1**   Components of a simple Exchange messaging infrastructure.

## Exchange Store

Exchange servers hold and route messages for individual recipients and for public folders. Each Exchange server has a set of databases called *stores*. Collectively, you can refer to the various stores on an Exchange server as the *Exchange Store*. Exchange defines two types of stores:

- **Mailbox stores.** These stores hold private user messages, calendar entries, notes, journals items, and personal contacts. An e-mail recipient in Exchange gets one and only one mailbox in a mailbox store.
- **Public folder stores.** These stores hold the same type of items as those found in private mailboxes but make the items available for general viewing.

Exchange Server 2003 Standard Edition hosts one mailbox store and one public folder store. The Enterprise Edition of Exchange 2003 can have up to 20 stores of either type.

## E-Mail Clients

Exchange designates a user who receives an e-mail message as a *recipient*. To read messages, a recipient relies on an application called an *e-mail client* that knows how to communicate with the Exchange server to retrieve and display messages.

A quick search of the Internet yields dozens and dozens of e-mail client applications capable of reading messages stored on Exchange servers. Some popular examples include

- Microsoft Outlook
- Microsoft Outlook Express
- Qualcomm Eudora
- Pegasus Mail
- Netscape Mail
- Stata Laboratories Bloomba
- Ximian Evolution
- Incredimail (e-mail with personality)
- Mozilla Thunderbird Mail

E-mail client applications can nestle inside other applications. For example, a collaboration application that uses a Web interface might read and write messages to an Exchange server using special scripts. This application qualifies as an e-mail client.

E-mail clients use a special set of commands, called a *protocol*, to access the contents of a user's mailbox. These protocols resemble human communication protocols; no great surprise considering that humans (for the most part) develop applications. For example, when you meet someone on the street, you use a "greeting" protocol. Depending on your culture, this protocol might consist of making eye contact, extending your right hand with palm outstretched, shaking hands, exchanging verbal greetings, and then entering into a conversation at a speed controlled by minor facial nuances.

An e-mail protocol works in a similar fashion. It determines how an e-mail client makes its initial connection to the Exchange server, what the client needs to do to request the contents of a user's mailbox, and how the client downloads the contents so that the user can read the messages.

Outlook uses an e-mail protocol called the *Messaging Application Programming Interface*, or MAPI. You'll hear this in other ways such as, "Outlook is a MAPI client"; or "I'm monitoring the MAPI traffic between my Outlook client and the server"; or "Exchange 2003 supports all legacy MAPI clients including the original Exchange client." Outlook also supports Internet standard e-mail protocols such as Simple Mail Transfer Protocol (SMTP), Post Office Protocol Version 3 (POP3), and Internet Mail Access Protocol Version 4 (IMAP4).

## Active Directory

An e-mail client protocol must use some mechanism to validate a user's identity so that Exchange can grant access to the appropriate mailbox. Exchange 2003 uses authentication protocols controlled by the underlying Windows operating system. The user credentials, along with other operational parameters for the Exchange organization, reside in a directory service called Active Directory.

In addition to using Active Directory for authentication, Exchange 2003 uses information stored in Active Directory to find a recipient's home e-mail server and to hold information about the Exchange organization. If a recipient has a mailbox on another server in the organization, Exchange determines the best route by referring to a routing map derived from information stored in Active Directory. If the recipient lies outside the organization, Exchange uses *connector* objects in Active Directory to build a map for routing the message so that it can reach its intended destination.

Plain and simple: Although you can deploy Active Directory without Exchange, you can't have an Exchange 2003 organization without Active Directory.

## Global Catalog

Each domain in an Active Directory forest acts as a separate Lightweight Directory Access Protocol (LDAP) replication unit called a *naming context*. A domain controller answers LDAP queries using the content of its own domain naming context. In response to queries for information outside its own domain, a domain controller gives a referral to one or more domain controllers outside the domain.

This presents a challenge for an LDAP client in a forest consisting of multiple domains. Not only must the client chase down referrals, but if the domain controllers reside in various offices separated by WAN links, then chasing down the referrals costs time. Active Directory streamlines these searches by designating certain domain controllers as *Global Catalog* servers.

A Global Catalog server replicates a read-only copy of the other domain naming contexts in the forest so it can reply authoritatively (without referrals) to forest-wide queries. To prevent the Active Directory database from getting excessively large on the Global Catalog servers, the Active Directory schema limits the number of attributes that get included in the Global Catalog.

Exchange takes advantage of the Global Catalog in a couple of ways. For example, a message might be addressed to a *distribution list* containing recipients from multiple domains. Distribution lists are represented in Active Directory by group objects. It would be extraordinarily time-consuming for an Exchange server to communicate with domain controllers throughout the forest to determine the mailbox server for each member of a group. Instead, Exchange queries a single Global Catalog server to determine the recipients' mailbox servers. (This works only for Universal groups, which requires that each domain in the forest to be set for a functional level of Windows 2000 Native or higher. This is discussed in more detail a later in the chapter.)

The Global Catalog server also provides a *Global Address List* (GAL) containing all the e-mail recipients in an organization. Users can select names from the GAL rather than manually typing in the e-mail addresses.

## DNS

What you don't see in the diagram in Figure 1.1 are the DNS servers, a critical set of servers for the messaging system. DNS makes it possible for all the machines in the diagram—Exchange servers and e-mail clients, and domain controllers and Global Catalog servers—to find each other and carry out their functions. Without the DNS servers and properly configured DNS clients, you can't deploy Exchange.

It's rare to find an Exchange issue that doesn't involve a DNS failure or configuration error. Microsoft Product Support Services (PSS) classifies support calls based on the root cause of the problem, and it has a rule of thumb that goes something like this: 80 percent of all Exchange and Active Directory problems encountered in production systems have DNS as a root cause. Many of the other 20 percent also involve DNS in one way or another.

If you were to answer the phones in the Exchange queue at PSS, or accompany a Microsoft Rapid Onsite Support Service (ROSS) engineer as she tries to bring a critically ill messaging system back to life, or read the reports from Microsoft Consulting Services after they perform on-site reviews of customers with histories of severe and sustained Exchange outages, or listen to the war stories of Exchange specialists from Hewlett-Packard and IBM and CSC, I think you'll come away with one very firm conclusion: Get DNS right and keep it right or you're wasting your time trying to deploy Exchange Server 2003.

## Exchange Test Lab Configuration

As you read through this book, you should try to perform as many of the examples as possible in your test lab. Not only will this help you learn how Exchange 2003 operates, but you'll find that a well-designed lab provides an environment for testing changes prior to introducing them into the production Exchange system.

A test lab should simulate your production environment as closely as possible. If you do not have a production environment to use for comparison, incorporate the elements you know you'll need for supporting your users into your test configuration. To simulate the Exchange operations described in this book, you'll need at least ten machines, shown in Figure 1-2 and listed as follows. They don't need to be physical servers, though. You can use desktop-quality machines or even virtual machines. More about that later. First, here's the cast of characters:

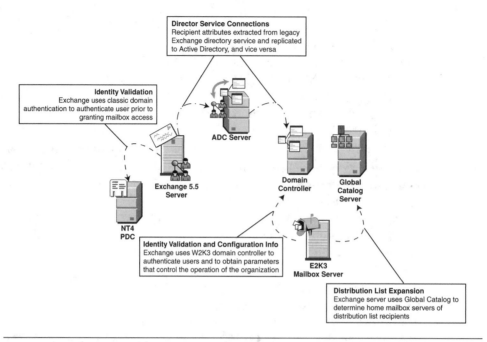

**Director Service Connections**
Recipient attributes extracted from legacy Exchange directory service and replicated to Active Directory, and vice versa

**Identity Validation**
Exchange uses classic domain authentication to authenticate user prior to granting mailbox access

ADC Server

Exchange 5.5 Server

NT4 PDC

Domain Controller

Global Catalog Server

**Identity Validation and Configuration Info**
Exchange uses W2K3 domain controller to authenticate users and to obtain parameters that control the operation of the organization

E2K3 Mailbox Server

**Distribution List Expansion**
Exchange server uses Global Catalog to determine home mailbox servers of distribution list recipients

**Figure 1.2**    Essential lab servers for testing Exchange 2003 operations.

- **Domain Controllers.** You'll need at least one Active Directory domain controller running DNS with an Active Directory integrated zone. This server holds the accounts and groups for the Exchange organization as well as the configuration settings for the Exchange servers, message repositories, and connectors.
- **Global Catalog server.** For best results, and to simulate a production environment, you'll need an additional domain controller configured to be a Global Catalog server. Exchange uses the Global Catalog to determine distribution list members and to route messages to users. The additional domain controller also gives you fault tolerance for Active Directory and DNS. In production, you should have at least three domain controllers, all of which would be Global Catalog servers unless you have a multiple domain forest. (See Appendix A for information about the relationship of the Infrastructure Master role holder and the Global Catalog.)
- **Exchange servers.** You'll need two Exchange 2003 servers so you can see how to move mailboxes between servers, share Internet e-mail between two servers, and how to replicate public folder content.

- **XP desktops.** You should install two XP desktops running Office System 2003 so you can test the connection features in Outlook using both Exchange servers simultaneously. In other words, you can send mail from one desktop and immediately see if you got it at the other desktop. You should never install Outlook on an Exchange server, so don't try to get around the need for desktops by using the Exchange servers as e-mail clients.

- **Windows 2000 or XP desktop running Outlook 2002 or Outlook 2000.** If you have legacy desktops and e-mail clients in your production environment, you should install sufficient clients in your lab to test how older clients react in an Exchange 2003 system. If you run other clients in production, or if you plan on migrating from another messaging system, you should have representatives of those applications, as well.

Throughout this book, the term "legacy Exchange" refers to all versions of Exchange prior to Exchange 2000.

In addition to these essential machines, if you plan on deploying Exchange 2003 into an existing Exchange 5.5 organization, you'll need to simulate the legacy Exchange machines. These include

- **Active Directory Connector (ADC) server.** You'll need an ADC server to synchronize e-mail attributes between objects in the legacy Exchange directory service and Active Directory.

- **NT Primary Domain Controller (PDC).** This server contains the NT accounts used to support access to the legacy Exchange mailboxes. If you have already migrated to Active Directory but still run Exchange 5.5, then you can eliminate this server.

- **Exchange 5.5 server.** You'll need an NT or Windows 2000 server running Exchange 5.5. In a pinch, you can install Exchange 5.5 on the NT PDC, but you'll get a better idea of production issues by using a separate server. If you run Exchange as a component of Small Business Server, then you'll need to configure your lab accordingly.

You may also want these additional servers to test special operations or features:

- **Exchange 2000 server and Windows 2000 Domain Controller.** If you have already deployed Exchange 2000 in production and you want to test migration scenarios in your lab, you should include at least one of each legacy server in your lab configuration.
- **Front-end Exchange 2003 server.** To follow the front-end–back-end server exercises in Chapter 10, "Managing Public Folders," you'll need an additional machine to act as a front-end server. This is also true if you are upgrading from Exchange 2000 and you have a front-end server in production.
- **Cluster server.** If you want to build the virtual cluster described in Chapter 13, "Service Continuity," you'll need a machine with sufficient memory and storage to host a couple of virtual machines with several 4GB virtual drives to use as shared cluster nodes.

## Virtual Machines as Test Servers

This probably sounds like a lot of machines to crowd into a lab, even if you could convince management to let you buy them. Putting together a quality lab does not require thousands of dollars of equipment, though. All you need is a couple of desktop-class machines with plenty of memory. Using these machines, you can build all the servers you need using *virtual machines*.

A virtual machine takes advantage of how an operating system views its hardware. When you think of a computer, you think of hard drives and RAM and motherboards and input-output devices. But from the perspective of the operating system, the physical computer exists only as a set of *devices*, each with one or more *drivers* that control access to the device.

You can see the logical representation of devices within the Windows operating system using the Device Manager. Right-click the My Computer icon, select Manage from the flyout menu, and then click Device Manager. Figure 1.3 shows an example.

Many of these device drivers live in the trusted portion of the operating system known as the Windows Executive where they communicate more or less directly with the Windows kernel, which works in concert with the Hardware Abstraction Layer (HAL) to move data to and from the hardware.

**Figure 1.3** Device Manager showing hardware abstracted as devices.

Applications such as Exchange and Outlook might appear to write to the screen or talk to the network, but in actuality they obtain these system services from device drivers residing within the Executive. The applications live in a separate portion of virtual memory where they cannot accidentally corrupt system memory.

It's possible to simulate hardware operation in order to give an operating system the impression that it's running on a physical computer, giving birth to a virtual machine. A host machine provides the hardware simulation for the virtual machine, and a guest operating system runs inside the virtual machine without the slightest idea that an entirely separate operating system actually owns the physical computer. A single virtual machine host can have many different guest operating systems running concurrently. For example, Figure 1.4 shows a Windows Server 2003 host running guest virtual machines containing Windows 2000 SP4, Windows 98 SR2, Windows NT SP6A, and SUSE Linux 8.2.

Virtual machines make ideal lab servers because of their flexibility. In the host environment, the virtual machine exists as a single file. You can copy these files to another physical computer and launch the virtual machine from there. The operating system inside the virtual machine would not know or care about the change.

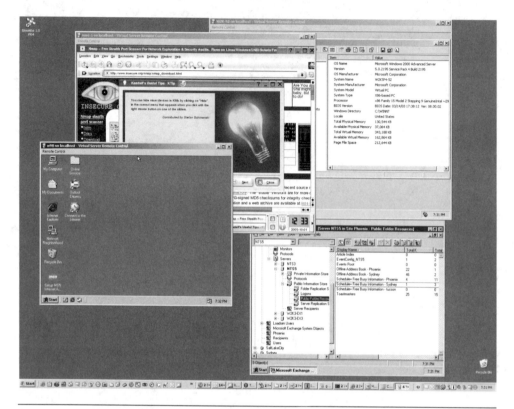

**Figure 1.4**   Virtual machine host running several guest sessions.

Virtual machines do have a disadvantage when it comes to testing performance or hardware compatibility. For those tests, you'll need to build a real server using real components. But the virtual machines can communicate with the real server, so you can easily incorporate your hardware-testing platform into an existing Exchange organization.

## Virtual Machine Vendors

If you decide to use virtual machines as servers to stock your lab, you have a choice of products from two vendors:

- **VMWare.** (www.vmware.com) The VMware company has a flagship product of the same name that is intended for use on a workstation-class host. VMWare also sells two enterprise products, GSX and ESX, intended for use in server consolidation. In January, 2004, EMC purchased VMware, so look for new products that make use of enterprise-class storage.

- **Microsoft.** (www.microsoft.com/virtualpc) Microsoft purchased virtual machine technology from a company called Connectix and used it to produce two products: Virtual PC and Virtual Server. Virtual Server product is intended for large-scale server consolidations.

Any of these products will work fine for building an Exchange test environment. The Virtual PC product has a $129 list price, while the VMWare product lists for $189 but sports more features and has broader support for third-party operating systems, both as the host and the guest. The Virtual Server product has not been given a price as of the publication of this book.

## Precautions When Cloning Test Servers

In addition to moving virtual machines from one host to another, you can also clone copies of a virtual machine by copying the support files, like Agent Smith replicates himself in *The Matrix Revolutions*. By taking a few simple precautions, you can create a fleet of virtual servers limited only by your server's available drive space and memory.

- **Each cloned machine must have a unique computer name and IP address.** Launch each cloned virtual machine one at a time, and change the name and IP address. Otherwise, you'll get duplicate IP address errors when the virtual machine initializes its network interface, and you'll get duplicate name errors when the Windows networking drivers attempt to bind to the network interface.
- **Each cloned server must have a unique Security ID, or SID.** Setup assigns a unique SID to a computer using an algorithm that virtually guarantees its uniqueness. If you copy the virtual machine to another file, the new virtual server has the same SID. This can cause subtle operational difficulties that can be difficult to troubleshoot. For example, if you attempt to promote two servers with the same SID to be domain controllers, the second server will give an error saying that it already exists in Active Directory. My favorite utility for changing SIDs is NewSID from SysInternals (**www.sysinternals.com**). NewSID permits you to assign a new name when you change the SID so you can combine this step with the first bullet.

- **Don't clone domain controllers or Exchange servers.** Create basic servers first, clone them, change their SID, and then promote them to domain controllers or install Exchange. Cloning domain controllers will cause a failure of the replication and authentication mechanisms in Active Directory, which are tied to unique SIDs and Globally Unique Identifiers (GUIDs) for domain controllers. Cloning Exchange servers will cause a failure in the routing and message handling infrastructure for Exchange. If you clone a server and then promote it to be a domain controller without first changing its SID, you'll get errors that say the server already exists. If you attempt to install Exchange in a cloned server with the same SID as an existing server, Setup will either fail with a series of relatively inscrutable errors or, worse yet, Setup will succeed but message handling will fail for no apparent reason.

Follow all licensing requirements when cloning servers.

## Virtual Machine Hardware Requirements

Virtual machines consume memory from the host computer along with storage space and CPU time. A Pentium 4 desktop with 2GB of RAM and a 120GB drive can host six to eight virtual machines without seeing much of a performance drag. (Older versions of VMWare can use only 1GB of physical RAM, so consult with EMC before purchasing additional memory.)

If your workstation motherboard can hold only 1GB of RAM, then you can install multiple host machines in your lab and put a few virtual machines on each host. If you have machines that can hold only 512MB of RAM or less, you do not need to abandon the flexibility of virtual machines. Collect enough older desktops to stock the lab with the 10 machines you require and then install a virtual machine on each one. This enables you to move the virtual machine files to another machine should it crash, something that could easily happen if you collect castoff hardware for your lab.

Virtual machine files can grow as large as 3GB to 4GB, so get sufficient storage to hold all your virtual machine files with a lot of free space to avoid fragmentation. Don't store the virtual machine files on the same logical drive as the operating system, also to avoid fragmentation.

## Installation Prerequisite Checklist

Before actually installing Exchange 2003, review the following prerequisites:

- **DNS.** First and foremost, you need a solid, reliable DNS infrastructure available to every networking entity in your environment.
- **Active Directory.** You need an Active Directory domain with either Windows 2000 SP3+ or Windows Server 2003 domain controllers (Windows Server 2003 is preferred).
- **Global Catalog.** You must have at least one Global Catalog server available both to the Exchange servers and to any Outlook clients.
- **Native functional level.** The domain functional level must be Windows 2000 Native or higher to permit creating Universal Security Groups.
- **Exchange server software.** You need at least one Windows 2000 SP3+ or Windows Server 2003 server on which to install Exchange 2003. (Windows Server 2003 is preferred.)
- **Application compatibility.** Uninstall (not just deactivate, but remove completely) any antivirus and backup agents you might have running on the machine. Reinstall them after you have installed Exchange. This avoids many problems that often trigger support calls to Microsoft.
- **Support Tools.** Install the Windows Server 2003 Support Tools (or the Windows 2000 Support Tools) to get the test utilities used during Setup. The Support Tools reside on the Setup CD in the Support folder.
- **Schema Master.** Ensure that the Schema Master server is running and available on the network. Exchange Setup makes a significant number of updates to the schema and to the content of the Global Catalog.

The schema and Global Catalog changes made during Exchange setup replicate outward to all other domain controllers in the forest. In a lab, this ripple of replication does not pose a problem. In production, however, a replication tsunami can occur that takes quite a while to dissipate and generates lots of traffic, depending on how many domain controllers you have and the bandwidth associated with the WAN links.

# Hardware Requirements

In the lab, you can squeak by with the minimum required hardware, either in the form of physical machines or virtual machines. In production, you should get the fastest and most capable servers you can afford.

## Minimum Requirements

Your lab machines, either physical or virtual, should at least meet Microsoft's minimum published requirements for Windows Server 2003 and Exchange 2003. Here are a few guidelines for outfitting your lab servers:

- **Processor.** The speed of a virtual machine depends primarily on the speed of the host processor. You'll get more done in your lab if you get the fastest processor you can afford. If you use physical machines, you can easily meet the minimum specification for an Exchange server with a 133MHz Pentium processor. For practical work, you shouldn't use anything less than a 1GHz processor if you want to do serious testing. If you prefer AMD processors, feel free to run Exchange on a K6 or higher processor. Exchange 2003 does not have a 64-bit binary, so you would only use an Opteron processor if you want to do separate experiments.
- **Memory.** The secret to getting good performance out of a virtual machine is to keep as much of the virtual machine file in memory as possible. For this reason, give each server at least 256MB of memory. If you plan on following along with exercises that cover how to use content indexing and message tracking, you should use 512MB for that virtual server. You can pare down the memory requirements for some of the auxiliary servers as long as you do not encounter slow performance. A Windows Server 2003 Active Directory domain controller can get by with 192MB of RAM. A

virtual XP or W2K desktop can survive with 96MB. A virtual NT server needs only 64MB. After you begin serious experiments, you might need to bump up these numbers to avoid excessive paging within the virtual machines.

- **Storage.** Each virtual server should have at least one virtual hard drive with a 4GB capacity for the operating system and another virtual hard drive with an 8GB capacity for the Active Directory or Exchange data files.
- **Network.** Virtual machines emulate a 100Mbps Ethernet connection regardless of the network card in the underlying host. For best results, use at least a 100Mbps Ethernet connection between the physical machines in your lab, whether or not they run virtual machines. If you plan on simulating production load on a physical server, feed the network connection to a high-quality switch rather than a hub.
- **Operating System.** Unless you have Windows 2000 in your production environment and you do not plan on upgrading, you should install Windows Server 2003 with the latest service pack and security updates on each lab server, virtual or physical. You can obtain 120-day evaluation copies of Windows Server 2003 and Exchange 2003 from Microsoft, which gives you plenty of time to practice the examples in this book, along with any experiments you might want to devise for your preproduction testing.

Download 180-day evaluation versions of Windows Server 2003 from www.microsoft.com/windowsserver2003/evaluation/trial/evalkit.mspx.

Download 120-day evaluation versions of Exchange Server 2003 from www.microsoft.com/exchange/evaluation/trial/2003.asp.

## Production Requirements

Precisely estimating your hardware needs for Exchange 2003 servers and other ancillary servers (domain controllers, Global Catalog servers, DNS services, firewalls, and so forth) requires a fairly good knowledge of how your users expect the system to perform. Putting issues of fault tolerance aside for a moment, here are some (very rough) rules of thumb to use when putting together a budget.

- **Processor speed.** Like any server, use the most capable processor you can afford. I don't imagine that you would purchase a new server in today's market with less than a 1.6GHz processor. You'll get better overall performance, all other things being equal, using a Xeon processor rather than a standard desktop-style processor. Although the latest crop of Prescott-core processors with a 400MHz front side bus and 3200Mhz of SDRAM memory will turn out respectable numbers.

- **Number of processors.** If your budget permits fast processors or multiple processors, but not both, then opt for more processors. On a heavily loaded server, you might get better performance with dual 1GHz Xeon processors than with a single 2GHz processor, depending on the bottlenecks in your system. Exchange 2003 scales well up to eight processors, but any additional processors give only slight performance advantages. At the current writing, an 8-way SMP server from HP or IBM costs in the neighborhood of $25,000 to $30,000, not bad for a machine that can handle several thousand recipients. You'll need to run Windows Server 2003 Enterprise Edition or Windows 2000 Advanced Server to take advantage of more than two processors.

- **Hyperthreaded Pentium processors.** Intel has published a presentation (available at `www.intel.com/idf/us/fall2003/presentations/F03USOSAS29_OS.pdf`) that compares Exchange performance between two machines, one with hyperthreaded Xeon MP processors and one with standard Xeon processors. The comparison identifies several healthy performance improvements in the MP server. Intel has incorporated MP technology into their desktop processors, as well, with only a slight price difference, so you might as well take advantage of hyperthreading regardless of the size of server you want to build.

- **Processor cache.** You might get some measurable improvements in performance by purchasing processors with larger caches. For example, in a report titled "The Effect of L3 Cache Size on MMB2 Workloads," Dell was able to document several crucial performance improvements by increasing the processor L3 cache from 512K to 1MB. However, the impact was truly felt only at extreme loads, which you should not experience in production if you size your servers effectively.

- **Memory.** With memory prices hovering around $200 per GB for a top-quality PC3200 SDRAM, you wouldn't want to spec out a production Exchange server with less than 2GB of memory unless you have a small number of mailboxes, or you use the server exclusively for connectors or public folder access. Exchange does not take advantage of any physical memory over the standard 4GB limit.
- **Storage.** Except for the smallest systems, you should place Exchange data files onto their own RAID array (or separate Logical Unit Number (LUN) in a Storage Area Network (SAN). For the best blend of performance and reliability, use RAID 1+0 or RAID 0+1, depending on which flavor your RAID controller supports. Avoid RAID 5 unless you absolutely can't afford the additional disks required by the other two options. See Chapter 7, "Managing Storage and Mailboxes," for more information.
- **Network.** You should use nothing less than a 100Mbps network card on a production Exchange server, and you'll see a definite performance boost when using 1Gbps adapters. Look for servers that can team dual adapters for fault tolerance. Some adapters can offload items such as TCP checksums and Secure Socket Layer (SSL) decryption from the CPU, which leaves free cycles for more important chores.

Table 1.1 Shows Microsoft's recommendations for sizing servers based on the average number of mailboxes. If you deploy Outlook 2003 in cached mode (see Chapter 2, "Understanding and Using Messaging Protocols"), you can effectively double the number of users.

**Table 1.1**   Approximate Users per Server (From Microsoft Recommendations)

| Number of Users | CPUs | Memory |
|---|---|---|
| Fewer than 500 | 1 to 2 | 512MB to 1GB |
| 500 to 1,000 | 2 to 4 | 1GB to 2GB |
| 1,000 to 2,500 | 4 to 8 | 2GB to 4GB |
| 2,500 or more | 4 to 8 | 4GB |

## Internet Connectivity

To send and receive Internet e-mail to and from the Exchange servers in your lab, you'll need to connect to a part of the network that has access to either a broadband connection (cable modem or DSL) or a dedicated high-speed line such as a frame relay connection.

**Avoid using dial-up connections to test e-mail, even if your dial-up connection can stay active continuously.** During various exercises in this book, you'll expose your lab servers to the Internet. Hosting an e-mail server behind a dial-up connection runs the risk of having your e-mail domain blacklisted. If this occurs, mail services subscribing to the blacklist will refuse to accept e-mail from your domain. If you're using your employer's domain for testing, this interruption in services could damage your reputation and possibly your résumé.

When the time comes to set up your production network, the only major connectivity difference involves bandwidth. A test lab works acceptably with a 56Kbps Internet connection, whereas your production environment might need a full T-1 (1.544Mbps) or more to handle the e-mail traffic.

## Firewalls

Unless you want to combine your Exchange studies with real-world intrusion-defense operations, make absolutely certain that your Internet connection has a functioning firewall.

Windows Server 2003 comes with a built-in firewall, so you could use one as a router-firewall in your lab, but you take the risk of opening up your network during a test evolution that involves the machine. You get more reliable protection by using a hardware firewall that sits right behind your broadband connection or the link to your production network. A suitable small office/home office (SOHO) router-firewall can be had for less than $75.

At some point during your lab testing for Exchange, you'll need to open up ports on the firewall for DNS and Simple Mail Transfer Protocol (SMTP) and possibly a few others, depending on how you configure your lab. If your firewall does not permit this sort of configuration, get another firewall.

Getting a production Exchange deployment to work behind a firewall involves a considerable amount of planning and careful execution. Throughout this book you'll find hints on setting up connections through a firewall and security precautions to prevent granting too much access. See Chapter 11, "Deploying a Distibuted Architecture," for a discussion of firewall operations when supporting Outlook clients over the public Internet.

### Server Hardening

Keep in mind that any open port on a firewall represents a potential exploit path, so put prudent defense measures in place in your lab. Keep all servers fully patched, even the test machines you don't expect to use very often. For tests that expose your lab to the Internet, harden any public facing servers using the guidelines published by Microsoft at www.microsoft.com/security.

An Exchange 2003 server also runs Internet services, so pay particular attention to security bulletins involving attacks on Internet Information Services (IIS). Regularly monitor the event logs on your public facing servers and take immediate action if you get any indication of abnormal activity. This would include unscheduled restarts of the w3wp.exe (Windows Server 2003) or dllhost.exe (Windows 2000) processes, repeated crashes of any Web application, or a mountain of failed connection requests in the IIS log, which is located in %windir%\System32\Logfiles.

# Version Selection

If you think trying to buy a gift for a loved one on the eve of an event like a birthday or holiday presents a wicked challenge, try choosing the right version of Exchange running on the right version of Windows, with the right client running on desktops with the right service packs.

### Exchange 2003 Enterprise Edition versus Standard Edition

Your first decision concerns the flavor of Exchange 2003 to install. You have two choices: Enterprise Edition or Standard Edition. Standard Edition goes for $699 retail, while Enterprise Edition goes for $3,999. These prices do not include Client Access Licenses (CALs), which retail for $67 per seat, with significant discounts for volume purchases and upgrades.

For an organization with modest message storage needs, Standard Edition is completely adequate. If you start to get slow performance or you exhaust the storage allocation on a Standard Edition server, install another one. You don't get a performance improvement with Enterprise Edition, just more features. Here is what you're paying for in Enterprise Edition:

- **Up to 20 stores.** Whereas Standard Edition has just two stores, one for mailboxes and one for public folders, Enterprise Edition can have up to 20 stores of either type, public folder or mailbox. (In practical terms, you would use only one store for public folders because the others cannot be accessed by Outlook.)
- **Up to four primary storage groups.** Exchange protects the integrity of a store by recording changes in special files called *transaction logs*. A group of stores on a server that share a common set of transaction logs is called a *storage group*. Exchange Standard Edition can have just one storage group with an additional storage group available for mailbox recoveries. Enterprise Edition can have up to four storage groups, with a fifth used for recovery.
- **Unlimited store size.** A store in Standard Edition can grow to a maximum of 16GB. Today, even a moderate number of users can fill up 16GB quickly. Stores in the Enterprise Edition have no size limits other than the physical restrictions of storage space and the ultimate restriction of NTFS addressing, which limits files to a maximum of 16TB (terabytes.)
- **Enterprise Edition can cluster.** If you want to maximize availability of your e-mail system, clusters can help you reduce maintenance downtime. Running Exchange 2003 Enterprise Edition on Windows Server 2003 Enterprise Edition permits you to have up to 8-node clusters. Not including the price of the hardware, the cost for an 8-node cluster with 1,000-user CALs would hover around $155,000. That's $155 per user, which compares favorably to the cost of other high-end, high-availability messaging systems.
- **X.400 connector.** The X.400 standard defines a suite of protocols for messaging systems. Exchange uses Simple Mail Transport Protocol (SMTP) instead of X.400, but if you have a legacy system that requires X.400 connectivity, you can purchase the Enterprise Edition of Exchange to get the X.400 connector.

If you have already deployed Exchange 2000 Enterprise Edition, you cannot upgrade to Exchange 2003 Standard Edition. This turns out to be a fairly substantial limitation because many organizations deployed Exchange 2000 Enterprise Edition as a front-end server for Outlook Web Access or POP3/IMAP4. Because Enterprise Edition has such a large difference in price compared to Standard Edition, if you have existing Exchange 2000 front-end servers, you should outline a migration plan that moves all front-end functionality to new Exchange Server 2003 Standard Edition front-end servers.

If you exceed the 16GB storage limit of Standard Edition, you can temporarily get an additional 1GB of storage to give yourself some breathing room while you place your order for Enterprise Edition, move mailboxes off the server, or compact the database. See Microsoft Knowledge-Base Article 828070 for details.

## Small Business Server 2003

If you plan to run Exchange 2003 as a component of Small Business Server 2003 (SBS 2003), you'll get a great package at a great price but at the cost of little flexibility. SBS 2003 supports up to 75 users with the capability to place mailboxes on other Exchange 2003 servers, if desired. You can also have additional Active Directory domain controllers, but the 75-user-limit stays in effect.

If it looks as if you will exceed the 75-user limit, you can convert the various components of SBS 2003 to their Standard Edition counterparts using the SBS 2003 Transition Pack. This involves a considerable expense, so consider your initial deployment carefully. If you have over 50 users and plan on growing at all, do a standard deployment rather than installing SBS 2003.

If you already run SBS 2000, you can upgrade directly to SBS 2003, but have a strategic plan in mind in case something goes wrong. You should do a full backup, of course, but you should also test the restore to make sure your tapes are readable and make an image of the operating system partition to speed the recovery, should that become necessary.

You cannot upgrade directly from SBS 4.5. You must perform a migration to a new SBS 2003 domain. Microsoft has a 48-page document

detailing the required steps. Download it from www.microsoft.com/
downloads/details.aspx?FamilyID=1c39e0a0-ac03-43a6-a457-
81e1695e5bb6&displaylang=en.

## Exchange 2003 and Windows Server Versions

Figuring out which version of Exchange can run on specific versions of
Windows can get a bit confusing. Here are the guidelines:

- **Yes to Exchange 2003 in a Windows Server 2003 domain.**
  You can install an Exchange 2003 server in a Windows Server
  2003 Active Directory domain. The schema and domain updates
  performed by Exchange 2003 Setup are completely compatible
  with Windows Server 2003 Active Directory. You do not need any
  special service packs or hot fixes.
- **Yes to Exchange 2003 in a Windows 2000 domain.** You can
  place an Exchange 2003 server in a Windows 2000 Active Directory domain. The schema and domain updates performed by
  Exchange 2003 Setup are completely compatible with Windows
  2000 Active Directory. That said, Windows 2000 SP3 is highly
  recommended for every domain controller in the forest. This
  ensures that the schema updates do not cause inordinately long
  reindexing. Microsoft has eliminated Windows 2000 SP2 from its
  test matrix. Do not install Exchange 2003 in a domain that has
  Windows 2000 SP2 domain controllers because Microsoft will not
  be able to help you if something unexpected happens.
- **Yes to Exchange 2003 Enterprise Edition on Windows
  Server 2003 Enterprise Edition.** The only advantage to using
  the Enterprise Edition of the two products, Windows Server 2003
  and Exchange 2003, is to get 8-node clustering and 8-way pro-
  cessing. Exchange 2003 Standard Edition running on Windows
  Server 2003 Enterprise Edition supports only 2-node clusters.
  You do not get any additional memory headroom in the Enter-
  prise Edition of Exchange. Exchange 2003 can use only 4GB of
  RAM. It's also a waste of money to run Exchange on the Datacen-
  ter Edition of Windows Server 2003.
- **Yes to Exchange 2003 in a mixed forest.** You can install an
  Exchange 2003 server in any domain in a forest regardless of the
  Windows Server versions in the other domains. Keep in mind that

configuration and schema naming context changes replicate to all domain controllers in the forest, so every W2K domain controller in the forest should have SP3 installed.

- **No to Exchange 5.5 on Windows Server 2003.** As the Wizard of Oz would say, "Not no way. Not no how." If you try to install Exchange 5.5 on a Windows Server 2003 server, you'll be blocked at the outset by a warning message from the operating system that refuses to let Setup continue. If you try to upgrade a Windows 2000 server that already has Exchange 5.5 installed, you'll be notified by Windows Server 2003 Setup that Exchange 5.5 is not supported.

- **No to Exchange 2000 on Windows Server 2003.** You'll hear stories that you can upgrade a Windows 2000 server running Exchange 2000 to Windows Server 2003 and it "works great." You can believe those stories if you like, but do you really want to put your production Exchange servers into an unsupported configuration?

- **Yes to Exchange 2003 on Windows 2000 SP3.** You can install Exchange 2003 on Windows 2000 as long as you have W2K SP3 or higher installed on Windows.

- **Yes to Exchange 2003 on Windows Server 2003.** Microsoft recommends this configuration as the most stable and secure messaging platform.

- **No to Exchange 2000 on Windows Server 2003 Web Edition.** Windows Server 2003 has a Web Edition designed for inexpensive blade servers running Web services. You cannot install Exchange 2003 on Windows Server 2003 Web Edition. Setup will refuse to let you do it.

# Install and Configure IIS

Exchange and IIS are as inextricably married together as fudge chunks in a Starbucks brownie. Windows Server 2003 Setup does not install IIS by default, so you need to install the services manually before beginning the Exchange 2003 installation.

1. Launch Control Panel and open the Add/Remove Programs applet.

2. Click **Add/Remove Windows Components**. This starts the Windows Components Wizard.
3. Check the Application Server option. This leaves a dimmed checkmark, indicating that not all subcomponents are enabled by default (Figure 1.5.)

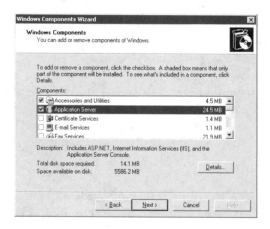

**Figure 1.5**    Windows Components Wizard showing Application Server selection.

4. Click **Details**. The Application Server window opens.
5. Check the **ASP.NET** option, a required component for Exchange.
6. Highlight the **Internet Information Services (IIS)** option and click **Details**.
7. Check the **NNTP Service** option and the **SMTP Service** option (Figure 1.6.). Both are required components for Exchange. The NNTP service is disabled by default on a fresh installation of Exchange Server 2003. The SMTP service must remain operational.
8. Click **OK** to save the change and close the IIS window.
9. Click **OK** to close the Application Server window.
10. Click **Next** in the Windows Components window to install the components. Point the installation program at the Windows Server 2003 CD or a network share holding the installation files. Be sure to apply the latest service pack or use a slipstreamed set of installation files.
11. Click **Finish** to exit the Windows Components Wizard.

Following the IIS installation, open a browser window and enter an address of `http://localhost`. This brings up an Under Construction page as shown in Figure 1.7. With that, you're ready to begin the Exchange installation.

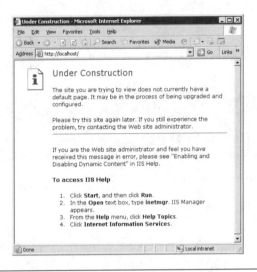

**Figure 1.6**    IIS Components showing SMTP and NNTP selected.

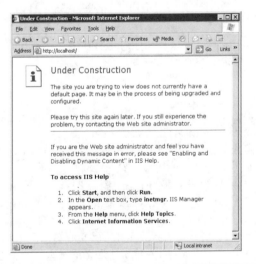

**Figure 1.7**    Accessing the default web page for Windows Server 2003 indicates that the IIS services are functional.

# Install Exchange 2003

The Exchange 2003 setup program includes a feature Microsoft calls a *prescriptive checklist* that guides you through the installation. To access the prescriptive checklist, either put the Setup CD in the caddy of the server, or connect to a share point that contains the installation files and launch Setup.exe from the root of the CD. This opens the Exchange Server 2003 Welcome window, as shown in Figure 1.8.

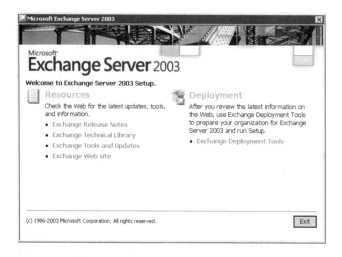

**Figure 1.8**    Initial Exchange Server 2003 installation window. The Deployment option launches the prescriptive checklist.

1. Click **Deployment Tools**. This opens a Welcome window for the deployment tools (Figure 1.9.)
2. Click **Deploy the First Exchange 2003 server**. This opens the Deploy the First Exchange 2003 Server window (Figure 1.10.)
3. Click **New Exchange 2003 Installation**. This opens the prescriptive checklist at the New Exchange 2003 Installation window.
4. Verify that you have installed Windows Server 2003, the proper IIS components, and the Windows Support Tools.
5. Run Dcdiag and Netdiag to make sure you have no errors. For details on the operation of these utilities, see Appendix A, "Building A Stable Exchange 2003 Deployment Infrastructure."

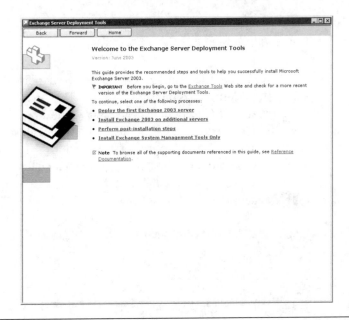

**Figure 1.9**   Exchange Server 2003 Server Deployment Tools welcome window.

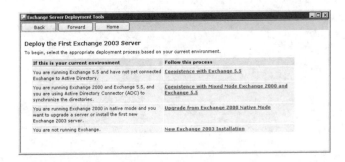

**Figure 1.10**   Initial steps of the prescriptive checklist for installing the first
Exchange 2003 server in an organization.

   **6.** The next two steps in the prescriptive checklist, ForestPrep and
      DomainPrep, can be combined with the final step, installing
      Exchange, as long as you have a single domain and you possess
      full administrator privileges in the forest and in the domain. In
      production, it's best practice to run each stage of the installation
      separately and verify its completion prior to proceeding.

7.  Click the **Run Setup Now** link. A notification tells you that Setup is loading files, and the Exchange Installation Wizard starts.
8.  Click **Next**. The License Agreement window opens.
9.  Select the **I Agree** radio button.
10. Click **Next**. The Component Selection window opens. If you did everything correctly, including all the prerequisites, you'll get a window similar to that shown in Figure 1.11. The **Action** column shows **Typical** for the Microsoft Exchange line, and **Install** on the Messaging and Collaboration Services line and the System Management Tools line.

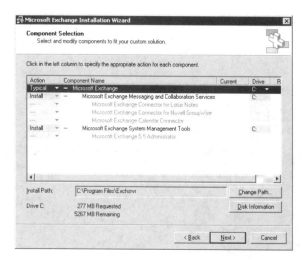

**Figure 1.11**   Component Selection window showing a Typical install, the default selection if all prerequisites are met.

If you neglected to complete one of the prerequisites, Setup will notify you of the deficiency; then stop and exit once you acknowledge it. Correct the problem; then start Setup from the beginning.

11. Pay particular attention to the **Install Path** entry. Note that the default path points at the C drive, which is suitable only in a test environment, not for a production server. In production, you should always install Exchange onto a separate logical drive. In addition, the Exchange data files and transaction logs should go onto their own drives to enhance performance and recoverability.
12. Click **Next**.
13. Select the **I Agree** radio button.
14. Click **Next**. A Summary window appears.
15. Click **Next** to begin the installation. A Component Progress window shows you each stage of the installation. If Setup stalls at any time during this final stage, you will be given the opportunity to correct the problem and move on.

After Setup has completed, close the Exchange Installation Wizard. You do not need to restart the machine. All the Exchange services start at the end of Setup.

You're not quite done, though. You need to install the most current service pack. Installing SP1 in Exchange Server 2003 requires hotfix KB831464. This hotfix corrects a problem with compression on temporary files. Download the hotfix and the service pack from the Exchange download site at www.microsoft.com/exchange/downloads.

Unfortunately, installing Exchange is a little like joining the military; beyond a certain point, there's no going back. If Setup fails and you can't correct the problem, often the server is left betwixt-and-between (as we say in southern New Mexico), and you might need to completely reinstall the operating system before commencing the Exchange installation again. The best way to avoid this situation is to carefully follow the prerequisites in the Setup checklists and make sure that DNS is working so that the server can communicate with domain controllers holding configuration information for the organization.

# Introducing Exchange System Manager

Part of Exchange setup includes an MMC console called the *Exchange System Manager*, or ESM. Launch the console from the Start menu via Start | All Programs | Microsoft Exchange | System Manager. Figure 1.12 shows an example ESM console for an Exchange organization with a half-dozen servers in various locations.

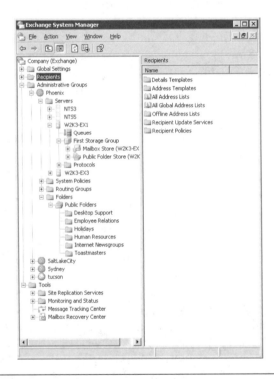

**Figure 1.12**   ESM console window showing contents of new organization.

Personally, I find it a little tedious to navigate through the Start menu each time I launch ESM, so I use a little feature in Windows Server 2003 Explorer that allows me to *pin* a Start menu item directly to the main menu. Right-click the System Manager icon and select Pin To Start Menu from the flyout menu, as shown in Figure 1.13. You can also add the icon to the quick launch bar.

Do the same for the Active Directory Users and Computers (ADUC) icon under the Microsoft Exchange folder in the Start Menu. This version of ADUC has add-ins that expose Exchange features when working with users and groups. You won't see Exchange options in ADUC on domain controllers and administrative workstations until you install ESM. This does not require installing Exchange, just the tools.

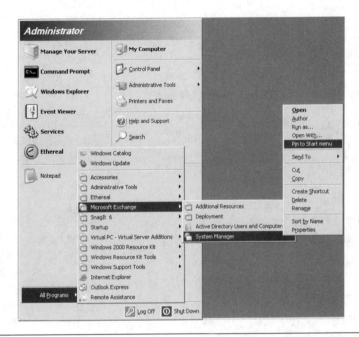

**Figure 1.13** Pin the Exchange System Manager launch shortcuts to the main Start menu.

Chapter 4, "Managing Exchange 2003 Servers," covers ESM operation in detail. For now, it's enough to know that you can see the content of an organization, including servers, mailboxes, public folders, and all the myriad settings that control message routing, storage, and handling.

## Assigning Mailboxes

At this point, you should check the operation of your Exchange server to make sure users can send and receive e-mail. Let's create a couple of accounts to use as e-mail recipients. An account that can receive and store e-mail is called a *mailbox-enabled user*. A user account with an e-mail address that points to a mailbox on an outside messaging system is called a *mail-enabled user*. You would create a mail-enabled user in situations where you have an outside user (a consultant, perhaps, or a visiting auditor) who has an account in Active Directory but who wants to receive e-mail at her home location.

You can mailbox-enable a user either when you create the user account or after the user account already exists. The following sections show how to do both.

## Mailbox-Enabling New Users

When you install Exchange, Setup adds additional functionality to the Active Directory Users and Computers (ADUC) console for displaying Exchange extensions in property menus and Exchange tabs in the property windows.

> You will not see the Exchange settings in the ADUC on a domain controller or on a management workstation until you install the Exchange tools. See Chapter 4 for details.

To complete the following steps, log on as an administrator at the console of the newly installed Exchange server. The account you use to create the new user must have permission to create new user objects in Active Directory and to access server information in the Exchange organization. For now, you can use the domain Administrator account, although you would not do this in a production environment.

1. Launch Active Directory Users and Computers at the console of the Exchange server.
2. Right-click the **Users** container and select **New | User** from the flyout menu. The New Object User window opens.
3. Fill in the naming information for the user account, as shown in Figure 1.14.
4. Click **Next**. A window opens for entering the user's password and account status information. Enter a password that meets the complexity requirements for the domain (Figure 1.15.) The default complexity for Windows Server 2003 is seven characters with at least one uppercase letter and one special character or numeral.

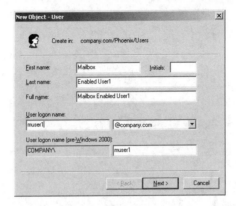

**Figure 1.14**     User name information when creating a new user account in Active Directory.

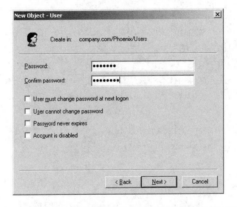

**Figure 1.15**     Password information for new user account.

5. Click **Next**. After a few seconds' pause, a window opens where you can select e-mail configuration settings for the user, as shown in Figure 1.16. For right now, you have only one Exchange server with one mailbox store, so the select couldn't get simpler. If you had multiple Exchange servers, or multiple mailbox stores on one Exchange server, you would select the correct destination for the mailbox.

6. Click **Next** to get a summary window.

7. Click **Finish** to create a user and assign the user a mailbox.

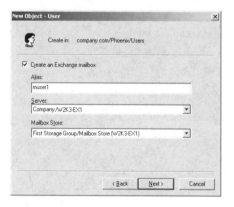

**Figure 1.16**    E-mail configuration for new mailbox-enabled user.

At this point, the user's mailbox does not yet exist. Exchange creates the mailbox the first time the user gets an e-mail, logs onto Outlook, or receives a meeting request, task assignment, or some other object that resides within the Outlook folders within the Exchange store.

In a few moments, check the object's Properties window to see the e-mail addresses assigned to the user. Figure 1.17 shows an example.

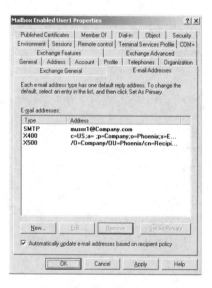

**Figure 1.17**    E-mail address information for new user account.

An Exchange service called the Recipient Update Service (RUS) applies e-mail addresses to new mailbox-enabled users and mail-enabled users, groups, and contacts. See Chapter 5, "Managing Recipients and Distribution Lists," for details on how RUS knows which e-mail suffixes to use. Sometimes RUS doesn't react as quickly as you'd want it to. If the e-mail address list is empty, try again in a minute or so.

## Mailbox-Enabling Existing Users

You can add a mailbox to any user in Active Directory. To test this capability, you'll need to create a new user who does not have a mailbox. The simplest way to create a new user is with the NET command-line utility. Here's the syntax:

```
net user <user_name> <password> /add /domain
```

For example, to create a user name standarduser1 with a password of Password!, the entry would look like this:

```
net user standarduser1 Password! /add /domain
```

Now give the user a mailbox as follows:

1. Launch Active Directory Users and Computers from the console of the Exchange server. Track down to the **Users** container.
2. Right-click the **standarduser1** account and select **Exchange Tasks** from the flyout menu. This launches the Exchange Task Wizard. Click past the welcome screen to the Available Tasks window, shown in Figure 1.18.

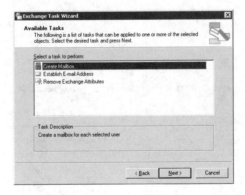

**Figure 1.18**    Exchange Task Wizard showing Create Mailbox option.

3. Highlight **Create Mailbox**.
4. Click **Next**. This opens the Create Mailbox window, shown in Figure 1.19.

**Figure 1.19** Create Mailbox window showing the selection for server and mailbox store for a new mailbox-enabled user.

5. Click **Next**. This begins the mailbox creation. The wizard presents a progress screen, shown in Figure 1.20. If you get an error, this window closes and a summary window allows you to display an XML-based error report.

**Figure 1.20** New user mailbox creation progress window.

6. After the mailbox has been created, the wizard presents a Success window and you're done.

## Mail-Enabling Contacts

Situations often arise when users want to send e-mail to recipients in other organizations. Rather than force users to enter the full e-mail address (`user@domain.root`) of an outside recipient, you might want to include the outside recipient in the GAL so users can simply select the name.

Active Directory contains a Contact object that Exchange can use to represent an outside recipient. A Contact object does not have a Security ID (SID) and therefore cannot act as a Windows security principal or have a mailbox.

A mail-enabled contact has an e-mail address corresponding to the user's address in the outside organization. For example, a mail-enabled contact called Nancy Consultant could have the e-mail address *nancy.consultant@outsidefirm.com*. A user who selects the Nancy Consultant item from the GAL would have the outgoing e-mail routed to the e-mail server for Outsidefirm.com. Mail-enabled contacts can also be included in the distribution lists.

Mail-enabled contacts also come in handy if you want to connect two Exchange organizations. You can use the Galsync utility in the Microsoft Identity Integration Server (MIIS) Feature Pack to create contacts in one organization corresponding to mailbox-enabled users in the other organization. In this way, each organization has a comprehensive GAL without the need to share mailboxes. (You can download the free MIIS Feature Pack from Microsoft's download site. The accompanying documentation walks you through installing and configuring Galsync.)

You can mail-enable a contact when you create the object or after the object as been created. You need sufficient permissions in Active Directory to create Contact objects. Figure 1.21 shows the configuration window for mail-enabling a Contact object when first creating the object.

Typically, the address you enter in the window would conform to the standard Simple Mail Transfer Protocol (SMTP) address format. You can use a specialized format such as an X.400 address or a third-party format, but you would need to install a special connector in Exchange to use that address for message routing.

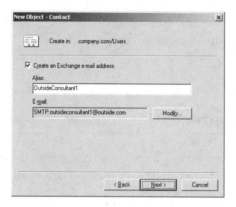

**Figure 1.21**    E-mail attributes for new mail-enabled contact.

If the contact object already exists, right-click on the object in Active Directory, select Exchange Tasks from the flyout menu, and walk through the Exchange Task Wizard to assign an e-mail address to the object. Figure 1.22 shows the Establish E-mail Address window in the Exchange Task Wizard contact.

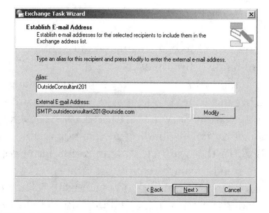

**Figure 1.22**    E-mail address to assign to a new mail-enabled contact.

When the Recipient Update Service notices that a new mail-enabled contact exists, it uses the External E-mail Address to assign an e-mail address to the object in Active Directory. You can open the Properties window for the contact and select the E-mail Addresses tab to see the address. Figure 1.23 shows an example.

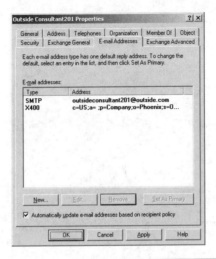

**Figure 1.23** Proxy e-mail addresses assigned to mail-enabled contact by the Recipient Update Service.

# Mail-Enabling Groups

Exchange uses mail-enabled groups in Active Directory as distribution lists. If you address a message to a mail-enabled group, the Exchange server determines which members have mailboxes and which members represent mail-enabled users or mail-enabled contacts with outside e-mail addresses. It then sends a copy of the message to each of those recipients.

It turns out that managing groups used for e-mail distribution lists quickly becomes a non-trivial exercise, even in a modestly-sized organization. Chapter 5 gives lots of details on how Exchange determines group membership, how it expands distribution lists, how it reacts in a multiple domain forest with group members from several domains, and so forth. For right now, let's forgo the complexity and simply create a mail-enabled group or two that we can use to test e-mail delivery.

## Mail-Enable New Groups

When you create a new group in Active Directory Users and Computers, you have the option to make it either a Security Group or a Distribution group. Figure 1.24 shows the New Object–Group window.

**Figure 1.24**    Configuration information Group.

Active Directory defines two group types:

- **Security groups.** These groups can be placed on Access Control Lists (ACLs) to control access to files, folders, Registry keys, public folders, and other secured resources
- **Distribution groups.** These groups function solely as e-mail distribution lists. They cannot be used to control access to resources.

Active Directory also defines three group scopes:

- **Domain Local.** This group scope accepts members from any domain, but can be placed only on ACLs for resources in the group's own domain. This group is intended for use on the ACL of a resource.
- **Global.** This group scope accepts members only from its own domain, but can be placed into Domain Local groups in any domain.
- **Universal.** This group scope accepts members from any domain and can be placed in domain local groups in any domain.

Both Security Groups and Distribution Groups can have e-mail addresses. This makes them a *mail-enabled group*, capable of receiving messages and appearing on the GAL.

The Group Type determines whether or not you can place the group on the Access Control List of a security object such as an NTFS folder or file, Registry key, or Active Directory object. Only Security groups can appear on Access Control Lists. Windows won't even offer you the option of selecting a Distribution Group in the pick lists for these objects. A Distribution Group has no security roles and only serves as a distribution list for Exchange.

The Group Scope option gets a little more complicated. In a nutshell, here are the differences between the groups:

- A Domain Local group can have members from any domain, but can only be placed on Access Control Lists within its own domain.
- A Global group can have members only from its own domain, but can be placed on Access Control lists in any domain.
- A Universal group can have members from any domain and can be placed on Access Control lists in any domain.

In addition to these three basic group types supported by Windows, Exchange 2003 adds a fourth group type called the Query-Based Distribution Group, or QDG. This group can be used only for e-mail distribution, not security. A QDG has a dynamic membership that relies on an LDAP query. For example, you could create a QDG that specifies a query such as, "Send to all mailbox-enabled users whose last name starts with K." If you work for the Men in Black, sending a message to that QDG would result in only one user getting an e-mail. If you work for the U.S. Navy, sending a message using the same QDG criteria might result in sending ten thousand e-mails. If a new sailor named Klem Kadiddlehopper gets a mailbox, the next time someone sends a message to that QDG, Exchange would send 10,001 e-mails.

Until you get to Chapter 5 to learn more about how Exchange handles all the various combinations of group scopes and group types, it's best just to create Universal Distribution Groups (UDGs) and be done with it. Try to keep things tidy by collecting your groups under Organizational Units rather than simply loading them into the Users container.

## Group Types Interchangeable, to a Point

If you create a Distribution Group, you can change your mind later and convert it to a Security Group by opening the Properties window and changing the Group Type option to Security. You can then place the group on an Access Control List or public folder permission list.

You can also convert a Security Group to a Distribution group, but use caution. Someone might have placed the group on an ACL somewhere, so therefore the system does not have the ability to scan for that configuration. You have no way of knowing if a security group has been used on an ACL or public folder permission list unless you do a full scan of the security settings on every security object on every server and workstation in the entire forest—a considerable undertaking. For this reason, you should convert a Security Group to a Distribution Group only in the most controlled circumstances you can arrange.

## Automatic Group Promotion

If you create a Distribution Group, Windows does not permit you to put the group on an Access Control List. The user interface does not even present you with the option.

But Exchange does permit you to put a Distribution Group on the permissions list for a public folder or user mailbox. Figure 1.25 shows an example for a group called Distro1.

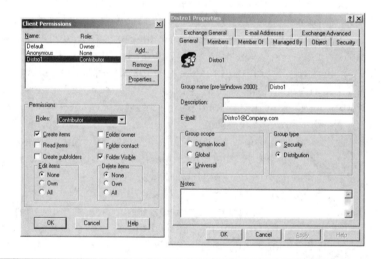

**Figure 1.25**   MAPI permissions showing a Universal Distribution Group as a role owner.

After you add a distribution group to the permissions list, the Exchange Information Store automatically promotes the group to a Security Group. It might take a couple of minutes for the promotion to occur.

## Mail-Enable Groups

Groups do not have mailboxes, and mail-enabling a group does not mail-enable the group members. Instead, mail-enabling a group tells

Exchange that a message addressed to the group should send to the group's members. Figure 1.26 shows the configuration information to mail-enable a group. Like other operations involving recipients, this configuration is done in Active Directory Users and Computers.

**Figure 1.26**    E-mail alias assigned to new mail-enabled group.

### For More Information

As I said at the beginning of this section, the chore of selecting the right types of groups to use for Exchange involves quite a bit of planning. Unless you're the only Exchange administrator in your organization, you'll be spending more than a few hours discussing all the possible options. Chapter 5 examines these options in detail.

## Test Exchange with Outlook 2003

Virtually any standard e-mail client can read and send messages using an Exchange server, but in a production-messaging system, Outlook and Exchange quickly become yin and yang. Many of the productivity features in Exchange come into play only when using Outlook as a MAPI client. Because this book covers the latest version of Exchange, it makes sense to use the most current version of Outlook as well, Outlook 2003.

You can install Outlook 2003 as a standalone product or as a component of Office System 2003. You can obtain a 180-day evaluation copy of Office System 2003 from Microsoft or just about any Microsoft software reseller.

Outlook 2003 requires XP or Windows 2000 Service Pack 3 (SP3) or higher. To use Outlook as a MAPI client, join the desktop to a domain in the same forest as the Exchange server. In the lab, I recommend using XP SP2 to get all the Outlook features and the increased security in SP2. In production, where you may need to install hundreds or thousands of copies of Office System 2003, you can create unattended installation files and deploy the installations or upgrades using software deployment group policies. For details, see Jeremy Moskowitz's book *Group Policy, Profiles, and IntelliMirror for Windows 2003, Windows 2000, and Windows XP*, published by Sybex.

In a production system, you must purchase a Client Access License (CAL) for each client that accesses an Exchange server from any type of client. The purchase price of Outlook 2003, Office System 2003, or the bundled version of Outlook on handheld devices and smart phones, does not include the CAL. You can purchase the CAL separately through a Microsoft reseller. Microsoft sets a retail price for an Exchange CAL at $67, but you can get lower prices depending on how many CALs you purchase and whether you own significant numbers of other Microsoft products.

*Don't install Outlook on a server where you intend to install Exchange.* This rule applies to any version of Outlook and any version of Exchange. Don't mix them on the same machine. Both Outlook and Exchange use a MAPI library stored in file called Mapi32.dll. However, Exchange uses a different version of Mapi32.dll than Outlook uses. You can cause some devilish problems by mixing the two applications on the same platform. Enabling the MAPI features in Eudora or Domino can cause the same compatibility issues.

If you need to use an e-mail client to access Exchange at the console of an Exchange server, use Outlook Express, Outlook Web Access, or a third-party application that does not have a MAPI component.

## Outlook 2003 Hotfixes

You can encounter problems in deploying Outlook 2003 if you do not have the most current set of hotfixes. The following is a list of the primary hotfixes required for proper operation. Each hotfix number corresponds to a Microsoft Knowledge-Base article.

- **Hotfix 828041.** Office 2003 Critical Update
- **Hotfix 823343.** Collaborative Data Objects Heap Corruption Occurs When You Try to Access an Exchange Mailbox
- **Hotfix 829418.** Information Store Intermittently Stops Responding and an Access Violation Occurs in EcDSDNFromSz

## Outlook 2003 Installation Procedure

1. Launch Setup from the CD or a network share containing the installation files. After a brief initialization, you'll be prompted for the 25-character Product Key.
2. Assuming you type the key correctly the first time (I rarely do), the next window prompts you for your name and initials. Your current logon name is inserted, but you'll probably want to use your full name.
3. Click **Next**. The End User License Agreement window opens.
4. Check **I Accept The Terms In The Licensing Agreement**.
5. Click **Next**. The Type of Installation window opens. If you want to test only messaging, you can limit your installation to Outlook, but I suggest that you install the entire suite so you can get a feel for what your users will encounter. For example, Office System automatically configures Word as the Outlook e-mail editor if you do a full installation.
6. Click **Next**. A summary window opens.
7. Click **Install** to perform the installation.

After the product is installed, run Office update (or the Windows Update Service, when available) to get the latest hotfixes and security patches. Then launch Word or Excel to initialize the system and get activated. You won't be able to do much with Outlook yet because you don't have an Exchange server. Hold off on configuring Outlook as a personal e-mail client. You'll do that in the next chapter.

## Outlook 2003 Features

If you aren't familiar with the Outlook 2003, it has several advantages over previous versions.

### Kerberos Authentication

Earlier versions of Outlook use NTLM (NT LanMan) authentication when connecting to an Exchange server. Outlook 2003 improves security considerably by supporting Kerberized connections to Exchange services.

You can configure Outlook strictly to use either Kerberos or NTLM, but the default configuration permits Outlook to negotiate a protocol with its Exchange server. You'll find this setting in the in the Security tab of the account Properties window in Outlook, as shown in Figure 1.27.

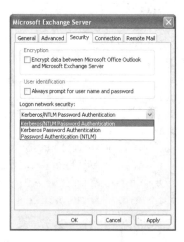

**Figure 1.27**    Authentication selection in Outlook 2003.

### Cached Exchange Mode

Outlook 2003 caches all messages and other e-mail elements in a local OST file, located in the user's profile folder under Local Settings\Application Data\Microsoft\Outlook. Caching improves performance and smoothes out the number of MAPI requests sent to the server after the client has initially downloaded all stored messages. You can turn off caching in Outlook as follows:

1. From the main menu, select **Tools | E-mail Accounts**. This opens the E-mail Accounts window.
2. Click **Next** and then click **Change**.
3. In the Exchange Server Settings window, uncheck the **Used Cached Exchange Mode** option, shown in Figure 1.28.

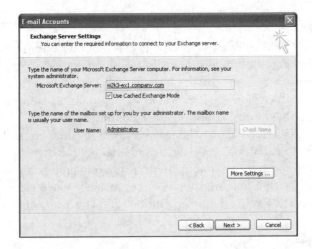

**Figure 1.28**  E-mail account properties in Outlook 2003 showing cached mode option.

The local cache is stored in an offline folder (OST) file. You can view and modify the file location as follows:

4. Click **More Settings**. This opens the Microsoft Exchange Server window.
5. Select the **Advanced** tab.
6. Click **Offline Folder File Settings**. This opens the Offline Folder File Settings window (Figure 1.29).

**Figure 1.29**  Offline file settings in Outlook 2003 showing option to move the location of the OST file.

7. Click **Browse** to select a new location for the OST file.
8. Click **OK** to save the change and close the windows.

### Intelligent Synchronization

Outlook 2003 refreshes its local cache by downloading messages from the Exchange server periodically throughout the logon session. If the download gets interrupted, Outlook picks up where it left off. This contrasts to all earlier versions of Outlook, which insisted on starting over from the beginning when refreshing offline folders.

Outlook 2003 shows the synchronization progress in the lower-right corner of the Outlook window. If client has not fully synchronized, the display lists new headers queued for transfer, remaining messages to transfer.

Also, rather than transfer an entire message when a change is made to flags such as the Read marker, Outlook 2003 transfers only a new header.

### Resilient Synchronization

If Outlook 2003 encounters a bad item in a mail transfer, it simply marks the item as bad, puts it in the Sync Issues folder, and then continues with the transfer. This contrasts with earlier versions, which often crash or get unstable when faced with a bad mail item.

You can view any synchronization problems by opening the Sync Issues folder, as shown in Figure 1.30.

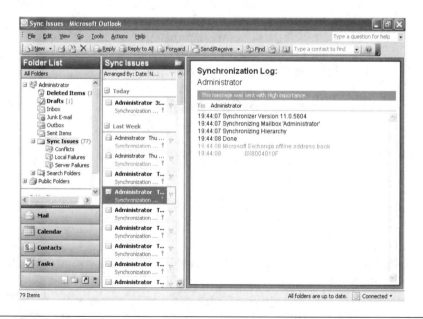

**Figure 1.30**   Outlook 2003 showing synchronization problem listed in Sync Issues folder.

### MAPI compression and Buffer Packing

Exchange 2003 servers and Outlook 2003 clients compress the bodies of messages to reduce the load on WAN connections and increase the number of remote clients that a single Exchange server can handle.

When a network client has a message to send to a server, it sends a software interrupt to the CPU so the CPU can schedule a timeslice for handling the transfer. The client tries to optimize these interrupts by doing as much work as possible during each timeslice. Part of this optimization includes filling a buffer with messages prior to issuing the software interrupt.

When an Outlook 2003 client has messages to send, rather than filling a buffer, and then compressing the contents and issuing the interrupt, it compresses the messages first and then puts them in the buffer. This "buffer stuffing" improves performance and reduces the number of packets involved in transferring a given block of information.

### Outlook Performance Monitoring

Outlook 2003 clients communicate latency and error information to their Exchange servers. The Exchange server stores this information where monitoring applications such as Microsoft Operations Manager can tap into it and produce reports.

### Antispam

Outlook 2003 includes a junk mail filter that categorizes inbound messages as Unsolicited Bulk E-mail (UBE) and sends it to a designated junk mail folder where the user can check to make sure the filter did not catch an important message by mistake before deleting them.

Users can also choose to filter their incoming messages so that only messages from their contacts or specific SMTP domains get accepted.

Some messages contain HTML content that has hyperlinks to graphic files on external servers. Spammers use these hyperlinks as *beacons* because the target server sees if a client touches the graphic file. Outlook 2003 blocks connections to hyperlinks in HTML messages to disrupt these beacons.

See Chapter 13 for details on the Outlook junk mail filter and how you can improve the filter operation by deploying Microsoft's Intelligent Mail Filter at your Exchange 2003 servers.

### Send Test Message From Outlook

You should now be able to connect to your Exchange server using the
Outlook client you previously installed. Also, if your Exchange server
can communicate to the Internet through your firewall, you should be
able to send a message to your public e-mail account from an Outlook
account.

1. Launch Outlook using the domain Administrator account or the
   account you entered during Exchange setup.
2. At the Outlook 2003 Startup window, click **Next**. The E-mail
   Accounts window opens.
3. Leave the **Yes** radio button selected.
4. Click **Next**. The Server Type window opens (Figure 1.31.)
5. Select the **Microsoft Exchange Server** radio button.

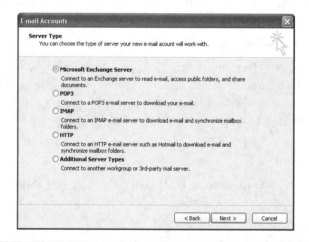

**Figure 1.31**    Server Type window for selecting which e-mail client protocol
to use in Outlook.

6. Click **Next**. The Exchange Server Settings window opens, as
   shown in Figure 1.32. Enter the fully qualified DNS name of the
   Exchange server you just installed. The Fully Qualified Domain
   Name (FQDN) of the example server is `W2K3-EX1.company.`
   `com`. The name is not case sensitive. For User Name, enter the
   name of a mailbox-enabled user account.

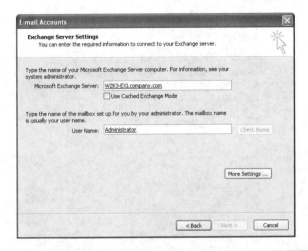

**Figure 1.32**   Exchange Server Settings window for a new Outlook profile showing entries for user name and Exchange server.

7.  Uncheck the **Use Cached Exchange Mode** option. Although this highly useful option should be kept enabled in production, in a lab it can be helpful to always see what is on the server, not in the local cache.

8.  Click **Check Name**. If Outlook can find the Exchange server and validate the name of the Administrator account, then both the server name and user name get an underline. If this does not happen, you'll get an error message explaining the problem. The most likely cause is a DNS configuration error. See the Troubleshooting section following this section for recommendations.

9.  Click **Next**. A Congratulations window opens.

10. Click **Finish** to close the wizard and open Outlook.

11. If this is the first Office application you've opened, you'll be prompted for a full name and initials. Enter them and click **OK**.

At this point, you can create a new mail message to send a test message. Do this as follows:

12. Click the **New** button or press Ctrl+N to start a new message.

13. Click the **To** button to open the Global Address List, shown in Figure 1.33. The mailbox-enabled account you created will be on the list.

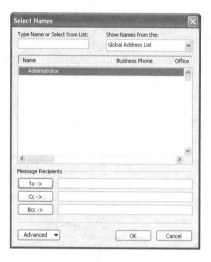

**Figure 1.33**    Initial Global Address List showing Administrator account.

14. Select the account and click **OK**.
15. Compose a message and then click **Send**.
16. In a couple of seconds, the notification area at the bottom of the main desktop window shows a balloon (sometimes called "toast" because of the way it pops up) containing the sender's name, the subject, and a line of the body. Figure 1.34 shows an example.

**Figure 1.34**    New e-mail notification in Outlook 2003.

17. Click the link in the balloon to open the message.
18. Close the message.
19. Send a few more messages to yourself, some of them with attachments.
20. Now send a message to your public e-mail account by entering your public e-mail address (such as **user@outsidedomain.com**) in the To field of a new message. Check your public inbox to see if the message arrives.

You won't be able to receive Internet e-mail in your Outlook account quite yet because you haven't created a connector from the Exchange server to the Internet, and because nobody on the Internet knows that your Exchange server exists. Chapter 8, "Message Routing," shows how to create this configuration.

# Test Exchange with Outlook Express

You might want to run an e-mail client on the console of an Exchange server where you can't run Outlook. Also, during testing, you'll want a quick and simple way to test access to Internet mail servers.

Microsoft provides a non-MAPI client in the form of Outlook Express. You'll find Outlook Express on every Windows platform that hosts a modern version of Internet Explorer. This includes Windows Server 2003 and XP.

## Enable POP3 Service

If you plan on using Internet clients to access your Exchange server, you can use Outlook Express to do a quick test of POP3 access. Windows Server 2003 disables the POP3 service by default. Enable and start the service from the command line using the SC (Service Controller) utility as follows:

```
sc config pop3svc start= auto
sc start pop3svc
```

## Outlook Express 6.0 Installation

1. Launch Outlook Express via the Start menu: **Start | All Programs | Outlook Express**. Because you haven't used Outlook Express before, this starts the Internet Connection Wizard. Cancel out of the initial portions that define the Internet connection and proceed with the Your Name window.

2. Enter the name **Administrator** or the account you specified during Exchange installation (Figure 1.35).

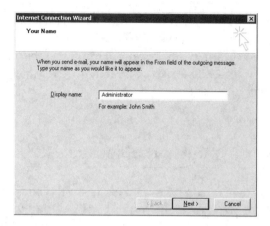

**Figure 1.35**    Outlook Express account setup showing the Your Name window for entering an account name.

3. Click **Next**. In the Internet E-mail Address window, enter the e-mail address of the Administrator account (Figure 1.36.)

**Figure 1.36**    Internet e-mail address of new Outlook Express account.

4. Click **Next**. In the E-mail Server Names window, leave the **My Incoming Mail Server...** option set for POP3. Enter the fully qualified DNS name of your Exchange server in both the **Incoming Mail** field and the **Outgoing Mail** field, as shown in Figure 1.37.

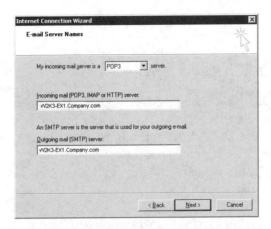

**Figure 1.37**    POP3 and SMTP server configuration information for Outlook Express client.

5. Click **Next**. In the Internet Mail Logon window, enter the full account name of the test account and the e-mail password (Figure 1.38.) If you check the Remember Password option, then Outlook Express saves an encrypted form of the password in Registry under HKCU\Software\Microsoft\Protected Storage System Provider.

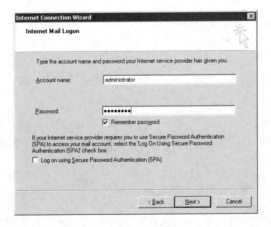

**Figure 1.38**    E-mail logon credentials for new Outlook Express account.

6. Click **Next**. A summary window opens.
7. Click **Finish** to save the configuration, and open the main Outlook Express window.

## Send Test Message Using Outlook Express

Now send a message from Outlook Express to your public e-mail account via the Exchange server as follows:

1. Click the **Create Mail** button. This opens a New Message window.
2. In the **To** field, enter the Internet e-mail address corresponding to your corporate account.
3. In the **Subject** and **Body**, enter test text. The final result looks similar to Figure 1.39.

**Figure 1.39** Sample outgoing e-mail in Outlook Express showing an Internet e-mail address.

4. Click **Send**. Outlook Express sends the message to your ISP, which then routes it to your corporate mail server. In a few seconds, you should see the message in your e-mail inbox.

If your corporate firewall blocks outbound SMTP connections, the test described above would fail. You can try making arrangements with your colleagues in network services to permit outbound SMTP from your test server.

# Troubleshooting Test E-mails

If you get an error during any of the tests, follow the hints in the error message to see if you mistyped an entry. It's easy to put a typo in the server name or to type the word `adminstritator` when you meant to type `administrator`. If you entered the correct account and server name but you get a message saying that the Exchange server cannot be found or is not available, try the following checks.

## Exchange Services Running

Make sure the Exchange services have started. You can use the `sc query` command or launch the Services console from the Run window by typing `Services.msc` and clicking OK. Navigate to the Microsoft Exchange services, as shown in Figure 1.40.

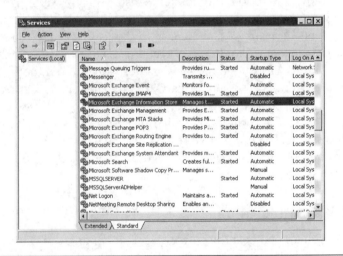

**Figure 1.40**   Services console showing status of Exchange services.

If you find any of the following services stopped, start them by right-clicking the name and selecting Start from the flyout menu:

- Microsoft Exchange Information Store
- Microsoft Exchange System Attendant
- Microsoft Exchange Routing Engine
- Microsoft Exchange MTA Stacks (not absolutely required, but it should automatically start)

Starting the Information Store should start the System Attendant and Routing Engine, but not vice versa. The Exchange Event service only starts when it's needed. Don't worry about its status for right now.

The POP3 and IMAP4 services are disabled by default on a fresh installation of Windows Server 2003 and they remain disabled after the Exchange installation. You will need to enable one or the other to use Outlook Express to connect to the Exchange server. They are not required for Outlook when used as a MAPI client, but you would need to enable them if you use Outlook as a POP3 or IMAP4 client.

### Exchange Server Available

Start by pinging the FQDN of the Exchange server from the desktop running the e-mail client. If this does not succeed, you might have a DNS configuration error at the client, although this is unlikely because you were able to join the domain. (Also, your firewall might block outbound ICMP.)

Type `ipconfig /all` and verify in the listing that the client points at the domain controller that is also acting as your DNS server. Correct the entry if it is wrong, and then try again. If you entered the IP address of a production DNS server instead of your lab server, it's likely that the client received a No Record reply back from the DNS server. The client caches this for 5 minutes, which can make you crazy if you're troubleshooting. Clear the DNS resolver cache using `ipconfig /flushdns` after making any changes to DNS configuration or the DNS zone file contents at the server.

### DNS Configuration

If the client points at the correct DNS server and you can ping the DNS server, check to make sure the Exchange server has Host (A) record in the zone and that the record has the correct IP address. Do this by opening the DNS management console at the domain controller and highlighting the name of the domain, as shown in Figure 1.41.

You should see a lot of folders holding SRV records and the name and IP address of the Exchange server. If you don't see the SRV records, then your domain controller is not configured to point at itself for DNS lookups. Make this change in the TCP/IP configuration of the Local Area Connection then either stop and start the Netlogon service or run `netdiag /fix`. (This utility is located in the Windows Server 2003 Support Tools.)

deploy new Exchange 2003 servers running on Windows Server 2003, but you might not have that luxury. You also want to decommission all legacy Exchange servers as quickly as possible, but you might need to keep them in service for a considerable period of time. Here is some information about Exchange features that require Windows Server 2003 and features that require Exchange Native Mode, which can be implemented only when all legacy Exchange servers have been removed from service.

## Exchange 2003 Features Requiring Windows Server 2003

You can install Exchange Server 2003 on Windows 2000 SP3 or higher, but several Exchange 2003 features rely on Windows Server 2003.

### IPSec between Front-end and Back-end Clusters

IP Security (IPSec) can protect password transactions between front-end and back-end servers, but Windows 2000 clusters do not support Kerberos transactions between nodes in the cluster, so using IPSec prevents the cluster from failing.

### Cross-Forest Kerberos Authentication with Outlook 2003

Windows Server 2003 supports two-way transitive Kerberos trusts between forests. Outlook 2003 uses Kerberos for authentication, so you can take advantage of an inter-forest trust to access mailboxes on Exchange servers in trusted forests.

### IIS 6.0 Security, Isolation Mode, and Health Monitoring

I can't say enough good things about IIS 6.0. Its improved reliability, scalability, and serviceability surpass its predecessor in every respect. This makes the combination of Exchange 2003 and IIS 6.0 a compelling partnership.

### Volume Shadow Backups

This feature, available only on Windows Server 2003, makes it possible to do nearly instantaneous snapshot backups of an Exchange mailbox or public folder store.

### Databases Stored Behind Mount Points

Windows often gets scoffed at for its reliance on letters as handles to drive volumes. The Roman alphabet imposes an ultimate limit of 26 letters, with 3 already in use for floppy drives and the operating system boot drive. A large Exchange server with many storage groups that require separate drives might run out of drive letters.

Exchange Server 2003 permits using mount points to store databases. A mount point installs a stub file on an empty folder in one volume that acts as a kind of redirector to a file system on another volume. In this way, you can put a database on D:\Mount1 instead of using a logical drive letter.

### RPC over HTTP

Outlook clients use Remote Procedure Calls (RPCs) to send and retrieve messages with an Exchange server. Windows Server 2003 provides an RPC Proxy that permits connecting to the RPC End-Point Mapper and getting a connection to an RPC-based service over a secure HTTP port (TCP port 443).

Outlook 2003 and Exchange 2003 can take advantage of this feature to improve the traveling user's Outlook experience by avoiding the need to provision a VPN to connect to an Exchange server in the home office. The user points Outlook 2003 at a public IP address with an open port 443 that connects to the Exchange server. Outlook uses RPC over HTTP to negotiate an RPC connection to the Exchange server and to a Global Catalog server to get a GAL.

### Advanced Memory Tuning

Ordinarily, virtual memory gets divided evenly between the operating system and an application: 2GB apiece. Windows 2000 introduced a memory tuning option called the /3gb switch that gives 3GB of virtual memory to an application while leaving 1GB for the operating system.

The /3gb option has a slight problem, though. It takes too much memory from the operating system so that a heavily loaded Exchange server could run out of file-handle space. Windows Server 2003 solves this problem with a /USERVA switch that permits specifying exactly how much memory to assign to applications.

Microsoft recommends a USERVA value in the range of 2970 to 3030, with 3030 as the preferred value.

### Improved Hyperthreading Support

The MP line of Intel processors sport dual input queues with an intelligent Thread Manager that presents two logical processors to the operating system. Intel calls this *hyperthreading*.

Windows 2000 does not know about hyperthreading and assumes that a machine with four hyperthreaded CPUs actually has eight processors. If you install Windows 2000 Standard Edition on a four-way machine, the operating system sees only the four physical processors, not the additional four logical processors.

Windows Server 2003 understands hyperthreading and gives you the logical processors for free.

### Linked Value Replication

In Windows 2000 Active Directory, when you change the membership of a group, the entire membership list gets replicated to the other domain controllers. This has two ramifications: It increases replication traffic, and it increases the likelihood of a collision caused by two administrators making a change to the same group during the same replication interval.

Windows Server 2003 Active Directory resolves this problem by replicating individual members of a group, something called "Linked Value Replication." Every domain in the forest, along with the forest itself, must be at full Windows Server 2003 functional level to get LVR replication.

## Exchange 2003 Features Requiring Exchange Native Mode

A couple of Exchange 2003 features cannot be implemented as long as you have legacy Exchange 5.x servers in your organization. This is called Exchange Mixed mode. After you decommission the legacy servers and shift to Exchange Native mode, you get the following features:

### 8BITMIME

When communicating with each other, Exchange 2003 servers in a Native mode organization use a full 8 bits when transferring characters in MIME messages using SMTP. Exchange 2000 uses 7-bit characters to assure full compatibility with Internet servers.

Adding the 8th bit to each character increases the data transfer rate over 10 percent, a significant improvement. If you're upgrading from Exchange 2000 while in Exchange Native mode, you should upgrade your bridgehead servers first so that the Exchange 2003 servers use 8BITMIME when communicating with each other.

### Zombie Removal

If you upgrade an Exchange 5.5 organization to Exchange 2003, you might run into problems with users who can't access public folders or delegated mailboxes. These problems generally stem from the presence of invalid recipients on the MAPI access list.

For example, a MAPI access list might specify that user Donald-Duck has Author access, but a user called DonaldDuck does not exist in Active Directory. Such an invalid recipient is called a *zombie*. Zombies can be created in a variety of ways. Exchange 2003, running in Native mode, automatically removes zombies if it finds them.

## Looking Forward

Completing this first chapter probably turned out to be more work that you expected, but the final result puts you in a good position to proceed. You have an Exchange 2003 server in a Windows Server 2003 domain, and you've verified that the server can receive and send e-mail to its own recipients and to Internet recipients.

In the next chapter, you'll get a good understanding of how e-mail clients communicate with an Exchange server. You'll use this information to help you design your production deployment and to troubleshoot any problems that might crop up along the way.

# CHAPTER 2

# Understanding and Using Messaging Protocols

The primary job of a messaging system consists of reliably routing e-mail between senders and recipients; then storing those e-mails for later retrieval. Oh sure, Microsoft includes other features such as calendaring, collaboration tools, task lists and so forth, but those services take second chair to the bread-and-butter mission of moving the mail.

Figure 2.1 shows a typical e-mail transaction. A user sits down at an e-mail client application and composes a message such as, "Hey, dude, whassssuuuuppp????" The user specifies the name of a recipient and presses the Send button. The e-mail client application delivers the completed message to the user's Exchange server. The server reads the recipient's address, determines the recipient's e-mail server, and sends the message to that server, which stores the message until the recipient downloads a copy of the message to read it. (The example does not include any antivirus or antispam filtering that would be included ordinarily in a production e-mail system.)

All across this planet (and possibly a few others), millions and millions and millions of transactions just like this occur every day. Compose, send, route, store, and read: Each of these operations requires that the e-mail client and its messaging server, or two messaging servers communicating with each other, obey a set of rules called a *protocol*. If you understand those protocols, you understand why and how Exchange works. Based on this understanding, you can design your messaging infrastructure to move the mail rapidly, reliably, and responsibly; then declare your tenure as e-mail administrator to be a success.

This chapter covers the protocols used by Internet clients to read and send e-mail, the protocols used by Outlook to read and send mail, and the protocols used by alternative clients such as Outlook Web Access. You'll see how these clients authenticate, how they formulate message requests, and how they interact with users.

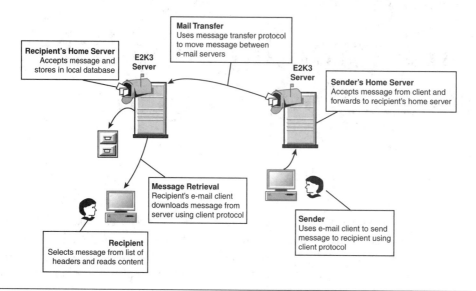

**Figure 2.1**    Simple mail transfer transaction involving Exchange servers and generic clients.

Outlook Web Access, an HTTP-based client, is covered in detail in Chapter 9, "Outlook Web Access."

# Client Protocol Overview

The Internet has been completely integrated into modern life, and e-mail has changed people's lives more than any other Internet technology. People in virtually every industry and profession rate e-mail as one of their most essential work tools, right up there with telephones and morning coffee.

Exchange supports three primary client protocols for retrieving e-mail. Two of these protocols use standards developed by the Internet community, and the other uses a proprietary protocol developed by Microsoft.

## Internet Standard E-mail Client Protocols

Internet clients use one of two protocols to retrieve messages from messaging servers like Exchange:

- **Post Office Protocol Version 3 (POP3)**, documented in RFC 1939, "Post Office Protocol–Version 3," and updated by RFC 1957, "Some Observations on Implementations of the Post Office Protocol (POP3)," and RFC 2449, "POP3 Extension Mechanism."
- **Internet Message Access Protocol Version 4 (IMAP4)**, documented in RFC 2060, "Internet Message Access Protocol–Version 4 rev1," and updated by a variety of RFCs describing nuances of namespace mapping, authentication, and security extensions.

The two protocols use entirely different methods for retrieving the list of queued messages from the server and downloading messages selected by the user.

Briefly here's how they work. A POP3 client accesses a user's inbox and downloads all the messages it finds, including their attachments. As it downloads each message, it removes the copy at the server unless the application has been configured to retain a central copy. An IMAP4 client, on the other hand, downloads just the message headers from the server. It then waits for the user to select a message before downloading a copy. The original messages stay at the server until the user marks them for deletion and purges them.

There are other differences between the protocols, as well. Table 2.1 shows a quick feature comparison. For more detail, see www.imap.org/ papers/imap.vs.pop.brief.html.

**Table 2.1**   Feature comparison between POP3 and IMAP4

| POP3 | IMAP4 |
|---|---|
| Client copies messages to local message store and deletes copy on server, unless specifically configured to do otherwise. | Client copies message headers from server and retrieves copy of message only when requested by user. |
| Local message copy handled by e-mail client. Deleted messages could be gone permanently. | Server retains original message. Deleted messages merely flagged for deletion and not permanently removed until purged by user. |
| If user runs client application on several machines, each machine has separate message repository. | Messages remain centralized on e-mail server. |
| Server has one inbox for each user. | Users can have multiple mail folders with a hierarchical arrangement. |
| No provision for accessing shared (public) folders. | Able to access shared (public) folders that comply with IMAP4 requirements. |
| No status information about queued inbox messages available to client. Client simply downloads any messages in the inbox. | Server-based messages have flags such as "Sent," "Opened," "Marked for Deletion," and even user-defined flags. |
| Attachments are downloaded with messages. | Attachments can be selectively downloaded. |

As you can see, POP3 favors the server operator, who needs to set aside only sufficient storage capacity to queue messages prior to delivery. IMAP4 favors users, who can access their messages and shared (public) folders from any location because a copy remains at the server.

Outlook users can choose to store inbound POP3 mail in their Exchange inbox rather than a local personal storage (pst) file. This keeps the messages available from multiple locations. POP3 connectors are available that automatically download messages from POP3 servers into the recipient's Exchange account. An example is the connector from MAPI Lab, www.mapilab.com/exchange/pop3_connector. Small Business Server also includes a POP3 connector.

## Messaging API (MAPI) Clients

An Application Programming Interface, or API, is a set of functions exposed by a program that can be used when coding other programs. The Exchange Information Store service exposes an API called the Messaging API, or MAPI. E-mail clients such as Outlook use MAPI functions to read and write to a user's mailbox.

Ordinarily, you'll configure Outlook to use MAPI as its client protocol when connecting with an Exchange server. Like its Internet cousins, the MAPI protocol includes commands for retrieving messages, viewing messages, annotating messages, sending messages, and so on. It also has specialized commands for accessing calendars, notes, tasks, and other proprietary items in Exchange.

The Exchange Software Developers Kit (SDK) contains the documentation for MAPI. You can download the Exchange SDK from Microsoft's download center, www.microsoft.com/downloads. Search for Exchange and SDK.

Very few third-party e-mail client applications use MAPI, and those that do support only a rudimentary form of the protocol. Eudora has a MAPI option. So does the Lotus Notes e-mail client. The most significant MAPI client, other than Outlook, is Ximian Evolution, a Linux application that mimics many Outlook features and has a MAPI connector to improve the user experience. Novell owns Ximian. Visit www.ximian.com for more information.

## Network News Transfer Protocol (NNTP)

I thought I'd sneak in this final protocol. NNTP permits users to interact directly with content on an Exchange server, so it fits the spirit of the definition for an e-mail client protocol. Although you cannot, strictly speaking, use it to send e-mails between two recipients (unless they don't mind the public reading their messages).

NNTP is an Internet standard protocol documented in RFC 977, "Network News Transfer Protocol, A Proposed Standard for the Stream-Based Transmission of News."

An NNTP client allows a user to post information into forum called a *newsgroup*. Exchange has a similar feature called *public folders*, which it exposes to NNTP clients as well as to MAPI and IMAP4 clients.

NNTP also defines how servers can stream newsfeeds to and from each other. Exchange servers can act as bidirectional newsfeeds.

Outlook does not support NNTP, but Outlook Express does. Popular third-party NNTP clients for Windows include NewsPro from Usenetopia (www.usenetopia.com) and Forte Agent (www.forteinc.com/agent/index.php).

A company called ghytred has released a beta of an NNTP add-on for Outlook called NewsLook. This application requires version 1.1 of the .NET Framework and Collaboration Data Objects (CDO) installed at the client machine. It features cross-posting checks and on-line searches using Google groups. Take a look at www.ghytred.com/NewsLook/screenshots.html.

## Message Formats

Long ago, researchers for the Advanced Research Project Agency (ARPA) wanted an easy way to send electronic notes to each other. The legendary Jon Postel defined a protocol for moving electronic messages across the Internet and documented the protocol in RFC 821, "Simple Mail Transfer Protocol." The SMTP standard has since been updated by RFC 2821.

For remembrances of Jon Postel, visit www.isoc.org/postel/condolences.shtml. For a lively and informative narrative on the history of e-mail, visit livinginternet.com/e/ei.htm.

During this same period, Dave Crocker, John Vittal, Kenneth Pogran, and D. Austin Henderson developed a format for e-mail messages that Dave Crocker later revised and documented in RFC 822, "Standard for the Format of ARPA Internet Text Messages." The Internet text message standard has been updated by RFC 2822. I'll refer to messages with formats that conform to the current standard as *RFC 2822 messages*.

It's no surprise that the general form and format of Internet messages in RFC 2822, and the way they get delivered as defined by RFC 2821, mimic the way paper mail gets written and delivered. After all, human beings have been sending written thoughts to each other via postal delivery for a very long time. Practically as soon as we learn to write, we learn how to format a piece of written mail. Why change the paradigm?

Figure 2.2 shows an example of paper business correspondence. The one-page message has a body that contains some information, and a header that specifies the name and address of the sender and the recipient. The correspondence has a signature that indicates the end of the message body.

The message goes into an envelope that also shows the sender and recipient. The envelope gets sealed and handed to an authorized agent for transport to the recipient's address where the recipient can retrieve it.

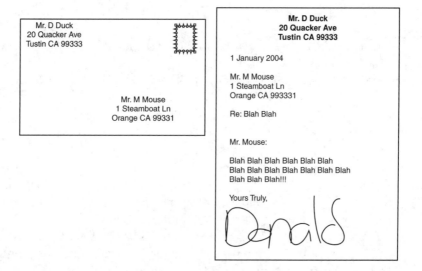

**Figure 2.2** Example paper message showing similarities between postal mail and e-mail.

## RFC 2822 Message Format

The format and structure of a basic Internet e-mail message, as defined in RFC 2822, looks like this:

```
From: Donald@duck.com
To: mickey@mouse.com
Subject: Blah blah

Blah blah blah blah blah blah blah
```

An Exchange server can deliver a message in this format without any additional information and without any intervention by a client. Test this yourself with your newly installed Exchange server:

1. Use Notepad to create a text file with contents similar to the listing except replace the **To:** entry with your own public e-mail address.
2. Save the file as **test.txt** in the following folder: **\Exchsrvr\Mailroot\VS 1\Pickup**.
3. In less than a second, you'll see the file disappear from the Pickup folder.
4. Check your public e-mail mailbox, and you'll see a new message appear.

The Simple Mail Transport Protocol (SMTP) service on the Exchange server does the grunt work of converting the RFC 2822 message into a format suitable for Internet delivery; then sends it to the recipient identified by the To entry in the text file.

You can see what SMTP does to the address information in an RFC 2822 message by viewing the raw header content in Outlook. Highlight the message in the Inbox and select **Options** from the flyout menu. This opens a Message Options window. The Internet Headers field at the bottom of the window shows addressing information added by SMTP servers that handled the message:

```
Return-Path: <Donald@duck.com>
Received: from xp-pro1 ([222.22.22.22])
        by w2k3-ex1.company.com with ESMTP id SAA05061
        for <mickey@mouse.com>; Fri, 18 Jul 2004 18:10:13 -0500
```

```
From: Donald@duck.com
Received: from mail pickup service by smtpsvr1 with Microsoft
➥SMTPSVC;
       Fri, 18 Jul 2004 19:10:08 -0400
To: mickey@mouse.com
Subject: Blah blah
Message-ID: <aqbC8wSA100000003@w2k3-ex1>
X-OriginalArrivalTime: 18 Jul 2004 23:10:08.0705 (UTC)
FILETIME=[BB6C1B10:01C34D81]
Date: 18 Jul 2004 19:10:08 -0400
```

You'll get details on how to interpret an SMTP header later in this chapter. For now, it's enough to know that the SMTP service on an Exchange server knows how to convert a simple address and a few lines of text into a format that it can transmit across town or around the planet.

This trick of dropping a simple RFC 2822 text file into the Pickup folder comes in handy for troubleshooting. You should practice creating a few files for various recipients and keep a couple of these files in your utility folder for use when mail messages don't seem to be moving correctly.

## Message Headers

You can use Outlook Express to send SMTP messages via an Exchange server. Figure 2.3 shows an outbound message just before you click the Send button. Note that you can format the recipient addresses to include a full name in addition to the standard e-mail format.

In addition to specifying one or more primary recipients, you can specify Carbon Copy (Cc) recipients and Blind Carbon Copy (BCc) recipients. The primary and carbon copy recipients can see names of the primary recipient but not the names of the bcc recipients. Hence, the word "blind" in blind carbon copy.

**Figure 2.3**    Sample e-mail showing the various recipient options.

Compose a message similar to that in the figure using Outlook Express and save the message without sending it. Outlook Express saves a file with an EML (e-mail) extension. If you view the content directly using Notepad, you'll see content resembling the following listing:

```
From: "Donald Duck" <donald@duck.com>
To: "Mickey Mouse" <mickey@mouse.com>
Cc: "Scrooge McDuck" <scroogemc@duck.com>
Bcc: "Hughie Duck" <hughie@duck.com>,
     "Dewey Duck" <dewey@duck.com>,
     "Louis Duck" <louis@duck.com>
Subject: My Heirs
Date: Wed, 17 Jul 2004 08:14:22 -0700
MIME-Version: 1.0
Content-Type: text/plain;
     charset="iso-8859-1"
Content-Transfer-Encoding: 7bit
X-Priority: 3
X-MSMail-Priority: Normal
X-Unsent: 1
X-MimeOLE: Produced By Microsoft MimeOLE V6.00.3790.0

blah blah
```

The additional header lines, starting with MIME-Version, comprise a set of Multipart Internet Mail Extensions (MIME) headers. You'll see more about MIME headers in upcoming sections.

RFC 2822 defines a standard set of headers for Internet mail messages. Table 2.2 lists the most commonly used headers and what they do. (The list does not include X-Headers, which are often present in messages but are not included in the RFC 2822 standard.) You can include any of the headers listed in Table 2.2 in the SMTP test message sample shown.

**Table 2.2** Commonly used RFC 2822 headers and their functions

| Header | Function |
| --- | --- |
| From | Sender's e-mail address |
| To | Recipient's e-mail address |
| Subject | Subject line |
| Sender | Sender's e-mail address |
| Reply-To | E-mail address for replies |
| Received | Trace information listing the SMTP server that handled the message |
| Return-Path | Trace information listing the sender's address |
| Date | Timestamp applied by SMTP service |
| Return-Receipt-To | When this option is selected, the field typically gets populated with sender's e-mail address |
| Cc | Carbon-copy: e-mail addresses of additional recipients |
| Bcc | Blind carbon-copy: e-mail address of hidden recipients |
| Message-ID | Unique number assigned to the message |

## Blind Carbon Copy Handling

When Outlook Express delivers an RFC 2822 message to the SMTP service on the Exchange server, SMTP converts the message to a format suitable for Internet delivery. In doing so, it removes the Bcc recipients from the headers, as shown here:

```
Received: from mail pickup service by smtpsvrl with Microsoft SMTPSVC;
        Thu, 17 Jul 2004 08:14:28 -0400
From: "Donald Duck" <donald@duck.com>
To: "Mickey Mouse" <mickey@mouse.com>
Cc: "Scrooge McDuck" <scroogemc@duck.com>
Subject: My heirs
Sender: Donald T. Duck
Message-ID: <WCG-PRO13bJeurIBwqv00000001@wcg-pro1>
Date: 17 Jul 2004 08:14:28 -0400

blah blah blah blah
blah blah blah blah
blah blah blah blah
```

Removing Bcc recipients protects their identities. In a Windows SMTP server, such as Exchange, the SMTP service keeps track of who gets a Bcc copy by making a list of addresses in a special named data stream inside the NTFS file that holds the outbound message.

When SMTP sends a copy of the message to a Bcc recipient, instead of putting the Bcc recipient's name and e-mail address in the To field of the header, it puts the name and e-mail address of the primary recipient. If all recipients are Bcc, then SMTP leaves the To field blank.

So, in the previous example, Mickey would see no mention of the Bcc copies sent to Donald's nephews. When Dewey gets the message, the To field shows Mickey Mouse <mickey@mouse.com> as the recipient rather than Dewey Duck <dewey@duck.com>.

## Additional Header Options

If you use Outlook to send a message to an Internet client, you can click the Options button in the new message window to open a Message Options window where you can select additional operations that affect message headers. Figure 2.4 shows an example.

The additional options that affect message headers include

- **Request a Read Receipt for This Message** adds a Return-Receipt-To header field. The recipient e-mail client uses the e-mail address in this field to send a message when the recipient opens the message. Outlook provides an option for the recipient to reject the return receipt.
- **Request A Delivery Receipt for This Message** adds a Disposition-Notification-To header field. If the final destination server supports this header type, it notifies the sender when the

message arrives. RFC 2298, "An Extensible Message Format for Message Disposition Notifications," defines the operation of the Disposition-Notification-To header.

■ **Have Replies Sent To** adds a Reply-To field. This could be a different e-mail address than the sender's address.

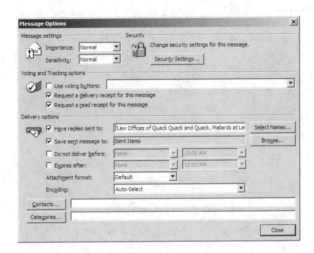

**Figure 2.4** Additional message options in Outlook for delivery receipts, read receipts, and an alternative return address.

The following listing shows how the SMTP service would create headers based on those optional entries:

```
Received: from mail pickup service by smtpsvr1 with Microsoft SMTPSVC;
        Wed, 16 Jul 2004 07:34:15 -0400
Return-Receipt-To: "Donald Duck" <Donald@duck.com>
Reply-To: "Law Offices of Quack Quack and Quack, Mallards at Law"
<client203@quackpartners.com>
From: "Donald Duck" <Donald@duck.com>
To: "Mickey Mouse" <mickey@mouse.com>
Disposition-Notification-To: "Donald Duck" <donald@duck.com>
Return-Path: donald@duck.com
```

When this message arrives at Mickey's e-mail server, the server sends a delivery receipt message to Donald, not the address in the **Reply-To** field.

When Mickey opens the message, the e-mail client sends a read receipt to Donald. Outlook and Outlook Express present an option to decline sending a read receipt.

When Mickey presses **Ctrl+R** to reply to the message, Outlook and Outlook Express populate the **To** field with the contents of the **Reply-To** field, in this case the e-mail address defined for the QuackPartners law firm.

### Key Points to Remember about Message Headers

If you're the kind of person who skips past a lot of tables and listings on a page, then here's a quick list of the important things to keep in mind about message headers. You'll need to know this information to see how the message-routing features work in Exchange 2003:

- Simple Internet messages use a format defined by RFC 2822 (obsoletes RFC 822).
- The Microsoft SMTP service can parse an RFC 2822–formatted text file to create a file suitable for delivery to the designated recipients.
- A message contains a set of headers used to identify the sender and the message's primary recipients, carbon copy (Cc) recipients, and blind carbon copy (BCc) recipients.
- Blind carbon copy recipients see the primary recipient's address in the **To** field rather than their own address. Other recipients do not see the BCc recipients.
- Outlook has additional delivery options for specifying delivery receipts, read receipts, and reply-to addresses.

# Formatted Text in Messages

RFC 2822 requires the body of an e-mail message to contain human readable, unformatted ASCII text. But as you probably know, you can put a lot of formatting and effects into an Outlook or Outlook Express message to liven up the text. For example, something like this:

*"Congratulations*!! You're getting married. **Wow, like AWESOME**."

A lively and often vociferous debate exists about whether to use anything other than simple ASCII text in e-mail, especially when sending messages to Internet users. The opponents to formatted text point out that

- Many popular e-mail programs do not understand formatted messages.
- Formatted messages add bulk to e-mail, especially when you consider that Outlook and Outlook Express send both a formatted and a plain text version of the message.
- Formatting consumes resources at the client for rendering. Formatting also encourages users to embed graphics, furthering the load on the e-mail servers.
- Even more important, from a security perspective, HTML formatted messages can hide embedded nasties like links back to spammer Web sites (beacons) and JavaScript trace routines and viruses, and so forth.

If you agree with these points and you want to restrict your users from sending formatting text, see the topic titled "Disabling Text Formatting" later in this chapter.

## HTML Formatting

Figure 2.5 shows a new message that uses HTML formatting. The actual content, based on the characters you see in the body, comprises only a few bytes of information.

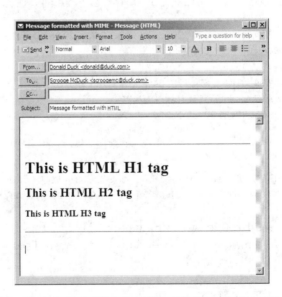

**Figure 2.5** Example e-mail that contains HTML-formatted text.

If you create a file similar to that in the figure and save it as an EML file, you can open the file in Notepad to view the contents directly. The following listing shows the body of the file:

```
Content-Type: text/html;
    charset="us-ascii"
Content-Transfer-Encoding: quoted-printable

<!DOCTYPE HTML PUBLIC "-//W3C//DTD HTML 4.0 Transitional//EN">
<HTML><HEAD>
<META HTTP-EQUIV=3D"Content-Type" CONTENT=3D"text/html; =
charset=3Dus-ascii">
<TITLE>Message</TITLE>

<META content=3D"MSHTML 6.00.2800.1170" name=3DGENERATOR></HEAD>
<BODY>
<DIV><SPAN class=3D179015123-17072003><FONT face=3DArial=20
size=3D2></FONT></SPAN> </DIV>
<DIV><SPAN class=3D179015123-17072003><FONT face=3DArial =
size=3D2> </DIV>
<DIV>
<HR>
</DIV></FONT>
<H1></SPAN><SPAN class=3D179015123-17072003>This is HTML H1 =
tag</SPAN></H1>
<H2><SPAN class=3D179015123-17072003>This is HTML H2 =
tag</SPAN></H2><SPAN=20
class=3D179015123-17072003>
<H3><SPAN class=3D179015123-17072003>This is HTML H3 =
tag</SPAN></H3></SPAN><SPAN=20
class=3D179015123-17072003>
<H2>
<HR>
</H2>
<DIV><SPAN class=3D179015123-17072003><FONT face=3DArial=20
size=3D2></FONT></SPAN> </DIV></SPAN></BODY></HTML>
```

Even if you know nothing about HTML tags, you can see that the formatted message uses over 850 characters and spaces to deliver a message with this basic content:

```
This is HTML H1 tag
This is HTML H2 tag
This is HTML H3 tag
```

It might seem a bit insincere to complain about a few extra characters in a message body when the sender might have attached a 2MB
Excel spreadsheet, but the cumulative effect of all that HTML formatting in thousands and thousands of messages can add significantly to
your storage requirements.

That said, after users see pretty text in e-mail messages, you aren't
likely to be able to take it away from them. I'd rather snatch a bone from
the mouth of a pit bull than try to take away text formatting from a CEO
who just loves to use special fonts in the "State of the Company" e-mail.

## Rich Text Formatting

Prior to the widespread use of HTML, Microsoft provided a proprietary
formatting mechanism called Rich Text Format (RTF). An RTF message consists of a set of headers, the plain text body, and an attachment
called Winmail.dat. The Winmail.dat file contains the text formatting
and any pictures or binary content converted into raw text using a technique called Base64 encoding. The following listing shows the content of
a message that has RTF content. The bolded lines show the handling
instructions for the Winmail.dat file.

```
Received: from smtpsvr1 ([222.22.22.222]) by xp-pro1 with Microsoft
➥SMTPSVC(6.0.2600.1106);
        Wed, 16 Jul 2004 07:29:21 -0400
From: "Mickey Mouse" <mickey@mouse.com>
To: <bozo@clown.com>
Subject: Your ears are bigger than mine
Date: Wed, 16 Jul 2004 07:29:21 -0400
Message-ID: <!~!UAAAAkFzJz6cHaEi07L4zYwEVUgEAAAAA@cox.net>
MIME-Version: 1.0
Content-Type: application/ms-tnef;
      name="winmail.dat"
Content-Transfer-Encoding: base64
Content-Disposition: attachment;
      filename="winmail.dat"
X-Priority: 3 (Normal)
X-MSMail-Priority: Normal
X-Mailer: Microsoft Outlook, Build 10.0.4024
Importance: Normal
X-MimeOLE: Produced By Microsoft MimeOLE V6.00.2800.1165
X-MS-TNEF-Correlator: 0000000032BBC601BD69034DA101B759613194E14446A500
```

```
X-OriginalArrivalTime: 16 Jul 2003 11:29:21.0237 (UTC)
FILETIME=[805A2850:01C34B8D]
```

```
IhULAQaQCAAEAAAAAAABAAQeQBgAIAAAA5AQAAAAAAADoAAEIgAcAGAAAAElQTS5NaWNy
ZnQgTWFpbC50b3RlADEIABAACAAAAgACAAEGgAMADgAAANMHBwAQAAcAGgAAAMAFQEB
AIQEAAAnAAAACwACAAEAAACMAAAAAAAMAJgAAAAACwApAAAAAAADAC4AAAAAAIBMQAB
... (additional 20 lines of Base64 encoding)
```

> Microsoft uses the phrase *Transport Neutral Encapsulation Format*, or TNEF, to describe the technique of converting a rich text message body into a Base64-encoded Winmail.dat attachment. A non-Outlook e-mail client might not know how to handle TNEF messages, so an RTF message usually contains a plain-text version in the message body.
>
> If you think HTML formatting yields tubby messages, imagine what RTF does. Fortunately, newer Outlook clients do not use RTF unless configured to do so.

> To get help with unpacking MS-TNEF messages in non-Microsoft clients, take a look at the TNEF project at SourceForge, `sourceforge.net/projects/tnef`.

# Disabling Text Formatting

You have the choice as an administrator to configure your clients' mail to send plain text messages. You can also choose to permit formatted text within your organization but configure the clients to convert messages to plain text when sent to Internet clients.

Rather than configuring individual clients, you can also configure your Exchange servers to convert messages to plain text when sent to Internet clients. This section shows you how to use all three methods.

## Configuring Outlook to Send Plain Text Messages

Configure Outlook to send plain text messages rather than HTML messages as follows:

1. From the main Outlook menu, select **Tools | Options**.
2. Select the **Mail Format** tab.
3. Change the **Compose in This Message Format** option from **HTML** to **Plain Text**, shown in Figure 2.6.

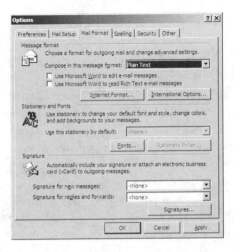

**Figure 2.6**   Outlook Options window showing Mail Format options for sending plain text messages.

**4.** Click OK to save the change.

## Configure Outlook to Convert Internet Messages

If you'd rather convert RTF messages to plain text when sent to recipients outside your organization, click the **Internet Format** button in the **Mail Format** tab in the Options window. This opens an Internet Format window, shown in Figure 2.7.

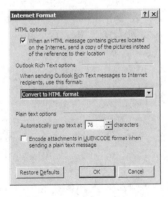

**Figure 2.7**   Outlook option to send plain text messages only to Internet recipients.

The Internet Format window has three sections:

- **HTML options.** Select this option to send a copy of an embedded picture rather than a reference. This prevents the recipient from getting a hyperlink to a file on one of your internal servers.
- **Outlook Rich Text options.** Select the **Convert to Plain Text Format** option. This maintains maximum compatibility when communicating with users outside your organization.
- **Plain Text options.** Leave the automatic wrapping setting at 76 characters. This standard format maintains compatibility with text-based e-mail clients such as PINE. For maximum compatibility, select the option to **Encode Attachments in UUENCODE** to render binary files into text.

## Manage Plain Text Settings with Group Policies

In an Active Directory domain with modern Outlook clients, you can avoid making configuration changes individually at each desktop by using Group Policies. The Office Resource Kit has Administrative (ADM) template files that you can load into a Group Policy Object (GPO) using the Group Policy Editor (GP Editor.) You must load the Outlook ADM file manually into the GPO before you can use the policy settings it contains. Load the ADM file as follows:

1. Load the Office Resource Kit on the machine you use to manage group policies. As an alternative, copy the Office ADM files to the **%windir%\Inf** folder on the machine where you manage group policies.
2. Open the GP Editor, right-click the **Administrative Templates** icon under **User Settings**, and select **Add/Remove Templates** from the flyout menu.
3. In the Add/Remove Templates window, click **Add**.
4. In the Policy Templates browse window, open the **Outlk##.adm** file where **##** represents the Outlook version. Figure 2.8 shows the list of available ADM files.
5. Close the Add/Remove Templates window to save the settings.
6. Drill down to the Microsoft Outlook folder and view the settings under the folder.

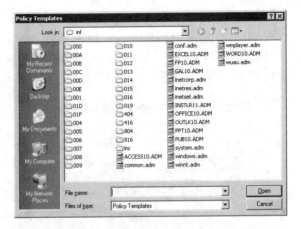

**Figure 2.8** Windows INF folder showing ADM files from Office Resource Kit.

7. To change the format of all messages to plain text, drill down to **Tools | Options | Mail** Format and change the **Message Format/Editor** setting to **Enabled | Plain Text/Outlook**. You should also deselect the **Use Microsoft Word to Read Rich Text E-Mail Messages** to avoid inadvertently launching a macro virus. See Figure 2.9 for an example.

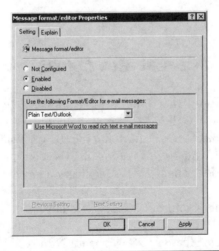

**Figure 2.9** Group Policy Editor with policy loaded to tell Outlook to use plain text formatting.

8. To change the format of Internet messages to plain text, select **Tools | Options | Mail Format | Internet Format | Outlook Rich Text Options**. Change the setting to **Enabled | Convert to Plain Text Format**. Figure 2.10 shows an example.

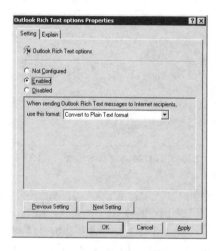

**Figure 2.10**    Group policy setting to force Internet e-mail to plain text in Outlook clients.

# MIME (Multipart Internet Message Extensions)

Rather than send the rather simple message body format defined in RFC 2822, nearly all modern e-mail clients use Multipurpose Internet Mail Extensions (MIME) as defined in RFCs 2045-2049. (You can find a full list of message-related RFCs at `asg.web.cmu.edu/rfc/smtplist.html`.) The MIME specification has five parts:

- Format of Internet Message Bodies
- Media Types
- Message Header Extensions for Non-ASCII Text
- Registration Procedures
- Conformance Criteria and Examples

MIME permits divvying the body of a message into separate sections, each of which has content that requires different handling. For example, one section might contain the plain text of the message while another section contains the HTML formatted text of the message while still another section contains an attachment encoded in Base64. MIME messages can also contain routing instructions and alternate message versions and other useful information.

Consider, for example, a short message generated using Eudora, as shown in Figure 2.11.

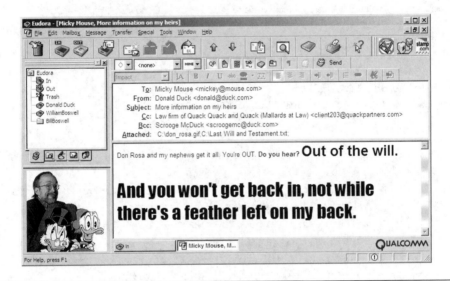

**Figure 2.11**   Sample Eudora message containing HTML formatted text.

The message consists of a formatted body and two attachments:

- A GIF image of Don Rosa, the legendary Donald Duck illustrator (see duckman.pettho.com/drinfo/drwork.html)
- A text document containing Donald's last will and testament

Let's see how this message looks when examined as raw MIME-formatted text.

## MIME Headers

The following listing shows the MIME headers in the e-mail message. As you can see, MIME headers look quite a bit like RFC 2822 headers.

```
Received: from wcg-pro1.duck.com ([222.22.22.222]) by w2k3-ex1 with
➥Microsoft SMTPSVC(6.0.2600.1106);
        Fri, 18 Jul 2004 23:03:18 -0400
Message-Id: <5.2.1.1.0.20030718225950.00b7ade8@mail.duck.com>
X-Sender: donald@mail.duck.com
X-Mailer: QUALCOMM Windows Eudora Version 5.2.1
Date: Fri, 18 Jul 2004 23:03:16 -0400
To: Micky Mouse <mickey@mouse.com>
From: Donald Duck <donald@duck.com>
Subject: More information on my heirs
Cc: Law firm of Quack Quack and Quack (Mallards at Law)
<client203@quackpartners.com>
```
**Mime-Version: 1.0**
**Content-Type: multipart/mixed;**
       **boundary="=====================_23966552==_"**
```
Return-Path: donald@duck.com
X-OriginalArrivalTime: 19 Jul 2003 03:03:18.0791 (UTC)
➥FILETIME=[4E29D170:01C34DA2]
```

The three lines in bold warrant special attention.

- **MIME-Version** identifies this as a MIME message. The current MIME standard is version 1.0, a testament to its fortitude.
- **Content-Type** defines the message type. The MIME standard defines a broad range of content types for use in a variety of circumstances. In this case, the **multipart/mixed** content type tells the e-mail client to expect just about anything.
- **Boundary** defines a unique number used to delimit sections of the message. The string can be any unique set of characters and numbers.

## MIME Body - First Section

The first section of the body of the message, and every new section after it, starts with the Boundary ID specified in the header prefixed by two dashes. The dashes indicate a section break.

```
--=====================_23966552==_
```

The remainder of the first section contains the plain text of the message. Many e-mail applications include the plain text for e-mail clients that don't understand formatted text.

```
Content-Type: text/plain; charset="us-ascii"; format=flowed
```

```
Don Rosa and my nephews get it all. You're OUT. Do you hear? Out
➥of the will.
```

```
And you won't get back in, not while there's a feather left on
➥my back.
```

The `Content-Type` entry of `text/plain; charset="us-ascii"` tells the recipient e-mail application to process this section as standard text. The `Format=Flowed` entry tells the recipient to ignore white space between lines.

## MIME Body-Second Section

The second and final section of the message body contains the same text as the plain-text section but with the addition of HTML formatting. Notice that the section starts with a Boundary ID prefixed by two dashes.

```
—=====================_23966552==_
Content-Type: text/html; charset="us-ascii"
```

```
<html>
<body>
Don Rosa and my nephews get it all. You're OUT. <b>Do you hear?
<font size=6>Out of the will. <br><br>
</b></font><font face="Impact" size=7>And you won't get back in,
➥not while there's a feather left on my back. </font></body>
</html>
```

The `Content-Type` entry notifies the recipient's e-mail client to use HTML rendering, if it supports that feature. If an e-mail application does not support a particular MIME content type, it's up to the application developer to decide what the application does. Most commonly, the application simply ignores that section of the message.

## MIME Attachments

By incorporating attachments into the same overall e-mail message as the body, MIME permits SMTP to send the entire contents of a message with a single command, eliminating the possibility that an attachment might accidentally get clipped onto some other message.

In the example message, the first of the two attachments contains a binary image, Don Rosa's picture. SMTP requires that all messages contain plain text. Binary information containing control codes can spoil transmission.

Internet e-mail clients encode binary content using Base64, which results in long text strings that can be handled by SMTP. The following listing shows a brief sample of a Base64-encoded attachment. The actual attachment consumes 64K of space in the message.

```
—=====================_23966552==_
Content-Type: image/gif; name="don_rosa.gif";
 x-mac-type="47494666"; x-mac-creator="4A565752"
Content-Transfer-Encoding: base64
Content-Disposition: attachment; filename="don_rosa.gif"

lhDgFFAfcLAPnIMaGWYa6GSitKRiNBMQExJAYmCyFJESEjFhAYGBMjE/////yspCypEKyIi
AYEAEDERAGEQQTE/fIKBgwIEotDGkuBolmKWlMKI1RJWxIDS0uKZyNF0pJK0psaRAQEKZN
32M4yRiyY1Mp9iE6uELwQjIsZwLY2KbRgoIAgIABYVExIUAwgQEMyHSxAgGCgQBFAyJwIS
```

The second attachment, a text document, does not require special encoding, so Eudora specifies a plain text content type. The numbers that start with an equal sign (=) represent special characters taken from the ISO 8859 character set. See **www.utoronto.ca/webdocs/HTMLdocs/NewHTML/iso_table.html** for a full set of Latin characters and their hex equivalents, or use the Charmap utility in Windows (Start | Run | Charmap).

```
—=====================_23966552==_
Content-Type: text/plain; charset="iso-8859-1"
Content-Transfer-Encoding: quoted-printable
Content-Disposition: attachment; filename="Last Will and
Testament.txt"

=EF=BB=BFLast Will and Testament of Donald Duck=20
My nephews get everything.=20
Don Rosa gets my stills and archives.=20
Mickey's OUT!!!
```

```
By my wing this 29th day of February
Donald Duck, Esq.=20
```

```
-===================_23966552==_-
```

The final entry signals the end of the message. It has a double-dash at the end of the boundary string.

### Key Points to Remember about MIME

The technique used by MIME to handle so many combinations of content types and attachment types is impressive in its simplicity. Define a beginning and ending boundary string; then stuff information into the message in a way that a client can interpret.

Here are the areas you should remember to help you do troubleshooting that involves MIME-based messages:

- MIME formatting divides messages into separate sections. Each section handles content in different ways.
- All sections of a MIME message get transmitted as a single DATA element in SMTP.
- Clients convert graphic attachments into Base64-encoded sections in a MIME message to facilitate transfer across the Internet.
- Outlook Express and Outlook (when used as an SMTP rather than a MAPI client) use MIME to format messages.

Now that we've seen how messages look on the inside, let's take a look at the types of e-mail clients that can send and retrieve messages with an Exchange server.

## MAPI Message Format

When Outlook clients communicate to Exchange servers, they do not format their messages using MIME. Outlook 2003 uses XML to format content. XML is an extension to the standard Hypertext Markup Language (HTML). It permits a developer to define tags that describe how to handle the body of a document.

Here is an example of a MAPI message stored in Exchange by an Outlook 2003 client:

```
<html xmlns:o="urn:schemas-microsoft-com:office:office"
xmlns:w="urn:schemas-microsoft-com:office:word"
xmlns="http://www.w3.org/TR/REC-html40">

<head>
<meta http-equiv=Content-Type content="text/html; charset=us-
➥ascii">
<meta name=Generator content="Microsoft Word 11 (filtered
➥medium)">
<style>

<!--
 /* Style Definitions */
 p.MsoNormal, li.MsoNormal, div.MsoNormal
     {margin:0in;
     margin-bottom:.0001pt;
     font-size:12.0pt;
     font-family:"Times New Roman";}
a:link, span.MsoHyperlink
     {color:blue;
     text-decoration:underline;}
a:visited, span.MsoHyperlinkFollowed
     {color:purple;
     text-decoration:underline;}
span.EmailStyle17
     {mso-style-type:personal-compose;
     font-family:Arial;
     color:windowtext;}
@page Section1
     {size:8.5in 11.0in;
     margin:1.0in 1.25in 1.0in 1.25in;}
div.Section1
     {page:Section1;}
-->
</style>
</head>
<body lang=EN-US link=blue vlink=purple>
<div class=Section1>
```

```
<p class=MsoNormal><font size=2 face=Arial><span style='font-
size:10.0pt;font-family:Arial'>
This is an example of formatted MAPI text as it appears in
➥the EDB database.
<o:p></o:p></span></font></p>

<p class=MsoNormal><font size=2 face=Arial><span style='font-
➥size:10.0pt;font-family:Arial'>
Notice that this format bears no resemblance to the MIME
➥format used by Internet standard clients. <o:p></o:p></span>
➥</font></p>

</div>
</body>
</html>
```

Notice that the message looks like an HTML message. That's because XML uses the same tag structure as HTML. The message header defines a schema where the elements used in the message body can be found.

The portion of the message that starts with `/* Style Definitions */` defines additional classes that can be used to format portions of the message. Notice that each line of text in the message starts with a class identification from the style definition. Essentially, each Outlook 2003 message includes a style sheet that tells Exchange how to render the message upon delivery to a client.

# Message Retrieval Overview

You're all done peering inside the content of message bodies and headers, at least for now. It's time to see how e-mail clients connect to an Exchange server and retrieve those artfully formatted messages. Here's an outline of the processes described in the next few topics.

- **Home server identification.** An e-mail client needs to know where to find the Exchange server that holds the user's mailbox. This requires configuring the client application with the server's name and making sure the client can resolve that name into an IP address. (Once again, DNS plays a vital role in your messaging infrastructure.)

- **Port selection.** The client selects a port to use when making a TCP connection to the Exchange server. The port number corresponds to the e-mail protocol used by the client: POP3, IMAP4, or MAPI.

- **Initial connection.** The client makes its initial connection to the port on the Exchange server. It receives a set of headers that it uses to begin the message transactions.

- **Authentication.** The client must provide credentials for the user so that the Exchange server can authenticate the user and select the proper mailbox for access by the user.

- **Message retrieval.** The client then uses a protocol to retrieve messages from the user's mailbox at the Exchange server.

## Enable POP3 and IMAP4 Services

A standard installation of Windows Server 2003 does not enable the POP3 or IMAP4 services. If Exchange Setup sees that the services are disabled, it installs the service extensions but does not enable the services. If you want an Exchange 2003 server running on Windows Server 2003 to respond to POP3 or IMAP4 requests, you must enable the services. This is also true when upgrading from Exchange 2000 to 2003.

You can use the Services console to enable and start the services, but I prefer using the command-line utility called SC. Here is the syntax for using SC to enable and start the POP3 service along with replies from the Service Control Manager (SCM):

```
C:\>sc config pop3svc start= auto
[SC] ChangeServiceConfig SUCCESS

C:\>sc start pop3svc

SERVICE_NAME: pop3svc
        TYPE               : 20   WIN32_SHARE_PROCESS
        STATE              : 2    START_PENDING
                                  (NOT_STOPPABLE, NOT_PAUSABLE,
IGNORES_SHUTDOWN))

        WIN32_EXIT_CODE    : 0   (0x0)
        SERVICE_EXIT_CODE  : 0   (0x0)
        CHECKPOINT         : 0x0
        WAIT_HINT          : 0x7d0
```

```
        PID                 : 1368
        FLAGS               :
```

Here is the syntax used to enable and start the IMAP4 service and the SCM
replies:

```
C:\>sc config imap4svc start= auto
[SC] ChangeServiceConfig SUCCESS

C:\>sc start imap4svc

SERVICE_NAME: imap4svc
        TYPE                : 20  WIN32_SHARE_PROCESS
        STATE               : 2   START_PENDING
                                  (NOT_STOPPABLE, NOT_PAUSABLE,
IGNORES_SHUTDOWN))

        WIN32_EXIT_CODE     : 0   (0x0)
        SERVICE_EXIT_CODE   : 0   (0x0)
        CHECKPOINT          : 0x0
        WAIT_HINT           : 0x7d0
        PID                 : 1368
        FLAGS               :
```

# Home Server Identification

An e-mail client such as Outlook, Outlook Express, or Eudora must
know the name of the user's home Exchange server before it can make a
connection to that server. This requires configuring the client application with the required information. The details of this configuration vary
with the client.

Figure 2.12 shows the server configuration when using Outlook as a
POP3 client. Access this window by right-clicking the Outlook icon on
the desktop and selecting Properties to open the Properties window.
Click **E-Mail Accounts**, select **View or Change Existing E-Mail
Accounts**, click **Next**, and then highlight the POP3 account and click
**Change**.

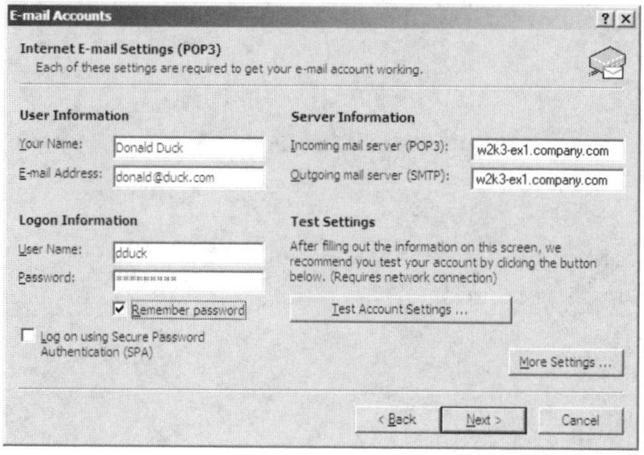

**Figure 2.12** Outlook e-mail settings specifying the home mailbox server for a POP3 client.

Outlook stores this configuration information, along with many other e-mail parameters, in a special place in the Registry called a *MAPI profile*. Each e-mail user on a machine gets a unique MAPI profile. Outlook stores its MAPI profiles in Registry entries under **HKCU | Software | Windows NT | CurrentVersion | Windows Messaging Subsystem | Profiles | Outlook**.

If you use Outlook as a MAPI client, the server configuration window changes. Figure 2.13 shows an example.

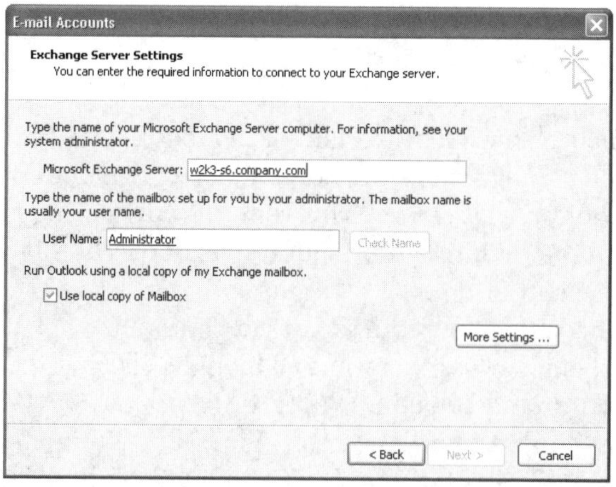

**Figure 2.13** Outlook e-mail settings specifying the home server for a MAPI client.

In the **Microsoft Exchange Server** field, you can enter the name of any Exchange server in the organization. The client retrieves the recipient's actual home server information from Exchange and updates the home server information in the MAPI profile. You can click **Check Now** to do the verification. Valid user and server names get underlined. Invalid entries prompt Outlook to open a new window where you can enter corrected values.

A small but significant difference exists in the server name format displayed by Outlook 2003 clients compared with previous versions of Outlook. For example, Figure 2.14 shows the Server Information window for Outlook 2000.

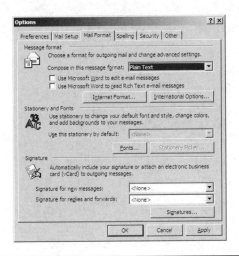

**Figure 2.14**    Outlook 2000 settings selecting the home server for a MAPI clientl with a flat name as the server name.

Notice that the earlier Outlook version displays the flat NetBIOS name of the Exchange server. Outlook 2003, on the other hand, uses Kerberos for authentication and therefore stores the Fully Qualified Domain Name (FQDN) of the Exchange server. This is part of Microsoft's ongoing effort to remove reliance on NetBIOS naming from its products.

## Protocols and Port Selection

Each e-mail client protocol uses a separate TCP port. This permits different services to listen for client connections without stepping on each other.

Exchange registers e-mail services like a hotel guest leaving instructions at the front desk. "If you get a FedEx for Bill Boswell, please call me immediately in room 110."

After a service registers a port number, it listens on that port for incoming connections. For example, Exchange listens for POP3 connections on TCP port 110.

### Well-Known Messaging Ports

The Internet Assigned Numbers Association (IANA) reserves port numbers between 1 and 1024 for well-known Internet services. IANA has set aside the following ports for Internet messaging:

- POP3-TCP port 110
- IMAP4-TCP port 143
- WebDAV (HTTP)-TCP port 80
- SMTP-TCP port 25

Each of these protocols has a version that runs over Secure Socket Layer (SSL). All but one of the e-mail protocols use a different port so the service can easily distinguish between the two connection types:

- POP3 over SSL-TCP port 995
- IMAP4 over SSL-TCP port 993 (was 585)
- HTTP over SSL-TCP port 443
- SMTP over SSL-TCP port 25

Note that SSL-enabled SMTP uses the same port as standard SMTP. The server must make the determination if an incoming request uses SSL. Some vendors use TCP port 465 for SSL-enabled SMTP based on a now-defunct IANA number registration.

For a partial list of services and their port numbers, refer to the Services file in `\Windows\System32\Drivers\etc`. Download a full list from the IANA Web site, `www.iana.org/assignments/port-numbers`.

## Viewing Active Ports

You can see a list of the active listens on a server using the command `netstat -ano`, where `-a` tells Netstat to list all listening ports, `-n` lists the bare port numbers instead of friendly names, and `-o` lists the Process ID (PID) of the listening service. (Only Windows Server 2003 and XP support the `-o` switch.) The following listing shows a few Netstat entries from a typical Exchange server where POP3 and IMAP4 have been enabled:

```
Active Connections

  Proto  Local Address    Foreign Address  State        PID
  TCP    0.0.0.0:25       0.0.0.0:0        LISTENING    3728
  TCP    0.0.0.0:80       0.0.0.0:0        LISTENING    5336
  TCP    0.0.0.0:110      0.0.0.0:0        LISTENING    3728
  TCP    0.0.0.0:135      0.0.0.0:0        LISTENING     704
  TCP    0.0.0.0:143      0.0.0.0:0        LISTENING    3728
  TCP    0.0.0.0:445      0.0.0.0:0        LISTENING       4
  TCP    0.0.0.0:593      0.0.0.0:0        LISTENING     704
  TCP    0.0.0.0:691      0.0.0.0:0        LISTENING    3728
  TCP    0.0.0.0:993      0.0.0.0:0        LISTENING    3728
  TCP    0.0.0.0:995      0.0.0.0:0        LISTENING    3728
```

To find the process name that corresponds to the PID entry in each line, use the **Tasklist** utility in Windows Server 2003 and XP or the Task utility in the Windows 2000 Resource Kit.

A handy third-party utility called TCPView from `www.sysinternals.com` lists the processes and the executable name and path in a GUI interface. Figure 2.15 shows an example that lists listens by the following Exchange services:

- **Emsmta.exe.** Exchange Message Transfer Agent
- **Mad.exe.** Exchange System Attendant
- **Store.exe.** Exchange Information Store
- **Inetinfo.exe.** Internet Information Service

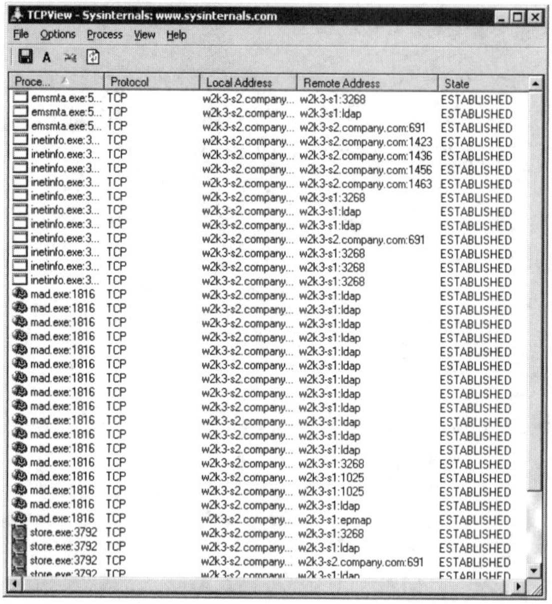

**Figure 2.15**   TCPView utility from SysInternals showing a list of services with active TCP port listens on an Exchange 2003 server.

## Remote Procedure Calls and Port Selection

When an application requires services from the Windows operating system, it often makes a *procedure call*. If the procedure call uses a service that runs on the same machine, it's a Local Procedure Call (LPC). In contrast, a Remote Procedure Call (RPC) connects to a service on another machine via a network protocol of some sort. The remote service processes the call and returns the result to the client. From the point of view of the client application, the RPC might just as well have connected to a local process. The only difference involves the latency of the reply

Developers love RPCs because they can abstract the complexity of the network into a neat set of procedure calls. However, from the viewpoint of a system administrator, RPCs have a reputation for being finicky and difficult to manage. You'll see error messages involving RPCs quite often in the Event Log. That doesn't mean that RPCs have inherent problems. They rely on the underlying network, so they become like canaries that start blacking out when the network has a problem. Also, several high-profile security vulnerabilities have been uncovered in RPC, which has led to its being blocked at nearly all ISPs and corporate firewalls, even though the specific problems have been patched.

When you configure Outlook to connect to an Exchange server via MAPI, Outlook uses RPCs to ferry messages back and forth. Port selection for an RPC-based client such as Outlook works quite a bit differently than port select for Internet e-mail clients because RPC-based services do not use well-known ports. Instead, they register their port selection dynamically when you install them on a server. For example, the Exchange Information Store service might use TCP port 1190 on one server and TCP port 1340 on another.

It's possible to lock down Outlook and Exchange to use specific ports for RPC connections, but this is generally not an issue behind a firewall. You can use Outlook as a POP3 or IMAP4 client, or use OWA, to make a non-RPC connections through a firewall. You can also use RPC over HTTP to use Outlook as a MAPI client through a firewall. See Chapter 11, "Deploying a Distributed Architecture," for details.

Outlook connects to several Exchange services using RPC, so it needs a way to determine the port registered by each of these services. For this purpose, the client queries a service called the RPC End-Point Mapper (EPM). The EPM runs on the server, where it listens for client requests on well-known TCP port 135.

When the EPM gets a client request for the endpoint registered by a particular service, the EPM looks up the port registration in the Registry and returns that number to the client, which then directs a connection request to that port number.

## Key Points to Remember about Port Selection

When you cover MAPI client connections later in this chapter, and RPC over HTTP connections in Chapter 11, you should keep these items in mind:

- TCP-based applications listen for client connections on specific ports.
- Netstat lists the services that have current listens on a server.

- Internet e-mail clients connect using well-known TCP port 110 (POP3) or TCP port 143. IMAP4/SSL-enabled Internet e-mail clients use TCP port 995 (POP3/SSL) and TCP port 993 (IMAP4/SSL).
- MAPI clients use RPCs to communicate with the Exchange server. They select ports dynamically with the help of the RPC EPM service.
- Windows Server 2003 disables POP3 and IMAP4 by default. The services remain disabled even after installing Exchange.

# Initial Client Connections

Because all of the e-mail services use TCP to get guaranteed delivery, the initial connection made by any of the e-mail clients starts with a three-part TCP handshake.

- The client sends a SYN request at the port where the server listens for connection requests.
- The server returns a SYN-ACK to indicate that it received the connection request and has set aside a buffer and assigned a session ID to the connection.
- The client replies with an ACK to indicate that it has also set aside a buffer and is ready to proceed with communications.

With the TCP handshake out of the way, the nature of the next set of transactions depends on the client protocol.

## Initial POP3 Connection

A POP3 client connects to TCP port 110. At the completion of the TCP handshake, the server returns a banner message showing the vendor, version, and Fully Qualified Domain Name (FQDN) of the server. You can see the banner returned by the server by connecting to the port using telnet. The syntax would be `telnet w2k3-ex2 110`. Here's an example listing:

```
+OK Microsoft Exchange Server 2003 POP3 server version
➥6.5.6940.0 (w2k3-ex2.company.com) ready.
```

In addition to a connection banner, the POP3 service has a disconnect banner that reads like this:

```
+OK Microsoft Exchange Server 2003 POP3 server version
➥6.5.6940.0 signing off.
```

## Initial IMAP4 Connection

An IMAP4 client connects to TCP port 143. When the TCP handshake completes, the IMAP4 service returns a banner like this:

```
* OK Microsoft Exchange Server 2003 IMAP4rev1 server version
➥6.5.6940.0 (w2k3-ex2.company.com) ready.
```

At the completion of the session, IMAP4 sends a signoff banner that looks like this:

```
* BYE Microsoft Exchange Server 2003 IMAP4rev1 server version
➥6.5.6940.0 signing off.
```

You can change the POP3 and IMAP4 banners if you don't like the fact that the service type is advertised in the clear. See the section titled "Disabling Banners" later in this chapter.

## Initial Outlook Connection

Outlook uses RPC to transfer messages to and from Exchange, so the first step taken by the client is to make a TCP connection to the RPC EPM service on TCP port 135 at the Exchange server. After this connection has been made, the client requests the Globally Unique Identifier (GUID) of the target Exchange service. A GUID is a long number generated in such a way as to guarantee its uniqueness. Developers such as Microsoft assign GUIDs to their services to prevent them from colliding with services from other vendors. For example, the Exchange Information Store service uses the GUID `0e4a0156-dd5d-11d2-8c2f-00c04fb6bcde`. (You'll sometimes see a GUID referred to as a UUID, or Universally Unique Identifier.)

From a functional perspective, the GUID used by an RPC connection resembles a TCP port number. When a client initiates an RPC connection—a transaction called a *bind request*—it specifies the IP address of the target server, the GUID of the service to which it wants to bind, and the port number it obtained from the EPM service. If the service responds to the connection request, it establishes a connection over the dynamically assigned TCP port number.

You can view the registered RPC ports on a Windows server using the RPCDUMP utility in the Windows Server 2003 Resource Kit. Be prepared for a long, long list of services. Windows uses RPCs extensively, not just for Exchange.

RCPDUMP sorts the registrations based on the fives places an RPC service might listen: HTTP via a proxy, UDP ports, local RPC, named pipes, and TCP ports. The RPCDUMP headers look like this:

```
ncacn_http(Connection-oriented TCP/IP using IIS as HTTP proxy)
ncadg_ip_udp(Datagram (connectionless) UDP/IP)
ncalrpc(Local Rpc)
ncacn_np(Connection-oriented named pipes)
ncacn_ip_tcp(Connection-oriented TCP/IP)
```

You can run RPCDUMP in standard mode (no switches) or you can get lots of information using verbose mode (/v), and you can check to see for an active endpoint using ping mode (/i). The format of a RPC-DUMP entry for a TCP registration looks like this:

```
192.168.0.6[1190] [0e4a0156-dd5d-11d2-8c2f-00c04fb6bcde]
➥Microsoft Information Store :NOT_PINGED
```

The format for a verbose RPCDUMP ping report looks like this:

```
ProtSeq:ncacn_ip_tcp
Endpoint:1190
NetOpt:
Annotation:Microsoft Information Store
IsListening:YES
StringBinding:ncacn_ip_tcp:192.168.0.6[1190]
UUID:0e4a0156-dd5d-11d2-8c2f-00c04fb6bcde
ComTimeOutValue:RPC_C_BINDING_DEFAULT_TIMEOUT
VersMajor 1  VersMinor 0
```

The first number represents a *socket ID*, a combination of IP address and port number, such as **192.168.0.6[1190]**. The long number represents the GUID of the service. The following list shows the common GUIDs registered by Exchange services:

```
1A190310-BB9C-11CD-90F8-00AA00466520: Database
F5CC5A18-4264-101A-8C59-08002B2F8426: Directory NSP
1544F5E0-613C-11D1-93DF-00C04FD7BD09: Directory RFR
F5CC5A7C-4264-101A-8C59-08002B2F8426: Directory XDS
0E4A0156-DD5D-11D2-8C2F-00C04FB6BCDE: Information Store (1)
1453C42C-0FA6-11D2-A910-00C04F990F3B: Information Store (2)
10F24E8E-0FA6-11D2-A910-00C04F990F3B: Information Store (3)
9E8EE830-4459-11CE-979B-00AA005FFEBE: MTA
38A94E72-A9BC-11D2-8FAF-00C04fA378FF: MTA 'QAdmin'
99E64010-B032-11D0-97A4-00C04FD6551D: Store admin (1)
89742ACE-A9ED-11CF-9C0C-08002BE7AE86: Store admin (2)
A4F1DB00-CA47-1067-B31E-00DD010662DA: Store admin (3)
A4F1DB00-CA47-1067-B31F-00DD010662DA: Store EMSMDB
F930C514-1215-11D3-99A5-00A0C9B61B04: System Attendant Cluster
83D72BF0-0D89-11CE-B13F-00AA003BAC6C: System Attendant Private
469D6EC0-0D87-11CE-B13F-00AA003BAC6C: System Attendant Public
➡Interface
f5cc5a18-4264-101a-8c59-08002b2f8426: MS Exchange Directory NSPI
➡Proxy
5ad70572-184b-11d3-be89-0000f87a9296: SRS SSL Registration
```

You absolutely do not need to remember any of these GUIDs. The key thing to remember, however, is that each RPC-based service you encounter in this book (and Exchange has many more than you see here) registers itself with the operating system, obtains a free port above 1024, and listens at that port for RPC connections directed at its GUID.

## Changing Banners

Many administrators feel that putting a lot of information about a POP3 or IMAP4 server in a publicly accessible banner constitutes a security breach. You can alter the banner contents by modifying the IIS Metabase.

If you're running Exchange 2003 on Windows Server 2003, you can use the Metabase Explorer utility from the IIS 6.0 Resource Kit to change the banner. The resource kit is a free download from Microsoft. If you're running Exchange 2003 on Windows 2000, use the MetaEdit utility from the Exchange 2003 Resource Kit. Before modifying the Metabase, always make a backup.

## Backing Up the IIS Metabase

Before changing the Metabase contents, back up the Metabase using the IIS Manager console as follows:

1. Right-click the server name and select **All Tasks | Backup/ Restore Configuration** from the flyout menu, as shown in Figure 2.16.

**Figure 2.16**    IIS Console menu selection to initiate a backup of the IIS Metabase on IIS 6.0.

2. In the Configuration Backup/Restore window (shown in Figure 2.17), click **Create Backup**. This opens the Configuration Backup window.

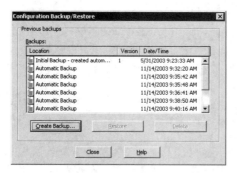

**Figure 2.17**    IIS Configuration Backup/Restore window showing the backup history.

3. Give the backup a friendly name that you'll recognize if you need to use it for a restore. Figure 2.18 shows an example.

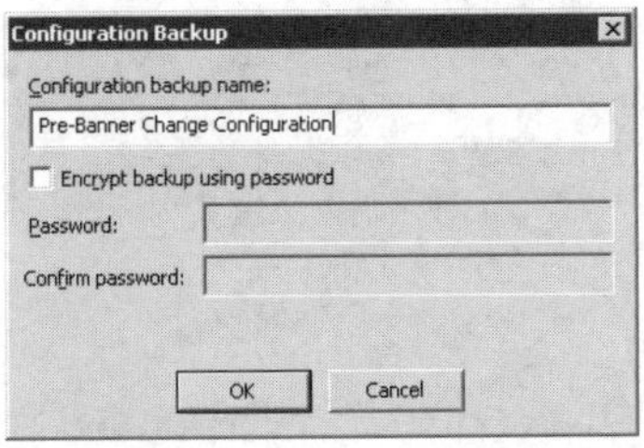

**Figure 2.18** IIS Configuration Backup window showing option to enter a backup name.

4. Click **OK** in the Configuration Backup window. This backs up the Metabase. You'll see the backup name in the Backups list.
5. Click **Close**.

You can also do a Metabase backup from the command line using the IIS-Back.vbs script, located in %windir%\System32. The IISBack utility places its backups in the %windir%\inetsrv\metaback folder. Confirm this prior to making changes to the Metabase.

## Changing POP3 Banners

The Metabase Explorer in the IIS 6.0 Resource Kit is the simplest way to change the contents of the Metabase. Load the IIS 6.0 Resource Kit on your Exchange server; then launch the Metabase Explorer from the Start menu. You don't need to make any configuration preparations in IIS because the utility takes care of that for you. Proceed as follows:

1. Open the Metabase Explorer and drill down to **LM | POP3SVC | 1**, as shown in Figure 2.19.
2. Right-click the 1 icon (it represents POP3 Virtual Server 1) and select **New | String Record** from the flyout menu. This opens the New Record window as shown in Figure 2.20.

**Figure 2.19** IIS 6.0 Metabase Explorer main window showing content of POP3 virtual server.

**Figure 2.20** IIS Metabase Explorer editor for string entries.

3. In the Record Name or Identifier field, enter the code `41661` and click **OK**. This adds the value to the Metabase.

4. Double-click the new value line to open the Properties window as shown in Figure 2.21. In the **Value Data** field, enter a string such as **POP3 Service Available**.

5. Select the **General** tab (shown in Figure 2.22) and change **User Type** to **Server**. Leave the **Attributes** option unchecked.

6. Use the same procedure to enter a new string record with an ID of **41662** and a value suitable for a signoff message, such as **POP3 Connection Terminated**.

7. Make a telnet connection to the POP3 service port as follows: **telnet <server_name> 110**. Verify that the banner reads the way you entered it in Metabase Explorer.

8. Type **Quit** and verify that the exit banner displays correctly.

**Figure 2.21**    Metabase Explorer properties editor showing new string to use for POP3 banner.

**Figure 2.22**    Metabase Explorer properties editor showing configuration settings for the POP3 banner.

### Changing IMAP4 Banners

You can change the content of the IMAP4 banners by modifying the IIS Metabase using the Metabase Explorer. Always back up the Metabase before making changes. Proceed as follows:

1. Launch the Metabase Explorer.
2. Drill down to **LM | IMAP4SVC | 1**.
3. Right-click the **1** icon
4. Select **New | String Record** from the flyout menu.
5. In the **Record Name or Identifier** field, enter the code **49884** and click **OK**. This adds the value to the Metabase.
6. Double-click the new value line to open the Properties window. In the **Value Data** field, enter a string such as **IMAP4 Service Available**.
7. Select the **General** tab and change **User Type** to **Server**. Leave the **Attributes** option unchecked.
8. Use the same procedure to enter a new string record with an ID of **49885** and a value suitable for a signoff message, such as **IMAP4 Connection Terminated**.
9. Make a telnet connection to the IMAP4 service port as follows: **telnet <server_name> 143**. Verify the banner content.
10. Type **0001 LOGOUT** to end the connection and verify the contents of the disconnect banner.

You can also change POP3 and IMAP4 banners from the command line using the smtpmd utility. See Microsoft Knowledge Base article 303513.

# Client Authentication

After an e-mail client connects to its complementary service on the server, it submits credentials on behalf of the user who wants to access a particular mailbox. The server uses these credentials to authenticate the user, thereby validating the user's identity. The authentication methods vary depending on the client protocol.

## POP3 Authentication

Following the receipt of the POP3 banner, the e-mail client sends a USER statement to the server containing the user's name in clear text. In a Windows domain, the name includes the user's domain in the format domain\username, such as `company\user1`. The server acknowledges this message with an OK.

The client now sends a PASS statement containing the user's password in clear text. In other words, if you observe this transaction with a packet sniffer, you'd see the user name and password in words as clear and plain as a traffic citation.

When an Exchange server gets a plain-text authentication request, it uses a secure connection with a domain controller to validate the user's credentials. This differs from a standard challenge-response pass-through transaction because a domain controller does not store passwords in clear text. Instead, Exchange does a sleight-of-hand by taking the user's clear text credentials and initiating a standard NTLMv2 authentication transaction, essentially doing a domain logon as if it were the user. If a domain controller validates the user's credentials, the Exchange server connects the client to the mailbox owned by the user with the validated credentials.

### Avoid Clear Text POP3 Passwords

The POP3 service at the Exchange server controls the authentication mechanism used by the client. You can view the setting as follows:

1. Launch the ESM console.
2. Drill down through the server name to the **Protocols | POP3** icon.
3. Open the **Properties** window for the **POP3 Virtual Server**.
4. Select the **Access** tab.
5. Click **Authentication** to open an Authentication window. Figure 2.23 shows an example. As you can see, the POP3 service not only supports Basic Authentication, it supports a method called Simple Authentication and Security Layer, otherwise known as SASL. The SASL mechanism permits a client and server to come to an agreement on an authentication mechanism.
6. Click **Edit** under the **SASL** option. The Acceptable SASL Mechanisms window opens as shown in Figure 2.24. Note that the list under SASL Mechanisms includes only one option, NTLM. This means that a POP3 client can authenticate using either plain text or NTLM.

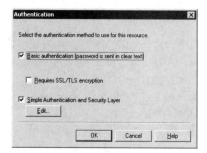

**Figure 2.23** POP3 authentication options showing SASL option.

**Figure 2.24** SASL options showing NTLM as the sole option that IIS will offer during an authentication negotiation.

Ordinarily, Outlook and Outlook Express use plain text for authentication. Each client has a configuration setting exposed in the Servers tab of the Account Properties window called Secure Password Authentication. Figure 2.25 shows an example. If you select this option, the client uses SASL to negotiate an authentication method. Because POP3 has only one option for SASL, the client uses NTLM.

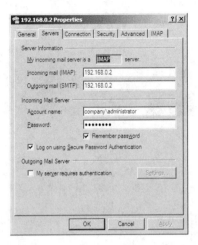

**Figure 2.25**   POP3 authentication setting at an e-mail client showing the Log on using Secure Password Authentication option.

### Limitations of Secure Password Authentication

Faced with the prospect of using clear text passwords that can be sniffed on your network, you might decide to use Secure Password Authentication for Outlook Express clients. However, this option does not guarantee security, as NTLM authentication has a variety of weaknesses. You get better authentication by using SSL to protect the POP3 connection and plain text password exchange. The transaction between the Exchange server and the domain controller cannot be sniffed effectively because the Exchange server uses NTLMv2 to validate the plain text credentials.

Also, third-party clients such as Eudora use protected authentication options that do not work when accessing Exchange mailboxes. For example, Figure 2.26 shows the IMAP/POP configuration window in Eudora. The **Passwords** option sends passwords in clear text. The **Kerberos** option does not work with a Windows Active Directory domain controller because of the difference in password hashes uses by Eudora and Windows. And Windows does not support the CRAM-MD5 mechanism.

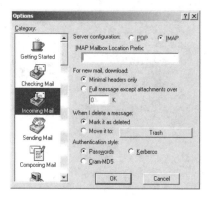

**Figure 2.26** Eudora client authentication settings showing a plain text option (Passwords).

## IMAP4 Authentication

Following the initial TCP connection and the receipt of the service banner, an IMAP4 client sends a CAPABILITY request to the server. Each IMAP request starts with a 4-byte alphanumeric value known as a tag, so the CAPABILITY request line starts with a tag of 0000. The server responds with a list of supported options. For Exchange, these options include

- IMAP4
- IMAPrev1
- Idle
- Logon Referrals
- Mailbox Referrals
- Namespace
- Literal+
- UID Plus
- Children
- Auth=NTLM

The client now sends a LOGIN request, which the server acknowledges.

The client sends the user's name followed by the user's clear-text password. The Exchange server passes these credentials to its logon server using the same NTLMv2 authentication process used by POP3. If the server validates the credentials, the IMAP4 service sends the client an **OK LOGIN Completed** message.

If you examine the capabilities list returned by the Exchange server, you'll see that the server supports NTLM authentication. You can configure the Outlook or Outlook Express client for Secure Password Authentication to take advantage of NTLM, but you get better overall security protecting the IMAP4 connection with SSL and using plain text passwords that the Exchange server validates with NTLMv2. This also supports third-party clients that can't use NTLM.

If you want to learn more about the specific commands used in IMAP4, take a look at Microsoft Knowledge Base article 189325.

### Outlook Authentication

When an RPC client such as Outlook initiates a connection with an RPC service such as the Exchange Information Store, it presents its credentials in the form of a *bind request*.

Outlook 2003 uses Kerberos for authentication to Exchange, so the client must first obtain a Kerberos session ticket from a domain controller to attach to the bind request. Earlier versions of Outlook initiate a challenge-response passthrough authentication during the bind phase of the RPC connection.

If you want to see the Kerberos session tickets obtained by Outlook, launch the Kerbtray utility that comes in the Windows Server 2003 Resource Kit. This utility puts a small green icon in the Notification Area (née System Tray). Double-click the icon to view a window that shows all the Kerberos tickets obtained on behalf of the user. Figure 2.27 shows an example.

An Outlook 2003 client needs three Kerberos session tickets to connect to an Exchange 2003 server, one for each of the three Exchange services it uses:

- **ExchangeAB.** The Exchange Address Book service, also known as the Name Service Provider Interface (NSPI), provides access to the GAL. If you look closely at the Kerbtray entry, you'll see that this session ticket specifies the name of a Global Catalog server.

**Figure 2.27** Kerbtray utility showing Kerberos tickets and ticket-granting tickets obtained by Outlook user.

- **ExchangeMDB.** The Exchange Information Store service provides access to the user's mailbox. The letters MDB stand for Message Database. This is the connection you generally think of when you say, "Outlook makes a MAPI connection to Exchange."
- **ExchangeRFR.** The Exchange Referral service gives the Outlook client the name of a Global Catalog server to use for accessing the GAL. It also acts as a proxy for older clients that don't know how to query a Global Catalog showing Kerberos tickets and server.

## Client Message Retrieval

You have now arrived at the point where you can analyze what happens when each of the clients protocols (POP3, IMAP4, or MAPI) ask to retrieve a message or messages from an Exchange 2003 server. (Using Outlook Web Access as an e-mail client is covered in Chapter 9, "Outlook Web Access.")

To see the details of the transactions for POP3 and IMAP4, let's take advantage of a feature in Outlook Express that permits logging protocol transactions.

1. From the main menu, select **Tools | Options**.
2. Select the **Maintenance** tab and find the **Troubleshooting** area at the bottom of the window. Figure 2.28 shows an example.

**Figure 2.28** Outlook configuration for POP3 client that shows logging enabled for all interfaces.

3. Check the **Mail** (another word for POP3) option and **IMAP** option to save logs for these protocols. Be sure to uncheck them after you have run your tests. Outlook Express puts the log files in the user profile under Local Settings\Application Data\Identities\{guid}\Microsoft\Outlook Express.

## POP3 Message Retrieval

For this test, open Outlook Express and connect to an Exchange server using a POP3 account. If you have no messages waiting, create a short RFC 2822 message addressed to your POP3 account and put it in the Pickup folder of your Exchange server. Give it a few seconds to get delivered; then press F5 in Outlook Express to refresh the view and retrieve any queued messages.

Open the POP3 log and find the start of the transaction. It begins with a banner line. The following listing shows a sample logon transaction. The listing shows client messages in bold.

```
POP3: 13:14:14 [rx] +OK Microsoft Exchange Server 2003 POP3 server version
↦6.5.6940.0 (w2k3-s2.company.com) ready.
POP3: 13:14:14 [tx] USER company\administrator
POP3: 13:14:14 [rx] +OK
POP3: 13:14:14 [tx] PASS ********
POP3: 13:14:14 [rx] +OK User successfully logged on.
```

The log makes it appear as if Outlook Express protected the user's password. Don't let this fool you. It sent the password in clear text on the wire. You can see it using a packet sniffer like Ethereal (www.ethereal.com), which is open source and free, or eEye's Retina (www.eeye.com) which costs a little money (starts at $995) but includes intrusion detection capabilities and has some nifty reporting features.

After the client successfully authenticates, it sends a STAT request to the server asking for messages. The server replies with a count of queued messages and their total size. For example, in this listing, the message queue for the user holds three messages of 1314 bytes each, so the server responds with **3 3492**.

```
POP3: 13:14:14 [tx] STAT
POP3: 13:14:14 [rx] +OK 3 3942
```

The client now sends a LIST request to get statistics for individual messages. The server replies with a numerical ID and size for each queued message. The server indicates the end of the queue with a dot.

```
POP3: 13:14:14 [tx] LIST
POP3: 13:14:14 [rx] +OK 3 3942
POP3: 13:14:14 [rx] 1 1314
POP3: 13:14:14 [rx] 2 1314
POP3: 13:14:14 [rx] 3 1314
POP3: 13:14:14 [rx] .
```

The client now sends a series of RETR (Retrieve) requests, one for each queued message. The server replies with the entire content of the message, header, and body. The log shows only the +OK response from the server, not the message contents.

```
POP3: 13:14:14 [tx] RETR 1
POP3: 13:14:14 [rx] +OK
POP3: 13:14:14 [tx] RETR 2
```

```
POP3: 13:14:14 [rx] +OK
POP3: 13:14:14 [tx] RETR 3
POP3: 13:14:14 [rx] +OK
```

By default, POP3 clients do not leave messages on the server. The client now sends a series of DELE (Delete) commands, one for each message.

```
POP3: 13:14:14 [tx] DELE 1
POP3: 13:14:14 [rx] +OK
POP3: 13:14:14 [tx] DELE 2
POP3: 13:14:14 [rx] +OK
POP3: 13:14:14 [tx] DELE 3
POP3: 13:14:14 [rx] +OK
```

Satisfied with a job well done, the client sends a QUIT, and the server replies with a disconnect banner.

```
POP3: 13:14:14 [tx] QUIT
POP3: 13:14:14 [rx] +OK Microsoft Exchange Server 2003 POP3
server version 6.5.6940.0 signing off.
```

The client now tears down the TCP session, something you won't see in the log, but you will see in Ethereal.

### POP3 and Server Message Storage

You can configure most POP3 clients to leave messages on the Exchange server. Figure 2.29 shows this setting for Outlook Express. Outlook has a similar setting in Advanced Properties.

If the user wants to see new incoming messages, she must manually refresh the client to retrieve the new messages. This repeats the entire connection transaction, including the TCP setup, user logon, message retrieval, message deletion, user signoff, and TCP teardown.

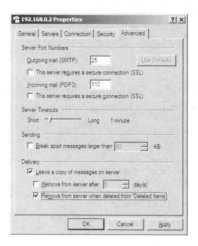

**Figure 2.29** Outlook configuration showing the option to leave messages at the server rather than deleting them as part of the retrieval.

### *Local POP3 Message Storage*

When a POP3 client retrieves messages, it stores them in a local database. Outlook either puts messages in a Personal Storage (pst) file in the user profile under \Local Settings\Application Data\Microsoft\Outlook or places them in the user's Exchange mailbox. Outlook Express puts them in a dbx file in the user profile under Local Settings\Application Data\Identities\{guid}\Microsoft.

Microsoft puts the message files in Local Settings because this folder, and its contents, does not form a part of a roaming profile. Local mailbox stores can grow quite large, and replicating them to and from the central profile server can slow down logon and logoff transactions and possibly corrupt the databases. Keep this in mind if you configure roaming profiles for your users.

Mobile users who connect to their Exchange mailboxes using a POP3 client often encounter a situation where they use a POP3 client to read their e-mail while on the road; then return to the office only to find no mail in their inbox. They freak out and run to your desk and stare at you with the look of a forest animal whose habitat has been leveled to make room for a housing development.

You patiently explain that a POP3 client downloads messages into a local file; then removes them from the server. This does not placate them, let me assure you. To avoid these types of confrontations, always configure your POP3 clients to leave messages on the Exchange server.

If you have a lot of POP3 clients and you place a premium on storage, you can configure the Delivery option in Outlook Express to **Remove From Server When Deleted From 'Deleted Items'**. This option automates the message deletion once the user has decided that the message is no longer needed. The Deleted Items folder does not actually exist at the server. POP3 has only one server-based inbox.

### Key Points to Remember about POP3 Message Retrieval

When the time comes to troubleshoot a POP3 connection to an Exchange server, these items can help you figure out if you have a connection problem, an authentication problem, or a configuration problem.

- A POP3 client uses TCP port 110 to connect to the Exchange server, or TCP port 995 when using POP3 over SSL.
- A POP3 client sends the user's password in clear text unless configured to do otherwise.
- Exchange only exposes the user's Inbox to a POP3 client, which is a limitation of POP3, not of Exchange.
- A POP3 client transfers messages from the server to a local database repository (pst for Outlook and dbx for Outlook Express) unless you configure Outlook to send incoming POP3 mail to the user's Exchange folders. The local databases do not form part of a roaming profile.
- A POP3 client deletes messages from the server once they have been transferred to the local mailbox store unless configured to do otherwise.

## IMAP4 Message Retrieval

For this next test, configure Outlook Express to use another account; then set that account to use IMAP4. Use your Administrator account to send a few messages to the test account. Then open the test user's inbox and read one of the queued messages.

Now open the IMAP4 log saved by the protocol logging feature in Outlook Express. You'll find the log files in the user profile under Local Settings\Application Data\Identities\{guid}\Microsoft\Outlook Express.

Locate the start of this transaction by finding the connection banner. Client commands show as **tx** and the server replies show as **rx**, while **db** acts as a status marker. The initial **db** entry immediately before the banner shows the client connecting to the server on well-known IMAP4 port 143.

```
IMAP: 15:59:49 [db] Connecting to '192.168.0.2' on port 143.
IMAP: 15:59:49 [rx] * OK Microsoft Exchange Server 2003
↪IMAP4rev1 server version 6.5.6940.0 (w2k3-s2.company.com) ready.
```

The client now sends a CAPABILITY request to the server. The server replies with a list of commands it supports. Each client request starts with a four-character alphanumeric value called a *tag*. The listing below starts with the tag 000F. When the server fulfills the client request, it replies with the same tag. A * indicates a partial response with more data to come. A + indicates that the server is waiting for more information.

```
IMAP: 15:59:49 [tx] 000F CAPABILITY
IMAP: 15:59:49 [rx] * CAPABILITY IMAP4 IMAP4rev1 IDLE LOGIN-
↪REFERRALS MAILBOX-REFERRALS NAMESPACE LITERAL+ UIDPLUS
↪CHILDREN AUTH=NTLM
IMAP: 15:59:49 [rx] 000F OK CAPABILITY completed.
```

The client now sends a LOGIN request to the server. We've already seen that this transaction involves a plain text password. The log shows that the server validates the password but does not display the tag for a LOGIN transaction. The client does use one, as you can see when the server includes it in the reply.

```
IMAP: 15:59:49 [tx] LOGIN command sent
IMAP: 15:59:49 [rx] 000G OK LOGIN completed.
```

The client now sends a SELECT command to the server along with a folder name. Unlike POP3, which assumes a single message queue at the server, an IMAP4 server knows that the server can have multiple folders. The primary folder is Inbox. The example log listing shows a

SELECT INBOX statement. The server responds with the number of messages in the Inbox folder.

```
IMAP: 15:59:49 [tx] 000H SELECT "INBOX"
IMAP: 15:59:49 [rx] * 5 EXISTS
IMAP: 15:59:49 [rx] * 0 RECENT
IMAP: 15:59:49 [rx] * FLAGS (\Seen \Answered \Flagged \Deleted
➥\Draft $MDNSent)
IMAP: 15:59:49 [rx] * OK [PERMANENTFLAGS (\Seen \Answered
➥\Flagged \Deleted \Draft $MDNSent)] Permanent flags
IMAP: 15:59:49 [rx] * OK [UIDVALIDITY 88] UIDVALIDITY value
IMAP: 15:59:49 [rx] 000H OK [READ-WRITE] SELECT completed.
```

In its reply, the server includes a list of flags that the client can request to indicate message status. RFC 2060 defines these flags:

- **\Seen.** Message has been read
- **\Answered.** Message has been answered
- **\Flagged.** Message requires urgent/special attention
- **\Deleted.** Message selected for removal
- **\Draft.** Message has not completed composition
- **\Recent.** Message arrived in mailbox since last connection

The client now uses a FETCH command to get information about the messages themselves. The example Inbox has three queued messages. The client asks to see a list of all message identifiers (**1:***), the size of each message (**RFC822.SIZE**), the status of each message (**FLAGS**), some selected message headers (**BODY.PEEK[HEADER.FIELDS…]**), any RFC 2822 headers (**ENVELOPE**), and the send date (**INTERNALDATE**). The server replies with the requested information. The example listing shows one of the replies.

```
IMAP: 15:59:49 [tx] 000I UID FETCH 1:* (BODY.PEEK[HEADER.FIELDS
➥(References X-Ref X-Priority X-MSMail-Priority X-MSOESRec Newsgroups)]
➥ENVELOPE RFC822.SIZE UID FLAGS INTERNALDATE)
IMAP: 15:59:49 [rx] * 8 FETCH (BODY[HEADER.FIELDS (References X-Ref X-
➥Priority X-MSMail-Priority X-MSOESRec Newsgroups)] {2}
IMAP: 15:59:49 [rx] Buffer (literal) of length 2
IMAP: 15:59:49 [rx]  ENVELOPE ("Sun, 20 Jul 2003 14:37:50 -0700" "test
➥message delivered to IMAP4 client" (("Administrator" NIL "Administrator"
➥"company.com")) (("Administrator" NIL "Administrator" "company.com"))
```

```
➡(("Administrator" NIL "Administrator" "company.com")) (("Administrator"
➡NIL "Administrator" "company.com")) NIL NIL NIL
➡"<954703A8CE5D314292754304526DF20E1B13@w2k3-s2.company.com>")
➡RFC822.SIZE 1411 UID 20 FLAGS (\Recent) INTERNALDATE "20-Jul-2003
➡14:37:50 -0700")
```

An IMAP client typically displays the header information in the user interface with an icon that indicates the message status. At this point, unlike a POP3 transaction where all the queued messages get downloaded, only a few message headers and flags have traversed the wire. When a user selects one of the messages, Outlook Express sends a **FETCH** (**BODY.PEEK** []) command to retrieve the message but leave the status as \Unseen. (Other clients such as Eudora read the message and set the \Seen flag in a single transaction.)

```
IMAP: 15:59:49 [tx] 000J UID FETCH 15 (BODY.PEEK [] UID)
IMAP: 15:59:49 [rx] * 6 FETCH (BODY[] {1373}
IMAP: 15:59:49 [rx] Buffer (literal) of length 1373
IMAP: 15:59:49 [rx]  UID 15)
IMAP: 15:59:49 [rx] 000J OK FETCH completed.
```

The Outlook Express client now sends a STORE command with a +FLAGS.SILENT \Seen argument to the server. This changes the message flag to \Seen.

```
IMAP: 15:59:49 [tx] 000K UID STORE 15 +FLAGS.SILENT (\Seen)
IMAP: 15:59:49 [rx] 000K OK STORE completed.
```

As you can see, the beauty of **IMAP4** lies in its server-based storage, even though the transactions themselves get a little more complex than POP3.

### IMAP4 Message Deletions

Unlike POP3, which deletes a message from the server after the client downloads it, IMAP4 leaves the messages on the server. When a user highlights a message and presses the Delete key or selects Delete from the property menu, IMAP4 clients do not actually delete the messages. They merely send a STORE command flagging the message as \Deleted.

When the server acknowledges this transaction, Outlook Express puts a line through the message header and a red X through the message icon. Eudora puts a red X in the status icon. Because the message still exists at the server, the user can undelete it with a simple selection from the Property menu.

Permanently removing deleted message in IMAP4 requires an EXPUNGE command from the client. Outlook Express sends this command when you select **Edit | Purge Deleted Messages** from the main menu. In Eudora, use the main menu option **Message | Purge Messages**.

### IMAP4 IDLE Command

Recall that POP3 required polling the server to find any newly queued incoming messages. This either requires action on the part of the user or a configuration setting telling the client application to periodically poll for new messages.

An IMAP4 client can avoid this silliness by telling the server to send a notification when new mail arrives. RFC 2177 documents a special IMAP4 command called IDLE for this function. In essence, the IDLE command tells the server, "Call me when new mail arrives. I promise to hear you."

Keep this behavior in mind when designing Exchange servers to act as IMAP4 servers. If you have thousands and thousands of clients all maintaining a connection with IDLE, you will need additional server resources to keep the connections open.

### IMAP4 and Public Folders

Unlike POP3 clients, an IMAP4 client can read and post items to public folders on an Exchange server. The only caveat is that the public folder content must be available at the user's home server. The IMAP4 protocol does not include the ability to follow up on public folder referrals. As you'll see in Chapter 11, you can work around this limitation by using front-end servers to host IMAP4 clients.

### Key Points to Remember about IMAP4 Message Retrieval

Not many organizations use IMAP4 to support their Internet users, but I hope what you've learned in this topic might convince you to give it a try. Here are the high points:

- An IMAP4 client uses TCP port 143 to connect to the Exchange server, or TCP port 993 when using IMAP4 over SSL.

- An IMAP4 client sends the user's password in clear text unless configured to do otherwise.
- Exchange exposes the user's entire folder collection to an IMAP4 client, but the client must elect to view them. The user can also read and post items to public folders as long as the content is available on the user's home server.
- An IMAP4 client downloads message headers first; then opens a copy of a message and its attachments when the user selects it. The original message remains on the server.
- When an IMAP4 client deletes a message, it remains available at the server until the deleted messages have been purged by the user.

## MAPI Message Retrieval

When Outlook (configured as a MAPI Exchange client) retrieves messages from an Exchange server, the transaction uses RPCs. This complicates our ability to view details of a MAPI transaction. You cannot use Telnet to simulate an RPC connection, and you won't see much in an Ethereal trace because because Outlook 2003 compresses the message contents to conserve bandwidth.

So, skipping a detailed analysis of the message transaction, here are some important things to remember about MAPI message retrieval.

- MAPI clients communicate directly with the Exchange Information Store service without intervention by any IIS-based services.
- MAPI clients can store local copies of messages if offline folders are enabled. The original message stays at the Exchange server.
- Outlook 2003 MAPI clients (in their default configuration) download all messages and their attachments at logon and store them in an offline folder cache.
- Outlook 2002 and earlier MAPI clients first download message headers; then retrieve each message as the client reads it.
- When an Outlook user sends a message, if the ultimate recipient has a mailbox on the user's Exchange server, the message goes more or less directly into the recipient's mailbox.
- If the ultimate recipient of a MAPI message has a mailbox on another Exchange server, or on an outside mail server, then Exchange converts the message from MAPI to MIME and hands it over to SMTP for routing.

- If the ultimate recipient of a MAPI message has a mailbox on a mail system that uses a protocol other than SMTP, Exchange hands the message to the MTA.
- MAPI clients do not use fixed ports. They negotiate a dynamic port using the RPC End-Point Mapper.

## Looking Forward

Take a deep breath. You just covered some of the toughest material in message administration. You don't see the inner workings of the e-mail clients very often, so it's easy to forget that a problem can occur to affect any or all of those myriad transactions.

Don't forget that e-mail clients come in some unlikely places. You'll probably be asked to configure all sorts of specialized clients buried inside database front ends and Web services and a variety of vendor applications. The better you understand the basics of the client transactions, the faster you'll be able to get those specialized clients working properly.

When you learn about spam and mail-borne viruses, you'll be glad that you know the secrets of RFC 2822 message formats so you'll see how they can be borked and smurfed to fool you and your messaging system. And when you learn more about message routing, you'll be glad that you understand how clients interact with Exchange so you can trace and troubleshoot routing errors.

In the next chapter, you'll see how to manage the recipients who will connect to your Exchange server to get e-mail using the client protocols you just read about. For now, though, it' time to take a break. Go outside. Watch the stars. Think about all those aliens hovering just out of sight who wait for us to develop a way to send e-mail across the subether so we can be considered mature enough to join the galactic empire. (Do you think they have spam on Beta Lyrae?)

# CHAPTER 3

# Exchange 2003 Service Architecture

Once you get into full production with Exchange, you'll put a lot of work into managing the servers, databases, message transports, recipients, and public folders in your Exchange organization. You'll do this in addition to the daily grind of running backups, fighting viruses, blocking spam, and dealing with users who never seem to quite catch on to setting appointments or purging old e-mail.

All of this information is covered in later chapters. At this point, though, let's take some time to see how the services that comprise Exchange fit together. Think of this chapter as an exploded diagram of Exchange that you might find in a repair manual. If you like, you can skip forward and refer back here when you have questions about how a particular service interacts with another service or with the operating system.

## Exchange Store

Arguably the most important component of Exchange is the databases that hold the e-mail messages and public folders. Microsoft calls these databases the *Exchange Store*.

Exchange exposes the content of the store using a variety of services. Figure 3.1 shows how these services connect to the store.

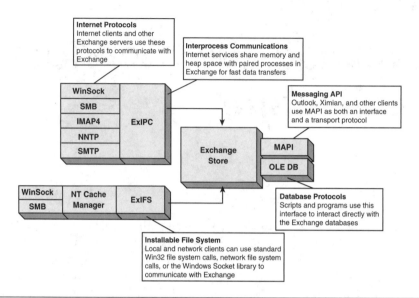

**Figure 3.1**    Diagram of services that interface with the Exchange Store.

## Internet Messaging Protocols

The Internet messaging protocols covered in the last chapter—POP3, IMAP4, NNTP, and SMTP—do not actually belong to Exchange. Instead, they run as part of the suite of services Microsoft calls *Internet Information Services*, or IIS. The services are extended and enhanced when you install Exchange.

You can see these service for yourself using the Tasklist utility that comes with Windows Server 2003. Run the utility from the command line with the syntax `tasklist /svc`. This dumps the executable names of all running processes and any services hosted by those processes. Here's a partial listing showing the processes that host Exchange-related services.

```
C:\>tasklist /svc

Image Name                      PID    Services
========================= ===== ===================================
inetinfo.exe               1328  IISADMIN, POP3Svc, IMAP4Svc,
                                 RESvc, SMTPSVC
srsmain.exe                1352  MSExchangeSRS
mssearch.exe               1884  MSSEARCH
```

```
svchost.exe                  172 W3SVC
w3wp.exe                     1931 <not applicable>
mad.exe                      2640 MSExchangeSA
store.exe                    2428 MSExchangeIS
```

Note that a single process, Inetinfo, contains the Iisadmin service that controls access to the IIS configuration settings along with the client e-mail services, POP3 and IMAP4; and mail transfer service, SMTP and the SMTP Routing Engine (RESvc).

If you run Exchange 2003 on a Windows 2000 platform rather than Windows Server 2003, you'll see several important differences in the task list. In Windows 2000, the World Wide Web service (W3SVC) runs as part of Inetinfo. In Windows Server 2003, the core HTTP handling for Internet services lives in the kernel (Http.sys), and the World Wide Web service runs independently of Inetinfo under the general purpose services process, Svchost.

More important, the core Internet processes used for Exchange on Windows Server 2003 reside in their own application pool hosted by a separate instance of the Worker Process executable, W3wp.exe. Figure 3.2 shows the IIS Manager console with the content of the Exchange ApplicationPool listed in the right pane.

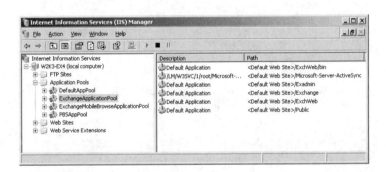

**Figure 3.2**   IIS Manager console showing virtual Exchange folders.

By separating Web sites into distinct application pools, IIS 6.0 prevents a failure in one application from causing an application in another pool to crash. Even with that separation, you should not host other Web sites on an Exchange server. Consider IIS simply as a support application for Exchange, and use other Windows Server 2003 servers to host your Web pages.

## *Epoxy*

Internet services such as SMTP, POP3, and IMAP4 act as *transports* that ferry data between clients and Exchange and, in the case of SMTP, between Exchange servers themselves. Although these transport services belong to IIS, Exchange tethers them to peer services running under the main Store process via an inter-process communication layer called *Epoxy*. As shown in Figure 3.3, this layer consists of shared memory areas, shared heap space, and shared message queues.

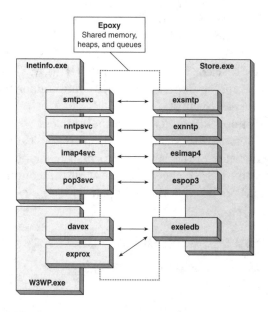

**Figure 3.3**    Diagram of shared IIS and Exchange processes connected via Epoxy.

You don't have to know the gory details of the symbiotic relationship between IIS and Exchange. Just remember to monitor the health of the IIS services on your Exchange server every bit as diligently as you monitor the health of the main Exchange services. Don't ignore Event Log entries that come from any IIS service, and by all means don't put off applying IIS security patches.

### *Distributed Authoring and Versioning (DAV)*

You may not have heard the term Web-Based Distributed Authoring and Versioning (WebDAV, or often simply DAV), but its use has become widespread in collaborative applications.

An open standard, WebDAV is documented in RFC 2518, "HTTP Extensions for Distributed Authoring—WEBDAV." The standard defines extensions to the HTTP protocol to permit more sophisticated file handling than you get from the standard GET and POST commands in HTTP.

Outlook Web Access (OWA) uses WebDAV to access the content of a user's mailbox and to display the content of public folders. Exchange System Manager also uses WebDAV to display public folder content.

Ordinarily, IIS handles the additional HTTP commands in a Web-DAV connection using a WebDAV extension filter called Httpext.dll. Windows Server 2003 sets the status of this extension filter to Prohibited to reduce the attack surface of a Web server. You can view this status using the IIS Manager console. Select the Web Services Extension icon, as shown in Figure 3.4.

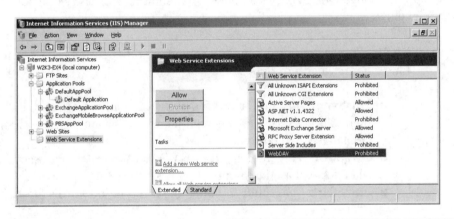

**Figure 3.4**   IIS Manager console showing status of Web Services Extensions.

You don't need to enable the WebDAV extension. Exchange does not use it. Instead, Exchange loads its own extensions, including one for WebDAV. You can view the list of Exchange extensions by highlighting the Microsoft Exchange Server extension icon and clicking Properties, as shown in Figure 3.5.

The Davex.dll filter provides the WebDAV functions for Exchange in its standard configuration. If you configure an Exchange server to act as a front-end server (described in Chapter 11, "Deploying a Distributed Architecture,"), the server proxies incoming Outlook Web Access connections to the back-end server that hosts the user's mailbox. In this configuration, Exchange replaces the Davex.dll extension filter with a filter called Exprox.dll.

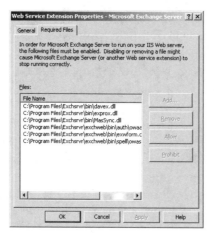

**Figure 3.5** Exchange Web Services Extension list showing WebDAV extension, Davex, and others.

Just in case you were wondering about the other Exchange extension filters, here's what they do:

- **MasSync.** This filter allows a mobile user with a handheld device such as a PocketPC or SmartPhone to synchronize mail with the Exchange server automatically.
- **Owaauth.** This filter handles OWA authentication transactions when forms-based authentication has been enabled.
- **Exwform.** This filter renders the Web-based forms used by Exchange.
- **Owaspell.** This filter provides online spell checking for messages created in OWA.

## Messaging Application Programming Interface (MAPI)

The last chapter introduced you to MAPI, one of the protocols used by Outlook and a few third-party e-mail clients for connecting to an Exchange server. Exchange System Manager uses MAPI to access a variety of information about mailbox and public folder settings, such as the permissions on a public folder, as shown in Figure 3.6.

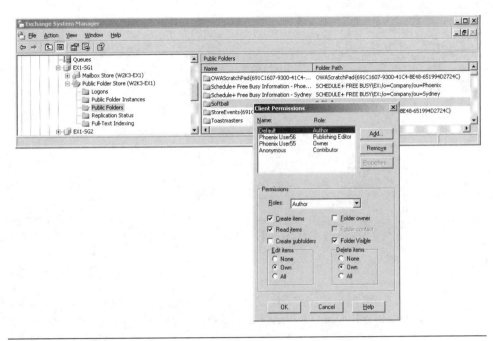

**Figure 3.6**    MAPI permissions in ESM.

### OLE DB

Microsoft defines a suite of technologies and design criteria for database access that it calls Object Linking and Embedding Database, or OLE DB. Applications can access a Microsoft database via an OLE DB *provider*. Exchange has an OLE DB provider that exposes the content of the Exchange Store.

You won't necessarily interact directly with the Exchange OLE DB provider unless you write scripts using one of the collaboration libraries provided by Microsoft. But you will definitely use applications that make OLE DB connections to the Exchange store. For example, when you touch one of the Mailbox Store icons in ESM, as shown in Figure 3.7, the information about mailbox size and item count come from the store's OLE DB provider.

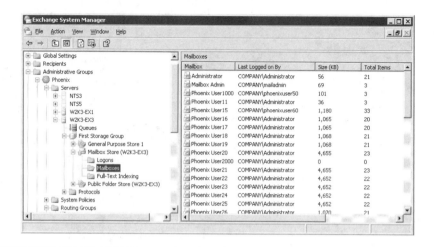

**Figure 3.7** Mailbox list in ESM obtained via OLE DB connection to Exchange Store.

If ESM cannot make OLE DB contact to an Exchange mailbox store or public folder store, either on a local server or a remote server, it will hang for a long time; then give up and display an error of one form or another. Your first action when you see this kind of behavior? Connect to the server using terminal services and verify that all Exchange services are running. Check the Event Log to see if it contains any errors from the Information Store.

If you run a monitoring application such as Microsoft Operations Manager, you will be informed immediately when a server experiences this kind of connection problem.

You should also check Task Manager to see if one of the Exchange services has begun taking 100 percent of the CPU time, indicating a malformed message, a corrupted element within the store, or a logic error in one of the Exchange management services. If you restart the server, and CPU utilization goes right back to 100 percent, it might be worth your while to call Microsoft Product Support Services and have them walk you through doing integrity checks of your databases.

## ExIFS

Operating systems talk to hardware via kernel-mode device drivers. When the operating system loads a device driver, it assigns a name to the place in memory where the driver resides. For example, the memory holding the device that represents the first volume on the first hard drive gets the name \Device\HardDiskVolume1.

When the operating system mounts a device, it provides a handle that user-mode applications can use when accessing the device. For example, the operating system assigns a handle of C: to \Device\Hard-DiskVolume1. This handle is called a symbolic link.

A Windows file system, such as NTFS, FASTFAT, or CDFS, takes the form of a device driver that Microsoft calls an Installable File System, or IFS. An IFS does not necessarily communicate directly to a piece of hardware. For example, Exchange exposes the content of the Exchange Store using an IFS driver called Exifs.sys. This device goes by the name \device\ExchangeIfsDevice, and it has a symbolic link called BackOfficeStorage.

All these memory tags and symbolic links are stored in a data structure called the Object Namespace. You can see the structure of the Object Namespace, including the ExchangeIfsDevice and the BackOfficeStorage symbolic link, using a free utility called Winobj, available from the SysInternals Web site, www.sysinternals.com. Figure 3.8 shows an example.

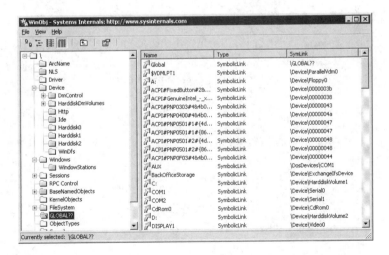

**Figure 3.8** Object Namespace seen via Winobj that shows BackOfficeStorage symbolic link to ExchangeIfsDevice.

You'll occasionally see the BackOfficeStorage symbolic link in Event Log entries or error messages, or if you go poking around in the background of configuration settings involving Exchange. For example, the Exchange virtual folders in IIS connect to the Exchange Store using the BackOfficeStorage symbolic link, as shown in Figure 3.9.

**Figure 3.9**   Exchange virtual folder in IIS with path using a BackOfficeStorage link to Exchange Store contents.

### Using ExIFS to View Mailboxes and Public Folders

You can view a list of mailboxes in the Exchange Store via the BackOfficeStorage symbolic link by opening a command prompt on your Exchange server and running DIR with the following syntax:

```
dir \\.\backofficestorage\<fully_qualified_domain_name>\mbx
```

Here's an abbreviated listing:

```
C:\>dir \\.\backofficestorage\company.com\mbx

Volume in drive \\.\backofficestorage is Exchange
Volume Serial Number is 00A9-8AC7
```

```
Directory of \\.\backofficestorage\company.com\mbx

4/4/2004   08:19 AM    <DIR>          .
4/4/2004   08:19 AM    <DIR>          ..
4/4/2004   08:19 AM    <DIR>          phoenixuser50
4/4/2004   08:19 AM    <DIR>          phoenixuser51
4/4/2004   08:19 AM    <DIR>          phoenixuser52
4/4/2004   08:19 AM    <DIR>          SystemMailbox
```

You can also list the items in a public folder via ExIFS using the path
\\.\backofficestorage\<fully_qualified_domain_name>\public folders\
<public folder name>. Here's an example for a public folder called
Toastmasters:

```
C:\>dir "\\.\backofficestorage\company.com\public
➥folders\toastmasters"

Volume in drive \\.\backofficestorage is Exchange
Volume Serial Number is 00A9-8AC7

Directory of \\.\backofficestorage\company.com\public
➥folders\toastmasters

4/4/2004   09:22 AM    <DIR>          .
4/4/2004   09:22 AM    <DIR>          ..
4/4/2004   05:20 PM              1,277 Thursday Meeting-
➥610294F6-58BC-457A-AB14-A99D9B33E861-19C5E-M.EML
              1 File(s)          1,277 bytes
              2 Dir(s)   5,773,104,128 bytes free
```

You can't actually open or modify an item in a mailbox or public
folder within Explorer using ExIFS. The interface exists primarily for
Exchange services and tools. If you want to experiment with ExIFS, use
extreme caution and **never make changes to file permissions.** This
could render Exchange incapable of mapping permissions and result in a
complete loss of access to mailboxes and public folders.

Exchange 2000 caused a lot of problems for administrators by automatically mapping a logical drive, the M: drive, to the same device as the BackOfficeStorage symbolic link. Microsoft intended this as a convenient way to access the Exchange Store contents when building applications. Instead, it caused no end of headaches because antivirus and backup programs would treat items in the M: drive as if they were actual files and make changes to the security descriptors that prevented Exchange from mapping standard MAPI permissions to the items.

Microsoft removed the M: drive by default in Exchange 2003. Knowledge-Base article 821836 discusses a Registry change you can use to put back the M: drive mapping and to select a different drive letter. Don't expose ExIFS with a drive letter until you verify that your antivirus and antispam solutions will not corrupt your Exchange store.

# Exchange Services

A process designed to run without direct interaction with a user is called a *service*. Services run as threads under a parent executable called a *process*. You can see the running processes on a machine using Task Manager.

Launch Task Manager by pressing Ctrl+Alt+Del and clicking the Task Manager button in the Windows Security window, by right-clicking the status bar in Explorer and selecting Task Manager from the flyout menu, or by pressing Ctrl+Shift+Esc. Figure 3.10 shows an example with the Exchange services highlighted.

You can stop and start Exchange services using the Services console, launched from Start | All Programs | Administrative Tools. Figure 3.11 shows an example.

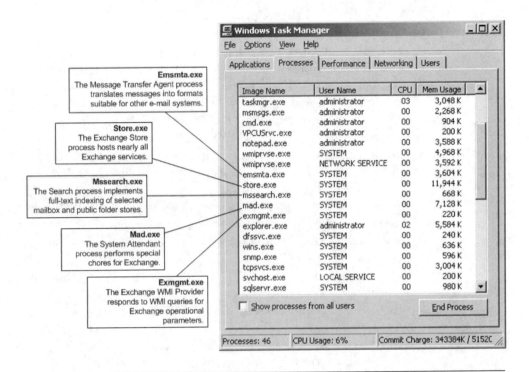

**Figure 3.10**   Process list in Task Manager showing Exchange 2003 processes and their functions.

**Figure 3.11**   Services console showing Exchange services and their status.

The following list gives a brief description of each Exchange service:

- **IMAP4 and POP3.** The Imap4svc and Pop3svc services provide access to the Exchange store for Internet clients.
- **Event.** The MSExchangeES service is hosted by its own process, Events.exe. This service provides an interface for event monitoring and logging.

- **Information Store.** The MSExchangeIS service, hosted by Store.exe, exposes the Exchange databases.
- **MTA Stacks.** The MSExchangeMTA service is hosted by its own executable process, Emsmta.exe. This service translates messages between different transport protocols. For example, messages sent from an Exchange 2003 server to an Exchange 5.5 server require conversion from SMTP to RPC.
- **Routing Engine.** The RESvc service, hosted by Inetinfo.exe, enhances the standard SMTP routing performed by Windows Server 2003. The enhanced routing engine knows how to query Active Directory for recipient information and can interact directly with the Exchange Store.
- **Active Directory Connector (ADC).** The ADC service isn't a core part of Exchange, per se. The ADC maintains synchronization between the contents of the legacy directory service in Exchange 5.5 and Active Directory.
- **Site Replication Service.** The MSExchangeSRS service is hosted by its own executable process, Srsmain.exe. This service maintains a functional copy of the legacy Exchange directory service so that an Exchange 2003 server can pretend to be an Exchange 5.5 server. This simplifies the transition to Exchange 2003.

Throughout this book, the term "legacy Exchange" refers to all versions of Exchange prior to Exchange 2000.

## System Attendant

The System Attendant service, hosted by the Mad.exe process, has extensive responsibilities and deserves a topic of its own.

MAD stands for Management and Administration Daemon.

If Exchange were a military organization, then the System Attendant services would be the enlisted men, doing all the System Attendant services grunt work with little or no fanfare. Here are the MAD services:

- **Recipient Update Service (RUS)**. This service applies e-mail attributes to objects in Active Directory and ensures that mail-enabled objects are included in the proper address lists.
- **DS2MB**. When you change the settings for a transport protocol (POP3, IMAP4, HTTP, NNTP, or SMTP) in Exchange System Manager, Exchange first writes the changes to Active Directory; then the DS2MB service plucks out the changes and applies them to the IIS Metabase.
- **Offline Address List (OAL) Generator**. Outlook users rely heavily on the comprehensive list of users, distribution lists, and contacts that go by the name Global Address List (GAL). Ordinarily, Outlook gets a fresh copy of the GAL from the Global Catalog each time the user checks the list. This can consume lots of time over a dial-up connection. A dial-up user can download a snapshot of the GAL called an Offline Address List. The OAL Generator service creates this offline address list and periodically refreshes it. It is also used by Outlook 2003 when operating in Cached Exchange mode, the default configuration.
- **Referral (RFR) service**. When an Outlook user wants to view the GAL, Outlook sends special Name Server Provider Interface (NSPI) requests to a Global Catalog server. It obtains the name of this Global Server from the RFR service on its home Exchange server.
- **NSPI Proxy**. Older Outlook clients (Outlook 98 SR1 and below) do not know how to request a Global Catalog server name using RFR. They send NSPI requests to the user's home server, and that's that. The NSPI Proxy service forwards these requests to a Global Catalog server and returns the responses back to the clients.
- **Free/Busy Service**. When Outlook makes a change to a user's calendar, Exchange places this change into a special system folder called Free/Busy Schedule+ so that other Outlook clients can check the user's availability when scheduling meetings. OWA clients can't update the Free/Busy Schedule+ folder directly, so OWA sends calendar updates to the System Attendant mailbox. From there, the System Attendant Free/Busy service (MadFB) forwards the calendar information to the Free/Busy Schedule+ system folder.

- **Mailbox Manager**. This service handles mailbox cleanup. For example, you could set a policy to remove or archive messages larger than 50K and older than 30 days. The Mailbox Manager would run periodically and enforce this policy by deleting or archiving as necessary in each user's mailbox.
- **Message Tracking**. If enabled, this service tracks messages sent and received by each server. It reads the message headers and writes tracking information to a log. Exchange System Manager displays the content of this log in a format that makes it simple to trace the message through the system.

## Service Diagnostics

You can view the operation of Exchange system services, including the services hosted by the System Attendant, using Diagnostics Logging. Launch ESM and open the Properties window for a server and select the Diagnostics Logging tab.

When you highlight a service, the right pane shows the functions performed by that service. Highlight MSExchangeSA to see the System Attendant functions available for diagnostics logging. Figure 3.12 shows an example. If you elect to log the activity of a service, the service writes information to the Event Log where you can survey the entries for problems.

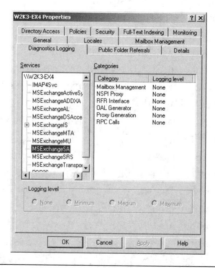

**Figure 3.12** Diagnostic Logging tab in ESM showing the System Attendant services.

## Service Dependencies

If you open the Properties window for the Microsoft Exchange Information Store service in the Services console, you'll see a tab labeled Dependencies (Figure 3.13.) Select this tab to view the services that must be running before the Information Store service can start.

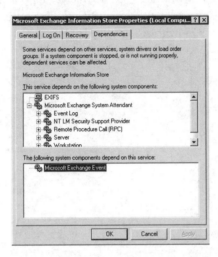

**Figure 3.13**    Service details for the Information Store service showing dependencies.

Notice that the System Attendant and the ExIFS (Exchange Installable File System) services must start before the Information Store service can start and that the Event service can't start until the Information Store starts. Also, the System Attendant service relies on quite a few operating system services.

These services form a line of dominos that must fall before the Information Store service can start. If you restart an Exchange server and you get a console message saying "One or more services did not start. See the Event Log for details," then you should first look to see if all the Exchange services started.

If a service does not start, check the Event Log to see if it recorded a reason. Try to start the service manually to see if it will initialize. Sometimes a startup condition forces a service to time out waiting to start, but it works just fine when started a little later.

## Looking Forward

This chapter was a tough slog. It's time to start taking action rather than studying, as I'm sure you'll agree. In the next few chapters, you'll learn how to manage the Exchange server that you've installed, how to manage the recipients who keep their mailboxes on that server, and how to deploy other servers that can route messages between themselves and between your organization and the Internet.

# CHAPTER 4

# Managing Exchange 2003 Servers

This chapter introduces Exchange System Manager (ESM), the primary management console for Exchange 2003, and shows the principles behind the operation of the various services that comprise Exchange. You'll see how the moving parts are knitted together using Windows object-based security and Active Directory delegation.

Armed with this knowledge, you'll discover how to define administrative roles in an organization and how to delegate those roles to selected administrators. Finally, you'll see how to compartmentalize the management of a large or diverse Exchange organization.

## Exchange System Manager

You first saw ESM in Chapter 1, "Installing an Exchange 2003 Server," but you haven't really needed to dive into the internals until now. Launch ESM from the console of your Exchange server via **Start | All Programs | Microsoft Exchange | System Manager**. Figure 4.1 shows the content of the ESM console for an organization with several servers in various locations.

Here's a quick rundown of the main items at the top of the ESM tree:

- **Global Settings.** These icons control general message formatting, delivery, and mobile services. The particular processes controlled by these settings are covered in their respective chapters. The key thing to remember about Global Settings is that the parameters you set in this area affect connections and message delivery throughout an entire organization. They override similar settings made on individual servers.

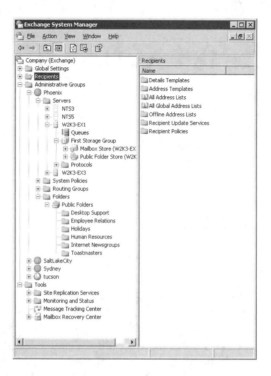

**Figure 4.1**    ESM console window showing contents of new organization.

- **Recipients.** This container holds templates, address lists, and policies to control recipient settings such as mailbox size. Like Global Settings, any policies you set at this level affect the entire organization, so use caution in your lab so that you don't set a policy here and then forget about it and wonder why some feature isn't functioning properly.
- **Administrative Groups.** This container is not ordinarily visible if you do a pristine installation of Exchange 2003. That's because a pristine installation has only a single Administrative Group, so ESM does not bother showing a hierarchy. To view the Administrative Group container, open the Properties window for the organization and select **Show Administrative Groups**, as shown in Figure 4.2.

With this change in place, the ESM view shows the Administrative Groups container with a single container under it called First Administrative Group.

**Figure 4.2**   Using Organization properties in ESM to display Routing Groups and Administrative Groups.

When you install Exchange 2003 for the first time, either as a pristine installation or to migrate from legacy Exchange, the first administrative group created in Active Directory gets a special flag called msExchDefaultAdminGroup. This flag denotes this administrative group as the sole repository of public folder hierarchy information. If you accidentally delete the default administrative group, Exchange selects another one to take its place.

## Servers

Under the Administrative Group icon you'll find a Servers icon that contains yet another icon representing your Exchange server, which exposes quite a few parameters for the server.

### Queue Viewer

Clicking the **Queues** icon opens a Queue Viewer, shown in Figure 4.3. The Queue Viewer shows the various inbound and outbound message queues on the server. This permits you to quickly assess mail routing failures.

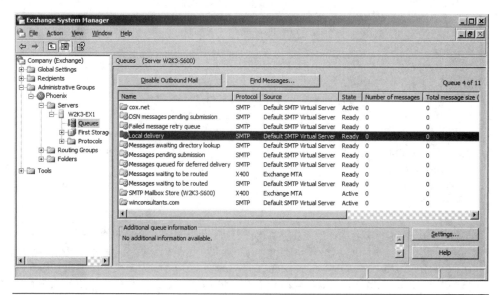

**Figure 4.3**    Queue Viewer in Exchange System Manager.

When users send mail to Internet recipients, the queue list expands to include the destination domain (**yahoo.com**, for example). After the message gets delivered, the queue entry stays in place for awhile and then goes away if no one sends mail to the same destination domain. If the routing engine has more than one message queued up for the same destination, the Number of Messages column will have a number larger than 1. For more information on message routing, see Chapter 8, "Message Routing."

### Find Messages

If a queue gets backed up—indicated by the Number of Messages column in the Queue Viewer staying above 1 for a long period of time—a potential cause is a malformed message that is caught in the queue, causing all other messages to pile up behind it like a marble stuck in a garden hose. To view individual messages in the queue, proceed as follows:

1. Right-click on a queue and select **Find Messages** from the flyout menu. The Find Messages window opens, as shown in Figure 4.4.

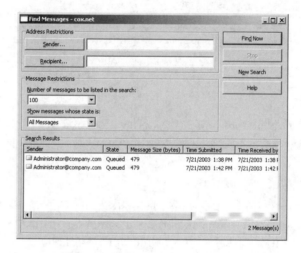

**Figure 4.4**    Find Messages window in Queue Viewer.

2. Click the **Find Now** button to list all the messages in the queue. The example shows a message from Administrator2.
3. Double-click the listing to see the content of the message header, shown in Figure 4.5. You cannot view the message content from this interface. Exchange blocks the content of messages to avoid potential security and performance issues.

**Figure 4.5**    Detailed contents of message headers in Queue Viewer.

## Tools

The Tools container in ESM holds a variety of items useful for managing and monitoring Exchange server functions.

### Monitoring and Status

One of your most important duties as an Exchange administrator is to keep track of the status of all the Exchange servers in your organization, so that you can take actions to recover from failures before users start calling the Help Desk (or your desk, if they know where it is). Proactive management should be one of your highest priorities.

The Monitoring and Status tools in ESM enable you to view the status of the services running on each Exchange server and to create ways to notify you and your colleagues if one of those services should stop or fail.

For example, Figure 4.6 shows an enterprise deployment of Exchange 2003 with several servers in a variety of locations. On server W2K3-EX2, one or more critical services are not running. Depending on the service, this could impair message routing to the server, and users with mailboxes on that server might not be able to access their mail.

To determine the actual cause of the error, open the Properties window for the server icon. This shows the list of monitored items that have been defined for the server, as shown in Figure 4.7.

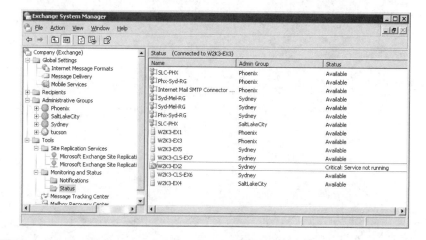

**Figure 4.6**   Status monitor in ESM showing failure of a critical service on an Exchange server.

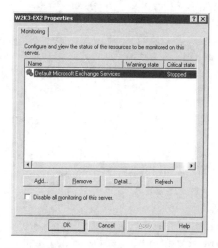

**Figure 4.7**   Properties window of a monitored server showing the list of service states that the monitoring service is looking for.

By default, Exchange defines a monitored item that looks at the status of the Exchange services running on a server. To see the list of services in this monitored item, click the item name, which is a hyperlink that opens the list of services, as shown in Figure 4.8. The figure shows that the Microsoft Exchange Information Store service has stopped.

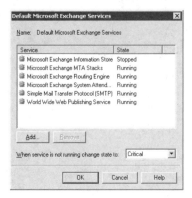

**Figure 4.8**   List of services obtained from the monitoring service showing the stopped service on a remote Exchange server.

The Information Store service exposes the contents of the mailboxes and public folders on an Exchange server. If the service is not running, the Exchange server is offline for all intents and purposes. Your most likely course of action would be to start the service, but you would also want to investigate why the service stopped in the first place. Diagnostic tips for finding and correcting problems like this are scattered throughout this book.

### *Alerts*

You probably don't want to sit in front of your console all day looking for changes to the icons under Status in ESM Tools. You want to be notified automatically in the event of a failure. That's the purpose of the Notifications icon.

Right-click the **Notifications** icon and select **New | E-mail Notification** from the flyout menu. This opens a Properties window, as shown in Figure 4.9. Using this window, you can send yourself an e-mail containing details of the event.

Also, if you have a paging service that accepts e-mail, you can create a second notification item that sends a message to your text pager.

E-mail notification has its limitations, however. If your mailbox is on the failed server, for example, you won't get a notification. Or events might occur that require immediate attention. For example, you might want to simply start the service and get notification that the service is running normally. You can script automatic actions that will initiate when the alert occurs. To do so, right-click the **Notifications** icon and select **New | Script Notification** from the flyout menu. This opens the Properties window shown in Figure 4.10.

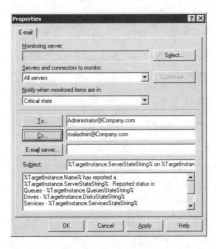

**Figure 4.9**   Notifications properties for the monitoring service showing a canned message to send if a server should trigger a critical or warning event in the monitoring service.

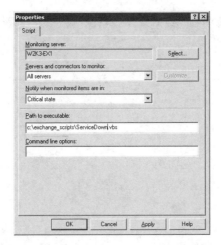

**Figure 4.10**   Script tab of a monitored server showing the ability to trigger automated actions in response to an event.

Writing scripts to take automated actions on Exchange servers falls outside the scope of this book. I highly recommend these three references if you want to do any sort of scripting in a Windows or Exchange environment:

- *Microsoft Windows 2000 Scripting Guide*, by The Scripting Guys at Microsoft (Microsoft Press)

- *Programming Microsoft Outlook and Microsoft Exchange*, Third Edition, by Thomas Rizzo (Microsoft Press)
- *Exchange 2003 Cookbook*, by Paul Robichaux, Missy Koslosky, et al (O'Reilly)

### Message Tracking Center

The message tracking feature in Exchange makes it possible to trace the path of any message handled by any server in the organization. This helps identify routing problems caused by incorrect addressing or other internal message configuration errors.

At this point, you've only installed one Exchange server, so message tracking is pretty simple. But once you have a production deployment with several servers in remote locations, message tracking gets somewhat more difficult. Figure 4.11 shows an example of a search performed in the Message Tracking Center window, and Figure 4.12 shows the routing information stored by the system for the message.

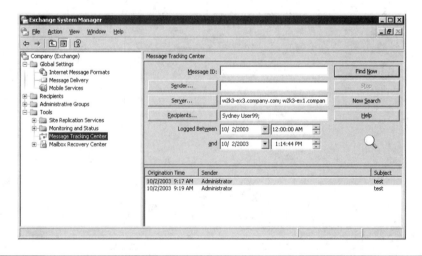

**Figure 4.11**   Message Tracking Center with list of messages captured from an Exchange server's tracking log.

The ability to analyze the path of a message through each component of Exchange helps to identify and isolate problems. This feature requires enabling message tracking logging at all Exchange servers and making sure that you have sufficient storage capacity to hold the log files.

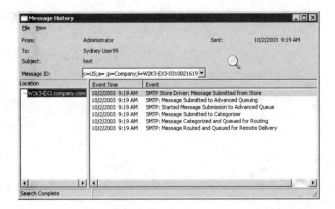

**Figure 4.12** Routing information extracted from a tracking log for a selected message.

## Legacy Exchange Servers

In Chapter 12, "Migrating From Legacy Exchange," you'll install an Exchange 2003 server into an existing Exchange 5.5 organization. When operating in this mode, ESM displays legacy servers as plain, black-and-white icons and does the same for legacy sites that do not contain Exchange 2000 or Exchange 2003 servers.

Throughout this book, the term "legacy Exchange" refers to all versions of Exchange prior to Exchange 2000.

ESM also allows you to see certain parameters in legacy Exchange servers. For example, Figure 4.13 shows the mailboxes on a legacy server called NTS3.

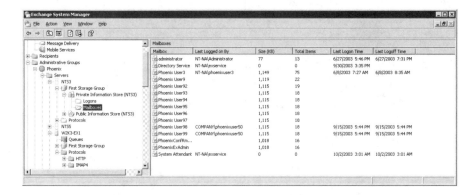

**Figure 4.13**   Legacy Exchange server shown in ESM.

You can't use ESM to add new recipients or distribution lists to legacy servers, or to modify the properties of existing objects, but you can use ESM to move mailboxes from a legacy Exchange server to an Exchange 2003 server. To get full administrative control over the legacy servers, you need the legacy Admin.exe tool. You can install a copy of this tool from the Exchange 2003 Setup menu.

# Installing ESM on a Workstation

ESM can be installed independently of Exchange. You can install ESM on any server or workstation where you manage accounts. Be sure to install ESM on domain controllers if you want to see the Exchange parameters in Active Directory Users and Computers.

## Prerequisites for Installing ESM

Here are the prerequisites for installing ESM separately from Exchange:

- **Operating system.** ESM requires either Windows Server 2003, Windows 2000 SP3 or higher, or XP SP1 or higher. You can install ESM on a workstation along with any version of Outlook or no Outlook at all. Unlike the core Exchange binaries, ESM does not conflict with the MAPI binaries used by Outlook.
- **Domain membership.** The workstation or server where you install ESM must belong to a domain in the same forest as the Exchange organization you want to manage.

- **IIS**. Install the following IIS components on your workstation or domain controller before you can install ESM. Exchange Setup checks for their presence and will refuse to proceed without them:

    - Network COM+ access
    - Common files
    - IIS manager
    - NNTP service
    - SMTP service
    - World Wide Web service

If running IIS on a domain controller violates an internal IT policy, you can disable the NNTP, SMTP, and WWW services after you have installed ESM. In fact, you should disable these services on any machine when they are not needed.

- **Active Directory management tools**. The Active Directory management tools (such as Active Directory Users and Computers) must be installed. ESM makes use of their DLLs. The tools come in a file called Adminpak.msi. For XP SP1, install the Windows Server 2003 administration tools. For Windows 2000 Professional SP3 or higher, install the Windows 2000 administration tools.

The Exchange 2003 prescriptive checklist states that the Windows Server 2003 admin tools must be loaded on a Windows 2000 server prior to installing ESM. This is not correct. Refer to Microsoft Knowledge Base article 826966 for clarification.

If you want to run Exchange 2000 ESM on an XP workstation, you have a challenge because Exchange 2000 ESM does not work with the Windows Server 2003 admin tools, and you can't install Windows 2000 admin tools in an XP workstation. Here's a trick to break the deadlock. Download a patch from Microsoft called Exchange2000-KB815529-x86-ENU.exe. The patch registers a Globally Unique Identifier (GUID) in the XP desktop that fools ESM into thinking that the Windows 2000 admin tools are loaded. Install the Windows Server 2003 admin tools, install the patch, and then install Exchange 2000 ESM.

If this seems like too much work, you always have the option of connecting to the Exchange server via Remote Desktop (also known as Terminal Services) to run ESM.

### Installing ESM

Put the Exchange 2003 CD in the caddy, or connect to a share point that has the installation files and double-click on the Setup.exe file at the root of the CD. This opens the Exchange Server 2003 Welcome window.

1. Click **Deployment Tools**. This opens a Welcome window for the deployment tools.
2. At the bottom of the list of installation options, click **Install Exchange System Management Tools Only**.
3. Under Step 4 of the prescriptive checklist, click **Run Setup Now**.
4. When the Component Selection window opens, select **Custom** next to **Microsoft Exchange** and **Install** next to **Microsoft Exchange System Management Tools**.
5. Click **Next**. A Summary window opens.
6. Click **Next**. This begins the installation.

ESM installation replaces the Active Directory Users and Computers (ADUC) console with a new version that exposes Exchange attributes and processes.

## Exchange Services and Security

Authentication and authorization are concepts that don't get much attention until something goes wrong. Then they take center stage, at least for awhile, until the problem gets resolved, and that's when they fade into the wings again. For example, think of the messages that get routed between Exchange servers. As you saw in Chapter 2, "Understanding and Using Messaging Protocols," an Exchange server does not allow an anonymous connection to route SMTP messages. This means that one Exchange server must have a way to authenticate with another Exchange server in order to route messages.

Here's another example. Let's say you install Exchange Server 2003 on a newly created Windows Server 2003 server in a Windows Server 2003 domain. When you restart the machine, you notice that none of the

Exchange services start, and you get a series of Event Log messages telling you that one service after another experienced errors with long and inscrutable error codes. You spend a few hours sifting through the Microsoft Knowledge Base, but nothing jumps out at you except the mention in a few places of an Exchange Enterprise Servers group and an Exchange Domain Servers group. You eventually determine that Setup did not update the group memberships correctly, a somewhat common error in Exchange Server 2003, and for this reason the entire suite of Exchange services failed to operate properly.

Microsoft Product Support Services (PSS) routinely deals with Exchange problems caused by improper configurations that result in authentication or authorization failures. Let's take a few minutes and see how an Exchange server interacts with other Exchange servers in an organization. Knowing how this works will help you understand the fixes you might need to apply when communications break down. You'll also get a firmer grasp on the architectural requirements for Exchange, and this will help you stand your ground when the Active Directory administrators want to play games with the structure of their domains.

## Special Exchange Groups

Every Exchange server belongs to a Global group called Exchange Domain Servers and a Domain Local group called Exchange Enterprise Servers in each domain in which Setup /Domainprep has been run. You'll find these two groups in the Users container in Active Directory Users and Computers.

If you move either the Exchange Domain Servers or Exchange Enterprise Servers group out of the Users container, or rename them, then Exchange fails to operate properly.

Take a look at the membership list for the Exchange Domain Servers group. Figure 4.14 shows an example. See how the membership includes all the Exchange servers in the domain? When you install Exchange 2003 on a server, the Recipient Update Service adds the server to the membership list of the Exchange Domain Servers group within in its domain. If RUS fails to update the membership correctly, the server cannot connect to items in Active Directory. This causes the Exchange services to fail.

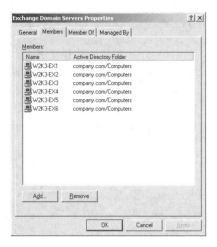

**Figure 4.14**   Exchange Domain Servers member list showing Exchange servers from local domain.

The membership of the Exchange Enterprise Servers group (Figure 4.15) shows the Exchange Domain Servers group from each domain that contains at least one Exchange server. Because of the way Windows handles nested groups, every Exchange server in a forest belongs to the Exchange Enterprise Servers group in every domain. As you'll see in the next section, the Exchange Enterprise Servers group has extensive privileges in a domain.

**Figure 4.15**   Exchange Enterprise Servers group showing membership of Exchange Domain Servers groups from each domain.

## Permissions Delegated to Exchange Groups

As part of Exchange Setup, the Exchange Domain Servers and Exchange Enterprise Servers groups are created and delegated permissions in the Exchange organization and in each domain. Here is a list of the Exchange organization permissions delegated to the Exchange Domain Servers group:

- List the contents, read properties, create subobjects, read and write access permissions for all objects in an organization.
- Change any attribute in the Public Information property set and the Private Information property set for all objects in the organization.
- Full control of all properties and permissions on Site Addressing objects.

Here is a list of the domain permissions delegated to the Exchange Enterprise Servers group:

- Write any attribute in the Public Information and Private Information property set and the DisplayName attribute for all objects in the domain.
- Read and write permissions and read any properties of group objects, user objects, and InetOrgPerson objects.

A *property set* defines a list of Active Directory attributes treated as a single attribute for purposes of delegating access. The Public Information and Private Information property sets contain a variety of attributes, such as a user's e-mail address, User Principal Name (UPN), and group membership.

If you look at the security permissions for the root container in the domain, you'll find the Exchange Enterprise Servers group, as shown in Figure 4.16.

Also, if you look at the security list for the Microsoft Exchange System Objects container (visible if you select **View | Advanced Features** from the console menu) you'll see that both the Exchange Enterprise Servers group and the Exchange Domain Servers group have Full Control access to any and all objects in that container. This container holds Public Folder objects for mail-enabled public folders and system folders along with User objects for Exchange system accounts.

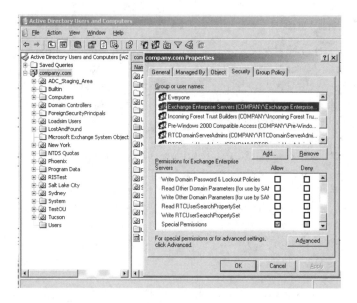

**Figure 4.16** Permissions assigned to a Domain object in Active Directory contain Exchange Enterprise Servers.

## Security Implications of Delegated Exchange Permissions

A member of the Exchange Enterprise Servers group can read just about any property on User, Group, and InetOrgPerson objects, and it can set the group type for any group. From a security standpoint, an Exchange server represents a significant security threat if it ever gets compromised.

You can demonstrate this to yourself using a quick experiment. First, log on at the console of an Exchange server using credentials with domain administrator privileges. Change the local security setting to give Authenticated Users local logon rights. Do this by launching the local Group Policy Editor, Gpedit.msc. Drill down to **Computer Configuration | Windows Settings | Security Settings | User Rights Assignments** and open the properties window for the **Allow Log On Locally** setting. Use the **Add** button to add the Authenticated Users group to the **Allowed Access** list.

The default configuration of the Log On Locally privilege allows access only to administrators and administrator equivalents. This experiment changes the default configuration only for demonstration purposes. This important security setting should never be changed in production.

Now, while logged on as an administrator, use the AT command to open an empty command prompt window in a few minutes from the current time. If the current time is 5:17 pm, the AT syntax would be:

```
at 17:19 /interactive cmd
```

Now log off and log on as an average user. Let a couple of minutes roll by and watch as an empty command prompt window springs open. By default, this console runs in the security context of the local system. At this point, you have given yourself the same sort of privilege elevation that a bad guy might get using an exploit that allows installing a root kit on your server.

From the command prompt, launch ADUC by typing dsa.msc and pressing **Enter**. By launching ADUC from a window running in the security context of Local System, the MMC console also runs in same security context.

Drill down to an OU that has users in it. You'll notice that you cannot create a user or delete one, but you can right-click and select Exchange Tasks and use the wizard to change the user's mailbox location or to remove the mailbox entirely.

Now go back to the command console window and change directory to the **\Exchsrvr\bin** directory. Launch ESM from there. Drill down to another Exchange server in the same Administrative Group and open the **Protocols | SMTP** folder. Right-click the **Default SMTP Virtual Server** icon and select **Stop** from the flyout menu. The service stops. This demonstrates that the Local System account on one Exchange server can access processes on another Exchange server.

Here's a quick question. If Exchange services run in the Local System security context, how do they exercise privileges on other servers and in Active Directory? After all, the Local System account does not have a domain SID, right?

*continues*

The answer lies with Kerberos. When an Exchange service connects to the network, it obtains a Kerberos ticket using the computer account of the Exchange server. When the Local System account reaches out to touch an Exchange service on another machine, it uses a copy of this Kerberos ticket to get a valid security connection to the server.

### Bottom Line on Exchange Permissions

Microsoft changed the security context for Exchange services in response to problems caused by using discrete service accounts in legacy Exchange. This service account had ultimate privileges in the Exchange organization and often became a back door to the Exchange servers in a way that invited abuse, either deliberately or by accident.

Because the Local System account runs all Exchange services, you don't need to worry about giving someone a back door to your Exchange organization. But you need to use particular caution to protect Exchange servers. Never permit unfettered physical access and never allow console logon to anyone except authorized administrators.

Also, use caution when adding new applications to an Exchange server or when doing such innocent things as browsing the Internet. If you accidentally introduce a Trojan onto an Exchange server, it would gain a tremendous foothold in your organization. Keep a current list of the services running on each Exchange server and refer to the Microsoft security white papers and prescriptive checklists for guidelines in keeping the servers secure. You'll find these documents at `www.microsoft.com/exchange/techinfo/security`.

## Management Components

Exchange makes use of a variety of information repositories in addition to the Exchange Store. Each of these repositories requires a different set of technologies for retrieving information. Exchange has core administrative business logic that knows how to access each of these target repositories, and ESM taps into that core logic to display information and control operations.

Figure 4.17 shows the repositories and their interfaces. Because you work with ESM every day, you need at least a passing familiarity with each of the data repositories it accesses and the interfaces it uses to get that access.

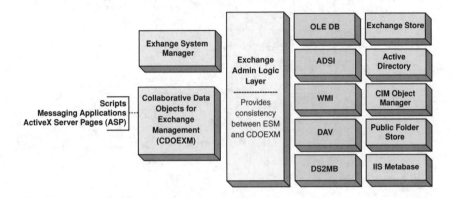

**Figure 4.17**     Exchange Admin Logic with interfaces that connect ESM and CDOEXM to various data repositories that support Exchange operations.

## ADSI and Active Directory

Active Directory holds configuration information for the Exchange organization along with e-mail parameters for users, groups, and contacts. Exchange accesses Active Directory information using the Active Directory Services Interface, or ADSI.

Try this experiment. Open Notepad and enter the following lines of VBScript. Save the file with the name ADSITest.vbs.

```
set RootDSE = GetObject("LDAP://RootDSE")
domainName = RootDSE.Get("DefaultNamingContext")
set adsiDomain = GetObject("LDAP://" & domainName)

Set connection = CreateObject("ADODB.Connection")
connection.Provider = "ADsDSOObject"
connection.open
```

```
Set command = CreateObject("ADODB.Command")
Set command.ActiveConnection = connection

Command.Properties("Page Size") = 1000
Command.Properties("Timeout") = 30
Command.Properties("searchscope") = 2
Command.Properties("Chase referrals") = 0
Command.Properties("Cache Results") = False

command.CommandText = "SELECT AdsPath,cn,mailnickname,homeMDB " &_
                      "FROM 'LDAP://dc=company,DC=com' " &_
                      "WHERE objectcategory = 'user' " &_
                      "AND mailnickname='*'"

Set rs = command.Execute

On Error Resume Next
Do Until rs.EOF
    WScript.Echo("User " & rs.fields("cn") &_
                " has a mailbox on " & rs.fields("homemdb"))
    rs.MoveNext
Loop
```

Execute the script by typing `cscript adsitest.vbs`. (The default wscript script engine will give you many pop-up windows.)

When you execute the script, you'll get a list of all the mailbox-enabled users in the organization. You'll get the same result whether you're logged on as an administrator or an average user. Any authenticated user has permission to view the values assigned to most of the attributes of Active Directory objects.

The script uses ADSI to access Active Directory. ESM also uses ADSI when it accesses Active Directory information; it formulates an ADSI query that searches for existing information or writes new information. For example, when you use ESM to access user information such as the Exchange features shown in Figure 4.18, the console uses ADSI to send LDAP queries to a domain controller.

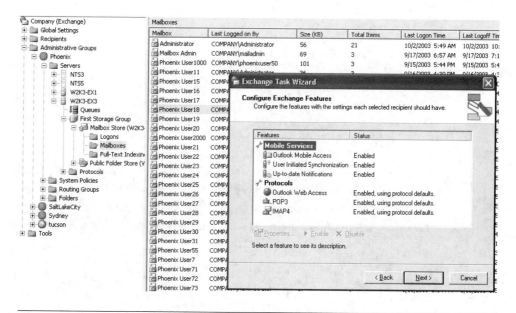

**Figure 4.18**    ESM accesses feature information for a user via ADSI.

## WMI and Server Status Monitoring

Windows Management Instrumentation (WMI) provides a way to access a variety of hardware configurations and application parameters on a Windows server. For example, you can get a quick assessment of the processor configuration on a Windows Server 2003 server or XP desktop by using a command-line WMI utility called WMIC. Use this syntax:

```
wmic cpu list full
```

Here's an excerpt from the listing:

```
C:\>wmic cpu list full
AddressWidth=32
Caption=x86 Family 15 Model 2 Stepping 9
CreationClassName=Win32_Processor
CurrentVoltage=15
ExtClock=800
L2CacheSize=512
```

```
L2CacheSpeed=2992
Manufacturer=GenuineIntel
MaxClockSpeed=2992
Name= Intel(R) Pentium(R) 4 CPU 3.00GHz
```

Applications that query for WMI information are called WMI consumers. Applications such as Exchange that contribute information to WMI consumers are called WMI providers. The Microsoft Exchange Management service, MSExchangeMGMT, running under the Exmgmt.exe process, acts as the WMI provider for Exchange.

ESM acts as a WMI consumer and uses information obtained via WMI in quite a few places. For example, when you select the Status icon under Tools | Monitoring and Status, ESM displays information it collects from making WMI queries to the various servers and connectors in the organization, as shown in Figure 4.19.

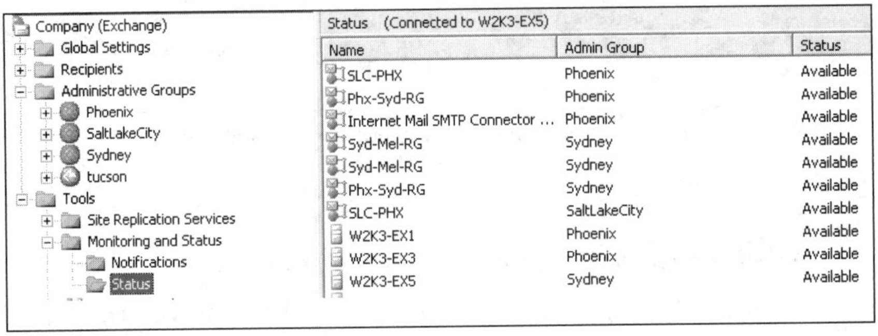

**Figure 4.19** ESM gets status information for other servers and connectors via WMI.

ESM also uses WMI to obtain queue information for display in the Queue Viewer. And when you use the Message Tracking Center (shown in Figure 4.20) in ESM to query for message history from the tracking log, ESM gets this information using WMI.

You can see that WMI provides critical services to ESM, and to Exchange itself. If you find Event Log entries on an Exchange server that contain errors associated with WMI or that originate from the Windows Server 2003 WMI service (WinMgmt) or the Exchange WMI provider (MSExchangeMGMT), take immediate action to isolate and correct the problem. For example, let's say you install a management utility such as a SNMP agent on an Exchange server.

A while later, you notice a console message that the Application Event Log is full, and you open it to find hundreds of these errors:

`MSExchangeMGMT Event ID 6 - "Could not start the Microsoft Exchange Management service on Local Computer. The service did not return error. This could be an internal Windows error or an internal service error. If problem persists, contact your system administrator."`

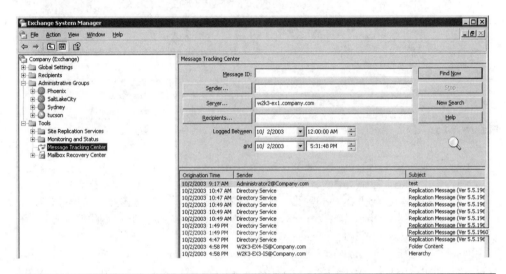

**Figure 4.20**    ESM obtains access to message tracking log via WMI.

This failure probably won't interfere with the operation of the critical Exchange services, but you won't be able to monitor the server using WMI, which is arguably more flexible than SNMP in many cases, but try convincing the networking group. You'll need to correct the problem so you can use the SNMP agent and Exchange WMI simultaneously. Future Microsoft utilities will leverage WMI more fully in regards to Exchange troubleshooting, and third-party monitoring and reporting applications also include WMI scripts to return valuable information, so don't ignore problems involving the Exchange WMI provider.

## WebDAV and Public Folder Access

ESM lets you access the public folder hierarchy and the contents of public folders. Figure 4.21 shows an example. Although this seems like a natural thing for an Exchange management utility to do, Exchange 2003 ESM represents the first time Microsoft has rolled this functionality into the main Exchange administrative interface.

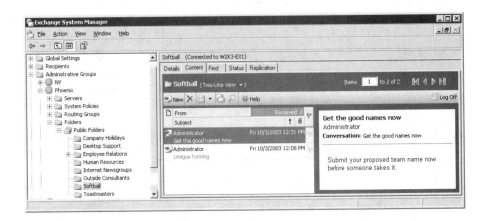

**Figure 4.21**    ESM accesses public folder content via WebDAV.

ESM uses WebDAV to access public folder content, the same protocol used by Outlook Web Access. Because WebDAV uses HTTP, it
accesses Exchange via the virtual folders hosted by IIS. (A virtual folder
in IIS has the same function as a share point in a network file system. It
provides a handle for accessing content.)

You can view the Exchange folders under Default Web Site in the
Internet Information Services Manager console, as shown in Figure
4.22. Don't make changes to virtual folders properties in the IIS Manager console. Use ESM to manage Exchange Web folders.

The IIS Manager console displays a virtual folder using an icon with
a folder and a globe. You can access a virtual folder directly from a
browser by inputting its name along with the name of the Web server in
Uniform Resource Locator (URL) format. For example, to access the
Exchange virtual folder on a server named W2K3-EX1, you would enter
the following URL in a browser: `http://w2k3-ex1/exchange`.

If you look at the Path column for virtual folders in IIS, you'll see that several of the Exchange folders use the `\\.\backofficestorage` symbolic link
exposed by the Exchange Installable File System (IFS). This means that
WebDAV applications such as ESM draw their content directly from the
Exchange Store.

IIS considers a folder containing executable code to be a Web application.
It uses a gear icon to indicate a virtual folder where users have Execute
permissions. For example, the OMA (Outlook Mobile Access) folder contains a Bin folder with a set of Dynamic Link Libraries (DLLs) that users
execute when they access the folder, so its icon has a gear.

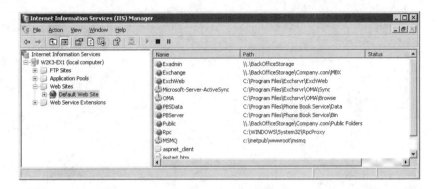

**Figure 4.22**    Exchange virtual folders in the Default Web Site displayed in the IIS Manager console.

You'll encounter references in quite a few places to WebDAV and the way ESM and OWA use WebDAV for accessing the Exchange Store. Keep this functionality in mind when you encounter situations where the connection does not work. For example, if you attempt WebDAV access to a public folder from one Exchange server, but the content of the public folder is hosted by another Exchange server, the connection might fail if it must traverse a firewall, or if DNS is not configured correctly.

## DS2MB and IIS Metabase

You've already seen how you can change the settings of IIS services from within ESM. In fact, on an Exchange server, you should use ESM only to modify IIS service settings. That's because ESM first writes its changes to Active Directory and then copies those changes to the local IIS Metabase (the database that contains IIS parameters). The service responsible for copying settings from Active Directory to the IIS Metabase is called DS2MB. Understanding the operation of the DS2MB (Directory Service to Metabase) service requires a bit of pre-liminary explanation of IIS configuration.

Recall that many services critical to the operation of Exchange actu-ally run under IIS, which stores configuration information in a repository called the IIS Metabase. In Windows Server 2003, the IIS Metabase is an XML file located in %windir%\System32\Inetsrv. In Windows 2000, the Metabase is a binary file located in the same folder.

The IIS 6.0 Resource Kit has a utility called the IIS Metabase Explorer that allows you to browse the content of the Metabase. Figure 4.23 shows an example listing for the attributes associated with the default SMTP virtual server.

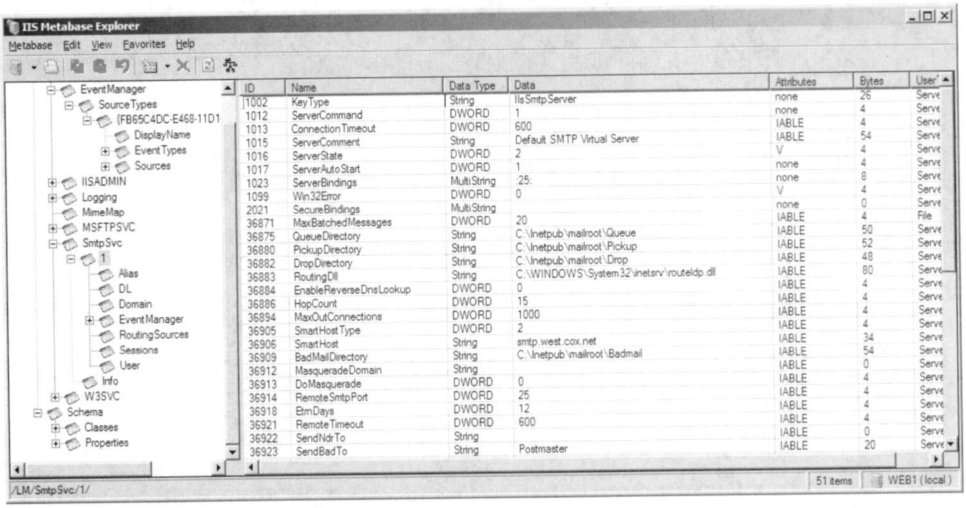

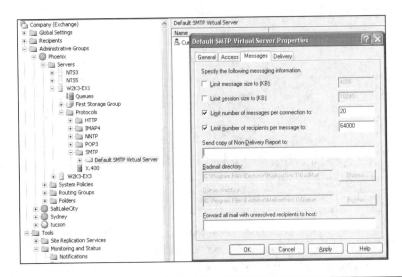

**Figure 4.23** IIS Metabase Explorer showing settings for SMTP virtual server.

Figure 4.24 shows SMTP configuration settings displayed in ESM. Although it looks as if you directly control IIS parameters from within ESM, in actuality, the parameters you see actually reside in a set of Protocol Configuration objects in Active Directory, not in the IIS Metabase.

**Figure 4.24** SMPT virtual server parameters displayed in ESM, parameters obtained from Active Directory.

You can verify this using the ADSI Editor, Adsiedit.msc, located in the Windows Server 2003 Support Tools.

Drill down through the Configuration container to **Services | Microsoft Exchange | <Organization_Name> | Administrative Groups | <admin_group_name> | Servers | <server_name> | Protocols | SMTP**. Open the Properties of the CN=1 object and find the list of attributes that start with msExchSmtp. Figure 4.25 shows an example.

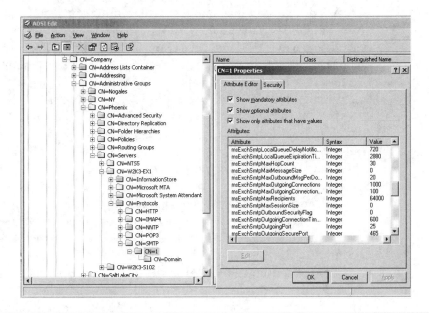

**Figure 4.25**    ADSI Editor showing Metabase-related attributes associated with Protocol objects in Active Directory.

So, with this in mind, here's the magic performed by DS2MB. When you make a change to a protocol in ESM, the change first gets written to a Protocol Configuration object in Active Directory. Periodically, the DS2MB service reads the content of the Protocol Configuration objects and writes any property changes it finds into the corresponding values in the IIS Metabase.

By placing all this IIS information in Active Directory, Exchange ensures that every Exchange server in the organization knows the protocol settings of every transport on every other Exchange server.

## Summary

Before moving forward to see how to manage all these Exchange services, here's a quick summary of the important points covered so far:

- **Exchange System Manager (ESM).** ESM is the primary tool for managing an Exchange organization. It gives you a central platform for configuring server parameters, storage parameters, recipient parameters, and message routing on any Exchange server in the organization.
- **Active Directory Users and Computers (ADUC).** As useful as ESM is, you also need ADUC to manage Exchange parameters on users, groups, and contacts.
- **Exchange and IIS tightly coupled.** The POP3, IMAP4, NNTP, SMTP, and HTTP transports run as part of IIS but have extensions in Exchange that expose additional features. SMTP is especially crucial to Exchange operation. If IIS fails to operate, an Exchange server cannot route mail.
- **Exchange services can be stopped and started via the Services console.** You do not necessarily need to restart an Exchange server if a single service hangs or misbehaves. You can stop and start that service individually, either using the Services console or the SC command-line utility.
- **System Attendant has *a lot* of duties.** Throughout the remainder of this book, you'll spend much of your time either configuring services controlled by the System Attendant or monitoring their operation. If you experience a failure in Mad.exe on a server, you will not have a good day as an Exchange administrator.

# Assigning Administrative Permissions

Once you get the first few Exchange servers deployed in production, it won't take long before you'll want other administrators to take over some of the operational duties. First, though, you need to make sure that only authorized administrators can make changes to Exchange servers, recipients, and other e-mail-related objects.

## Operations Requiring Administrative Permissions

Exchange defines quite a few permissions that can be assigned to administrators. Here is a list of their titles, which should be fairly self-explanatory:

- Administer Information Store
- Create named properties in the Information Store
- Create public folder
- Create top level public folder
- Modify public folder ACL (Access Control List)
- Modify public folder admin ACL
- Modify public folder deleted item retention
- Modify public folder expiry
- Modify public folder quotas
- Modify public folder replica list
- Open mail send queue
- Read Metabase properties (this refers to the IIS Metabase)
- Receive As
- Send As
- View Information Store status

You'll see items from this list in the Security tab for various Exchange-related objects in ADUC and Active Directory Sites and Services. Only permissions related to that particular object's class get put on the list.

## Administrative Roles

You don't ordinarily assign individual Exchange permissions to an administrator. Instead, Exchange collects permissions together and gives them a name, called a role. Exchange 2003 defines three administrative roles:

- Exchange Full Administrator
- Exchange Administrator
- Exchange View-Only Administrator

The following sections contain details about each role and a description of what the role can do in an Exchange organization.

Classic Exchange also uses roles to define permission sets, but it has many more roles that are often confusing to implement. You'll see these roles appear throughout the Exchange 5.x documentation, so it doesn't hurt to know their names, but you don't need to memorize their permission sets. They are Service Account Admin, Permission Admin, Admin, View-Only Admin, User, and Send As.

### Exchange Full Administrator

As you might expect from the name, the Exchange Full Administrator role has full access permissions on all objects in an Exchange organization, including the ability to change permission settings. This means that an administrator with the Exchange Full Administrator role can grant administrative permissions to another administrator. From a security perspective, this privilege should be given only to a select few individuals.

In addition, the Exchange Full Administrator role has Read and Change permissions on the Deleted Objects container in each Domain naming context. This permits an administrator who has been assigned the Exchange Full Administrator role to use ESM to reassign the mailbox of a deleted user. This permission *does not* permit restoring a deleted user.

### Exchange Administrator

The Exchange Administrator role has the same rights as the Exchange Full Administrator role, with one exception: An Exchange Administrator cannot modify security permissions. This means you can assign the Enterprise Administrator role to a colleague without worrying that he or she will turn around and delegate an administrative role or permission to someone else.

### Exchange View Only Administrator

An administrator assigned the Exchange View Only role can see the contents of the Exchange organization but cannot make any changes. Assign this role to Windows administrators if you want them to mailbox-enable users or mail-enable groups and contacts when they create the objects in Active Directory. Otherwise, you'll have to come along later and do the mail configuration yourself.

## Administrators Denied Access to User Mailboxes

The default security permissions assigned to an organization specifically deny mailbox access to anyone who has the Exchange Full Administrators or Exchange Administrators role (except for the administrator's personal mailbox.) This prevents administrators from indiscriminately opening user mailboxes and getting inappropriate access to a user's private information.

For example, let's say that you delegate the Full Exchange Administrator role to an account called Exchange Administrator (logon name: Exadmin). Figure 4.26 shows the Security settings for a mailbox owned by a user in the organization.

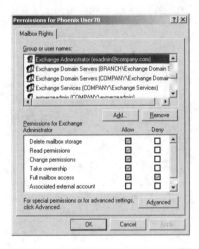

**Figure 4.26**  Access Control List for a user showing that administrators are denied access to mailboxes by default.

Note that Exchange assigned the Exadmin account full control of all objects in the organization (that's why you see all the Allow checkboxes) but it also specifically set a Deny on the Full Mailbox Access permission for User objects. A Deny permission overrides an Allow permission if they get assigned at the same level in Active Directory, so this blocks administrators from accessing any user's mailbox anywhere in the organization.

### *Granting Selective Mailbox Access*

If you want an administrator to open a user's mailbox, you can specifically override the Deny setting via the user's object in Active Directory. This requires Exchange Full Administrator permissions.

1. Launch ADUC and drill down to a user object.
2. Open the Properties window for the user object.
3. Select the **Exchange Advanced** tab.
4. Click **Mailbox Rights**. This opens the Mailbox Rights window that shows the ACL for the user's mailbox.
5. Click **Advanced** to open the detailed view of the ACL. This view shows each individual entry on the ACL.
6. Click **Add** to open the Select Users or Groups window.
7. Add the Exchange Administrator (`exadmin@company.com`) account to the ACL. This opens a Permission Entry window that allows you to select individual permission entries, shown in Figure 4.27.

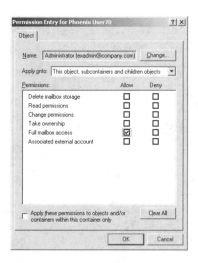

**Figure 4.27**    Addition to user permissions that directly apply an Allow to mailbox access.

8. Check the **Allow Full Mailbox Access** option; then click **OK** to save this setting.
9. Click **OK** in the Advanced window of the ACL Editor to return to the general window. The Exchange Administrator (exadmin) entry now shows a directly applied Allow (no gray behind the check) for Full Mailbox Access and an inherited Deny (gray behind the check) for the same permission, as shown in Figure 4.28.

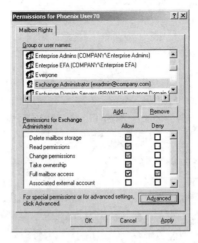

**Figure 4.28** Revised ACL for user object showing that the directly applied Allow takes precedence over the inherited Deny.

In Windows object security, a directly applied Allow overrides an inherited Deny, so the Exchange Administrator can now get access to the user's mailbox. Don't forget to remove this entry when the administrator has completed the work. You don't want to leave little security bread crumbs that might cause problems for you later if someone gets unauthorized access.

# Role Delegation

An Exchange organization forms a miniature tree inside the larger directory service controlled by Active Directory. At the top of the Exchange tree sits the Organization container itself. The lower branches hold objects that represent servers, with their mailbox and public folder stores and protocols, global settings, recipient policies, monitoring tools and so forth.

Windows protects objects in Active Directory by providing them with a security descriptor that contains an ACL defining who can access the object and what they can do once they have access. You can view this security descriptor in ESM, but first you have to set a special Registry entry. Note that the Registry entry resides in the Current User hive, so each administrator who uses ESM on the machine must enter this setting.

```
Key: HKCU | Software | Microsoft | Exchange | ExAdmin
Value: ShowSecurityPage
Data: 1 (RegDWORD)
```

Don't make changes to security descriptors directly. You could end up dis-abling every server in your organization with one poorly chosen change to an ACL. Always use the Delegation wizard, described in the next section, to assign administrative roles.

Once you've put the Registry change in place, launch ESM and open the **Properties window** for the Organization object at the top of the tree, and select the **Security tab**. Figure 4.29 shows an example. The entries you see on the ACL were added by Exchange during Setup. Now let's see how to add additional administrators to this list to give them access to objects in the Exchange organization.

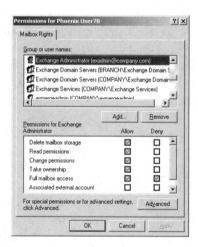

**Figure 4.29** Security tab for the Organization object after Registry change to expose security page.

## Delegation Wizard

Microsoft developers must have read a lot of Harry Potter books in their formative years, because just about every configuration interface uses a wizard of one sort or another, and Exchange is no exception. Exchange System Manager uses a Delegation Wizard to assign administrative roles.

Best practices dictate that you do not delegate a role to an individual user. Instead, create a group for your Exchange administrators, and then delegate a role to that group. This avoids putting a lot of individual accounts on the ACLs of the Exchange objects, which simplifies administration and reduces the domain controller processing necessary to evaluate access rights.

To demonstrate how delegation works, first create a Universal Security Group that represents the central Exchange administrators in the organization. Call this group anything you wish. I'll call the group Enterprise EFA.

Also create a user account to act as an Exchange administrator for the entire organization. I'll call it Org Admin with a logon ID of orgadmin. Make this account a member of the Enterprise EFA group. To delegate Exchange Full Administrator permissions for the organization to the Enterprise EFA group, proceed as follows:

1. Open ESM.
2. Right-click the **Organization** icon at the top of the tree and select **Delegate Control** from the flyout menu, as shown in Figure 4.30. This starts the Exchange Administration Delegation Wizard.

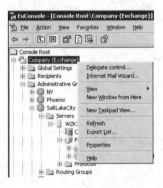

**Figure 4.30**    Delegation option in flyout menu of Exchange organization object.

3. Click **Next**. The Users or Groups window opens. This window lists the principals who currently have been delegated access permissions, as shown in Figure 4.31.
4. Click **Add** to open the Delegate Control window.
5. Browse for the Enterprise EFA group by clicking **Browse**, then **Advanced**, and then **Find Now**.
6. Select the group from the pick list, as shown in Figure 4.32.

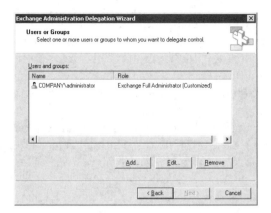

**Figure 4.31** Existing delegations shown in the Delegation Wizard.

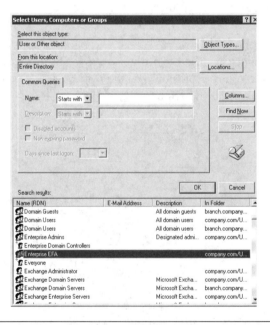

**Figure 4.32** Selection of an Exchange administrator group using the Select Users, Groups, and Computer interface in the Delegation Wizard.

7. Click **OK** in each window until you get back to the Delegate Control window.

8. Assign the Exchange Full Administrator role, as shown in Figure 4.33; then click **OK** to save the change and return to the Users and Groups window.

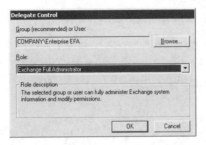

**Figure 4.33** Delegation Wizard showing the Exchange Full Administrator role assignment.

> **9.** Click **Next**. The wizard displays a summary window.
>
> **10.** Click **Finish** to save the changes. The wizard presents an informational warning (Figure 4.34) that the selected user or group must also have local Admin rights on the Exchange servers the group must administer.

**Figure 4.34** Warning that administrator must also have local server administrator permissions.

> **11.** Click OK to acknowledge the warning and to close the window.

Now log on to a workstation where you've installed ESM using the organization administrative account you created. In my example, that would be orgadmin. Verify that **orgadmin** can manage parameters on servers, stores, and protocols by adding a few words to the Details tab of selected objects.

## Local Server Admin Rights

If you focus your attention on Active Directory too much, it's easy to forget that you also need local access rights on the Exchange servers themselves. To accomplish this, you should first create a Global or Universal Security Group and populate the group with the accounts of your Exchange administrators. You can use the same group you created for role delegation in ESM. Then, nest that group into the local Administrators group on each Exchange server. You can do this in a variety of ways.

### Computer Management Console

If you have only one or two Exchange servers and you're comfortable using graphical tools, you can use the Computer Management console to assign a group from a domain to the local Administrators group on the Exchange as follows:

1. Log onto the Exchange server using an account in the Domain Admin group or some other group that already has local administrator rights on the computer.
2. Open the Computer Management console by right-clicking the **My Computer** object and selecting **Manage** from the flyout menu.
3. Drill down to the **Groups** icon under **Local Users and Groups**. Figure 4.35 shows an example.

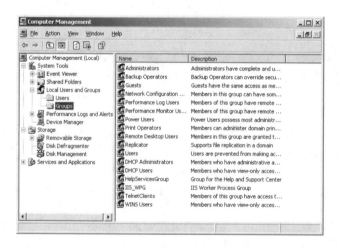

**Figure 4.35** Computer Management console showing list of groups in the local SAM of an Exchange server.

4. Double-click the Administrators group to open the Properties window.
5. Click **Add**, and then browse Active Directory to select the Exchange group you just created.
6. Log on as the administrator to make sure you have full admin rights on the server.

If you have installed Exchange on a domain controller, you will use the ADUC console rather than the Computer Management console to add the group to the Administrators local group. It is not considered best practice to run Exchange on a domain controller, but it happens quite a bit, and is the default configuration of Small Business Server.

### NET Command

If you prefer command-line tools, you can add the Exchange group you just created to the local Administrators group using the NET command with the following syntax:

```
net localgroup administrators <domain>\<group_name> /add
```

For example, to add a group called Exchange EFA in the Company domain to the local Administrators group, the command would look like this:

```
net localgroup administrators "company\exchange efa" /add
```

### Restricted Groups

If you have quite a few Exchange servers and you want to get sophisticated about managing local group membership, you can create a Restricted Group policy that designates the membership of the Administrators group on your Exchange servers.

If you haven't already created a separate OU to hold your Exchange servers, you should do so now. This has a couple of advantages. First, it prevents someone from creating a Group Policy Object (GPO) in their OU that interferes with the operation of your Exchange servers. Second, it provides a handy place for you to link your own GPOs that you want to use for managing your Exchange servers. Once you've created this OU, move all the Computer objects representing your Exchange servers into the OU using drag and drop in Active Directory Users and Computers. Unless you've already moved them once, you'll find the Computer objects representing the Exchange servers in the Computers container.

You should use the Group Policy Management Console (GPMC) for managing group policies. GPMC does not get installed by default. You can run it on Windows Server 2003 or XP SP1+. Download the GPMC installer for free from Microsoft's Web site at www.microsoft.com/windowsserver2003/gpmc/default.mspx.

The installation file for GPMC comes as an MSI (Microsoft Installer) package. Just double-click and run through the installation. Once it's installed, launch the console from the Administrative Tools section of the Start menu and proceed as follows to create and link a GPO:

1. Drill down to the **Group Policy Objects** icon, as shown in Figure 4.36. There you'll find a list of all the GPOs that exist in the domain. The example shows the two default GPOs, the Default Domain Controllers Policy, and the Default Domain policy.

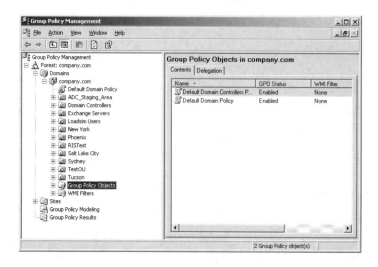

**Figure 4.36** Group Policy Management Console (GPMC) showing default GPOs.

2. Right-click the OU you created to hold the Exchange Servers and select **Create And Link A GPO Here** from the flyout menu.

3. When prompted for a name, give the GPO a friendly name such as **Exchange Server Management**. The GPMC creates the GPO, and it appears as an icon under the Exchange Servers OU.

4. Right-click the new GPO and select **Edit** from the flyout menu. This opens the Group Policy Object Editor.

5. Drill down to **Computer Configuration | Windows Settings | Security Setting | Restricted Groups**, as shown in Figure 4.37.

6. Right-click the **Restricted Groups** icon and select **New Group** from the flyout menu. The Add Group window opens.

7. Type the word **Administrators**. Don't browse for a group name, because the object picker will default to the domain, not the local computer, and you can't convince it to do otherwise.

**Figure 4.37**    Restricted Groups folder in Group Policy Editor.

8. Click **OK**. The Properties window for the Restricted Group policy opens. This window has one tab, **Configure Membership**.
9. Next to the Members Of This Group field, click **Add**. This opens an Add Member window.
10. Click **Browse** and use the Select Users or Groups window to locate the Exchange Administrators group you created earlier (or whatever name you used). The Add Member window should look like Figure 4.38 when you've finished.

**Figure 4.38**    Add Member window inn Restricted Groups policy setting.

11. Click **OK** to add the name to the member list in the Restricted Groups policy.
12. Wait. You're not done. The member list in this policy overwrites the local membership, so you need to add the standard members of the Administrators local group, which includes the local Administrator account and the Domain Admins global group.
13. When you add the Domain Admins group, browse for it using the Select Users or Groups window. When you add the Administrator account, simply type that name into the Add Member

window. This tells the machine that gets the policy to use the local Administrator account.

14. When you've finished adding members, the Properties window for the Restricted Groups policy should look like Figure 4.39. Click **OK** to save the policy.

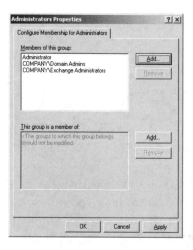

**Figure 4.39**     List of groups that will be applied to local SAM of any computers in the OU linked to the GPO that contains the Restricted Groups setting.

Within the next 90 to 120 minutes, each Exchange server will download the policy and apply the membership changes to its local Administrators group. You can speed up the process by running GPUPDATE at the console of each Exchange server and then verifying that the Administrators group membership has changed. Do this by opening a command prompt and typing gpupdate. Wait for a minute or so and look for a response saying that all updates have been applied.

## Administrative Groups

In an Exchange organization of moderate size, where a single group of administrators work closely together to manage all Exchange servers, the default organization configuration works just fine.

But Exchange administrators in a large and geographically diverse enterprise often want to divvy up their management chores. For example, an organization with branches in North America, Europe, and Asia Pacific might have autonomous e-mail administrators in each region who all say, "Don't mess with my servers." during their telephone conferences. ("Finger weg von meinen Servern!" for administrators in Frankfurt and "Wu Yong Fu Wu Xi Xie Xie!" for administrators in Taipei.)

King Solomon, as it turns out, had a good solution for problems involving custody disputes—simply split up the target of the dispute. Exchange implements this solution by permitting you to divide an organization into separate Administrative Groups and to delegate administrative roles to different administrators for each group. Figure 4.40 shows an example of how you might divide an organization into Administrative Groups based on the geographic location of the administrators.

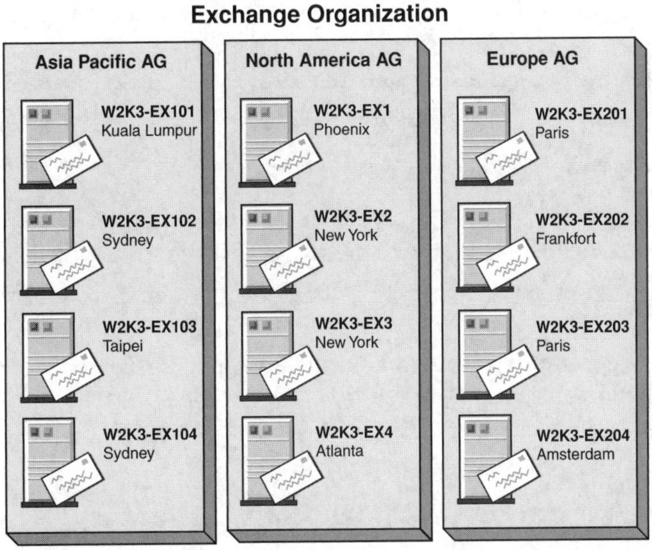

**Exchange Organization**

| Asia Pacific AG | North America AG | Europe AG |
|---|---|---|
| W2K3-EX101 Kuala Lumpur | W2K3-EX1 Phoenix | W2K3-EX201 Paris |
| W2K3-EX102 Sydney | W2K3-EX2 New York | W2K3-EX202 Frankfort |
| W2K3-EX103 Taipei | W2K3-EX3 New York | W2K3-EX203 Paris |
| W2K3-EX104 Sydney | W2K3-EX4 Atlanta | W2K3-EX204 Amsterdam |

**Figure 4.40** Native mode Exchange organization divided into Administrative Groups based on location of Exchange administrators.

## Administrative Groups Don't Control Message Routing

You don't necessarily need to assign Administrative Groups by location. Exchange 2003 uses an entirely separate set of Active Directory objects, called Routing Groups, to define how messages move around in an organization. (A Routing Group defines an area of high-speed interconnection between Exchange servers.)

You might work in a company with subsidiaries, each with its own IT staff and Exchange administrators. You can create an Administrative Group for each subsidiary, even if their servers reside in the same server room. (I might even say *especially* if their servers reside in the same server room.) The Routing Groups could overlap the administrative boundaries, as shown in Figure 4.41.

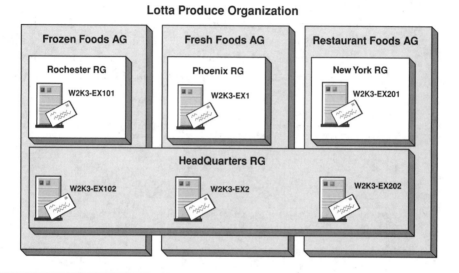

**Figure 4.41**    Organization with Administrative Groups assigned by business unit and Routing Groups assigned by office.

## Administrative Groups in Active Directory

Each Administrative Group exists in Active Directory as a container that holds servers, public folder trees, and system policies. Figure 4.42 shows an ESM console window containing several Administrative Groups.

In essence, Administrative Group containers have the same function in an Exchange organization that OUs have in a domain. They impose a hierarchy on the contents of the organization and provide a place for assigning administrative permissions on the objects within them.

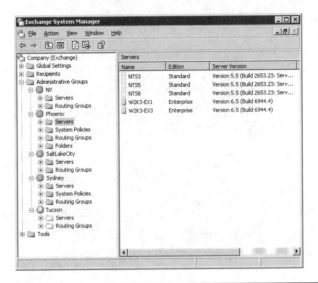

**Figure 4.42**    ESM showing multiple Administrative Groups.

## Administrative Groups and Legacy Sites

If you have an organization with a mix of Exchange 5.5 servers or earlier (which I'll call legacy Exchange servers) and Exchange 2003 servers, then you'll need to respect several operational restrictions on the use of Administrative Groups:

- Each legacy site forms a separate Administrative Group.
- Administrative Groups and Routing Groups must encompass the same servers. In other words, if a server falls under the Phoenix Administrative Group in Active Directory, it must also fall under the Phoenix Routing Group and no others.
- Mailboxes cannot move between servers in different Administrative Groups.
- To signal the presence of legacy servers, Exchange sets a Mixed Mode attribute in the Exchange organization object to TRUE. Exchange System Manager displays this configuration with an informational blurb in the Properties window for the organization, as shown in Figure 4.43.

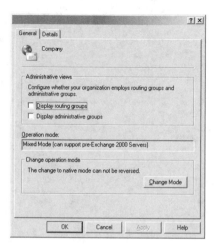

**Figure 4.43**   Organization Properties window has a setting to display
Routing Groups.

You must then decommission and remove all legacy Exchange
servers and remove the Site Replication Service from any Exchange
2003 server (more about this in Chapter 12) before you can shift the
organization to Native Mode. Once you're in Native mode, the dimmed
option to display Administrative groups will be available.

If you do a pristine deployment of Exchange 2003, you do not face
these limitations. You can shift Exchange to Native Mode immediately
after installing the first Exchange 2003 server.

## Creating New Administrative Groups

If you decide that you need additional Administrative Groups, you can
create new ones using Exchange System Manager. By default, the tree
view of the organization in ESM does not display Administrative
Groups. Open the **Properties** window for the Organization object and
check the **Display Administrative Groups** option and then click **OK**.

To create a new Administrative Groups, right-click the **Administrative Groups** folder and select **New Administrative Group** from the
flyout menu. Give it a name and the job is done.

When you have more than one Administrative Group in an organization, any new Exchange servers you install will get a window during
Setup prompting you to select an Administrative Group to hold the
server, as shown in Figure 4.44.

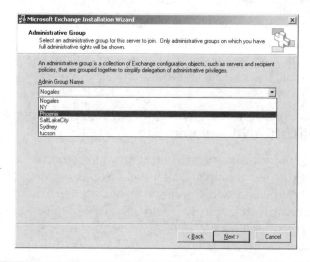

**Figure 4.44**    Administrative Group selection when installing new Exchange server in an organization with multiple Administrative Groups.

If you install an Exchange server in one Administrative Group and then decide later that you want to put it in another, you must move all the mailboxes and connectors from the server, de-install Exchange, and then re-install Exchange, and select another Administrative Group during setup. Not a fun way to spend a Saturday afternoon.

### Delegating Administrative Group Permissions

The whole purpose of having separate Administrative Groups is to divide up the administrative duties, so as soon as you create a new Administrative Group, you'll want to delegate administrative roles to it.

For the sake of being tidy, you should create a group to represent the administrators for a particular Administrative group. Put this group in an Active Directory OU where the central Exchange administrators have access to it. Don't put it in a location where the local Exchange administrators can change the membership. Otherwise, you'll lose control over who can manage the local Exchange servers.

Now that you've created a group representing the Exchange administrators, use the Exchange Delegation wizard to assign an administrative role to the group. The delegation steps parallel the steps you used to delegate a role for the organization except that you right-click the Administrative Group to start the Delegation Wizard.

An administrator who has an administrative role for an Administrative Group can open Exchange System Manager and drill down to the servers in that Administrative Group and manage the settings on those servers and their Exchange stores.

## Crossing the Line—Moving Mailboxes between Administrative Groups

You cannot move a server from one Administrative Group to another, whether or not the organization is in Mixed or Native mode. You can move user mailboxes between servers in separate Administrative Groups if you have switched to Exchange Native Mode or installed Exchange SP1. This simplifies user management. If a user gets transferred from Phoenix to New York, all you need to do is move the user's mailbox to the new server.

But…If you want the mailbox move to succeed, you need Exchange Administrator permissions in both the source and target Administrative Group. In addition, because the mailbox move changes the user's e-mail attributes in Active Directory, you need read and write access for the user's Active Directory objects.

In many enterprises, user and group management falls under the purview of Windows system administrators, not Exchange administrators. By the same token, most Exchange administrators take a dim view of Windows administrators who try to make changes in the Exchange organization. The two sets of administrators might play on the same softball team and eat lunch in the same server room, but when it comes to sharing admin rights, they turn grim and start pointing fingers.

Still, you need to find some way to let each set of administrators do their jobs. Windows administrators need to create new user, group, and contact objects, and it would make their life a lot easier if they could mailbox or mail-enable them at the same time. Exchange administrators need the ability to work with the e-mail attributes assigned to a user or group account without the ability to create new accounts or delete them or change their passwords.

### Giving E-mail Permissions to Windows Administrators

It doesn't take much work to satisfy the Windows administrators. About the only privilege they need is one that enables them to see information about servers in an Administrative Group so that they select the right storage group when mailbox-enabling a user and select the right Administrative Group when mail-enabling a group or contact.

If you give a Windows administrator Exchange View Only permissions in the organization, or in selected Administrative Groups, that will do the trick.

### Giving Domain Permissions to Exchange Administrators

Giving the Exchange administrators permission to change e-mail attributes on user, group, and contact objects without giving them the ability to create and delete the objects, or modify other attributes, involves a little more work. You need to delegate access rights for a long list of attributes. You can do this for the entire domain or in selected OUs.

If you want to see the exact permissions that are required to perform a particular Exchange task, try doing the task and letting it fail; then look at the detailed failure report generated by the Exchange Task wizard. This XML file lists all the permissions necessary to perform the task. For example, Figure 4.45 shows the failure report when attempting to mailbox-enable a user without any special rights in the domain.

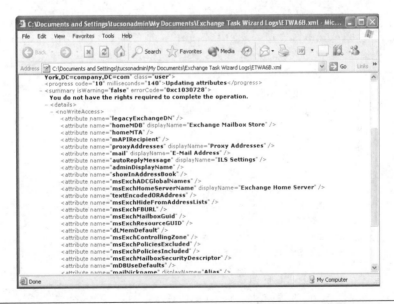

Figure 4.45    Failure report following mailbox move between Administrative Groups. XML report lists attributes for which administrator must have access permissions.

You can save this file or cut and paste the attribute list so you can assign the necessary permissions in Active Directory.

Selecting each and every one of these attributes using the Delegation of Control Wizard in ADUC gets awfully tedious. You can do the same work from the command line using the DSACLS utility.

For your initial testing, create a new OU and put a few test users in it. You don't want to accidentally render your test lab (or worse, your production domain) unavailable with a poorly chosen set of DSACL switches.

DSACLS has a rather extensive parameter list, but the syntax to grant permission for a particular attribute to a specified account doesn't involve many entries. For example, the following entry grants Read and Write permission to the Exadmins group for the HomeMTA attribute on User objects:

```
dsacls ou=testou,dc=company,dc=com /I:S /G Exadmins:RPWP;HomeMTA;user
```

The /I:S switch controls inheritance and applies the change to subobjects only. This switch is required so that you can apply the change only to User objects under the OU.

The /G switch grants permission. The example syntax says, "Grant the Exadmins group Read Property and Write Property permission for the HomeMTA property and apply this only to User objects."

Once you know the attributes you need to modify, you can build a batch file to apply the changes in one swoop. Here's an example for a few of the attributes involved with mailbox-enabling a user object:

```
dsacls ou=testou,dc=company,dc=com /I:S /G
➡Exadmins:RPWP;legacyExchangeDN;user
    dsacls ou=testou,dc=company,dc=com /I:S /G Exadmins:RPWP;homeMDB;user
    dsacls ou=testou,dc=company,dc=com /I:S /G Exadmins:RPWP;homeMTA;user
    dsacls ou=testou,dc=company,dc=com /I:S /G
    ➡Exadmins:RPWP;mAPIRecipient;user
    dsacls ou=testou,dc=company,dc=com /I:S /G
    ➡Exadmins:RPWP;ProxyAddresses;user
```

After you assign all the necessary permissions, test your configuration by mailbox-enabling a test account using an Exchange administrator account that does not have any other Active Directory admin privileges.

## Key Points for Administrative Group Permission Delegation

Here are the important things to keep in mind about Administrative Groups:

- An Administrative Group defines a management boundary. Administrators delegated to manage one Administrative Group do not get access to servers in another Administrative Group.
- In a Mixed mode organization, each legacy site becomes a separate Administrative Group.
- In a Mixed mode organization, you cannot move mailboxes directly between servers in different sites unless you install Exchange 2003 SP1 on the servers. You must have at least one Exchange 5.5 SP3 server in your organization.
- Don't make changes directly to the security settings of a container in an Exchange organization. Always use the Delegation Wizard to assign administrator permissions.

# Looking Forward

At this point, you've seen how ESM works, how it interfaces to Exchange and other critical services, and how you can delegate administrative permissions in an entire organization or an individual Administrative Group. This is enough information to start doing some practical administrative tasks, like enabling users in the Active Directory domain to access mailboxes and to send messages to distribution groups, and fun things like that.

# CHAPTER 5

# Managing Recipients and Distribution Lists

In his book, *Zen and the Art of Motorcycle Maintenance*, Robert Pirsig contends that quality is an intrinsic element of any structure. To make his point, he lays out the parts of a motorcycle on a garage floor and then patiently describes, not the reassembly process, but the attitude toward Quality necessary to perform a successful reassembly. During this discussion, he draws your attention to a small sheet metal screw used to attach the oil pan cover. "If this screw gets stripped," he says, "the motorcycle cannot be ridden." Thus, the value of the smallest part on the motorcycle equals the value of the motorcycle itself. That knowledge helps you to maintain a good attitude toward the Quality inherent in every part.

This lesson comes in handy when managing recipients. You can spend weeks, even months, building a fully functional Exchange infrastructure filled with top-notch servers and redundant network connections and state-of-the-art storage systems, but all that work, every single erg of energy you expended, could go completely to waste if the users aren't happy with the result. In this chapter, you'll see how to configure Exchange in a way that gives your users a Quality experience. If they still don't appreciate your efforts, you can ask them to help you with a little blindfolded archery practice.

## Security Groups and Exchange

Windows servers use groups to control access to security objects such as NTFS files and folders, Registry keys, and Active Directory objects. Exchange 2003 uses groups to control access to public folders and user mailboxes as well as to act as distribution lists.

For example, Figure 5.1 shows how you can put a Security group called Engineering on the permission list for a public folder so that only members of the Engineering group can read or contribute to the folder.

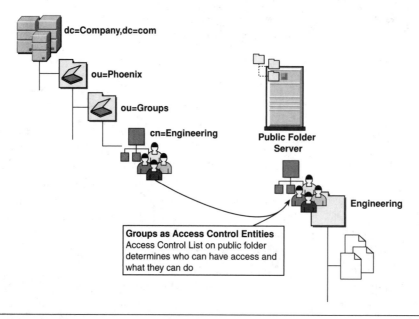

**Figure 5.1**    Exchange can use Active Directory Security groups to control access to resources such as public folders and mailboxes.

You can also use Security groups to control access to an individual user's private mailbox. For example, if the Forensics team wants access to the mailbox of an employee under suspicion of industrial espionage, you could create a Security group called Forensics and put that group on the permission list for the user's mailbox without the user's knowledge.

As you saw in the previous chapter, you can use Security groups to delegate administrative roles for your entire Exchange organization or for individual Administrative Groups.

## Issues with Mail-enabled Security Groups

At first, using Security groups both to protect Exchange resources and to support e-mail distribution doesn't appear to present any difficulties. But the devil lies in the details, as they say, and if you don't plan your group management correctly, both your users and your Windows system administrator colleagues down the hall might not like the results.

Most Windows administrators consider the ability to create Security groups in Active Directory something of a special privilege and they tightly control that privilege, granting it only to administrators who agree to abide by a strict set of business practices or risk getting shamed at a Monday meeting.

"After all," reason the Windows administrators, "we spent a lot of time and sat down at a lot of meetings to come up with a strategy for naming and nesting groups that meets all of our users' business requirements with the fewest groups possible. We don't want outsiders coming in and messing things up."

The outsiders, in this case, include e-mail users who have an entirely different set of business practices, not to mention their own personal eccentricities, which affect their attitude toward distribution lists. E-mail users have a love affair with distribution lists. They want *lots* of them, and they want to give them all sorts of names to please executives, managers, clients, vendors, government regulators, secret agents, and just about anybody else who interacts with the messaging system in any capacity whatsoever.

And if they want a new distribution list, they want it *now*. Not tomorrow. Not by the end of the day. Not in response to filling out an online work order. *NOW!*

Because an Exchange distribution list is really an Active Directory group, and the Windows administrators don't want to see groups created willy-nilly, you might find yourself at something of an impasse. Statesmanship demands a compromise. You need a group that can act as a distribution list but cannot reside on an Access Control List where it could cause problems for Windows administrators. You need a Distribution group.

If you can get IT management and the user's managers to agree on a naming scheme, then life gets simple in this area.

## Distribution Group Advantages

Distribution groups have their limits, but those limits become their strength. Windows administrators might not care about groups that can't end up on file and printer ACLs, so they can loosen the reins a bit on who can create them or modify their membership.

Okay, the Windows admins probably do care about Distribution group names, but at least the meetings to agree on Distribution group standards won't get nearly as rancorous as the meetings to agree on Security group standards.

For example, you might want junior Exchange administrators or even department gurus to create Distribution groups, with the understanding that group names such as "Executives I Loathe" had better not show up in the Global Address List (GAL). You could even grant permission to Help Desk technicians to modify the membership of Distribution groups in response to a phone call from designated users, something you would not ordinarily want to do with Security groups.

Active Directory does permit nesting a Distribution group into a Security group, but this does not assign access permissions to members of the Distribution group. For example, consider a user named TinaTurner who belongs to a Distribution group called DynamiteDivas. You nest the DynamiteDivas group into a Security group called OnStageProduction, and you grant the OnStageProduction group access permissions for an NTFS folder called LightsAndCameraControls. In this configuration, the TinaTurner account cannot access the LightsAndCameraControls folder.

## Watch Out for Automatic Promotions

Your idyllic compromise to permit Exchange administrators to create Distribution groups using a different set of business practices and standards than the Windows administrators use for Security groups could get you into trouble if you don't watch out for a feature in Exchange 2003.

ESM and Outlook permit you to place a Distribution group on the permission list for a public folder or a user's mailbox, as shown in Figure 5.2.

If you take advantage of this capability, when the Exchange Information Store notices that the group appears on a permission list, it automatically promotes the Distribution group to a Security group.

Once the group becomes a Security group, it begins to appear in the Select Users and Groups control used to add security principals to Access Control Lists in Windows. Very soon after that occurs, your phone rings. It's the manager of the Windows administration team calling you to a meeting to discuss why you have violated your agreement not to create Security groups. Personally, I'd rather lock the senior representatives of the national Republican and Democratic parties in a cage for a six-hour, no-holds-barred policy fight over gun control than be present at that meeting.

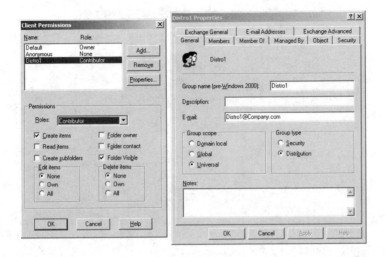

**Figure 5.2**    Exchange permits Distribution groups on MAPI permissions, but will subsequently promote the group to a Security group.

To avoid those situations, it's important that you make anyone with Author permissions on a public folder aware of the security group promotion feature and urge them to be absolutely sure that they only add Security groups onto a permission list.

## Delegating Group Membership Management

You might decide to permit non-administrators to manage the membership of Distribution groups without allowing them to create groups, delete them, or change their scope or type. Active Directory has a "Modify Group Membership" permission intended for this purpose.

Unfortunately, Active Directory does not have a filter that applies the "Modify Group Membership" permission solely to Distribution groups. You need to collect your Distribution groups into a separate OU (Figure 5.3 shows an example) and then delegate the "Modify Group Membership" permission to a Security group on the ACL of that OU. Do so as follows:

1. Right-click the **OU** icon and select **Delegate Control** from the flyout menu. This starts the Delegation of Control Wizard.
2. Click **Next**. The Users and Groups window opens.
3. Click **Add** and use the object picker to select the **Distro Managers** group. The result looks like Figure 5.4.

**Figure 5.3**   Congregate Universal Distribution Groups into their own OU to simplify delegating permission to change membership.

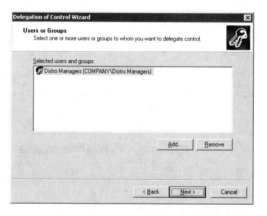

**Figure 5.4**   Select a group to delegate admin permissions.

4. Click **Next**. The Tasks to Delegate window opens.
5. Check the **Modify the Membership of a Group** option, as shown in Figure 5.5
6. Click **Next**. This opens a Summary window.
7. Click **Finish** to exit the wizard.

With this delegation in place, any user you put in the Distro Managers group can change the membership of a Distribution group in the Distribution Groups OU. You do not need to train those users to use Active Directory Users and Computers and you don't need to install the Adminpak.msi tools on their desktops. They can do the work via Outlook.

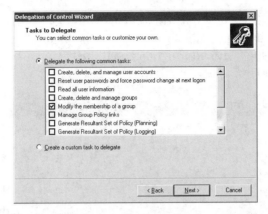

**Figure 5.5** Delegation of Control Wizard showing permission to assign to selected group.

## Managing Distribution List Membership in Outlook

A user who has "Modify Group Membership" permissions on a group in Active Directory can use Outlook to manage members of that group. Here's the procedure:

1. From the main Outlook window, open the Address Book either by selecting **Tools | Address Book** from the main menu or by pressing **Ctrl+Shift+B**.
2. In the **Show Names** dropdown field, select **Global Address List**. Figure 5.6 shows an example.

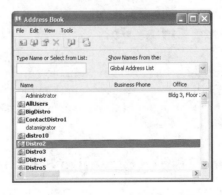

**Figure 5.6** Distribution list as it appears in the GAL in Outlook.

**3.** Right-click a distribution list and select **Properties** from the fly-out menu. This shows the membership list of the distribution list along with information about the owner, if any. Figure 5.7 shows an example.

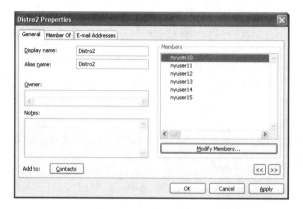

**Figure 5.7**    Properties of a distribution list in Outlook showing group members.

**4.** Click the **Modify Members** button to open a Distribution List Membership window.

**5.** Click **Add** to open a browse list for the GAL from which you can select new members. The member can be a user account, another group, or a contact.

**6.** Click **OK** and then **OK** again to save the change.

**7.** Close the Address Book.

# Group Membership Expansion

When you send a message to a mail-enabled group, the Exchange server sends a copy of the message to each mail-enabled user and contact in the group. The process of finding those mail-enabled group members is called *expansion*.

## Description of Group Expansion Process

Figure 5.8 shows a diagram of the expansion process. During this discussion, I'll use the term "ultimate recipients" to mean mailbox-enabled users, mail-enabled users, and mail-enabled contacts.

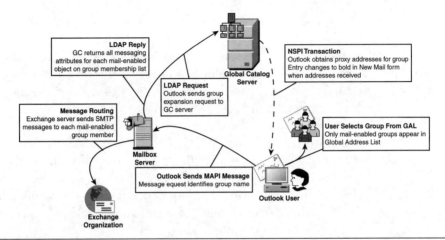

**Figure 5.8** Required processes for selecting a group and sending a message to the group.

1. **User selects group from Global Address List (GAL).** The process starts when an Outlook user selects a distribution list from the GAL to be the recipient of an e-mail message. Outlook obtains the GAL via a Name Service Provider Interface (NSPI) request sent to a Global Catalog server. The user could also simply enter the distribution list name in the To field of the message.

2. **Name Server Provider Interface (NSPI) transaction.** Outlook uses NSPI to verify the group name in the Global Catalog and, if the verification succeeds, it bolds the name in the To field.

3. **MAPI Send.** When the user clicks the Send button, Outlook uses MAPI to transmit the message to the user's home Exchange server.

4. **Group Expansion.** The Exchange server sees that the recipient is a group, and it sends an LDAP query to a Global Catalog server asking for the ultimate recipients who are members of the group, along with a list of e-mail attributes that it needs for each of those recipients.

The Global Catalog server obtains the names of the ultimate recipients from its copy of Active Directory, along with the requested e-mail attributes. If the list includes any mail-enabled groups, the Global Catalog server expands the membership of each of those groups and repeats the process recursively until it has assembled a full list of all ultimate recipients in each of the nested groups. It returns this list to the Exchange server.

5. **Message Routing.** The Exchange server then sends a copy of the message to each of the ultimate recipients. If multiple recipients have mailboxes on the same server, the Exchange server sends a single message tagged for delivery to the recipients. This "single instance messaging" complements the "single instance storage" for messages on the target server.

This process of expanding group membership lists and returning the results to an Exchange server happens hundreds, if not thousands, of times a day. You want to support Exchange with good-quality, high-powered Global Catalog servers, and you need enough of them to handle both expansion requests and the GAL requests coming from Outlook clients.

In production, start with a minimum of two Global Catalog servers for each Exchange server. To scale from there, Microsoft recommends a 4:1 ratio between the number of processors in your Exchange servers and the number of available Global Catalog servers. For example, if you have two 4-way Exchange servers in an office, you should have two Global Catalog servers in the same location.

## Designating Expansion Servers

When an Outlook user sends a message to a group, the user's home Exchange server works with a local Global Catalog server to expand the group's membership. Under most circumstances, the user's home Exchange server does the expansion by working with a local Global Catalog server. The term "local," in this case, means local to the Exchange server, not necessarily local to the user. In some circumstances, you might want to specify a specific Exchange server to handle the group expansion. These circumstances include

- **Mail-enabled global groups.** If you have multiple domains in your forest, you want to use Universal groups for e-mail distribution because the Global Catalog contains the membership list. If you use a Global group instead, you should target the expansion of that group to an Exchange server in the same domain. Otherwise, if a user in another domain sends a message to the Global group, the Exchange server in that user's domain cannot expand the group membership because the Global Catalog does not contain the membership list for Global groups.
- **Localized mail delivery.** If all members of a particular Universal group reside in the Asia Pacific region, it might make sense to specify an Exchange server in Taipei as the expansion server rather than letting an Exchange server in Phoenix or Amsterdam expand the membership and send the messages.

If you decide that you need to designate an expansion server for a group, do so using Active Directory Users and Computers (ADUC). Open the group's Exchange Advanced Properties window, shown in Figure 5.9. Notice that a group is assigned to an Administrative Group. The expansion server must reside in the same Administrative Group.

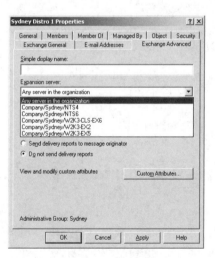

**Figure 5.9**    Selecting an expansion server for a group.

### Single Point of Failure

If you designate an Exchange server as an expansion server for a group or groups, e-mail sent to that group does not arrive when you take that server down for maintenance. The Exchange server will log a warning about the inability to find the expansion server, and messages queue up for delivery to the recipients. Keep this in mind as you schedule maintenance on your Exchange servers.

You might want to determine whether groups have been assigned to a single expansion server. The Active Directory Users and Computers console does not have a standard query to find groups with expansion servers. You can use the Saved Query option to create a custom LDAP search using the Active Directory attribute that stores the expansion server name. This attribute is called msExchangeExpansionServerName.

The msExchangeExpansionServerName attribute stores the distinguished name of the expansion server in X.521 format; for example, o=organization,ou=site,cn=configuration,cn=servers,cn=servername. You can't just match the first few letters, so the search must use a wildcard to represent the initial part of the name. Here's the LDAP filter syntax that searches for every group that uses W2K3-EX1 as an expansion server:

```
(&(objectCategory=group)(mailnickname=*)
➥(msExchangeExpansionServerName=*w2k3-ex1)
```

If you have thousands and thousands of mail-enabled groups, this search could take a while to run because it uses a wildcard at the start of the attribute string.

# Managing Group E-Mail Properties

You can control the way Exchange distributes mail to members of groups used as distribution lists. To start, select a mail-enabled group in Active Directory Users and Computers and open the Properties window. The Exchange General tab comes up first, as shown in Figure 5.10.

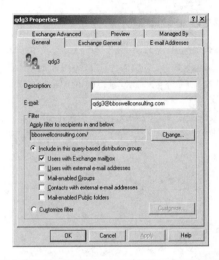

**Figure 5.10**     General properties for a mail-enabled group.

## General Properties

In most circumstances, you don't want a user sending the latest Star Wars Kid AVI to a distribution list with thousands of recipients. In fact, you don't want users sending indiscriminate messages to any group they happen to pick from the GAL.

The Message Restrictions settings give you control over these and other situations. For example, let's say you have a group titled Corporate Executives that contains the accounts of, well, corporate executives. You probably don't want folks sending messages to this group saying, "This company *really* sucks!" unless that person has been authorized to voice such an opinion. You can set the Message Restrictions so that only members of specified groups can send messages to the Corporate Executives group.

If you don't want users from outside the company to send messages to a particular group, you can check the **From Authenticated Users Only** option. This prevents spammers from targeting a corporate distribution list on a public-facing Exchange server.

If a sender does not meet the Message Restrictions criteria, Exchange returns a Non-Delivery Report (NDR) stating that the sender does not have permission to send to this recipient.

## Advanced Properties

Select the Exchange Advanced tab in the group's Properties window. Figure 5.11 shows an example. Use settings in this tab to hide groups from the GAL and to specify NDR handling.

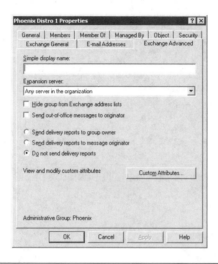

**Figure 5.11**    Advanced Exchange properties of a mail-enabled group.

### Hiding Groups

You can help prevent users from sending inappropriate messages to a group by hiding the group from the GAL. You can still send messages to the group (or any mail-enabled object that has been hidden from the GAL) by entering the recipient's full SMTP address; for example, executives@company.com.

### Do Not Send Delivery Reports

If the system fails to deliver a message to one or more members of a group, you might want the sender to get an NDR. Exchange disables this option by default because it exposes the distribution lists to spammers and other unauthorized persons. If you send a message to a distribution list and get an NDR for each invalid address, you now have a clue about who is and isn't in the company, both a security violation and a privacy violation.

### Administrative Group Affiliation

Groups do not have mailboxes, so it might surprise you to see that a group has an Administrative Group associated with it. Exchange uses this Administrative Group to build an X.400 proxy address for mail-enabled objects. This is true even if the organization has been shifted to Exchange Native mode.

If you do not use X.400 connectors, then this requirement doesn't have an impact on production. If you do use X.400 connectors, then be sure to affiliate a mail-enabled group with the correct Administrative Group, so that messages sent to the group get routed correctly through the connector.

## Hiding Group Members

When you mail-enable a group, you expose the group's membership list to MAPI clients. An Outlook user can open the GAL, right-click a group, and select **Properties** to see the group members, as shown in Figure 5.12.

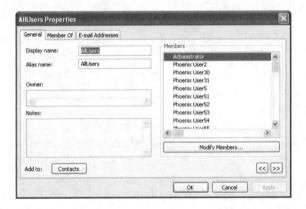

**Figure 5.12**    Outlook exposes members of a group, which could create a privacy or a security issue.

You might not want Outlook users to see a group's membership because of privacy concerns for the members or because the Windows administrators don't want to expose the contents of mail-enabled Security groups.

You can hide the group membership using the Exchange Tasks Wizard for the group. Right-click the group in Active Directory Users and

Computers, select Exchange Tasks from the flyout menu, then select Hide Membership in the Exchange Task Wizard, as shown in Figure 5.13.

**Figure 5.13**    Exchange Task Wizard showing the Hide Membership option.

Hiding group membership requires some fancy footwork on the part of Exchange. Here's why.

An Active Directory group object has an attribute called Member that holds the list of accounts that belong to the group. If you want to block all Outlook users from seeing the group's membership, Exchange must set a Deny Read permission on the Member attribute for the Everyone group.

But it's not that simple. An Exchange server needs to see the Member attribute so it can send e-mail to the members. That means Exchange can't simply deny access to the Everyone group, because Everyone includes the Exchange server's account.

Exchange solves this problem by changing the sort order for the Access Control List entries on a group object with hidden membership. You can see this for yourself. Use the Exchange Task Wizard to hide the membership of a group; then open the Properties window for that group in Active Directory Users and Computer, and select the Security tab. You'll get a warning that the contents can't be modified. Acknowledge the warning and proceed.

Click **Advanced** to view the Advanced view of the Security tab, as shown in Figure 5.14. This view shows the access control entries in the order that the operating system evaluates them when determining access authorization. Each line corresponds to an access control entry

(ACE), which contains the SID of a user or group and the permissions assigned to that SID. (The interface communicates with a Global Catalog server to replace the bare SIDs with their friendly names.)

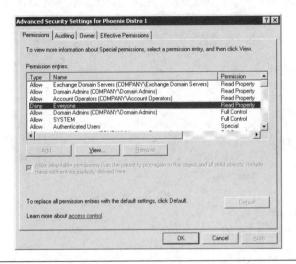

**Figure 5.14**   Advanced view of ACL for group with hidden membership showing non-canonical sorting of permissions.

You'll see that Exchange played a little shell game with the access list. It did indeed give the Everyone group a Deny Read on the Member attribute, but it also put an Allow Read on the same attribute for the Exchange Domain Servers group, the Domain Admins group, and the Account Operators group.

The security subsystem in Windows evaluates access control entries in the order you see them in the ACL Editor. Because the security subsystem encounters the Allow Read assigned to an Exchange server before it encounters the Deny Read assigned to the Everyone group, it gives the Exchange server access to the Member attribute while blocking users and other computers.

This is called *non-canonical sorting*. As shown in Figure 5.14, you can recognize non-canonical sorting when you see a Deny ACE placed below Allow ACEs in the same level of the hierarchy.

Because the ACL Editor always enforces canonical sorting when changing security settings, don't use the Security tab in the Properties page of a group to change the permission settings if the group has been configured to have hidden membership in Exchange.

# Query-Based Distribution Groups

Exchange 2003 introduced a new group type called a Query-Based Distribution group, or QDG. Instead of a static Member attribute that you must manually populate with accounts, a QDG uses an LDAP query to build a membership list dynamically.

The power of a QDG lies in its flexibility. For example, let's say you plan to take an Exchange server down for maintenance. You want to notify users of the maintenance, but you don't want to bother users on other servers.

You can create a QDG that includes an LDAP filter specifying mailbox-enabled users who have their mailbox on the designated server. You can then mail-enable the group and send it a message. The Exchange server works with a Global Catalog server to expand the group membership by executing the LDAP search.

## Creating a QDG

You can use a QDG if you run Exchange 2003 on Windows 2000 or Windows Server 2003. The QDG class is added during the Forestprep stage of Exchange Setup, when new attributes and classes are added to the Active Directory schema.

Throughout this book, the term "legacy Exchange" refers to all versions of Exchange prior to Exchange 2000.

To create a QDG, the Exchange organization must be in Native mode. Legacy Exchange servers don't know how to process QDGs. If you attempt to create a QDG in Mixed mode, you'll get an error message even though the option exists on the property menu. Create a QDG as follows:

1. Launch Active Directory Users and Computers.
2. Right-click an OU where you want to create the group and select **New | Query-based Distribution Group** from the flyout menu. This opens a New Object window, as shown in Figure 5.15.
3. Enter a name for the group, such as QDG5 or Phoenix Recipients or something that reflects the nature of the LDAP query you'll be using.

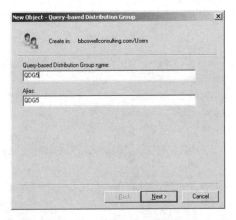

**Figure 5.15** New Object window showing alias for Query-Based Distribution Group.

4. Click **Next**. A filter selection window opens, as shown in Figure 5.16.

**Figure 5.16** Selecting criteria for membership in a QDG involves creating LDAP query.

5. Check the options you want to include in your search. For example, you might want just users with mailboxes, or just mail-enabled contacts.

6. If you want to be more selective, click **Customize Filter** and then click **Customize** to open a Find Exchange Recipients window. Figure 5.17 shows an example with the **Storage** tab selected.

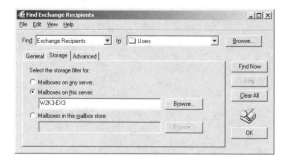

**Figure 5.17**   QDG selection criteria can target users on certain Exchange servers.

7. The **Advanced** tab of the Find Exchange Recipients window exposes an even more detailed set of search options, shown in Figure 5.18. You can select search criteria that include any attribute of any type of recipient—user, group, contact, or public folder. In the example, the QDG members would include all Exchange recipients (mail-enabled user; mailbox-enabled user; and mail-enabled groups, contacts, and public folders) who work in the Phoenix office. (For this query to work, you would need to have a work process that populates the Office Location field for user objects in Active Directory.)

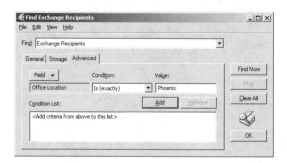

**Figure 5.18**   LDAP query builder showing advanced selection features that enable selecting a variety of object attributes.

8. Click **OK**, then **Next**, and then **Finish** to create the group. Always preview the result of the LDAP query before using the group by opening the Properties window for the group and selecting the **Preview** tab, as shown in *s*Figure 5.19.

**Figure 5.19**    Result of an LDAP query shown in the Preview window for a QDG.

It's important that the LDAP search you define for the QDG produces at least one result. If the preview tab does not list at least one recipient, anyone sending a message to the group will get a NDR.

It's also important that you formulate the LDAP query so that only users, groups, and contacts that are able to receive e-mail get included in the result. If the query results in even one invalid recipient, Exchange cannot send a message to anyone in the group. Checking the search results in the preview window can be difficult for a large QDG, so always test the QDG by sending it an e-mail.

## QDG Caveats

When a user addresses a message to a QDG, the Exchange server plucks the LDAP search criteria from the QDG definition and sends it to a Global Catalog server, along with a list of e-mail attributes it needs for the group's members. The Global Catalog server executes the LDAP search, looks up the e-mail attributes for each member, and returns the result to the Exchange server. The Exchange server then sends the message to each member.

You can put fairly complex queries into a QDG, and the result could include a large number of recipients, so using a lot of QDGs could overload your Global Catalog servers. Until you get a feel for their performance impact in your system, use QDGs sparingly. You can nest QDGs into other groups, so be on the lookout for performance and execution issues with standard groups that have QDGs as members.

If you run Exchange 2003 on Windows 2000, you'll need to adjust the SMTP service to adapt to LDAP page handling to avoid performance problems when using QDGs. This requires a Registry change (documented in Microsoft Knowledge Base article 822897):

```
Key: HKLM | SYSTEM |CurrentControlSet | Services | SMTPSVC
➥| Parameters
Value: DynamicDLPageSize
Data: 31 (REG_DWORD)
```

# DSAccess

Exchange needs access to Active Directory domain controllers for a variety of reasons (see Figure 5.20):

- **Configuration information for the Organization.** Exchange stores server parameters, mailbox and public folder store parameters, public folder hierarchy, tool parameters, and much more in the Configuration naming context of Active Directory.
- **Recipient information in the Global Catalog.** Exchange and Outlook need access to a Global Catalog server to expand group memberships for mail-enabled groups, to obtain address lists such as the GAL, and to obtain recipient information necessary for message handling and routing.
- **Recipient information in a Domain.** If Exchange can get the information it needs about a recipient from a standard domain controller in its own domain rather than a Global Catalog server, it will do so. This reduces load on the Global Catalog servers.

An Exchange service called DSAccess has the task of finding domain controllers and Global Catalog servers suitable for use by Exchange. Think of DSAccess as a nightclub owner who books stage talent. It applies a series of tests, the details of which you'll see in a minute, to determine which servers it wants to use. It then selects up to ten domain controllers and ten Global Catalog servers and puts them in a local DSAccess profile. It also selects one domain controller to use for a configuration server. This avoids replication latency issues.

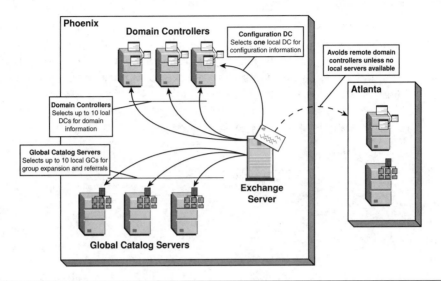

**Figure 5.20**    Diagram of DSAccess selection based on location.

DSAccess keeps an open connection to each server in the DSAccess profile. This avoids the expensive chore of building up and tearing down RPC and TCP connections each time the Exchange server needs information.

Other Exchange services, such as the SMTP Routing Engine Categorizer and DSProxy, send their LDAP and NSPI requests to DSAccess, which selects a target domain controller or Global Catalog server from its profile and forwards the request to that server. It uses a round robin selection process for load balancing.

Because all LDAP queries funnel through DSAccess, Exchange dramatically improves performance by caching the query results. By default, Exchange gives 4MB of physical memory to the DSAccess cache.

DSAccess refreshes its cache periodically. You can manually flush the cache during troubleshooting using the Dscflush utility, a free download from Microsoft.

## Global Catalog Advertising and DSAccess

DSAccess uses DNS to locate domain controllers and Global Catalog servers. Figure 5.21 shows an example DNS zone with three GC SRV records located in the _msdcs.dc.gc._tcp folder. Active Directory domain controllers also place copies of these SRV records into individual site folders underneath the _msdcs.dc.gc._sites folder. By looking in the folder corresponding to its own Active Directory site, DSAccess can locate local Global Catalog servers.

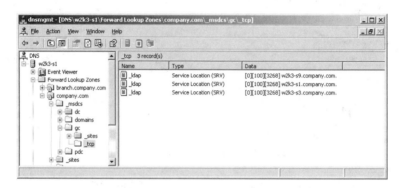

**Figure 5.21**   SRV records for Global Catalog servers in DNS.

When you configure a domain controller to be a Global Catalog server, the server must replicate the Domain naming contexts from the other domains before it can answer Global Catalog lookup requests authoritatively. Once a newly promoted Global Catalog server has replicated all domain naming contexts, it places an SRV record in DNS that "advertises" itself as available. You can verify the status of the Global Catalog promotion in several ways:

- Look for an Event log entry saying that the GC promotion has completed (Figure 5.22 shows an example).
- Look for a Registry entry called **HKLM | System | CurrentControlSet | Services | NTDS | Parameters | Global Catalog Promotion Complete** (shown in Figure 5.23.) and verify that the value is set to 1.
- Dump the RootDSE contents using the LDAP Browser (LDP) from the Windows Server 2003 Support Tools and look for the isGlobalCatalogReady attribute set to TRUE.
- Use the Nltest utility that comes in the Windows Server 2003 Support Tools. The following example shows that the server running Nltest was able to find a Global Catalog server in its local site (Phoenix) in its domain (Company.com):

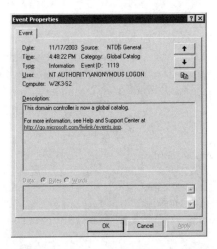

**Figure 5.22**  Event Log entry announcing that a domain controller has successfully begun operating as a Global Catalog server.

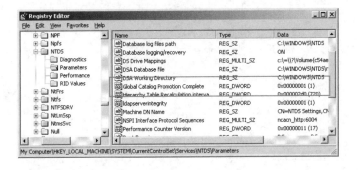

**Figure 5.23**  Registry entry on newly promoted Global Catalog server.

```
C:\>nltest /dsgetdc:company.com /gc
          DC: \\w2k3-s1.company.com
     Address: \\192.168.0.1
    Dom Guid: 01012378-a008-409d-9696-3c7f16bfbb62
    Dom Name: company.com
 Forest Name: company.com
Dc Site Name: Phoenix
Our Site Name: Phoenix
       Flags: GC DS LDAP KDC TIMESERV WRITABLE DNS_DC
➡DNS_DOMAIN DNS_FOREST CLOSE_SITE
The command completed successfully
```

- Use the Netdiag utility that comes in the Windows Server 2003 Support Tools. The following example shows that the server running Netdiag was able to enumerate all domain controllers, it was able to find a domain controller in the local site (W2K3-S1), and it was unable to contact one of the domain controllers (W2K3-S9):

```
C:\>netdiag /test:dclist /v

    Gathering IPX configuration information.
    Querying status of the Netcard drivers... Passed
    Testing Domain membership... Passed
    Gathering NetBT configuration information.
    Gathering the list of Domain Controllers for domain
➥'COMPANY'

<<<intermediate tests skipped>>>

DC list test . . . . . . . . . . . : Passed

    Find DC in domain 'COMPANY':
    Found this DC in domain 'COMPANY':
        DC. . . . . . . . . . . . : \\w2k3-s1.company.com
        Address . . . . . . . . : \\192.168.0.1
        Domain Guid . . . . . . : {01012378-A008-409D-9696-
➥3C7F16BFBB62}
        Domain Name . . . . . . : company.com
        Forest Name . . . . . . : company.com
        DC Site Name. . . . . . : Phoenix
        Our Site Name . . . . . : Phoenix
        Flags . . . . . . . . . : GC DS KDC TIMESERV WRITABLE
➥DNS_DC DNS_DOMAIN DNS_FOREST CLOSE_SITE 0x8
    List of DCs in Domain 'COMPANY':
        w2k3-s1.company.com
        W2K3-S2.company.com
        W2K3-S3.company.com
        W2K3-S4.company.com
        w2k3-s9.company.com  (this DC is down)
        [WARNING] Cannot ping 'w2k3-s9.company.com' (it may be
➥down).

The command completed successfully
```

## DSAccess Selection Criteria

DSAccess performs a series of tests to determine the suitability of a domain controller or Global Catalog server. The first tests determine whether the domain controller or Global Catalog server can respond to Exchange queries:

- **Reachability.** The server must respond to an LDAP bind request on TCP port 389 for domain controllers and TCP port 3268 for Global Catalog servers.
- **Replication current flag.** DSAccess checks RootDSE on the domain controller to verify that the isSynchronized attribute shows TRUE.
- **Global Catalog flag.** DSAccess checks RootDSE on a Global Catalog server to verify that the isGlobalCatalogReady attribute shows TRUE.
- **Server functional test (Netlogon).** In this somewhat time-consuming test, DSAccess makes an RPC connection to the Netlogon service at the domain controller and then checks available disk space, time synchronization, and whether the server participates in replication. You can disable this test for front-end servers in front of firewalls. See Chapter 11, "Deploying a Distibuted Architecture," for details.
- **Operating system version.** Exchange 2003 requires that all domain controllers used by DSAccess run at least Windows 2000 SP3 or higher.
- **Domain Exchange-Ready.** DSAccess looks to see if the Exchange Enterprise Servers group has Manage Auditing and Security Log permissions on the domain controller. This verifies that an administrator has run DomainPrep in the domain and that the changes have replicated to the target domain controller.

The Exchange Support Tools (free download from Microsoft) contains a utility called Policytest that runs the same test as DSAccess to verify that DomainPrep has fully replicated to all domain controllers. It checks to see if the Exchange Enterprise Servers group has been granted the Manage Auditing And Security Logs privilege on each domain controller. You'll need Domain Admin rights to run Policytest. Here's a sample listing for three domain controllers:

```
==========================================
Local domain is "Company.com" (COMPANY)
Account is "COMPANY\Exchange Enterprise Servers"
========================
  DC      = "W2K3-S1"
  In site = "Phoenix"
  Right found:  "SeSecurityPrivilege"
========================
  DC      = "W2K3-S4"
  In site = "Sydney"
  Right found:  "SeSecurityPrivilege"
========================
  DC      = "W2K3-S9"
  In site = "SaltLakeCity"
  Right found:  "SeSecurityPrivilege"
```

The next tests determine how DSAccess distributes queries once it has assembled the servers in its profile. DSAccess looks for these configuration settings:

- Weighting in the SRV records
- FSMO (Flexible Single Master Operations) roles (See Appendix A, "Building A Stable Exchange 2003 Deployment Infrastructure," for details.)
- Site where the server resides
- LDAP query performance
- LDAP loading based on current number of connections

All things being equal, DSAccess uses round robin to share load among domain controllers and Global Catalog servers. The final checks determine if a Global Catalog server can actually give authoritative answers to queries. DSAccess verifies the following:

- Global Catalog attribute in the NTDS Settings object for the server set to TRUE
- Correct number of naming contexts

### Viewing DSAccess Selection Results

Once DSAccess selects its domain controllers and Global Catalog servers, you can view the results in ESM by opening the Properties window for an Exchange server and then selecting the Directory Access tab, as shown in Figure 5.24.

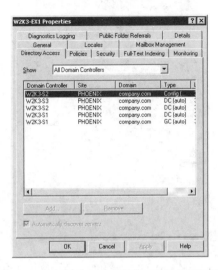

**Figure 5.24** Directory Access tab in Exchange server Properties window showing selection of domain controllers and Global Catalog servers.

If you change the selection in the Show dropdown list from **All Domain Controllers** to one of the other selection options, you can uncheck **Automatically Discover Servers** and manually select a server or servers for that operation. If you select servers manually, include more than one for fault tolerance. DSAccess does not dynamically select a server if it cannot contact any of the statically configured servers.

## Event Log Entries for DSAccess Selection Results

If you enable diagnostic logging for DSAccess in the server Properties window in ESM and set the logging level to Medium, you will see a log entry Event ID 2080 from the MSExchangeDSAccess showing the result of the DSAccess evaluation. Figure 5.25 demonstrates an example.

The evaluation includes 10 tests. It's difficult to see in the Event Properties window, but the test results are displayed as columns. You can click the Copy to Clipboard button and paste the result into Notepad if you want a clearer layout. The first column, Server Name, lists the server's Fully Qualified Domain Name (FQDN). Here's a brief description of the content under each column. For more details, see Microsoft Knowledge Base article 316300.

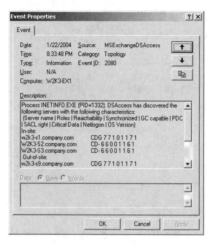

**Figure 5.25**   Event Log entry showing result of DSAccess domain controller evaluation.

- **Roles.** CDG stands for Configuration, Domain Controller, and Global Catalog.
- **Reachability.** DSAccess uses a numerical system to show whether it can connect to a server via TCP. A successful connection to a Global Catalog server is represented with a 1, 2 means a successful connection to a domain controller, 4 means a successful connection to a configuration domain controller, and 7 means the sum of the first three.
- **Synchronized.** Setting of isSynchronized flag in RootDSE.
- **GC Capable.** Setting of isGlobalCatalog flag in RootDSE.
- **PDC.** Result of "FSMO" check.
- **SACL Right.** Result of "Exchange Ready" check.
- **Critical Data.** Verifies that Exchange organization object exists in Configuration naming context.
- **Netlogon.** Result of "Netlogon"—numerical value must match Reachability value.
- **OS Version.** Must run at least Windows 2000 SP3 to support all features required by Exchange 2003.

# DS Proxy

In a modern Exchange system, the Global Catalog servers handle requests for the GAL or a custom address list. They do so using a special service called the Name Server Provider Interface, or NSPI.

As shown in Figure 5.26, the DSProxy service on an Exchange server decides how to handle Outlook clients who need a place to send their NSPI requests.

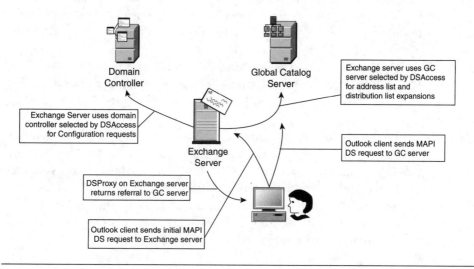

**Figure 5.26**    Diagram of DSProxy operation.

## Name Service Provider Interface (NSPI) Service

Outlook versions older than Outlook 98 service release 2 send their NSPI requests directly to the home Exchange server of the user. The DSProxy service exposes an NSPI interface to handle these requests. The original Exchange client uses MAPI to do name service lookups. DSProxy handles these requests, as well.

When an Exchange server receives an NSPI request from a legacy client, it passes the request to a Global Catalog server for processing. The Global Catalog server determines the content of the address list and returns the first few items to the Exchange server, which forwards the reply to the legacy Outlook client.

For reasons of security and performance, the Exchange server does not open or modify either the client's NSPI requests or the Global Catalog server's replies.

## Referral (RFR)

Modern Outlook clients, Outlook 2000 SR2 and higher, know that Global Catalog servers can handle NSPI requests. These clients connect to the user's home Exchange server and send a request to the RFR service, hosted by DSProxy.

RFR works with DSAccess to determine the name of a qualified Global Catalog server and returns that name to the Outlook client. The Outlook client sends its NSPI requests directly to that Global Catalog server.

Under normal circumstances, the Global Catalog server selected by DSAccess resides in the same site as the Exchange server. But the Outlook client might reside in another location, so the DSAccess choice forces the Outlook client to send its NSPI request across the WAN.

You can set a Registry entry at the desktop running the Outlook client that tells Outlook to use a Global Catalog server in the local site and to ignore the referral from the Exchange server:

```
Key: HKCU | Software | Microsoft | Exchange | Exchange Provider
Value: Closest GC
Data: 1 (REG_DWORD)
```

You can also hardcode the FQDN of a Global Catalog in the Exchange Provider key. The Value name is **DS Server** with a REG_SZ data type. You would not ordinarily want to make this entry except for testing.

To confirm that the **Closest GC** (or **DS Server**) Registry entry worked in Outlook 2003, hold the Ctrl key, right-click the Outlook icon in the Notification Area, and select **Connection Status** from the flyout menu. This opens a Connection Status window that lists the Directory servers selected by the client. To confirm that the entry worked in earlier versions of Outlook, follow these menu items and windows: **Tools | Address Book | Tools | Options | Global Address List | Properties**. This opens a properties window that lists the Global Catalog used by Outlook.

## Static DSProxy Port Mappings

If you have a firewall between your Outlook clients and a domain controller, the clients cannot send their NSPI requests directly to a Global Catalog server. You can force the clients to use the Proxy services of DSProxy rather than getting a referral to a Global Catalog server by setting a Registry entry at the Exchange server to disable referrals:

```
Key:
HKLM\System\CurrentControlSet\Services\MSExchangeSA\Parameters
Value: No RFR Service
Data: 0x1 (REG_DWORD)
```

For this to work, you'll need to open a conduit in the firewall to allow the Exchange server to query a Global Catalog server. This requires locking down the NSPI and RFR services to use specific ports. Use the following Registry entries to assign the ports. Work with your Network Services colleagues to select the ports. You might want to use port numbers in the stratosphere of the allowable number space to avoid conflicts. Port numbers from 1024 to 65535 are allowed.

### RFR

```
Key: HKLM | System | CurrentControlSet | Services | MSExchangeSA
➥| Parameters
Value: TCP/IP Port
Data: <port_number> (REG_DWORD)
```

### NSPI

```
Key: HKLM | System | CurrentControlSet | Services | MSExchangeSA
➥| Parameters
Value: TCP/IP NSPI Port
Data: <port_number> (REG_DWORD)
```

*Information Store*

```
Key: HKLM | System | CurrentControlSet | Services | MSExchangeIS
➡| Parameters
Value: TCP/IP Port
Data: <port_number> (REG_DWORD)
```

# Managing Recipient Policies

A user who wants to get e-mail from outside the Exchange organization needs an address that a foreign messaging system can understand. Microsoft calls this a *proxy address* because Exchange "stands proxy" for the foreign messaging system.

Because Exchange 2003 uses Simple Mail Transfer Protocol (SMTP) for internal and external mail routing, all e-mail objects in Active Directory get an SMTP proxy address. Exchange also assigns an X.400 proxy address, just in case you need to route messages to a legacy Exchange system. Legacy Exchange uses X.400 to route messages between sites.

You might also encounter outside messaging systems that use Lotus Notes, GroupWise, or some other application with unique addressing. These require special connectors that fall outside the scope of this book.

## Default Recipient Policy

You can view the proxy addresses assigned to a recipient using the Active Directory Users and Computers console. Open the Properties window for the recipient and select the E-mail Addresses tab. Figure 5.27 shows an example.

When you install Exchange for the first time, it determines the format of the SMTP address you'll want for your users based on your organization name and the DNS name of your domain. It places the result into an Active Directory object called a *Recipient Policy*.

A service called the Recipient Update Service, or RUS, reads the proxy addresses in that default recipient policy and applies them to the mail-enabled objects in Active Directory.

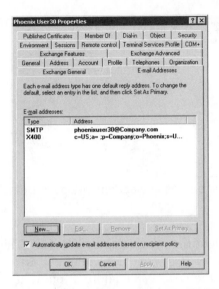

**Figure 5.27** Proxy e-mail addresses assigned based on Default Recipient Policy.

To access recipient policies in ESM, drill down under Recipients to the Recipient Policies container, as shown in Figure 5.28.

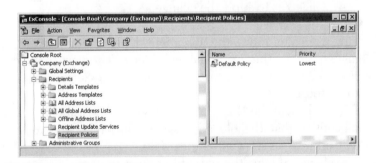

**Figure 5.28** ESM console showing Recipient Policies container and Default Policy.

To see how Exchange formulates a proxy address, open the Properties window for the Default Policy object. Figure 5.29 shows an example. If Exchange guessed wrong when formulating the default SMTP address for your organization, you can change the address as follows:

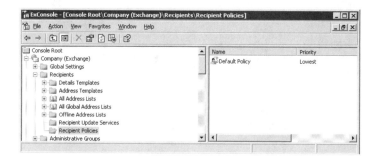

**Figure 5.29**    Proxy e-mail address selection options in Default Recipient Policy.

1. Highlight the address and click **Edit**. This opens an Edit window where you can enter a new address.
2. Enter the new SMTP address you want as the default for your organization.
3. Save the change. You'll get a warning message saying that **The e-mail Addresses of type(s) SMTP have been modified. Do you want to update all corresponding recipient e-mail addresses to match these new address(es)?**
4. Click **Yes** to apply the change.

In a few minutes, the Recipient Update Service will apply the change to all existing mail-enabled objects. The next time you create a new mail-enabled object, the Recipient Update Service applies the new address settings.

If you look at the E-mail Addresses tab of existing users and groups, you'll notice that the old address remains, relegated to a secondary SMTP address, as shown in Figure 5.30.

Exchange retains the old address just in case a user receives mail addressed to that SMTP domain. For example, if you have salespeople already getting mail addressed to subsidiary.com and you configure a recipient policy to give them an SMTP domain of company.com, you don't necessarily want mail addressed to subsidiary.com to bounce.

If you want the superseded addresses to go away, you must either remove the addresses manually in Active Directory Users and Computers or use an automated process of some sort. Microsoft Knowledge Base article 318774 describes how to dump the contents of the recipient's attributes using LDIFDE, and how to manipulate the ProxyAddresses attribute to get rid of the unwanted addresses to then import the result back into Active Directory. You can also write a script to replace the content of the ProxyAddresses attribute. These processes can get fairly complex, so you have to ask yourself if you *really* want those old addresses to go away.

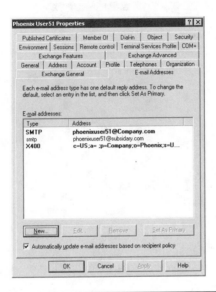

**Figure 5.30** Proxy address changes done as the result of changing the Default Recipient Policy.

## Policy Filter

Each Recipient Policy contains an LDAP filter that defines who gets the proxy addresses contained in the policy. (Recipient policies also control the Mailbox Management feature, covered later in this chapter.)

To see the LDAP filter for a Recipient Policy, select the General tab. Figure 5.31 shows the filter for the Default Recipient Policy. Note that the default policy applies to every mail-enabled object in Active Directory via the simple expedient of searching for any object with a mailnickname attribute.

You can create a new Recipient Policy and target it to specific types of recipients via an LDAP query. For example, let's say that the Sales department manager wants potential customers to try out a new corporate identity called WhizBang.com instead of the boring old

Company.com. She wants salespeople to give out their e-mail addresses as user@whizbang.com instead of user@company.com, but she does not want them to give up their old addresses because they have made valuable contacts with those addresses.

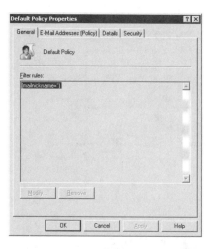

**Figure 5.31**   LDAP query associated with Default Recipient Policy, which selects all mail-enabled objects in Active Directory (mailnickname=*).

You work with your ISP to register the whizbang.com address and to install an MX record in the whizbang.com DNS zone so Internet clients can find the public interface of your Exchange front-end server. But if the front-end server gets an e-mail message addressed to sally@whizbang.com, it rejects the message unless it finds that proxy address in Sally's account.

You can configure a recipient policy to assign a second SMTP address suffix of @whizbang.com to members of the Sales group using this procedure:

1. Right-click the **Recipient Policies** icon and select **New | Recipient Policy** from the flyout menu. This opens the new Policy window, as shown in Figure 5.32.
2. Check the **E-Mail Addresses** option and click **OK**. This opens the Properties window for the policy.
3. In the **General** tab, give the policy a name.
4. Select the **E-Mail Addresses (Policy)** tab.
5. Click **New** to add a new e-mail address.

**Figure 5.32** New recipient policy with selection for policy type, either E-mail Addresses or Mailbox Manager Settings.

6. Select **SMTP Address** from the list of addresses and click **OK**.
7. In the SMTP Address window, enter the SMTP suffix for the domain, such as @whizbang.com. Figure 5.33 shows an example. Leave the **This Exchange Organization is responsible...** option selected.

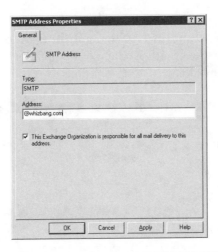

**Figure 5.33** SMTP address assigned to new recipient policy.

8. Click **OK** to save the address. The new address appears in the address list, as shown in Figure 5.34. Check the box to make the new address effective.
9. If you want the outbound mail sent by the salespeople to show company.com as the return address, highlight the address and click **Set As Primary**.
10. Click **OK** to save the new policy.
11. Double-click the new policy to open the Properties window.

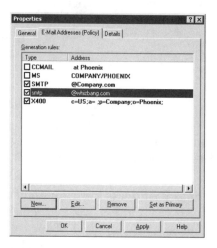

**Figure 5.34** Proxy address changes done as the result of adding a new recipient policy in addition to the default policy.

12. In the **General** tab, under **Filter Rules**, click **Modify**. This opens the Find Exchange Recipients window, as shown in Figure 5.35.

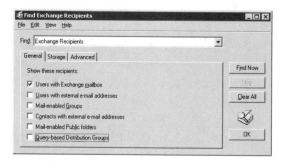

**Figure 5.35** LDAP query builder limiting the selection to mailbox-enabled users.

13. Uncheck all options except for **Users with Exchange Mailbox**.
14. Click the **Advanced** tab.
15. Click **Field** and then **Users**; then scroll down and select the **Member Of** option.
16. Leave the **Condition** field as **Is (exactly)**.
17. In the **Value** field, enter the distinguished name of the group that has members from the Sales department. You might need to

create this group. For example, the entry might read `cn=sales,ou=groups,ou=phoenix,dc=company,dc=com.` (See Appendix A for information about distinguished names.)

18. Click **Add** to add this set of selection criteria under **Condition List**.
19. Click **Find Now** to check your selection criteria. The list of users in the **Search Results** field should match your expectations.
20. Click **OK** to save the filter.
21. Click **OK** to close the Properties window. You'll be prompted that the policy does not apply right away.
22. Click **OK** to acknowledge the warning and close the window.
23. Right-click the new policy and select **Apply This Policy Now** from the flyout menu.

The next time the Recipient Update Service fires, it applies the new proxy addresses on the targeted recipients and changes the existing addresses to a secondary addresses.

## Multiple Recipient Policies

At this point, you should have two Recipient Policies, one you just created for the Sales group and the default. ESM displays the policies in the order that RUS evaluates them.

If you create several policies, stacked one on top of the other, RUS evaluates them in order, starting with the policy at the top of the list. If a selected target object does not fall within the LDAP filter criteria of the first policy, then RUS goes on to check the search criteria of the next policy. If the filter in the policy *does* include a particular object, though, then RUS applies that policy and no others.

You might have situations where you want to apply different e-mail addresses to different groups of users. For example, the Sales department might want to publish e-mail addresses using several different DNS domains, such as sales@companyinfo.com or info@newcompany.com. If you want a set of recipients to have multiple addresses, put all the required addresses into the policy that targets those users. If a recipient falls under several filter criteria, the first filter RUS finds that includes the recipient in the filter takes precedence. RUS ignores all other filter criteria for that recipient.

## Recipient Update Service and Proxy Addresses

The Recipient Update Service has responsibility for applying proxy addresses in Recipient Policies to target objects in Active Directory. To prevent conflicts, only one Exchange server in each domain can use RUS to perform updates. You can select this server, and configure other RUS parameters using ESM.

Drill down under Recipients to find the Recipient Update Services folder. In the right pane, you'll find at least two objects, one for Enterprise Configuration and one for each domain with an Exchange server. Figure 5.36 shows an example.

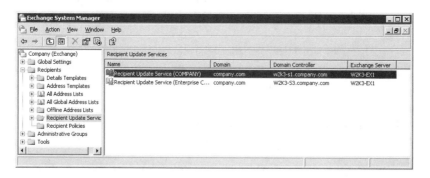

**Figure 5.36**    Recipient Update Service folder in ESM showing two RUS instances, one for Enterprise and one for the domain.

The Enterprise Configuration item controls the application of policies to system accounts for the Exchange servers. The domain item (or items) controls the application of policies to mail-enabled objects in the specified domain.

Note the Domain Controller and Exchange Server columns for each item. These columns list the Exchange server where RUS runs and the name of the domain controller where RUS sends its LDAP requests. Open the Properties window for the RUS instance to change the server selections and the update interval. Figure 5.37 shows an example.

Before taking an Exchange server offline, check first to see if it hosts a RUS instance. Exchange does not automatically select a new Exchange server to host RUS for a domain if the current server becomes unavailable. You must make this selection manually from the Properties window of the RUS instance. Click the Browse button next to Exchange Server and select another server that is operational and centrally located in your organization.

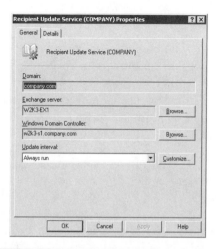

**Figure 5.37**    RUS instance properties showing server selected to run RUS instance, domain controller selected as the update server, and the update interval.

## RUS Intervals

RUS does not wait in the wings for you to change a recipient policy so it can leap out and apply the change. It wakes up periodically, does its chores, and then goes back to sleep. You can control the Update Interval using the setting in the Properties window for a RUS instance.

By default, Exchange sets the Update Interval for a RUS instance to Always Run, meaning that RUS fires once a minute.

The Always Run interval relies on an Active Directory attribute called msExchPollingInterval, which has a default value of 60 seconds.

You can select a longer update interval for RUS, but use caution. RUS has other duties in addition to applying recipient policies. For example, RUS also applies address list parameters to mail-enabled objects. If you set an Update Interval of four hours, new recipients will take quite a while to get those address list settings, which delays their appearance in the GAL.

## RUS and Multiple Domains

If you have more than one domain, you'll notice that ESM shows a separate RUS icon for each domain. This relates to the way Active Directory uses naming contexts. The users, groups, and contacts you normally deal with are stored in a Domain naming context, and the Exchange server running RUS must communicate with a domain controller in that domain.

RUS can't send updates to all domains via a Global Catalog server because the partial domain replicas in the Global Catalog are read-only.

Exchange system objects reside in the Configuration naming context. The Enterprise Configuration thread of RUS takes care of updating their proxy addresses.

## Forcing a Recipient Policy Update

You can force RUS to update Active Directory objects by right-clicking the RUS instance in ESM and selecting either Update Now or Rebuild from the flyout menu, shown in Figure 5.38.

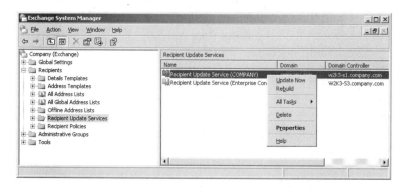

**Figure 5.38** RUS instance update options, Update Now or Rebuild.

These selections look simple, but they initiate an intricate set of processes. I'm warning you about this right up front, not to scare you away, but to keep you from wondering, "Why is he making this seem so darned complicated?" It actually *is* darned complicated.

### Standard Updates

Let's start with the default way RUS works. Every so often, RUS fires up and gets ready to do its thing. Remember that RUS runs on an Exchange server, so it starts by querying a domain controller for any objects that have been updated since the last time it ran.

Let's say you recently added a mail-enabled user called New User1 with a logon name of newuser1. RUS gets the name of that object and then performs an evaluation based on the Recipient Policies. Just for the sake of argument, let's say that only the Default Policy applies to this object. RUS sends an LDAP write request to Active Directory that assigns an SMTP and an X.400 proxy address based on the policy. In this case, that would be an SMTP address of newuser1@company.com and an X.400 address of c=US;a=  ;p=Company;o=Phoenix;s=newuser1;g=Phoenix. (The user is in the Phoenix OU of the domain Company.com.)

This is the behavior you get if you select the **Update Now** option from the flyout menu. RUS searches for a new or changed mail-enabled object and applies the first recipient policy that includes that object in its filter criteria. Key point: *Only new and modified objects get updated.*

### Policy Changes

Remember that I said this process gets complicated. Here's where the complications begin.

Let's say you want to add a new SMTP address, such as @companyinformation.com, to an existing Recipient Policy. You open the Properties for the policy and add the new address and check the box next to the new address to enable it. When you click OK to save the change, a little notification window pops up telling you that the e-mail addresses have been modified and asking if you want to update all corresponding recipient e-mail addresses to match the new address.

This is an important window. If you don't click Yes, then RUS won't see any changes to apply. If you click Yes, the new proxy addresses in the policy get added to an attribute called GatewayProxy in the Recipient Update Service object, as shown in this listing:

```
gatewayProxy: {98356E20-3000-
4F1DBB4B3852C423E766}smtp:@companyinformation.com;
{98356E20-3000-4F1DBB4B3852C423E766}smtp:@company.com;
{98356E20-3000-4F1DBB4B3852C423E766} X400:c=US;a=
;p=Company;o=Phoenix;;
```

The next time RUS fires, it applies the entries in GatewayProxy to the objects targeted by the search query in the Recipient Policy. It then clears the entries from GatewayProxy.

### Rebuilds

If you change the proxy addresses in a recipient policy and you want to apply the new addresses to all existing objects, select the Rebuild option. This sets a flag called msExchDoFullReplication in the Active Directory object that controls the RUS instance, which tells RUS to look at all current objects as well as any new or modified objects. You can see this flag using the ADSI Editor. Figure 5.39 shows an example.

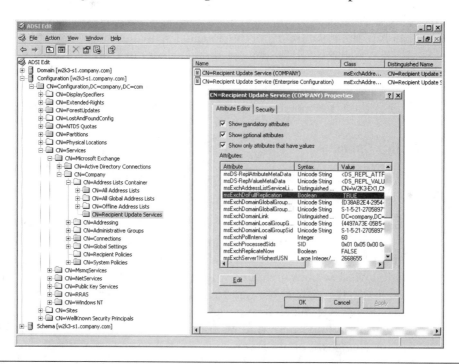

**Figure 5.39**   ADSI Editor showing msExchDoFullReplication attribute after setting RUS to Rebuild.

When you select Rebuild, you'll get a warning that this could take some time and that it could possibly update a significant number of objects, increasing replication traffic. But if you want to change existing objects, Rebuild is your only option.

But wait…It's not quite that simple.

The Rebuild option does not actually begin rebuilding immediately. It only sets the msExchDoFullReplication flag. Nothing happens until RUS reaches its next scheduled start interval.

When RUS fires, it sees the msExchDoFullReplication flag and commences the rebuild. This happens within a minute, if you left the RUS Update Interval set for Update Always, but takes longer if you set the Update Interval to a longer period. Key point: *Rebuild uses the standard RUS update schedule.* Don't expect the changes to take effect immediately if you do a manual rebuild.

### Applying Changes Right Away

If you change a proxy address and you want to apply the change to all existing mail-enabled objects, and you want the change to happen **right now**, first select Rebuild and then select Update Now. The Rebuild selection primes RUS with the msExchDoFullReplication flag and the Update Now option overrides the update interval.

### Policy Scope Changes

It's not over yet. Each recipient policy has a *scope* defined by the content of the LDAP filter. Let's say you define a filter that says, "apply to members of group name Executives." (You should not use group membership as filter criteria for recipient policies, and this example will eventually show you why.) You populate this policy with an SMTP suffix for use by executives and board members and the standard SMTP suffix for your organization.

Later on, you realize that the administrative assistants who work with the executives also need that executive SMTP suffix, so you expand the policy scope to include members of the Executive Admin Assistants group.

When you make a change to the scope of a recipient policy, a little warning window pops up. This window contains a different warning than the previous one, so don't just click it and go on about your business. This warning tells you that the change you just made does not take effect unless you specifically select "Apply This Policy Now" from the flyout menu of the policy. Clicking OK on this warning does not perform any action. It simply acknowledges the message.

This necessity to manually prime RUS with proxy addresses following a scope change makes it possible to have "stealth" scope changes that do not result in an update to the target objects. For example, if you add an existing user to the Executive Administrative Assistants group, that user will not get the addresses in the Executive recipient policy because nobody has primed RUS by selecting "Apply This Policy Now."

For this reason, you should avoid defining LDAP searches that include group membership as a search criterion when formulating recipient policies or any other feature that relies on RUS. This includes Mailbox Management and Address Lists.

If you experiment with applying group policies manually and you get a result that you don't expect, I recommend using the LDP from the Support Tools to view the current GatewayProxy attribute of the RUS object as part of your troubleshooting. To view the attributes for an object, bind using a standard set of user credentials and then select View | Tree and enter the distinguished name of your forest, such as `dc=company,dc=com`. Then drill down through the Configuration container and the Exchange organization container to the RUS objects.

## Key Points for Managing Recipient Policies

If the preceding process descriptions make you want change professions, here are a few simple rules of thumb for RUS:

- When creating a new recipient policy, include all addresses that apply to the target recipients. Remember that RUS evaluates each policy in order of precedence. The first policy whose search scope includes a mail-enabled object is the policy that RUS applies to that object.
- When changing the content or scope of a policy, be sure to select Apply This Policy Now from the flyout menu.
- When applying a policy to existing recipients in a domain, select Rebuild followed by Update Now on the RUS service icon for that domain.
- When taking an Exchange server down for maintenance, always check to see if the server hosts a RUS instance for a particular domain or the Enterprise Configuration. If so, select another Exchange server to host that instance until you complete the maintenance.

- Avoid using group membership as a filter for a recipient policy. Only use filters that interact directly with the LDAP search, such as the Department or the Location attributes.

# Restricting Mail Storage

Under normal circumstances, you want users to have as much access to your messaging system as possible. Circumstances arise, however, when users take advantage of the system by sending messages with huge attachments to hundreds of users or by storing every bit of e-mail they've received since the start of the Bush administration. (That's George H., not George W.)

In the first Matrix movie, the agent program named Smith whines to Morpheus that he, Smith, has tired of the Matrix and yearns to return to wherever programs live when they don't torture human spirits. Smith compares humanity to a virus, saying, "You move to an area and you multiply and multiply until every natural resource is consumed. The only way you can survive is to spread to another area."

I'm sure you'll agree that Smith had an ax to grind and therefore didn't exactly have an objective opinion, but to tell you the truth, when I look at storage on an Exchange server, I'm tempted to think that Smith stumbled on a bit of truth. No matter how much storage you provide to users, they quickly use it up and cry for more. If you try to draw a line and say, "You get this much storage and no more," users go around you and cry to executive management or buy their own servers and sneer at you in the lunchroom.

## Putting the Brakes on Storage Expansion

Users don't appreciate, of course, that the cost of storage starts only with the spindles and RAID cages. You have to back up the store every night and restore it if something goes wrong. If you have more than 16GB of data in your Exchange store, you have to invest in Exchange Enterprise Edition, at a $2,500 price differential. And above all, you have to address concerns about stability and reliability and service level agreements when you have a server with a huge store.

So, for better or worse, in spite of their bellyaching and complaining, the time eventually comes when you have to put limits on the size of your users' mailboxes. The sooner the better, really, before they get spoiled.

You can find the worst offenders by scanning down the list of mailbox sizes shown in ESM. Drill down to a Mailbox Store and see the sizes and item count in the right pane of the console, as shown in Figure 5.40.

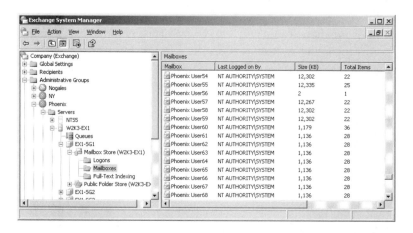

**Figure 5.40** Mailbox sizes displayed in ESM. Click the Size column heading to sort the largest mailboxes to the top.

When setting mailbox size limits, select a maximum size that accommodates average use while not overloading your storage capacity. If you have 200 users and a single Exchange Standard Edition server, you would need to impose a quota of 80MB per user to stay under the maximum storage limit of 16GB. If you invest in Enterprise Edition, calculate your quotas based on the maximum size of the databases you want to back up and restore.

There are a lot of ways to decide how to apportion storage. For example, you could use a economist's approach:

- **Capitalistic.** Track the storage consumed by a set of users and charge them for it. To keep data growth in check, economically punish any department that abuses your storage guidelines. "Sure, we'll give you another 16GB of storage. It will cost you $5,000."

■ **Socialistic.** Follow the dictum, "To each according to his need." The IT organization purchases spindles and backup equipment out of its own budget; then carves out quotas based on the total available storage and takes requests from departments who can prove they need more than their standard allotment. (Leaving chocolate chip cookies and fresh Arabica coffee beans at the entrance to the server room helps to get an allotment increase.)

## Storage Policies

You can assign storage limits on individual mailbox stores, but it makes more sense to set a System Policy and then assign the policy to the mailbox stores within an Administrative Group.

For example, if you have several Enterprise Edition servers, you can create multiple mailbox stores and use them to categorize users by mailbox usage. You can have a high-quota mailbox store for users who insist on having 500MB mailboxes, you can have moderate-quota stores for users who are happy with a 25MB limit, and you can have low-quota stores for users who infrequently use the messaging system and need only a 5MB mailbox. You would then create System Policies to enforce these limits and apply the policies to the appropriate mailbox stores.

If your account has been delegated the Exchange Administrator role in multiple Administrative Groups, or on the organization, you could create a System Policy in one Administrative Group and apply that policy to stores and servers in other Administrative Groups. In general, this does not conform to best practices. Compartmentalize your administrative settings whenever possible.

To create a System Policy to set storage limits, proceed as follows:

1. Launch ESM and drill down to the Administrative Group you want to manage.
2. Right-click the **System Policies** icon and select **New | Mailbox Store Policy** from the flyout menu. This opens the New Policy window.
3. Check the **Limits** option under **Property Pages** and click **OK**. This opens a Properties window where you can enter the name you want to apply to the policy. I'll use the name Moderate Quota User Storage Limits.

4. Select the **Limits (Policy)** tab, as shown in Figure 5.41. The policy in the example issues an e-mail warning to the user when the total size of the user's mailbox store exceeds 25MB. The policy prohibits the user from sending messages after exceeding 35MB and essentially turns off the mailbox after exceeding 40MB.

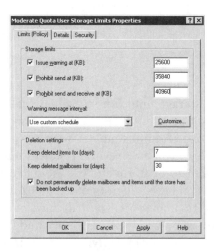

**Figure 5.41**    Mailbox size limits imposed by storage policy.

5. Click **OK** to save the policy. It will not affect any storage yet. You must first link the policy to a mailbox store before it takes effect.
6. Right-click the new policy in ESM and select **Add Mailbox Store** from the flyout menu.
7. Use the object picker to select the store or stores from your Administrative Group that you want to manage.
8. Click **OK** to save the change. If you want to apply the policy settings immediately, right-click the policy icon in ESM and select **Apply Now** from the flyout menu.

Of the three escalation options, prohibiting incoming mail receipt is the most drastic. Some organizations don't like to block incoming mail for any reason because an important message might get bounced. For example, if a user has exceeded the upper storage limit and has been blocked from receiving messages, a sender will get a NDR similar to the one shown in Figure 5.42.

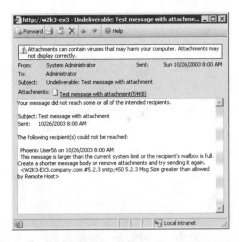

**Figure 5.42** NDR sent to user when recipient's mailbox has exceeded quota.

The user gets a warning that the storage limit has been exceeded, but does not get notified when individual messages begin bouncing back to the sender. Before implementing this policy, it's a good idea to get specific approval from management. Your manager's mail could get bounced.

## Local Archiving

It doesn't do any good to have quotas if you don't give users a place to put their overflow messages. The Exchange server does not have an offline storage feature for old items. Instead, each Outlook recipient keeps a repository of older messages in an *archive*.

The Outlook archive consists of a PST file called Archive.pst by default. This file contains messages placed there by an Autoarchive service that runs periodically within Outlook. I'm sure you've seen the popup message that asks, "Do you want to archive your messages now?"

To change the autoarchive settings, go to **Tools | Options** on the main menu and then select the Other tab. Look for the second set of options, labeled AutoArchive, shown in Figure 5.43.

Click the **AutoArchive** button. This opens the AutoArchive settings window, as shown in Figure 5.44.

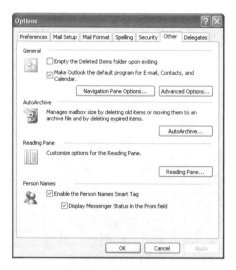

**Figure 5.43**   Outlook options showing AutoArchive button (second section).

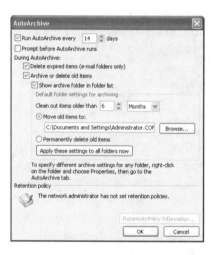

**Figure 5.44**   Outlook configuration for AutoArchive feature.

Every 14 days (the default interval), the autoarchive process cleans out old messages from the user's mailbox and places them into the archive.pst file. This has several ramifications for desktop support technicians:

■ Archive.pst resides in the user's profile. If the technician deletes the profile, all archived messages go bye-bye.

- The archive file resides in a special section of the user's profile called Local Settings. This section does not form a part of a roaming profile. This means that roaming users see different archive contents depending on the machine they use.
- Outlook displays archived items in a separate folder, so users of older Outlook clients who do not have Folder View enabled do not see the archive folder and think their mail has disappeared.

The archive process in Outlook copies an item to Archive.pst and then deletes the archived item directly from the folder where it resides. This so-called "hard" delete means that the item does not pass through the Deleted Items container. As you'll see in a bit, you can recover hard deleted items, even when deleted via archiving, if you get to them during the retention interval, seven days by default.

The option to **Prompt Before AutoArchive Runs** keeps the user informed of the archiving process, but it also provides the user with the option to say "No, Don't Archive." By archiving in the background, you are more likely to achieve 100 percent compliance with your storage policy. The user can still access the archived messages, but they need to look in the archive folder. This will require a little end-user education. Make sure that any archiving/deletion policy you implement adheres to corporate information retention-compliance issues.

## Mailbox Management

You might want to take more sweeping enforcement action to limit mailbox sizes. If users can't do their own archiving and cleanup, you can do it for them. The Mailbox Management service cleans out old messages by either deleting them completely or moving them to a cleanup folder for eventual deletion.

The decision whether to impose automated mailbox management depends a lot on money and corporate culture. If you are an administrator in a small company where everyone likes to function with as few rules as possible, and you can convince management to buy as much storage (and backup capacity) as necessary to accommodate the users' needs, then you don't need to control mailbox size. But if you work in a company where you have to fight for every nickel to buy storage, and your backup window is stretched to the limit and you can't convince your users that messages they received during the halftime of Superbowl XX can be safely deleted, then automated mailbox management starts to look pretty good.

## Mailbox Manager Recipient Policies

A Mailbox Manager Recipient policy controls the selection of items that the Mailbox Management service deletes or archives. To create a Mailbox Manager policy, open ESM and drill down to the Recipients container. Right-click the Recipient Policies folder and select **New | Recipient Policy** from the flyout menu. This opens a New Policy window as shown in Figure 5.45.

**Figure 5.45** New Policy window showing option to select Mailbox Manager Settings instead of E-Mail Addresses setting.

Select the Mailbox Manager Settings option and click OK to open the Properties window for the new policy. Give the policy a name, such as **Mailbox Manager Policy**. Figure 5.46 shows an example of the default settings. The policy allows a user to keep all messages received in the last 30 days and to keep older messages if less than 1MB in size.

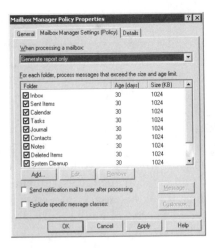

**Figure 5.46** Mailbox Manager policy settings.

The **When Processing a Mailbox** dropdown box defines the following actions:

- **Generate report only.** The Mailbox Management service evaluates the content of a user's mailbox against the policy settings and e-mails a report to the user and to an administrator. It does not take any actions to move or delete the messages.
- **Move to Deleted Items folder.** The Mailbox Management service takes each item that exceeds the policy settings and moves it to the Deleted Items folder in the user's mailbox. Users must purge their Deleted Items folders occasionally for this option to have an impact on mailbox size.
- **Move to System Cleanup folders.** If you select this option, items identified by the Mailbox Management service get moved into a new folder called System Cleanup. The folder structure under System Cleanup mimics the folder structure in the user's Inbox so users can find a message quickly if they need to retrieve it. You can create another policy targeted at the System Cleanup folder with a slightly longer interval that deletes the contents.
- **Delete Immediately.** The Mailbox Management service removes the item entirely. This will get your user's attention, I guarantee.

## Informing Users of Automated Mailbox Actions

When you enforce mailbox limits, be sure to configure the Mailbox Manager recipient policy to inform the user what happened. Select the **Send Notification Mail to User after Processing** option and modify the message to tell your users the purpose of the scan and the actions they should take.

If you decide to forego playing Mr. or Ms. Nice Guy, you can elect to move the items to a cleanup folder and tell the users where to look for their mail. Figure 5.47 shows an example message.

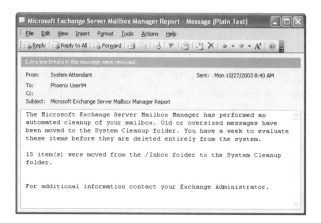

**Figure 5.47**    Example message sent to user following a Mailbox Manager cleanup.

## Targeting Mailbox Manager Policies

You can have separate Mailbox Manager recipient policies for different types of users. For example, you can choose to simply notify some users, to move items into the System Cleanup folders for the majority of users, and to delete items completely for those users singled out as e-mail storage abusers.

To do this kind of targeting, you need to have a way to identify the recipients by a unique attribute that they share in common. The Mailbox Manager recipient policy uses an LDAP filter to identify target users, and you can use the LDAP query builder in the policy to help you create a filter.

## Applying Mailbox Manager Policies

The settings you select in a Mailbox Manager policy get applied to a user's mailbox in two stages:

- In the first stage, the RUS finds users who meet the filter rule in the policy. When the RUS fires, it performs an LDAP search using the Filter Rules in the Mailbox Manager recipient policy. If it finds a user who matches the search criteria in the filter rules, it marks the user's Active Directory object with an attribute called MsExchPoliciesIncluded. This attribute contains the Globally Unique Identifier of the Mailbox Manager recipient policy. In other words, RUS acts a little like a county code inspector who determines that a building does not comply with some statute and places a big red tag on the front door.

- In the second stage, the Mailbox Management service goes through each mailbox in a mailbox store, finds the associated user object for each mailbox, determines if RUS has flagged it with a Mailbox Manager recipient policy, and then takes the action defined by the policy.

The next section describes how to configure when the Mailbox Management service runs and where to send a summary report.

## Configuring the Mailbox Management Service

The Mailbox Management service runs periodically on each Exchange server with a schedule that you can configure via the Properties window for the server object in ESM. Select the Mailbox Management tab, as shown in Figure 5.48.

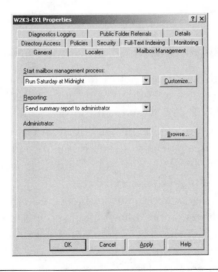

**Figure 5.48**     Mailbox Management settings on an Exchange server.

The default setting tells the Mailbox Management service not to not run at all. The **Start Mailbox Management Process** dropdown list has two primary options: run each **Saturday at Midnight** or each **Sunday at Midnight**. You can establish a custom schedule if those times interfere with other processes running on the server.

In the Reporting dropdown list, you can choose to send a report to a selected administrator. You have the option of a Summary or Detailed report. Figure 5.49 shows an example of a summary report. Choose the detailed report option only if you want lots and lots of data.

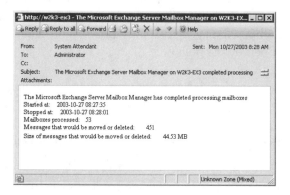

**Figure 5.49**    Example summary message sent to the administrator at the end of a Mailbox Management session.

## Manually Initiating Mailbox Management

If you want to test a new set of mailbox management policies, start by right-clicking the new Mailbox Management recipient policy and selecting Apply This Policy Now from the flyout menu. Then right-click the Recipient Update Service instance for that domain, select Update Now, and then do it again and select Rebuild. This primes the Recipient Update Service with the new policy and then applies the policy to existing objects that meet the search criteria.

Once you've flagged the user objects in Active Directory using RUS, you can run the Mailbox Management service manually on a server using ESM. Right-click the server icon and select the **Start Mailbox Management Process** option, as shown in Figure 5.50.

The system does not give you any progress bars or any other indication that the Mailbox Management process has completed. Instead, look for a summary report in your inbox. For troubleshooting, you can increase the diagnostics logging for the Mailbox Management item under MSExchangeSA in the properties window of an Exchange server in ESM.

**Figure 5.50**    Manual initiation of Mailbox Management using Exchange server property menu.

# Blocking a User's E-Mail Access

It sometimes happens that a user needs educating that access to corporate e-mail is a *privilege*, not a *right*, and that you can revoke this privilege if it gets used improperly. For example, consider a user who sends an e-mail to the entire GAL announcing that the user's manager is capable of performing certain improbable acts of personal gymnastics. If the user retains his or her job, you might want to restrict the user's e-mail access for a while. Exchange offers a variety of alternatives for temporarily or permanently removing a user's e-mail access.

## Disable the User's Active Directory Account

One particularly draconian way to block a user from getting access to a mailbox is to disable the entire user account, as shown in Figure 5.51. Users who have been denied access to the network cannot access their e-mail through any client protocol, including HTTP/WebDAV (Outlook Web Access) and POP3/IMAP4.

This option has the unfortunate (depending on your perspective) result of causing Exchange to bounce any incoming messages to the user. This sometimes causes a problem when the user interacts with customers or vendors. If this is the case, use one of the other options or refer to Microsoft Knowledge Base article 278966 for hints on avoiding message bounces.

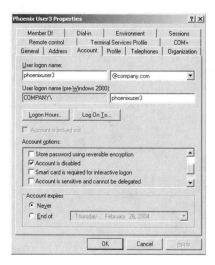

**Figure 5.51**   User properties in Active Directory showing Account Disabled flag.

### Remove the User's Mailbox

You can remove the link between a user's object in Active Directory and the user's mailbox in Exchange by using the Delete Mailbox option in the Exchange Task Wizard. Right-click the user's object in Active Directory Users and Computers, select Exchange Tasks from the flyout menu, and then select Delete Mailbox from the list of tasks. (You can access this same task list from the property menu for a mailbox in Exchange System Manager.) Figure 5.52 shows an example.

The Delete Mailbox option results in the removal of the user's name from the Global Address List, the digital equivalent of banishment. Users sometimes get perturbed when you do this to them. Get written permission first.

By default, deleting a user's mailbox does not actually delete the user's messages in the mailbox store. Exchange retains a user's mailbox for 30 days, by default, before deleting the mailbox and its contents. (This value can be changed. See "Deleted Mailbox Retention" later in this chapter.) Any mail sent to the SMTP address of a deleted user gets bounced with a "Recipient Not Found" message.

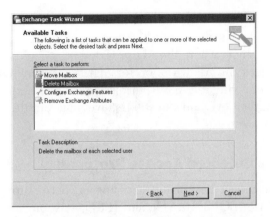

**Figure 5.52**    Exchange Task Wizard showing option to delete user's mailbox.

## Deny Access Permission to the User's Mailbox

If you want the user to continue to receive mail but you don't want the user to read that mail, you can block access using mailbox permissions.

Open the Properties window for a user, select the Exchange Advanced tab then click Mailbox Rights. The Permissions window for the selected user opens with the Mailbox Rights tab selected, as shown in Figure 5.53.

**Figure 5.53**    Mailbox Rights window for user mailbox showing how to remove Full Mailbox Access from user.

The permission list contains an entry called SELF. This well-known SID acts as a placeholder for the user account represented by the Active Directory object where the ACL resides.

Uncheck the Allow option for SELF and click OK to save the setting. By removing the Allow permission for SELF, the user continues to appear in the GAL and can still receive mail, but the user cannot access his or her messages.

## Remove Selected Access Protocols

Users can access their mailboxes using any of the supported client protocols—MAP , POP3, IMAP4, and HTTP—as long as the corresponding service has been enabled at the Exchange server. A user can always make a MAPI connection using Outlook, but you can restrict access by the other protocols.

To change the protocol setting for a user, open the user's Properties window in Active Directory Users and Computers and select the Exchange Features tab, as shown in Figure 5.54.

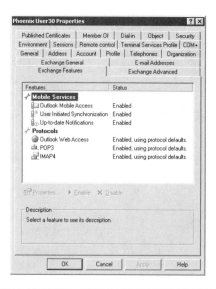

**Figure 5.54**   User Properties window in Active Directory showing that Exchange Features can be enabled and disabled individually.

If you only want a particular set of users to access Exchange using OWA, you can disable the protocol for all other users.

You can also use the Properties of a particular protocol to determine whether Exchange uses Multipurpose Internet Mail Extensions (MIME) with HTML message bodies or plain text. The Plain Text option prevents potentially harmful HTML content from getting delivered to a user.

### Remove the User's Exchange Configuration

If you get into a situation where Exchange refuses to remove the link between a mailbox and a user account due to a configuration error, you can elect to remove all Exchange attributes from the user object using an Exchange Task Wizard option called Remove Exchange Attributes (shown in Figure 5.55).

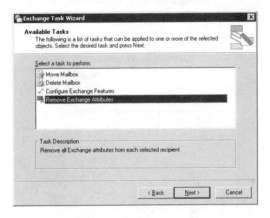

**Figure 5.55** Exchange Task Wizard showing option to Remove Exchange Attributes entirely.

If you take this action, the user loses mailbox access, but the mailbox remains in the store where you can link it to the same or another user. Use this option only if the attempt to delete the mailbox using the Delete Mailbox option fails.

## Accessing Another User's Mailbox

Situations arise when a user—maybe you—needs to access another user's mailbox. You can accomplish this in a variety of ways: The user can delegate access to you or another user, you can give access to yourself, or you can grant access to another user.

## Delegating Mailbox Access

When an executive or senior manager wants her administrative assistant to screen her e-mail and handle routine items, she can use Outlook to delegate access to her inbox and calendar. Or a user might go on vacation and want some other user to monitor his messages.

An Outlook user can delegate access permissions to another user. The Outlook Options window (Tools | Options in the Outlook menu) has a Delegates tab for this purpose. Figure 5.56 shows an example.

Click Add to add a delegate. Once you select a delegate from the Global Address List, the Delegate Permissions window opens, as shown in Figure 5.57.

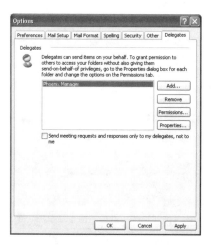

**Figure 5.56**  Outlook option to select a Delegate for access to user's mailbox.

**Figure 5.57**  Outlook delegate options permitting access to Calendar and Tasks (the default) and to the user's inbox, which enables Send As and Receive As access.

By default, a delegate gets Editor (read, create, modify) rights only to the Calendar and Tasks folders. The user can include other folders or change the level of access using the dropdown box next to the folder.

## Accessing a Delegated Mailbox

Once a user has been delegated access to another user's mailbox folders, the delegate can access the folders by selecting the File | Open | Other User's Folder option from the main menu, as shown in Figure 5.58.

If the mailbox owner delegates Editor rights for the Inbox, the delegate can use the From field in Outlook (shown in Figure 5.59) to send mail on behalf of the primary mailbox owner. This highly privileged operation should not be delegated without some thought as to the suitability (trustworthiness, maturity, and so forth) of the delegate.

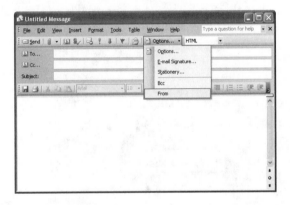

**Figure 5.58**    Outlook menu option for viewing another user's mailbox folders once delegation has been granted.

**Figure 5.59**    Outlook options showing the From field, which permits sending mail on behalf of another user.

## Granting Access to Another User

Sometimes you don't have the opportunity to ask a user to delegate mailbox access to you or someone else. The user might have been fired or the security team has the user under investigation. Also, human nature being what it is, sometimes you'll encounter situations where a manager wants to see a subordinate's mailbox without the subordinate being aware of this access. (Don't do this in production until you have a chat with someone in your legal department. You don't want to inadvertently violate a privacy law.)

Grant a user access to another user's mailbox via Active Directory Users and Computers as follows:

1. Open the Properties window for the user's mailbox to which you want to grant access.
2. Select the **Exchange Advanced** tab, as shown in Figure 5.60.

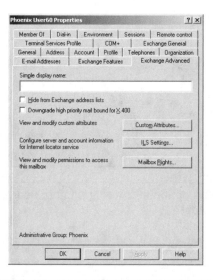

**Figure 5.60**    Exchange Advanced settings in Active Directory showing the Mailbox Rights button.

3. Click the **Mailbox Rights** button. This opens the Permissions window for the user's mailbox. If the permission list has only SELF, as shown in Figure 5.61, then the user has not yet received any messages and therefore does not have a mailbox. Send the user an e-mail and then the security list will include all the inherited permissions from the mailbox store.

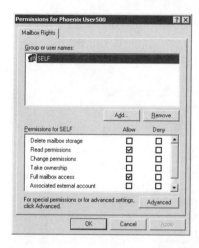

**Figure 5.61** Mailbox permissions for user showing a new user that has not yet received e-mail and therefore has only the default mailbox permission settings.

**4.** Click **Add** and select the name of the user you want to have access to the mailbox. Give this user **Read** permission if they just want to look at the messages and **Full Mailbox Access** if they need to send messages on behalf of the user.

Once you have assigned access to another user, the user can open the mailbox in Outlook using the procedure shown in the "Accessing a Delegated Mailbox" section of this chapter.

## Granting Yourself Access to a User's Mailbox

By default, Exchange denies mailbox access to any Domain Admin, Enterprise Admin, the Administrator account, and any account that has been delegated the Exchange Administrator or Exchange Full Administrator role. Figure 5.62 shows the Security tab of the Organization object in Active Directory where the Deny settings reside. If you delegate the Exchange a Full Administrator or an Exchange administrator role on an Administrative Group, then Exchange places the Deny entries on the Administrative Group object.

You can override a Deny inherited from the organization or an Administrative Group by placing an Allow permission on the mailbox itself in Active Directory Users and Computers. Because of the inheritance rules in Active Directory, an Allow applied directly to an object takes precedence over an inherited Deny. You can grant full access to mailboxes on a per-store or per-server basis as well. See Microsoft Knowledge Base article 262054 for details.

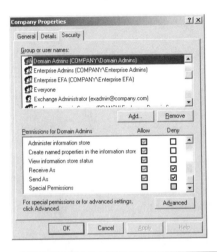

**Figure 5.62** Exchange organization object showing how to override default Deny for administrators by applying an Allow for Receive As and Send As permission on mailboxes.

# Mail Retention

Users call upon Exchange administrators for help with a variety of problems. Here is a brief list:

- "I deleted an important message, and you have to get it back for me right away."
- "I deleted all the stuff in my Junk Mail folder, but now I think there was an important message in there. How can I check?"
- "I cleaned out all my deleted items like you told me to and now I can't find some messages that I really, really, really need. Get them back for me."
- "I permanently deleted a message that I thought was spam, but it turned out to be from a new client and I really need it back because they want me to do something, and I'm going to get fired if I don't do it. Help me out, okay?"

- "I was archiving my inbox last night and Outlook blew up and now I can't see any of my messages. This e-mail system of yours really sucks."

- Finally, one that you might hear from a colleague: "I accidentally deleted a user last night and I re-created the account, but now he can't get his e-mail."

Some of these problems seem trivial, others complex, but they all could require considerable corrective work on your part if you don't take a few precautions.

For example, recovering a user's mailbox (or recovering a single deleted message within a mailbox) involves a lengthy tape restore of the entire mailbox store followed by an extraction and import of the user's mailbox contents. Instead, you can set a retention interval for mailboxes and mailbox items and simply grab the deleted mailbox or deleted item from a hidden container in Exchange and put it back to its original location.

Do you want to do hours of work or seconds of work? Not a tough choice.

## Deleted Mailbox Retention

When you delete a user from Active Directory, or remove the user's Exchange attributes by deleting a user's mailbox, Exchange does not immediately wipe the mailbox from the store. Instead, it retains the mailbox intact for a period of time to give you a chance to either change your mind or to assign the mailbox to another user.

Unless you have a regulatory or corporate policy against retaining e-mail, you should leave the deleted mailbox retention settings enabled. It is not uncommon for a user to leave the company and then return, or for the user's replacement to want access to the e-mail.

Each mailbox store has a setting that determines the deleted mailbox retention interval. By default, Exchange sets a 30 day interval. You can change the interval using the Limits page of the Properties window for a mailbox store, as shown in Figure 5.63. You can also set a System Policy to manage the retention interval for all mailbox stores in an Administrative Group.

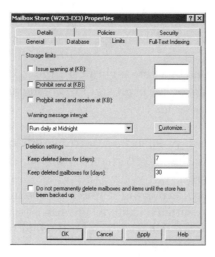

**Figure 5.63**   Mailbox Store Properties window showing default item and mailbox retention interval.

### Deleted User Identification in ESM

Exchange periodically monitors the status of Active Directory users to make sure they still have links to their mailboxes. The Mailbox Cleanup Agent does this work.

You can manually initiate a Mailbox Cleanup Agent session from ESM. Right-click the Mailboxes icon under a mailbox store and select Run Cleanup Agent from the flyout menu, as shown in Figure 5.64.

**Figure 5.64**   Manually initiating Cleanup Agent using Mailbox Store property menu.

If the Mailbox Cleanup Agent determines that a mailbox no longer has an owner, it flags the mailbox in ESM with a big X next to the original owner's name.

You might also notice that the "Last Logged On By" entry for the mailbox shows a bare SID, indicating that the system cannot resolve the SID to a friendly name because the user account has been removed from Active Directory.

### Recovering the Deleted Mailbox

Once the Mailbox Cleanup Agent has flagged a mailbox as having no link to a User object, you can then link the mailbox to another user who does not have a mailbox.

You must see a red X on the mailbox in ESM before you can relink the mailbox. If you delete a user but you do not see a red X, manually initiate the Mailbox Cleanup agent for the mailbox store. You might need to wait a few minutes and refresh the console before the red X appears.

Right-click the mailbox in ESM and select Reconnect from the flyout menu. Use the object picker to select a new account for the mailbox. Exchange updated the Active Directory account, and the mailbox and ESM shows the selected user as the new owner after you refresh the console. The process takes only a few seconds.

You must have Exchange Full Administrator privileges to link a mailbox to another user. This gives your account permission to scan the Deleted Objects container looking for the original user. If someone with simple Exchange Administrator permissions attempts to reconnect a mailbox, the system refuses to comply and displays an error saying that the administrator does not have the rights to complete the operation.

## Deleted Item Retention

Now let's deal with the users who accidentally delete a message, calendar appointment, or task item from their mailbox. Ordinarily, Outlook simply moves deleted items to the Deleted Items folder where the user can drag them back.

Things get a bit more complicated if the user empties the Deleted Items folder. You might get a panicked call when the user discovers that an important message got purged.

Exchange comes to the rescue in these situations by not actually deleting items when the user empties the Deleted Items container. Instead, Exchange gives the items a special mark that flags them as purged so that they do not display in Outlook or an Internet client. The messages remain available for recovery for a period of time—seven days by default—and you can do the recovery in Outlook and OWA.

### Recovering Purged Items from the Deleted Items Folder

You can walk a user through this process. Have the user highlight the Deleted Items container and then select Tools | Recover Deleted Items from the flyout menu, as shown in Figure 5.65.

**Figure 5.65**    Outlook menu option showing deleted item recovery option for Deleted Items folder.

This opens a Recover Deleted Items From—Deleted Items window, as shown in Figure 5.66.

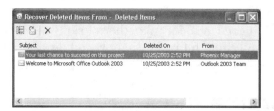

**Figure 5.66**    Recover Deleted Items From window showing items still marked for retention at Exchange server.

Highlight the item you want to recover and click the Recover Selected Items menu. This moves the item back into the **Deleted Items** folder where the user can then drag the item into another folder.

Deleted items obey the same single instance storage rules as any other item in the Exchange Store. If a message gets sent to 20 recipients who share the same mailbox store, only one copy of the item actually resides in the store, whether or not the item has been flagged for purging. This means you can increase the interval from seven days without getting a tremendous increase in the size of the Exchange store.

### Recovering from "Hard" Deletes

Ordinarily, deleted items pass through the Deleted Items folder on the way to oblivion, so recovering purged items from Deleted Items makes sense in most cases. Here are some exceptions:

- The user presses Shift+Del to delete the item.
- A POP3 user deletes a message, or an IMAP4 user purges a message without first deleting it.
- An offline user deletes an item and then purges the Deleted Items folder before syncing with Exchange.

Microsoft calls these "hard" deletes because they don't pass through the Deleted Items folder. As it turns out, though, Exchange treats hard deletes just like any other deleted item. It simply flags the item as purged and retains it for the duration of the Deleted Item Retention period, seven days by default.

If you want to recover hard deleted items, set a Registry entry that allows Outlook to expose the Recover Deleted Items window from any folder, not just the Deleted Items folder:

```
Key: HKLM | SOFTWARE | Microsoft | Exchange | Client | Options
Value: DumpsterAlwaysOn
Data: 1 (DWORD)
```

Ordinarily, it's not a good idea to let the users believe that a "hard" delete truly lasts forever because they might recover a virus-laden message that they originally deleted using Shift+Del.

## Managing Recipients with System Policies

Up to this point, you've configured recipient storage using settings on individual mailbox stores. You can avoid all that work by setting up system policies that control the same settings for all the mailbox stores on servers in an Administrative Group. These system policies override settings applied locally.

Create and manage system policies using ESM by drilling down under an Administrative Group to the System Policies folder. Figure 5.67 shows an example with a few policies already created.

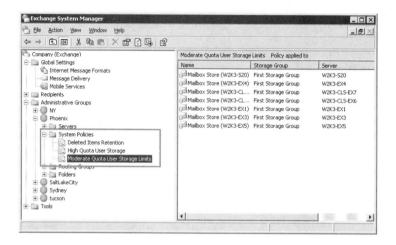

**Figure 5.67**  ESM showing the System Policies folder in an Administrative Group with a few policies already in place.

## Creating New System Policies

To create a new system policy, right-click the System Policies folder and select New; then select one of the object types to manage: Public Store Policy, Mailbox Store Policy, or Server Policy. Figure 5.68 shows the menu.

**Figure 5.68**  Options for creating new types of system policies in the System Policies property menu.

When you select an object type, a New Policy window opens. The window divides each policy into options that correspond to tabs on the Property window for the associated object type. For example, a Public Store policy can manage settings on the General, Database, Limits, and Full-Text Indexing tabs, as shown in Figure 5.69.

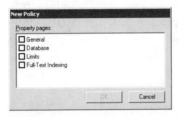

**Figure 5.69** Options for property tabs to include in the new system policy. Tabs can be added after the policy has been created.

Once you select a property page or pages to include in the policy, the resultant Properties window (example in Figure 5.70) shows the associated tabs and their settings.

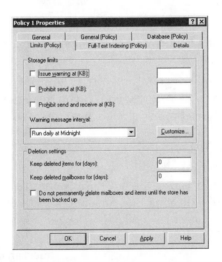

**Figure 5.70** System Properties settings showing that the tab in the properties mimics the tab in the local policy.

## Targeting a System Policy

System policies do not take effect until you link them to one or more mailbox stores, servers, or public folder stores. To do this, right-click the policy icon and select the Add option that matches the policy type you created. A Select Items window opens that lets you browse to the correct object type: mailbox store, public folder store, or server.

Once you link a policy to a particular object, the linked object appears under the policy icon in ESM, as shown in Figure 5.71. You can remove the linked object to return control back to the locally controlled settings.

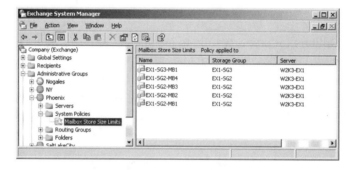

**Figure 5.71** ESM showing links from a System policy to selected mailbox stores.

You can link only one property page from one policy to any given property page on a store or server. If you try to link a second, you'll get a warning that the store has already been put under the control of a conflicting policy.

When you link a policy to a property page on a store or server, ESM locks you out from changing the settings locally. If you view the local property page in ESM, you'll see the values set by the policy with the fields dimmed, indicating that you cannot make changes.

To figure out which policy has locked a particular page, click the Policies tab. This lists any policies linked to the store and the property page affected by that policy. Figure 5.72 shows an example.

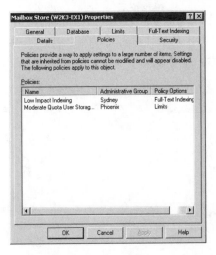

**Figure 5.72**    List of policies that affect the settings of a local mailbox store. The corresponding property pages would be dimmed in the local policy.

# Managing Recipients with Global Settings

The system policies you've worked with so far in this chapter affect only servers and stores within an individual Administrative Group. Some settings require a more universal influence.

Exchange defines a set of *Global Settings* to control certain operations throughout an entire organization. In ESM, the Global Settings container sits right under the root of the Organization.

Exchange defines three types of global settings: Internet message formats, Message Delivery, and Mobile Services. Let's see what each one does.

## Internet Message Settings

If you do business with a client from a certain SMTP domain and you want to manage the messages sent to that client, you can impose a policy for your entire organization that targets messages sent to anyone in that particular SMTP domain.

For example, you can create a Message Format policy that determines the format for messages traveling to and from that particular SMTP domain. Figure 5.73 shows an example.

**Figure 5.73**    Internet Message Settings showing default message encoding and character set parameters.

### Exchange Rich-Text Format

The body of a message from an older Outlook client might contain Rich Text formatting rather than HTML. You can disable this formatting, forcing Exchange to remove any portions of the message that contain Rich Text features. This significantly reduces the size of the message and makes it more compatible with third party e-mail clients.

### Message Text Word Wrap

This option is handy when the client application cannot word wrap a message and the line endings get truncated. The choice of 77 characters fits most text screens.

### Additional Messaging Options

The automatic messaging options are disabled by default so that you do not invite spam automatically by replying to an Internet message.

You might want to disable the option to **Preserve Sender's Display Name on Message** if you do not want the user's friendly name (LDAP display name) to show up on Internet messages. This also helps if your country of origin uses character sets that are not widely recognized. SMTP addresses are required to use ASCII, but your display name might use Unicode characters.

You should leave the delivery and non-delivery report options enabled. They provide helpful information for outside clients who might want an explanation of why their messages are not arriving. If you find that spammers use this information to gain data about your users, disable the options.

## Message Delivery Settings

As shown in Figure 5.74, you can specify message size limits to discourage soaking up bandwidth with frivolously large message attachments.

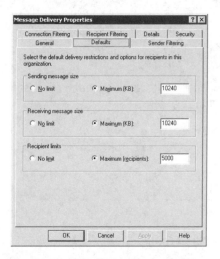

**Figure 5.74**    Global Message Delivery settings limiting size of mailboxes that affect all Exchange servers. Note the default setting of 10MB, which limits impact of Denial-of-Service (DoS) attacks.

The Default settings get applied to all messages. The filter settings—Sender, Recipient, and Connection—get applied only by selecting the filter at an individual SMTP virtual server or servers. See Chapter 13, "Service Continuity," for more information about using these filter options to block spam and other unwanted e-mail.

## Mobile Services Settings

If you want to take advantage of the ability in Exchange 2003 to synchronize e-mail with portable devices or to provide access by handheld devices using Outlook Mobile Access, you can use the Mobile Services settings to enable the services, as shown in Figure 5.75.

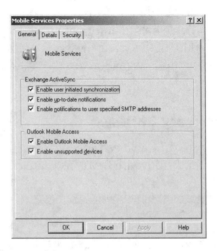

**Figure 5.75**    Mobile Services settings in Global Settings shown as enabled. Mobile services are disabled by default.

# Looking Forward

At this point, you've given users their mailboxes without giving them complete license to dump anything they want into those mailboxes. You gave them distribution lists and a process for managing them that doesn't require an MIS degree to understand. You put a set of controls in place to guide your users toward proper e-mail practices, and you lined the route with graceful landscaping (backed up with electrified barbed wire) just in case they veer too far outside the lines.

Now you're ready to make their life even simpler by giving them a flexible set of address lists that they can access from the office and from home.

# CHAPTER 6

# Publishing Address Lists

If you ask a set of users to list the features they like most about their corporate e-mail system, nearly every list would include the ability to easily find and select recipients from a common set of names that everyone can access. Exchange calls this the Global Address List, or GAL. The GAL contains all mailbox-enabled users, mail-enabled users, mail-enabled groups, mail-enabled contacts, and any mail-enabled public folders that have not been hidden from the address list (the default configuration).

Although Exchange can host any number of address lists, users care most about the GAL. The GAL takes on mystic properties in an organization. A user's presence on the GAL indicates his or her membership on the "team." If a user's name disappears from the GAL for some reason, his first reaction is to think that he's been fired, especially if the company is downsizing. His colleagues might think the same thing when they don't see his name on the GAL. For this reason, among others, you have a certain paternal/maternal responsibility to make sure the GAL, including all the other address lists, stays current and correct.

This chapter describes how Exchange derives address lists, how you can create and deploy custom address lists, how to hide selected users from address lists, and how to manage offline address lists for dialup users.

## Global Address List and Outlook

Outlook users access the GAL in a couple of ways. They can click the Address Book icon in the button bar, or they can open a new message and click the To button. Figure 6.1 shows the result.

If you right-click a user name in the GAL and select Properties from the flyout menu, you can view details about the recipient, as shown in Figure 6.2.

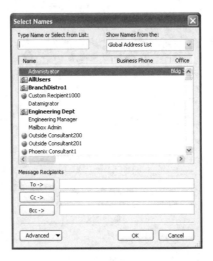

**Figure 6.1**    Global Address List as seen from Outlook.

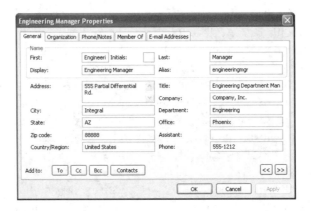

**Figure 6.2**    Recipient properties obtained, along with the recipient list in the GAL.

Outlook obtains the GAL by sending a Name Server Provider Interface (NSPI) request to a Global Catalog server. This request includes the address list name and a list of attributes that Outlook uses to populate the Properties window.

The Global Catalog server searches Active Directory for objects that belong in the address list and returns the list along with the requested attributes. If the list is fairly long, the Global Catalog returns only the first few names in the list, enough to populate the Select Names window (or the Address Book window if that's what the user selected to view the

GAL). If the user moves the slider in the window to view more names, Outlook goes back to the Global Catalog server to get additional items and their attributes.

# LDAP and Address Lists

An Exchange 2003 address list works something like the Sorting Hat in the Harry Potter series. When a student wizard first arrives at the Hogwarts School of Witchcraft and Wizardry, the Sorting Hat looks inside the student's head and heart and decides which house best suits the student's capabilities: the Gryffindor house for bravery, the Slytherin house for cunning, and so forth.

Exchange builds an address list using an Lightweight Directory Access Protocol (LDAP) query that examines the inside of Active Directory to find objects with messaging attributes that best suit the scope of the address list.

Once Exchange has determined which objects to include in an address list, it stamps those objects with an attribute that the Global Catalog server uses when asked to assemble the list. By controlling address lists with LDAP queries, Exchange keeps the contents current from one minute to the next. If you add a new mailbox-enabled user to Active Directory, in short order the user appears in the GAL with no additional work on your part. Powerful stuff.

## Address List Objects in Active Directory

Two Active Directory containers hold the address lists definitions used by Exchange: All Global Address Lists and All Address Lists. You can view the address lists in these containers and control the parameters of those lists using Exchange System Manager. Figure 6.3 shows an example.

If you open the Properties page for the Default Global Address List, you'll see that the General tab displays an LDAP query. Exchange uses this query to determine the content of the GAL. Figure 6.4 shows an example.

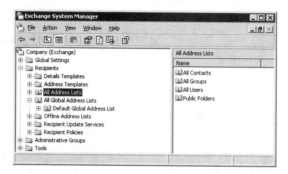

**Figure 6.3**  ESM showing Address Lists folders.

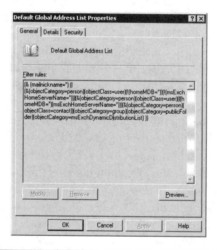

**Figure 6.4**  LDAP query in Default Global Address List used to produce GAL.

## Understanding Address List LDAP Queries

It's instructive to see how an address list LDAP query works because you might want to create custom address lists that use similar LDAP queries.

To unravel a long LDAP expression, you need to know that LDAP puts Boolean operators such as *and* (&) and *or* (|) and *not* (!) at the start of the sequence of items under comparison. For example, the expression (&(objectClass=User)(!sn=Johnson) yields a list of users who do not have a last name of Johnson.

If you want more information about how LDAP queries are structured and used, check out the documentation for the Windows Platform SDK available as a free download from Microsoft at `msdn.microsoft.com`. If you get to like the power of LDAP, and you want to see how a more comprehensive programming model looks, get the book *LDAP Programming with Java* by Rob Weltman and Tony Dahbura or *LDAP Directories Explained* by Brian Arkills (both published by Addison-Wesley).

With that in mind, you can lay out a long LDAP query like one that is used to create the GAL, but in a more readable format:

```
(&
(mailnickname=*)
(|
(&(objectCategory=person)(objectClass=user)(!(homeMDB=*))(!
➡ (msExchHomeServerName=*)))
(&(objectCategory=person)(objectClass=user)(|(homeMDB=*)
➡ (msExchHomeServerName=*)))
(&(objectCategory=person)(objectClass=contact))
(objectCategory=group)
(objectCategory=publicFolder)
(objectCategory=msExchDynamicDistributionList)
)
)
```

This query starts with a blanket statement: Give me every object with a mailnickname attribute. In other words, give me every mail-enabled object.

The remainder of the expression narrows the field a bit by limiting the search to objects that meet the following criteria:

- User objects without a mailbox
- User objects with a mailbox
- Contact objects
- Group objects
- Public Folder objects
- Query-based Distribution Group (QDG) objects

This expression should make sense to you in the overall context of what you know about Exchange up to this point. Based on this LDAP query, the GAL contains all mail-enabled users, mailbox-enabled users, mail-enabled groups, mail-enabled contacts, mail-enabled public folders, and mail-enabled QDGs.

### Alternate Address Lists

As you can see in Exchange System Manager (ESM), in addition to the Default GAL, Exchange hosts several alternate address lists with names that describe their contents. Essentially, these alternate address lists break down the GAL into its component parts. Each one contains an LDAP query that limits the search to a particular type of mail-enabled object.

Users can access these alternate address lists in Outlook by selecting them from the dropdown under Show Names From, as shown in Figure 6.5.

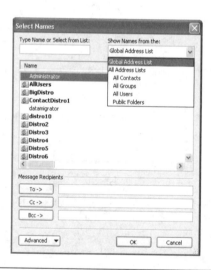

**Figure 6.5**    Alternate address lists as seen by Outlook.

## Custom Address Lists

You can create your own custom address lists to add to the canned lists that come with Exchange. For example, you might want to create an address list for the Engineering department so members of that department don't need to sift through thousands of other names to find their colleagues. Create a custom address list as follows:

1. Launch ESM.
2. Right-click the **All Address Lists** icon and select **New |
   Address List** from the flyout menu. This opens the Create
   Exchange Address List window as shown in Figure 6.6.

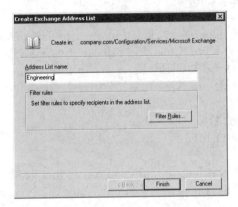

**Figure 6.6**   New Address List window with name of custom address list.

3. Give the list a name that describes its contents.
4. Click **Filter Rules**. This opens the Find Exchange Recipients
   window.
5. Leave all check blocks selected in the **General** tab.
6. Select the **Advanced** tab, as shown in Figure 6.7.

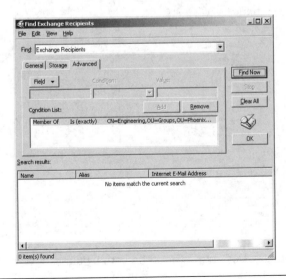

**Figure 6.7**   Selection criteria to build LDAP query for address list.

7. Click **Field** and select **User | Member Of** from the dropdown list.

8. Under **Condition**, select **Is (exactly)**.

9. Under **Value**, enter the distinguished name for a group. The example uses a group named Engineering with the distinguished name `cn=Engineering,ou=Groups,ou=Phoenix, dc=Company,dc=com`. (The entry is not case sensitive but it must have the correct distinguished name format.)

10. Click **Add** to add the search criteria under **Condition List**.

11. Click **Find Now** to verify that the search produces the expected results.

12. Click **OK** to save the query.

13. Click **Finish** to save the address list.

You can check the contents of the address list by clicking **Preview** in the address list Properties window. You can also open Outlook and view the contents of the list in the Outlook Address Book. It might take a few minutes for the address list to appear in Outlook.

If you have a lot of custom address lists, make a hierarchy for them by creating address lists with a name, but no filter rules, and then creating actual custom address lists under the empty lists. The result looks something like Figure 6.8.

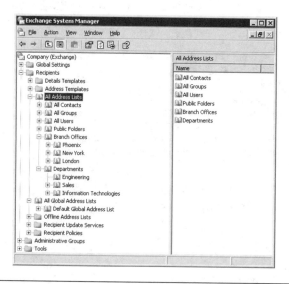

**Figure 6.8**    Creating a hierarchy of address lists by using custom lists with no recipients.

Putting the address lists in a hierarchy helps users to navigate the custom lists more efficiently in Outlook. Figure 6.9 shows an example of the hierarchy in the Select Names window.

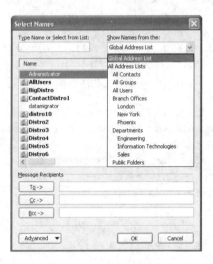

**Figure 6.9**    View of custom address list hierarchy in Outlook.

## Recipient Update Service and Address Lists

Remember the Recipient Update Service (RUS) from the previous chapter? It was responsible for applying proxy addresses and mailbox manager settings to mail-enabled objects based on the content of Recipient Policies.

RUS also has a part to play in creating address lists. Each time RUS runs (every minute, by default), it performs the LDAP queries stored in each of the address lists. If a particular object lies within the scope of an address list search, RUS populates an attribute called ShowInAddress-Book with the name of the address list.

The following listing shows the content of the ShowInAddressBook attribute for a user who falls within the scope of a variety of address list searches:

```
showInAddressBook:
```

```
CN=Engineering,CN=Departments,CN=All Address Lists,CN=Address
➥Lists Container,CN=Company,CN=Microsoft Exchange,CN=Services,
➥CN=Configuration,DC=company,DC=com;
```

```
CN=Phoenix,CN=Branch Offices,CN=All Address Lists,CN=Address
➥Lists Container,CN=Company,CN=Microsoft Exchange,CN=Services,
➥CN=Configuration,DC=company,DC=com;
```

```
CN=All Users,CN=All Address Lists,CN=Address Lists
➥Container,CN=Company,CN=Microsoft Exchange,CN=Services,
➥CN=Configuration,DC=company,DC=com;
CN=Default Global Address List,CN=All Global Address
➥Lists,CN=Address Lists Container,CN=Company,CN=Microsoft
➥Exchange,CN=Services, CN=Configuration,DC=company,DC=com;
```

These four address lists include two canned lists—Default Global Address List and All Users—and two custom lists—Phoenix and Engineering.

If you add a new mail-enabled object to Active Directory, and you want to add it to the address lists immediately, right-click the RUS instance for the domain that holds the mail-enabled object and select the Update Now option. This stamps the address lists onto the object. The next time you view the address list in Outlook, the new recipient appears on the list.

## Hiding Users and Groups from Address Lists

If you don't want a particular user or group to appear on an address list, you can set an option in the Exchange Advanced properties called Hide From Exchange Address Book. Figure 6.10 shows an example.

Selecting this option sets a Boolean attribute called msExchHide-FromAddressLists in the object to TRUE. The next time RUS scans Active Directory, it sees this flag and removes the ShowInAddressBook attribute from the object. This removes it from the search scope for any address list, canned or custom.

Hiding a user from all address lists has a ramification. Many Outlook operations validate a user's name by sending an Name Service Provider Interface (NSPI) request to the Global Catalog to find the user in the GAL. This validation fails for users who you've hidden from address lists.

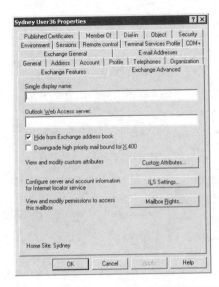

**Figure 6.10**    Properties to hide the user from all address lists.

For example, when you configure Outlook for the first time, you enter an Exchange server's name and the user's name. If Outlook cannot find the user in the GAL, it refuses to continue, and profile generation fails. You must uncheck the Hide from Exchange Address Book option long enough to set up Outlook for the user.

Hiding a user from address lists does not guarantee anonymity. Users can still send him e-mail if they know the his e-mail address. For example, if the Barry White account has been hidden from address lists, you can still send messages to bwhite@company.com.

## Offline Address Lists

When an Outlook user views the content of the GAL, long streams of packets travel back and forth between the Outlook client and the Global Catalog server. Dialup users who access Exchange can get frustrated quickly when trying to scroll through a long list of names in the GAL.

They can avoid this frustration by downloading a copy of the GAL to use when connected over a slow link. This static copy of the GAL is called an Offline Address Book, or OAB. The Offline Address Book service, OABGen, runs under the System Attendant, MAD.exe.

Download a copy in Outlook via the Tools menu: **Tools | Send/Receive | Download Address Book**. See Figure 6.11. Because this operation could consume quite a bit of bandwidth, the user must make this selection manually. If the user forgets, he will not see the most current copy of the GAL when sending messages offline.

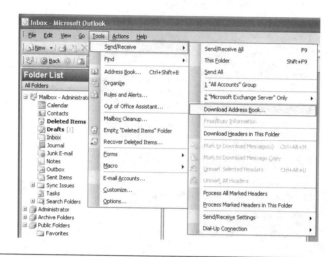

**Figure 6.11**    Outlook menu option for downloading the Offline Address Book.

Once you have a local copy of the GAL, you can take a laptop off the wire and send messages to recipients selected from the OAB. When you reconnect the laptop, Outlook sends the accumulated messages to the Exchange server.

Configuring earlier versions of Outlook to download an offline address book gets a little tricky. You must first create an offline storage (OST) file, configure a set of local send and receive groups to use offline folders, and then download the offline address book.

### Offline Address Book Download Options

When you elect to download an address book, a confirmation window called Offline Address Book opens to gives you a couple of download choices. See Figure 6.12.

**Figure 6.12**    Outlook options for either download bare recipient list or all associated properties.

Ordinarily, Outlook downloads only changes to the OAB. This conserves bandwidth if the user updates the file over a dialup connection. While in the office, if you want to do a complete refresh of the OAB, uncheck this option and download the entire address book.

If you want the fastest download possible, select the No Details radio button to omit the additional properties that Outlook normally requests when it asks the Global Catalog server for the GAL. If you select this option, the user won't see recipient phone numbers, though, which could cause them some inconvenience.

### Offline Address Book Local Storage

Outlook stores the OAB in the user's profile under Local Settings\Application Data\Microsoft\Outlook. The Local Settings folder does not roam with a roaming user. This prevents transferring large files as part of the roaming profile, which is a good thing. But a roaming user with two laptops will need to download the OAB on both laptops.

### Populating the Offline Address Book

Exchange supports the Offline Address Book feature in Outlook by taking a snapshot of the Global Address List and saving it to a file. Exchange calls this feature an *Offline Address List*. Set the parameters of an OAL using ESM. The objects are located under Recipients | Offline Address Lists, as shown in Figure 6.13.

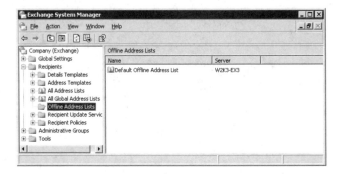

**Figure 6.13**    ESM showing Offline Address List location.

An Offline Address List consists of a pointer at an existing address list. Figure 6.14 shows the Properties window for the Default Offline Address List, which targets the GAL as its address list, as you might expect. Exchange performs the LDAP query defined in the address list and saves the result in a system folder called the Offline Address Book.

**Figure 6.14**    Properties of default Offline Address List.

Note that the OAL gets recalculated only once per day, before the start of the workday at 5 a.m. If you add 100 new mailbox-enabled users and mail-enabled groups to Active Directory at 8:30 a.m., dialup users do not see those new entries until the next day, assuming they choose to download OAB updates.

If you want to update the OAL manually, right-click the icon in ESM and select Rebuild from the flyout menu. A large OAL can take anywhere from several minutes to a half hour to build. Outlook 2003 Cached mode clients also download the OAB when they connect, so schedule the OAB to generate well in advance of the morning logon.

Only one server has responsibility for updating a particular OAL. If you plan on taking that server offline for maintenance during the OAL rebuild period, associate the OAL with another server.

## Create New Offline Address List

If you decide that you want your users to get a different address list than the GAL when they download the Offline Address Book, you can create a custom Offline Address List and link it to one or more mailbox stores as follows:

1. Launch ESM.
2. Right-click the **Offline Address List** icon and select **New | Offline Address List** from the flyout menu. This opens a New Object-Offline Address List window, as shown in Figure 6.15.

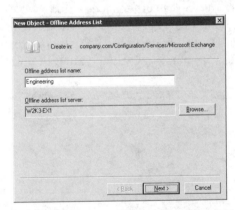

**Figure 6.15**   New Offline Address List window showing name of the server that will compile the list.

3. Enter a name for the offline address list, such as that shown in Figure 6.15. (It's usually a good idea to pick the same name as the address list.) Select a name for the server to do the OAL calculations.

4. Click **Next**.

5. Click **Add** to add a custom address list to the Offline Address List, as shown in Figure 6.16. You can add multiple address lists if you want users to get a wider selection.

**Figure 6.16**    Custom offline address list linked to a custom address list.

6. Click **Next**. A notification appears that you won't see the OAL until the next maintenance period (see Figure 6.17). As part of the maintenance, the OAL server runs the OAL calculations and creates a public folder to hold the results. Because this happens every 24 hours, you will need to wait until the next business day.

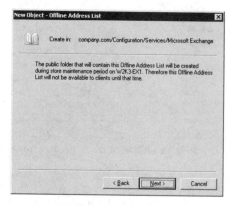

**Figure 6.17**    Notification window that Offline Address Book changes do not occur immediately.

7. With the custom OAL in place, open the Properties window for a mailbox store and select the new OAL. The next time users homed to that server begin to download the OAB, they get this list rather than the default OAL.

## Offline Address Book System Folder

Exchange saves the content of the OAL into a system folder called Offline Address Book. You can view the content of this folder in ESM by right-clicking the Public Folders icon and selecting View System Folders from the flyout menu. Figure 6.18 shows an example.

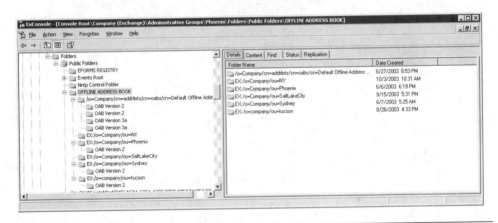

**Figure 6.18**   System folder containing Offline Address Books ready for downloading by Outlook users.

The mixed-mode Exchange organization shown in the figure has several legacy Exchange sites, each with its own OAB. The main OAB has the label Default Offline Address Book.

> Throughout this book, the term "legacy Exchange" refers to all versions of Exchange prior to Exchange 2000.

Exchange maintains different versions of an OAB to support legacy versions of Outlook and Exchange. (The system folder replicates throughout an organization, which could include legacy Exchange servers.) OAB Version 2 supports legacy Exchange servers and clients. OAB Version 3a contains Unicode content that only Exchange 2003 and Outlook 2003 can read.

Each mailbox store must have a link to an OAL so that users with mailboxes in that store can download the associated OAB. Figure 6.19 shows an example. Under normal circumstances, a mailbox store uses the Default OAL, so that dialup users see the same GAL as online users (with the understanding that the OAL represents a once-daily snapshot unless manually configured for multiple snapshots).

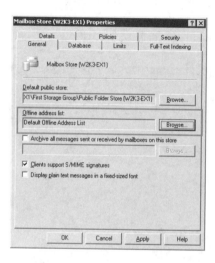

**Figure 6.19**   Each mailbox store linked to one and only one Offline Address List.

If you change the OAL linked to a mailbox store, users homed to that store get the new list the next time they download the Offline Address Book in Outlook.

Although you can create custom Offline Address Lists—because you can link only one OAL to a mailbox store—it makes more sense to simply add an existing address list to the current Default OAL, as shown in Figure 6.20.

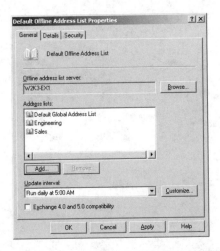

**Figure 6.20** Adding additional custom address lists to the Default Offline Address List.

The next time an Outlook user downloads the Offline Address Book, she sees these additional address lists.

## Looking Forward

The best part about working with Address Lists is that you don't have to do much work. Most users are perfectly satisfied with the GAL. Most dialup users are happy to have an Offline Address Book. They don't often ask for any custom work on your part.

Don't get complacent, though. The following chapter covers the operation, configuration, and management of the Exchange Store. (Deep, solemn drum beats.)

# CHAPTER 7

# Managing Storage and Mailboxes

My very first overseas trip in the U.S. Navy took me to Athens, where I stood on the steps of the Parthenon and pretended to be a latter-day Socrates, thwarting my enemies with barbed questions and avoiding honest work. I remember marveling at the excellent condition of the structure, considering its age. My barracks back in the States was only a year old and looked a thousand times worse. I commented on the workmanship to our Greek guide, who looked proud, as if he had designed it himself. He pointed to the base of the steps leading up to the columns and said in a wonderful, rolling Aegean accent, "Deep roots."

The foundations of Exchange also have deep roots, a set of database files capable of holding tens of thousands of mailboxes and public folders. Much of the work done by an Exchange server involves those database files: storing messages in them, reading existing messages from them, verifying permissions, checking internal consistency, and so forth.

At some point or another in your career as an Exchange administrator, you will encounter a situation that requires you to dig down into the foundation of your Exchange server and tend to the structural stability of those database files. A mailbox store might refuse to mount, or the Information Store service itself might refuse to start, or you might get a dreaded 1018 error in the Event Log, indicating that your hardware has done something tragic to the integrity of the database.

Microsoft diagnostic utilities and their documentation assume that you have a good understanding of the Exchange database internals. You're expected to use this understanding to determine when to perform corrective measures that, if done improperly, could permanently damage the store. For that reason, it's important to know the key elements in the Exchange database design and operation.

This chapter describes the architecture and structure of the Exchange database files and shows you how to configure disk storage that complements the operation of those files. You'll see how to move mailboxes between stores to take advantage of additional storage in

Exchange Server 2003 Enterprise Edition, and you'll see how to test servers to see if they can handle a production load. You'll also see how to speed up mailbox and public folder searches with full-text indexing.

# Exchange Store Architecture

An introduction to the internals of the Exchange Store sounds a little like the introduction to a *Law and Order* episode. The Exchange Store consists of two separate but important database files:

- **STM** file that contains the bodies and attachments of MIME messages
- **EDB** file that contains the body and attachment of MAPI messages and the header information for messages in the streaming file

### EDB File Layout

The EDB file uses a b+ tree structure to store information. Figure 7.1 shows a schematic of the data layout.

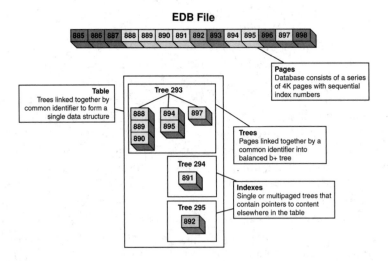

**Figure 7.1**  Diagram of tables, trees, and pages in the Exchange Store EDB file.

Each entry in the EDB database consists of a 4K *page*. This page contains a bit of header information and then some data, either an e-mail or a system message or an index or a pointer to another page. The first couple of pages in the database contain a catalog of the database itself. Each page after that gets a sequential index number starting with 1.

It's entirely possible that a given item consumes more than one page. The database then creates a *tree* of pages and assigns the ID number for the tree to each page.

In addition to a tree that contains messages, calendar items, tasks, and so forth, the system uses trees to hold index information and security permissions. The database links these related trees into a *table*.

## EDB Folders

Upper level processes in Exchange access data in the database files by referencing tables. The database gathers together the trees linked to the table and assembles the patchwork of pages in those trees into a block of data suitable for processing.

This assemblage of tables, trees, and pages doesn't give us as users much guidance in finding useful information in the database, though. We humans need a more practical representation of the data. Exchange provides this representation in the form of a hierarchy of folders and items within those folders. Exchange defines a hierarchy of folders for each user and calls this hierarchy a *mailbox*. Figure 7.2 shows a piece of the mailbox folder structure for a sample user.

The table representing the user's Inbox contains several trees. One of these trees contains message headers. The others have index entries. The message headers have pointers to entries in a master table called Msg. This table contains all the messages in the EDB file. Another table, called 1-24, contains all the message attachments. By dividing the database into special purpose tables, Exchange makes judicious use of the available space, minimizing fragmentation and improving performance.

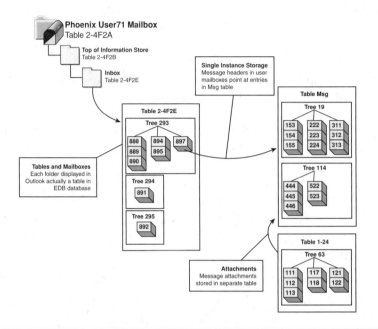

**Figure 7.2** Diagram of relationship between user folders, the tables in the EDB file, and central tables that store messages and attachments.

## User Mailbox Folders

An individual mailbox in Exchange turns out to be a fairly complex beast. It contains almost two dozen folders, any one of which could contain hundreds or even thousands of message headers and message content. Figure 7.3 shows the standard folder layout for a user mailbox.

The folders on the left of the diagram might not be familiar to you. They do not appear directly in Outlook. Instead, they provide support services for various Outlook features. For example, one of the cool new features in Outlook 2003 is the ability to create Search Folders that hold pointers to messages in other folders based on selection criteria such as Unread Mail or Large Messages.

These special folders are not visible in standard Exchange management tools. Keep them in mind, though, because if a user's mailbox gets corrupted, the error messages might contain the names of these folders.

## Single Instance Storage

Because messages and attachments physically reside in their own tables, with pointers from various mailboxes, a particular message or attachment sent to multiple recipients does not consume additional space as long as all recipients have their mailboxes in the same message store. This is called *single instance storage.*

Exchange uses single instance storage for attachments, as well, by keeping the attachments in a single table (Table 1-24) If a user opens an attachment and makes changes to it, Exchange creates a separate copy in the Attachments table.

Single instance storage not only conserves disk space, it also improves performance. When the store gets an incoming message addressed to multiple recipients, it writes the message to the database only one time. As users read then delete the message, the Exchange store simply flags the message pointer as "Deleted" in each mailbox and leaves the original alone. When the last mailbox breaks its link to the message, an online maintenance service removes the message from the Msg table and reclaims the table space, removing the empty lines from the tables (compacting the database).

### Mailbox Moves

If you move several users from one mailbox store to another, single instance storage is preserved. In other words, if two users were recipients of the same message, when you move the two users' mailboxes to another server, only one copy of the message is stored in the new message store with pointers from the two new mailboxes.

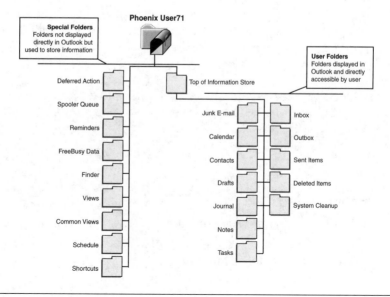

**Figure 7.3** Standard mailbox folders, showing both the folders available in Outlook and hidden folders used to support special features.

This is not the case if you manually move mailboxes using the Exmerge utility described later in this chapter. Exmerge works by dumping a mailbox to a Personal Storage (pst) file and then importing the pst contents into another mailbox. Each item imported by Exmerge gets a unique ID and a separate page in the EDB database. Single instance storage is not preserved.

### Multiple Message Stores

As you've seen, Exchange implements single instance storage by maintaining separate tables in a single EDB file. Exchange Server 2003 Enterprise Edition can have multiple mailbox stores, each with its own EDB file. For this reason, single instance storage does not apply to messages sent to recipients with mailboxes in different mailbox stores, even if they reside on the same server.

In other words, if you send a message with a 2MB attachment to five recipients, and each recipient has a mailbox in a different mailbox store, the Exchange server ends up with five different copies of the message and its attachment. The overall storage utilization grows by 10MB. This is true even if the stores reside in the same storage group.

When designing mailbox stores for an Enterprise Edition server, it ordinarily doesn't pay to get too worked up about the space savings involved with single instance storage. The primary advantage is performance. If you have departments with users who spend the majority of their time sending mail to each other, put them in the same mailbox store. Otherwise, purchase sufficient storage to accommodate possibly redundant storage between mailbox stores and be done with it.

A Performance Monitor counter called SIS Ratio will tell you how much the database would grow if the single instance storage feature were turned off.

## STM File Layout

Microsoft has molded MAPI to the requirements and operation of the EDB database file. The two of them together provide a high performance messaging infrastructure.

The same cannot be said for the combination of the EDB database file and Internet e-mail clients such as POP3 and IMAP4. Internet clients expect to see messages stored in individual files, not in little chunks inside a database. The overhead to convert messages back and forth degrades performance.

Starting with Exchange 2000 and continuing with Exchange 2003, Microsoft alleviated some of this conversion burden by including a second storage file in the Information Store with an internal format more suited to Internet clients. They called this a *streaming* file and gave it an STM extension.

The STM file also uses 4K pages, but unlike the pages in the EDB file, which are sorted and indexed using a b+ tree, the streaming file works more like NTFS. As you can see in Figure 7.4, Exchange places a message into the STM file using a contiguous set of pages called a *run* and then addresses the run by its offset and size. This permits the Information Store service to send the heads of the hard drives right to the start of the message and then scoop up the entire contents. The EDB file indexes the messages in the STM file by storing a copy of the header information for each item.

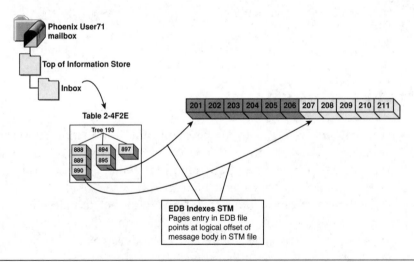

**Figure 7.4** Diagram showing relationship of index information stored in EDB file with item content stored in STM file.

### Content Conversion

The STM file improves performance when a message originates at an Internet client and gets read by an Internet client. But a message sent by an Internet client and read by an Outlook client requires conversion. For example, when an Outlook user requests the content of a message stored in the STM file, Exchange converts the MIME content in the Internet message to MAPI format and sends it on its way.

The Imail service within Exchange handles this content conversion. Under normal circumstances, Imail does a temporary conversion. But if a MAPI client forwards an Internet mail message to another user, Imail converts the message from MIME to MAPI and stores the result in the EDB file. For details, see Microsoft Knowledge Base article 259890, "Imail Service Conversion Scenarios."

Imail uses a temp file in the TMP folder on the server as a scratch pad during conversions. If your Outlook users receive significant numbers of messages from Internet clients, you can reduce processing time for the MIME-to-MAPI conversion by pointing the TMP folder at a separate fast disk.

## Transaction Processing

A new item that arrives for processing by the Information Store service remains in memory until the store can commit the item to the database on disk. Keeping all open transactions in memory is one reason why a busy Exchange server needs so much RAM.

When the Information Store service can get the attention of the CPU for a few cycles, it transfers the item from memory into the main database files. Exchange follows four dictums, called the ACID test, when processing items into the database files:

- **Atomic.** Every piece of an item, its headers and body and so forth, must commit in the same transaction. If the store cannot commit any single piece of the item for some reason, then it does not commit the item at all.

- **Consistent.** If you've ever tried to build a house of cards, you know that it's unwise to add a new card to the stack until the quivers caused by adding the last card die away. A database is no different. Each transaction must take the database from a consistent state to another consistent state.

- **Isolated.** The Information Store must not expose the contents of a new item until it has fully committed the item to the database. For example, if you search for all messages with a subject line that contains "hanta virus," and at that exact moment the system gets an incoming message from the Centers for Disease Control concerning a hanta virus outbreak, you don't want the database engine to give you a pointer to the message until the entire message with all portions of the body and its attachments have been fully committed to the Information Store. Otherwise, you might get an error if you attempt to open the message.

- **Durable.** If the server were to crash, the Information Store must be able to restore the database to a consistent state with all uncommitted pages properly added to the database files. To achieve this, the Information Store does not commit an item to the database until after it has first added the item to a separate storage file called a *transaction log*.

## Database Support Files

The primary database files (priv.edb and priv.stm, or pub.edb and pub.stm) have the following entourage of support files:

- **E00.log.** This is the transaction log. By default, Exchange starts with an empty 5MB log file that it fills as new items arrive. If you have multiple storage groups (covered later in this chapter), then the transaction log file in each storage group gets the next sequential number. The transaction log for the second storage group would have the name E01.log, and the next storage group transaction log would have the name E02.log, and so on.

- **E0000001.log.** When the transaction log fills with items, Exchange renames it by adding a sequence number starting with 0000001 and then creates a new E00.log file to hold the next set of transactions. In the second storage group, the additional log file names would start with E01000001.log.

- **E00.chk.** This is a checkpoint file that tells Exchange the location of the last committed transaction in the transaction logs.
- **Res1.log and Res2.log.** These are reserve logs that give Exchange a little elbow room if a drive should run out of space. The store most likely will crash if it must write to the reserve log files, but at least you can recover the store with all messages intact if that happens.
- **Tmp.edb.** This file acts as a scratch pad during online defragmentation.

## Transaction Logs and Exchange Backup

If an Exchange database file gets corrupted, you can restore a copy of the file from backup and continue with normal operations. Replaying the transaction logs forms an integral part of this restoration. Here's why.

Let's say you run a backup on Sunday and use that tape for a restoration on Wednesday. Your users would be upset if they lost three days of messages, but that won't happen. Once you restore the primary database files from the tape, Exchange replays the transaction logs from disk to get the database back to a current state.

This trick of keeping historical transaction logs for replay during restoration has a limit, though. You do not want to retain every single transaction log since the first day you installed the Exchange server. Exchange draws a line when you do a full backup. During a full backup, once the Exchange Backup API ensures that the Information Store has committed all items from the transaction logs, it tells the Information Store to delete the transaction logs. This frees up disk space for the next set of logs.

For this reason, it's very important to do full backups regularly. Don't be the administrator who spends $250 on a call to Microsoft Product Support services to complain about "out of disk space" errors on your Exchange server. If you get an Event Log entry saying that a logical volume is about to run out of space, and you look at the volume and you see hundreds and hundreds and hundreds of transaction logs, you will not suspect a failure of Exchange. Instead, you'll suspect a failure of your backup application.

## Database File Locations

By default, Exchange stores the primary database files—priv1.edb, priv1.stm, pub1.edb, and pub1.stm—in the folder \Exchsrvr\MDBData. During Setup, put this folder on a fast, stable disk array or a SAN.

After initial setup, you can change the location of the main database files for a store using the Properties window. Figure 7.5 shows an example. You must run ESM on the server that hosts the files to change their location.

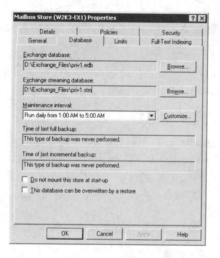

**Figure 7.5** Mailbox Store properties showing database file locations.

When you specify a new location for the database files, Exchange dismounts the store and then copies the database files to the new location and remounts the store. You'll get a warning like that shown in Figure 7.6. During the period of the dismount, users are cut off from all access to the mailbox or public folder store. You should avoid doing this during working hours. If you are running Enterprise Edition with multiple mailbox stores, the other stores are still available for use.

You have the option of putting the EDB file on a different drive than the STM file. This can help performance somewhat on a heavily loaded server that handles both Internet e-mail clients and MAPI clients. If all your users access the store with Outlook and only a small fraction of your message traffic comes from the Internet, don't waste time putting the STM file on a different drive.

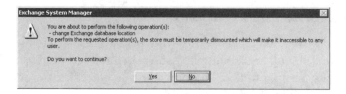

**Figure 7.6** ESM warning that a mailbox store is dismounted when moving database files.

## Changing Transaction Log File Location

Exchange aggregates mailbox and public folder stores into a structure called a *Storage Group*. This helps conserve resources, because all stores in a storage group share a common set of transaction logs.

The Standard Edition of Exchange 2003 has only one storage group plus a second used to recover a store. Enterprise Edition can have up to four storage groups plus the recovery storage group.

Use the Properties window of the storage group to view and manage the transaction log configuration. Figure 7.7 shows the default storage group configuration.

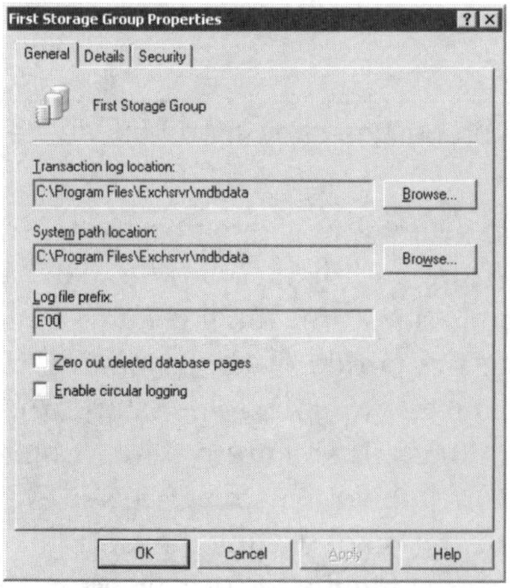

**Figure 7.7** Storage Group properties showing the location of the transaction logs and system files.

The **Transaction Log Location** entry designates the path to the main transaction log, E00.log, along with the E000000## logs created since the last full backup and the reserve logs, res1.log and res2.log.

The **System Path Location** entry designates the path to the E00.chk and tmp.edb files.

You'll gain no performance or recoverability advantage by designating separate spindles or logical drives for the System and Transaction Log locations. Put them on the same volume.

You can select a new location for the transaction logs and system files. If you enter a new path, Exchange dismounts *every store in the storage group* and then copies the transaction and system files to the specified location. You get the warning shown in Figure 7.8.

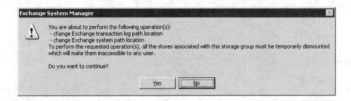

**Figure 7.8** ESM warning that all mailbox and public folder stores in a storage group are dismounted when moving transaction and system files.

Perform a full backup of the storage group before moving its transaction logs. This removes the old transaction logs, which limits the amount of data copied during the transfer.

## Mailbox Stores

On an Enterprise Edition server, you can add three more mailbox or public folder stores to the first storage group and up to five stores of either type on each of the other three storage groups for a maximum of twenty stores.

To create a new mailbox store, you'll need the Exchange Administrator role in the Administrative Group that holds the Exchange server. With that in mind, proceed as follows:

1. Right-click the storage group and select **New | Mailbox Store** from the flyout menu. This opens a Properties window for the new store, shown in Figure 7.9.

**Figure 7.9** Properties window for new mailbox store. This is one of the few evolutions in Exchange that does not involve a task wizard.

2. When you create a new mailbox store on a server, Exchange automatically makes an entry under **Default Public Store** that points to the same server. It also selects the Default Offline Address List for Outlook. You do not need to change these settings.

3. Give the mailbox store a name. You might want to consider including the storage group and server name in the mailbox store name, such as EX1-SG2-MB1, so that you can identify the source of every mailbox store just by looking at its name.

4. Select the **Database** tab, as shown in Figure 7.10.

5. Select the path for the database files.

6. Click **OK** to create the store.

Here are a few Do's and Don'ts when creating mailbox stores:

■ Don't place the database files on the same drive as the transaction log files for the storage group. This reduces performance by forcing the drives to handle both sequential transaction log operations and random mailbox item lookups. It also reduces recoverability should you lose the volume.

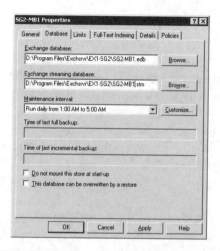

**Figure 7.10** Properties of new mailbox store showing that database files should be placed on a separate volume to enhance performance and recoverability.

- Do use separate drives for each mailbox store. This improves performance and recoverability. If you don't have sufficient drives or LUNs in a SAN, put mailbox stores from the same storage group on the same drive. This way, if you do lose a volume, you won't disturb other storage groups during the recovery.
- Do use separate drives for the EDB and STM file if you want maximum performance.
- Don't place Exchange database files on a NAS drive unless the drive has been specifically approved for use with Exchange Server 2003 and has a Microsoft logo to that effect.

## Online Maintenance

The Exchange IS service performs a series of maintenance operations every night sometime between 1 a.m. and 5 a.m., by default. These operations include

- **Index removal.** When an Outlook 2003 user creates a special view of a mailbox, Exchange creates an index of the folders in the user's mailbox (Inbox, Sent Items, and so forth.) If the index does not get used within a 40 day period, online maintenance deletes it. The 40-day value is fixed.

- **Deleted item removal.** When an item in the primary message table (Msg) has no links from any mailboxes, it is placed in a special table called the *tombstone* table. When items have been listed in the tombstone table for a period of time equaling the item retention period (seven days, by default), then online maintenance removes the items completely from the database and compacts (defrags) the database tables. This does *not* return free space to the file system but it does return free space to the Exchange store, which is limited to 16GB in Standard Edition. (The online maintenance compacts the public folder store as well.)

- **Public folder posting expiration.** If you define an age limit for postings in public folders, online maintenance removes outdated items.

- **Public Folder deletions.** When a public folder gets deleted, Exchange retains a copy for 180 days. Once that interval expires, online maintenance removes the folder permanently. The 180-day value is fixed.

- **Server version updates.** Online maintenance verifies the Exchange version of each server and adjusts the public folder replication mechanism based on the versions on its replication partners.

### Schedule Online Maintenance Around Backups

If you initiate a backup of any store in a storage group, online maintenance stops for all mailbox and public folder stores in the storage group. Once backup finishes, online maintenance picks up again. If the backup runs all night, you'll never defrag your stores. This would eventually cause performance issues and might cause database corruption.

Look at your backup logs and determine when the backups start and end. Change the times for online maintenance accordingly. If you have so many stores that a full backup consumes an entire night, then shift to running incremental or differential backups to reduce the backup window. Remember that you need to run a full backup periodically to clear out the transaction logs. If your backup application can take advantage of snapshot backups (see Chapter 13, "Service Continuity"), then the size of the backup window should not become an issue.

Don't schedule online maintenance for the middle of the work day. The maintenance process puts a significant load on the Global Catalog server as it validates user names and recipient information. It will also interfere with other scheduled Exchange processes such as Offline Address Book generation and Mailbox Management operations.

### Additional Mailbox Store Configuration Options

A couple of other settings in the mailbox store Properties window deserve mention.

- **Do Not Mount This Store at Start Up.** This is a diagnostic setting. Select this option if you have a corrupted store that you want to troubleshoot, and you don't want to wait for the Exchange IS service to time out trying to mount the store.
- **This Database Can Be Overwritten by a Restore.** This is a recovery option. It allows you to overwrite the store with the contents of a backup. By forcing you to flag the store for overwrites, Exchange prevents you from accidentally overwriting the wrong store.

## Storage Groups

One of Microsoft's major design goals for Exchange 2000 and Exchange Server 2003 was to increase the number of mailboxes that a single server could handle. Even though Enterprise Edition is capable of supporting individual stores with well over 16GB of content, the likelihood of performance and corruption problems increases with store size. A huge store is clumsier to manage and maintain than a slim store, all other things being equal.

So, from the point of view of manageability and performance, you're better off with lots of smaller stores than one huge store. For this reason, Microsoft allows creating up to 20 stores on the Enterprise Edition of Exchange 2000 and Exchange 2003.

This introduces another challenge, though. The Jet database engine used by Exchange is highly dependent on transaction logs. For performance reasons, it's desirable to put the transaction logs on a different drive than the main database files. Well, if every store has its own set of transaction logs, to have 20 stores, you'd need a server with 40 different logical drives (or LUNS from a SAN).

To reduce the storage management complexity, Microsoft aggregated stores into *storage groups*, with each storage group sharing a common set of transaction logs. The Enterprise Edition of Exchange 2003 can have up to four storage groups with five mailbox or public folder stores apiece. Standard Edition has one storage group with one mailbox store and one public folder store.

Both editions have the capability of creating an additional storage group to use for mailbox or public folder store recovery. Figure 7.11 shows a diagram of the storage group layout.

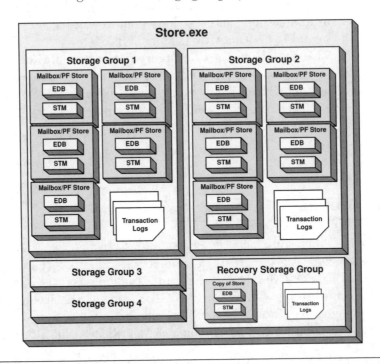

**Figure 7.11** Diagram of storage group constituents in Exchange Server 2003 Enterprise Edition.

Using multiple storage groups has several important advantages.

■ **Performance.** Each storage group has a separate set of transaction logs. Putting each set of logs on a different drive improves the overall message throughput for the server.

- **Stability.** An Exchange server with ten 5GB mailbox stores is less likely to encounter database problems than a server with one 50GB mailbox store.
- **Flexibility.** Individual stores within a storage group can be separately mounted and dismounted. This permits you to do maintenance on a single mailbox store, which limits the impact of an outage.
- **Backup.** You can back up and restore mailbox and public folder stores in separate storage groups simultaneously. With this feature, you can shorten your overall backup times considerably by using a backup application that supports multiple agents, each of which controls backup for a separate storage group. This trick works only if the backup device has multiple drives.

## Storage Groups Disadvantages

Although storage groups provide a great way to host lots of users on a single server, you need to watch out for a few potential problems.

- **Additional memory.** Each new storage group requires a big chunk of memory in addition to the memory required for each store in the group.
- **Temporary dismounts.** If a mailbox store or public folder store dismounts unexpectedly due to an error, the other stores in the storage group dismount and then remount. This causes a temporary loss of connection to mailboxes and might force users with older Outlook clients to close and restart Outlook.
- **Serial backups.** Although you can do simultaneous backups of stores in separate storage groups, the Backup API permits only one mailbox or public folder store in each storage group to get backed up at any one time. If you have five stores in a single storage group, you cannot take advantage of a multi-threaded backup application or a tape device with multiple drives.
- **Online maintenance interruption.** When any mailbox or public folder in a storage group is getting backed up, online maintenance stops for all the other stores in the storage group. This can hamper the ability of the Exchange server to completely defrag all the databases.

By evenly apportioning mailbox stores between all four available storage groups on an Enterprise Edition server, you get more flexibility in controlling your backups and a more fault-tolerant server, with the caveat that you'll consume more memory. At today's memory prices, you should not build a server with less than 2GB of RAM, so the additional memory used by the storage groups shouldn't cause a performance problem.

## Creating New Storage Groups

To create a new storage group on an Exchange server, right-click the server icon in ESM and select New | Storage Group from the flyout menu. This opens a Properties window for the storage group similar to that shown in Figure 7.12.

**Figure 7.12** Properties of new storage group showing transaction file locations different from the stores within the storage group.

It doesn't make sense to spend the additional two and a half thousand dollars for the Enterprise Edition of Exchange and then scrimp on storage spindles. To get the best performance, put the transaction log for each storage group onto its own RAID array or SAN LUN. If you absolutely can't find room in the budget to support additional storage, then buy a large enough array to hold the largest expected database size and a week of transaction logs with at least 30 percent free space. It's difficult to estimate the mailbox store size based on the number of users because the equation has too many variables. A quick post to an Internet newsgroup will get you at least a dozen responses from administrators with similar organizations to yours who can tell you their database sizes.

### Additional Configuration Options

Leave the other storage group configuration options at their default settings. These include

- **Zero Out Deleted Database Pages.** This option prevents access to deleted information by writing over the memory pages with zeros. This places an additional processing burden on the server and should only be used in secure environments.
- **Enable Circular Logging.** This option limits the use of disk space by reusing transaction log. **Never implement circular logging for mailbox stores.** This option is intended only for public folder stores that support NNTP newsfeeds.

The version of Exchange that comes on Small Business Server enables circular logging by default to conserve on disk space. For a small shop with a few users, this might make sense, but you sacrifice recoverability. I suggest making sure you have sufficient disk space to handle standard logging and run full backups at sufficient intervals to assure that you do not fill the transaction log disk. Track your disk utilization carefully to determine the maximum required size for a specific environment.

### Storage Group Names

When assigning a name to a storage group, include the server name in the storage group name; for example, EX1-SG1. In this way, if you have only a bare list of storage group names, you know the server that owns them.

Exchange assigns a name of First Storage Group to the default storage group created on a server. You can change this name by selecting Rename from the flyout menu of the storage group in ESM or by highlighting the name and pressing F2.

Renaming a storage group does *not* result in a dismount of the stores nor does it cause an interruption of message flow. It does, however, change the distinguished name of the mailbox stores in the storage group. If you have scripts hard coded with the old distinguished names, you'll need to change the code.

# Configuring Physical Storage

When you spec out the hardware for an Exchange server, pay particular attention to the storage configuration options at your disposal. You should use SCSI or Fibre Channel rather than ATA or SATA (serial ATA) to take advantage of the faster overall throughput and because you can put multiple drives on the same bus without degrading performance. If you have a single-channel RAID controller, put the server boot drives on a pair of mirrored ATA drives and reserve the RAID array for your Exchange files.

> Technology changes rapidly, and by the time you read this, the performance numbers for SATA drives might approach those of SCSI drives, at least in terms of raw I/O times. If you are pricing out an Exchange server on a strict budget for an organization with a few hundred mailboxes, then a set of SATA drives in a hardware-based RAID array will perform acceptably, assuming that you have an average set of users and do not have mail-enabled applications that make tremendous demands on I/O.

If you absolutely must use ATA drives for Exchange database storage, put one drive on each of the two IDE controller channels to avoid bottlenecks or use a hardware RAID controller. (Some ATA RAID controllers have four channels to give you more options for configuring large stripe sets.) Better yet, get a system with a motherboard that supports connecting SATA drives directly to the chipset rather than going through the PCI bus.

The software RAID that comes with Windows Server 2003 and Windows 2000 performs adequately, but the cost of ATA RAID controllers has gotten so low that it does not make sense to use software RAID for a server.

## Use RAID 1+0 or RAID 0+1

Most basic RAID controllers support mirroring (RAID 1) and striping with parity (RAID 5). Either method preserves file access if a single drive crashes. Mirrored drives exhibit average write performance and good read performance. RAID 5 arrays exhibit average read and relatively poor write performance unless you spread writes among several drives. A large RAID 5 array can also take quite a while to rebuild following an event. The data remains available during the rebuild, but performance slows considerably.

For a few dollars more, you can get a controller that supports RAID 1+0 or RAID 0+1. Both of these alternatives combine the good performance of RAID 0 (striping without parity) with the excellent recoverability of RAID 1 (mirroring).

- RAID 0+1 consists of two stripe sets mirrored together to form an array.
- RAID 1+0 consists of a series of mirrored drive sets striped together to form an array.

Both alternatives require more disks than standard RAID 5, but you get much better performance and improved fault tolerance should two drives fail at the same time. In RAID 5, a simultaneous drive failure brings down the array. In RAID 0+1, the two failed drives would need to belong to different mirrored sets before you would lose data. In RAID 1+0, the two failed drives would have to belong in the *same* mirrored set, which makes a catastrophic failure even more unlikely.

> The chances of two drives failing in the same array at the same time should be fairly remote, so the choice of using RAID 1+0 or RAID 0+1 pretty much depends on the RAID controller used by your server vendor. Simultaneous failures are not impossible, though. Ask anyone who has lived through a series of drive failures caused by a production line defect.

A RAID 1+0 array also regenerates faster following a drive replacement because only one drive needs to regenerate. In RAID 0+1, the entire stripe set must regenerate. You'll experience less performance degradation during regeneration, as well.

So, with all this in mind, when the time comes to spend your boss' money, what's the best way to go? Most top-tier server vendors include a RAID controller that supports either RAID 1+0 or 0+1 in addition to RAID 5, so you won't spend more money for the controller, just the disks and possibly the enclosure, depending on your hardware.

If you're building an Exchange 2003 Standard Edition server, the mailbox store can't grow larger than 16GB, and you probably don't have more than 200 to 500 users, so two RAID 1 arrays, one for transaction logs and one for the mailbox and public folder stores, are perfectly adequate. If you're building an Exchange 2003 Enterprise Edition server capably of handling 2000 to 6000 mailboxes, you should use RAID 1+0 or RAID 0+1 with at least 10,000-RPM SCSI 320 drives.

## Assign Similar Recipients to the Same Mailbox Stores

If you have a service level agreement (SLA) that specifies a certain amount of allowable downtime, calculate how long it will take you to restore a particular store during the work day and size your stores accordingly. For example, if it takes four hours to restore a 20GB mailbox store on a particular server, and your SLA stipulates only two hours of allowable down time, then you need to limit each mailbox store to a maximum size of 10GB.

You should try to keep your mailbox stores approximately equal in size so you don't end up with a Wednesday's Child that nobody dares to touch because it's too big or contains too many large mailboxes.

Here's one way to maintain fairly consistent mailbox store sizes. Divide your users based on the amount of storage they consume. Give the packrats their own mailbox stores and put the other users into the remaining stores. Distribute them so that the expected growth rate of each storage group stays within your storage capacity. Don't be afraid to impose storage limits. The users might curse your name, but they probably won't do you bodily harm.

It also helps to put executives into their own mailbox stores. This might not sound egalitarian, but when budget time comes around and you want more money for servers and software, it helps that the executives who approve your budget have not experienced frequent service interruptions. (For some reason, it doesn't seem to do any good to say, "If you give me more servers, you won't crash as often.") Keeping the "squeaky wheel gets the grease" admonition in mind, be sure to route the executives a weekly uptime report with trend lines showing that more storage/memory/CPU capacity will be needed in the next budget cycle. Also, putting executives in their own store permits you to assign separate retention and mailbox management policies, something that might be required by regulations or desirable for business management purposes.

# Moving Mailboxes Between Storage Groups

Once you create new mailbox stores, you can move mailboxes to the new stores using the Move Mailbox option in the Exchange Task Wizard in Active Directory Users and Computers. You can also launch the Exchange Task Wizard from ESM by drilling down to the mailboxes under the Mailbox Store. You must have the Exchange Administrator role or higher to move mailboxes.

The Mailbox Move feature in Exchange 2003 allows you to move mailboxes for multiple users at the same time. It also skips corrupted mail items, rather than hanging, and removes the corrupted item from the store. If you install Exchange Server 2003 SP1 and have at least one Exchange 5.5 server in your organization, you can move mailboxes between servers in different Administrative Groups (legacy sites). In Exchange Native mode, you can move mailboxes between mailbox stores on any server in any Administrative Group as long as you have the Exchange Administrator role on both sides.

Don't confuse Exchange Mixed mode with Windows Mixed mode. In Windows Mixed mode, an Active Directory domain controller can replicate with downlevel Backup Domain Controllers (BDCs), forcing Active Directory to obey certain restrictions for backward compatibility with NT. Exchange Mixed mode allows the legacy Exchange directory service to interact with Active Directory via the Active Directory Connector, which imposes certain restrictions on Exchange operations. See Chapter 12, "Migrating from Legacy Exchange," for details.

During the move, Exchange locks the user's mailbox. It makes no attempt to force the user off the system nor does it warn the user about the change in mailbox status. If you move a user's mailbox while the user has Outlook open, the user gets a popup message stating that the Exchange server is unavailable. The user must exit Outlook and log on again to connect to the new mailbox store.

If the user has mail en route to the old mailbox store, Exchange diverts it to the new store. Exchange caches recipient information, though, so it's possible that a message that arrives just after the mailbox has moved might get bounced.

To move a mailbox to another mailbox store, either on the same server or to another server, proceed as follows:

1. Right-click a user's icon in Active Directory Users and Computers or the mailbox icon in ESM and select **Exchange Tasks** from the flyout menu. Figure 7.13 shows an example.

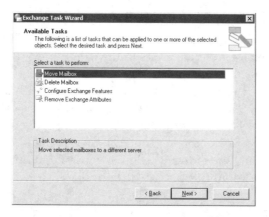

**Figure 7.13** Exchange Task Wizard showing the Move Mailbox option. Use this to populate a newly created store with existing mailboxes.

2. Highlight the **Move Mailbox** icon and click **Next** to open the Move Mailbox window, shown in Figure 7.14.

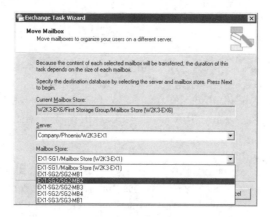

**Figure 7.14** Move Mailbox window showing selection options for any storage group on a selected server.

3. Select the server and the mailbox store where you want the user's mailbox to reside.
4. Click **Next** to initiate the move.
5. Once the mailbox has completed moving, notify the user to launch Outlook again to verify that the user can access the mailbox on the new server.

## Moving Multiple Mailboxes

You can move multiple mailboxes at the same time, as shown in Figure 7.15. Exchange uses up to four threads to handle the moves. Exchange 2000 and legacy Exchange use a single thread to move mailboxes, so a large migration takes a considerable amount of time.

Also, Exchange 2003 allows you to initiate multiple instances of a quad-threaded mailbox move, which speeds up the process even more. If the mailbox move encounters a corrupted item in the user's mailbox, it skips the item instead of hanging, deletes the item from the source mailbox, and logs the event.

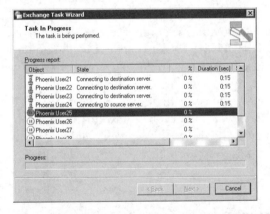

**Figure 7.15** Move Mailbox window showing four threads for moving mailboxes, making Exchange 2003 four time faster than Exchange 2000 in migrating users to new servers.

Just highlight a set of users in Active Directory Users and Computers, or highlight a set of mailboxes in ESM, and use the Exchange Task Wizard to specify a new server and mailbox store. The current mailboxes can reside on different home servers, but they must all go to the same destination.

As much as you'd like the mailbox moves to happen in an instant, it takes time to securely and safely transport large gobs of information between servers. It irritates users because they can't access their e-mail, so you have to do the work after hours. Third-party applications are available that can speed up the process essentially by dumping messages into an intermediate database as they move between servers and then allowing users to access their e-mail while the database engine presents any messages in transit. An example of this sort of application is the Exchange Migration Manager from Aelita Software, `www.aelita.com` (now a division of Quest Software).

### Moving Mailboxes Results in EDB Promotion

When you move a mailbox to a new mailbox store, Exchange places the incoming items into the EDB file, even if the original messages resided in the streaming (STM) file. This can degrade performance for POP3 and IMAP4 clients after the move.

If you plan on moving a considerable number of mailboxes that have content in the STM file, and the owners of those mailboxes use POP3 or IMAP4 clients, consider beefing up memory and processors on the new server to handle the additional conversion requirements.

Content conversion requires scratch space in a temp file. Exchange uses the TMP/TEMP folder specified by the operating system. You can find the location of this folder by typing **SET** at a command prompt. Prior to moving a significant number of mailboxes with streaming content to a new server or mailbox store, point the TMP/TEMP environment variable at folder on a fast drive to assure good conversion performance. Make sure this drive has at least twice as much free space as the size of the database that you're moving.

# Moving Mailboxes with Exmerge

In some circumstances, you can't use the Move Mailbox feature to transfer mailboxes between servers. You might need to save the contents of a user's mailbox to a flat file then import the file to a new location. Microsoft provides a utility called Exmerge for this purpose.

Exmerge dumps the content of a user's mailbox to a Personal Storage (PST) file. You can import this PST file into the same mailbox if you're using Exmerge for backups, or import it into a mailbox on another server. Here are a few examples of how this functionality can come in handy:

- **Mixed mode mailbox moves.** In Exchange Mixed mode, you cannot move mailboxes between servers in different Administrative Groups. This limitation stems from legacy Exchange, where each site represents a separate partition in the directory service.

- **Legacy mailbox moves.** If you have an existing legacy Exchange organization with only 20 or 30 users, you might not want to go through the work of creating an Active Directory Connector, monitoring replication, dealing with the limitations of Exchange Mixed mode, and so forth. You can set up a pristine Exchange 2003 organization and use Exmerge to import the mailboxes from the legacy organization.

- **Corrupted mailbox moves.** The Move Mailbox Wizard in Exchange might stop working if it encounters a corrupted message. Using Exmerge, you can dump the contents of the existing mailbox while skipping the corrupted message; then import the result into the user's new mailbox. You can also use this trick to recover access to a mailbox if the corrupted message prevents opening Outlook.

- **Individual mailbox restores.** To restore an individual mailbox, first restore the mailbox store containing the mailbox; then use Exmerge to dump the contents of the recovered mailbox to a file and import it into the user's production mailbox.

- **Brick-level backups.** If you don't like the thought of restoring an entire mailbox store every time a user accidentally or negligently messes up their mailbox, you can periodically use Exmerge to dump the entire content of the mailbox store to a set of files, one for each user. This takes LOTS of time and LOTS of storage, so you might be better off purchasing a third-party backup application that can backup individual mailboxes. Microsoft terms this a *brick-level* backup. See Chapter 13 for details. Many administrators use Exmerge to do brick-level backups of high-value mailboxes, such as executives and owners.

Microsoft provides Exmerge as a free download from
`download.microsoft.com/download/8/d/e/8ded36c6-ee38-43ca-9ab3-387603e7afe7/exalltools.exe`.

## One-Step and Two-Step Merges

Exmerge operates most efficiently in situations where you want to migrate a user's mailbox directly from one server to another. This can be done in a one-step process that dumps the mailbox to a file and then immediately imports it into the new location. This one-step Exmerge process works only if the source and destination mailboxes have the same distinguished name.

For example, you cannot use the one-step process to move a mailbox with the distinguished name `/o=company/ou=phoenix/cn=recipients/cn=phoenixuser72` to a mailbox with the distinguished name `/o=company/ou=sydney/cn=recipients/cn=phoenixuser72`. This means you can't use the Exmerge one-step process to move mailboxes between Administrative Groups.

In those cases, you can use a two-step process. Dump the mailbox from the old Administrative Group; then, during the import, specify a mailbox in the new Administrative Group. You can also run Exmerge in batch mode, which permits you to specify the target distinguished name. The Exmerge examples in this book use a two-step process.

## Exmerge Requires Mailbox Access

You must have Send As and Receive As permission on the user's source and target mailbox. Exchange administrators are specifically denied this permission, so you'll need to grant yourself access as follows:

1. Open a user's Properties window in Active Directory Users and Computers.
2. Select the **Exchange Advanced** tab.
3. Click **Mailbox Rights**.
4. Click **Advanced**.
5. Click **Add**.
6. Add your account. Grant yourself all permissions except for **Associated External Account**.
7. Click **OK** to save the change.

In production, be sure to remove these special permissions after you finish migrating the mailbox. Avoid leaving your account on the permission list for mailboxes just in case someone exploits your credentials.

## Exmerge Requires Access to Exchange Binaries

The simplest way to run Exmerge is to place the Exmerge.exe executable and Exmerge.ini file in the \Exchsrvr\bin folder. If you prefer not to mix additional files with the native binaries, you can modify the Path in the system environment to include the path to the Exchange binaries then run Exmerge from a separate folder.

## Exmerge Caveats

A user's mailbox contains a lot more than just an Inbox. It holds calendar information, tasks, journal entries, deleted messages, junk mail, and so forth. It also holds hidden content in the form of special-purpose folders such as free/busy information, search folders, inbox rules, and items purged from the Deleted Items container but not yet removed from the Information Store. Exmerge has the capability of exporting just about all this information to the PST file, with a few exceptions.

- **Exmerge does not include embedded attachments.** Exmerge does not open messages to search them. If a message has an embedded message, such as a reply to a distribution list, and the embedded message has an attachment, Exmerge does not know the attachment exists and does not include it in the export.
- **Loss of Free/Busy information.** An export retains the user's calendar items, but you'll lose the association between the user's calendar and the Schedule+ Free/Busy system folder that holds availability information.

Here's a workaround for the problem of losing free/busy information. Immediately after completing an Exmerge import, launch Outlook using the /cleanfreebusy switch. Do this by opening a command prompt, navigating to the location of the Outlook.exe executable, and then entering:

```
outlook /cleanfreebusy
```

Once Outlook opens, create a new calendar appointment. Outlook then extracts the current appointments in the user's Calendar folder and creates a new set of free/busy entries in the Free/Busy public folder.

### Imported Rules Might Be Lost

Let's say a user has an inbox rule that moves all messages with a certain subject line to a certain folder. The Exmerge import creates the folder but there's a slight catch to implementing the rule.

Although it appears that an inbox rule specifies a folder by name, in the background, Outlook identifies the folder by its Globally Unique Identifier (GUID). When you do an Exmerge import, it creates a new folder by the same name, but the folder has a different GUID.

Following the import, the first time the user opens the Rules and Alerts window, Outlook displays a notification that one or more rules have errors. The rules show red in the listing, and the "specified folders" section of the rule no longer displays the folder name.

To overcome this limitation, have the user go through each inbox rule and specify the name of the destination folder. This refreshes the rule with the correct GUID.

This process of cleaning up invalid rules can get tedious very quickly. You will almost certainly want to make up some instructions for your users and brief your Help Desk staff.

## Moving a Mailbox with Exmerge

The following steps use Exmerge to export a user's mailbox. It deletes the user and creates a new user by the same name with a mailbox store in a separate storage group and imports the mailbox. The example demonstrates the "merge" feature of Exmerge by placing a few messages in the new inbox before importing the PST file.

To create the initial conditions for this test, create a user account and send the account several e-mails. Then create several folders in the user's inbox and establish one or two inbox rules that move messages into the new folders. When you've finished, log off the user of Exchange.

### Mailbox Export

Make sure that you have access permissions to the user's mailbox and then proceed with the Exmerge dump as follows:

1. Launch Exmerge.
2. Click **Next** at the introductory window. This opens the Procedure Selection window, as shown in Figure 7.16.

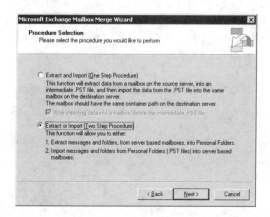

**Figure 7.16** Exmerge window showing option to use One-Step or Two-Step Procedure.

3. Select the **Extract or Import (Two Step Procedure)** radio button.
4. Click **Next**. The Two Step Procedure window opens as shown in Figure 7.17.

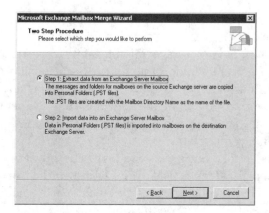

**Figure 7.17** Exmerge Two-Step window showing steps to either extract data or import data.

5. Select the **Step 1** radio button.
6. Click **Next**. The Source Server window opens, as shown in Figure 7.18. Enter the flat name of the Exchange server that hosts the user's mailbox, such as **W2K3-EX1**. If you have a very large organization, you can speed up the next few steps by specifying the name of a local domain controller that hosts the domain containing the user's Active Directory account.

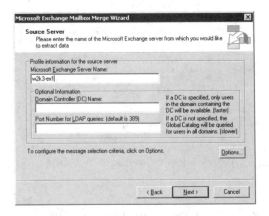

**Figure 7.18** Exmerge window showing option to select the source server and to specify a domain controller rather than a Global Catalog server.

7. Click **Options**. This opens the Data Selection Criteria window, as shown in Figure 7.19. The default selection is User Messages and Folders. If you want to export the inbox rules, select Associated Folder Messages. If you want to overwrite the permission on any target folders that share the same name, select the Folder Permissions option. If you want to export any items that have been purged from the Deleted Items container, but not yet removed from the Information Store, select the Items from Dumpster option.
8. Select the **Import Procedure** tab, shown in Figure 7.20. The default selection is **Merge Data into the Target Store**. If you prefer to copy or overwrite, select an alternate option. You can also elect to remove the item from the source store. This option, combined with the ability to filter for a particular message or attachment name, can be used to purge a virus-laden message from each person's mailbox.

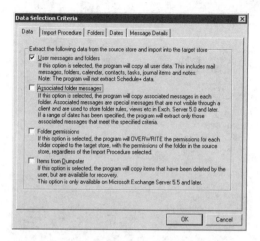

**Figure 7.19** Exmerge data export selection window.

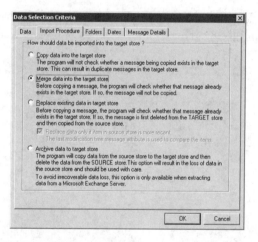

**Figure 7.20** Exmerge data import window.

9. Select the **Folders** tab, shown in Figure 7.21. You can specify folders that you do not want to export. For example, you can click **Modify** and elect to skip the **Deleted Items** and **Journal** containers. You can also type in your own folder paths. For example, the figure shows a manual entry for **Junk E-mail** to avoid exporting accumulated spam.

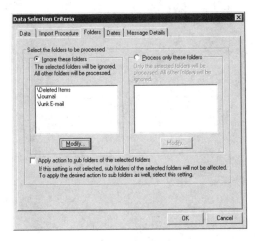

**Figure 7.21** Exmerge Folder selection window.

10. Select the **Dates** tab, shown in Figure 7.22. Use the options in this tab to select which messages you want to export.

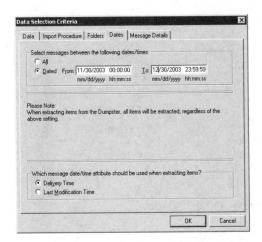

**Figure 7.22** Exmerge Dates window that permits including only a certain range of items.

11. Select the **Message Details** tab, shown in Figure 7.23. Use these options to export only selected messages. This is especially useful if you want to extract a message with a virus attachment.

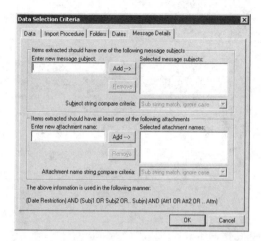

**Figure 7.23** Exmerge Message Details window that permits selecting items by their content.

> **12.** Click **OK** to close the Data Selection Criteria window and return to the Exmerge wizard.
>
> **13.** Click **Next**. The Database Selection window opens (Figure 7.24).

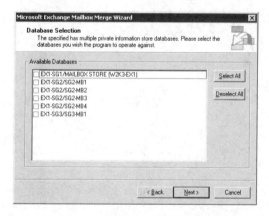

**Figure 7.24** Exmerge Database Selection window to select the source of the mailbox export.

> **14.** Select the mailbox store containing the mailboxes you are exporting. If you're not sure of the mailbox store, click **Select All** and let Exchange give you a list of the users in the next window.
>
> **15.** Click **Next**. The Mailbox Selection window opens (Figure 7.25). Select the user or users whose mailboxes you want to move.

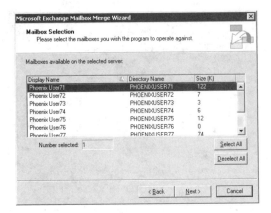

**Figure 7.25** Mailbox Selection window showing list of user mailbox in selected mailbox store.

> **16.** Click **Next**. The Locale Selection window opens (Figure 7.26). Select the locale where the mailbox is currently stored.

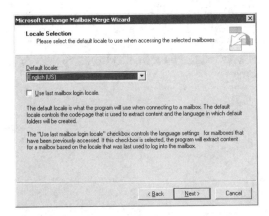

**Figure 7.26** Locale selection window that allows selecting country codes to control language and punctuation.

> **17.** Click **Next**. The Target Directory window opens. Navigate to a folder on the local machine (or a network share) where you want Exmerge to create the PST files. Be sure to have sufficient room on the drive to hold the PST files. They can get fairly large if you're going to export a lot of packrat users. Exmerge does not export Unicode PST files, so do not use it for mailboxes larger than 2GB.

18. Click **Next**. The Save Settings window opens (Figure 7.27). This option allows you to save your selections into an INI file used by Exmerge to perform the requested operations.

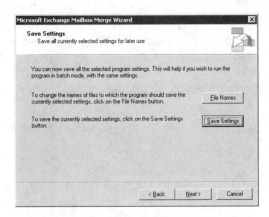

**Figure 7.27** Save Settings window that permits saving an Exmerge profile.

19. Click the **File Names** button. This opens a Change Settings Filenames window (Figure 7.28) that displays the various support files used by Exmerge. By default, Exmerge uses the folder where the executable was launched.

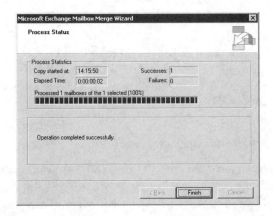

**Figure 7.28** File selection window permits alternate locations for the various support files used by Exmerge.

**20.** Click **OK** to close the Change Settings Filenames window and return to the Save Settings window.

**21.** Click **Save Settings**. This updates the Exmerge.ini file with the selections you made in the wizard.

**22.** Click **Next** to begin the export. A Process Status window opens to show you the steps as they occur. When the export has completed, the window displays the result, as shown in Figure 7.29.

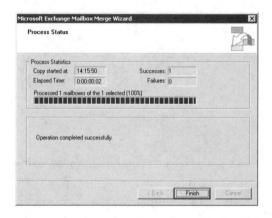

**Figure 7.29** Exmerge status window that can display errors if the export does not progress satisfactorily.

**23.** Click **Finish** to close the window and exit the wizard.

At this point, check the dump folder for the presence of the PST file. If the export operation succeeded, you should also see a series of messages in the Exmerge.log file stating that the contents of the user's mailbox was saved to the PST file via MAPI.

### Delete and Re-create User Account

Now use Active Directory Users and Computers to delete the user account. This breaks the link between the account and the mailbox. Let this replicate to the other domain controllers (especially the Global Catalog servers) and then create a new user with the same name. Mailbox-enable the user and specify a different mailbox store on the Exchange server.

When you delete a user account from Active Directory, the object representing the user is stripped of nearly all attributes and thrown into a hidden container called Deleted Objects where it lurks for 60 days before being completely removed by a garbage collection process. It's possible to reanimate a deleted object in Windows Server 2003, but without the attributes that define a user's identity, the undeleted object isn't of much worth. You can use third-party utilities to restore deleted objects from Active Directory. Look at Recovery Manager for Active Directory from Aelita Software (www.aelita.com) and ActiveRestore from Quest Software, www.quest.com. (Quest now owns Aelita and is determining if and how it will merge the two products.)

Log on to the domain as the new user. Launch Outlook. Use another client to send this user a couple of messages and verify that they appear in the user's inbox. Close Outlook.

### Import Mailbox

You're just about ready to import the contents of the PST file into the user's mailbox. First, though, you'll need to give your administrative account access permissions on the user's new mailbox. This is a brand-new account so your administrative account will be denied access by default.

Once you've granted yourself access to the user's new mailbox, proceed with the import as follows:

1. Launch Exmerge.
2. Click **Next** at the introductory window to open the Procedure Selection window.
3. Select the **Extract or Import (Two Step)** radio button.
4. Click **Next**. The Two Step Procedure window opens.
5. Select the radio button titled **Step 2: Import Data into an Exchange Server Mailbox**.
6. Click **Next**. The Destination Server window opens. The entry under **Microsoft Exchange Server Name** should already be entered.
7. Click **Next**. The Database Selection window opens. Select the mailbox store that holds the newly created mailbox.
8. Click **Next**. The Mailbox Selection window opens. Select the user name from the list.

9. Click **Next**. The Locale Selection window opens. Ensure that the locale is correct.
10. Click **Next**. The Target Directory window opens. Ensure that the folder name and path is the same that you entered when you did the export. The import function will match the user name on the PST file with the user name you selected as the destination mailbox.
11. Click **Next**. The Save Settings window opens.
12. Click **Next** to begin the import. The Process Status window opens.
13. When the import has succeeded, you'll be notified. If the process encountered errors, you can look in the Exmerge.log file to find the cause. Ordinarily, the cause of an import error is a failure to give yourself adequate access permissions on the target mailbox.

At this point, log on as the user and launch Outlook. The mailbox should contain the messages you imported from the old mailbox and the messages you sent to the new account.

### Bulk Exmerge Operations

You can automate these steps for multiple users by building a Mailbox.txt file that contains the distinguished names of the users. Run Exmerge in batch mode to perform the dumps and imports. Make sure you have sufficient storage capacity to hold all the PST files. Refer to the detailed document that accompanies the Exmerge utility.

# Full-Text Indexing

Once users have more than a few dozen messages into their mailboxes, you start hearing complaints about finding old e-mails. "My boss is yelling at me because I printed a report on yellow paper. I know he told me to use yellow paper and I can prove it if I can find the darned e-mail." You'll hear similar complaints about finding content in public folders.

You encourage your users to take advantage of the Advanced Find feature in Outlook, but they object that the searches "take too darned long."

Don't scoff. They have an excellent point. When you use Outlook to search for an item in a mailbox or public folder, the Information Store opens each item in the mailbox or public folder, one at a time, and parses through it looking for a match. This imposes a heavy I/O and CPU load on the server and produces quite a few network transactions between the Exchange server and Outlook.

You can alleviate these performance issues by indexing the mailbox and public folder stores using the Microsoft Search Service, or MSSearch. Once indexed, the Information Store service can reply to an Outlook search request using the index rather than searching each individual item. This dramatically reduces processor utilization and disk reads at the server and results in a much faster response to clients.

The really exciting part of this feature is that it requires virtually no change to the way the users currently do searches. They simply bring up the Advanced Find option just as they do now, and when Exchange gets the search request, it sees that the store is indexed and replies with the content of the index.

Exchange Setup installs MSSearch but does not enable the service, by default. When you configure the first store for indexing, Exchange enables MSSearch and configures it to start automatically. You can control the index settings using...you guessed it...Exchange System Manager (ESM).

## Indexing Prerequisites

Before enabling indexing, make sure you have sufficient memory on the server to handle building and updating the index and sufficient storage to hold the index catalog files.

A catalog can grow as large as 30 percent or more of the total store size, depending on the number of unique words that occur. So, the index catalog for a 12GB mailbox store might take up to 4GB of drive space plus an additional 15 to 20 percent to make room for index rebuilds. Put the catalog on a separate spindle from the Exchange database files and give the catalog lots of room to grow to avoid fragmentation.

Don't put the index files on a single disk. You don't want to rebuild the index if you have a single drive crash. To get the best mix of performance and fault tolerance, put the index files on a RAID 1+0 array. If you have multiple mailbox stores on an Enterprise Edition server, you can store the index files for all the mailbox stores on the same array.

Microsoft recommends no less than 512MB of RAM for an Exchange server that uses full-text indexing. Personally, I would not build an Exchange server with less than 2GB of RAM, regardless of whether or not indexing is enabled.

## Indexing and Performance

You're bound to see a performance drag during the initial index build. MSSearch does its work in the background but the process still consumes resources. If you have a mailbox store of considerable size, start the initial index late on a Saturday afternoon so the indexing can run the rest of the weekend.

Once the initial index has finished building, the incremental builds do not consume an inordinate amount of CPU time or disk I/O. Do incremental builds as often as possible because messages won't appear in a search until they get included in the index. Start with an hourly interval for index updates and then monitor the server for utilization problems.

## Difference between Full-Text Indexing and Standard Text Search

If your users are accustomed to the standard text-based searches in Outlook, some of the operational differences when searching against an indexed store might catch them off-guard. Here are some examples:

- **Word-based searches.** The standard Outlook search simply matches character combinations. If you search for the string "grass," you get messages that contain "grassland," "bluegrass," "Bruce Grassham," and so forth. An indexed search, on the other hand, looks for full words, not portions of words.
- **Stem analysis.** The search engine has a stem analyzer that strips off common suffixes, so that an indexed search for "grass" would return a hit for "grassy" but not "grassland."
- **No wildcards.** You can't use wildcards in searches. For example, you can't search for "*grass" to find "bluegrass."
- **Not case sensitive.** Searches are not case sensitive. A search for "grass" would turn up "Grass" and "gRASS."
- **Attachments included in search.** Full-text indexing includes attachments if MSSearch recognizes the document type, such as

Web files (.html, .htm, and .asp), Excel worksheets (.xls), Power-point (.ppt), Word and Wordpad (.doc), and text files (.txt). The search result listing does not indicate which attachment contains the hit, though. You might have to open each attachment to find the source of the hit.

- **No noise words.** The search engine classifies conjunctions, definite articles, and single letters as *noise words* and does not include them in the index to conserve disk space and improve indexing performance. You can use this feature to test for the presence of an index on a store. If a search for "and" results in a hit, you know the store is either not indexed or that the index service has stopped.
- **Limited attribute indexing.** The search engine only indexes these message attributes: sent-by, sent-to, subject, body, and attachments (if they are of the correct file type).

The users can also submit Boolean searches against an indexed store. The search engine responds to these Boolean operators:

- **OR.** Use the word "or" or a comma (,) or a pipe symbol (|). For example, use "grass or grassland | Grassham, bluegrass."
- **AND.** Use the word "and" or an ampersand (&) or a space (" "). For example, use "grass and grassland & Grassham."
- Use the word "not" or an exclamation point (!). For example, use "grass not Grassham ! grassland."

The stem analyzer does its work before the search operators, so a search for "steel, iron" would turn up documents with the word "steeler" and documents with the word "ironing."

## Enabling Full-Text Indexing

It takes two separate set of steps to put an index into production: Initiate indexing and then make the index available to users.

### Initiate Indexing

1. Right-click a mailbox or public folder store and select **Create Full-Text Index** from the flyout menu, as shown in Figure 7.30.

**Figure 7.30** Initializing a full-text index using Create Full-Text Index option in Mailbox Store property menu.

2. When prompted for a path to the catalog files for the index, put the catalog files on the RAID array you've installed for them. By default, the path is **\Program Files\Exchsrvr\Exchange-Server_W2K3-EX1\Projects**, which is the location of the Exchange application files and probably not suitable for catalog files.

3. Begin populating the index by right-clicking the mailbox store icon again and selecting **Start Full Population** from the flyout menu.

4. Answer **Yes** to the warnings that this will take a while and could take a lot longer than an incremental index.

5. To keep track of the indexing status, select the **Full-Text Indexing** icon under the mailbox store, as shown in Figure 7.31. Once the indexing has finished, the **Index State** will show **Idle**.

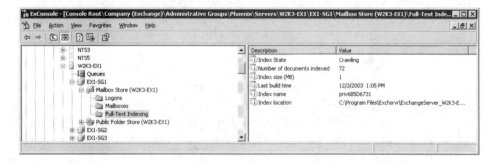

**Figure 7.31** ESM showing parameters and status of the full-text index on a mailbox store.

### Make Index Available to Users

Now that the index is ready, allow users to see it as follows:

1. Open the Properties window for the mailbox store and select the Full-Text tab, shown in Figure 7.32.
2. Open the Properties window for the mailbox store and select the **Full-Text** tab, shown in Figure 7.32.
3. Select the option to make the index available to clients and then change the update interval from **Never Run** to a time interval that makes sense in your organization. Start with an hourly update and see how that affects performance.

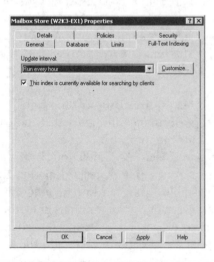

**Figure 7.32** Mailbox Store properties showing Full-Text Indexing tab with option to control Update Interval.

4. When prompted with the warning that the index must be up-to-date to assure that users get all the messages in a search, click **OK**.

Test that the index is available by using Outlook to perform a search. The results should appear very quickly. Now search for a noise word such as *the* or *and*. Nothing should appear. Unless you have no conjunctions in any of the mail in your inbox, this is proof that the search used the index.

The MSSearch engine runs as a service and does its indexing in the background. For the most part, this requires no intervention from an administrator. If you have reason to believe that the indexer is not behaving as it should (searches do not return results when it can be verified that messages contain the search items) then you can use ESM to check the status and look for MSSearch events in the Event Log. In the event that the indexing has gone completely awry, you can stop indexing a store, remove the indexes, and then start over.

# Performance Testing

If you're responsible for putting together the specs for an Exchange server, you'll probably get asked by your colleagues, "Is this hardware powerful enough to perform the tasks assigned to it?" (Actually, the question will probably get asked this way, "Can that bad boy cut the mustard?")

Meanwhile, management asks somewhat different questions. "Do we really need this amount of power? Can't we use something we already have? Didn't you just buy an Exchange server during the last Olympiad?"

One way to resolve this issue of "too much" versus "too little" is to get some good performance numbers that indicate whether or not the server...well...cuts the mustard.

Microsoft provides a free simulation tool called LoadSim 2003 that permits you to run a series of tests designed to yield a performance score. You can establish your hardware configurations, run the test, get a score, and then vary your configurations and run the test again to compare scores. Microsoft also provides specialized load-testing tools such as Medusa and Jetstress. LoadSim 2003 and the other tools are available from the Exchange download site at `www.microsoft.com/exchange/tools/2003.asp`.

LoadSim 2003 creates lots of users, mailboxes, distribution groups, and public folders; then pounds away at the server for hour after hour doing just about every type of MAPI operation imaginable. Figure 7.33 shows the list of operations performed by LoadSim 2003 and how many times per hour per user it performs the operation.

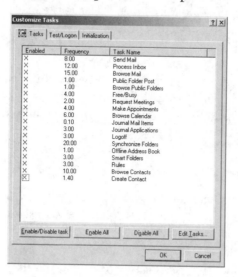

**Figure 7.33** LoadSim test list. The default configuration does not run all tests.

Here are few items to keep in mind as you prepare to install LoadSim:

- **Test environment only.** Run LoadSim only in your lab. It can create literally thousands of objects in Active Directory and thousands of mailboxes and public folders in the Exchange store. It also generates considerable load on the Exchange server and the Global Catalog servers, something you would not want to do to a production system.
- **Exchange 2003 only.** LoadSim 2003 assumes the availability of Exchange 2003 Schema objects. You can use it only in domains with at least one Exchange 2003 server. Microsoft provides older versions of LoadSim for Exchange 2000 and legacy Exchange, but they don't exercise the system nearly as much as LoadSim 2003.
- **Run on desktop.** Run LoadSim 2003 on a desktop, not directly on an Exchange server. The desktop must have Outlook 2003 installed. For an operating system, use XP SP1 with the Q331320 hotfix, XP SP2, or Windows Server 2003 (any edition).

- **Sufficient memory on workstation.** Make sure the desktop running LoadSim 2003 has at least 512MB of RAM and a 1GHz processor or faster. You'll need about a 1000MB of free disk space for logging. A 100 Mbps or faster network card helps.
- **Sufficient storage on server.** LoadSim creates many messages and public folder postings, so you can expect to see quite an increase in hard disk utilization at the Exchange server under test. Make sure your lab servers have plenty of storage to handle the number of users in your test run. You don't want to get 7 hours of the way through an 8 hour test and run out of disk space. A test simulating 1000 users can add over 5GB to the Exchange stores and an additional amount in transaction logs.

## Install LoadSim Performance Counters

You can download the LoadSim 2003 package from Microsoft for free. Expand the files into a folder on the test workstation. LoadSim 2003 has no setup program, but you need to do a few preliminary steps.

1. Install Registry entries for the LoadSim performance counters by double-clicking the **Lsperf.reg** icon in Explorer.
2. Install the LoadSim performance counters by opening a command prompt, changing to the directory holding the LoadSim files, and running this command: `lodctr lsperf.ini`.
3. Move the Lsperf.dll file to the %windir% folder, usually **\Windows** for XP.
4. In Performance Monitor, ensure that the LoadSim Action and LoadSim Global entries appear in the Performance Objects dropdown list.

## Configure LoadSim Test Topology

When you first launch LoadSim, you'll get a stark gray window that lists a few informational items. For example, if you do not meet a prerequisite, LoadSim lists the problem and suggests what you should do to correct it. If you get no errors, proceed as follows to create a test topology:

1. Select **Configuration | Topology Properties** from the main menu. This opens the Topology Properties window, as shown in Figure 7.34.
2. On each Exchange server you want to test, configure each mailbox store with the number of mailboxes you want to add.

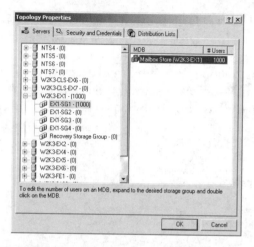

**Figure 7.34** LoadSim server selection window where you can set the number of synthetic users for each mailbox store in each storage group.

3. Select the **Security** tab, as shown in Figure 7.35. Simulate a real-world authentication environment by selecting the **Login to users using their respective accounts...** radio button and entering a complex password that each user will get assigned to him or her. (This doesn't exactly simulate the real world because the synthetic LoadSim users won't forget their passwords, complain about memorizing strong passwords, or write down their passwords on sticky notes attached to their monitors.)

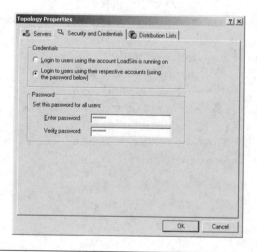

**Figure 7.35** LoadSim topology creation window showing the option to use a distinct password for synthetic users.

4. Select the **Distribution Lists** tab, as shown in Figure 7.36. Leave the **Distribution List (DLs)** settings at their default. Under Dynamic Distribution Lists, check the Use Dynamic Distribution Lists option and check **Create One For All Load-Sim Users** as a starting point. This tells LoadSim to create Query-Based Distribution Groups in Active Directory.

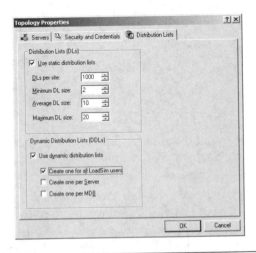

**Figure 7.36** LoadSim topology creation window showing the number of Distribution Lists to create and how to populate them. The option to use Query-Based Distribution Groups is not enabled by default.

5. Click **OK** to save the changes.
6. From the menu, select **Configuration | Test** Properties. This opens the Test Properties window shown in Figure 7.37. Leave the default duration settings.
7. Click **Add** to add a server and the test users to the list. The Add/Edit User Group window opens, as shown in Figure 7.38.
8. Leave the settings at their default and click **OK** to add this set of users to the test list.
9. Click **Customize Tasks**. Use the **Enable** button to enable the following public folder tests.

Performance Testing    **357**

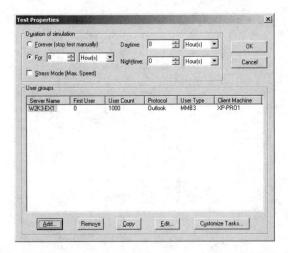

**Figure 7.37** LoadSim Test Properties window showing the default test interval, 8 hours, and the selection of a test server.

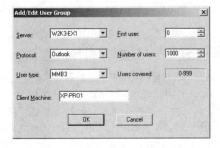

**Figure 7.38** LoadSim user selection window that specifies the properties of the test server. The default synthetic user type meets MMB3 specifications.

10. From the menu, select **Run I Create Topology**. LoadSim now creates the users, sets up their mailboxes, creates distribution groups, and sets up their membership. Figure 7.39 shows a view of Active Directory Users and Computers after LoadSim has finished creating objects. Each server gets a separate container in Active Directory that holds the associated users, so it's simple to remove the objects once you've completed your testing. All distribution groups go into the LoadSim Users container. LoadSim creates Global Distribution Groups to minimize impact on the Global Catalog.

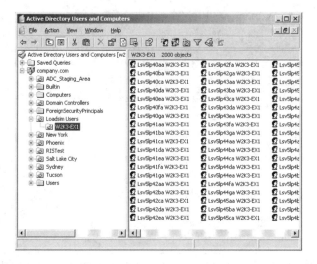

**Figure 7.39** LoadSim users created in Active Directory. This is one reason why you only want to run LoadSim in a test environment.

### Initialize and Run LoadSim Test

At this point, you're just about ready to begin testing. LoadSim now needs to initialize mailboxes and public folders. Select **Run | Initialize Test**. You will be prompted with a message to permit the LoadSim machine to create public folders. Click **Yes** to acknowledge.

The initialization stage can take considerable time depending on how many users you have. LoadSim logs on each user, sets up the user's mailbox, and creates a great many public folders and stocks them with postings. You can see the user mailboxes in ESM. Figure 7.40 shows an example.

Before starting the simulation, get the Performance Monitor logs in place and running. The documentation accompanying LoadSim lists the counters that have particular importance for Exchange operation.

To run the test, from the main menu, select **Run | Run Simulation**. LoadSim immediately starts the test runs. CPU load and I/O ramp up to a maximum and remain there for the duration of the test.

At the end of the test, LoadSim presents you with a score. This score is a little like an SAT score—in and of itself, it doesn't mean much. It takes on significance only in relation to scores of other servers in the same class as the server you tested. The performance monitor logs tell you much more than the MMB3 score, especially considering that you will someday operate this server in production.

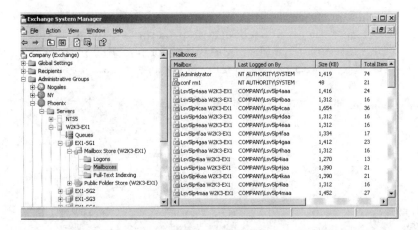

**Figure 7.40** ESM showing list of mailboxes created in target storage group at test server. You should create a test storage group to make it easier to get rid of the test mailboxes at the end of the test.

Carve out a long afternoon and sit down with the raw performance numbers, a big pot of coffee, a pile of Grandma's Original chocolate chip cookies, three six packs of Mountain Dew, and a copy of a Microsoft white paper called "Troubleshooting Exchange Server 2003 Performance." At the end of that session, you'll know more intimate details about this prospective Exchange server than Freud knew about Dora.

Once you complete the test, run a utility in the LoadSim 2003 suite called Lslog to get a score for the test run. Figure 7.41 shows a sample score listing.

Don't just go by the score. Analyze the performance logs, as well. Unless you spent considerable money to purchase an 8-way ccNUMA server connected via dual 64-bit PCI-X host bus adapters to the latest Fibre Channel fabric and from there to storage devices sporting dozens of SCSCI 320 drives in a huge RAID 10 array, you'll probably see some bottlenecks. Use the documentation that accompanies LoadSim to determine if the bottleneck will become a production issue.

The LoadSim documentation describes how to do a low-level analysis of the results. For the sake of comparison, you should run the tests on other hardware. Also, HP and Dell and IBM publish LoadSim numbers for many of their server platforms.

If you selected an appropriate number of users and the correct mix of operations in LoadSim compared to your production environment, and you see queue lengths and response times considerably higher than the recommended limits in the Microsoft white paper, you should consider spending a little more money on the server. If your boss (or client) says, "I gave you a budget and you spent it and that's that," at least you can keep an eye out in the future for potential performance issues related to the test results. You might even get to say, "I told you so."

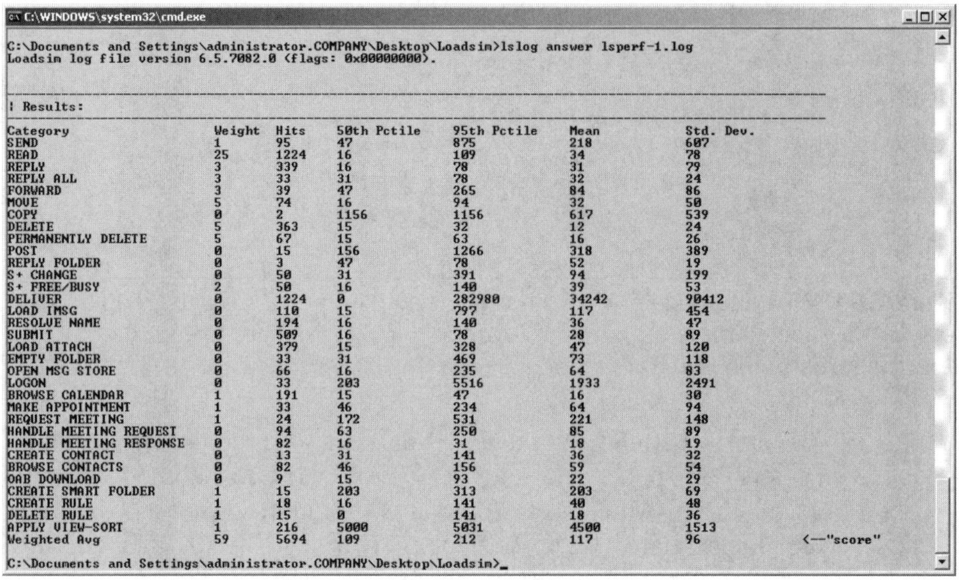
C:\WINDOWS\system32\cmd.exe

```
C:\Documents and Settings\administrator.COMPANY\Desktop\Loadsim>lslog answer lsperf-1.log
Loadsim log file version 6.5.7082.0 (flags: 0x00000000).

-------------------------------------------------------------------------------------
| Results:
-------------------------------------------------------------------------------------
Category                 Weight  Hits   50th Pctile   95th Pctile   Mean    Std. Dev.
SEND                     1       95     47            875           218     607
READ                     25      1224   16            109           34      78
REPLY                    3       339    16            78            31      79
REPLY ALL                3       33     31            78            32      24
FORWARD                  3       39     47            265           84      86
MOVE                     5       74     16            94            32      50
COPY                     0       2      1156          1156          617     539
DELETE                   5       363    15            32            12      24
PERMANENTLY DELETE       5       67     15            63            16      26
POST                     0       15     156           1266          318     389
REPLY FOLDER             0       3      47            78            52      19
S+ CHANGE                0       50     31            391           94      199
S+ FREE/BUSY             2       50     16            140           39      53
DELIVER                  0       1224   0             282980        34242   90412
LOAD IMSG                0       110    15            797           117     454
RESOLVE NAME             0       194    16            140           36      47
SUBMIT                   0       509    16            78            28      89
LOAD ATTACH              0       379    15            328           47      120
EMPTY FOLDER             0       33     31            469           73      118
OPEN MSG STORE           0       66     16            235           64      83
LOGON                    0       33     203           5516          1933    2491
BROWSE CALENDAR          1       191    15            47            16      30
MAKE APPOINTMENT         1       33     46            234           64      94
REQUEST MEETING          1       24     172           531           221     148
HANDLE MEETING REQUEST   0       94     63            250           85      89
HANDLE MEETING RESPONSE  0       82     16            31            18      19
CREATE CONTACT           0       13     31            141           36      32
BROWSE CONTACTS          0       82     46            156           59      54
OAB DOWNLOAD             0       9      15            93            22      29
CREATE SMART FOLDER      1       15     203           313           203     69
CREATE RULE              1       18     16            141           40      48
DELETE RULE              1       15     0             141           18      36
APPLY VIEW-SORT          1       216    5000          5031          4500    1513
Weighted Avg             59      5694   109           212           117     96        <--"score"

C:\Documents and Settings\administrator.COMPANY\Desktop\Loadsim>_
```

**Figure 7.41** Test results obtained using Lslog with final score calculated from test data.

## Looking Forward

You've now built an Exchange server that can accept client connections and deliver messages, but unless your users work in a single location, you're going to want more than one Exchange server. You also probably want to connect your Exchange server to the Internet so your users can send and receive e-mail beyond the bounds of their office.

To do all that, you'll need to configure message routing and SMTP connectors. That's what lies ahead in the next chapter.

# CHAPTER 8

# Message Routing

If you had to point to a single service on an Exchange server and say, "There it is. Right there. That's the most important service on this machine," then you would probably point at the SMTP service.

Exchange uses Simple Mail Transfer Protocol (SMTP) to move messages between Exchange servers and to route messages to and from the Internet. If it weren't for SMTP, an Exchange server could talk only to itself. Before long, it would begin eating junk food and watching Jerry Springer and making necklaces out of pop-tops.

This chapter describes how SMTP works and shows you typical SMTP configurations and flowpaths with lots of detail about SMTP transactions. But it's one thing to have the *ability* to communicate and another thing altogether to actually *communicate*, so the chapter also shows you how to define areas of reliable, low-latency network connectivity called Routing Groups and how to configure connectors between those Routing Groups so you can route messages anywhere within your organization.

You'll also see how to create SMTP connectors that let you route messages to and from the Internet, and how to plumb the inner workings of the Link State Table, which is used by Exchange to manage the routing topology, including how to troubleshoot routing problems.

Quite a bit of the information in this chapter refers to architectural topics and process mechanics. Because SMTP is so important to the smooth operation of an Exchange organization, you should learn as much about these topics as you can. But you don't need to swallow the information all at once. Work your way through the high points, set up a few servers and configure routing, and then move on. Revisit the chapter as you encounter routing issues that require a more detailed knowledge. I would recommend getting proficient at testing SMTP using telnet and at tracing SMTP transactions using a packet sniffer. You'll use these skills continually for troubleshooting and for analyzing your security configurations.

Throughout this book, the term "legacy Exchange" refers to all versions of Exchange prior to Exchange 2000.

# SMTP Message Routing Overview

Figure 8.1 shows a typical chain of SMTP transactions in an Exchange organization. The cast of characters in this example includes

- An Outlook client with the SMTP address user@company.com
- Exchange servers in two locations, London and Phoenix
- A three-way firewall that defines a perimeter network (DMZ)
- A public facing SMTP server residing in the DMZ
- An SMTP server at an Internet Server Provider (ISP) somewhere on the Internet
- An Internet user with an e-mail client configured to send messages to the ISP's SMTP server
- A public DNS server that hosts a zone file for Company.com

A final set of characters, omnipresent but not shown in the diagram, are the internal DNS servers that host the private zone file for Company.Com. These servers could be domain controllers with Active Directory-integrated DNS zones. Every internal server and client points at one of these DNS servers for name resolution.

The chain of transactions starts when the Internet user decides to send an e-mail to the Exchange user.

1. **Client to ISP SMTP Server.** The e-mail client uses SMTP to send the message to the server at the ISP. This transaction consists of a connection to TCP port 25 on the SMTP server followed by a few commands to transfer the data. Here is a short example of a telnet session that sends a short message:

```
ehlo
mail from: client@subsidiary.com
rcpt to: user@company.com
subject: Did you get those widgets?
data
Call our shipping department if you didn't get the delivery.
.
quit
```

2. **ISP finds Public Facing SMTP Server.** Based on the domain of the target recipient, the SMTP server at the ISP needs the IP address of an SMTP server in the Company.com domain. It obtains this information by querying the DNS server for any Mail eXchange (MX) records in the Company.com zone.

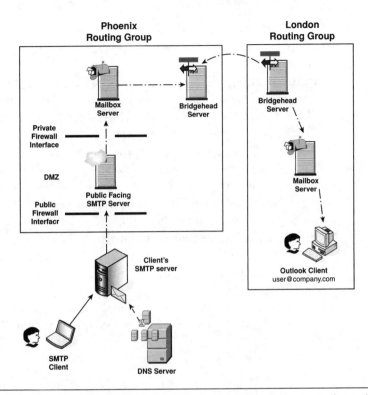

**Figure 8.1** Diagram showing Simple Mail Transfer Protocol transactions that move a message from an Internet client to an Outlook recipient.

The DNS server returns an MX record for the public facing SMTP server and the A (Host) record with the server's IP address that corresponds to the name in the MX record. (This is called a *glue* record.)

3. **ISP SMTP to Public Facing SMTP.** The ISP's SMTP server establishes a TCP connection to port 25 of the public facing SMTP server at Company.com. It transmits the message along with additional headers containing information about the transited SMTP server.

4. **Public Facing SMTP to Phoenix Exchange Server.** The public facing SMTP server at Company.com routes all incoming messages to the Exchange server in Phoenix. This limits the number of conduits the network administrators need to open in the firewall.

5. **Phoenix Exchange Server to Phoenix Bridgehead.** The Phoenix Exchange server refers to Active Directory and determines that the recipient's home Exchange server resides in London. It refers to a topology map for the organization called a

*Link State Table* to find a route to the London server and then sends the message to the bridgehead server between Phoenix and London.

6. **Phoenix Bridgehead to London Bridgehead.** The Phoenix bridgehead server refers to Active Directory and to its own copy of the Link State table and determines that it needs to forward the message to the bridgehead server in London.

7. **London Bridgehead to London Exchange Server.** The bridgehead server in London refers to Active Directory and its own copy of the Link State Table and determines that the recipient's home server resides right there in London. It sends the message directly to the recipient's home server.

8. **London Exchange Server to Outlook Client.** The recipient's home server places the message into the Exchange store and waits for the mailbox owner to request a copy.

Using these high-level transactions as a guide, let's delve into the inner workings of SMTP to see how Exchange uses it to handle message routing.

# SMTP Configuration Details

Like the other Internet protocols used by Exchange, SMTP runs under the auspices of Inetinfo as part of the Internet Information Services (IIS). Exchange enhances SMTP with a beefed-up routing engine that knows how to make link state routing calculations and a snazzy categorizer that knows how to do Active Directory lookups.

## SMTP Virtual Server

SMTP configuration information is stored in the IIS Metabase in the form of a *virtual server*. Figure 8.2 shows the SMTP virtual server parameters in Exchange System Manager (ESM). Navigate to **Administrative Groups | <admin_group> | Servers | <server_name> | Protocols | SMTP | Default SMTP Virtual Server**.

Exchange permits you to create multiple SMTP virtual servers, but you won't ordinarily gain any operational advantage by doing so. The SMTP service is multithreaded so you won't prevent bottlenecks by creating new virtual servers.

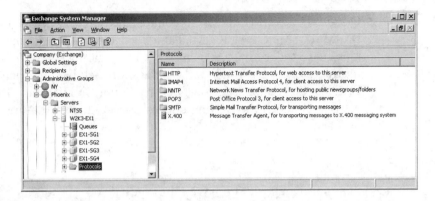

**Figure 8.2** ESM showing Protocols folder that contains the Default SMTP Virtual Server.

That being said, you might need to create a new virtual server if you want the Exchange server to use different routes to the Internet, or if you want to use SSL in one SMTP domain but not in another.

## SMTP File Locations

SMTP queues messages for delivery by storing them on disk in the form of an Electronic Mail (EML) file. It places these files in a location defined by parameters in the SMTP virtual server. Figure 8.3 shows the location settings for two of the folders, BadMail and Queue.

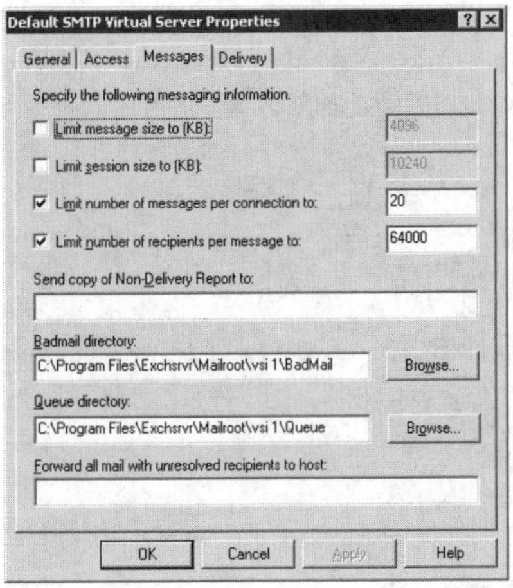

**Figure 8.3** Default SMTP Virtual Server properties showing BadMail and Queue folder and message-handling limits.

- **Queue.** Holds EML files for incoming and outgoing messages.
- **BadMail.** SMTP uses BadMail as a dead letter office. It contains messages that cannot be delivered to the ultimate recipient or returned to sender. You'll find two files for each bad message—a BAD file that contains a Non-Delivery Report (NDR) and a BDP file that contains the routing entries extracted from the original message.

---

The BadMail folder can fill up with garbage messages if you get quite a bit of spam. Feel free to delete the files in the folder every once in awhile. You can automate the process with a batch file launched by the Task Scheduler. For a great script to use for managing your Badmail folder, take a look at Neil Hobson's blog entry at `hellomate.typepad.com/exchange/2003/07/dealing_with_ba.html` or dowload the Badmail utility from Microsoft at `http://snipurl.com/6wnz`.

---

### Pickup Folder

SMTP also uses a third folder, Pickup, that is not shown in the Messages window. You can place a file formatted as an RFC 2822 message in this folder, and the SMTP service will deliver it. This is a handy feature if you have an application that needs to deliver mail but you don't want to code an e-mail client. Here is an example of a text message you can put in Pickup (this information is also covered in Chapter 2, "Understanding and Using Messaging Protocols"):

```
from: test@notarealdomain.com
to: administrator@company.com
subject: test message

This message was placed in the Pickup folder of Exchange server
W3K3-EX1.
```

### Queue Viewer

Internally, SMTP divides the content of the Queue folder into a variety of logical queues, and tags the EML files accordingly. You can see these queues on an Exchange server using ESM. Look for a Queues folder under each server, as shown in Figure 8.4.

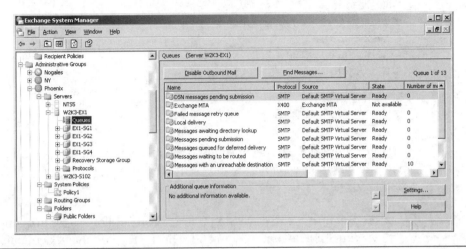

**Figure 8.4** ESM showing the Queue view containing messages held in the SMTP queue.

# SMTP Capabilities

The SMPT service, as enhanced by Exchange, can perform a variety of capabilities. You can list them using telnet. Connect to port 25 on the server and enter **EHLO (Extended Hello)**. Here is a sample response:

```
C:/>telnet w2k3-ex1 25
220 w2k3-ex1 Microsoft ESMTP MAIL Service, Version:
➥6.0.2600.1106 ready at Wed, 23 Jul 2004 14:32:31 -0400
ehlo
250-w2k3-ex1.company.com Hello [192.168.0.1]
250-TURN
250-SIZE
250-ETRN
250-PIPELINING
250-DSN
250-ENHANCEDSTATUSCODES
250-8bitmime
250-BINARYMIME
250-CHUNKING
250-VRFY
```

```
250-X-EXPS GSSAPI NTLM LOGIN
250-X-EXPS=LOGIN
250-AUTH GSSAPI NTLM LOGIN
250-AUTH=LOGIN
250-X-LINK2STATE
250-XEXCH50
250 OK
```

Here's a quick rundown of some of the more important capabilities. The authentication capabilities shown in the listing are covered a little later in the chapter:

- **TURN and ETRN.** An SMTP server can hold messages in queue waiting for a dequeue command. The TURN command dequeues messages, but it does not support authentication. The ETRN (Extended TURN) command includes the ability to authenticate and to specify a particular dequeue client.
- **Delivery Status Notification (DSN).** The Delivery Status Notification feature enables an SMTP server to notify the sender of the reason for a non-delivery. This feature enables servers to send detailed delivery and non-delivery notifications to clients to act as a troubleshooting aid.
- **X-LINK2STATE.** This command permits Exchange SMTP servers to send link state information in standard SMTP messages.
- **XEXCH50.** This command tells Windows SMTP servers that the SMTP on a server is owned by Exchange. This permits two Exchange servers to trade proprietary messages.
- **Pipelining.** Specifications for this command can be found in RFC 2920, "SMTP Service Extension for Command Pipelining." In brief, this feature permits the client or server to send all elements of the message header before expecting a reply. In legacy SMTP, each element of the header is sent and separately acknowledged.
- **Chunking.** Specifications for this command can be found in RFC 3030, "SMTP Service Extensions for Transmission of Large and Binary MIME Messages." This feature replaces the legacy SMTP method of parsing a document line by line looking for the final end-of-file character. When a client sends a message to an RFC 3030 SMTP server, it sends the number of octets in the message and then starts blasting away at the transmission, marking

the final octet as LAST. The end result is a streamlined transaction that doesn't get bogged down waiting for repeated ACKs from the receiving server.

# Inbound Message Handling

When a message arrives at an Exchange server, a variety of processes come into play to move the message onward to its intended destination. Figure 8.5 shows the major elements Exchange uses when it gets an inbound message. This message could come from another Exchange server, an Internet SMTP server, an Internet e-mail client using SMTP to send mail, or a MAPI client such as Outlook.

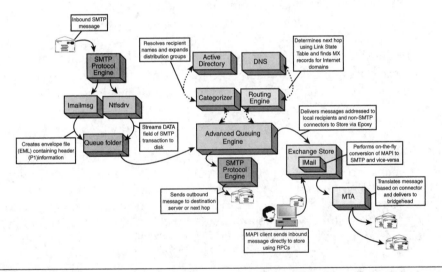

**Figure 8.5** Diagram of internal SMTP message flowpath for inbound messages.

The SMTP process starts when an outside entity (not shown) sends a connection request to TCP port 25 (SMTP port) on the Exchange server.

1. **Inbound Connection to Protocol Engine.** The *SMTP Protocol Engine* listens at TCP port 25 and accepts the connection request.
2. **Protocol Engine Accepts Connection.** The outside entity sends an EHLO, and the Protocol Engine replies with the list of capabilities you saw in the last topic.
3. **Message Transfer.** The outside entity sends the headers and body of the message; then it quits.
4. **Message Queued.** The Protocol Engine creates an envelope file (EML) in the Queue folder to hold the message headers and then streams the message body into the EML file. At this point, the Advanced Queuing Engine takes over the processing chores.

In contrast, inbound messages originating with MAPI clients start by going directly to the Information Store via Remote Procedure Calls (RPCs). The Information Store converts the message from MAPI to SMTP and then delivers it to the Advanced Queuing Engine. This ensures that event triggers (automated responses to incoming message streams) in the Advanced Queuing Engine apply to all messages, even those originating on the same Exchange server. This differs from legacy Exchange, which gave local messages special handling to keep them away from the Message Transfer Agent (MTA).

SMTP stores the message body and headers in ASCII format so you can read the message if gets stuck in the queue. You won't see any additional routing information in the file because SMTP stores that information in an alternate data stream called PROPERTIES. Alternate data streams are a feature of NTFS, so the SMTP Mailroot folder must be installed on an NTFS volume. For more information about alternate data streams, visit the Crucial Security Web site and download their white paper on ADS, `www.crucialsecurity.com/downloads.html`.

## Advanced Queuing Engine

The Advanced Queuing Engine contains two primary components: the Message Categorizer and the Routing Engine.

The Message Categorizer determines how to handle a message by looking up the recipients in Active Directory to find their home servers.

If the recipient is a group, the categorizer works with a Global Catalog server to expand the group membership.

The categorizer also checks to see if the message violates any policies. For example, if the organization contains a Recipient Policy that limits the size of outbound message attachments to 50K, the Message Categorizer checks the attachment size and refuses to send the message if the size exceeds the policy limit.

If the Exchange server loses access to its Global Catalog server, you might see Event Log entries from a service called Phatcat.dll indicating a problem with the connection. Phatcat.dll is the message categorizer. You can also get these types of errors when you have a problem with DNS.

Once the categorizer determines the recipient's location, the Advanced Queuing Engine hands the message to the Routing Engine, which takes the name of the recipient's home Exchange server and decides where to send the message. In making this decision, the Routing Engine relies on a map of the servers and connectors in the organization called a *Link State Table*.

- **Local delivery.** If the Exchange server hosting the recipient's mailbox resides in the same local network (called a *Routing Group*) as the Exchange server hosting the Routing Engine, the engine selects the recipient's home server as the next destination.
- **Remote delivery.** If the recipient's home server resides in a different Routing Group, the Routing Engine finds a *connector* to that Routing Group in the Link State Table and selects the *bridgehead server* for that connector as the next destination.

## Final Delivery

The Routing Engine returns its selection to the Advanced Queuing Engine for final delivery. If the Routing Engine identifies a destination server that uses SMTP, the Advanced Queuing Engine gives the message to the SMTP Protocol Engine for delivery.

If the Routing Engine identifies the local machine as the ultimate destination, the Advanced Queuing Engine delivers the message to the Information Store for delivery to the recipient's mailbox.

If the Routing Engine identifies a bridgehead server for a special-purpose connector as the destination, such as an X.400 connector or Lotus Notes or GroupWise, the Advanced Queuing Engine delivers the message to the Information Store, which converts the message from SMTP and hands it to the MTA for translation and delivery.

## Delivery Status Notifications

RFC 1893 defines a system of codes by which an SMTP server can communicate a wide range of message status reports to clients and other SMTP servers. The messages come in the form of three-part, dotted decimal codes. For example, 2.1.5 denotes a successful transaction in which the message address had a valid address. Newer specifications can be found in RFC 2852, *Deliver By SMTP Service Extension.*

The first number represents a status code:

```
2.x.x Success
4.x.x Persistent Transient Failure
5.x.x Permanent Failure
```

The next number represents a status sub-code:

```
x.0.x   Other or Undefined Status
x.1.x   Addressing Status
x.2.x   Mailbox Status
x.3.x   Mail System Status
x.4.x   Network and Routing Status
x.5.x   Mail Delivery Protocol Status
x.6.x   Message Content or Media Status
x.7.x   Security or Policy Status
```

The final number represents an enumerated status code. Each combination of sub-code and enumerated status code stands for a unique message. For example

```
x.1.1   Bad destination mailbox address
x.2.1   Mailbox disabled, not accepting messages
x.3.1   Mail system full
x.4.1   No answer from host
x.5.1   Invalid command
x.6.1   Media not supported
x.7.1   Delivery not authorized, message refused
```

Exchange uses these status codes to construct messages to notify senders of problems.

# Detailed SMTP Transaction

Now let's take a look at the SMTP message delivery mechanism itself with an eye toward seeing where the pieces fit together. To do these tests, use the telnet utility that comes with Windows.

You'll need to do couple of configuration changes to the telnet client. Type telnet at a command prompt then type set -? to get a list of parameters.

```
Microsoft Telnet> set ?
bsasdel        Backspace will be sent as delete
crlf           New line mode - Causes return key to send CR &
➥LF
delasbs        Delete will be sent as backspace
escape x       x is an escape character to enter telnet client
➥prompt
localecho      Turn on localecho.
logfile x      x is current client log file
logging        Turn on logging
mode x         x is console or stream
ntlm           Turn on NTLM authentication.
term x         x is ansi, vt100, vt52, or vtnt
```

First type set localecho. This lets you see what you're typing after you make telnet connection to a remote server. Then type set logfile telnet.log and set logging to save a copy of the commands you type and the server's responses. Exit the telnet configuration by typing quit.

## Use Telnet to Make Initial Connection

Now test your settings by pointing telnet at port 25 on your Exchange server as follows: telnet <server_name> 25. You should get a connection banner similar to this:

```
220 w2k3-ex1 Microsoft ESMTP MAIL Service, Version:
➥6.0.2600.1106 ready at Wed, 23 Jul 2004 14:32:31 -0400
```

You can now type commands in the window and see the results coming back from the server. First, though, let's do something about all that revealing information in the banner.

## Change the SMTP Connect Banner

You might not want to announce the vendor and version number of your SMTP service. Many so-called "hacking" utilities target Microsoft SMTP servers because…well…because they say Microsoft, I suppose.

You can change the content of the SMTP banner to remove the vendor name and version number, but you cannot remove the server name. The banner string resides in the IIS Metabase. Change the string using Metabase Explorer from the IIS 6.0 Resource Kit. Always back up the Metabase before making modifications.

### Back Up the IIS Metabase

Before changing the Metabase contents, back up the Metabase using the IIS Manager console as follows:

1. Right-click the server name and select **All Tasks | Backup/Restore Configuration** from the flyout menu, as shown in Figure 8.6.

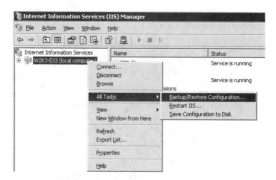

**Figure 8.6** IIS Manager console showing IIS Metabase backup selection in server property menu.

2. In the Configuration Backup/Restore window (shown in Figure 8.7), click **Create Backup**. This opens the Configuration Backup window.

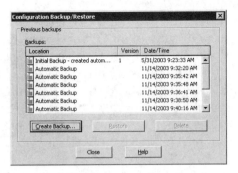

**Figure 8.7** Backup history for IIS Metabase.

3. Give the backup a friendly name that you'll recognize if you need to use it for a restore. Figure 8.8 shows an example.

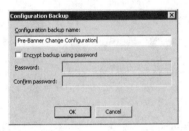

**Figure 8.8** Name of backup file. Use a name that gives useful information in the backup log listing.

4. Click **OK** in the Configuration Backup window. This backs up the Metabase. You'll see the backup name in the Backups list.
5. Click **Close**.

### Enter New SMTP Banner String

Now you're ready to change the SMTP banner string. Proceed as follows:

1. Open the Metabase Explorer and drill down to **LM | SMTPSVC | 1**.
2. Right-click the **1** icon (it represents SMTP Virtual Server 1) and select **New | String Record** from the flyout menu. This opens the New Record window.
3. In the **Record Name or Identifier** field, enter the code **36907** and click **OK**. This adds the value **ConnectResponse** to the Metabase.

4. Double-click the new value to open the Properties window and enter a string such as **SMTP Service Available**.

5. Select the **General** tab and change **User Type** to **Server**. Leave the **Attributes** option unchecked.

6. Save the changes to the Metabase by closing the record window.

7. Make a telnet connection to the SMTP service port as follows: `telnet <server_name> 25`. Verify that the banner reads the way you entered it in Metabase Explorer.

```
220 w2k3-ex1.company.com SMTP Service Available Thu, 24 Jul
➥2004 17:40:17 -0700
```

8. Type **Quit**.

## SMTP Authentication

Once you have a telnet connection to the SMTP port on the Exchange server, enter `ehlo` to get the server capabilities. You've already seen the list, but a couple of the capabilities involve authentication and warrant a closer look:

```
250-w2k3-ex1.company.com Hello [192.168.0.1]
250-X-EXPS GSSAPI NTLM LOGIN
250-X-EXPS=LOGIN
250-AUTH GSSAPI NTLM LOGIN
250-AUTH=LOGIN
250 OK
```

An SMTP client uses the AUTH command to initiate an authentication transaction. The server replies with the authentication methods it supports. In the example above, the server supports three methods:

- **GSSAPI.** This stands for *Generic Security Service Application Programming Interface*, documented in RFC 2743. Microsoft Exchange servers support GSSAPI, but Microsoft clients do not use it.

- **NTLM.** Microsoft Outlook and Outlook Express clients use this authentication method when configured to use Secure Password Authentication.

- **LOGIN.** This method, defined in RFC 2554, "SMTP Service Extension for Authentication" uses a name and password for credentials.

The LOGIN method obscures the password transaction somewhat by using Base64 encoding, but this is not intended to protect the transaction. Base64 encoding does not use a cipher. It simply converts a given input into a string of alpha text using a well-known algorithm. Microsoft provides the source code for a Base64 encoder/decoder called Base64.exe at the www.microsoft.com Web site. A compiled version is available at www.rtner.de/software/base64.html.

Outlook Express (and Outlook, when configured as an Internet client) uses the LOGIN method when configured to make an authenticated connection that does not involve Secure Password Authentication. The following listing shows a sample transaction with the decoded Base64 entries shown in angle brackets at the side of each line):

```
Client - AUTH LOGIN
Server - 334 VXNlcm5hbWU6                       <Username:>
Client - Y29tcGFueVxhZG1pbmlzdHJhdG9y
<company\administrator>
Server - 334 UGFzc3dvcmQ6                        <Password:>
Client - Y2xlYXJ0ZXh0cGFzc3dvcmQ=               <cleartextpassword>
Server - 235 2.7.0 Authentication successful.
```

The client starts by sending an AUTH request that specifies LOGIN as the authentication method. The server requests a user name and the client complies. (Note the domain context prefixed to the name. This is required for plain-text authentication in Windows.) The server now requests the user's password and the client complies. If you were to sniff this transaction on the wire, you would not have any problem seeing and decoding the password.

## Simulate an Authenticated SMTP Connection

You can use the Base64 encoder to help you simulate an authenticated SMTP connection using telnet. For example, let's say you want to send an SMTP message to a user called TedTurner@cnn.com using an Exchange server in the Company.com domain. You have an account in the Company.com domain with the logon name PhoenixUser1 and a password of Rumplestilt$kin. First, convert the credentials to Base64:

```
company\phoenixuser1 => Y29tcGFueVxwaG9lbml4dXNlcjE=
Rumplestilt$kin     => UnVtcGxlc3RpbHQka2lu
```

Now establish a telnet session to port 25 of an Exchange server and use the following listing as a guide for the transaction:

```
telnet w2k3-ex1 25
220 w2k3-ex1.company.com SMTP Service Available Tue, 29 Jul 2004
➥10:26:27 -0700
ehlo
250-w2k3-ex1.company.com Hello [192.168.0.1]
250-TURN
250-SIZE
250-ETRN
250-PIPELINING
250-DSN
250-ENHANCEDSTATUSCODES
250-8bitmime
250-BINARYMIME
250-CHUNKING
250-VRFY
250-X-EXPS GSSAPI NTLM LOGIN
250-X-EXPS=LOGIN
250-AUTH GSSAPI NTLM LOGIN
250-AUTH=LOGIN
250-X-LINK2STATE
250-XEXCH50
250 OK
auth login
334 VXNlcm5hbWU6
Y29tcGFueVxwaG9lbml4dXNlcjE=
334 UGFzc3dvcmQ6
UnVtcGxlc3RpbHQka2lu
235 2.7.0 Authentication successful.
mail from: broccoli@carrot.com
250 2.1.0 broccoli@carrot.com....Sender OK
rcpt to: tedturner@cnn.com
250 2.1.5 phoenixuser10@cox.net
data
354 Start mail input; end with <CRLF>.<CRLF>
Make Larry King wear different suspenders!
.
```

```
250 2.6.0 <W2K3-S6HM3SOlbpH71y00000008@w2k3-ex1.company.com>
➥Queued mail for delivery
quit
221 2.0.0 w2k3-ex1.company.com Service closing transmission
➥channel
Connection to host lost.
```

The dot on the final line of the message body signals SMTP that you've completed the DATA portion of the transmission.

Note that even though you use the PhoenixUser1 credentials to authenticate to the SMTP service, you can use another recipient's address in the MAIL FROM: portion of the message. SMTP does not validate the sender's name against the authentication credentials.

If you get an "access denied" error, make sure you encoded the full domain\user name and used the correct password. The user name is not case-sensitive but the password is.

Now that you've seen how SMTP authenticates incoming connections, let's see how an Exchange server makes use of these authentication methods to control access by other SMTP servers. This information will help you avoid accidentally configuring your server as an *open relay*, which invites exploitation by spammers.

# SMTP Authentication and Relaying

When an SMTP server outside your organization wants to forward e-mail to someone in your Exchange organization, it must either make a connection to the SMTP service on one of your Exchange servers, or it must connect to an SMTP server that has the ability to route messages to one of your Exchange servers.

You can view and modify the authentication requirements for these connections using ESM. Drill down through the server icon to **Protocols | SMTP** and then open the Properties window for the **Default SMTP Virtual Server**. Select the **Access** tab and then click **Authentication**. This opens the Authentication window shown in Figure 8.9.

**Figure 8.9** SMTP authentication options.

## Anonymous SMTP Relaying

By default, the SMTP service uses all three authentication methods supported by IIS: Anonymous, Basic, and Integrated Windows (negotiated). Basic authentication should be avoided because it exposes the user's password in clear text. You could configure your SMTP server to use Transport Layer Security (TLS)—virtually the same thing as Secure Socket Layer (SSL)—but that limits the service to connections from other SSL-enabled SMTP servers, and that's not a popular option because of the processing overhead.

So, the only two practical authentication options for SMTP are Anonymous Access and Integrated Windows Authentication. An SMTP service must accept anonymous connections so it can route mail from Internet servers to clients in the Exchange organization, as shown in Figure 8.10.

In this example, an Internet client addresses a message to a user in the Exchange organization using the organization's SMTP domain, Company.com.

- When the user presses Send, the e-mail client application sends the message to an SMTP server at the user's ISP.
- The SMTP server at the ISP uses DNS to locate the MX record for the public-facing SMTP server at Company.com. It also gets the glue record with the IP address of the SMTP server.

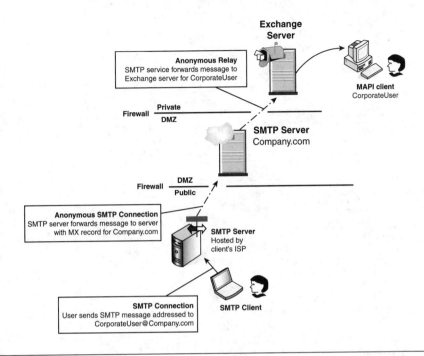

**Figure 8.10** Diagram of SMTP flowpath for anonymous connection and relaying of Internet mail to internal recipients.

- When the ISP's server forwards the message to the public-facing SMTP server at Company.com, it does not have an Active Directory account, so it makes an anonymous connection.
- The SMTP server at Company.com looks at the recipient name in the SMTP header and verifies that the account (or group) exists in Active Directory and that the SMTP domain in the address corresponds to one of the proxy addresses stored in the Active Directory object for the user.
- The SMTP server forwards the message to the mailbox server for the user, where it goes into the user's Inbox for retrieval.

## Open SMTP Relaying

This willingness to accept an anonymous connection puts the SMTP service in a position where it might be asked to send a message to a user that does not reside in the local Exchange organization. This is called *open relaying*. You would never deliberately configure an open SMTP relay, but it's useful to see why such a relay represents a problem. Figure 8.11 shows how an open relay works.

The following description is for illustrative purposes only. The default configuration of Windows SMTP **does not** permit open relaying.

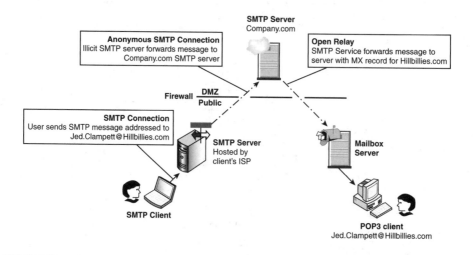

**Figure 8.11** Diagram of SMTP flowpath for anonymous connection and relaying of Internet mail to external recipients. The Windows SMTP service does not permit this type of relaying by default.

In this example, a bad guy has set up an SMTP server that forwards all messages to the Company.com SMTP server regardless of the recipient's SMTP domain.

- The bad guy sends a message addressed to a recipient in the Hillbillies.com domain rather than the Company.com domain.
- Rather than use the true SMTP server for the Hillbillies.com domain, the illicit SMTP server forwards the message to the public-facing SMTP server at Company.com using an anonymous connection.
- The Company.com SMTP server evaluates the user name and the destination SMTP address. In a production configuration, the

server would reject the address, but if an administrator accidentally configures the server to act as an open relay, the server forwards the message to the e-mail server for the Hillbillies.com domain.

■ The e-mail server in Hillbillies.com is unaware that the message has come from a relay and accepts it as if it were a standard piece of e-mail coming in from the Internet.

Imagine that the source of the SMTP traffic through the illicit SMTP server is a spammer sending hundreds of thousands of messages to users in all sorts of SMTP domains. Exposing an open relay like this to the public Internet can have unfortunate consequences. If the Company.com server gets identified as a potential source of spam, then the entire Company.com domain could get blacklisted. See Chapter 13, "Service Continuity," for details.

## Configuring Relay Settings

In the Properties window for the SMTP Virtual Server, select the Access tab and click Relay. Figure 8.12 shows an example. As you can see, the SMTP service does not relay for anonymous users. It relays only for computers that make an authenticated SMTP connection.

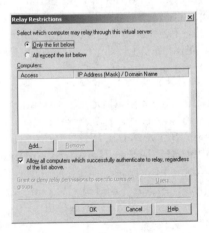

**Figure 8.12** Default SMTP relay options.

If the SMTP service on an Exchange server receives a message addressed to an SMTP domain outside its organization, or one that has not been included as a proxy address in a Recipient Policy, the service returns this error to the sender:

```
The message could not be sent because one of the recipients was
➡rejected by the server. The rejected e-mail address was
➡'JedClampett@Hillbillies.com'. Subject 'Way'll Doggies',
➡Account: 'w2k3-ex1.company.com', Server: 'w2k3-
➡ex1.company.com', Protocol: SMTP, Server Response: '550 5.7.1
➡Unable to relay for bigBHfan@yahoo.com', Port: 25,
➡Secure(SSL): No, Server Error: 550, Error Number: 0x800CCC79
```

Now turn your attention to the option with the inordinately long title, **Allow All Computers Which Successfully Authenticate to Relay, Regardless of the List Above**. This option, selected by default, tells the Exchange server to accept connections only from authenticated servers or clients. This allows other Exchange servers in the organization to use Windows Integrated authentication to make SMTP connections that can route messages to outside recipients.

## Configuring Internet Clients for Authorized Connections

You can configure an Internet e-mail client to make an authenticated SMTP connection to an Exchange server so that the client can send messages outside the Exchange organization. The user must have credentials in Active Directory. Configure Outlook Express for authenticated SMTP connections as follows:

1. Open the Account Properties window from the main menu using **Tools | Accounts | Properties**.
2. Select the **Servers** tab. (See Figure 8.13.)
3. Select the **My Server Requires Authentication** option.
4. If you want to provide a different set of credentials than those used for the POP3 or IMAP4 connection, click **Settings** and enter those credentials in the **Outgoing Mail Server** window.

Test the setting by sending an e-mail addressed to a user outside your organization using Outlook Express. You'll know the transaction succeeds when the outbox clears of messages. If the message stubbornly refuses to disappear, check the SMTP log at the Outlook Express client for errors. If the message disappears but you immediately get a NDR, check to make sure you typed your credentials correctly.

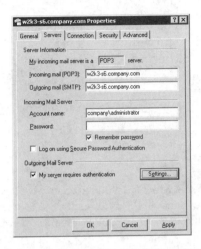

**Figure 8.13** POP3 client configuration that specifies an Exchange server as the mailbox server and SMTP server.


# Configuring an SMTP Internet Connector

Any Exchange server with access to the Internet over TCP port 25 can send and receive SMTP traffic. Most organizations prefer to control SMTP access, though, so if you will need to designate at least one Exchange server as the SMTP gateway to the Internet. This is done by installing an *SMTP Connector* that designates the server as a bridgehead. Other Exchange servers in the organization will then route SMTP traffic for Internet recipients to this bridgehead server.

Exchange 2003 has a wizard to help you configure an SMTP Internet connector, but before launching the wizard, you need to decide where the Internet side will route outgoing mail. You have a couple of choices. The connector can route mail directly to an e-mail server in the recipient's domain (DNS routing), or it can forward all Internet mail to an SMTP relay server (smart host) that does the necessary routing.

## DNS Routing

If you want your Exchange server to route messages directly to a recipient's SMTP domain, the server must obtain the name and IP address of at least one e-mail server in the destination domain. The SMTP service uses DNS for this purpose by querying for MX (Mail eXchange) records in the DNS zone for that domain.

An MX record contains the name of an SMTP server. You can see the MX records returned by DNS for a domain using Nslookup. For example, the following syntax returns the public SMTP servers for the Yahoo.com domain:

```
C:\>nslookup
Set type=mx
yahoo.com.

Non-authoritative answer:
yahoo.com       MX preference = 1, mail exchanger = mx2.mail.yahoo.com
yahoo.com       MX preference = 5, mail exchanger = mx4.mail.yahoo.com
yahoo.com       MX preference = 1, mail exchanger = mx1.mail.yahoo.com

yahoo.com           nameserver = ns4.yahoo.com
yahoo.com           nameserver = ns1.yahoo.com
yahoo.com           nameserver = ns2.yahoo.com
mx1.mail.yahoo.com      internet address = 64.156.215.5
mx1.mail.yahoo.com      internet address = 64.156.215.6
mx1.mail.yahoo.com      internet address = 64.157.4.78
mx2.mail.yahoo.com      internet address = 64.157.4.78
mx2.mail.yahoo.com      internet address = 64.157.4.79
mx2.mail.yahoo.com      internet address = 64.157.4.82
mx2.mail.yahoo.com      internet address = 64.156.215.5
mx2.mail.yahoo.com      internet address = 64.156.215.6
mx4.mail.yahoo.com      internet address = 66.218.86.254
mx4.mail.yahoo.com      internet address = 216.136.129.5
mx4.mail.yahoo.com      internet address = 66.218.86.253
```

After the Exchange server has identified an SMTP server in the target domain, it makes an SMTP connection to that server and delivers the message.

The advantage to DNS routing is its flexibility. The Exchange server is free to locate the target mail server and to communicate directly with it without intervention. There are a couple of disadvantages to DNS routing. One is the lack of a single pathway for mail out of the organization where the content can be scanned, analyzed, and possibly diverted. For example, if every Exchange server were configured for DNS routing, and you wanted to use a third-party utility to block outbound traffic to selected sites, you would have to place this utility on every Exchange server. The second disadvantage is security. If you use the Exchange server both for inbound and outbound SMTP traffic, you must permit SMTP traffic to enter through your firewall.

## Smart Hosts

Using a smart host alleviates some of the security concerns because it can reside in a protected location, either in your own DMZ, at an ISP, or at a service provider that specializes in SMTP handling. Such a service provider might also sell you antivirus and antispam scanning services. A smart host can also be a single point of failure, so either designate multiple smart hosts or diligently protect the one you have.

You can put a standalone Windows Server 2003 server (or some other platform) in the DMZ to act as an SMTP router for inbound and outbound traffic. It cannot run Exchange, but it can host third-party SMTP scanning products. You might even decide to use the SMTP services in a firewall such as an Internet Security and Acceleration (ISA) server or a third-party product with application firewall capabilities. Microsoft will soon provide an antispam/antivirus solution called the Microsoft Edge Server that will run on a smart host.

You should use a smart host whenever possible. Not only does it simplify message routing, but you can install antivirus and antispam applications on the server that traps inappropriate or dangerous messages before they enter the private side of your network. This is called *perimeter filtering*.

## Creating an Internet Connector with the Internet Mail Wizard

Exchange 2003 has an Internet Mail Wizard (IMW) that simplifies building connectors to the Internet. You can use the IMW to create one or more connectors, with a few caveats:

- **No legacy bridgeheads.** The IMW cannot create an SMTP connector to a server running Exchange 5.x or earlier.
- **No clusters.** The IMW will not run on an Exchange server that participates in a shared-disk or network cluster.
- **Single network interface.** The IMW will refuse to run if the Exchange server has multiple network cards configured for different subnets and RRAS is enabled for routing.

You could theoretically create an SMTP connector manually that would not take these limitations into account. However, because the limitations assure proper SMTP connector operation, you should use the IMW.

Once you've verified that you meet these requirements, configure an SMTP Internet connector using the IMW as follow:

1. In ESM, right-click the organization icon and select **Internet Mail Wizard** from the flyout menu.
2. Click **Next**. This opens the Prerequisites for Internet Mail window.
3. Verify that you meet the requirements to register your SMTP domain with an Internet registrar, to have an Internet IP address assigned to your Exchange server (or a NAT forwarder), and to place an MX record for the Exchange server in your Internet zone.
4. Click **Next**. The Server Selection window opens (Figure 8.14). Select the server you want to host the SMTP connector to the Internet.

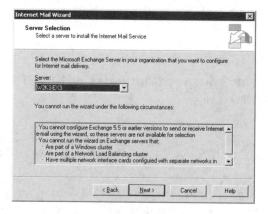

**Figure 8.14**  IMW Server Selection window.

5. Click **Next**. The wizard displays a Progress window while it creates the SMTP connector.
6. Once the server passes the prerequisite test, click **Next**.
7. In the Internet E-Mail Functions window, select both **Receive Internet E-Mail** and **Send Internet E-Mail** unless you want to separate these functions in your network.

8. Click **Next**. If you have more than one SMTP domain in the virtual SMTP server, select the one you want to use for Internet mail.
9. Click **Next**. The Outbound Bridgehead Server window opens. The server you selected at the start of the wizard now gets displayed as the bridgehead.
10. Click **Next**. The Outbound Mail Configuration window opens (Figure 8.15). You have two options. You can elect to use DNS to locate MX records for destination SMTP domains, or you can elect to use a smart host.

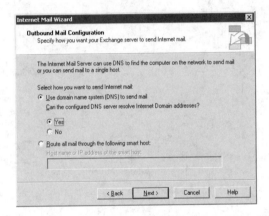

**Figure 8.15** IMW Outbound Mail Configuration window that allows you to specify routing alternatives: DNS or Smart Host.

11. Click **Next**. The Outbound SMTP Domain Restrictions window opens. If you want to block deliveries to selected SMTP domains, enter them here.
12. Click **Next**. A summary window opens.
13. Click **Next** to create the SMTP connector.
14. Click **Finish** to close the wizard.

Once the connector is in place, verify that you can send and receive Internet e-mail. If outbound mail does not get delivered, check the Queues window in ESM to see where the messages are piling up and then look for a possible configuration problem in the routing to or from that server. Start with verifying the DNS configuration. If inbound mail does not get delivered, check to make sure that the MX record in your public DNS zone has the correct information.

# Message Routing

When a set of Exchange servers shares a high-speed, reliable network with each other, you can configure them to belong to the same *Routing Group*. Exchange servers in the same Routing Group can send messages directly to each other. Figure 8.16 shows a diagram of a typical Routing Group arrangement.

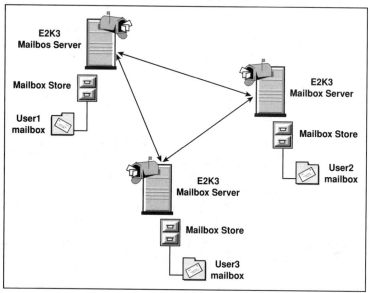

**Figure 8.16** Diagram showing point-to-point message routing between Exchange servers in the same Routing Group.

SMTP message routing requires a little more control if the Exchange servers reside in separate locations. Message routing in a large enterprise would become extraordinarily complex if Exchange servers could send mail directly to each other, no matter where they were located. Also, your colleagues in network services appreciate it when you exercise control over the WAN traffic caused by message routing between offices.

Exchange uses *Routing Group Connectors* to describe pathways between Routing Groups. These connectors define a set of *bridgehead servers* that route messages between the Routing Groups, as shown in Figure 8.17.

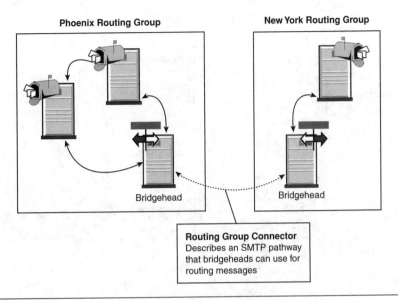

**Phoenix Routing Group**

**New York Routing Group**

Bridgehead

Bridgehead

**Routing Group Connector**
Describes an SMTP pathway
that bridgeheads can use for
routing messages

**Figure 8.17** Diagram showing message routing between Routing Groups using bridgeheads communicating via a Routing Group Connector.

Instead of using a Routing Group Connector to define a path between Routing Groups, you can use an SMTP connector, the same type of connector used for your Internet connections. This isn't a commonly used option but it does have the advantage of giving you a few more filters than the standard Routing Group Connector. Unless you have a specific reason to restrict traffic from a location in a way that only an SMTP connector supports, use Routing Group Connectors between all your Routing Groups.

## Routing Group Configurations

You can use Routing Group Connectors to create topologies that mimic your underlying WAN, but most administrators choose to implement a hub-and-spoke arrangement such as that shown in Figure 8.18. In this arrangement, the bridgehead servers in the outlying offices route messages to each other through the bridgehead at the company headquarters.

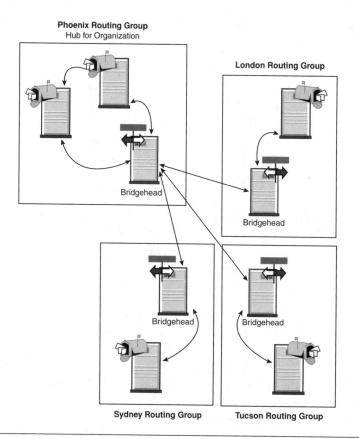

**Figure 8.18** Diagram of typical hub-and-spoke Routing Group configuration.

A larger organization might define several hubs, one for each continent perhaps, and then join the hubs using Routing Group Connectors.

In a hub-and-spoke arrangement, the central bridgehead server or servers can take quite a pounding. Depending on the message load, you might want to consider increasing the number of processors and RAM in the central bridgehead servers. Gather performance data regularly and look at for long-term trends that indicate insufficient memory, inordinately long SMTP queues, or excessive network traffic.

## Routing Group Connector Features

A Routing Group Connector has a variety of features that make it simple to configure and manage:

- **Legacy support.** A Routing Group Connector uses SMTP to connect modern Exchange servers (Exchange 2000 and Exchange Server 2003), but it can also use RPCs to connect a bridgehead in an Exchange 2003 Routing Group to an Exchange 5.5 SP3 bridgehead in a legacy Exchange Site.
- **Fault tolerance.** A Routing Group Connector can eliminate single points of failure by using multiple bridgehead and target servers.
- **Oversized message handling.** Messages over a certain size can be scheduled to transfer separately from standard messages. This permits delaying the transfer of large messages until after working hours. You can also block messages beyond a certain size to keep from overloading a WAN link.
- **Deny public folder referrals.** Normally Outlook clients ferret out the servers that host public folder replicas using referrals from their home Exchange servers. A Routing Group Connector can block these public folder referrals, which prevents users in one Routing Group from getting public folder content across an expensive WAN link.

The only reason you might want to avoid creating Routing Groups for each LAN in your WAN is to get more robust message routing. If you have a fat network pipe between two locations, it doesn't make much sense to force SMTP traffic to queue up at the bridgehead servers. On the other hand, if you want more control over message routing, then creating Routing Groups for each LAN makes a lot of sense.

## Creating and Configuring Routing Groups

If you're following along with the examples by doing tests in your lab, you should now install at least two additional Exchange servers so you can place them in Routing Groups to see how messages get routed through the bridgeheads.

### View Routing Groups in ESM

Before you can see any Routing Groups, configure the organization object to display them in ESM. Figure 8.19 shows the Properties window for the organization object. Place a check next to Display Routing Groups and click OK to save the change.

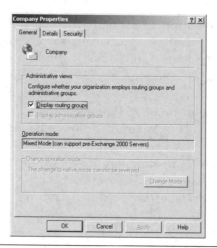

**Figure 8.19**  Routing Groups not displayed until configured in Organization properties.

## Create a Routing Group

Create a new Routing Group as follows:

1. Launch ESM and drill down to First Administrative Group.
2. Right-click the **Routing Groups** icon and select **New | Routing Group** from the flyout menu. This opens a Properties menu where you enter the name of the Routing Group. I'll call the example **Tucson**.
3. Rename the existing First Routing Group to the name Phoenix. Do this by right-clicking the icon and selecting **Rename** from the flyout menu. The final result looks like Figure 8.20.

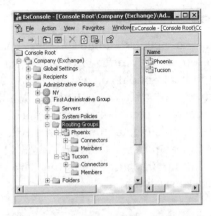

**Figure 8.20** ESM showing Routing Groups folder with newly created Routing Group and renamed First Routing Group.

## Move a Server to the New Routing Group

I once tried moving back to my home town only to discover that I didn't fit in very well anymore. For example, I was the sole liberal Democrat in a county where the second most liberal voter thought Herbert Hoover was a bit soft on communism. When asked about the loneliness of my political views, I would answer, "What good is it to have two parties in this town if one of them doesn't have any members?"

The same is true for the new Routing Group you just created. It needs at least one member server. You can move servers between Routing Groups using a simple drag and drop.

1. Highlight the **Members** icon under the newly renamed Phoenix Routing Group.
2. Drag one of the servers under Phoenix into the **Members** folder of the Tucson Routing Group. Voila, the move is done. No waiting. No service interruptions. If everything in e-mail administration were this simple, they wouldn't need administrators.

## Create a Routing Group Connector

Routing group connectors define one-way paths between Routing Groups. Therefore, each Routing Group must have a connector pointing at the other Routing Group if you want to send messages back and forth.

When you create a Routing Group Connector in one Routing Group, ESM creates a complementary connector in the other Routing Grou, if you have sufficient administrative privileges. Creating a Routing Group Connector requires Exchange Administrator privileges in the Administrative group. Create the Routing Group Connectors between Phoenix and Tucson as follows:

1. Right-click the **Connectors** icon under Phoenix and select **New | Routing Group Connector** from the flyout menu. This opens an empty Properties window.
2. I usually name Routing Group Connectors after the endpoints. This lets me run my thumb down a list of connectors and know exactly what they're used for. I'll name this connector **Phx-Tuc**.
3. In the **Connects This Routing Group with** dropdown list, select **Tucson**.
4. Select the **Remote Bridgeheads** tab.
5. Click **Add** and select the server from the pick list. You only have one server in the Tucson Routing Group, so only one option is available in the list.
6. Select the **Delivery Options** tab. Note that the **Connection Time Is Set to Always Run** option is checked by default. Leave this setting in place unless the underlying WAN connection is not available for long periods of time.
7. Click **OK** to create the connector.
8. When prompted to create the connector in the other Routing Group, click **Yes**. A pleasant but meaningless progress bar appears, complete with an elapsed time counter. A few seconds later, ESM displays the two connectors.

Verify that you can send messages between Exchange servers in the two Routing Groups. The best way to do that is to log on to Outlook using an account with a mailbox on the Phoenix server and then send a message to a user with a mailbox on the Tucson server.

## Configure Routing Group Connector Properties

When you create a Routing Group Connector, it's a good practice to designate multiple source and target bridgeheads. This minimizes the chance of losing connection between Routing Groups when a single server is unavailable. The SMTP routing engine implements load balancing and failover automatically.

Legacy Exchange does not support multiple bridgeheads between sites because the older routing protocol makes it possible to get truly stupendous routing loops if a bridgehead server or network connection goes down. Modern Exchange uses a more sophisticated routing algorithm, the Link State Algorithm, to decide on the best route between servers and to avoid circularities.

Figure 8.21 shows the Properties window for a sample Routing Group Connector in ESM.

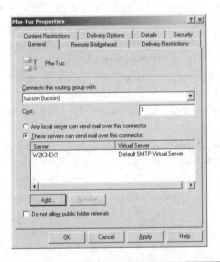

**Figure 8.21** Routing Group Connector properties showing a specified bridgehead and the connection cost. If more than one server can act as a bridgehead, it can be added to the list.

In general, you don't need to change any of the settings in the Routing Group Connector with the exception of the remote bridgeheads. You should designate multiple bridgeheads if they are available so that taking one server down doesn't stop message flow between the Routing Groups.

In a more complex organization with many Routing Groups, you can set the Cost on the Routing Group Connectors to help the routing engines decide on the proper primary and secondary pathways between locations. This requires a fairly detailed knowledge of the routing algorithm used by Exchange, and that's covered in the next section.

# Link State Routing

Imagine that you're Forrest Gump and you've decided to run across the country for no particular reason other than to get exercise and fresh air and to work off a few of the pounds you gained from eating chocolates.

You want to take the shortest route from coast to coast to minimize wear and tear on your sneakers and knees. Each night you lay out a map in front of you and select the town in which you want to sleep the following night. You might not follow a straight path to your destination, but you continue to move forward as expeditiously as possible.

Exchange uses a similar approach to message routing. If you're familiar with modern network routing algorithms, you'll recognize the Exchange mechanism as a form of Open-Shortest Path First, or OSPF. The more general term is *link state routing*.

In link state routing, every routing entity knows the entire routing topology and the status of each of the other routing entities. When given a message to route, the routing entity selects the next hop by calculating the least-costly route between itself and the message's final destination.

Link state routing uses an algorithm developed by a mathematician named Edsger Dijkstra. If you're interested in the math underlying the algorithm, or you want to view a little animation of how the Dijkstra algorithm works, visit `ciips.ee.uwa.edu.au/~morris/Year2/PLDS210/dijkstra.html`.

## Link State Table

Exchange servers act like nosy neighbors in a homeowner's association. They keep track of the status of their routing partners, either UP or DOWN, and they make sure that this status gets recorded in a special data structure called a *Link State Table*.

The Link State Table contains information about every Exchange server, Routing Group, and connector in the organization, including

- Distinguished names, GUIDs, and versions of each Exchange server
- Routing Group addresses (X.400, SMTP, and so forth)
- Routing Group members, their version, build number, and whether they can be contacted by the Routing Group Master
- Connector type, source and destination bridgeheads, restrictions, address spaces, and state: UP or DOWN

Each Exchange server has a copy of the Link State Table that it stores in memory, never on disk.

## Routing Group Master

Think of the Link State Table as a Chamber of Commerce map showing the location of all the major attractions in an area and how to get from one attraction to the other. If a new attraction opens, or an existing attraction shuts down, the Chamber must issue a new map and distribute it to all its members.

If every Exchange server were able to update its own copy of the Link State Table and then try to replicate it to every other Exchange server, the resulting replication frenzy would scare away great white sharks.

Instead, Exchange designates one Exchange server in each Routing Group to make updates to the Link State Table. This server is called the *Routing Group Master*.

You can find the identity of the Routing Group Master in ESM. Drill down to the Members folder under the Routing Group. The right pane of the window shows the Server Type designation, either Member or Master. Figure 8.22 shows an example. To select a different Routing Group Master, right-click the target server and select Set as Master from the flyout menu.

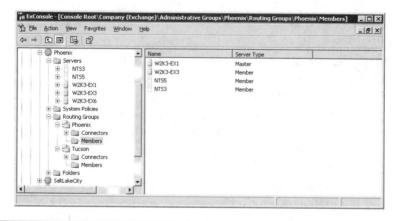

**Figure 8.22**  ESM showing Routing Group Master.

If the Routing Group Master goes down, the remaining servers in the Routing Group continue to use their current copy of the Link State Table. Any messages addressed to users with mailboxes on the Routing Group Master queue up at the sending server, which keeps retrying until the Routing Group Master comes back online or you select another Routing Group Master.

If the Routing Group Master goes down for a short time, then you gain very little by selecting another Master. However, if you plan on an extended maintenance outage, or the server crashes and must be rebuilt, then you should designate another Routing Group Master to ensure that the Routing Group remains up to date with link state changes.

## Orphaned Link State Entries

A Routing Group Master can update the Link State Table only for entities in its own Routing Group. In other words, if a server in the Phoenix Routing Group goes down, only the Phoenix Routing Group Master can change the server's state in the Link State Table. This prevents multiple Routing Group Masters from updating the table based on a single event.

This straightforward engineering decision turns out to have a left-handed consequence: Routing Groups can never disappear from the Link State Table.

For example, let's say you want to retire a Routing Group called Superior by creating a new Routing Group called Duluth. You can't delete a Routing Group while it has members, so you move all the servers from the Superior Routing Group into the Duluth Routing

Group and then delete Superior. That's a perfectly acceptable thing to do and it happens all the time.

But now the Superior Routing Group has no Routing Group Master. This means that no server exists that can remove Superior from the Link State Table. The other Exchange servers realize that the Routing Group no longer exists and they can safely ignore the entry in the Link State Table but the entry itself lingers on and on, like the picture you keep of your high school sweetheart.

### Problems Associated with Orphaned Link State Entries

The remnants of a few dead Routing Groups in the Link State Table doesn't constitute much of a problem, but a huge organization with an existing legacy Exchange deployment could potentially encounter replication issues owing to the size of the Link State Table.

As you'll see in Chapter 12, "Migrating From Legacy Exchange," when you connect the legacy Exchange directory service to Active Directory with the Active Directory Connector and install the first Exchange 2003 server, each of the legacy Exchange sites becomes a separate Routing Group in Exchange 2003.

After you complete the migration of mailboxes and connectors to new Exchange servers, you can decommission the legacy servers and shift to Exchange Native Mode. At that point, you can consolidate your servers into new, larger Routing Groups to take advantage of the improved mail-handling characteristics of SMTP.

But even though you delete the old Routing Group from the organization, their entries remain in the Link State Table. Each time a Routing Group Master updates its copy of the table, then the entire table must replicate to every other Exchange server, including its baggage of orphaned Routing Group entries.

Because the Link State Table resides in memory, the only way to remove these old Routing Groups is to **stop all the Exchange servers throughout the organization at the same time.** When you start up Exchange again after the outage, the first server reads the Routing Group entries in Active Directory and builds a fresh Link State Table that does not contain the deleted Routing Groups.

Microsoft has a way to avoid an entire organization shutdown to clean out the LST, but it involves precise timing of outages within each Administrative Group. Call Microsoft Product Support Services for details or see Dan Winter's blog entry titled "Thoughts on Stale Link State Information (Part 2)" at blogs.msdn.com/exchange/archive/2004/03/11/88037.aspx.

Microsoft does not supply a tool to remove orphaned link state entries from the Link State Table because doing so causes a problem for the algorithm used to calculate routes.

## Example of Link State Routing

The diagram in Figure 8.23 shows an example message routing topology. Within a Routing Group, Exchange servers send messages directly to each other. This results in a lot of short SMTP transactions, which is acceptable in a high-bandwidth, low-latency environment. Between Routing Groups, bridgehead servers send messages only to each other.

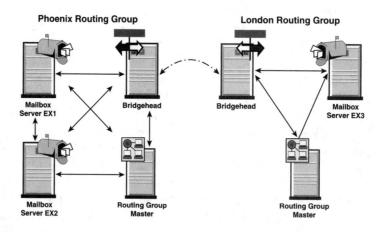

**Figure 8.23** SMTP message flowpaths within a Routing Group and between Routing Groups.

When a user with a home mailbox in Phoenix sends a message to a user with a home mailbox in London, the Phoenix mailbox server needs to decide where to route the message. It looks at its copy of the Link State Table to determine the least-costly route to the destination server.

Let's say a user homed on mailbox server EX2 sends a message to a user with a mailbox on server EX3.

1. **Recipient home server determination.** When the SMTP service on EX2 gets the message, it does a quick LDAP query to a Global Catalog server and determines that the recipient's home server is EX3.

2. **Link State Table lookup.** EX2 refers to its copy of the Link State Table and determines that the best route to EX3 lies through the bridgehead server in its Routing Group. It immediately opens an SMTP transaction with the Phoenix bridgehead server and sends it the message.

3. **Link State Table lookup.** The SMTP service on the Phoenix bridgehead server looks at its copy of the Link State Table and decides that the bridgehead server in London represents the shortest path to the target server. It opens an SMTP connection to the London bridgehead server and sends the message.

4. **Link State Table lookup.** The London bridgehead server refers to its copy of the Link State Table and sees that EX3 resides in its own Routing Group. It opens an SMTP connection directly to EX3 and sends the message.

5. **Final delivery.** EX3 sees that the recipient of the message resides in a local mailbox store. The SMTP service hands the message to the Information Store service, which tucks it into the user's Inbox folder.

## Link State Table Updates

Now refer to Figure 8.24 to see what happens if an Exchange server goes down. Recall that each server maintains a copy of the Link State Table in memory and that only the Routing Group Master can change the content of that table.

In this example, an administrator takes server EX2 down for maintenance. Here's what happens:

1. **Link State Change.** A member of the Phoenix Routing Group discovers that EX2 has stopped responding and immediately informs the Routing Master by communicating to the SMTP Routing service (RESVC) over TCP port 691.

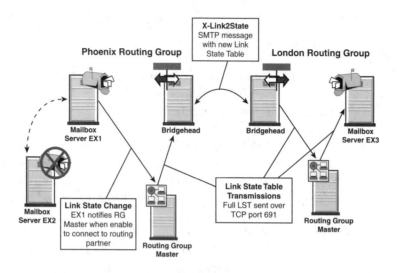

**Figure 8.24** Diagram of Link State Table update flowpaths when an Exchange server goes down.

TCP port 691 has been registered with the Internet Assigned Numbers Association (IANA) for use in Exchange routing. You can view the latest list of registered port numbers at www.iana.org/assignments/port-numbers.

2. **LST Transmission within Routing Group.** The Routing Group Master marks EX2 as DOWN in the Link State Table and then transmits the entire table to the other members of the Phoenix Routing Group using TCP port 691.

3. **LST Transmission between Routing Groups.** When the bridgehead server in Phoenix gets the copy of the new Link State Table, it uses a special SMTP command called X-Link2State to send a copy of the Link State Table to the London bridgehead server.

4. **LST Updates at Second Routing Group.** The London bridgehead forwards the message containing the Link State Table to the Routing Group Master in London. The London Routing Group Master transmits the Link State Table to the other members of the London Routing Group over TCP port 691. (That's when the Routing Engine at the London bridgehead server sees the content.)

## Link State Oscillations

When an Exchange server goes down cleanly, as EX2 did in the previous example, the Link State Table changes propagate out as smoothly as a small pebble thrown in a mountain pond. But what happens if a WAN link starts to hiccup? Each time the link goes down, the bridgehead reports the status change to the Routing Group Master, which updates and transmits a new Link State Table. The link goes up, and the process repeats.

The entire Link State Table propagates to every Exchange server in the entire organization each time any item in the table changes. Imagine what would happen if a WAN link goes up and down at five-second intervals for an hour. Link State Table updates would flood the network.

To mitigate the consequences of erratic changes in link state, if the Routing Group Master sees the link state change a few times in a given interval, it simply leaves the link state value at UP and lets the bridgehead servers or Routing Group partners queue up messages as they deal with the intermittent availability of the connection.

If a connection goes down and no alternate path exists, the Routing Group Master also leaves the connection marked UP. This avoids instabilities that could result if other Routing Group Masters try to find a way around the down connection.

## Loss of Bridgehead or WAN Link

If a bridgehead server cannot contact one of its partners on the other side of the Routing Group Connector, it keeps trying for 10 minutes then tags the bridgehead as DOWN and tries another. If it cannot connect to any of the target bridgeheads, it flags the connector as DOWN and notifies the Routing Group Master.

The Routing Group Master updates the Link State Table and communicates the new table to the other members of the Routing Group. This happens quickly to minimize the number of messages sent to the bridgehead server, where they would queue up waiting for the connector to come back. You can use the queue viewer in ESM to view the messages in the queue.

The bridgehead now tries to open a zero-message connection to the target bridgehead. It keeps trying until the underlying WAN link returns to service and the connection succeeds. It then empties its queue and informs the Routing Group Master of the link state change.

## WinRoute

Microsoft provides a diagnostic tool called WinRoute that shows the content of the Link State Table. Figure 8.25 shows an example Win-Route display for an organization with five Exchange 5.5 servers and ten Exchange 2003 servers in seven Routing Groups. As you can see, the Link State Table can get complex fairly quickly. Winroute is available from the Exchange download site as part of the Alltools.exe download, `www.microsoft.com/exchange/downloads/2003.asp`.

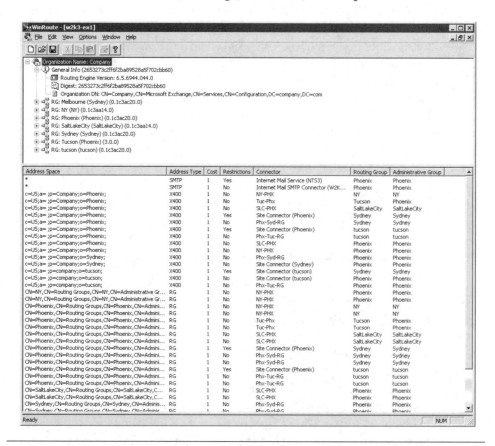

**Figure 8.25** Main window of WinRoute showing Routing Groups and details on organization link configuration.

WinRoute makes it simple to identify a problem. For example, Figure 8.26 shows a WinRoute display for a Routing Group with one server, W2K3-EX3, in a DOWN state.

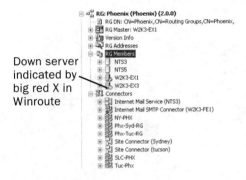

Down server indicated by big red X in Winroute

**Figure 8.26** WinRoute interface showing server tagged as DOWN in Link State Table.

It's a good idea to get familiar with the typical Winroute listings during normal operations. You'll find that getting familiar with Winroute will reward you time and time again by making it simple to diagnose and correct routing problems.

## Looking Forward

You can take a well-deserved rest at this point. You have Exchange servers in several locations, and they can route messages to each other and to the Internet. Your next job consists of delivering the content of your Exchange servers in specialized ways. In next two chapters, you'll configure an Exchange server to deliver e-mail to a Web browser via Outlook Web Access, and you'll see how to put content into public folders so that users throughout the organization can share their ideas in a common forum.

# CHAPTER 9

# Outlook Web Access

U p until this point, the e-mail clients you've used to view the contents of an Exchange mailbox have required a special application running on the user's desktop. As you are no doubt aware, deploying applications requires planning, training, time, and tools. Deploying Outlook is especially difficult because of its reliance on pesky, overly complicated, nearly undocumented MAPI profiles.

You can avoid deploying an e-mail client entirely by having your users access their e-mail, calendars, and public folders using a standard Web browser. The Exchange service that supports this functionality is called Outlook Web Access, or OWA.

If you've seen or used OWA in previous versions of Exchange, you'll be pleasantly surprised by the look and feel of OWA in Exchange 2003. It makes the older versions of OWA look like clunky Hanna-Barbara cartoons compared to modern anime.

This chapter describes how to configure OWA so that your users get all the available features (or as many as you want to give them). You'll also see how to protect OWA with Secure Socket Layer (SSL) and how to permit users to change their domain passwords using OWA, a handy feature for road warriors who never touch the network except to check their mail.

In Chapter 11, "Deploying a Distibuted Architecture," you'll see how to use OWA in a distributed Exchange architecture where a single front-end OWA server can handle thousands of user connections without hosting one single mailbox. Stay tuned.

## Outlook Web Access Overview

You don't need to make any special configurations on an Exchange 2003 server to enable OWA. Just fire up a browser and connect to the server using the following URL:

```
http://<server_name>/exchange
```

Figure 9.1 shows an example of the interface, which is a near-perfect rendering of an Outlook 2003 window. Note the right-side preview pane, the flexible Inbox sorting, the ability to assign lots and lots of flags, and the folder view selection options in the lower-left corner.

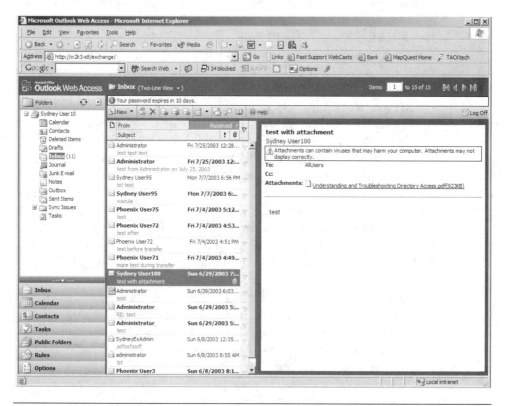

**Figure 9.1**    Outlook 2003 main window showing new elements such as right-side preview and simplified navigation buttons.

In addition to the feature-rich interface, Exchange 2003 OWA includes plug-ins that render most attachments at the server rather than the client, making this the thinnest browser-based e-mail client Microsoft has ever provided. Because it might be years before you can fully deploy Office System 2003, OWA provides a great way to give your users a taste of the future today (sizzling sound effects).

Exchange 2003 OWA has only a few limitations compared to Outlook 2003:

- **No client-side rules.** OWA can only access server-side rules for automating incoming message handling. This presents a minor (or perhaps not so minor) inconvenience to users who expect inbox actions in OWA to mimic the actions in Outlook. The client-side rules will take effect the next time they connect to their mailboxes from Outlook. The list of server-side rules exposed to OWA is also fairly limited.
- **Cannot copy between inbox and public folders.** OWA uses two different interfaces to access mailboxes and public folders, so a user cannot use drag and drop to move items between the two.
- **Clunky Global Address List selection.** An OWA user doesn't get a slick address book interface for selecting recipients from the GAL.
- **HTML composition.** You can create new messages only in the HTML interface provided by OWA. This means that users don't get the same set of features that they might expect from Outlook, especially when using Word as their e-mail editor.
- **No access to message headers.** Although Outlook will show you the full header of a message, OWA shows you only the standard From/To/Subject headers and the message body.
- **No add-ons.** Outlook supports extensive add-ons for use in spam filtering, RSS aggregators (used for getting information from blogs and Web sites), and video e-mail, among others. These add-ons do not apply to e-mail access via OWA.
- **Limited junk mail filtering.** If your users currently rely on client-side filtering in Outlook, then they'll be disappointed to see lots of spam in their OWA inbox. You can resolve this by deploying a server-side filter, a perimeter filter, or by installing Microsoft's Intelligent Message Filter (IMF) for Exchange.
- **Limited spell check languages.** Although Exchange 2003 SP1 adds quite a few languages to the dictionary, OWA still does not have the extensive country coverage of Outlook.

There are no workarounds for these limitations. Perhaps many of the third-party applications will find their way into OWA add-ons.

As this book was going to press, Microsoft released the Intelligent Message Filter (IMF) along with other updates associated with Exchange Server 2003 Service Pack 1. Download the IMF from `http://snipurl.com/6ot3`.

## Browser Support

Exchange 2003 classifies browsers into two categories: those delivering a Premium Experience and those delivering a Basic Experience. To get the Premium Experience, you'll need a…drum roll…Microsoft browser. More specifically, you'll need Internet Explorer 5.01 or higher. (This does not include IE 5.01 for UNIX.) Figure 9.2 shows an example of the Premium calendar display.

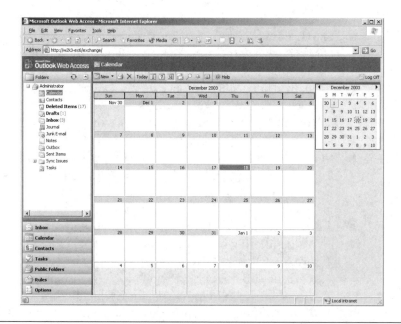

**Figure 9.2**    Outlook Web Access Calendar in Premium browser.

All other browsers deliver a subset of the Premium features, which Microsoft calls a Basic experience. For example, Figure 9.3 shows the Calendar window using Opera 7.0. There's very little essential difference except in look and feel. It's like buying an Acura instead of a Lexus. You get all the important functions and forgo a few luxuries.

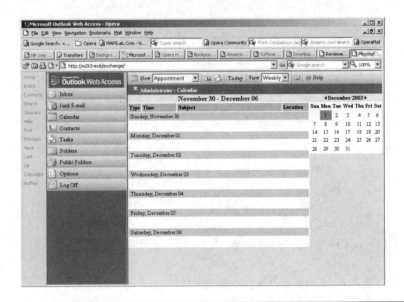

**Figure 9.3** Outlook Web Access Calendar in Basic browser.

Some OWA features, not strictly classified as Premium, require IE 6.0 or higher. These features include the following:

- **S/MIME.** Secure messaging using S/MIME allows you to encrypt and digitally sign messages. For more information, download the "Exchange Server 2003 Message Security Guide" from the Exchange download site. This white paper was written by the Exchange Team's senior security specialist and covers all the steps for deploying secure messaging.
- **Compression.** When you use Internet Explorer 6.01 or higher on a Windows 2000 desktop or higher to connect to an Exchange 2003 OWA server running on a Windows Server 2003 platform, and forms-based authentication has been enabled, then OWA compresses the stream of traffic to and from the server using the

same gzip algorithm that Microsoft uses to compress files. This puts a bit of load on the server, but it radically reduces the traffic on the wire, often a critical consideration for traveling users.

- **Clear credential at logoff.** A security issue can crop up in Exchange 2000 OWA because user credentials are attached to the browser process itself, not the particular window where the user connects to OWA. If the user does not close every single window, the credentials can be used by another user in a later connection as long as the browser process remains in memory. Exchange 2003 uses cookie-based authentication to overcome this problem, but to take advantage of the feature, you need IE 6.0 SP1 or higher.

# OWA Features

This section outlines the important and/or popular Outlook 2003 features that users will find in Exchange 2003 OWA.

## Server-Side Inbox Rules

Users quickly become addicted to manipulating their incoming messages with rules. They don't like to give up those rules when they use OWA. The OWA client supports some server-based rules, but not all of them, and it does not support client-side rules stored in the user's local MAPI profile.

Unfortunately for users, and those of us who must support them, Outlook does not do a good job of indicating whether a particular rule runs at the server or at the client. In general, rules that scan the **header** of a message run at the server, whereas rules that scan the **contents** of a message run at the client.

You can create and modify server-side rules in OWA. Click the Rules bar in the lower-left corner of the window and then select one of the rules in the list in the right pane of the window. Figure 9.4 shows an example.

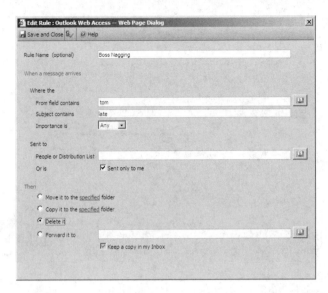

**Figure 9.4**    OWA rules editor. This editor works only with server-side rules.

### Spell Checker

Spell checking was one of the most requested feature upgrades for Exchange 2003. When a user selects the Spell Checker option for a message, if the Spell Checker finds an error, a separate window opens with the offending word highlighted in context. Figure 9.5 shows an example.

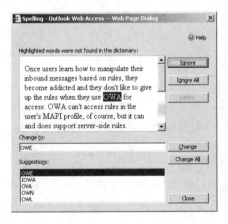

**Figure 9.5**    OWA Spell Checker. Special words and acronyms cannot be added to the dictionary.

The OWA Spell Checker can use any of several languages. OWA prompts the user to select a language the first time the user selects the Spell Checker option and then stores the setting in a cookie. Figure 9.6 shows the selection window.

**Figure 9.6**   Spell Checker prompts for language the first time it gets used. The OWA Options window also has a language setting.

The Spell Checker has a few limitations:

- **No custom dictionaries.** The OWA Spell Checker runs at the server, so a user cannot add items to the main dictionary and cannot configure custom dictionaries.
- **Limited languages.** Exchange 2003 SP1 adds quite a few languages, but not all that you would find in Outlook.
- **Message bodies only.** The Spell Checker does not examine the Subject line of a message.
- **No meeting requests.** The Spell Checker does not scan the messages you write to accompany meeting requests.
- **No grammar checking.** The Spell Checker does not scan for grammatical errors, so it's perfectly possible to give the impression that you are a complete imbecile with impeccable spelling skills.

## Keyboard and Mouse Shortcuts

This feature is my personal favorite. Many of the keyboard shortcuts in Outlook work exactly the same in OWA. Ctrl+N creates a new mail message. Alt+S sends the message. Ctrl+R replies to a message. Ctrl+K does a name lookup when the cursor is in a To, Cc, or Bcc field.

If you prefer a mouse, you'll be happy to know that most of the property menus exposed by the right mouse button in Outlook 2003 also appear in OWA. Figure 9.7 shows an example.

**Figure 9.7**    A right-click of the mouse presents a standard property menu.

## Recipient Selection

The interface to select recipients in Exchange 2003 OWA has improved considerably over its predecessors, but it is still fairly clunky. You click the To button to launch a Global Address List selection window, just as in Outlook, but instead of scrolling through list of recipients, you have to enter a few letters and click Find to bring up a partial recipient list, as shown in Figure 9.8.

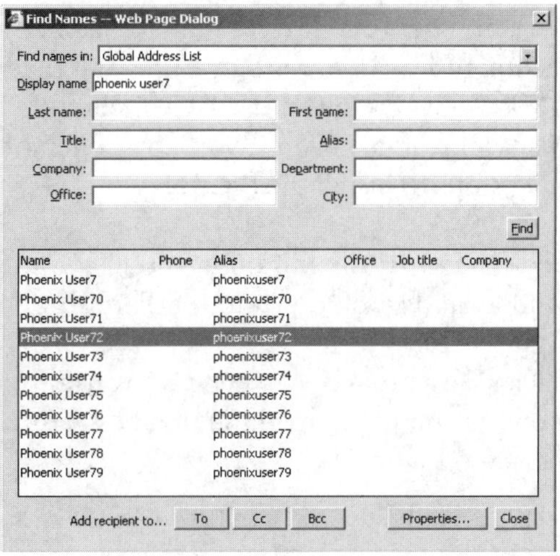

**Figure 9.8**    GAL selection window does not have an interactive mode.

You can view the Properties of a user by clicking the Properties button, but OWA won't show you the members of a group.

## File Attachment Handling

Attaching a file to a message in OWA also gets a little clunky, although there are ways to make the process more efficient. In a normal configuration, click the paper clip icon in a message, which brings up an Attachments dialog box, as shown in Figure 9.9.

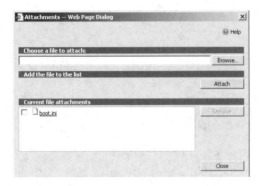

**Figure 9.9**    Standard file attachment window has only simple click-and-select functionality.

To select a file, click Browse to open a standard file navigation interface. Select a file from the interface and then click Attach to add the file to the attachment list. If you prefer to skip all that clicking, here's a tip. The S/MIME ActiveX control in OWA includes a scrollable file search window that you can use even if you don't encrypt your messages. Use the following steps to install the control:

1. Click the **Options** button at the lower-left corner of the OWA window and scroll down to the **E-mail Security** field shown in Figure 9.10.
2. Click **Download**. A Security Warning window opens that prompts you to approve the digital sigature on the ActiveX control. (See Figure 9.11.)

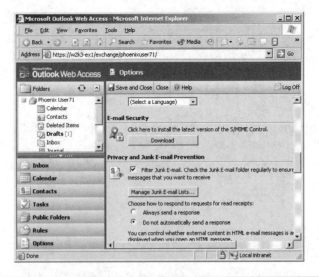

**Figure 9.10** OWA Options window showing S/MIME installation option, which installs an ActiveX control that permits interactive file browsing.

**Figure 9.11** ActiveX Control installation verifier for the S/MIME control.

**3.** Click **Yes** to approve the signature and install the control.

With the control installed, when you click the paperclip icon in a new message, you get a standard file navigation window rather than the Web page dialog box.

Installing the S/MIME controls also gives you these additional features (thanks to Neil Hobson for digging up this information):

1. You can now drag and drop existing messages into new messages that you are currently composing. You then see those messages added as .eml attachments.
2. When composing a new message, you can drag and drop files from Explorer directly into the new message.
3. All installed fonts on your system are now available rather than the default five fonts.

### Antispam Features

OWA contains several of the antispam features used by Outlook.

- **No read receipts.** You can block all read reciepts, which spammers use to discover if they have a live e-mail address.
- **Beacon blocking.** OWA blocks hyperlink connections to embedded graphics in HTML messages, also known as "beacons" because they notify a spammer that a particular message has been opened.
- **Intelligent Mail Filter.** The IMF comes with OWA plug-ins that give the user access to the spam filters.

## OWA Authentication

You can see the authentication settings used by OWA in Exchange System Manager (ESM) by drilling down through the server name to **Protocols | HTTP | Exchange Virtual Server**, as shown in Figure 9.12.

The right pane of the window shows the virtual folders inside the Exchange virtual server. Open the Properties window for the Exchange virtual folder. Select the **Access** tab and then click **Authentication**. Figure 9.13 shows an example.

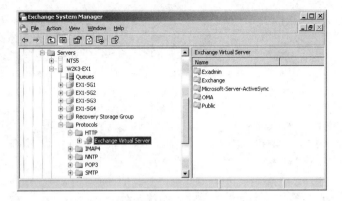

**Figure 9.12**    ESM showing Exchange Virtual Server under Protocols for an Exchange 2003 server.

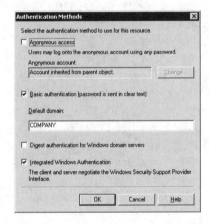

**Figure 9.13**    Exchange HTTP Virtual Server authentication methods.

Note that the Anonymous Access option is not checked by default. A user cannot make an anonymous connection to OWA. When a browser tries to connect as an anonymous user, the Web service returns a list of acceptable authentication mechanisms:

- Negotiate (permits client to select an authentication method)
- NTLM
- Basic

Third-party browsers such as Opera and Netscape use Basic authentication. Internet Explorer prior to version 5.0 uses NTLM if the desktop belongs to the same domain as the Exchange server. Current versions of Internet Explorer use Kerberos when launched from a modern Windows desktop that belongs to the same forest as the Exchange organization; otherwise, they use Basic authentication. Basic authentication passes the user's name and password across the wire in clear text. You should always protect Basic authentications using SSL. This is covered later in the chapter.

### Forms-Based OWA Authentication

The OWA authentication negotiation could theoretically be manipulated by a man-in-the-middle attack, either to obtain the user's credentials (Basic authentication) or to redirect the user to a bogus Web site by manipulating the HTTP data stream.

Using SSL to protect the OWA connection avoids these kinds of exploits. In addition, Exchange 2003 has a feature called Forms-Based Authentication that replaces the standard negotiation process with a credentials window that uses Basic authentication over SSL.

Exchange does not enable forms-based authentication by default. Enable it manually from ESM. Drill down through the server name to **Protocols | HTTP | Exchange Virtual Server**. Figure 9.14 shows an example. Leave the **Compression** option at **None** if you don't want to put any additional load on the server, or select a higher level of compression if you want to speed up transfers to your dial-up users.

If you select this option, you'll get a warning message telling you to configure the virtual server to use SSL. This is covered a little further in the chapter in a section titled "Configuring OWA to Use SSL." First, let's get familiar with the forms-based authentication functionality.

Forms-based authentication is not available on clustered Exchange servers.

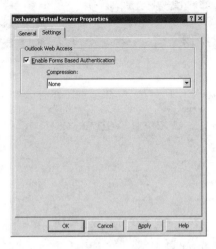

**Figure 9.14**   Exchange HTTP Virtual Server properties showing Forms Based Authentication option.

### Forms-Based Authentication Page

When you enable forms-based authentication, Exchange adds an ISAPI filter called OWALogon.dll to the Web services hosted by IIS and replaces the default OWA window with a new page, OwaLogon.asp. Figure 9.15 shows the OWALogon page.

You can modify the look of the OWALogon.asp page to suit your corporate standard. For example, you could replace the logo and background elements with your own organizational ID.

OWALogon requires that users enter their credentials in *domain\username* format even if they run a current browser version and belong to the same domain as the Exchange server. OwaLogon uses only Basic authentication and protects the plain text password with SSL.

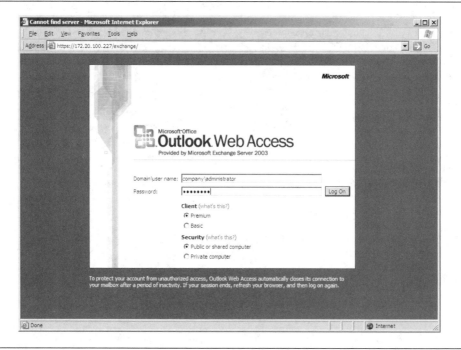

**Figure 9.15**    OWA authentication form.

Unlike the Basic authentication used by IIS for other Web sites, you cannot specify a default domain for forms-based authentication. The entry is set to "\" by default. If you try to hack the IIS Metabase to change the default domain, Exchange System Manager changes it right back to "\" the next time you touch the virtual server settings.

### *Forms-Based Authentication Options*

Users can select an option in the OWA logon window to view Basic rather than Premium content. For dial-up users, this speeds up access at the cost of a few premium-viewing features, such as two-line mail view, keyboard shortcuts, and popup notifications.

Users can also stipulate whether they're using a browser on a private or public machine. This determines the inactivity interval before the user gets forcibly logged off. OWA controls this feature with an authentication cookie. The inactivity interval is 15 minutes for public connections and 24 hours for private connections. You can change these settings with a couple of Registry entries:

```
Key: HKLM | SYSTEM | CurrentControlSet | Services |
➡MSExchangeWeb | OWA
Value: PublicClientTimeout
Data: <1-4320 minutes in decimal> REG_DWORD

Value: TrustedClientTimeout
Value Data: <1-4320 minutes decimal> REG_DWORD
```

### Cookie-Based Authentication

In addition to a more secure logon process, the OwaLogon filter provides additional security by controlling how a browser maintains connection with an OWA server.

Ordinarily, when a user authenticates using the negotiation process in IIS, Internet Explorer caches the authentication credentials so that they remain in effect as long as Internet Explorer (Iexplore.exe) remains in memory.

Many users do not know of this feature. They think that closing a browser window also breaks the connection to the OWA server. Users of older OWA versions sometimes find out to their dismay that another user can sit down at their machine and open a browser window and go right to their OWA mailbox because Iexplore.exe was still running in the background.

The OwaLogon filter solves this problem by storing information about the browser session in a cookie issued to the client. The cookie controls the session authentication. When the user closes the OWA window, Iexplore deletes the cookie and the OWA session lapses, even if Iexplore remains running. If the user opens an OWA window again, the user must logon once more.

This feature **does not** work if the user has configured Internet Explorer to reject cookies.

## Configuring OWA Options

If you've used Outlook for any period of time, you've probably come to love it for its wealth of options and hate it for the confusing way the options are presented in the user interface. OWA exposes quite a few configuration options, as well, but it lays them out much more plainly, in my opinion. Just click the Options icon in the lower-left corner of the OWA window to open a configuration page, as shown in Figure 9.16.

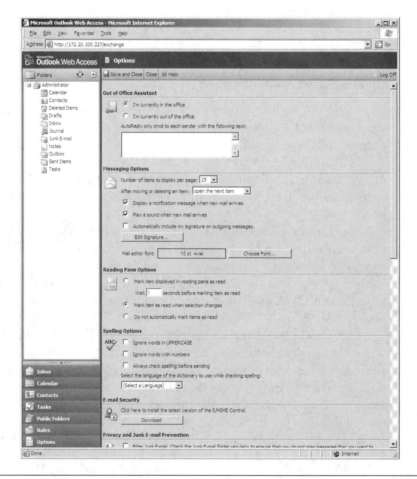

**Figure 9.16**    OWA Options page with a variety of control settings for OWA features.

Most of these options are self-explanatory. Here's a quick list just to give you an idea of the available functionality.

- **Out of Office Assistant.** Sends an autoreply. Encourage your users not to enable this option. Autoreplies encourage spammers.
- **Messaging options.** OWA can display visual and audible alerts when messages arrive and it can sign all outgoing messages. Use these options to set the editor font and to set the number of messages to display.
- **Reading Pane options.** OWA, like regular Outlook, can display a preview pane showing the message contents. Previewing raises security concerns because it can fire off a macro virus or embedded code. This is not as likely to occur in a browser session, but you can disable the feature if it makes you nervous.
- **Spelling options.** This set of options includes the capability to ignore uppercase words, words that contain numbers, and to specify whether or not to always check spelling.
- **E-Mail Security.** This option allows you to enable S/MIME support in OWA.
- **Privacy and Junk E-Mail Prevention.** This set of options allows you to block read receipts and HTML beacons (embedded hyperlinks that point at a sender's Web site). OWA can also take advantage of the Intelligent Mail Filter (IMF) running on an Exchange server.
- **Appearance.** This option allows you to select a color scheme for OWA.
- **Calendar options.** These settings allow you to determine the starting day of the week, 12 or 24 hour time display, and long or short dates.
- **Reminder options.** These settings allow you to use audible alerts for calendar and task items.
- **Contact options.** This setting allows you to check your personal contact list first instead of the GAL.
- **Recover Deleted Items.** This option allows you to recover items purged from the Deleted Items container.

You can also use OWA to recover "hard deletes" from other folders. A "hard delete" occurs when you use Shift+Delete to delete an item. To see the deleted items in a folder other than the Deleted Items folder, open OWA with the following syntax:

```
http://<exchange_server>/exchange/<mailbox_name>/<folder_name>/
➥?cmd=showdeleted
```

For example, to see hard deletes in the inbox of a user named Administrator on a server named W2K3-EX1, use this syntax:

```
http://w2k3-ex1/exchange/administrator/inbox/?cmd=showdeleted
```

## Blocking OWA Options

If you want to give your users a different OWA experience than that described in the previous section, you can disable selected features. Microsoft calls this OWA segmentation. You can control segmentation on a server-by-server basis or for individual users.

Microsoft also provides a Web-based tool for managing OWA options. It is included in the Exchange Server 2003 All-In-One Tools download package available at **`http://snipurl.com/6xmt`**.

### OWA Segmentation by Server

To segment OWA features for all users on a particular server, use this Registry key:

```
Key: HKLM | System | CurrentControlSet | Services |
➥MsExchangeWEB | OWA
Value: DefaultMailboxFolderSet
Data: Mask ID (see table)
```

The Mask ID is a 32-bit binary mask representing the flags that control OWA features. Table 9.1 lists the bit numbers.

**Table 9-1**    OWA Segmentation Bit Numbers

| Feature | 512 | 256 | 128 | 64 | 32 | 16 | 8 | 4 | 2 | 1 |
|---|---|---|---|---|---|---|---|---|---|---|
| Messaging (Inbox, Outbox, Sent Items) | 0 | 0 | 0 | 0 | 0 | 0 | 0 | 0 | 0 | 1 |
| Calendar | 0 | 0 | 0 | 0 | 0 | 0 | 0 | 0 | 1 | 1 |
| Contacts | 0 | 0 | 0 | 0 | 0 | 0 | 0 | 1 | 0 | 1 |
| Tasks | 0 | 0 | 0 | 0 | 0 | 0 | 1 | 0 | 0 | 1 |
| Journal | 0 | 0 | 0 | 0 | 0 | 1 | 0 | 0 | 0 | 1 |
| Notes | 0 | 0 | 0 | 0 | 1 | 0 | 0 | 0 | 0 | 1 |
| Public Folders | 0 | 0 | 0 | 1 | 0 | 0 | 0 | 0 | 0 | 1 |
| Reminders | 0 | 0 | 1 | 0 | 0 | 0 | 0 | 0 | 1 | 1 |
| New Mail | 0 | 1 | 0 | 0 | 0 | 0 | 0 | 0 | 0 | 1 |
| Premium Experience | 1 | 0 | 0 | 0 | 0 | 0 | 0 | 0 | 0 | 1 |
| All | 1 | 1 | 1 | 1 | 1 | 1 | 1 | 1 | 1 | 1 |

To expose a particular set of features, add up the decimal equivalents of the bit flags and then enter that number in the Registry entry.

Here's one example. Let's say you want to display just the Inbox, Outbox, and Sent Items folders with the full Premium experience. Find the selection under **Feature** and then write down the decimal equivalent of the bit setting:

```
Messaging                  1
Premium Experience       512
------------------       ---
Total                    513
```

Launch Regedit and drill down to **HKLM | System | CurrentControlSet | Services | MsExchangeWEB | OWA | DefaultMailboxFolderSet**. Change the DWord Editor to use Decimal rather than Hex and enter **513**. Restart the HTTP service.

If you also wanted to show the Calendar folder and Public Folders with a Premium Experience, you'd add **1 + 2 + 64 + 512** to get **579**. Again, be sure to enter the number using the Decimal setting of the Dword Editor.

## OWA Segmentation by Individual User

Instead of changing the OWA content for all users on a server, you can elect to change the content for specific users. This involves manipulating a bit flag in the user's Active Directory object. The attribute containing the flag is called msExchangeMailboxFolderSet.

Use the chart in Table 9.1 to determine a segmentation setting; then put that value into the msExchangeMailboxFolderSet attribute using the ADSI Editor console, Adsiedit.msc. This utility comes in the Windows Server 2003 Support Tools.

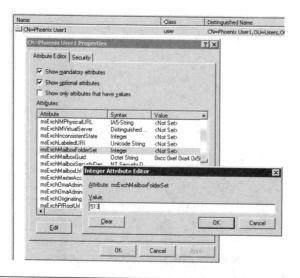

**Figure 9.17** ADSI Editor showing OWA Segmentation entry for msExchangeMailboxFolderSet attribute.

# Configuring OWA to Use SSL

You should always use secure connections when connecting to a public-facing OWA server. This prevents exposing authentication traffic and message content to bad guys watching your Internet traffic.

For Web services such as OWA, the term "secure connection" is virtually synonymous with Secure Socket Layer (SSL). The latest version of SSL, version 3.1, goes by the name Transport Layer Security (TLS). To avoid confusion, I'll use SSL when referring to secure Web connections.

SSL relies on public/private key pairs to produce a session key that the Web server uses to create a series of ciphers for encrypting traffic to and from the Web site. A public/private key pair is the yin and yang of cryptography. Anything encrypted by one key can be decrypted only by the other.

Part of the SSL transaction involves delivering a public key to the Web client. The public key is embedded in a secure data structure called an X.509 certificate, as shown in Figure 9.18.

**Figure 9.18**   Sample X.509 certificate as displayed by Windows certificate viewer. The public key is displayed in clear text, and the thumbprint represents a hash of the certificate encrypted with the private key of issuing authority.

A certificate is issued and digitally signed by a *Certification Authority*. You can either purchase a certificate from a vendor that specializes in certificate management, or you can deploy your own Certification Authority servers in what's called a *Public Key Infrastructure*, or PKI.

Costs for commercial certificates vary widely, from below $100 to over $300 per server with annual subscription fees on top of the initial costs. Rates also vary with encryption level. Take a look at `www.sslreview.com` for comparison information. Examples of certificate vendors include

- **Verisign.** `www.verisign.com`
- **Baltimore.** `www.baltimore.com`
- **Entrust.** `www.entrust.com`

Windows Server 2003 and Windows 2000 include a PKI as part of the operating system. You can deploy as many Certification Authority servers and issue as many certificates as you like at no cost except for the hardware to host the servers. For information on how to deploy a PKI using Windows servers, see my book, *Inside Windows Server 2003*, or take a look at Microsoft's documentation in TechNet.

Your primary concern when you purchase certificates or deploy your own CAs is to make sure that your clients have a copy of the public key certificate for the Root CA in the PKI. Without a Root CA certificate, a client cannot validate the authenticity of public key certificates purportedly issued by that CA or any of its child CAs.

Commercial CA vendors give Microsoft a copy of their Root CA certificates to include on the Windows Setup CD and to put on the Microsoft Update site. In a private PKI, your Enterprise CAs put copies of their public key certificates in Active Directory where the clients can retrieve them and store a copy locally.

The next few topics give you an overview of how a Web server uses SSL and shows you how to obtain a certificate from either a third-party vendor or a Windows PKI. The final section describes how to require SSL for all OWA connections to an OWA server.

## SSL Overview

It's not necessary to understand an SSL transaction in excruciating detail, but it helps considerably to have a good idea of the overall process. Figure 9.19 shows the principal elements of an SSL transaction. The Web server has already obtained an X.509 certificate for its public key from a Certification Authority. The server stores the private key in a secure location on its hard drive.

The process begins when a user launches a browser and points it at a secure Web site on a Web server, such as `https://w2k3-ex1.company.com`.

1. **TCP connection.** The client browser makes a TCP connection to port 443 at the target server, the port owned by HTTP over SSL.
2. **TLS handshake initiated.** Following the initial TCP connection, the browser initiates the SSL transaction by sending a Hello message, the first part of the TLS Handshake protocol.

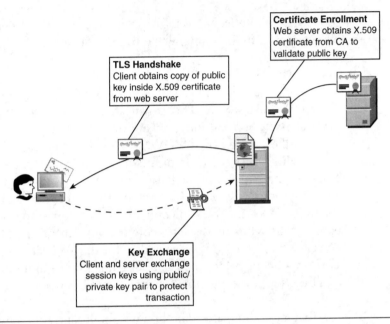

**Certificate Enrollment**
Web server obtains X.509 certificate from CA to validate public key

**TLS Handshake**
Client obtains copy of public key inside X.509 certificate from web server

**Key Exchange**
Client and server exchange session keys using public/private key pair to protect transaction

**Figure 9.19** Diagram of typical SSL authentication. The Web server obtains its X.509 certificate prior to the transaction.

3. **TLS handshake completed.** The server responds with its own Hello message that includes a copy of the server's public key certificate obtained from the CA. The security subsystem at the desktop validates the certificate by checking its local certificate store for the root CA certificate

4. **Key exchange.** The browser uses the public key in the certificate to initiate a transaction with the Web server to obtain a session key. Only the Web server has the private key associated with the public key. This assures the privacy of the key exchange.

5. **Secure data transfer.** Once the Web server and client have agreed on a session key, they begin exchanging messages encrypted with ciphers derived from the session key. Each message uses a different cipher so an attacker cannot perform a cryptanalytic attack on the data stream.

If process descriptions like this give you a piercing headache, here are a few high points to remember while you fumble for the aspirin:

- HTTP over SSL uses TCP port 443.
- You must obtain an X.509 certificate for any Exchange server that hosts OWA using SSL. This certificate can come from a third-party Certification Authority or your own Windows CA server.
- The certificate used by the OWA server must be trusted by the client. This "trust" consists of a copy of the root CA certificate stored in the Registry of the local client.
- The user must use `https://` rather than `http://` to make a secure connection. You can configure a Web server to reject any connections other than secure connections. In the IIS Manager console, open the properties window for the Web site, select the Directory Security tab, click Edit under Secure Communications, and then select the Require Secure Channel (SSL) option.

The next two sections describe how to obtain an X.509 certificate either from a commercial vendor or from a Windows PKI. You'll need to do only one of the processes. They contain similar steps.

One of the steps in each process asks you to enter a common name for the Web server. The format you use must match the format your users enter in the browser to connect to the OWA server. For example, if you enter a common name of w2k3-ex1.company.com, and the user connects by entering the name w2k3-ex1, the SSL connection succeeds but the user gets a warning window stating "The Name on the Security Certificate Is Invalid or Does Not Match the Site Name." This does not prevent access. It merely warns (and confuses) the user.

The best way to avoid this error is to give your users a URL shortcut to the Exchange server that you've configured with the correct name, or put a link from an unsecured Web site that has the correct URL. You could also include a Hosts entry with the correct name format if you need to resolve a problem quickly.

No, you can't assign multiple certificates to the server, one for each name format. Sorry.

## Obtaining a Commercial Certificate

To obtain a third-party certificate, go to the vendor's Web site and sign up for the service. You pay a few hundred dollars, and as soon as your credit card gets debited, the Web site delivers a certificate to your browser. Save the certificate and install it into your Web server and you're done. The following steps show an example using a 30-day sample certificate obtained from Thawte, a division of Verisign.

If you're lucky, you'll have a colleague experienced with managing a Web server who is willing to help you with this work. If not, it really doesn't take much to get the certificate. Once you do it in the lab, it becomes second nature in production. The major steps are

- Download a copy of the Commercial Root CA Certificate.
- Trust the Commercial Root CA.
- Generate a certificate request at the OWA server.
- Transfer the certificate request to the vendor and get the certificate.
- Install the certificate in IIS.

### Download Copy of Commercial Root CA Certificate

Your first step is to download a copy of the vendor's Root CA certificate. This might not be necessary in all cases. Many commercial CAs already have a copy of their Root CA certificate in Windows.

The vendor's Web site will have a pointer to a copy of the Root CA certificate. It comes in the form of a file with a CER extension. Save this file to a convenient location such as your desktop and then double-click the file icon. This opens the Windows certificate viewer, which shows you the contents of the certificate. Figure 9.20 shows an example.

**Figure 9.20** General information on test Root CA certificate obtained from the Thawte. The X on the certificate icon indicates that the client has not yet installed the certificate.

### Trust the Commercial Root CA

Trusting a CA essentially consists of putting a copy of the CA's certificate into the Trusted Certification Authority key in the local Registry. Do this as follows:

1. Click the **Install Certificate** button. This starts the Certificate Import Wizard.
2. Click **Next** to open the Certificate Store window, as shown in Figure 9.21.
3. Leave the radio button selected that reads **Automatically Select the Certificate Store Based on the Type of Certificate**. The wizard recognizes root certificates and will install it into the Trusted Certification Authority portion of the Registry.
4. Click **Next**. This opens a summary window.
5. Click **Finish**. A Security Warning window opens telling you that the certificate cannot be verified to come from the listed root CA (shown in Figure 9.22). If this were a production root certificate, you would compare the thumbprint in the certificate to the list of thumbprints on the vendor's Web site.

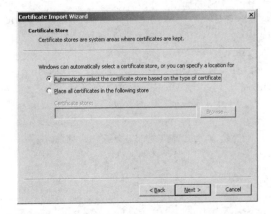

**Figure 9.21** Certificate Import Wizard showing the Certificate Store window where you can elect to let the wizard select the local repository or select it manually.

**Figure 9.22** Warning that Root CA certificate cannot be verified and should be manually verified using thumbprint.

6. Click **Yes** to install the certificate. The wizard responds with a Success window.

### Generate Certificate Request at OWA Server

Return to the vendor's Web site and navigate to the page that contains a certificate request form.

1. Launch the IIS Manager console. This is one of the few times that you'll use this console to change Web service settings on an Exchange server.
2. Drill down to the **Default Web Site** icon and open the Properties window for the Default Web Site.
3. Select the **Directory Security** tab, as shown in Figure 9.23.

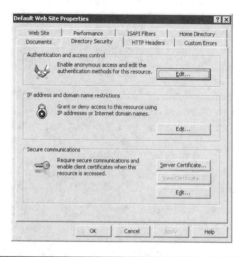

**Figure 9.23** Default Web Site Properties window with Server Certificate button for installing an X.509 certificate.

4. Click **Server Certificate**. This starts the Web Server Certificate wizard.
5. Click **Next**. The Server Certificate window opens, as shown in Figure 9.24. Leave the **Create a New Certificate** radio button selected.
6. Click **Next**. The Delayed or Immediate Request window opens as shown in Figure 9.25. Leave the **Prepare the Request Now, but Send It Later** radio button selected.

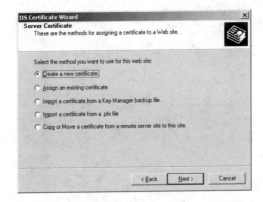

**Figure 9.24**    Server Certificate window with selection options for creating a new certificate or importing or copying an existing certificate.

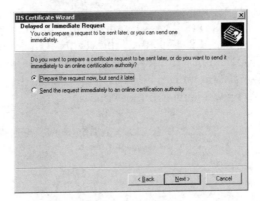

**Figure 9.25**    Delayed or Immediate Request window showing option to prepare a certificate request that can be submitted separately.

7. Click Next. The Name and Security Settings window opens (Figure 9.26). Change the Bit Length entry to 2048. This assures that you have sufficient strength in the SSL Session key to withstand all known cryptanalytic attacks.

**Figure 9.26**    Name and Security Settings window with field for naming the certificate and selecting a bit length.

> 8. Click **Next**. The Organization Information window opens (Figure 9.27). Enter the Fully Qualified Domain Name (FQDN) of your organization and a name for the Organization Unit. This information is placed into the certificate so users who get a copy can find you.

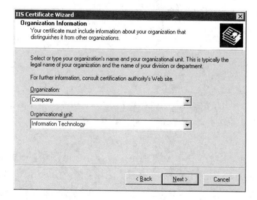

**Figure 9.27**    Organization Information window with options for entering the organization name and local business unit name.

> 9. Click **Next**. The window titled Your Site's Common Name opens, as shown in Figure 9.28. Enter the FQDN of your Exchange server. A browser uses this name to validate the Web

server's name in an SSL transaction, so if the user enters the flat name and you register the FQDN, the user gets an error but can still connect to the Web service. If you think your users will enter a flat name more often, register the flat name to avoid confusing them, or train them to do otherwise.

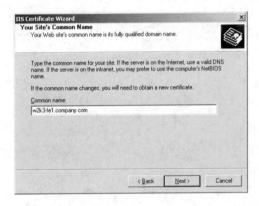

**Figure 9.28**    Your Site's Common Name window with field for entering name of Web server. Name format must match the name format the user enters in the Web browser to avoid caution window.

10. Click **Next**. The Geographical Information window opens, as shown in Figure 9.29. Enter your locality information. This gets included in the certificate, so be accurate with the spelling.

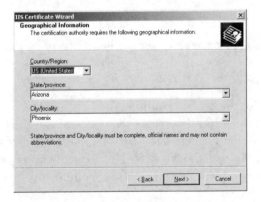

**Figure 9.29**    Geographical Information window with fields for entering location information that will be included in the certificate.

11. Click **Next**. The Certificate Request File Name window opens, as shown in Figure 9.30. Place the file in a convenient location. Don't put it in a public place, though, because somebody could use it to obtain a certificate while you're getting ready to do the same.

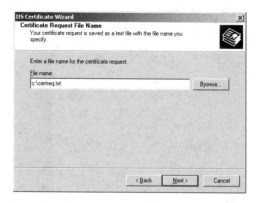

**Figure 9.30** Certificate Request File Name window with field for specifying path and name for certificate request.

12. Click **Next**. A Request File Summary window opens.
13. Click **Next**.
14. Click **Finish** to complete the first stage of the certificate request.

### Transfer Certificate Request to Vendor and Get Certificate

1. Use Notepad to open the certificate request. Figure 9.31 shows an example. Use caution not to change any of the contents.
2. Highlight and copy the contents of the **certreq.txt** file to the clipboard. Include the BEGIN and END lines.
3. At the vendor's Web site, look for the empty field in the certificate request page. Paste the contents of the clipboard into this field.
4. When the vendor's server finishes processing the certificate request, the Web site will present the contents of an X.509 certificate in text form. Figure 9.32 shows an example.

**Figure 9.31**    Notepad showing content of certificate request. Inside this request is the public key from the Web server.

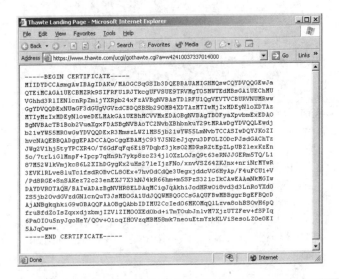

**Figure 9.32**    Notepad showing content of certificate issued by the Certification Authority. The Windows certificate viewer interprets this information to display a certificate.

5. Copy the contents of the certificate to the clipboard.
6. Open an empty instance of Notepad and paste the clipboard into the window. Save this file with a CER extension in a convenient location.

### Install Certificate in IIS

1. In the IIS Manager console, open the Properties window for the Default Web Site icon and select the **Directory Security** tab.
2. Click **Server Certificate**. This starts the Web Server Certificate Wizard.
3. Click **Next**. This time the Pending Certificate Request window opens, as shown in Figure 9.33. Leave the **Process the Pending Request and Install the Certificate** radio button selected.

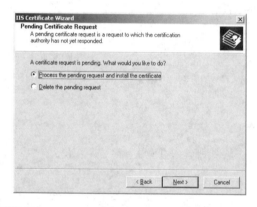

**Figure 9.33** Pending Certificate Request window with option to process a pending request selected.

4. Click **Next**. The Process a Pending Request window opens, as shown in Figure 9.34. Browse to the location of the file containing the certificate you obtained from the vendor's Web site.
5. Click **Next**. The SSL Port window opens, as shown in Figure 9.35. Leave the port setting at 443, the default port for HTTP over SSL.

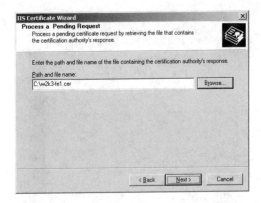

**Figure 9.34**    Process a Pending Request window with field for entering certificate path and name.

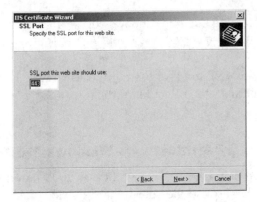

**Figure 9.35**    SSL Port window showing standard HTTP over SSL port number 443.

6. Click **Next**. A Certificate Summary window opens.
7. Click **Next**.
8 Click **Finish** to install the certificate and return to the **Directory Security** tab.
9. Click **View Certificate** to see the contents of the certificate in the Windows certificate viewer. Figure 9.36 shows an example.

**Figure 9.36**    Certificate as seen by Windows certificate viewer. Certificate shows as valid because client has a copy of the Root CA certificate.

> 10. Click **OK** to close the certificate viewer. Leave the **Directory Security** tab selected for the next steps.

## Obtaining a Certificate via Windows PKI

If you have deployed a Windows Server 2003-based PKI, you'll have at least one Enterprise Certification Authority (CA). An IIS server can obtain its certificate directly from the Enterprise CA. This is true for IIS5 and II6. To obtain the certificate, proceed as follows:

> 1. In the IIS console, open the Properties window for the Default Web Site.
> 2. Select the **Directory Security** tab (Figure 9.37).
> 3. Click **Server Certificate**. This opens the IIS Certificate Wizard.
> 4. Click **Next**. The Server Certificate window opens (Figure 9.38).

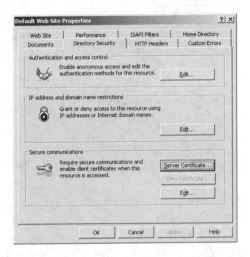

**Figure 9.37**    Default Web Site Properties window showing Server Certificate button for installing an X.509 certificate.

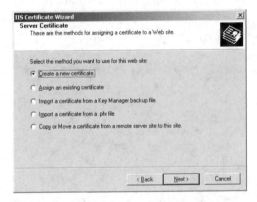

**Figure 9.38**    Server Certificate window with selection options for creating a new certificate or importing or copying an existing certificate.

5. Select the **Create a New Certificate** radio button.
6. Click **Next**. The Delayed Or Immediate Request window opens.
7. Select the **Send Request Immediately to an Online Certification Authority** radio button.
8. Click **Next**. The Name and Security Settings window opens (Figure 9.39). Select a **Bit Length** of 2048. Recent advances in cryptology have made a 1024-bit key potentially vulnerable to cryptanalytic attack. Don't use excessively long keys, though, because this slows down processing.

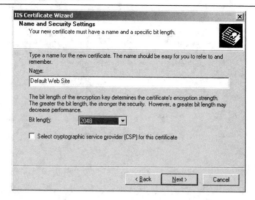

**Figure 9.39** Name and Security Settings window with field for naming the certificate and selecting a bit length.

9. Click **Next**. The Organization Information window opens (Figure 9.40). Enter the name of the Exchange organization and the name of the department that owns the Exchange server. The exact names do not matter. This information is stored in the certificate, so make sure it makes sense to a user viewing the certificate contents.

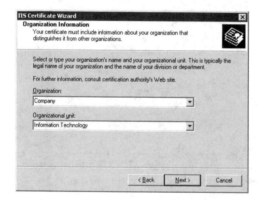

**Figure 9.40** Organization Information window with options for entering the organization name and local business unit name.

10. Click **Next**. The Your Site's Common Name window opens (Figure 9.41). Enter the FQDN of the Exchange server.

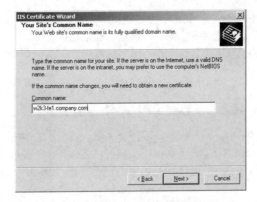

**Figure 9.41**    Your Site's Common Name window with field for entering name of Web server. Name format must match the name format user enters in Web browser to avoid caution window.

> 11. Click **Next**. The Geographical Information window opens (Figure 9.42). Enter the full, unabbreviated name of your state and city.

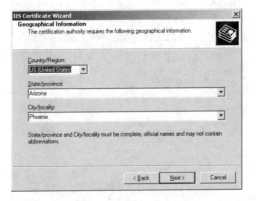

**Figure 9.42**    Geographical Information window with fields for entering location information that will be included in certificate.

> 12. Click **Next**. The SSL Port window opens. Leave the entry at the default port number of 443.
> 13. Click **Next**. The Choose a Certification Authority window opens. If you have more than one issuing CA, select it from the dropdown list. Otherwise, leave the entry at the default.

**14.** Click **Next**. This opens a summary window.
**15.** Click **Next** to obtain the certificate.
**16.** Click **Finish** to close the wizard.

### Require SSL for Default Web Server

Now that you've enabled SSL for the Web services on the Exchange server, require that all Web connections to the server use SSL. Otherwise, users might inadvertently enter Basic credentials in a non-secure window and expose their passwords.

You can require SSL for individual virtual folders, but the simplest way to secure the entire server is to require SSL for the Default Web Site. This is one of the few times you will use the IIS Manager console to make changes on an Exchange server.

**1.** Open the Properties window for the default Web server.
**2.** Select the **Directory Security** tab.
**3.** In the **Secure Communications** field, click **Edit**. This opens the Secure Communications window (Figure 9.43).

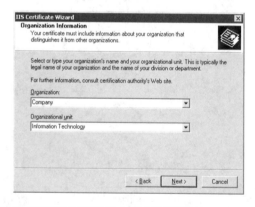

**Figure 9.43**   Secure Communications window for the Default Web Site showing the option to require SSL for all connections and to use 128-bit encryption on every connection.

**4.** Check the **Require Secure Channel (SSL)** option and the **Require 128-bit Encryption** option.
**5.** Click **OK** to save the change. An Inheritance Overrides window opens (Figure 9.44) listing the child nodes in the Web server.

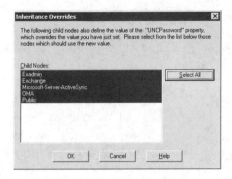

**Figure 9.44**    Inheritance Override window that allows you to apply the SSL connection requirement to all virtual folders in the Default Web Site.

6. Click **Select All** and then click **OK** to save the changes.

With this configuration in place, attempt to connect using standard HTTP to the Exchange server. Verify that this results in a 403.4 error (Figure 9.45) with a message that SSL is required.

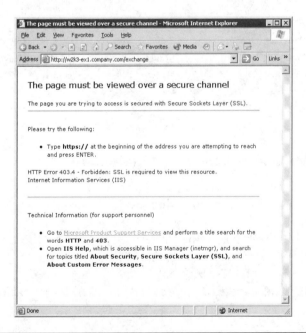

**Figure 9.45**    Test of a standard connection to the newly secured Web site. A 403.4 page indicates that the Web server rejects standard HTTP connections, which is what you want to see.

## Verify Secure Connection

At this point, any HTTP connection to this Exchange server must use SSL. Verify this as follows:

1. Launch a browser and point it at the FQDN of the Exchange server using a URL that includes https rather than http; for example, `https://w3k3-ex1.company.com`. This brings up an Under Construction window. In the Internet Explorer status bar at the bottom of the window, you'll see a little closed padlock. This indicates that you've made secure connection.
2. Enter the address again and leave out the "s" in https to verify that you get a 403.4 error stating that the page must be viewed over a secure channel.
3. If you have recipient mailboxes on this server, connect to one of those mailboxes using explicit authentication by entering an URL that includes the mailbox name; for example, `https://w2k3-ex1.company.com/exchange/phoenixuser77`. This should open the user's mailbox once you enter the user's credentials.

> You can't connect to a mailbox on another server unless the second server also has a certificate. This is because OWA will redirect you to the home server through the secure connection.

## Enable Forms-Based Authentication

Once you have assigned a certificate to the Web site, you can configure it to use forms-based authentication as follows.

1. In ESM, open the Properties window for the Exchange Virtual Server under **Protocols | HTTP**.
2. Select the **Settings** tab.
3. Check the **Enable Forms-Based Authentication** option.

4. Enable compression only if bandwidth is at a premium. This option can have a performance impact due to increased load on the server.

5. Click **OK** to save the change.

At this point, check the configuration by connecting to the OWA server using the following syntax: `https://server_name/exchange`. The logon form page appears. The padlock in the status bar at the bottom of the browser (Figure 9.46) should be closed, indicating that the connection uses SSL.

**Figure 9.46**    SSL connection indicator in status bar of Internet Explorer. Double-click this icon to view Web server's X.509 certificate.

## OWA Password Changes

When users spend a long time on the road away from the office, their passwords get stale. If your organization enforces a password expiration interval, then users need a way to reset their passwords to maintain access to their e-mail via OWA. If you do not provide VPN access to your network, it helps to have an option within OWA for a user to reset a password.

Both IIS 5.0 and 6.0 have password-reset options, but they are not enabled by default. The IIS 5.0 password-reset option uses HTR files, which have been the focus of several infamous exploits over the years. The most current Windows 2000 patches have resolved these issues. The IIS 6.0 password-reset option uses ASP.NET code with no documented vulnerabilities. This section shows you how to enable the OWA password-reset option using IIS 6.0.

Using the Web for password resets requires the use of SSL to protect the transaction from prying eyes. Enable SSL as described previously in this chapter. The remaining steps for installing and configuring the Web-based password-reset function in OWA are described as follows. The major steps are

- Create a Password Reset Virtual folder. This folder holds the ASP files that handle the password reset.
- Modify the Registry to Expose the Password Change option. This step will display the option in OWA.

Once you've enabled the Web-based password change option in OWA, you'll need to test it and see how it works if the user's password has already expired. This will help you train your users in performing the steps.

## Create a Password Reset Virtual Folder

You do not need to install additional Windows components to get the password reset files. A standard installation of IIS 6.0 Web services includes the files. Create a virtual folder for the files as follows:

1. Launch the IIS Manager console.
2. Drill down to the **Default Web Site** icon.
3. Right-click the **Default Web Site** icon and select **New | Virtual Directory** from the flyout menu. This opens the Virtual Directory Creation wizard.
4. Click **Next** to open the Virtual Directory Alias window, shown in Figure 9.47.

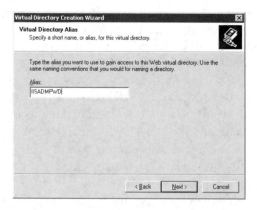

**Figure 9.47** Virtual Directory Alias window showing field for entering the name of the new virtual directory, IISADMPWD.

5. In the **Alias** field, enter **IISADMPWD**. The entry is not case sensitive.

6. Click **Next**. The Web Site Content Directory window opens. Browse for the path to the Iisadmpwd folder, which is located in **C:\Windows\System32\Inetsrv\Iisadmpwd**.

7. Click **Next**. The Virtual Directory Access Permissions window opens (Figure 9.48). By default, the **Read** and **Run Scripts** options are selected.

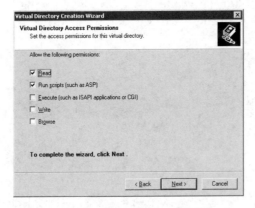

**Figure 9.48**   Virtual Directory Access Permissions window showing options to permit only Read and Run Scripts access to the new virtual folder.

8. Click **Next** to save the configuration and close the wizard.

## Modify the Registry to Expose Password Change Option

OWA does not display a password-reset option by default. This requires a Registry change on the Exchange server as follows:

```
Key: HKLM | System | CurrentControlSet | Services |
➥MSExchangeWeb
Value: DisablePassword
Data: 0 (REG_DWORD)
```

The value will be presented by default with a Data entry of 1 to hide the option. You do **not** need to restart IIS or Exchange to enable the change.

## Changing Passwords in OWA

Now you need to test the password change feature in OWA. Get familiar with this functionality so you can train your users and Help Desk personnel.

1. Start by launching OWA in a browser. You should see a **Password** section in the **Options** list. This section contains a **Change Password** button. Figure 9.49 shows the location. You do not need to make the OWA connection using SSL. As soon as you click **Change Password**, the connection shifts to using HTTPS.

**Figure 9.49**   Outlook Web Access Options window showing Change Password button after making Registry change.

2. Click the **Change Password** button. This opens a new browser window titled Internet Service Manager, as shown in Figure 9.50. (This page is also customizable.)
3. Enter your current credentials and new password.
4. Click **OK** to save the new password. A Success window opens to verify the change.

**Figure 9.50** Internet Services Manager window showing option to change password in OWA.

The new password is passed to the Exchange server over the SSL connection, which keeps it from being seen. The Exchange server handles secure communication with a domain controller to actually change the password.

## Handling Password Expirations in OWA

It sometimes happens that a user's password expires between the time the user was last on the network and the time the user attempted to access a mailbox via OWA. This presents a problem to an OWA user because the password reset option resides in the OWA pages, which cannot be accessed unless you log on. When a user enters the 14-day notification period prior to password expiration, OWA begins counting down the days, but users often ignore this until it's too late.

There is no workaround for this Catch 22 logon problem. Inform your OWA users that they need to refresh their passwords regularly to avoid losing access to their e-mail.

If a user does lose OWA access due to an expired password, the user can call the Help Desk to reset the password. Train your Help Desk technicians to reset the password, but not to check the User Must Change Password at Next Logon option in the password reset window. This prevents access to OWA.

Have the Help Desk technician instruct users to change their password as soon as the OWA window opens. One way to encourage this behavior is to give the user a temporary password that is so excruciatingly long and complex that they would never want to retain it.

## Looking Forward

That wraps up the discussion of browser-based access to mailboxes using OWA. Many organizations, once they see the features and performance in Exchange 2003 OWA, start to think seriously about deploying it as their primary client messaging platform. Frankly, I still prefer the Outlook client because of its snappiness, but I would not hesitate to use OWA rather than a POP3 or IMAP4 client, given the choice, if for nothing else than to get the calendar features. I want to see all the appointments I'm missing.

In the next chapter, you'll see how to provide content to your users in a common forum called public folders.

# CHAPTER 10

# Managing Public Folders

In this chapter, you're going to see how to create and manage public folders. This isn't as easy as it sounds. The problem with public folders is that they're...well...public. When you think about it, when you put the word "public" in front of something, it immediately starts collecting layers of grime and streaks of spray paint and piles of rubbish.

Frankly, when it comes to managing public folders, the job of being an Exchange administrator becomes part technologist and part janitor. You can minimize the hours you'll spend with a scrub brush in your hand by keeping tight control over your public folders, letting people add content to them only when you either absolutely trust them or when you have influence over the person who signs their paycheck.

This chapter will show you how to create and manage public folder structures, content, and permissions in ways that discourage untidy behavior on the part of the users. You'll also see how to replicate public folders in Native and Mixed mode organizations and how to recognize and troubleshoot permission replication problems with legacy Exchange servers.

Don't skip this chapter, even if you don't plan on deploying public-folders. Exchange maintains a wide variety of folders that, although they might not be available to public view, play a critical role in the operation of popular features such as shared calendars and offline address books. You don't want to have your first experience with public folders be a troubleshooting session following a loss of free/busy information in everyone's appointment lists.

## Public Folder Architecture

Like a mailbox store, a public folder store consists of a pair of primary data files: an EDB file containing a set of pages sorted in a b+ tree and an STM file containing streaming files from Internet clients. The default file location is Exchsrvr\MDBData, as shown in Figure 10.1. You can change this location at any time after installing Exchange.

Each Exchange server hosts at least one public folder store, called the *Default Public Folder Store*. This is often called the MAPI store because Outlook clients can view the contents.

Exchange 2003 Enterprise Edition can host additional public folder stores, called *general purpose* public folder stores. General purpose stores cannot be read by MAPI clients, so Outlook cannot display their contents. Also, MAPI will only use the default public folder tree. You cannot point it at another tree.

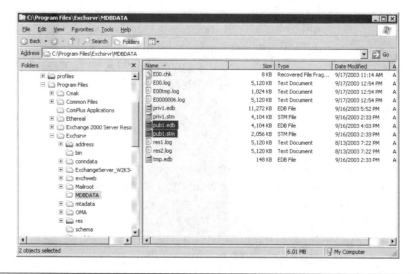

**Figure 10.1** Default location of public folder database files. Like a mailbox store, the public folder store consists of an EDB and an STM file.

## Hierarchies and Content

The internal structure of a public folder store has two major components:

- **Public Folder Hierarchy (PFH).** The folder structure you see in the left pane of the Outlook window under Folder List acts as an index to the content of the public folder store. This folder list is called the Public Folder Hierarchy, often abbreviated as PFH. Every Exchange server in the organization gets a copy of the Public Folder Hierarchy.

■ **Public folder content.** The items you see in the middle pane of the Outlook window come from the public folder store of the Exchange server that hosts the folder's content. You can configure multiple servers to host the content of a given public folder, and they replicate changes among each other.

You'll see references in Microsoft documentation to the Top Level Hierarchy and to the Public Folder Tree. These terms mean the same thing as Public Folder Hierarchy and can be used interchangeably.

You can view public folders in Outlook by clicking the Folder List icon in the lower-left corner and then expanding the tree. Figure 10.2 shows a sample set of public folders in Outlook 2003.

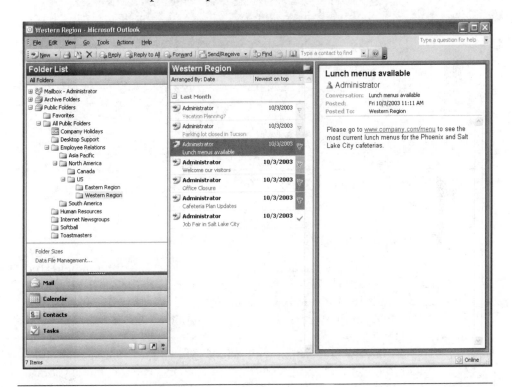

**Figure 10.2** Outlook 2003 view of public folders.

The left pane of the Outlook window, under Folder List, shows the Public Folder Hierarchy. The middle pane of the Outlook window shows the content for a selected folder in the hierarchy. If you have sufficient permissions, you can create and delete folders in the hierarchy and add and remove content in each folder.

You can also view and modify the content of public folders in Exchange System Manager (ESM). ESM connects to the public folder using WebDAV, the same connection made by Outlook Web Access (OWA), so you see the same display in ESM that you see in OWA. Figure 10.3 shows an example.

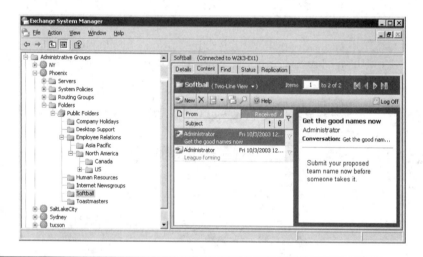

**Figure 10.3** ESM showing public folder content.

## System Folders

There are actually two public folder hierarchies. One of them holds the public folders you see in Outlook. This is called the IPM hierarchy. (IPM stands for Inter-Personal Messaging.) The other hierarchy holds system folders that are not visible in Outlook. This is the non-IPM hierarchy.

You can view the system folders in ESM by right-clicking the Public Folders icon and selecting View System Folders. The result looks something like the example in Figure 10.4.

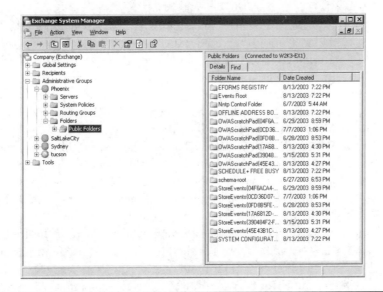

**Figure 10.4** System folder view of public folders in ESM.

Here is the function of each type of system folder:

- **EForms Registry.** This is where organizational forms created by Outlook admins reside. By publishing these custom organizational forms in a public folder, Outlook users can select the forms from the Organizational Forms option and use them when creating items such as custom tasks, postings, or messages.
- **Events Root.** This folder holds configuration information for event sinks installed by Exchange 5.x compatible applications. An event sink is a piece of code that waits for a particular type of message to arrive and then performs an action based on the content of the message or its headers. Exchange 2003 also uses event sinks, but it manages them from Active Directory and does not need a public folder.
- **NNTP Control.** This folder contains NNTP control messages.
- **Offline Address Book.** This folder contains the OAB generated by the Offline Address List in ESM. Exchange 2003 supports OAB version 2 for legacy support and Unicode OAB version 3 for Outlook 2003.

- **OWAScratchPad.** This folder contains public folder attachments added from OWA. Each attachment gets a system folder with a unique GUID. System folders are limited to 1024KB, so if you try to attach a larger file, you'll get an error saying that the maximum size has been exceeded, even if quotas have not been defined for the store. If you want to change the OWAScratchpad value, see Microsoft Knowledge-Base article 304307.
- **Schedule+ Free Busy.** This crucial system folder holds the calendar information published by Outlook so that users can see each other's calendar appointments. Each recipient who has published free/busy information will have an item in the Schedule+ Free Busy folder. If a client cannot access this folder, or one or more recipients have information missing from the folder, then the recipients show a hashed bar for free-busy information when scheduling an appointment.
- **Schema-Root**. This folder contains schema information and registrations from various Exchange applications and third-party add-ons.
- **StoreEvents**. This folder contains event sink registrations.
- **System Configuration**. This folder contains a set of items that lists the various Exchange servers in the organization.

The content of several of these folders gets replicated to every Exchange server. When you add a new Exchange server to the organization, Exchange adds the server to the replica list.

## Exchange Explorer

The Exchange Software Developer's Kit (SDK) has a utility called Exchange Explorer that shows details of the content of the Public Folder Hierarchy and the items in each public folder. Figure 10.5 shows an example listing of a public folder with some test content.

This type of information might not be terribly useful for troubleshooting, but you can use it to gain an insight into the way Exchange stores and modifies public folders, which helps hone your diagnostic skills and gives you something to do on a Friday afternoon.

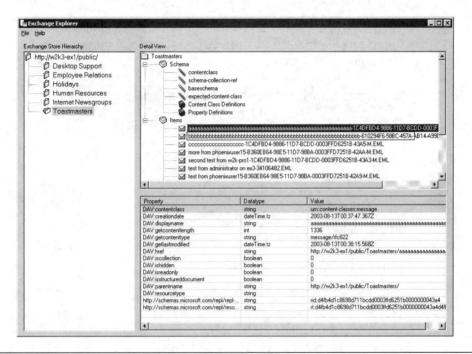

**Figure 10.5** Exchange Explorer showing details of public folder content.

# Public Folder Hierarchy

Exchange stores the Public Folder Hierarchy inside the public folder store itself. Every Exchange server in the organization gets a copy. You can view the Public Folder Hierarchy stored in a particular server using ESM, as shown in Figure 10.6.

From the point of view of Active Directory, the default Public Folder Hierarchy resides in the first Administrative Group you created in the organization. If you migrated from legacy Exchange, this would be the Administrative Group corresponding to the site where you installed the first Exchange 2003 server.

ESM displays the Public Folder Hierarchy stored on a selected Exchange server. The right pane of the console (next to the words Public Folders above the tabbed display) show you which Exchange server you're using to view the hierarchy. You can select another server by right-clicking the Public Folders icon and selecting Connect To from the flyout menu.

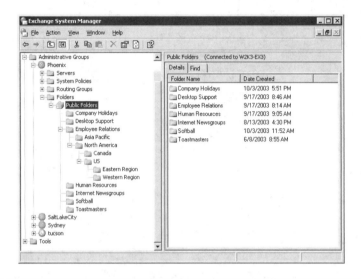

**Figure 10.6** Public Folder Hierarchy displayed in Folders | Public folders under the first Administrative Group created in the organization.

## Public Folder Hierarchy Replication

When a user creates a new public folder, Outlook writes the change to the Public Folder Hierarchy replica at the user's home Exchange server. This server then packages the change into an e-mail message and sends the message to the other Exchange servers in the organization. When an Exchange server receives a Public Folder Hierarchy update message, it extracts the content and updates its local replica.

Because Public Folder Hierarchy replication uses e-mail messages, if you have a problem with connectors between Routing Groups, you might find that some users don't see updates to the hierarchy. If you get reports that users aren't getting a full list of public folders in Outlook, check Queue Viewer in ESM for clogged queues and check the Status window under Tools | Monitoring and Status to make sure the bridge-heads are up and functioning.

An Exchange server replicates changes to its copy of the Public Folder Hierarchy within five minutes after making the change.

## Public Folder Hierarchy and Stores

Each folder in the Public Folder Hierarchy contains a pointer that identifies the location of the folder's contents in the public folder store. Therefore, a Public Folder Hierarchy must be associated with a public folder store. You can see this link in the properties of a particular store, as shown in Figure 10.7. For this reason, each new server you create in the organization must have a default public folder store.

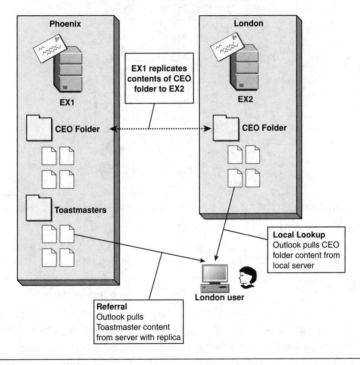

**Figure 10.7**  Each Public Folder Hierarchy is linked to a public folder store.

# Creating Top-Level Folders

The folders at the top of the Public Folder Hierarchy are called top-level folders. By default, Exchange 2003 allows only Exchange Administrators and Exchange Full Administrators to create top-level folders. (This is a change from Exchange 2000, where anyone could create top-level folders.) You can add other groups or administrators to the permission list.

To see the Access Control List (ACL) for the Public Folder Hierarchy in ESM, right-click the Public Folders folder and select the Security tab. This opens the standard Windows ACL Editor. Figure 10.8 shows an example.

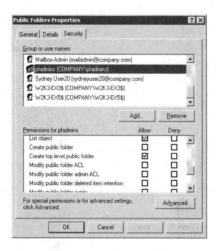

**Figure 10.8** Public Folder Hierarchy permissions displayed as standard Windows ACL in ESM.

To add a group to the list, click Add, select the group from the object picker, and assign Create Top Level Folder permissions.

Work closely with your colleagues and representatives of the user community to decide on the number and names of the top-level folders. Don't create more than you need, but don't scrimp, either. Only changes replicate, so you won't create excessive network traffic by maintaining a large Public Folder Hierarchy. This works something like Active Directory, where only the changed objects are replicated, not the entire structure of the directory.

## Creating Subordinate Public Folders

If you highlight the Everyone group in the ACL Editor, you'll see that the default security settings do not permit members of the Everyone group to create top-level folders, but they can create public folders underneath the top-level folders. The two permissions are called Create Public Folder and Create Named Properties in the Information Store.

These permissions start at the Organization container and flow down to the Public Folder container.

The ability to create public folders on a whim represents a significant responsibility, more responsibility than some users can handle. ("What do you mean, I shouldn't create a folder called Used Car For Sale in West Parking Lot.") Although the external ACLs in the organization permit creating public folders, Exchange automatically restricts this ability with the MAPI permissions assigned to a folder.

> Folders in the Exchange store use Windows object security with ACLs, but public folders use MAPI permission lists. Exchange must translate MAPI permissions and ACLs. This is probably the most confusing part of managing public folders in Exchange, and it can cause you a lot of grief if the translation doesn't work correctly. This topic is covered in much greater detail later in the chapter.

A user must have Author permission on a public folder to create additional child folders. As an administrator with the Exchange Administrator role, you can grant a user Author permission using either Outlook or ESM. To use ESM, open the Properties window for the public folder, select the Permissions tab, and then click Client Permissions. This opens a Client Permission window (Figure 10.9) where you can add recipients and groups (distribution lists) from the GAL and grant them permission to perform the functions displayed in the lower half of the window.

**Figure 10.9** MAPI permissions (aka Client Permissions) assigned to public folder.

The Default permission applies to any authenticated user. Anonymous applies to OWA users who have not authenticated. The other entries in the example were added after the folder was created.

Don't give Owner permission to users unless you are willing to let them create new subfolders. It's best to include a little training as part of bestowing this honor, and don't forget to monitor the content of their folders every once in awhile just in case they need refresher training. And absolutely don't give the Default user any higher role than Author. You could end up with a real mess very quickly.

## General Purpose Public Folder Trees

Outlook can display only the contents of Default Public Folder Tree, also called the MAPI public folder tree. Exchange 2003 Enterprise Edition has the capability of hosting additional public folder trees. Microsoft calls these general purpose trees. A better name would be "No Particular Purpose" trees. (You can pretty much guess that a feature doesn't get used very much if a search in Google comes up with only Microsoft sites and certification references.)

Future versions of Microsoft server products might take advantage of the storage offered by general purpose trees. For now, it's enough to know they exist and how to create one for testing.

### Storage for General Purpose Trees

Recall that a Public Folder Hierarchy is really nothing more than an index of the contents of a public folder store. When you create a general purpose public folder tree, you cannot put content in the folders until you link the tree to a public folder store. When you create a new public folder store, you'll be prompted to link the store to a general purpose public folder tree. Figure 10.10 shows an example.

A storage group can hold only five stores, either mailbox stores or public folder stores. Don't create a public folder store if you don't need it or won't use it. Leave the slot available for a mailbox store.

**Figure 10.10** General purpose public folder trees can be linked to a public folder store. MAPI clients cannot view these trees.

### *Referral Limitations of General Purpose Public Folders*

You can replicate the contents of a general purpose public folder tree and the folders in the tree to multiple Exchange servers, but Exchange does not perform referrals. In other words, a server must contain a replica of the contents of a folder in a general purpose tree before it can expose the contents to a query.

## Public Folder Replication

Public folder contents do not replicate between Exchange servers by default. The initial folder contents reside in the public folder store of the Exchange server where Outlook or ESM was pointed when creating the folder. You can designate additional servers to host the folder's contents.

For example, refer to Figure 10.11. Let's say the leader of the Toast-masters club in Phoenix wants a public folder so the club members can post information about meetings and hints for public speaking and so forth. Users do not have permission to create new top-level folders, so she contacts you to create the folder. You use ESM to create the folder on the Exchange server in Phoenix.

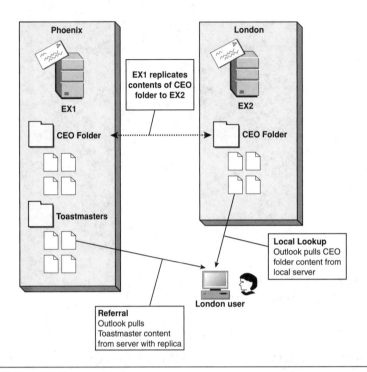

**Figure 10.11** Clients access public folder content either from the user's home server or from the closest server with replica of folder content.

A user homed to a server in London who wants to see posts in the Toastmasters public folder would click the folder in Outlook. The Outlook client sends a MAPI lookup request to the London user's home server, but that server does not have a replica of the contents. The London server returns a referral naming the Exchange server in Phoenix as a replica holder. Outlook follows up on the referral by sending a MAPI lookup request to the Phoenix server.

This works fine for a public folder where the majority of the users reside in the same location as the Exchange server. But what if the CEO wants a public folder to hold announcements that affect all employees? You could place the public folder on an Exchange server in headquarters, but this would generate quite a bit of network traffic as users from all the outlying offices pounce on the headquarters server to see if the CEO has posted anything interesting.

It makes more sense to replicate a copy of the CEO's folder to a local Exchange server in each office. The replication necessary to keep the content refreshed consumes very little bandwidth in relation to all the read requests coming in from across the globe.

In addition to saving bandwidth, maintaining multiple copies of public folders also gives a degree of fault tolerance to your public folder infrastructure. If you take a server hosting a public folder down for maintenance, clients can still access the content from another server.

Replicating public folder content does have a drawback. You increase the data storage requirements on your Exchange servers. Minimize this impact by replicating only those folders that have wide audiences. Host very large public folders with rapidly changing content on a single server or perhaps replicate between two servers in the same routing group for fault tolerance.

Content of replicated folders can get out of sync for a while until modifications converge. If you have a public folder where the users must see a consistent set of items at any given point in time, you should not replicate the folder. Sometimes a better option is to have a dedicated public folder server that can handle lots of public folder connections because it does not need to manage mailboxes.

## Public Folder Replication Agent

Public folder replication does not rely on the Windows File Replication Service, nor does it use the replication topology generated for Active Directory replication.

Public folder replication uses standard message routing. When a user posts a new item to a public folder, the item gets written to the public folder store on the user's Exchange server, and then that server mails the change to the other replica holders.

The Public Folder Replication Agent (a component of Store.exe) tracks modifications to replicated public folders, notifies replication partners of changes, generates replication messages, and guarantees delivery of those replication messages.

## Item-Level Replication

When a user modifies an item in a public folder, the Public Folder Replication Agent replicates the entire item along with any attachments, not just the changed portion of the item. Keep this behavior in mind as you train your users how to post information to public folders.

For example, consider a posting in a public folder that says "Read this to get news about the upcoming merger." The posting has a 400K PDF attachment. The public folder author changes the wording of the posting to read, "Read this to get *exciting* news about the upcoming merger." The Replication Agent replicates the new body *and* the 400K attachment.

The Replication Agent tracks messages that have been modified and how many times they have been modified using a *change number*, a separate counter maintained by each server's public folder store. Each time an addition, deletion, or modification to an item arrives at a server, it increments the local change number and stores it along with the updated item and a unique identifier for the originating server.

When a message gets modified at several different Exchange servers, it accumulates a set of change numbers and the names of the servers that made the changes. This acts like a kind of revision history with the fancy name of *predecessor change list.* When a replication partner sends out a copy of a modified message, it includes the message's predecessor change list, just like a tech writer would include a revision history for each new update.

Each server receiving the public folder update message checks its local copy of the predecessor change list to see if it already received the change from another Exchange server. This prevents changes from circulating over and over through an organization.

## Enabling Replication for a Folder

If you configure replication at a top-level folder, the child folders inherit the replication settings. You can specify different replication servers on a child folder if you wish, but that can get complex if you aren't careful. Enable replication on a top-level folder as follows:

1. Open the Properties window for a public folder in ESM and select the **Replication** tab (Figure 10.12).
2. The initial configuration shows a single Exchange server, the server where the folder was first created. The example in the figure shows that the administrator created the Employee Relations folder on server W2K3-EX4.
3. Click **Add** to open the Select a Public Store window (Figure 10.13).

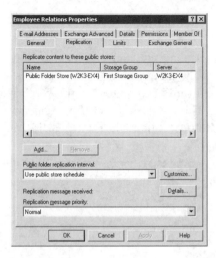

**Figure 10.12** Public folder replication settings.

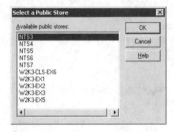

**Figure 10.13** Select a Public Store window showing all Exchange servers in an organization. Public folders can replicate between Administrative Groups.

4. Select the server where you want to replicate the contents of the public folder and click **OK**. For example, in the screen shot, you could select W2K3-EX1.
5. Click **OK** to add the server to the replication list.
6. Click **OK** again to save the change.

The replication entry gets written to the Public Folder Hierarchy, which W2K3-EX4 sends to all the other Exchange servers via a replication message. When W2K3-EX1 receives the Public Folder Hierarchy update, it discovers that it has been assigned to have a copy of a public folder. It sets to work replicating a copy of the current contents. See the topic titled "Public Folder Backfill" for details on what happens next.

You can verify that the server has replicated the full content of the public folder by checking the replication Status window using ESM. Highlight the public folder and select the Status tab in the right pane. Figure 10.14 shows an example.

If the item number matches for the replica servers, then you know you're in sync. You can also select the Replication tab to check the synchronization status, as shown in Figure 10.15.

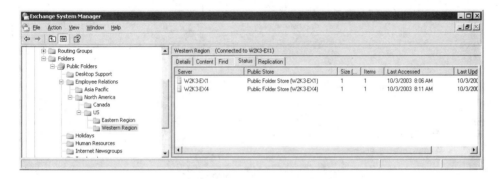

**Figure 10.14** ESM showing status of the replica on each server that hosts a copy of a public folder.

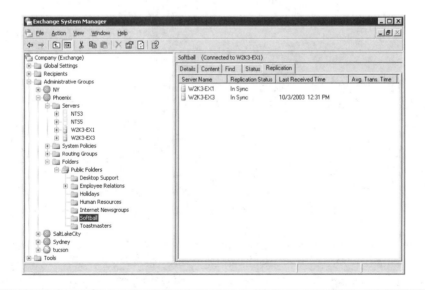

**Figure 10.15** ESM showing replication status of a public folder on each host.

## Replication Intervals

Each public folder store has a replication interval. By default, Exchange sets this interval to Always Run, meaning that replication occurs every 15 minutes at any time of the day or night. Figure 10.16 shows an example.

Public folders themselves ordinarily replicate at an interval specified by the public folder store hosting the folder, as shown in Figure 10.17.

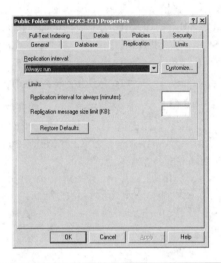

**Figure 10.16** Replication properties for a public folder store showing default replication interval of Always Run.

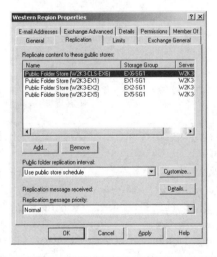

**Figure 10.17** Replication properties of a public folder showing a default replication interval that relies on public folder store settings.

Unless you have a very large folder and a certain period of the day when WAN bandwidth gets tight, leave the replication interval for the folders set to use the store schedule.

## Manual Replication

Exchange 2003 has the capability to force replication of public folder hierarchies and public folder content. This handy feature helps you to send out changes immediately to satisfy a service level commitment or to keep a user from calling the Help Desk over and over again.

### Manually Replicating Public Folder Hierarchy

Recall that the Public Folder Hierarchy (PFH) is the set of all public folders, but not their content. Think of the PFH as having an index to the public folder structure. Each Exchange server in the organization gets a copy of the PFH.

To push out changes you made to the public folder hierarchy, right-click the Public Folders icon and select Send Hierarchy from the flyout menu (shown in Figure 10.18).

**Figure 10.18** Public Folders property menu showing Send Hierarchy option, which initiates replication manually.

This opens a Send Hierarchy window (Figure 10.19) where you can select the server to use as the source for the hierarchy and the servers to which you want to send the hierarchy. You must select a value for Resend Changes Made in the Last (Days); unless you're trying to get caught up after a lengthy outage, enter 1 Day.

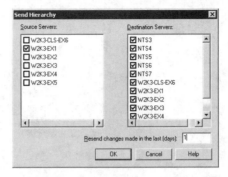

**Figure 10.19** Send Hierarchy window showing options to select source and target servers for Public Folder Hierarchy replication.

When you click OK, the system warns you that this can cause considerable replication traffic. Click OK again to initiate the replication.

Give the system a few minutes, then check the Public Folder Store on the target servers to verify that they see the new hierarchy.

### Manually Replicating Public Folder Content

Situations arise when you have important changes made to the content of a public folder that you want to send to the other replica holders immediately. To force replicate the content of a folder, right-click the folder in ESM and select **All Tasks | Send Contents** from the flyout menu (shown in Figure 10.20).

**Figure 10.20** Public folder property menu showing the Send Contents option that manually initiates replication of items in the folder.

This opens a Send Contents window (Figure 10.21) that looks identical to the Send Hierarchy window except that it lists only the replica holders.

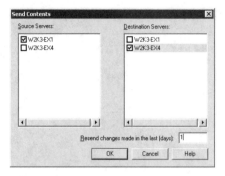

**Figure 10.21** Send Contents window that allows specifying the source and target servers for content replication.

Select the source and target server or servers and enter a value in Resend Changes Made in the Last (Days) and click OK. Acknowledge the warning that this can cause a lot of network traffic. Give the system a few minutes and then check that the Public Folder Store on the target server has the new contents.

### Public Folder Backfill

When you configure an Exchange 2003 server to host a replica of an existing public folder, the server backfills the contents from servers that already host a replica. Figure 10.22 shows an example of how the server would backfill the folder contents.

Backfill can sop up quite a bit of bandwidth, especially if you have quite a few items in the folders. To minimize the impact, Exchange 2003 servers wait six hours before sending a backfill request with the hope that standard replication might deliver some or all of the content to the new server. After six hours, the server sends a backfill request based on a few simple selection rules:

- **Local servers.** Backfill starts by pulling content from any local server that has items in the folder, even if the item list is incomplete and even if the server runs some other version of Exchange. Exchange 2003 prefers to replicate from Exchange 2003 servers if it can find them, but it is willing to settle on some other version.
- **Lowest cost connections.** If local servers do not have all the required items in the folder, Exchange then looks for servers in nearby Routing Groups; "nearby" meaning those with the lowest transport cost assigned to the Routing Group Connector. When

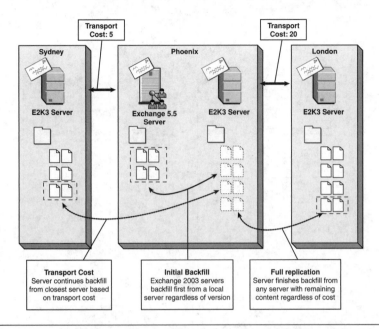

**Figure 10.22** Diagram of example backfill scenario where an Exchange server must obtain latest contents of public folder after being configured to host a replica.

selecting between Routing Groups with equal connector costs, Exchange 2003 prefers Exchange 2003 servers and then Exchange 2000 servers and then legacy Exchange servers. When selecting between servers of the same version, it prefers servers with the most items.

- **Final top-off from any server.** If the Exchange server is not able to get the remaining items in the folder from a nearby server, it goes to any server regardless of location to finish the backfill.

## Public Folder Referrals

When a user opens a public folder in Outlook, a chain of events ensues that eventually points the user at a server with a replica of the folder contents, as shown in Figure 10.23.

When the user clicks on a folder in the Public Folder Hierarchy, Outlook requests the content from the user's home server. If the home server has a replica of the selected public folder, it replies with a collection of headers for items in the folder.

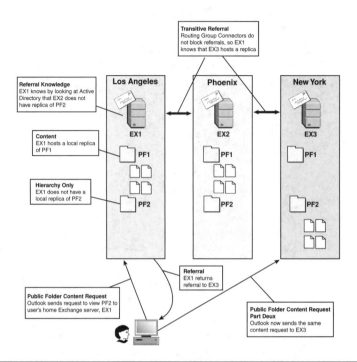

**Figure 10.23** Diagram of example public folder referral where a client obtains the name of the closest server that hosts the content of a requested public folder.

If the user's home server does not have a local replica, it returns a referral to a server that does. The Information Store service knows each server that hosts a replica of the requested folder. It derives a referral by sending the replica list to the Routing Engine, which returns the transport cost to each server and whether a route exists to the server based on the current Link State Table entries.

If a server within the same routing group hosts a replica, the Information Store returns that name to Outlook. If no servers within the routing group have a replica, then the referral contains a list of the least costly servers. The client selects one of these servers at random for load balancing.

The client remembers the name of the server it used the last time it accessed a public folder so it can go there again the next time without a referral. This information does not get written to disk, so the next time Outlook starts it must once again determine a target server for each public folder selected by a user. You can also flush bad referrals from the local cache by stopping and starting Outlook.

## Referral Failures

When Outlook receives the name of a server in a referral, it sends a MAPI request to open a session. If Outlook 2003 cannot make contact, it notifies the user using a bubble message in the Notification Area, as shown in Figure 10.24. In the example, the only replica of the folder resides on an Exchange 5.5 server running on NT, which sometimes causes a lookup problem if the server is slow to respond.

If an Outlook client cannot contact *any* server that hosts a replica of the selected public folder, it notifies the user with a message in the right pane of the folder view, as shown in Figure 10.25.

**Figure 10.24** Notification balloon when Outlook is unable to locate a server that hosts a replica of a public folder.

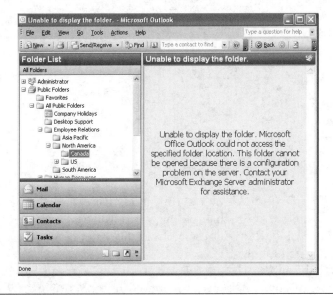

**Figure 10.25** Outlook displays error message when unable to locate replica.

If you see this window, check for a possible WAN failure that has disrupted communications between the client and the replica server. You might have also inadvertently disabled public folder referrals through a Routing Group Connector, as discussed in the next section.

## Transitive Referrals

The public folder referral mechanism in Exchange 2003 supports transitive referrals. For example, as shown in the diagram in Figure 10.23, the Los Angeles routing group connects to Phoenix, and Phoenix connects to New York, so an Outlook client in Los Angeles can seamlessly access a public folder hosted on a New York Exchange server.

You can block public folder referrals in the Properties window for a Routing Group Connector, as shown in Figure 10.26.

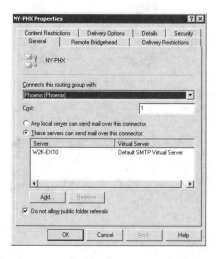

**Figure 10.26** Routing Group Connector properties showing the option to disallow public folder referrals to block access across expensive connection.

The **Do Not Allow Public Folder Referrals** setting blocks referrals to any servers in that routing group. You can also select the Disallow Public Folder Referrals option from the flyout menu of a routing group, as shown in Figure 10.27.

Use caution when disallowing referrals. You can cause users to lose access to public folder information. This option is mostly valuable for troubleshooting or for preventing large amounts of traffic through a remote site. For example, if you want users in Malaysia to see public folder content only from their local servers and not to go across an expensive satellite connection to North America, you can block public folder referrals on the Routing Group Connector that represents the satellite-based WAN connection.

**Figure 10.27** Routing Group Connector property menu showing the option to Disallow Public Folder Referrals without forcing the administrator to open the Properties window.

## Specifying Referral Servers

There might come a time when the standard referral mechanism of calculating transport costs does not yield a satisfactory referral path. For example, you might want messages to route a certain way in your organization and you design your routing group connectors accordingly. But the most efficient message routing might not make for the most efficient public folder referral path. Exchange 2003 permits you to specify one or more servers by name to use for public folder referrals, as shown in Figure 10.28.

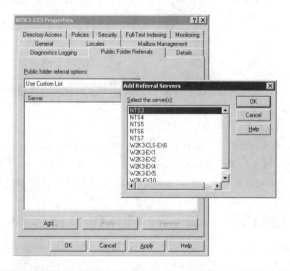

**Figure 10.28** Exchange server properties showing option to specify certain servers as referral targets.

## Referral Limitations

The public folder referral mechanism used by Exchange 2003 has a few limitations:

- **IMAP4 does not use referrals.** Only MAPI clients understand public folder referrals. IMAP4 clients do not. An IMAP4 client always goes to the user's home server to look at a folder. You can work around this limitation with a front-end server for IMAP4 clients. The front-end server follows up on referrals when locating public folder content and simply delivers the data stream back to the IMAP4 client. See Chapter 11, "Deploying a Distributed Architecture," for more information on front-end and back-end servers.
- **Possible RPC failures.** MAPI clients use RPCs to download public folder content. RPCs have a notorious propensity for ill-tempered behavior when used over slow or unreliable connections. If you experience timeout and connection problems using referrals to servers in other Routing Groups, you should replicate a copy of the public folder to a local server. The replication uses standard SMTP messaging, which has a better chance of working over an unreliable connection.
- **No referrals for general purpose folders.** The public folder referral mechanism works only for the MAPI (default) public folder tree. Exchange does not provide referrals for general purpose public folder trees.

# Recovering Deleted Items from Public Folders

If a user inadvertently deletes an item from a public folder, you can recover it without resorting to a tape restore. You can even walk the user through the restoration on the phone as long as the individual has at least Editor permissions on the folder (read, write, or delete).

## Setting Public Folder Deleted Item Retention Intervals

By default, an Exchange 2003 public folder store retains deleted items for seven days (the default interval for Exchange 2000 is zero days). You can modify the interval using the Properties window of the public folder store in ESM. Figure 10.29 shows an example.

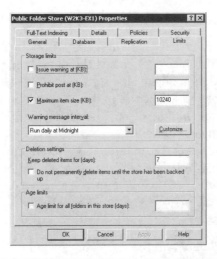

**Figure 10.29** Public Folder Store properties showing default deleted item retention period of seven days.

Keep in mind that each Public Folder Store has its own Deletion Settings option. A folder might get replicated between servers with different retention settings. This is especially true if you have a mix of Exchange 2000 and Exchange 2003 servers. You can avoid this situation by setting a System Policy in each Administrative Group that defines a value for Deletion Settings. This imposes a consistent value on all servers in the AG.

As an added precaution against losing valuable information in public folders, select the option titled Do Not Permanently Delete Items Until the Store Has Been Backed Up. Be sure that you regularly run backups of your public folder store. If you do not, the backlog of deleted items can cause your storage requirements to exceed the capacity of your drives.

While you're looking at the Limits tab of the Public Folder Store properties, notice that the standard Exchange 2003 settings do not permit a user to post an item to a public folder if the item size exceeds 10MB. (This setting can be changed.) The message-size limit helps prevent a denial-of-service attack in which a user could post hundreds of huge files and exhaust the storage capacity of your Exchange server. You can and should augment this limit by configuring warning limits to monitor growth of a public folder and, if you have limited storage, a final limit that prohibits additional posts.

## Restoring a Deleted Item in a Public Folder

You can restore a deleted item using Outlook. You cannot restore the item using ESM or OWA. To test the operation, post a few entries in a test folder and then delete all the entries.

In Outlook, highlight the folder from which the item was deleted. From the main menu, select Tools | Recover Deleted Items. Figure 10.30 shows the menu item.

When you select this menu option, the Recover Deleted Items window opens. Figure 10.31 shows a few retained items in a public folder.

**Figure 10.30** Tools menu in Outlook showing the ability to recover deleted items in a public folder.

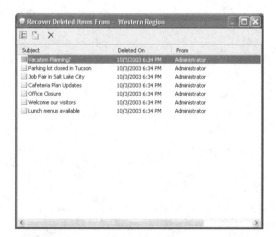

**Figure 10.31** Recover Deleted Items from window in Outlook showing deleted items still marked for retention in the public folder store.

Select the items you want to bring back then click the Recover Selected Items button (second from the left). The items get restored to their original location and even retain their original flag colors. Be careful not to select the Purge Selected Items button or you'll lose all the entries. You can use this same technique to recover deleted calendar entries from Calendar public folders.

# Public Folder Permissions

As I'm sure you'll agree, the ability of a public folder to display a variety of items from many different folks in your organization can be a tremendous benefit. It can also become a support nightmare when users make unauthorized changes to postings or add inappropriate postings or generally muck around with something they don't or won't understand.

Exchange 2003 protects folders using standard Windows security by assigning each item a security descriptor that contains an ACL defining who can access the folder and what they can do. Each entry on the ACL is identified by a Security ID, or SID.

The Information Store maps these ACL entries to MAPI permissions for the folder. MAPI permissions correspond to roles. For example, a user with the Reviewer role can see a list of items in a folder and can read those items, but can't modify them or add new items.

ESM exposes both the MAPI and ACL permissions on a public folder in the Properties window of the folder. Figure 10.32 shows an example for a public folder called Toastmasters.

The Permissions tab for a public folder has three buttons:

- Client Permissions
- Directory Rights
- Administrative Rights

Let's see what each of these buttons reveals and why Exchange needs to play Three-Card Monte with permissions in the first place.

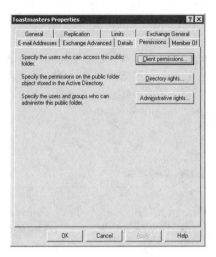

**Figure 10.32** Public folder properties showing three permission options: Client Permissions, Directory Rights, and Administrative Rights.

## Client Permissions

Click the Client Permissions button. This opens the same window you would see if you viewed the folder permissions in Outlook. Figure 10.33 shows an example. The roles you see on the list are also called MAPI permissions.

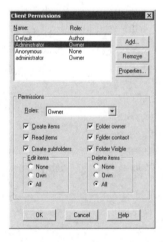

**Figure 10.33** Client permissions for a public folder showing role holders and their permissions.

The MAPI permissions assigned in this window form a part of the Public Folder Hierarchy entries for the folder. They replicate to every other Exchange server in the organization, whether or not that server actually hosts a replica of the folder content.

Exchange 2003 stores permissions for a public folder in two special attributes within the public folder store:

- ptagNTSD stores client permissions.
- ptagAdminNTSD stores admin permissions.

When you view MAPI permissions for a user, Exchange converts the content of ptagNTSD into its associated MAPI permissions. The presence of legacy Exchange servers in an organization complicates this conversion somewhat. See the "Public Folder Permission Mapping" topic at the end of the chapter for details.

You can display the raw security permissions in ptagNTSD by pressing the Ctrl key when you click the Client Permissions button in ESM. **Never change permissions using this view**. You will lose the mapping between ACL permissions and MAPI permissions.

### MAPI Permissions

The MAPI permission list displayed in the Client Permissions window defines these access rights:

- Create Items
- Read Items
- Edit Items (with options for All or Own)
- Delete Items (with options for All or Own)
- Create Subfolders
- Owner (controls permissions on the folder)
- Contact (gets notified when problems occur with the folder)

### MAPI Roles

Exchange mixes and matches these permissions to define a slew of roles. Table 10.1 lists the MAPI roles and their permissions.

**Table 10.1  MAPI** Roles and Permissions

| Role | Create Items | Read Items | Edit Items | Delete Items | Create Subfolders | Owner | Contact |
|------|--------------|------------|------------|--------------|-------------------|-------|---------|
| Owner | X | X | All | All | X | X | X |
| Publishing Editor | X | X | All | All | X | | |
| Publishing Author | X | X | Own | Own | X | | |
| Editor | X | X | All | All | | | |
| Author | X | X | Own | Own | | | |
| Non-editing Author | X | X | None | Own | | | |
| Contributor | X | | None | None | | | |
| Reviewer | | X | None | None | | | |

Some of these roles have odd capabilities. A Contributor, for example, can create an item but not read it once it's created. This makes sense if you use an automated process to simply dump items into a folder. A Non-editing Author can create and read an item but not modify it. This keeps a user from modifying an item once they've posted it.

You don't have to conform to the preset roles. You can assign additional permissions to an existing role, making it a Custom role.

If you uncheck the Folder Visible option in the Client Permission list and save the settings, and then open the permissions again, you might find that the option once again has a check. You cannot deny permission to view a folder if you have permission to read it, or if the user is an owner of the folder.

## Directory Rights

Close the Client Permissions window and click the Directory Rights button. This opens a Permissions window similar to that in Figure 10.34.

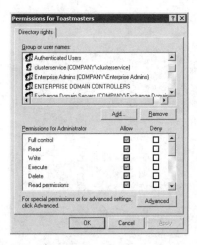

**Figure 10.34** Directory Rights listing for a public folder, showing the contents of the ACL for the Public Folder object in Active Directory that represents a mail-enabled public folder.

The Directory Rights button shows you the security descriptor contents for Public Folder object in Active Directory. All MAPI public folders have a Public Folder object to enable them to receive e-mail. Do not change permissions from this interface. Always use the MAPI permissions interface to assign permissions. ESM displays them solely for informational purposes.

## Administrative Rights

Close the Permissions window and click the Administrative Rights button. This opens a window that is also titled Permissions but has a different set of entries, as shown in Figure 10.35.

In addition to the MAPI permissions that control client access to a public folder, Exchange stores a separate set of admin permissions. These permissions include

- Modify Public Folder ACL
- Modify Public Folder Admin ACL
- Modify Public Folder Deleted Item Retention
- Modify Public Folder Expiry
- Modify Public Folder Quotas
- Modify Public Folder Replica List
- Administer Information Store
- View Information Store Status

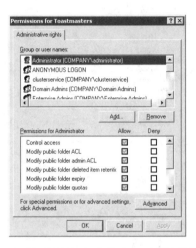

**Figure 10.35** Administrative Rights listing for a public folder showing the contents of the special administrative security descriptor stored in the public folder store.

Each public folder inherits its admin permission settings from the public folder hierarchy. It's best to leave those settings alone. Only define separate admin permissions on a public folder for testing. Use role delegation in the Administrative Group to grant access to the public folder hierarchy.

# Public Folder Permission Mapping

If you install Exchange Server 2003 into an existing Exchange 5.x organization, you face a distinct challenge. Public folders that replicate back and forth between legacy Exchange servers and Exchange 2003 servers require special handling to ensure that the permissions assigned to the folders remain intact.

A large number of Exchange deployments have come to grief when public folder permission mapping went awry. The administrators of those organizations went from being folk heroes to pariahs in one stroke.

This subject isn't simple. In fact, it's one of the most complex areas of Exchange integration. It is well worth the effort to understand this process so you can be prepared for potential problems. If you wait until you are deluged with support calls and your boss is staring over your shoulder while you troubleshoot, you'll have a difficult time figuring out how to use the tools that Microsoft provides to help you fix mapping errors.

## Legacy Permission Mapping

Exchange 2003 stores folder permissions using two special attributes within the public folder store, **ptagNTSD** for client permissions and **ptagAdminNTSD** for admin permissions. Legacy Exchange uses a somewhat more complicated arrangement.

Legacy Exchange stores public folder permissions in an Access Control List ID (ACLID) table. As shown in Figure 10.36, each folder in the Public Folder Hierarchy has a pointer to an entry in the ACLID table. If two folders have the same set of permissions, then they point at the same ACLID table entry.

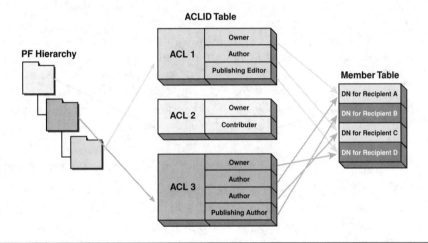

**Figure 10.36** Access Control List ID table for legacy Exchange showing links between the MAPI roles assigned to a folder and the Member Table, which lists the Distinguished Names of the role-holders.

To conserve space and to simplify internal references, the ACLID table lists recipients by a reference number stored in another table called the Member Table. The Member Table contains, among other things, the Distinguished Name (DN) of each recipient and distribution list.

The end result of all this cross-referencing is a mechanism that identifies role holders by their Distinguished Names. This contrasts with the security descriptors used by modern Exchange, which identify access control entries by their Security ID (SID).

When the MAPI permissions change on a folder, legacy Exchange makes the necessary changes to the local ACLID table, and it also updates a little binary data structure called *ptagACLData*, which converts the ACLID entry for the folder into a form that Exchange can replicate. The Exchange server includes the ptagACLData attribute in the Public Folder Hierarchy update message it sends out to replicate the change.

### Permission Conversion from Legacy Exchange to Exchange 2003

When an Exchange 2003 server receives the update message, it converts the legacy DNs in the ptagACLData entry into the SIDs of the corresponding recipients. Then it uses that information to update its local copy of ptagNTSD.

Ordinarily, this conversion goes without a hitch. Each mail-enabled object in Active Directory has an attribute called LegacyExchangeDN that contains the object's legacy Exchange Distinguished Name. The Exchange 2003 server simply searches for the object with a certain LegacyExchangeDN, obtains the corresponding SID for the object, and maps the permissions accordingly.

### Permission Conversion from Exchange 2003 to legacy Exchange

When the replication goes the other way, that is, when a modern Exchange server replicates public folder permission changes to a legacy Exchange server, the process works a bit differently.

The Exchange 2003 server calculates the contents of the ptagACLData attribute by mapping the SIDs in ptagNTSD with their corresponding legacy DNs and then includes this synthetic ptagACLData in the replication message it sends to the legacy Exchange server. (It does not bother including this information in replication messages sent to modern Exchange servers.)

The legacy Exchange server treats this synthetic ptagNTSD attribute as if it came from another legacy Exchange server and applies the attribute to its copy of the folder and then updates the ACLID table accordingly.

Exchange 2003 also includes a copy of ptagNTSD and ptagAdminNTSD, even though the legacy Exchange server doesn't know what to do with them. This ensures that the public folder stores remain in sync.

## Potential Failure Possibilities

There are a couple of things that can cause a failure when converting a legacy DN within the ptagACLData coming from legacy Exchange into a corresponding SID for ptagNTSD:

- **Distribution Groups.** Exchange relies on Windows object management, and therefore every entry in ptagNTSD must represent a security principal. It's possible for legacy Exchange to put a distribution list into ptagACLData that corresponds to a Distribution Group in Active Directory. Distribution Groups cannot appear on an ACL, and therefore they do not qualify for inclusion in ptagNTSD. The Information Store handles this problem by promoting the Distribution Group to a Security Group.
- **No legacy DN.** If the Information Store searches for an Active Directory object with a legacy DN that matches an entry in ptagACLData and comes up empty, it has a problem. Essentially, this means that a legacy recipient or distribution list does not have a complementary mailbox-enabled user or mail-enabled group in Active Directory.

## Slaying Zombies

When a permission list contains an entry for a non-existent user or group, Microsoft calls this a zombie. If you're a fan of Buffy, the Vampire Slayer, (and who isn't?), you know that having zombies in your neighborhood is never good news. In the original release of Exchange 2000, the presence of just one zombie would cause the entire ptagACLData-to-ptagNTSD conversion to fail, resulting in all users (except the owner) losing access to the folder. The phones would start to ring at the Help Desk and some poor Exchange administrator would have a very bad day.

In the post-SP3 roll-up for Exchange 2000, Microsoft introduced a new Registry key called Ignore Zombie Users that helped minimize the problems associated with invalid public folder permissions.

### Mixed-Mode Zombie Handling

Exchange 2003 (and Exchange 2000 with a current service pack) shows a bit more gumption in handling zombies. Instead of simply giving up and applying default permissions, Exchange 2003 ignores zombies completely if they appear any time after initial public folder replication. This exacts a performance penalty, though, because Exchange must wait for a timeout from Active Directory (after which it tries again a couple of times) before realizing that it has a zombie on its hands. Symptoms of failed ACL conversions include

- Lengthy "Requesting information from Exchange Server" errors when clicking on public folders in Outlook
- Very long delays (from 20 seconds up to several minutes) when opening public folders
- E-mail stuck in outbox for a long time and then delivered
- Access denied to public folders or not even visible
- Messages queued in "Local Delivery" queue
- Delegates denied access to a target mailbox to which they have been granted access

### Native-Mode Zombie Handling

A Native mode Exchange 2003 organization takes a different corrective action in response to zombies on a public folder permission list. It slays them altogether. In other words, Exchange 2003 removes a zombie entirely the first time it encounters one during a ptagACLData-to-ptagNTSD conversion. This cleans up invalid entries on the fly and eliminates subsequent performance problems.

The updated ptagNTSD entry replicates back to the legacy Exchange servers in the form of a new ptagACLData attribute, thus removing the source of the problem.

Deleting zombies can cause a security infraction if an administrator originally intended on denying access but didn't configure the entry correctly. Keep an eye on Event Log entries that indicate the presence of a zombie so you can take corrective action, if required.

rectly. Keep an eye on Event Log entries that indicate the presence of a zombie so you can take corrective action, if required.

### DS/IS Consistency

Rather than wait for Exchange 2003 to prune zombies, especially because it might take a while to shift the organization to Native mode, you might want to take it on yourself to act as a slayer.

Legacy Exchange has a utility called the DS/IS Consistency Adjuster that goes through the ACLID tables and removes any entries that refer to invalid or missing recipients. The ADC Tools in Exchange 2003 Setup include a step for running the DS/IS Consistency Adjuster to clean up permissions. You can also run it manually before installing the ADC.

**Use considerable caution when running the DS/IS Consistency Adjuster.** If the local replica of the information store does not contain an up-to-date list of recipients, then you might strip public folder permissions unintentionally. See the latest Microsoft Knowledge Base articles before running the DS/IS Consistency Adjuster independently of the ADC Tools.

## Looking Forward

If you're able to get your public folder structure built and presented to your users without spending too many hours listening to their advice/complaints, then you have some time on your hands. Spend a while in the lab dumping content into the folders, and watching it replicate and seeing the way the queues react. This will help you prepare for any production issues that come up. Pay particular attention to calendar appointments that use free/busy information.

CHAPTER 11

# Deploying a Distributed Architecture

When you go to a restaurant, you expect a certain routine. You get seated by a hostess, served drinks by a bartender or wine by a sommelier, served food by a waiter or waitress, and served with a check by someone interested in your comments.

You probably wouldn't be too upset if the same person seated you and then took your order. Anyone eating at Denny's comes to expect that. But down the road from me is a place called Roman's where the same person takes your order, runs back to the kitchen to cook your food, dashes out to your table periodically to offer you drinks and appetizers, and washes the dishes when you're finished.

Forget about problems with sanitation and the fact that a good service person isn't necessarily a good cook (although the chili at this place is terrific). Even if the person serving you were a world-class expert on every job in the restaurant, making one person do all the work just isn't efficient.

In the same way, when you ask an Exchange server to handle e-mail retrievals, accept and route outgoing mail, authenticate users, do database lookups, render Web pages, and do all the other assorted tasks that go along with managing a messaging platform, hey, you're talking about a pretty busy machine.

If you have a few hundred, or even a couple of thousand users homed to a server, you might not notice a performance drag. But if the server has 5,000 mailboxes, it could bog down considerably, especially if it is required to handle secure OWA connections and S/MIME.

Because the transport protocols used by Exchange do not reside in Exchange itself, it's possible to split the duties of mailbox storage and message transport and assign the transports to a front-end server. You could place this front-end server in a public-facing perimeter network and where it could proxy all the incoming mail requests to the back-end servers who own the mailboxes. This makes effective use of the resources on the machines and multiplies productivity.

In this chapter, you'll see how to configure a front-end/back-end topology for Outlook Web Access, SMTP, POP/IMAP; and how to proxy Outlook 2003 clients through a firewall using RPC over HTTP.

# Advantages of Using Front-End Servers

As shown in Figure 11.1, when you configure an Exchange server to act as front-end server, it does nothing more than accept e-mail requests from clients and pass those requests to back-end servers. Using a front-end server to handle e-mail requests from Internet clients makes a lot of sense from a security perspective as well to enhance performance and convenience.

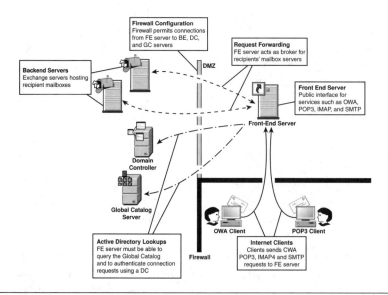

**Figure 11.1**  Principal constituents of a distributed architecture using a front-end server to proxy clients to back-end mailbox servers.

## Security Advantages

If you want to send and receive Internet e-mail, you must expose at least one server to the public Internet. Without a front-end server, you would need to poke holes in your firewall to allow each Exchange server to send and receive SMTP traffic with any and every e-mail server on the Internet, and to accept e-mail client connection requests from all quarters.

Even if you use an SMTP connector and select one server in the private network as an Internet bridgehead, the server represents a potential exploit point if an attacker were able to get root via a rogue SMTP connection or some other subterfuge.

By placing a front-end server that handles only transport duties in the DMZ, you can harden the machine so that it only accepts connections for certain ports, and then throttle the private side of the perimeter network firewall to pass traffic only to those ports. You can even use application-layer firewalls, such as Internet Security and Acceleration (ISA ) server, to provide an additional barrier between the public interface of your DMZ and the front-end server. Small Business Server even runs ISA and Exchange on the same server.

For OWA connections and Outlook clients using RPC over HTTP, you can configure the front-end server to accept only Secure Socket Layer (SSL) connections, making it into a secure corridor to the mailbox servers in the private network.

## Performance

Because you free the front-end server from the drudgery of doing mailbox lookups, it becomes much more nimble when processing client e-mail requests. Give a front-end server a couple of fast processors and enough memory to handle a pile of concurrent connections (1GB is more than sufficient), and you have an appliance that can handle thousands of simultaneous users, even if they connect using SSL.

If you use a front-end server to host OWA or POP3 sessions, you can service four back-end mailbox servers. Because an Exchange 2003 server with moderately powerful hardware can easily host a couple of thousand mailboxes, a single front-end server could route traffic for 8,000 or more users. You get an even better performance advantage if your clients use IMAP4 to connect to their mailboxes and public folders. You can use a ratio of one front-end server for every eight back-end mailbox servers. A lot of variables control the actual traffic you can expect to get. These numbers are for average users, if there is such a thing.

If your users access public folders using OWA, you'll like the way that front-end servers automatically load balance public folder requests if a particular folder is hosted on multiple Exchange servers. This ensures that all public folder requests coming to the front-end server don't go to a single back-end server.

If you need to support a spectacular number of concurrent connections, you can use Network Load Balancing (NLB) to cluster multiple front-end servers into a single virtual server with a single IP address. The only caveat to this configuration is that you don't want users jumping from one server to another after they have made their initial connection. SSL certificates and forms-based authentication cookies are tied to a specific front-end server. You could overcome this limitation by fronting the server farm with an SSL director such as F5's BigIP, www.f5.com.

## Convenience

By providing a single server (or cluster of servers) as a front-end server, you can place one MX record and one glue record in the public DNS zone that your users can enter for virtually all of their e-mail configurations. This simplifies user configurations and reduces support costs.

One particularly handy front-end feature improves support for IMAP4 clients who use public folders. A standard IMAP4 application does not know how to handle folder referrals. But in a distributed topology, the front-end server handles the public folder referrals, giving your IMAP4 users a single point of access to all the distributed public folders in your organization.

Exchange 2003 includes mobility features to support smart phones and Pocket PCs, and the front-end server can proxy these devices as well, giving your users the convenience of pointing all their clients, large and small, at the same front-end server.

## Front-End Server Caveats

When you use front-end servers, you need to adjust your thinking a bit on some of the operations performed by users in the public space.

- **Front-end servers support only Basic authentication.** A front-end uses IIS to accept client connections, and IIS does not accept Windows integrated authentication from a public client. This leaves Basic authentication, which uses plain-text passwords. You must protect Basic authentication transactions using SSL.
- **Front-end OWA servers communicate to back-end servers only over TCP port 80.** In other words, you cannot require SSL on the back-end servers and you cannot use alternate port numbers on the back-end servers to support multiple virtual HTTP servers.

- **Front-end servers must be domain members.** You cannot run Exchange on a standalone server, so the front-end server must be a member of a domain in the forest that hosts the Exchange organization. You cannot use a Windows Server 2003 forest root trust. You can create a separate domain for the perimeter network, but the domain must be a part of the forest that holds Exchange.
- **SMTP servers require the Information Store service.** A front-end server does not host user mailboxes, so ordinarily you could dismount and delete mailbox and public folder stores and disable the Information Store service to reduce the attack surface of the machine. However, the SMTP service needs the Information Store service, one mailbox store, and the default public folder store so that it can send Non-Delivery Reports and reliably route mail to public folders on back-end servers.
- **SMTP front-end servers might require MTA.** An SMTP front-end server can deliver messages to legacy Exchange servers, but the MTA service must be running at the front-end server and the firewall must permit RPC connections between the front-end server and the legacy Exchange servers. This takes quite a bit of security out of the secured DMZ, and few people opt to deploy this configuration.

# Authentication and Front-End Servers

When a user makes connection to a front end server, the server obtains the user's credentials using basic authentication. You should always protect this transaction with SSL. Chapter 9, "Outlook Web Access," shows you how to configure a server to use SSL.

A front-end server merely proxies client requests. When the user presents a name and password as part of the Basic authentication transaction, the front-end server uses those credentials to *become* the user and to authenticate either in the domain or through the back-end server. The nature of this authentication transaction depends on the protocol used by the e-mail client:

- **Outlook Web Access.** An OWA front-end server uses Kerberos to connect with a back-end server. The front-end server obtains a

Kerberos session ticket on the user's behalf using the credentials obtained via plain-text authentication. By using Kerberos, the back-end server has no need to communicate with a domain controller to validate the user's credentials. This makes the connection very quick, and you only need to open a Kerberos port (TCP port 88) through the firewall to get it to work.

- **POP3 and IMAP4.** For Internet e-mail clients, the front-end server uses Basic authentication to connect to a back-end server. To avoid revealing plain-text passwords, you can establish an IPSec connection between the front-end and back-end servers. Exchange 2003 permits connecting to a clustered back-end server using IPSec, and Windows Server 2003 permits tunneling IPSec through a NAT firewall.

### Implicit OWA Authentication

Because a front-end server uses Basic authentication, a user must provide credentials that include the user's domain name. This can be in domain\username format or the User Principal Name (UPN), such as user@domain.root.

Now, there's no question that users hate entering passwords. Sure, they realize the necessity of passwords, but they hate entering them all the same, and you don't want to force your users to enter their password twice. OWA avoids dual authentication transactions by using *implicit authentication* to log on to the back-end server. As you'll see, this does not expose security vulnerabilities. It simply uses the inherent authentication features in Windows to simplify the experience for the user. Here's how it works.

In a typical OWA front-end server configuration, you would configure the Exchange virtual folder in the Default Web Site to accept only Basic authentication, as shown in Figure 11.2.

After the front-end server validates the user's authentication credentials, the server constructs a URL to connect to OWA on the back-end server. It formats this URL using the Fully Qualified Domain Name (FQDN) of the back-end server (obtained from a Global Catalog lookup) and the user's mailbox name extracted from the user's logon name.

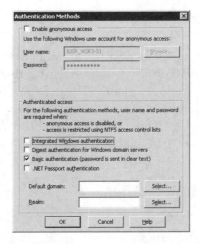

**Figure 11.2** When configuring a front-end OWA server, strip out all authentication mechanisms except for Basic.

For example, a user named Phoenix User71 with a logon name of phoenixuser71 and a home mailbox server of W2K3-EX1 in the domain Company.com could connect to the front-end OWA server and enter simply:

```
http://w2k3-ex1.company.com/exchange
```

The front-end server would add the user name to the URL and connect to the back-end server.

When the front-end server makes the initial HTTP connection to the back-end server using this URL, it includes the Kerberos session ticket it obtained on behalf of the user. Because you've already opened a port for Kerberos through the firewall separating the DMZ from the private network, this mechanism for implicit authentication should work seamlessly.

It sometimes happens that you can't get the cooperation of your network services folks to open the necessary ports to permit the front-end server to authenticate the user. In this case, the users must enter an explicit logon by including their logon name in the URL. The front-end server sends that information to the back-end server and then proxies the authentication transaction. This imposes a performance penalty on the front-end and back-end servers and limits the number of simultaneous connections you can create.

# Necessary Firewall Ports for Front-End Servers

The two most common distributed configurations use the front-end server to proxy either OWA or SMTP, sometimes both. The front-end server must belong to a domain in the same forest as the Exchange organization, so several firewall ports must be open to permit the server to authenticate and get a full domain logon. Figure 11.3 shows an example configuration, but certainly not the only option. Many organizations choose to protect the Exchange server with an ISA firewall and to put the Exchange servers in the private network.

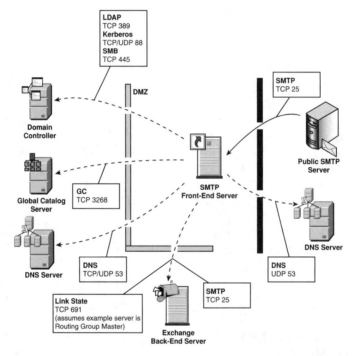

**Figure 11.3**  Firewall ports required to operate an Exchange SMTP front-end server in a perimeter network.

### SMTP Front-End

The public interface on the firewall must have two access points:

- **SMTP** (TCP port 25). Must accept inbound and outbound connections.
- **DNS** (UDP port 53). Must be able to find MX records for Internet domains.

The front-end server must authenticate itself, so the following ports must be open on the private side of the DMZ:

■ **LDAP** (TCP port 389). Necessary for logon.
■ **GC** (TCP port 3268). Necessary for logon in Native mode domain.
■ **Kerberos** (TCP port 88). Necessary to get authenticated.
■ **DNS** (TCP/UDP port 53). Necessary to resolve IP address of DC and GC and back-end server.
■ **SMB** (TCP port 445). Necessary to download group policies from Sysvol.

The front-end server must find and connect with Exchange back-end servers in the private network, which requires the following ports on the private side:

■ **SMTP** (TCP port 25). Must accept inbound and outbound connections.
■ **GC** (TCP port 3268). Required to find home servers of recipients. Not necessarily required if SMTP connector bridgehead can handle routing.

Finally, the Routing Engine on the front-end server must be able to get link statue table updates, which requires this port:

■ **Link State** (TCP port 691). Must accept inbound and outbound connections.

## OWA Front End

The other popular front-end server is one running Outlook Web Access. The port requirements for OWA are somewhat less than for SMTP, unless you want to combine SMTP and OWA on the same front-end server. Figure 11.4 shows the basic requirements for an OWA server in a perimeter network.

OWA clients make SSL connection to the front-end server, so only one open port is required on the public side of the DMZ:

■ **HTTP over SSL** (TCP port 443). Accepts inbound connections only.

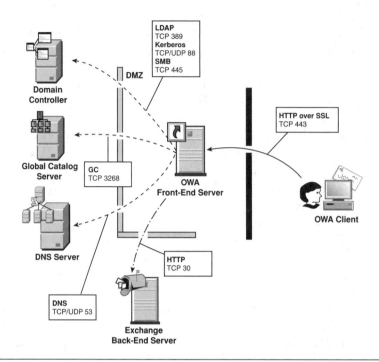

**Figure 11.4**   Firewall ports required to operate an Exchange OWA front-end server in a perimeter network.

Like SMTP, the front-end server must authenticate and log on to the domain, which requires the following ports:

- **LDAP** (TCP port 389). Necessary for logon.
- **GC** (TCP port 3268). Necessary for logon in Native mode domain.
- **Kerberos** (TCP port 88). Necessary to get authenticated.
- **DNS** (TCP/UDP port 53). Necessary to resolve IP address of DC and GC and back-end server.
- **SMB** (TCP port 445). Necessary to download group policies from Sysvol.

These ports should be locked down so that only the front-end and back-end servers can use them.

Finally, the front-end server must connect to OWA on each back-end server, so the following port must be open on the private side for each back-end server:

- **HTTP** (TCP port 80). Must accept inbound connections.

# Configuring a Front-End Server

Start by placing the domain member server in the DMZ and making arrangements with your network services colleagues to open the required ports to support the server. If you plan on using the server for Outlook Web Access, configure the Default Web Server to use SSL as described in Chapter 9.

After you've verified that the server can log on to the domain through the firewall, proceed with the next steps.

## Set the Front-End Flag for the Server

The Active Directory attributes for an Exchange server contain a flag that identifies the server as a front-end server. Set this flag in the server Properties window in ESM as follows:

1. Launch ESM.
2. Drill down to the server icon under its associated Administrative Group icon.
3. Open the Properties window for the server, as shown in Figure 11.5.

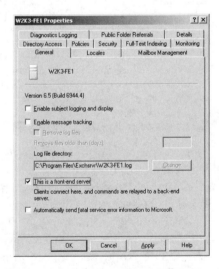

**Figure 11.5** General properties of an Exchange server showing the Front-end server flag.

4. Select the **This Is a Front-End Server** option.

5. Click **OK** to save the change.
6. ESM prompts you to restart the server or to restart POP3, IMAP4, HTTP, and all Exchange services. It's simpler to restart the server. Do so now.

## Remove Unnecessary Exchange Services

If the front-end server does not provide SMTP services, perform these remaining checklist items to remove information store components. This cuts the attack surface to its absolute minimum with respect to Exchange services.

1. **Dismount the Mailbox store.** Right-click Mailbox Store under the First Storage Group icon and select Dismount from the flyout menu.
2. **Dismount the Public Folder store.** Right-click Public Information Store under the First Storage Group icon and select Dismount from the flyout menu.
3. **Delete the Mailbox store.** Right-click the Private Information Store icon and select Delete from the flyout menu.
4. **Delete the Public Folder store.** Right-click the Public Information Store icon and select Delete from the flyout menu.
5. **Stop and disable the Information Store service.** Launch the Services console from the Administrative Tools menu, open the Properties window for the Microsoft Exchange Information Store service, stop the service, and set the status to Disabled.

## Configure DSAccess to Avoid Using RPCs

The DSAccess service on a front-end server uses LDAP to identify domain controllers and Global Catalog servers that it can use to perform lookups. This ordinarily does not cause a firewall problem because you have already opened up TCP port 389 so the server can authenticate.

But unless you configure it to do otherwise, DSAccess insists on verifying the status of a domain controller by making an RPC connection to the Netlogon service. This Netlogon connection fails through a firewall because it uses a random port. Disable the Netlogon test on front-end servers using the following Registry entry:

```
Key: HKLM\System\CurrentControlSet\Services\MSExchangeDSAccess
Value: DisableNetlogonCheck
Data: 1 (REG_DWORD)
```

### Verify Operation of Front-End Server

At this point, you should be able to make an OWA connection to the front-end server, provide your credentials, and get immediately connected to the back-end server that hosts your mailbox. You should also verify that you can access public folders through the OWA connection.

If you're setting up a front-end server to host POP3 or IMAP4, make sure that you can connect to your mailbox from a client session that points at the front-end server.

If you're setting up an SMTP server as a front-end server, you should now create an SMTP connector that specifies one or more bridgeheads within the private network and the front-end server as the smart host. You should now test that you can send mail to Internet clients from Outlook clients in the test organization.

Make sure that your public DNS zone contains an MX record for the front-end server's public interface. Use several Internet clients to send e-mail to your test domain. Consider the use of message tracking if you need to diagnose a routing problem.

## RPC over HTTP Front-End Servers

Imagine a world where your traveling users simply dial into a local network access point, or connect to the Internet from their hotel room via broadband, launch Outlook, and get their new e-mail. No VPNs. No browsers. No special configuration changes. No change at all from their normal routine. That's the whole premise behind configuring Outlook to use RPC over HTTP.

Like so many aspects of technology, something that makes the user's experience slam-dunk simple can get a little complicated for administrators to configure, but the end result is worth it.

## Remote Procedure Call Fundamentals

When an Outlook client views the content of a mailbox or peruses items in a public folder, the requests go to the Exchange server in the form of Remote Procedure Calls, or RPCs.

If you're accustomed to thinking of single-purpose network protocols such as ftp, DNS, or LDAP, each with its own well-known ports, it can be a little difficult to visualize the operation of RPCs.

Consider the Exchange Information Store, for instance. An Outlook client connects to the Information Store service using MAPI. The Outlook client uses a set of commands called *procedure calls* designed to communicate instructions to the Information Store and to handle the responses. Because the service responding to these procedure calls runs on a separate machine, they're implemented as *remote procedure calls*, meaning that the underlying network gets involved to ferry the procedure calls to and from the pair of machines involved in the transaction.

Here's where the process gets interesting. An RPC-based application does not use a well-known TCP port. It registers a port dynamically when the service starts on the server.

But that presents a problem for the client. How does it discover the port registered by the server?

The client enlists the help of a special service running at the server called the RPC Endpoint Mapper, or EPM. The EPM acts like a receptionist with an attitude. When someone calls and asks for an employee by name, the receptionist says curtly, "Here's her extension. Thank you for calling. Goodbye." It's up to the caller to dial the extension.

Here's a more concrete example. Refer to Figure 11.6. When an Outlook client first starts up, it makes its initial connection to the Referral service on the server so it can get the name of a Global Catalog server. Outlook doesn't know the port used by the Referral service on that particular Exchange server, so it first makes a connection to the RPC Endpoint Mapper service using well-known TCP port 135.

Outlook asks EPM for the TCP port number registered by the msExchangeRFR service. (I'm simplifying this just a bit. In reality, Exchange services register a variety of interfaces, each identified by a Globally Unique Identifier, or GUID.)

EPM replies to the request with the port number registered by the Referral service. Outlook breaks the connection to the EPM and immediately connects to the port registered by the Referral service. What happens after that depends on the nature of the service.

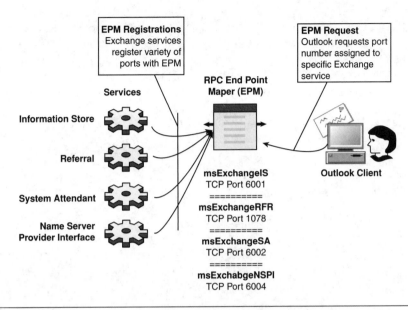

**Figure 11.6** Outlook client obtains dynamically registered port numbers of Exchange services by querying RPC Endpoint Mapper service (EPM).

You don't need an in-depth knowledge of Remote Procedure Call technology to deploy or troubleshoot RPC over HTTP, but it helps to know a few key elements of RPC communication.

### RPC-Based Service Identifiers

When an RPC service initializes, it identifies itself with a Universally Unique Identifier, or UUID. Each interface used by the service gets a different UUID, and a particular service can register several interfaces. (The word "interface" in this case is a logical interface, the combination of a protocol and a port number.)

You can use the RPCDump utility in the Windows Server 2003 Resource Kit (also in the Windows 2000 Resource Kit) to list the RPC services and their UUIDs. Here are the UUIDs registered by the Exchange Server Store Admin interface for a server with the IP address of 192.168.0.13:

```
192.168.0.13[6001] [99e64010-b032-11d0-97a4-00c04fd6551d]
➥Exchange Server STORE ADMIN Interface

192.168.0.13[6001] [89742ace-a9ed-11cf-9c0c-08002be7ae86]
➥Exchange Server STORE ADMIN Interface

192.168.0.13[6001] [a4f1db00-ca47-1067-b31e-00dd010662da]
➥Exchange Server STORE ADMIN Interface
```

### RPC Client Protocols

If you picture the ISO networking model, an RPC-based service sits right up there at the top, at the Application layer. It makes use of the underlying network services to move procedure calls across the network, in the same way that the network redirector relies on the TCP/IP drivers to move file system calls around the network.

Windows has several network services, and a particular RPC service can use any or all of them. Microsoft calls them *RPC client protocols.*

Exchange uses five RPC client protocols, each of which has an identifier called a "protocol sequence." I'll list them here because you'll need to configure an RPC Proxy server to recognize these protocols when an Outlook client requests them:

- TCP (ncacn_ip_tcp)
- UDP (ncadg_ip_udp)
- Named Pipes (ncacn_np)
- HTTP (ncacn_http)
- Local Procedure Call (ncalrpc)

### RPC Endpoints

When an RPC service launches, it registers the client protocol (or protocols) it supports and an entry point for each protocol. The combination of a client protocol and an entry point is called an *endpoint.* Of the endpoint types used by Exchange, only those with wire protocols that require port numbers concern us. Unlike standard Internet services such as ftp or DNS, which use specific, well-known ports for communication, an RPC service selects its port based either on a Registry entry or by choosing a port dynamically from the non-registered ports above 1024.

Because of this dynamic port registration, an RPC client needs a way to determine the port number registered by the RPC service. It makes this determination by querying the Endpoint Mapper (EPM) service on the target server.

The EPM listens on two ports: TCP port 135 and TCP port 593. (The original DCOM standard assigned TCP port 593 specifically to ncacn_http requests, but Exchange and most other applications register their ncacn_http interfaces with TCP port 135.)

You can use a tool from the Windows Server 2003 Support Tools called Portqry to list the ports that have registered with the Endpoint Mapper. Microsoft Knowledge-Base article 310298 has a good list of the RPC ports. You'll get a fairly long listing so pipe the output to a text file using this syntax:

```
portqry -n <server_name> -p tcp -e 135 > portqry.txt
```

The Portqry output resembles Rpcdump, but you can run Portqry against any server. Here's a sample listing showing the ports registered by the Exchange Referral (RFR) service:

```
C:\>portqry -n w2k3-ex3 -p tcp -e 135
Querying target system called:
 w2k3-ex3

Attempting to resolve name to IP address...
Name resolved to 192.168.0.13
TCP port 135 (epmap service): LISTENING
Querying Endpoint Mapper Database...
Server's response:

UUID: 1544f5e0-613c-11d1-93df-00c04fd7bd09 MS Exchange Directory RFR
➥Interface
ncacn_np:\\\\W2K3-EX1[\\pipe\\E60E3840067D1C87]

UUID: 1544f5e0-613c-11d1-93df-00c04fd7bd09 MS Exchange Directory RFR
➥Interface
ncalrpc:[LRPC00000784.00000001]

UUID: 1544f5e0-613c-11d1-93df-00c04fd7bd09 MS Exchange Directory RFR
➥Interface
ncacn_ip_tcp:192.168.0.6[1067]
```

```
UUID: 1544f5e0-613c-11d1-93df-00c04fd7bd09 MS Exchange Directory RFR
➥Interface
ncadg_ip_udp:192.168.0.6[1068]

UUID: 1544f5e0-613c-11d1-93df-00c04fd7bd09 MS Exchange Directory RFR
➥Interface
ncacn_http:192.168.0.6[6002]

UUID: 1544f5e0-613c-11d1-93df-00c04fd7bd09 MS Exchange Directory RFR
➥Interface
ncalrpc:[OLE86D8B80CA5B44FDB8E1B7FF4C784]

==== End of RPC Endpoint Mapper query response ====
```

### *More Detailed End-Point Mapper Operation*

When an Outlook client connects to an Exchange server, it asks the EPM for the port associated with a particular service. To continue with the example of the Exchange Referral (RFR) service, the client directs a query at TCP port 135 on the Exchange server, a query that contains these elements:

- UUID of the target service:
  1544F5E0-613C-11D1-93DF-00C04FD7BD09
- Type of client protocol: Connection Oriented

The EPM replies with the port number registered by the service. In the previous Portqry listing, for example, the RFR service registered the ncacn_ip_tcp client protocol to use TCP port 1067, so the EPM returns that port number to the Outlook client.

Outlook repeats this process for the Information Store Admin interface and the Information Store mailbox interface. Then, armed with the port numbers for those services, Outlook proceeds to open the user's mailbox and obtain messages.

### *RPC Endpoints Used By RPC over HTTP*

Each of the Exchange services required by a client registers an ncacn_http endpoint. In other words, these services listen for HTTP requests at specified ports. The ports are not dynamically determined.

Instead, they are statically mapped in the Registry to simplify setup at the RPC Proxy server. These ports are as follows:

- Information Store: TCP port 6001
- System Attendant: TCP port 6002
- Referral (RFR) service: TCP port 6002
- NSPI (Name Server Provider Interface): TPC port 6004 (As a reminder, this service provides access to address lists such as the GAL)

## Sample RPC over HTTP Process

Figure 11.7 shows a simplified set of transactions that describes how an Outlook client configured to use RPC over HTTP communicates with the user's Exchange mailbox server. The actual process is a bit more complex, as we'll see in a minute, owing to the need for firewalls and global catalog servers and so forth. For now, though, let's take a look at the essentials of the process.

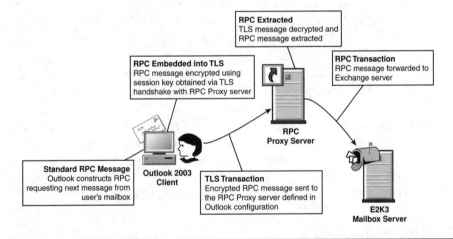

**RPC Extracted**
TLS message decrypted and RPC message extracted

**RPC Embedded into TLS**
RPC message encrypted using session key obtained via TLS handshake with RPC Proxy server

**RPC Transaction**
RPC message forwarded to Exchange server

**RPC Proxy Server**

**Standard RPC Message**
Outlook constructs RPC requesting next message from user's mailbox

**Outlook 2003 Client**

**TLS Transaction**
Encrypted RPC message sent to the RPC Proxy server defined in Outlook configuration

**E2K3 Mailbox Server**

**Figure 11.7** Diagram of basic RPC over HTTP transactions with an Outlook client connecting directly to the RPC Proxy server in a private network.

1. First, the user launches Outlook. This results in a series of RPC messages that contain instructions for the Exchange server to open the user's mailbox and deliver any new message headers. Because Outlook has been configured to use RPC over HTTP, it embeds the RPC message into a standard HTTP message with a header that contains instructions for the RPC Proxy service.

2. Outlook will not send a bare RPC over HTTP message due to the possibility of interception in transit. Instead, Outlook establishes an SSL session with the RPC Proxy service. This service is a feature of Windows Server 2003, not of Exchange, so the proxy server does not need to be running Exchange. As part of the SSL handshake, Outlook obtains a session key that it uses to encrypt the contents of the RPC.

3. Outlook sends the encrypted HTTP traffic to the RPC Proxy server using TCP port 443, the SSL port. Think of this as a SSL "tunnel" for the RPC traffic.

4. The RPC Proxy server decrypts the traffic, yielding a stream of HTTP messages that contain an RPC payload. These messages specify the name of the final destination, which in this case is the Exchange server hosting the user's mailbox.

5. The RPC Proxy server establishes an HTTP connection to the Exchange server and uses it to send the RPC over HTTP traffic to the server.

6. The Exchange server extracts the RPC instructions from the HTTP data stream and performs the requested operations.

As you can see from this process description, the term "RPC over HTTP" is something of a misnomer. Outlook 2003 *requires* the use of SSL when communicating with an RPC Proxy server, so the true term should be "RPC over a Secure Socket Layer Tunnel" or RPC over HTTPS. I suppose that's not sufficiently euphonious.

## Key Points So Far

I'm sure you're getting weary of long process descriptions. Exchange sure has its share of them. Here's the key point to keep in mind.

The RPC Proxy service on Windows Server 2003 acts as an intermediary between an Outlook client and an Exchange server. The proxy needs to know the Exchange server's IP address and the exact port number where each Exchange service is listening for HTTP connections. The majority of the configuration work you're about to do involves locking down these settings in the Registry and in the configuration parameters.

The RPC Proxy service could actually run on the Exchange server itself, but this is not a best practice because it would require putting the mailbox server in the DMZ. A more common configuration uses ISA server to protect the RPC Proxy or uses ISA as the RPC Proxy itself.

## RPC Limitations for Internet Use

Although RPCs are ideally suited for use in a LAN environment where the machines share a reliable, high-speed data communication path, when you try to use them across slow and unreliable WAN, they have a few distinct disadvantages:

- **Sensitive to network latencies.** When an RPC process initiates a transaction with its partner, it expects a quick response. If network latency delays the reply longer than a few tenths of a millisecond, the RPC connection could time out. After a few timeouts, RPC applications get fed up and break connections, and you have to restart the application or otherwise refresh the connection.
- **EPM no longer available on the Internet.** If you lived through the MSBlast worm and its many variants, you're aware that the RPC protocol driver that originally shipped with Windows had several unchecked buffers that made it the target of buffer overflow exploits. These vulnerabilities have long since been patched, but ISPs blocked TCP port 135 at their firewalls and blocked it will stay. It is now virtually impossible to make RPC connections across the Internet.
- **Chatty.** RPCs make a tacit assumption that bandwidth is highly available. If you look at a packet trace for a typical RPC transaction, you'll see many, many small packets generated as the client and server trade configuration information, status checks, parameter changes, and so forth. Many of these transactions involve synchronous communications, requiring either side to ACK the message before the next transaction can proceed. This causes extremely slow performance if the WAN connections in between get congested.

- **Open to inspection.** There is nothing inherently secure in the operation of an RPC-based application. Sure, an application developer can decide to encrypt the contents of the messages traded between the RPC client and server, but you cannot guarantee that every application does this. By the same token, RPC transactions perform only rudimentary consistency checking, so it's theoretically possible to modify the contents of an RPC message in transit without the two endpoint processes being aware of the changes. In a nutshell, you cannot guarantee the end-to-end confidentiality or integrity of RPC communications.

### RPC over HTTP Resolves Limitations

The RPC Proxy service on Windows Server 2003 alleviates most of these problems. By embedding RPC messages into a standard HTTP stream, it's possible to create a tunnel between an RPC client and server that does not require connection to an Endpoint Mapper and is much more resilient in the face of uncertain network latencies.

When the RPC Proxy service is used to support Outlook, it acts just like an Exchange front-end server in that it passes messages to and from Outlook 2003 and Exchange 2003 without modifying the message contents.

The RPC Proxy service also overcomes the inherent insecurity of RPC transactions by using the encryption and integrity validation features of SSL. This ensures that the user credentials and mailbox content are not exposed over the Internet.

## Deploying RPC over HTTP

You're just about ready to configure the necessary services to support RPC over HTTP. As you can see in Figure 11.8, the cast of characters has expanded somewhat compared to the simple process description.

It's worth repeating here that most production deployments of RPC over HTTP use Microsoft's ISA Server to protect the RPC Proxy server or use ISA as the RPC proxy itself. In Exchange 2003 SP1, Microsoft simplified the steps for deploying RPC over HTTP. See the web page for this book at the Addison-Wesley website, www.aw.com, for updates.

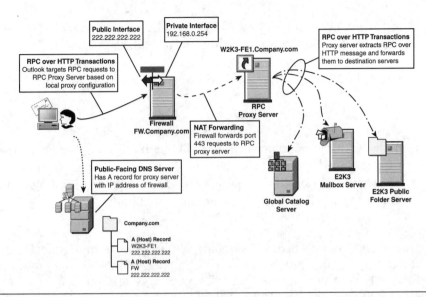

**Figure 11.8** Practical example of using RPC over HTTP to connect an Outlook client in the Internet to a back-end server via an RPC Proxy server in a perimeter network.

You have five principal players that you need to get prepped and on stage, ready to perform:

- **RPC over HTTP clients.** These clients must be running Outlook 2003 on either XP SP2 or XP SP1 with QFE 331320.
- **Firewall.** This can be any firewall capable of tunneling SSL through TCP port 443 to a server on the private side.
- **RPC Proxy server.** This is a server running Windows Server 2003 and IIS with RPC over HTTP enabled. It could also be ISA server acting as an RPC Proxy.
- **Exchange 2003 mailbox and public folder servers.** These servers must be running Windows Server 2003. You cannot connect to mailboxes on an Exchange 2000 server from the RPC Proxy server.
- **Windows Server 2003 Global Catalog servers.** Any Global Catalog server that might be referred to an Outlook client by an Exchange server must be running Windows Server 2003 and have IIS installed with RPC over HTTP enabled.

In addition, the Outlook clients must have some way of resolving the name of the RPC Proxy server into an IP address. You have a couple of options in this regard. You could configure a local Host file on each client, but a better solution is to put an A record in your public DNS zone.

In either case, the IP address associated with the RPC Proxy server must be a public address at the firewall interface, not the server's private address. In the example, TCP port 443 on the firewall has been configured to tunnel through to TCP port 443 at the RPC Proxy server.

Depending on your firewall, you can publish a different port number, a special IP address, or a combination of both.

Most organizations who decide to deploy RPC over HTTP in production do not put the RPC Proxy server directly in the DMZ. Instead, they protect the RPC Proxy using Internet Security and Acceleration (ISA) Server. Using ISA falls outside the scope of this book. See Dr. Thomas Shinder's procedure for using ISA Server and the RPC Proxy at `www.tacteam.net/isaserverorg/exchangekit/2003rpchttp/2003rpchttp.htm`.

## RPC over HTTP Prerequisites

RPC over HTTP is a feature of Windows Server 2003 and XP SP2 or XP SP1 with QFE 331320. (QFE stands for Quick Fix Engineering, a Microsoft term for product updates issued between service pack releases.) You can obtain QFE 331320 by downloading it from Microsoft's Web site. Search for Knowledge-Base article 331320.

There is no general-purpose interface for RPC over HTTP, no "redirector" capable of nabbing standard RPCs and transferring them via HTTP. Both the client application and the server application must know how to construct RPC over HTTP messages.

In the messaging arena, only Outlook 2003 and Exchange 2003 know how to take advantage of RPC over HTTP, so you must first upgrade your messaging infrastructure. This includes Public Folder servers if you want your RPC over HTTP clients to view public folder content across the Internet.

You must run Exchange 2003 on Windows Server 2003 servers with IIS installed and RPC over HTTP enabled. Although you can run Exchange 2003 on Windows 2000, you cannot use RPC over HTTP in that configuration. (Windows 2000 has a rudimentary form of RPC over

HTTP but it is too limited for production use and Microsoft has no plans for upgrading it.)

Because Outlook clients interact directly with Global Catalog servers to obtain address lists, you must also upgrade all Global Catalog servers to Windows Server 2003. Standard domain controllers can continue to run Windows 2000, if required.

### Installing and Configuring the RPC over HTTP Service

Because IIS owns the HTTP over SSL protocol, you must install IIS and enable RPC over HTTP on any server that will participate in RPC over HTTP transactions. The service is not installed by default. Install the service as follows:

1. Launch **Control Panel**.
2. Open the **Add/Remove Programs** applet.
3. Click **Add/Remove Windows Components**.
4. Highlight **Networking Services** and click **Details**.
5. Check the **RPC over HTTP Proxy** option.
6. Click **OK** to return to the Windows Components window.
7. Scroll up to see that there is now a dimmed checkmark next to **Application Server**.
8. Click **OK** again to save the changes.

The checkmark next to Application server indicates that a set of IIS components gets enabled automatically to support RPC over HTTP. These components include the following:

- World Wide Web Service
- IIS Manager
- IIS Common Files
- Network COM+ Access

Repeat these same steps on every Exchange server and Global Catalog server. Although IIS 6.0 is much more secure than its predecessors, you should take precautions to make sure that the servers get patched whenever Web service vulnerabilities are announced.

You'll know that you have RPC over HTTP installed on a server if the IIS Manager console shows an RPC virtual folder, as shown in Figure 11.9. You could also confirm the RPC Proxy Server Extension is 'Allowed' in the Web Service Extension list.

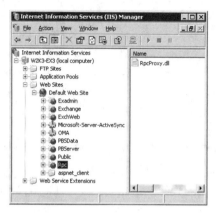

**Figure 11.9** IIS Manager console showing RPC virtual folder. The RPC proxy uses Rpcproxy.dll within that virtual folder.

## Configure the RPC Proxy Server

The RPC Proxy server must support an SSL connection and it must know where to find the ncacn_http ports on the Exchange and Global Catalog servers in the organization.

To support SSL, you must issue a Server certificate to configure the Web services in order to use this certificate. See Chapter 9 for details on issuing Server certificates using a Microsoft PKI. If you decide to use a third-party certificate, it must be issued by a Certification Authority trusted by the client. Examples include Verisign, Baltimore, and Entrust.

### Configure RPC Virtual Folder Security

The RPC virtual folder must be configured to reject all but Basic authentication and to accept only SSL connections with 128-bit encryption. Perform both configurations using IIS Manager. Open the Properties window for the RPC virtual folder and select Directory Security.

Under Authentication and Access Control, click Edit to open the Authentication Methods window, as shown in Figure 11.10. Uncheck everything except Basic Authentication and click OK to save the change. You don't need to worry about exposing the clear-text password in Basic authentication because SSL protects the transaction.

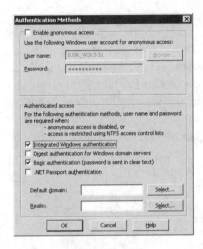

**Figure 11.10** RPC over HTTP for Outlook and Exchange requires Basic authentication.

Back in the Directory Security tab, under Secure Communications, click Edit to open the Secure Communications window as shown in Figure 11.11. Check the Require Secure Channel (SSL) option and the Require 128-bit Encryption option, and click OK to save the change. Then click OK to exit the Directory Security window.

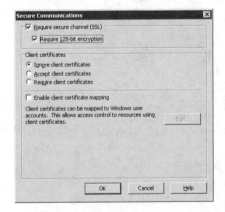

**Figure 11.11** RPC over HTTP for Outlook and Exchange requires SSL.

### Configure RPC Endpoint Mapping

When the RPC Proxy server decrypts the SSL traffic to reveal the HTTP messages inside, it finds the name of the destination server, but it doesn't see the port used by the Exchange service. That's because the Outlook client has no way of knowing this information. You must statically configure the RPC Proxy server with the name of each Exchange 2003 and Global Catalog server in your organization and the ports they use for ncacn_http RPC transactions. This requires an update to an existing Registry entry. Here's the information:

```
Key: HKLM | Software | Microsoft | RPC | RPCProxy
Value: ValidPorts
Type: Reg_SZ
Data: See Below
```

The Data entry for the Registry value includes the name and port number for each ncacn_http endpoint in the form of `<server_name>:<port_number>`; for example, `W2K3-EX1:6001`.

An Exchange server listens for ncacn_http requests on ports 593, 6001, 6002, and 6004. Each port requires its own entry, except that contiguous ports can be joined with a dash; for example, `W2K3-EX1:6001-6002`.

To make things even more complicated, the RPC Proxy does not append DNS suffixes onto flat names, so each port must be entered twice, once with the server's flat name and once with its FQDN. Here's an example for a single Exchange server:

```
W2K3-EX1:593
W2K3-EX1.Company.com :593
W2K3-EX1:6001-6002
W2K3-EX1.Company.com:6001-6002
W2K3-EX1:6004
W2K3-EX1.Company.com :6004
```

The entry for a Global Catalog server would look like this:

```
W2K3-GC1:593
W2K3-GC1.Company.com :593
W2K3-GC1:6004
W2K3-GC1.Company.com:6004
```

If the thought of typing all those entries for several servers (or several dozen, or several hundred servers) makes you want to say "Not in this lifetime," don't give up hope. Microsoft provides a Visual Basic script called Rpchttp_setup.vbs that finds all the Exchange and Global Catalog servers in your organization and adds them to the VirtualPorts value on a designated RPC Proxy server.

Like so many nifty tools, this one comes to us from the friendly folks at Microsoft Product Support Services, who devised the script rather than walk customers through the tedious updating of their Registries. Service Pack 1 for Exchange 2003 simplifies the configuration so that the script is not required.

## Configure NSPI at Global Catalog Servers

Modern Outlook clients such as Outlook 2003 send their address list requests directly to the NSPI interface on a Global Catalog server. For this reason, a critical part of configuring RPC over HTTP involves statically mapping the ncacn_http client protocol for the NSPI service on your Global Catalog servers to a port number known to the RPC Proxy server. Do this by adding a new value to the Registry. Here's the information:

```
Key: HKLM | System | CurrentControlSet | Services | NTDS |
Parameters
Value: NSPI Interface Protocol Sequence
Type: Reg_Multi_SZ (multi string)
Data: ncacn_http:6004
```

Microsoft recommends using TCP port 6004 because that is the default ncacn_http port used for NSPI on Exchange servers. You could, if necessary, select another port.

The Rpchttp_setup.vbs script does not make Registry changes to Global Catalog servers. You must do this update separately. If you don't feel like manually adding the change to every GC server, try using the Reg utility that accompanies Windows Server 2003. The following syntax will make the required Registry change to the destination server (the entire command should be on one line):

```
reg add \\<server_name>\hklm\system\currentcontrolset\
➥service\ntds\parameters /v NSPI "Interface Protocol
➥Sequence" /t REG_MULTI_SZ /d ncacn_http:6004
```

You can put this command in a batch file and feed it a list of your GC servers to do the updates in a single step.

## Configure Firewalls for SSL Passthrough

There are far too many types of firewalls to discuss specific changes necessary to permit Outlook to connect to the RPC Proxy server. However, if you meet a few general conditions, just about any firewall can provide the right access without giving up any security.

Ideally, the RPC Proxy server would reside in a DMZ, or protected perimeter network, rather than directly in the private network. This gives you more control over the traffic from the server in case it should get compromised. The server must be a member of a trusted domain in the forest so it can authenticate the user connections.

If your organization cannot afford a three-legged firewall or you simply do not want the hassle of configuring a DMZ, you can open a TCP port on the external interface of your firewall and point the port specifically at port 443 of the RPC Proxy server. Keep in mind that this makes the other virtual folders on the server available to the public, so do not place sensitive information on the server, and especially do not put untested scripts or CGI tools where they might be executed in an inappropriate manner.

Outlook must be able to establish an SSL connection to the RPC Proxy server. This means that Outlook must be able to resolve the name of the server into an IP address. For this reason, you'll need to publish an A record in your public DNS zone that maps the RPC Proxy server name to the SSL port you opened on the firewall. You can't use the name of the firewall or the firewall's IP address because the client needs to match the server's name to the name in the certificate it gets during the SSL handshake.

For example, in Figure 11.11, the public interface on the firewall has an address of 222.222.222.222. The public DNZ zone contains two A records: one for the firewall itself and one with the name of the RPC Proxy server, but with the IP address of the firewall. You won't need to publish the IP addresses of your Exchange or Global Catalog servers as long as the RPC Proxy server can resolve the names it finds in the decrypted RPC over HTTP messages.

## Configure Outlook for RPC over HTTP

At last we've arrived at the Outlook client itself. Recall that it must be running on XP SP2 or SP1 with QFE 331320. After you meet the pre-requisites, configure Outlook 2003 to use RPC over HTTP as follows:

1. From the main menu, select **Tools | E-mail Accounts**. This opens the E-mail Accounts window.
2. Select the **View or Change Existing E-mail Accounts** radio button.
3. Click **Next** to open an e-mail configuration window.
4. In the list of e-mail accounts, highlight **Microsoft Exchange Server** and click **Change**. This opens the Exchange Server Settings window.
5. Click **More Settings**. This opens the Microsoft Exchange Server window.
6. Select the **Connection** tab.
7. Check the **Connect to My Exchange Mailbox Using HTTP** option, as shown in Figure 11.12.

**Figure 11.12** Exchange Server settings in Outlook 2003 showing the HTTP connection option.

8. Click **Exchange Proxy Settings**. This opens the Exchange Proxy Settings window, as shown in Figure 11.13.

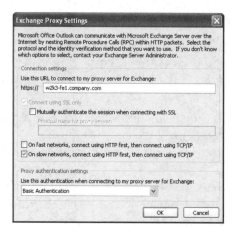

**Figure 11.13** Exchange Proxy Settings on Outlook 2003 showing the URL to the front-end server.

9. In the Connection Settings field, enter the FQDN of the RPC proxy server. The example shows the front-end server W2K3-FE1.Company.com. If you are not using a front-end server, you can enter the name of your Exchange server.

10. The format for the name you enter here must match the format of the name in the SSL certificate **exactly**. If it does not, the connection will fail with no error messages. For example, the entry in Figure 11.13 uses the FQDN of W2K3-FE1.Company.com. If the SSL certificate has the name W2K3-FE1, then the connection will fail. There are no error messages, so this type of problem can be tough to troubleshoot.

11. In the **Proxy Authentication Settings** field, select **NTLM Authentication** from the drop-down list. This gives a seamless experience to the user by taking the current logon credentials and using them to connect to the RPC Proxy server. For configurations involving home computers or non-domain members, use Basic authentication.

The authentication method submitted by a desktop is controlled by a Registry value called LMCompatibilityLevel. By default, XP sets this value to 0, meaning that the desktop submits whatever the application requests. A setting of 0, however, prevents RPC over HTTP from using NTLM authentication. So, you must set it to 3, forcing the desktop to use NTLM authentication. Here is the Registry information:

```
Key: HKLM | System | CurrentControlSet | Control | LSA
Value: LMCompatibilityLevel
Data: 3 (REG_DWORD)
```

## Make RPC over HTTP Connection

After you've configured the Outlook client, launch Outlook and make sure you can open your mailbox. Keep in mind that you're outside the firewall so you cannot authenticate to the domain. You must already have authenticated once inside the firewall to get cached credentials.

Because you configured Outlook to use Basic authentication, when you launch Outlook you'll get a prompt for a name and password. Make sure you specify your name using domain\username format. Basic authentication through a proxy cannot accept a UPN (username@ domain.root) format.

If you get prompted over and over and over again for credentials, you have a problem validating the certificate from the RPC Proxy server. This typically happens if the server name or the format used for the name in Outlook does not match the name or the name format in the SSL certificate.

Here's a quick way to check the configuration. Open a browser at the client and enter the path to the RPC virtual folder in IIS. An example of the syntax is as follows:

```
https://w2k3-fe1.company.com/rpc
```

If the port on the firewall is configured correctly and the SSL configuration at the server is correct, you should connect but get a 403.2 error, indicating Access Denied. That's because the browser is requesting Read access to a folder that only permits Execute. This is normal and exactly what you want to see. If you get a 404 error, indicating that the client cannot find the server, then you have a DNS problem.

In the page that contains the 403.2 error, double-click the little padlock at the bottom of the window in the status bar. This opens the SSL certificate. Compare the name in the certificate with the name you used when configuring RPC over HTTP in Outlook. Make sure they match.

## Test Without a Firewall

If you want to test RPC over HTTP connections without going through the bother of configuring a firewall and a separate RPC Proxy server, you can make the RPC VirtualFolder registry updates on the Exchange 2003 server then point the Outlook client directly at the server. Make sure you select the On Fast Networks, Connect Using HTTP First, Then Connect Using TCP/IP option. If you leave this unchecked, the client will connect using TCP/IP because that's the fastest option.

To make sure you've made an HTTPS connection after you successfully open Outlook, hold down the Ctrl key, right-click the Outlook icon in the Notification Area, and select Connection Status from the flyout menu as shown in Figure 11.14.

**Figure 11.14**  Outlook 2003 Connection Status option in property menu of Outlook icon in the Notification Area.

This opens a Connection Status window as shown in Figure 11.15. This window should show a HTTPS connection for each Mail, Directory, and Public Folders connection.

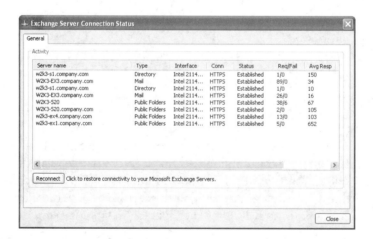

**Figure 11.15**  Exchange Server Connection Status window in Outlook 2003 showing HTTPS connections for all RPC connections: Directory, Mail, and Public Folders.

### Verify Mutual Authentication

The SSL protocol includes the ability for the client to validate the identity of the SSL server. This prevents man-in-the-middle exploits. One possible scenario for such an exploit involves hijacking or poisoning your public DNS zone so that the A record representing your RPC Proxy server has an IP address of a bad guy's server rather than your server. Such a scenario is not unthinkable, so it's best to provide defense in depth. Always require mutual authentication when configuring an Outlook client to use RPC over HTTP.

Configure mutual authentication using the Exchange Proxy Settings window (Tools | E-mail Accounts | View or Change Existing E-mail Accounts | Change | More Settings | Connection | Exchange Proxy Settings). Check the **Mutually Authenticate the Session When Connecting with SSL** option and enter the principal name for the proxy server.

All member servers in an Active Directory domain have several Service Principal Names (SPNs), or principal name, for short. A principal name can have many formats, but in general, it uses the FQDN preceded by the service that registered the SPN. You can use the Setspn utility in the Windows Server 2003 Support Tools to list the SPNs registered for a particular machine. The syntax is `setspn   -L <server_flat_name>`. Here's a sample listing:

```
C:\>setspn -l w2k3-fe1
Registered ServicePrincipalNames for CN=W2K3-
➥FE1,CN=Computers,DC=company,DC=com:
    exchangeRFR/w2k3-fe1.company.com
    exchangeMDB/w2k3-fe1.company.com
    SMTPSVC/w2k3-fe1.company.com
    HOST/w2k3-fe1.company.com
    exchangeRFR/W2K3-FE1
    exchangeMDB/W2K3-FE1
    SMTPSVC/W2K3-FE1
    HOST/W2K3-FE1
```

Fortunately, you don't need to know the exact SPN of the service on the RPC Proxy. Instead, Microsoft provides a standard form for a principal name used in conjunction with SSL. The syntax is `msstd:<server_FQDN>` ; for example, `msstd:w2k3-fe1.company.com`. Figure 11.16 shows an example of the Exchange Proxy Settings window with mutual authentication enabled, and a properly formatted principal name supplied for the proxy server.

**Figure 11.16** Exchange Proxy Settings showing the requirement to do mutual authentication with the front-end proxy server.

If you make a typo in the name, or forget to use the msstd format, the client will not successfully connect. You'll be prompted repeatedly for a password.

## RPC Over HTTP—Final Thoughts

As you can see, making the decision to deploy RPC over HTTP to your organization is going to take a while. After you do the grunt work, though, the payoff is substantial in terms of reduced support costs and greater user satisfaction. As for the security of the configuration, you're essentially creating a special-purpose SSL VPN into the DMZ of your network. In this respect, using RPC over HTTP is not better and no worse than any other SSL VPN solution.

What could reduce security is laxity in hardening the RPC Proxy server. Make certain that the server has all patches and lock down unneeded services. If you decide to deploy a front-end server for OWA or POP3/IMAP4, you should use the same server for RPC over HTTP to reduce your overall attack surface in the DMZ.

If you connect directly to an RPC Proxy server or an Exchange server behind the firewall in the private network, keep in mind that an exploit that exposes the server will let an attacker into your private network. Monitor closely and consider installing a host-based Intrusion Detection Service (IDS) on the server to notify you if it suddenly begins misbehaving.

# Looking Forward

At this point, if you have a pristine production environment, you're now all set to deploy Exchange Server 2003 from scratch. You have to be concerned with service continuity, spam, virus prevention, and backups so you'll want to take a look at Chapter 13, "Service Continuity." But other than that, you can go over your lab notes and then start planning your production deployment.

But if you belong to one of the many organizations that already have a production deployment of Exchange 5.x, your job is only just starting. In the next chapter, you will learn how to migrate those legacy servers to Exchange 2003 and maybe even have fun at the same time.

Or maybe not.

# CHAPTER 12

# Migrating from Legacy Exchange

U p to this point in the book, you've worked with a pristine installation of Exchange 2003 in either a Windows Server 2003 or Windows 2000 forest. But while you've worked through the examples and studied the process descriptions and configured your lab, you've probably been wondering how you're going to put this information to use in a production environment that already contains legacy Exchange servers.

Throughout this chapter, the term "legacy Exchange server" refers to servers running Exchange 5.5 or earlier. Features and options that apply solely to Exchange 2000 servers are called out separately.

Before taking on the complex task of migrating your Exchange organization, I invite you to relax and take a few moments to consider the broad expanse of history before computers and digital communications and e-mail, before even the advent of the printed word itself. Back to a simpler time when common folk such as ourselves found inspiration in tales of great heroes who battled mighty foes in pursuit of lofty goals.

One ancient character embodied the very definition of heroism itself, the Greek warrior Heracles. Overcome by madness in his early life, Heracles killed his wife and children. When he sought purification for this act, he was given 12 deadly labors, which he undertook while prepared to die. Instead, he overcame the odds and bested all his opponents. In his maturity, Heracles went on to avenge many evils and eventually had his own action figure and a slot in the AWWF (Ancient World Wrestling Federation).

The story of Heracles puts me in mind of an Exchange 2003 migration because one of the 12 deadly labors involved in defeating the many-headed Hydra. The Hydra posed a special challenge for Heracles.

Not only was each individual head of the monster especially ferocious, but if he lopped off one of the heads, two more would grow back in its place. Every apparent success put him closer to defeat, a perfect metaphor for e-mail administration, regardless of the messaging platform you use.

When you get in the middle of your Exchange migration and you face problems that seem to multiply geometrically like the heads of the Hydra, you might want to take a hint from the way Heracles solved the problem. He didn't try to do the job himself. He sought help from his nephew, who cauterized each neck as Heracles swooped off the head, preventing a new head from growing. Thus they were able to bring down the monster and move on to the next labor.

I'm not telling you to hire your nephew for your Exchange 2003 migration. What I'm advising is this: Approach the migration with all due respect and work with your colleagues to prepare for unexpected calamities. Set reasonable expectations for your management and users. Don't promise a completely transparent and problem-free transition, although that might very well happen. Instead, promise that you'll do your best to stand between your users and any monsters as you make the transition. When everything goes smoothly, your users might not declare you a hero like Heracles, but they'll be happy enough with the experience to continue bringing you cookies and chocolate cake when they want you to do something special with their e-mail. What more could an Exchange administrator want?

## Pre-Migration Operational Evaluations

At some point early in your migration planning, you're going to need to sit down with a clean sheet of paper (or a blank computer screen) and figure out what you're going to do. You should test all your actions in a lab first before rolling them out into production. You might also want to arrange for a pilot program where selected users are placed in a separate forest where you perform the entire migration in an environment that more closely matches the production configurations than might be possible in a lab.

It's also important to document your current configurations. You would be surprised how often you'll need to know where a user's mailbox *used* to be, or what server used to be located in Sheboygan, or what information is available only on old backup tapes buried in a mountain somewhere.

Here is a list of items that you should include in your pre-migration planning. You'll also find a prerequisite list later on in the chapter along with a roadmap for the major steps in the migration.

## Active Directory Domains

Evaluate your current domain configuration with an eye toward making sure that it will support Exchange 2003 operations. The deployment tools that come with Exchange 2003 help you to test for these conditions, but it's a good idea to get familiar with the requirements in advance. Here are some items to consider:

- **Domain controller location.** You'll need at least one domain controller in each office that has an Exchange 2003 server.
- **Global Catalog server location.** You'll need at least one Global Catalog server in each office that has an Exchange 2003 server. This can also act as the local domain controller. The simplest way to accomplish this is to make all branch office DCs into GCs. Microsoft recommends a minimum of one Global Catalog server for every four Exchange *processors*, not servers.
- **DNS configuration.** Make certain that DNSLint shows no errors. See Chapter 1, "Installing an Exchange 2003 Server," for details.
- **Active Directory Native Mode.** The Active Directory domain containing the Exchange servers must be in Native Mode so that you can use Universal Security Groups for e-mail distribution.
- **Replication or authentication problems.** Verify by a sweep of the event logs that you have no errors from directory service replication, KCC topology calculations, or authentication errors originating from domain controller accounts. You can use the EventCombMT utility, a free download from Microsoft, to perform this sweep. EventCombMT is part of the Account Lockout and Management and Lockout, available at `http://snipurl.com/5z37`.

If you're willing to spend a few dollars and a couple of weekends learning the configuration, you'll find that Microsoft Operations Manager (MOM) or a third-party product will do a better job of monitoring your event logs.

## Current Exchange Organization

Evaluate your current production Exchange organization to make sure that you don't have any outstanding issues that might cause a problem during the transition to Exchange 2003.

The ExMap utility from the Exchange Resource Kit and the ExInfo utility (a free download—see Microsoft Knowledge-Base article 305816) can assist in this information-gathering phase. Here are some key points:

- **Exchange server version.** You'll need at least one Exchange 5.5 server with SP3 or higher in each site.
- **Site configuration.** Verify that you have an active Exchange server in each site. If you have sites that are no longer used, remove them from the legacy Exchange directory service prior to commencing the Exchange 2003 deployment. It is extraordinarily difficult to remove a site from the Link State Table once it has been placed there.
- **Site connectors and Directory Replication connectors.** Make sure that you get proper message routing and directory service updates through your existing connectors. Resolve any problems prior to commencing the Exchange 2003 deployment.
- **Internet connectors.** Identify the servers that are acting as Internet Messaging Service (IMS) bridgeheads. You'll want to plan on replacing these servers with Exchange 2003 servers early in your deployment.
- **Unsupported connectors.** If you have connectors to third-party messaging systems that do not have Exchange 2003 connectors, such as PROFS and SNADS, you'll need to find another way to connect the systems or plan on installing at least one Exchange 2000 server to act as the gateway.
- **Key Management Services.** If you are using digital certificates issued by an Exchange Key Management Service to encrypt and digitally sign e-mail, then you'll need to deploy a Windows Server 2003 PKI and migrate the KMS database to a Windows Server 2003 Configuration Authority. This procedure falls outside the scope of this book. Microsoft has an excellent white paper on migrating a legacy KMS.
- **Compatible backup.** Make sure the backup software you're using supports Exchange 2003 and that you have the most current backup agents installed on the Exchange 2003 servers. You can

use NTBackup that comes with Windows Server 2003 until your vendor gets a compatible agent. See Chapter 13, "Service Continuity," for details.

■ **Antivirus and antispam software.** Make sure that your centrally managed antivirus and antispam solutions have agents for both legacy Exchange and Exchange 2003. Make sure that any new servers are included in signature distribution. If your antispam solution runs at a smart host in the perimeter, make sure that any tagging done by the application is compatible with the Exchange 2003 antispam API. See Chapter 13 for more information.

■ **E-mail dependent applications.** If you use third-party applications that depend on Exchange, such as fax, telephony, or collaboration services, make sure that the application has a version that runs on Exchange 2003. Check their product databases for special configuration requirements and any known problems.

■ **Exchange 2000 instant messaging.** Must be isolated from Exchange 2000 mailbox/public folder servers that are going to be upgraded to 2003.

## Network Infrastructure

Evaluate your WAN connections and network routing topology to make sure that you have sufficient capacity for Exchange 2003 and to give you an idea where to create Routing groups. Here are some important considerations:

■ **Traffic patterns.** If your WAN infrastructure handles the current Exchange message traffic with no problems or errors, you should not experience problems with Exchange 2003. However, keep in mind that the combination of Outlook 2003 in cached mode and Exchange 2003 can result in a significant amount of traffic on Monday mornings when users refresh their local message cache with e-mails received over the weekend. Warn your network services colleagues and check the Microsoft white paper titled "Client Network Traffic with Microsoft Exchange Server 2003." Download it from `www.microsoft.com/exchange/techinfo/outlook/CliNetTraf.asp`.

■ **Outages.** Have you experienced any significant outages in the last six months that might recur and impact your deployment? Instabilities in WAN connections can also cause message routing issues as you make the transition from legacy Exchange routing based on the Gateway Address Routing Table and the Link State Table used by Exchange 2003.

- **Remote users.** If remote Outlook users currently connect to the Exchange system via a VPN or dial-up to get their e-mail, you might want to consider deploying RPC over HTTP to support remote e-mail access, especially if e-mail is the only reason that users need a VPN. See Chapter 11, "Deploying a Distibuted Architecture," for more information.
- **Routing groups.** Use your Active Directory site map to help define your routing group topology. You don't need to follow them slavishly, though. SMTP works fine over high-latency connections that might cause a problem for Active Directory. Consider consolidating existing sites into a single Routing group based on the traffic volume you see after the deployment. For example, you might have several campuses in the same city connected by fractional T1s in a frame relay cloud. You might have defined separate legacy sites to control bandwidth, but with Exchange 2003, you can use a single Routing group for the entire city. This simplifies mail routing and makes it simpler to manage public folder access.

## Costs

Deploying Exchange 2003 requires money, time, and people.

- **Server software.** Exchange 2003 Standard Edition lists for $699. Enterprise Edition lists for $3,999. You'll need to purchase Exchange 2003 Enterprise Edition if you want to set up shared-disk clusters or if you need multiple mailbox stores with virtually an unlimited database size. (Standard Edition allows only one mailbox store and limits it to 16GB.)
- **Client Access Licenses (CALs).** You do not need to deploy a new client, but you will need to pay for and upgrade your CALs. Each CAL lists at $67 with substantial discounts for upgrade licenses and volume purchases. If you deploy Exchange in several business units, it's theoretically possible to delay the upgrade for a particular business unit until they have the money for the CALs. But in practical terms, you should purchase your licenses up front before you begin deployment.
- **Additional personnel.** When estimating the personnel component of your deployment costs, don't forget to factor in a consult-

ant or two who can help you streamline the deployment as well as budgeting for support calls to Microsoft Product Support Services (PSS) if something doesn't go well.

- **Training.** Budget for in-depth training for the Exchange administrators and high-level summary training for the Windows system administrators, since they interact with Active Directory objects that affect Exchange operation. End-user training is important, too, if you are going to roll out new clients.

- **Client software.** When deciding whether to deploy a new client in conjunction with the Exchange 2003 deployment, keep in mind that you get the full range of features, including cached message handling, if you roll out Office System 2003 or Outlook 2003. (The standalone version of Outlook 2003 can be used for no additional change once you pay for the Exchange 2003 Client Access License.)

When deciding how to size your servers, take a look at the Microsoft white paper titled "Server Consolidation Using Exchange Server 2003." This paper takes a fair look at the factors that affect server sizing and gives you a good baseline to start your testing.

## Additional Considerations

Categorize and define the potential problems and challenges you might face during the upgrade. Here are some of the more important items to consider:

- **Directory service connection failures.** If you have underlying DNS issues, either with client configuration or the DNS server itself, you can find yourself in situations where the Exchange servers can't locate domain controllers and Global Catalog servers. This results in a variety of errors. See Appendix A, "Building a Stable Exchange 2003 Deployment Infrastructure," for more information about DNS configuration and troubleshooting.

- **Inability to access public folders.** If public folder permission mapping fails for some reason, such as invalid permission list entries, then users might lose access to their public folders. See Appendix B, "Legacy Exchange Operation," for more details about permission mapping.

- **Inability to replicate public folders with legacy Exchange.** Before you can decommission your legacy Exchange servers, you must move all public folder content to the new Exchange 2003 servers. This includes system folders that contain critical calendaring and offline address book information. It sometimes happens that this replication fails, so part of your testing should monitor for correct content of all folders prior to removing a legacy server from operation.

■ **Incompatible historical backups.** If you deploy Exchange 2003 and decommission all your legacy servers, and then need to restore a mailbox from a date preceding the deployment, you won't be able to restore the legacy Exchange mailbox database onto an Exchange 2003 server. Leave the Exchange organization in Exchange Native mode until you're sure that you won't need the old backups.

■ **Hardware failures.** You're going to be deploying new servers running Exchange 2003. There's always the likelihood that you'll find incompatibilities in the new hardware or component drivers. Be prepared to get quick help in the event of a failure, and make sure all hardware is listed in the Windows Server Catalog (which used to be the Hardware Compatibility List).

■ **Software compatibility failures.** You could find that your selection of backup, antivirus, and antispam tools or other server utilities causes the server to become unstable. If you encounter problems keeping the server operating, one of your first steps should be to deactivate all third-party software, just to see if that makes the problem go away.

## Goals

■ **No service interruptions**. In today's IT environment, messaging is supposed to be as pervasive and available as a dial tone. The major contributors to downtime during a typical Exchange migration are incorrectly configured DNS settings, unstable Active Directory replication, improper hardware, improperly configured Routing groups, and lack of coordination between the Exchange administrators and the other IT staff.

■ **Single mailbox-enabled account for each user**. In your existing Exchange environment, you might have many legacy mailboxes owned by a single user. Or you might have mailboxes that have no owner. During the migration to Exchange 2003, you will normalize your mailbox ownership so that each legacy mailbox has one and only one valid user. This is done as part of the ADC deployment.

- **Retain existing mailbox and public folder permissions**. Exchange maps legacy Exchange MAPI permissions to the ACL-based security descriptors in Exchange 2003. It's important that this mapping work correctly. Be cautious and do lots of testing before making any large-scale changes to permissions.

- **Fastest possible introduction of new features.** To take full advantage of the new features in Exchange 2003, you need to complete the Exchange migration and decommission all legacy Exchange servers. Don't let weeks turn into months turn into years. Until you shift to Native mode, you won't be able to take full advantage of the features you paid for.

- **Maximize existing hardware**. It's one thing to pay for the Exchange 2003 server software and CALs. It's quite another to pay for a new fleet of servers to run Exchange. Be sure to inventory your server hardware with an eye toward adding RAM, faster disks, more storage, and possibly an updated network adapter that can offload SSL and TCP/IP services.

# Exchange Migration Roadmap

You cannot do an in-place upgrade from Exchange 5.5 to Exchange 2003. This applies even if you run Exchange 5.5 on Windows 2000. All upgrades from Exchange 5.5 to Exchange 2003 involve setting up new Exchange 2003 servers and moving mailboxes and connectors to those servers.

A basic migration has three phases: upgrade the domain to Windows Server 2003 (or Windows 2000, if you want to use the older operating system), deploy new Exchange 2003 servers, and then decommission the legacy servers. Here are the high-level details for each phase. The remainder of the chapter describes the details for performing each stage.

## Domain Upgrade

The roadmap for a typical single domain upgrade looks like this:

1. **Upgrade the current PDC to Windows Server 2003.** Use a leapfrog upgrade so that you have fresh hardware on the newly upgraded server. A leapfrog upgrade involves installing a new NT BDC, promoting it to PDC, and then upgrading it to Windows Server 2003. This puts the domain (and forest) at an Interim functional level, which enables certain replication features in Windows Server 2003 (such as replicating individual group members rather than the entire Member attribute) while retaining backward compatibility with NT domain controllers.

2. **Install additional Windows Server 2003 domain controllers.** Don't tempt fate by having fewer than three domain controllers in a domain. This lets you take one domain controller down for maintenance and still have two up and running. Make as many of those domain controllers into GC servers as possible.

3. **Decommission all NT BDCs.** This eliminates the need to support legacy LanMan replication.

4. **Shift the domain and forest to Windows Server 2003 functional level.** This enables you to create Universal Security Groups, a requirement in a multiple domain forest.


## Exchange 2003 Server Deployment

In the second phase, you'll deploy Exchange Server 2003 alongside your legacy Exchange servers. The roadmap looks like this:

1. **Install SP4 and the latest security patches on all Exchange 5.5 servers.** The ADC requires that any legacy Exchange server that acts as a Connection Agreement endpoint runs Exchange 5.5 SP3 or higher. This gives it the ADC the ability to read and write the legacy directory service via LDAP.

2. **Normalize mailboxes.** You need to spend an afternoon, maybe a long afternoon, validating that you have a one-to-one match between each legacy Exchange mailbox and an Active Directory user. At the same time, verify that each mailbox owner actually exists in Active Directory. The ADC tools perform this check, but you don't want to wait until the middle of the deployment to

find out that you have a problem. Download the NTDSNoMatch utility from Microsoft to help with this work. See Knowledge-Base article 274173 for download and configuration information.

3. **Verify public folder permissions.** Spend another long afternoon going through the permission list for each public folder to ensure that the recipients and distribution lists actually exist. This avoids having *zombies* on the permission lists; that is, distinguished names that do not point at a valid account in the legacy Exchange directory service. Exchange 2003 contains safeguards against problems caused by zombies, but you'll have more success in your deployment if you avoid the problem completely. The Pfadmin tool is great for doing this work. Microsoft Knowledge Base article 188629 discusses how to remove invalid permission entries using Pfadmin.

4. **Install the ADC.** This updates the Active Directory schema to include all changes required by Exchange Server 2003, so it takes some preparation on the Windows side. This chapter describes those preparations.

5. **Configure Recipient and Public Folder connection agreements.** A Connection Agreement (CA) defines a pathway between Active Directory and the legacy Exchange directory service. The ADC uses CAs to transfer mailbox information from legacy Exchange to mailbox-enabled users in Active Directory and to create Distribution groups and Contact objects in Active Directory that match the distribution lists and custom recipients in legacy Exchange.

6. **Install the first Exchange 2003 server.** This creates a Configuration connection agreement in the ADC that copies information about the legacy Exchange organization into Active Directory. This server also runs an instance of the Site Replication Service (SRS) so the Exchange 2003 server can replicate directly with legacy Exchange servers in its site.

7. **Move Connection Agreement endpoints.** An Exchange 2003 server running SRS can act as an endpoint for connection agreements. The ADC Connection Agreement Wizard initially assigns endpoints to legacy Exchange servers. You have to manually move the endpoints of Recipient and Public Folder CAs to an Exchange 2003 SRS server.

## Legacy Exchange Server Decommissioning

The final phase includes moving all Exchange operations over to the new servers and removing the legacy servers from the organization. Here's the roadmap:

1. **Move mailboxes.** Now that you have a fully functional Exchange 2003 server, you can move mailboxes to it from the legacy Exchange servers in the same site. You might want to install additional Exchange 2003 servers if you need the additional storage capacity and horsepower, or you can install Exchange 2003 Enterprise Edition and create additional storage groups and mailbox stores. Exchange is still in Mixed mode, so you cannot move mailboxes directly between servers in different legacy sites, which correspond to Exchange 2003 Administrative Groups.

2. **Move connectors.** The legacy Exchange server probably hosts a variety of connectors, such as the Internet Mail Connector (IMC), Site connector, Directory Replication connector, and possibly additional connectors for X.400 or third-party e-mail systems. You'll need to create new connectors on the Exchange 2003 server and make sure that those connectors work satisfactorily before removing the legacy connectors. You'll need Enterprise Edition if you have an X.400 connector.

3. **Decommission legacy servers.** At this point, you no longer need the legacy Exchange servers in this particular site. Uninstall Exchange from the servers. This removes their objects from the organization both in the legacy Exchange directory service and from Active Directory.

4. **Repeat for all other sites.** During the time that you're upgrading the first Exchange site to Exchange 2003, you can start upgrading the other sites using the same steps. You'll wake up one morning and all the legacy Exchange servers will be gone. This stage invariably takes twice as long as you originally had in the schedule.

5. **Shift to Exchange Native mode.** This step involves removing the Site Replication Service from all Exchange 2003 servers then setting a flag in the organization that releases it from compatibility with legacy Exchange.

6. **Celebration.** Don't forget this very important final step. Your Mode Shift Party (MSP) does not necessarily need to feature the unconscious forms of grinning Exchange administrators draped over piles of empty pizza boxes outside the server room, but that's certainly a possibility.

## Special Considerations

The basic roadmap I'm following assumes that you start with a single domain and all legacy Exchange servers. Just a few of the possible scenarios include the following:

- Legacy Exchange servers running in several NT domains
- Legacy Exchange servers running in a Windows 2000 forest
- Mix of legacy Exchange servers and Exchange 2000 servers running in a Windows 2000 forest

Here are the additional considerations you need to include in your planning for these more complex situations.

### Multiple NT Domains

If you have multiple NT4 domains and you choose to consolidate them into a single, pristine Windows Server 2003 domain, then your Exchange 2003 deployment roadmap changes just a little.

In an in-place migration, your efforts focus on transferring recipient and configuration information from the legacy Exchange directory service to Active Directory via the ADC. In a domain migration, you must first concern yourself with migrating security principals (user accounts, servers and desktops, and groups) from the NT domain to the Active Directory domain. Then you can set up the ADC and start your Exchange 2003 deployment.

An Active Directory attribute called SIDHistory contains the SID from the legacy NT domain so that users retain access to NT domain resources, such as their legacy Exchange mailboxes. Always migrate accounts using a tool that populates SIDHistory. Microsoft provides a free tool called the Active Directory Migration Tool (ADMT v2) on the Windows Server 2003 CD. You can get additional features and reporting capabilities by using third-party tools such as Domain Migration Wizard from Aelita Software or NetIQ's Domain and Exchange Migration Administrator.

Don't use the ADC to populate Active Directory with user accounts from the NT domain. The ADC does not populate SIDHistory and does not migrate user passwords, two critical features of a migration tool such as ADMT. Once you've migrated user accounts into Active Directory, then you can use the ADC to transfer legacy Exchange mailbox information to the objects, in the same way you did for an in-place migration.

From there, the roadmap matches an in-place upgrade. You install Exchange 2003 servers, move mailboxes and public folders and connectors to the new servers, decommission the old servers, shift to Native mode, and celebrate.

### Legacy Exchange in a Windows 2000 Forest

If you have already deployed Windows 2000 but you still run legacy Exchange, you have a somewhat easier deployment roadmap. You can run Exchange 2003 in a Windows 2000 forest, but without some of the features you might want. (The feature set is detailed later in the chapter.) You should strongly consider upgrading your forest to Windows Server 2003 prior to deploying Exchange 2003 to get all the new features.

The details of upgrading your forest lie outside the scope of this book. (See my book, *Inside Windows Server 2003*, or *The Ultimate Windows Server 2003 System Administrator's Guide* by Robert Williams and Mark Walla. Both books are from Addison-Wesley.)

In general, the upgrade consists of modifying the Windows 2000 schema by running a tool called Adprep, and then either upgrading your Windows 2000 domain controllers to Windows Server 2003, or introducing new Windows Server 2003 domain controllers and decommissioning the old domain controllers.

An upgrade leaves the domain functional level at its current state. For example, if the Windows 2000 domain were in Mixed mode, the Windows Server 2003 domain and forest would be set to Windows 2000 Mixed functional level. You'll need to shift to a Windows 2000 Native functional level to get the ability to create Universal Security Groups prior to deploying Exchange 2003.

Once you've completed the Windows Server 2003 upgrade, you can begin deploying Exchange 2003. I do not recommend doing both upgrades at the same time because this introduces too much complexity into the deployment plan, makes recoverability more problematical, and complicates troubleshooting.

### Mix of Exchange 5.5 and Exchange 2000 Servers

Speaking of keeping things simple, you should avoid deploying Exchange 2003 in the midst of an Exchange 2000 deployment that involves an upgrade from Exchange 5.5. Microsoft refers to this as a TIPTOS deployment, derived from the chemical symbols of the code names for the three Exchange products: Titanium for Exchange 2003, Platinum for Exchange 2000, and Osmium for Exchange 5.5.

Imagine the Monday meetings where you discuss configuration changes in sites with servers that have one, two, or all three versions of Exchange, maybe running with different service packs and security patches. You would need to include multiple strategies for directory service replication and multiple strategies for message routing; and you would need to keep track of the eccentricities of each type of server with your mix of antivirus, antispam, and backup agents.

Now imagine diagnosing and fixing problems caused when those servers don't want to interoperate for some inexplicable reason.

Now imagine what your resume might look like after you explain to your boss for the hundredth time why the CIO didn't get her e-mail.

If you decide to get a head start by deploying Windows Server 2003 in a mixed environment of Exchange 2000 and Windows 2000, before running Adprep, it's important that you correct an issue with the InetOrgPerson attributes in the Schema. The syntax for several attributes does not follow RFC guidelines, and if you update the schema without doing the fix, you'll "scramble" the attributes, and they cannot be fixed later on. Look at Microsoft Knowledge-Base article 325379 for more details.

# Prerequisites and Precautions

Include the following items in your preparation checklist as you begin planning your upgrade:

- **Security patches.** I'm sure you don't need me to tell you to put the most current security patches on a server prior to putting it into production. This reminder is here for the "other guy" who neglects this rudimentary precaution.
- **Windows service packs.** Exchange 2003 runs fine on Windows Server 2003 without service packs, but you might want to install SP1 on your Exchange servers and domain controllers to get the security rollups. If you install Exchange 2003 on Windows 2000, you must be running Service Pack 3 or higher.
- **Exchange service packs.** Exchange 2003 SP1 should be installed as part of your deployment plan
- **Schema Master availability.** Installing Exchange 2003 requires updating the Active Directory schema. Only one domain controller can change the schema—the Schema Master. You can find the identity of the Schema Master using the Dumpfsmos utility in the Resource Kit or the Exchange Deployment Tools, which can be run anytime.
- **Upgrade domain controllers.** You can deploy Exchange 2003 into a Windows 2000 forest, but if you have many sites that have slow WAN connections, you might want to first upgrade the forest to Windows Server 2003. This lessens the impact of the Global Catalog updates performed by Exchange 2003.
- **Mobile Information Server (MIS).** Exchange 2003 has no direct upgrade path for MIS 2000. If you want to preserve functionality for existing mobile users during the Exchange 2003 deployment, keep at least one MIS 2000 server running as you migrate your mobile users to Exchange 2003.
- **Instant Messaging (IM) and Chat.** Exchange 2003 has no upgrade path for Exchange 2000 IM or Chat. This functionality has been replaced by Live Communication Server (LCS), which has a per-user license fee. If you decide to deploy LCS, keep at least one Exchange 2000 IM server running as you migrate your users to LCS.
- **ccMail connector.** Exchange 2003 does not include a ccMail connector. If you still run ccMail in your organization along with Exchange, it's time to finally make the transition.

- **Backup, antivirus, and antispam compatibility.** Your current backup, antivirus, and antispam solutions must have full compatibility with Exchange 2003 and Windows Server 2003. De-install these applications prior to performing an in-place upgrade to prevent possible compatibility problems during Setup.
- **ADC upgrades.** You should avoid TIPTOS deployments (combination of Exchange 5.5, Exchange 2000, and Exchange 2003), but circumstances might require you to begin preparations for your Exchange 2003 deployment during the final stages of the migration away from Exchange 5.5. You *must* upgrade the ADC servers to Exchange 2003 ADC prior to introducing any Exchange 2003 servers into the organization. The ADC upgrade modifies the schema, so make sure that the Schema Master is available.
- **Front-end/back-end upgrades.** If you have an existing deployment of Exchange 2000 that uses a distributed architecture, upgrade the front-end servers first and then upgrade the back-end servers. Upgrade Exchange first, and then Windows.

Many organizations choose to replace their Exchange 2000 front-end servers rather than upgrade them. Exchange 2000 requires Enterprise Edition for a front-end server, a considerable expense. Exchange 2003 supports front-end servers on Standard Edition. You cannot upgrade Exchange 2000 Enterprise Edition to Exchange 2003 Standard Edition, so it makes economic sense to replace the front-end servers completely. Minimize the hardware expense by using a "swing" upgrade—introduce a new Exchange 2003 front-end server to replace the Exchange 2000 front-end server, and then wipe the drives of the old server. Do a pristine install of Windows Server 2003 and Exchange 2003, and then redeploy it.

# Active Directory Connector Operation

One of the challenges in making the transition to Exchange 2003 consists of extracting all the operational parameters for e-mail recipients, distribution lists, custom recipients, public folders, address lists, and message routing parameters from the existing legacy Exchange directory service and putting that information into Active Directory. You as the administrator can move mailboxes and connectors off the old Exchange 5.x servers and onto sleek, new Exchange 2003 servers with minimal service disruption.

The tool Microsoft supplies to perform this operation is called the *Active Directory Connector*, or ADC. As illustrated in Figure 12.1, the ADC locates objects of interest in both directory services—legacy Exchange and Active Directory—and copies attributes for those objects back and forth to keep the objects in sync. An exception would be a one-way Connection agreement, used in specialized circumstances.

- Legacy mailbox owners replicate to Active Directory as mailbox-enabled user objects.
- Legacy distribution lists become mail-enabled Universal Distribution Groups, which get promoted to Universal Security Groups if used to control access to public folders or user mailboxes.
- Legacy custom recipients become mail-enabled contacts.

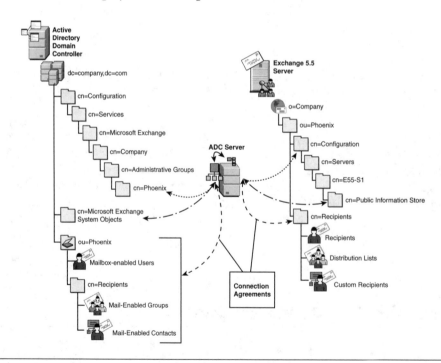

**Figure 12.1**   Diagram of object replication to and from the legacy Exchange directory service and Active Directory.

With the ADC working in the background, you can manage legacy Exchange objects from the Active Directory Users and Computers console. Once all mailboxes, public folders, and connectors have been moved, you can decommission the legacy servers and remove the ADC from service.

Don't use the ADC that comes on the Windows 2000 or Windows Server 2003 Setup CD. That version of ADC does not map special attributes required by Exchange recipients and public folders. If you have already installed the operating system version of the ADC, remove it before installing the Exchange version. Also, unlike the Exchange files themselves, you can do the initial installation of the ADC using the Exchange service pack files.

## Connection Agreements

The ADC stores configuration parameters in Active Directory objects called Connection Agreements (CAs). A CA defines object types for the ADC to copy, the source and target containers for the objects, a replication schedule, credentials to use for making inter-server replication connections, and the name of an Exchange server to act as an endpoint on the legacy side of the CA.

The ADC uses LDAP to query and update servers on both sides of a CA, so the legacy Exchange server must run Exchange 5.5 SP3 or higher to support LDAP writes and paged results.

Exchange servers that do not form the endpoint of a CA can run earlier versions of Exchange, but you should try to run the same version on all servers to minimize potential compatibility issues and increase flexibility.

The ADC uses three types of CAs:

- **Recipient.** This CA maps the attributes of User, Group, and Contact objects in Active Directory with Recipient, Distribution List, and Custom Recipient objects in the legacy Exchange directory service.

- **Public Folder.** This CA maps legacy public folders with Public Folder objects in Active Directory to permit Exchange 2003 to accept e-mail on behalf of the public folders.
- **Configuration.** This CA maps some of the objects in the legacy Configuration container with objects in the Exchange 2003 Organization container in Active Directory. You cannot create this CA manually. Exchange Setup configures the CA as part of installing the first server in each legacy site.

Because each site forms a separate naming context in the legacy Exchange directory service, you must create a separate User and Public Folder CA for each site. The Connection Agreement Wizard in Exchange 2003 automates this process. You can use the same ADC for multiple sites. Consider installing multiple ADCs if you have large geographical separations or so many sites that you would overload a single ADC server.

## ADC Mailbox Mapping

To build a mental picture of the way the ADC operates, it helps to understand the function of certain critical attributes that tell the ADC how to select objects and which e-mail parameters to copy between the objects.

Let's assume that you do an in-place upgrade of an NT4 domain to Active Directory. This transfers user account information from the PDC's SAM into Active Directory, including the users' original SIDs and passwords. As shown in Figure 12.2, a user's SID provides the initial link between the user's domain account and the user's legacy Exchange mailbox. Legacy Exchange stores this SID in the Primary Windows NT Account attribute. Active Directory stores the SID in an attribute called ObjectSID.

### Initial ADC Attribute Copy

When you configure a Recipient Connection Agreement, the ADC makes an LDAP connection between the two directory services and, for each recipient object in the legacy Exchange directory service, it reads the Primary Windows NT Account attribute and then searches for a user object in Active Directory with a matching ObjectSID attribute.

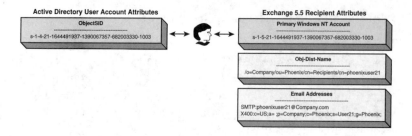

**Figure 12.2**    Initial linkage of user object in Active Directory to legacy mailbox via user SID.

Once the ADC makes this match, it copies the e-mail attributes from legacy Exchange to the Active Directory object. Figure 12.3 shows a few of the copied attributes. An ADC Policy object in Active Directory determines which attributes to copy and maps the legacy Exchange attribute names to their Active Directory equivalents.

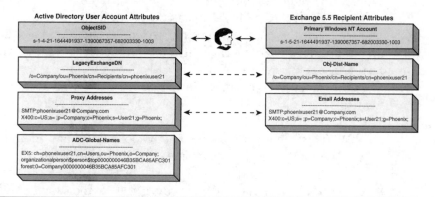

**Figure 12.3**    Following initial ADC replication, e-mail attributes copied to Active Directory object and ADC-Global-Names created.

### ADC-Global-Names Attribute Creation

In addition to copying attributes from legacy Exchange, the ADC assigns a new attribute called ADC-Global-Names to the Active Directory object. This permits the ADC to store detailed matching information that simplifies subsequent searches and reduces the LDAP traffic required to perform object mapping. The initial content of the ADC-Global-Names attribute includes two elements:

- **EX5.** This element contains the Distinguished Name and object class of the legacy Exchange object along with a timestamp of the last update and a set of flags that control the update methods used by the ADC.
- **Forest.** This element contains the Distinguished Name of the Active Directory forest along with an update timestamp and some flags.

The next time the Connection Agreement runs, the ADC looks for User objects that have an ADC-Global-Names attribute, uses the EX5 element to locate the complementary object in legacy Exchange, and then replicates any updated e-mail attributes to the legacy object. This transaction also replicates the ADC-Global-Names attribute.

After this replication, as shown in Figure 12.4, the ADC then adds two elements to the legacy Exchange copy of ADC-Global-Names:

- **NT5.** This element contains the Globally Unique Identifier (GUID) of the legacy Exchange organization along with an update timestamp and some flags.
- **FOREST.** This element contains the GUID of the Configuration container in Active Directory along with an update timestamp and some flags.

The next time the Connection Agreement runs, these new elements replicate from legacy Exchange to Active Directory. At this point, the ADC can match users to mailbox owners based solely on their ADC-Global-Names attributes and no longer needs their SIDs.

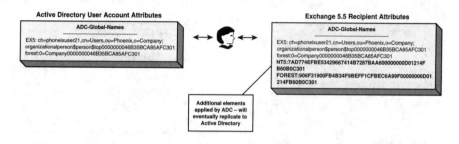

**Figure 12.4** Following replication back to legacy Exchange, the ADC-Global-Names provides all mapping information needed to keep objects in sync.

## NT Account Migrations

Not all transitions from NT to Active Directory involve an in-place upgrade of the PDC, though. Many organizations create a pristine Active Directory domain and then use a utility such as the Active Directory Migration Tool (ADMT), or a third-party migration utility, to move user, group, and computer account information into the Active Directory domain.

Unlike an in-place upgrade, which retains the users' original domain SIDs, a migration creates new user accounts with new SIDs. It also saves the original NT domain SIDs into a special Active Directory attribute called SIDHistory.

When a user authenticates in the Active Directory domain, the SID-History value gets included in the user's access token. Essentially, this gives the user two account identities: the new Active Directory account, represented by the ObjectSID attribute, and the old NT account, represented by the SIDHistory attribute.

In a migration involving Exchange, first create the user accounts in Active Directory using the migration utility of your choice, and then install and run the ADC to populate these objects with e-mail attributes. As shown in Figure 12.5, the ADC starts off by matching a mailbox owner's SID with a SID stored in SIDHistory. Once the ADC completes this initial match and copies the e-mail attributes, it can then use ADC-Global-Names to permanently link the two objects.

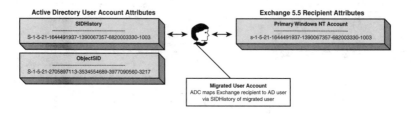

**Figure 12.5**   Migrated user maps to legacy Exchange mailbox via SIDHistory attribute.

## Invalid User Accounts

The ADC matching process might seem straightforward, but if you read between the lines, you'll see that the ADC makes a couple of critical assumptions:

- **Valid mailbox owner.** Every mailbox in the legacy Exchange directory service has an owner that exists in Active Directory.
- **Unique mailbox owner.** No two mailboxes have the same owner.

One or both of these assumptions might prove invalid in a production environment. For example, although it's unusual to have a mailbox with no owner, it's possible for someone to create a mailbox and deliberately not put an entry in the Primary Windows NT Account field. Or the mailbox owner might be assigned to a group, something not supported by Active Directory. Missing owners can also occur in domain migrations, where an NT account might not successfully copy to Active Directory for one reason or another. Keep in mind that a mailbox can be assigned only to a single user.

If a legacy mailbox owner does not exist as a user object in Active Directory, the ADC creates a *disabled* user object to represent the recipient. As shown in Figure 12.6, this disabled user object has no legacy NT domain SID, so the ADC creates an attribute called msExchangeMasterAccountSID and populates it with the user's legacy SID. It then uses this attribute as the initial match between the disabled user object and the legacy mailbox owner so it can populate the object with e-mail attributes and set up the ADC-Global-Names link.

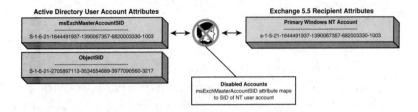

**Figure 12.6** ADC creates a disabled user object when confronted with a legacy Exchange mailbox without a direct match in Active Directory.

### *Don't Enable the Disabled User Objects*

A disabled user object created by the ADC acts solely as a placeholder. It has no authentication functions. As shown in Figure 12.7, the disabled object has a scrambled logon name and no User Principal Name (UPN), indicating that it should not be used for logon purposes. (You can't see it in the user interface, but the account also gets a randomly generated complex password.)

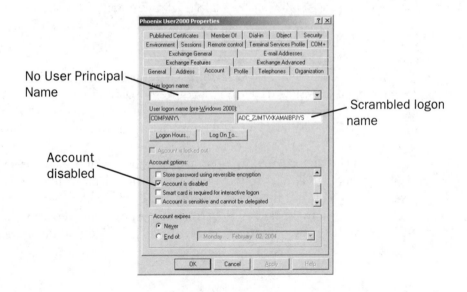

**Figure 12.7** Disabled mailbox created by ADC not intended for authentication purposes. It's simply a placeholder for a resource mailbox.

If you do a thorough job of migrating user accounts from each NT domain to Active Directory, you should not see any disabled user accounts after installing the ADC. If you *do* get a disabled user account, don't simply change the logon name and enable the account. Determine why the legacy mailbox did not have a valid owner, correct the condition, and then delete the disabled user account and let the ADC find the correct object. Microsoft Knowledge-Base article 316047 discusses the various negative effects of enabling a disabled ADC placeholder account and offers several workarounds.

### *Multiple Mailbox Owners*

Another common ADC matching issue involves so-called resource mailboxes. These mailboxes don't represent users. Instead, they represent conference rooms, projectors, audio equipment, laptop computers, and so forth. By creating mailboxes for these items, you can use the free/busy information in Outlook calendars to schedule access to the resources.

Resource mailboxes tend to have the same owner. For example, a single admin assistant in an office might own all the resource mailboxes for the conference rooms and audio-visual equipment. This presents a problem for the ADC, because Exchange 2003 permits users to have only one mailbox. You can resolve this problem using an ADC feature called NTDSNoMatch. Here's how it works.

Consider a user who has ownership of a primary mailbox and several resource mailboxes. The ADC Tools has a Resource Mailbox Wizard that looks for multiple mailboxes owned by the same user. It presents these mailboxes in a tree with the suggested primary mailbox shown in bold, as shown in Figure 12.8.

The wizard determines its candidate for the primary mailbox by matching the mailbox alias to the user name. If the wizard makes a mistake, you can highlight the actual primary mailbox and click Set as Primary. (The Resource Mailbox Wizard in the ADC Tools replaces the NTDSNoMatch utility described in Microsoft Knowledge-Base article 274173.)

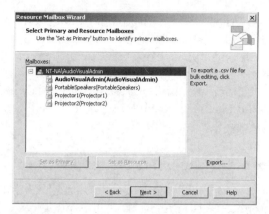

**Figure 12.8** Primary mailbox can be mapped to user account separately from resource mailboxes using Resource Mailbox Wizard in ADC Tools.

The wizard takes the settings you configure in the tree and marks each resource mailbox by placing the word NTDSNoMatch in Custom Attribute 10 of the mailbox object in legacy Exchange. Figure 12.9 shows an example.

**Figure 12.9** Resource mailboxes marked with NTDSNoMatch entry in Custom Attribute 10 of legacy Exchange object.

When the ADC runs the Recipient Connection Agreement the first time, it copies the e-mail attributes from the primary mailbox to the matching user object in Active Directory. It then creates disabled user accounts for each resource mailbox and places the original owner on the permission list for those mailboxes, so the original owner retains the ability to open the mailboxes, even though they are now owned by the disabled user accounts.

## Active Directory Account Cleanup Wizard

If you should accidentally or deliberately use the ADC to create a set of disabled user accounts in Active Directory prior to migrating users from one or more legacy domains, you can recover full functionality in two stages.

- First, migrate user accounts using ADMT or a third-party migration tool. Because the migrated accounts have actual logon names, not the scrambled logon names assigned by the ADC, the migration succeeds so long as you don't target the new user objects to the same container that holds the disabled user objects.
- Second, use the Active Directory Account Cleanup Wizard that accompanies the ADC to merge the e-mail attributes from the disabled user objects to the actual user objects and then delete the disabled objects.

The AD Account Cleanup Wizard is installed along with Exchange 2003 and can be accessed via the Start menu using the path **Start | All Programs | Microsoft Exchange | Deployment**. Run the Active Directory Cleanup Wizard as follows:

1. At the initial welcome screen, click **Next**. The Identify Merging Accounts window opens, as shown in Figure 12.10.

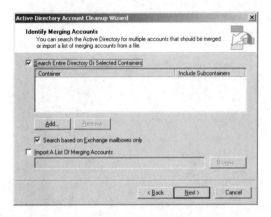

**Figure 12.10**    AD Cleanup Wizard showing Identify Merging Accounts window where you select a search container for the cleanup.

>    2. Leave the **Search Entire Directory or Selected Containers** option selected along with the **Search Based on Exchange Mailboxes Only**.
>    3. Click **Next**. After a period of searching, the Review Merging Accounts window opens to display the list of disabled accounts that match enabled accounts. Figure 12.11 shows an example.

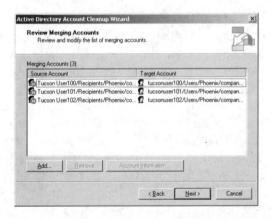

**Figure 12.11**    Review Merging Accounts window gives side-by-side comparison of disabled user object and live user object.

>    4. Click **Next**. The Begin Merging Accounts window opens, as shown in Figure 12.12.

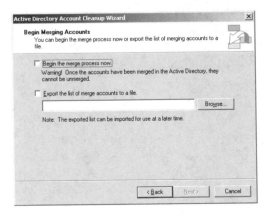

**Figure 12.12** Begin Merging Accounts window provides options to do the merge or save to a file.

5. Check the **Begin the Merge Process Now** box.
6. Click **Next** to begin the merge. Acknowledge the warning that pops up.
7. Once the merge has completed, a Summary window opens. If you see any errors, follow up by checking the Adclean.log file in the \Exchsrvr\bin folder.

Now check the Recipients folder that originally held the disabled user accounts and verify that the accounts have disappeared. You might need to press F5 to refresh the display. Check the Properties window of a user account to verify the presence of the Exchange tabs and that the Exchange information looks correct.

As a recap, you should not need to use the Active Directory Cleanup Wizard if you perform the migration steps in the proper order (migrate and then install the ADC.) If you have a few accounts that did not migrate the first time, you can use the Active Directory Cleanup Wizard to merge the e-mail attributes and avoid a remigration. You can also run Adclean.exe from the command line. The utility has several switches. See Microsoft Knowledge-Base article 270655 for details.

## ADC and Distribution Lists

Exchange 2003 uses Distribution groups and Security groups in Active Directory to represent distribution lists. When the ADC encounters a distribution list in the legacy Exchange directory service, it creates a Universal Distribution Group in Active Directory.

The ADC creates Universal groups so that the members can get mail from any user in any domain in the forest. Universal group membership replicates in the Global Catalog so that membership expansion works correctly.

The ADC creates Distribution groups rather than Security groups just in case the target domain has not been upgraded to Windows 2000 Native functional level or higher. Distribution groups have an SID, but they cannot be used on Access Control Lists (ACLs) for security objects such as NTFS files and folders, Registry keys, and Active Directory objects. Creating Universal groups also avoids conflict with Windows administrators, who might not want a pile of new Security groups to appear in Active Directory following the e-mail migration.

### Automatic Security Group Upgrades

Populating Active Directory with Universal Distribution Groups can lead to a problem, though. Legacy Exchange allows distribution lists to control access to resources such as public folders and user mailboxes.

In Exchange 2003, MAPI permissions on a public folder correspond to Access Control Entries (ACEs) on an ACL for the folder. Figure 12.13 shows a comparison of the MAPI permissions and ACEs for an example public folder. The example shows that a group called TucsonDistro1 appears on the MAPI permission list with the Author role, and that Exchange converts this to a set of ALLOW and DENY entries for two ACEs in the ACL for the folder.

It's this correlation of MAPI permissions to ACL entries that causes a problem when the ADC creates a Universal Distribution Group. If the distribution list represented by that group appears on the MAPI permissions of a public folder, then the Exchange 2003 Information Store can't create an Access Control Entry for the group to put on the ACL for the folder.

Exchange 2003 resolves this in the same way that your mother resolved arguments with you. It doesn't take no for an answer. If the Information Store sees that a Universal Distribution Group has been placed on the MAPI permissions for a public folder or user mailbox, it automatically promotes the group to a Universal Security Group and then puts the SID of the group in the ACL.

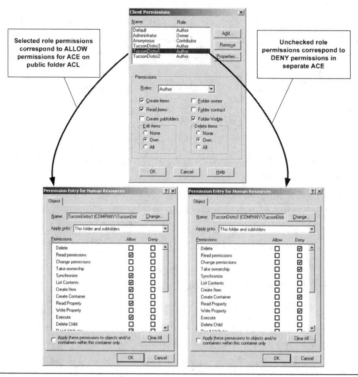

**Figure 12.13**    MAPI role corresponds to a set of Allow and Deny permissions in standard Windows ACL.

### Distribution List Membership

When the ADC creates a new Universal Distribution Group, it populates the group with members based on the membership of the legacy Exchange distribution list.

For example, if the legacy Exchange directory service contains a distribution list called South Park that holds a recipient named Kenney, the ADC creates a Universal Distribution Group called South Park and links the group's Member attribute to the Kenney object.

If a distribution list contains an invalid recipient—for example, if someone deletes the Kenny object from Active Directory (the b#°$%ds)—the ADC would create a disabled user account to represent the recipient and then would create the Universal Distribution Group with a link between the Member attribute and the disabled account.

Subsequent changes to the group membership in Active Directory replicate to legacy Exchange as a change to the distribution list members.

If you permanently delete the newly created Kenny account from Active Directory and remove him from the membership of the South Park group, then the ADC removes him from the legacy distribution list, as well.

## Forest and Domain Preparation

The first major stage of the deployment involves modifying the Active Directory schema and creating the top-level containers in the Configuration naming context. This is done as part of installing the ADC. Figure 12.14 shows the Exchange organization objects following the installation of the ADC and before installing the first Exchange server.

The Forestprep and Domainprep steps can be run anytime in advance of actually starting the upgrade and installing the ADC. You can also run the deployment tools several times in preparation for deploying the ADC.

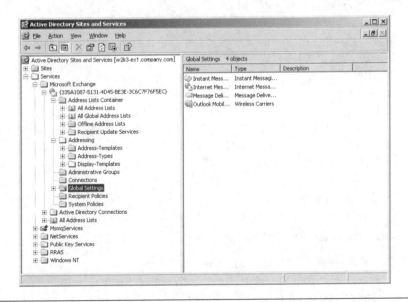

**Figure 12.14** The ADC will create Organization placeholders but does not populate servers or connections until the first Exchange 2003 server is installed.

This method for preparing the organization avoids the necessity for running ADC Setup with an account that has both full administrator rights in the legacy Exchange organization and Enterprise Admin permissions in the Active Directory forest. Many enterprises do not permit combining these two functions into a single administrator. This issue is independent of installing the ADC, and becomes a factor only because the ADC requires Forestprep and Domainprep.

## ADC Setup Permissions

The account you use to install the first ADC must meet the following requirements:

- **Belong to the Enterprise Admins group.** This allows Setup to modify the Configuration naming context.
- **Belong to the Schema Admins group.** This allows Setup to modify the schema.
- **Belong to the Domain Admins group in the domain where the ADC resides.** This allows Setup to create the Exchange Services group in the domain and to write to the Registry of the server hosting the ADC service.

Installing subsequent ADCs requires Domain Admin rights only in the domain that hosts the server.

Because ADC Setup performs all the necessary schema modifications for Exchange 2003, installing the first Exchange 2003 server after installing the ADC requires Domain Admin permissions only in the domain hosting the server along with Exchange Full Administrator permissions in the Exchange organization.

Subsequent Exchange 2003 server installations requires Exchange Full Administrator permissions only in the Administrative Group (legacy site) containing the server.

## ADC Server Selection

The Exchange 2003 ADC service can run on Windows 2000 SP3+, Windows Server 2003 Standard, or Enterprise Edition as long as the server belongs to the same forest as the Exchange 2003 organization. The service communicates with Active Directory, but it does not need to run on a domain controller.

If you have a large organization with many Exchange sites, you should dedicate a server exclusively to running the ADC so that it can handle connections to the various sites without interruption. If you have a medium-sized organization with a few sites, you can run the ADC service on a domain controller or directly on the Exchange 2003 server.

If possible, install the ADC server in the forest root domain where administrators have full rights to the Configuration naming context and the schema.

If you cannot install the ADC server in the forest root domain, before you install the ADC, extend the schema in the forest root domain using **setup /schemaonly** while logged on as an Enterprise Admin and a member of Schema Admin group. This step is not included in the Exchange 2003 prescriptive checklist.

If you choose to deploy Exchange 2003 in the midst of a migration to Exchange 2000, either upgrade your existing Exchange 2000 ADC or install an Exchange 2003 ADC on a Windows Server 2003 server; then create new connection agreements and tear down the old ones.

## ADC Service Account Selection

During ADC Setup, you must designate a service account for the ADC that it can use when connecting to a legacy Exchange server. The service account you designate during Setup becomes the Logon Account for the service, as shown in Figure 12.15.

You should not use the domain Administrator account for the ADC service account. It's too likely that you'll forget you did this and change the password. Also, most security experts agree that the domain Administrator account should be avoided as a service account to minimize the impact of a successful penetration. Instead, use the following criteria to select the service account:

- If the ADC server belongs to the same domain as the legacy Exchange servers (for example, after performing an in-place upgrade), then you can use the same service account as that used by the legacy Exchange servers. (And if that's the domain Administrator account, well, shame on you.)

**Figure 12.15**   ADC requires a service account with access to legacy Exchange directory service.

- If the ADC resides in a different domain than the legacy Exchange servers, create a new account in Active Directory and grant this account Service Account Admin permissions on the Organization, Site, and Configuration containers in each legacy Exchange site.

On the Active Directory side, ADC Setup creates a group called Exchange Services with Full Control access rights to the Exchange organization. It makes the ADC service account a member of this group.

## Domain Prerequisites

Windows 2000 introduced the concept of a "mode change" to differentiate between a domain that can support NT BDCs (Mixed mode) and one that has full functionality (Native mode). Windows Server 2003 extends the mode concept to include backward compatibility with Windows 2000 but the term is now "functionality level." The highest functional level is *Windows Server 2003*. This functional level enables certain critical features helpful for Exchange 2003 operation, such as replicating individual members of groups and reducing the replication interval within a site from five minutes to five seconds.

Exchange 2003 does not require a functional level of Windows Server 2003, but it does require at least one domain to be set at the functional level of Windows 2000 Compatible. This enables Universal Security Groups.

If you are consolidating multiple NT4 domains into a single Active Directory domain, you must have a trust between each NT4 domain, the Active Directory forest root domain, and each domain hosting users with mailboxes on NT4 Exchange servers.

You'll also need to perform a few operations in each domain that hosts mail-enabled objects:

- **Name Resolution.** Verify proper DNS name resolution at each server you intend to use for ADC and Exchange 2003. It's important that the servers find domain controller and Global Catalog servers. You should also verify proper WINS registration for Exchange server candidates. Legacy Exchange servers and downlevel Exchange clients use WINS to locate Exchange services. WINS has a couple of other minor functions, as well. See **hellomate.typepad.com/exchange/2004/03/exchange_200x_r.html** for details.

- **ADC Staging OU.** You'll need an OU to act as a repository for groups and contacts created by the ADC when it replicates distribution lists and custom recipients along with disabled user accounts representing resource mailboxes. In the examples, I'll call this OU the ADC_Staging_Area.

- **Verify Trusts.** The trust relationships between the Active Directory domains and any downlevel domains must be intact. Use Nltest from the Windows Server 2003 Support Tools to verify the trust.

- **Global Catalog locations.** You should have at least one Global Catalog server in each site that has an Exchange 2003 server. Microsoft recommends a 4-to-1 ratio for the number of processors in your Exchange servers to the number of Global Catalog servers. For example, if you have two 4-way Exchange servers in the same site, you should have two Global Catalog servers. If you have a single domain, enable the Global Catalog on all domain controllers. This does not increase the size of the Active Directory file. It merely ensures that the server listens on TCP port 3268 for LDAP queries directed at the Global Catalog.

- **Active Directory Replication topology.** Identify each Active Directory bridgehead server and map out the inter-site replication links. This helps you diagnose replication problems that might occur when you upgrade the Schema. Also, Exchange 2003 depends on Active Directory replication to inform other Exchange servers about configuration changes, so you want to document your configuration and get proactive about monitoring for critical events.
- **Remove Internet Explorer Enhanced Security.** ADC Setup (and Exchange 2003 Setup) make extensive use of Internet files (.html, .hta, and so forth). This can cause you a bit of irritation because Windows Server 2003 has a feature called Internet Explorer Enhanced Security that forces to you accept the location for each of the screens launched by the wizard. Do yourself a favor and remove this feature from the server, at least for the duration of the ADC and Exchange setup.

> You can run Exchange Setup without going through the prescriptive checklist and the deployment tools. Run Setup from the \Setup\I386 folder on the CD.

To remove the Internet Explorer Enhance Security feature:

1. Launch **Control Panel**.
2. Open the **Add/Remove Programs** applet.
3. Click **Add/Remove Windows Components**.
4. Uncheck the **Internet Explorer Enhanced Security Configuration** option, shown in Figure 12.16.
5. Click **Next** to accept the change.

When you've finished installing the ADC and/or Exchange on the server, feel free to install the Internet Explorer Enhanced Security Configuration service again. It does not interfere with Exchange operations, and it prevents other administrators from using your Exchange server to browse the Internet and possibly download something that performs an unfortunate activity on your server.

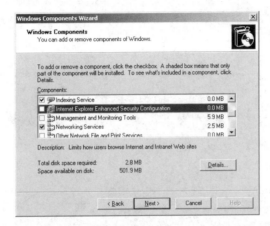

**Figure 12.16**    Simplify ADC and Exchange Setup by removing Internet Explorer Enhanced Security Configuration for the duration of the Internet Explorer Enhanced Security Configuration service installation.

## ADC Installation

I recommend installing the ADC using the prescriptive checklist in Exchange Server 2003 Setup rather than using the ADC Setup directly. Following the prescriptive checklist ensures that you run all the preliminary tests to validate your configuration and the operation of your infrastructure. You can also take full advantage of the ADC Tools and the Connection Agreement Wizard.

The checklist appears as part of the standard Exchange and ADC Setup. Figure 12.17 shows an example of the checklist.

You'll need to install the Windows Server 2003 Support Tools prior to starting the ADC installation so that you have the Dcdiag and Netdiag utilities available. These are required components of the prescriptive checklist.

You can do the installation in an admin-mode remote desktop session, if that's your normal way of managing your servers. In Windows Server 2003, you might want to connect directly to the console by running mstsc /console. This puts a warning message on the regular console display to warn your colleagues if they select the server with a KVM switch.

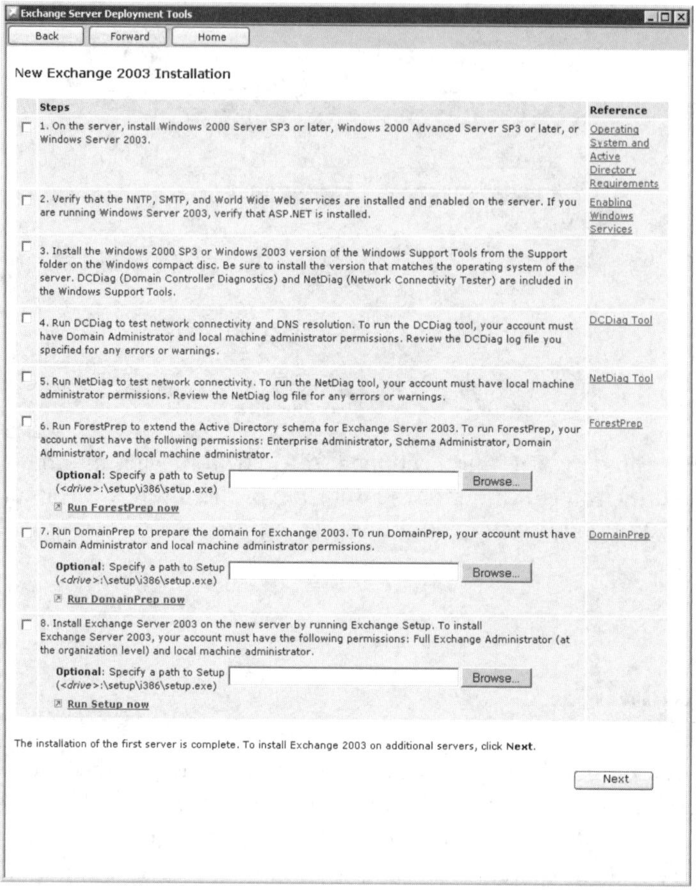

**Figure 12.17**    Component Selection window showing ForestPrep selected under Action if all prerequisites are met.

The prescriptive checklist prompts you to run Forestprep to modify the Active Directory schema. If you do not use the checklist, the ADC Setup Wizard updates the schema using its own files. The end result is the same. Unlike Exchange 2000, the ADC in Exchange Server 2003 performs the same schema modifications as the Exchange server setup.

This section does not contain a step-by-step procedure for installing the ADC. That's provided by the prescriptive checklist. It gives you an overview the of the more important elements of the checklist along with pointers about the information you'll need to enter, and it shows you what a clean set of deployment log entries would look like.

1. To start the ADC installation, insert the Exchange Server 2003 CD and launch Setup from the root of the CD.
2. At the main welcome screen, under the **Deployment** column, select **Exchange Deployment Tools**. The Welcome to the Exchange Server Deployment Tools window opens.
3. Click **Deploy**, the first Exchange 2003 Server option. The Deploy the First Exchange 2003 Server window opens.
4. Select the **Coexistence with Exchange 5.5** option. This opens the prescriptive checklist. Follow the numbered items in the checklist. Make sure you specify the log file location on a handy local folder so you can review the logs frequently during the process.

## Initial Testing

The first major item on the prescriptive checklist runs a comprehensive suite of tests called DSScopeScan. This suite includes the following tests (detailed a little later in this section):

- **DSConfigSum.** This test reports the total number of sites and the number of servers in each site.
- **DSObjectSum.** This utility reports the total number of public folders, distribution lists, distribution lists with hidden membership, and custom recipients.
- **UserCount.** This test reports the total number of recipients (users) in the organization, broken down by site.
- **VerCheck.** This test verifies that you have the right Exchange version and service pack level on your Exchange servers.

You must specify the name of an Exchange 5.5 SP3 (or higher) server, an Active Directory domain controller, and a location for the deployment log files. If you enter an incorrect path for the log files, each element of DSScopeScan errors out and you'll see that the log folder holds no files. If this happens, simply correct the entry for the path and run the tool again.

The main log file for the deployment is Exdeploy.log. It shows the result of each test performed by DSScopeScan. (The other deployment tools have their own detailed logs with summaries appended to Exdeploy.log.) For example, if your logon account does not have sufficient legacy Exchange permissions, you get an error message like this in the Exdeploy.log file:

```
Warning: Either you do not have permission to view
➡hidden objects in the Exchange 5.5 directory, or the
➡directory is not Exchange 5.5 SP1 or later. Returned
➡information may be inaccurate.
```

A file called Exdeploy-Progress.log gives a blow-by-blow account of the installation, useful only if something entirely unexpected and strange goes wrong. Be sure to resolve all error messages prior to continuing. New messages append to the end of each log, so you won't lose any diagnostic information by running DSScopeScan over and over. See Appendix C, "Detailed Deployment Log Contents," for details on the expected content of the individual logs.

After you have resolved any errors that came up in DSScopeScan, go to the next page of the prescriptive checklist.

## ForestPrep

The next major step in the prescriptive checklist runs Forestprep. This modifies the Active Directory schema to include new attributes and classes used by Exchange and also installs the top-level objects for a placeholder organization tree in the Configuration naming context in the Active Directory forest.

Clicking ForestPrep in the prescriptive checklist launches Exchange Setup, which takes you through an End-User License Agreement (EULA) window to the Component Selection window shown in Figure 12.18.

If you properly completed all prerequisites, the Action column automatically fills in with the word Forestprep. If the Action column remains empty, you neglected to fulfill one of the prerequisites. To see what you missed, manually select Forestprep in the Action column. An error window will appear describing what you forgot to do.

During ForestPrep, you'll get prompted for the name of the Microsoft Exchange Server Administrator Account, as shown in Figure 12.19. This account gets Exchange Full Administrator privileges in the skeleton Organization container created by ForestPrep. Enter the domain name and the name of the account that you want to act as the initial Exchange administrator.

When ForestPrep completes, return to the prescriptive checklist.

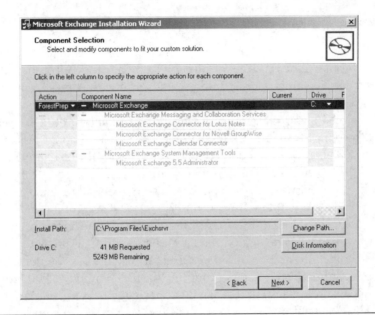

**Figure 12.18**    Component Selection window showing ForestPrep selected under Action, if all prerequisites are met.

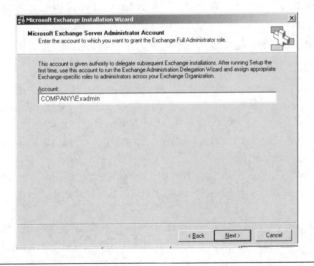

**Figure 12.19**    Exchange Server administrator account given Exchange Full Administrator role in organization.

## DomainPrep

The next step in the prescriptive checklist runs DomainPrep. This creates objects in the Active Directory domain that represent Exchange service accounts, public folders, and groups that represent Exchange servers in the domain and the enterprise.

When you click on DomainPrep, Exchange Setup launches and takes you through a EULA window to the Component Selection window. This time the Action column is filled in with word DomainPrep.

If the Action column remains empty, you neglected to fulfill one of the prerequisites. To see what you missed, manually select DomainPrep, and an error window appears describing what you forgot to do.

During DomainPrep, a warning message appears informing you that the domain has been identified as insecure for mail-enabled groups. The default configuration of Active Directory in Windows Server 2003 places the Authenticated Users group in the Pre-Windows 2000 Compatible Access group. This group has Read permissions for group membership. This does not override the Deny Read permissions used to hide group membership, but Setup doesn't seem to know that. Click OK to acknowledge the message.

When DomainPrep finishes, return to the prescriptive checklist.

## Verification Tests

At this point, let's take a breather and figure out where we stand. As part of the preparation steps to installing the ADC, you've updated the schema, made significant changes to the Global Catalog, and added quite a few objects to the Domain naming context. You want to make sure that all these changes fully propagate to all domain controllers and Global Catalog servers in the enterprise before you proceed. For this purpose, the next step of the prescriptive checklist presents a tool called OrgPrepCheck. This tool runs two tests, Orgcheck and Polcheck.

- **OrgCheck.** This test verifies that Setup created the proper Exchange objects in the Configuration naming context and Domain naming context. For example, it verifies that the Exchange Domain Servers group, Exchange Enterprise Servers group, and Exchange Services group exist. It also verifies that the schema changes have fully propagated and that it can find a Global Catalog server in the same site as the ADC server.

- **PolCheck.** This test queries each domain controller in the domain to determine if the Exchange Enterprise Servers group has been given the Manage Auditing and Security Logs privilege. If this has not yet occurred, then the Domainprep changes have not yet replicated to that domain controller, or an error prevented the changes from applying. You can use Active Directory Sites and Services to force replication to the affected domain then run OrgPrepCheck again.

A successful run of these two tests indicate that the schema changes have fully replicated and that every domain has been properly updated to include the necessary Exchange objects. You're ready to proceed to the next step in the prescriptive checklist.

## ADC Setup

You're now ready for the meat and potatoes part of the ADC installation. Click the Run ADC Setup Now option in the prescriptive checklist to launch ADC Setup. (You can run Forestprep and Domainprep on a different server than where you install the ADC.)

1. At the welcome window, click **Next**. A EULA window opens.
2. Click **Next**. The Component Selection window opens, as shown in Figure 12.20. Select both options to install the ADC and the ADC Management components.

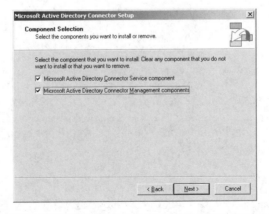

**Figure 12.20** Component Selection window permits installing the ADC and the ADC Tools, or just the tools.

3. Click **Next**. The Install Location window opens. Enter a path for the ADC executable files. The ADC does not use a database, but it does store error logs in this location.

4. Click **Next**. Setup installs the ADC and keeps you notified via a status window. At the completion of ADC Setup, return to the prescriptive checklist. This could take quite a while. Go grab a sandwich and come back in a half hour or so.

## ADC Tools

The next step in the prescriptive checklist prompts you to open the ADC management console and select the ADC Tools option, as shown in Figure 12.21.

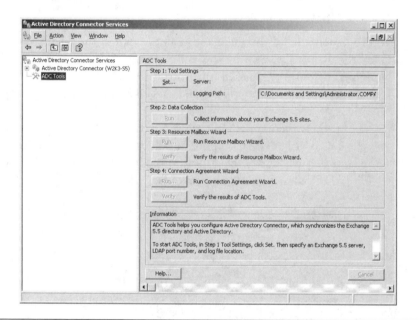

**Figure 12.21** ADC Tools simplify the process of testing prerequisites and installing Connection Agreements.

The ADC Tools consists of a suite of utilities designed to report on inconsistencies in the legacy Exchange directory service, to automate the process of marking resource mailboxes with NTDSNoMatch, and to automate the process of creating Recipient and Public Folder Connection Agreements. The user interface divides these chores into four steps:

- **Step 1: Tool Settings.** In this step, you specify the name of the Exchange 5.5 server to use for data collection and a location for the ADC logs.
- **Step 2: Data Collection.** This step runs a suite of utilities that scans both Active Directory and the legacy Exchange directory service to find parameters that will be synchronized by the ADC.
- **Step 3: Resource Mailbox Wizard.** This step determines if the same user owns multiple mailboxes and gives you the opportunity to identify the user's primary mailbox so that the other mailboxes can be designated as resource mailboxes and given new, disabled accounts in Active Directory.
- **Step 4: Connection Agreement Wizard.** This step creates Connection Agreements that define the replication endpoints of the ADC and determine how attributes will be mapped between the endpoints.

The ADC reads and writes to the legacy Exchange directory service using LDAP. The server must be running Exchange 5.5 SP3 or higher so that it supports LDAP writes and LDAP queries that use paged results.

### Step 1: Tool Settings

Click Set. The Tool Settings window opens. Here you specify the name of an Exchange 5.5 server to use for data collection. You do not necessarily need to select the server you will use for Connection Agreements, but you could. Select a location for the ADC logs. The default location puts the files in your user profile.

### Step 2: Data Collection

Click Run to query the Exchange 5.5 server and collect information about the Exchange organization. ADC Tools performs a series of four tests that check for objects and attributes in legacy Exchange and Active Directory. These tests also build XML database files used by later steps for resource mailbox marking.

#### Resource Mailbox Scan

This test looks for mailboxes that have the same owner. If it finds them, it puts an entry in the ADCTools.log file similar to the following:

```
Pass 1 of 4: Resource Mailbox Scan 01/09/2004 13:37:35
Warning: The Data Collection tool found objects that must be marked as
➡resource mailboxes before they can be replicated to Active Directory.
➡Running the Resource Mailbox Wizard in Step 3 will resolve these issues.
```

### Active Directory Connector Object Replication Check

This test verifies that each mailbox owner has a match to an Active Directory user object. If it finds unmatched objects, it identifies them in the ADCTools.log file. Here's a sample listing:

```
Pass 2 of 4: Active Directory Connector Object Replication Check
➡01/09/2004 13:37:48
Matched 'cn=PhoenixUser1,cn=Recipients,ou=Phoenix,o=Company' to
'cn=Phoenix User1,ou=Phoenix,dc=Company,dc=com' based on SID.
Could not find match to 'cn=PhoenixUser2,cn=Recipients,ou=Phoenix,
➡o=Company'.
Could not find match to 'cn=phoenixuser3,cn=Recipients,ou=Phoenix,
➡o=Company'.
```

```
Warning: The Data Collection tool found objects that are not replicated
➡from the Exchange 5.5 directory to Active Directory. Running the
➡Connection Agreement Wizard in Step 4 will resolve these issues.
```

The log might reassure you that the Connection Agreement Wizard will resolve replication issues for the matched entries, but you should not proceed until you resolve any unmatched entries. You do not want the ADC to create disabled user accounts in Active Directory for any mailboxes other than resource mailboxes. The presence of other unmatched objects indicates a possible error in the user account migration, if you migrated from a separate NT domain, or user accounts that someone deleted without deleting the mailboxes.

### Active Directory Object Replication Scan

This test looks for mail-enabled objects in Active Directory that do not have corresponding recipient objects in legacy Exchange. You have not yet run a Connection Agreement, so this test does not find any invalid entries. Here's a sample listing:

```
Pass 3 of 4: Active Directory Object Replication Scan 06/09/2003 13:38:17
No mail enabled objects found in Active Directory.
Active Directory Object Replication Scan completed.  No unreplicated
➡objects found.
```

If you run this test once you've deployed Exchange 2003 servers, you might get an error such as this:

```
Warning: The Data Collection tool found mail-enabled users,
➥contacts, or groups that are not replicated from Active
➥Directory to the Exchange 5.5 directory. Running the
➥Connection Agreement wizard in Step 4 will resolve these
➥issues.
```

This error indicates that you created a mail-enabled object in Active Directory, but the ADC has not yet replicated that object to the legacy Exchange directory service. Resolve this by determining why the CA has not replicated the object. The most likely cause involves a failure of the CA to locate the two endpoint servers.

### Active Directory Unmarked Resource Mailbox Scan

This test checks for potential resource mailboxes that do not have an NTDSNoMatch entry. Since you have not yet run the ADC or deployed Exchange 2003 servers, this check comes up clean. If you run the test after you have been operating awhile, you might get an error about mismatched accounts. This indicates that the ADC cannot match a potential resource mailbox to a disabled user account. The most likely cause involves a failure to properly mark the primary and resource mailboxes assigned to the same owner in legacy Exchange. Correct the problem and repeat the test.

### Step 3: Resource Mailbox wizard

The next step in the ADC Tools identifies and marks resource mailboxes using the Resource Mailbox Wizard. Larger enterprises might have hundreds of these resource mailboxes. You can use the bulk edit capabilities to create .csv files for doing the mailbox marking.

1. Click **Run** to start the Resource Mailbox Wizard. The Welcome window opens.
2. Click **Next**. The Select Primary and Resource Mailboxes window opens, shown in Figure 12.22. This window lists owners of multiple mailboxes along with the mailboxes they own. The wizard makes a guess about the primary mailbox based on the user's account name and mailbox alias. It indicates the primary mailbox in bold.

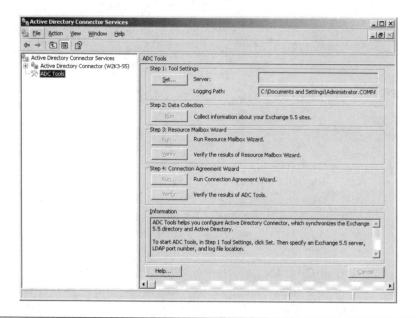

**Figure 12.22**    Resource Mailbox Wizard searches out mailboxes with the same owner and allows you to specify which mailbox is the user's primary mailbox and designates the remainder as resource mailboxes.

>   3. If the wizard guesses wrong about the primary mailbox, high-light the true primary mailbox and click **Set as Primary**. The other mailboxes automatically shift to resource mailboxes.
>   4. Click **Next**. The Site Credentials window opens, as shown in Figure 12.23.

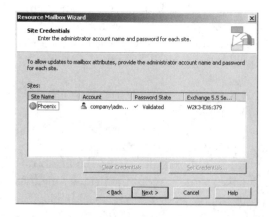

**Figure 12.23**    Site Credentials window validates the account you select to install the ADC.

5. Click **Set Credentials** and browse for an account that has administrative permissions in the legacy Exchange organization. Use the Exchange service account, because you know it has Service Account Admin permissions. If the Password State column indicates Validated, you know you entered the correct password, but that does not guarantee that the account has sufficient admin permissions.

6. Click **Next**. A Summary window opens. Verify that all settings are correct.

7. Click **Next**. This applies the changes.

8. Click **Finish** to return to the ADC Tools window.

9. In the ADC Tools window, click **Verify** to test that each resource mailbox has been marked with NTDSNoMatch.

### Step 4: Connection Agreement wizard

You've arrived at the point where you'll create Connection Agreements that replicate the e-mail attributes to the Active Directory objects. The Connection Agreement Wizard asks you a few questions then sets up sufficient Recipient and Public Folder CAs to connect each site to Active Directory.

1. Click **Run** to start the CA Wizard.

2. At the main welcome window, click **Next** to open the Staging Area window, shown in Figure 12.24.

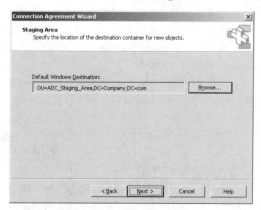

**Figure 12.24**    Staging Area allows you to enter the OU in Active Directory where Distribution Groups, Contacts, and disabled User accounts will be created.

3. Browse to the **ADC_Staging_Area** OU (or whatever OU you created to act as the repository for group and contact objects replicated from legacy Exchange).

4. Click **Next**. The Site Connections window opens (Figure 12.25). The **Two-Way Connections** pane of the window should list every legacy site. If you don't see a site, stop and determine the problem. Replication failure at the legacy Exchange server used by the ADC can cause this problem.

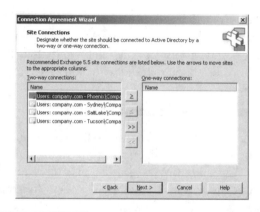

**Figure 12.25**    Site Connections shows the Connection Agreements suggested by the Connection Agreement Wizard.

5. Click **Next**. The Site Credentials window opens, shown in Figure 12.26. Use the **Set Credentials** button to enter the name and password for an account with Service Account Admin permissions in each site. In the example, each site uses the **company\exservice** account.

6. Click **Next**. The Domain Credentials window opens. Enter a set of administrator credentials for each domain in the Active Directory forest.

7. Click **Next**. The Connection Agreement Selection window opens, shown in Figure 12.27. Leave all the entries checked.

8. Click **Next** to get a summary window.

9. Click **Next** again to build the Connection Agreements.

10. When the CA Wizard has completed its tasks, check the final window for reported errors.

11. Click **Finish** to return to the ADC Tools interface.

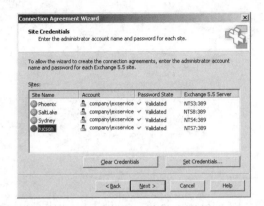

**Figure 12.26**    Site Credentials window validates the account you provide to install the Connection Agreements.

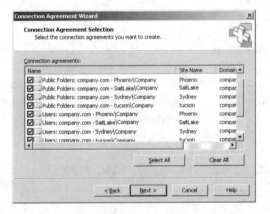

**Figure 12.27**    Connection Agreement Selection window allows you to not install one or more Connection Agreements suggested by the wizard.

12. Click **Verify** to initialize the Connection Agreements. This verifies that all necessary updates were applied to both directory services.

13. In the ADC Services console, select the Active Directory Connector icon and press F5 to refresh the display. The listing now includes the Connection Agreements created by the wizard, as shown in Figure 12.28.

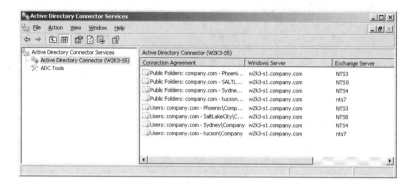

**Figure 12.28**    ADC Services console showing Connection Agreements created by the wizard and their endpoint servers.

## Final Checks

At this point, now that you've completed installing the ADC, you should check a few Active Directory users to make sure the Exchange attributes appear in their properties using the Active Directory Users and Computers console. Also, check the staging area to make sure you have objects representing the legacy distribution lists and custom recipients. Figure 12.29 shows an example.

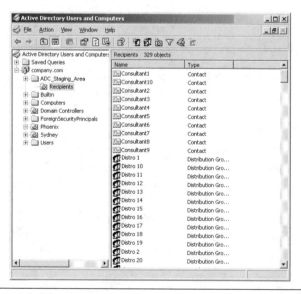

**Figure 12.29**    Active Directory Users and Computers showing the Universal Distribution Groups and Contacts created by the ADC.

Once you get an Exchange 2003 server up and running, you can familiarize yourself with the operation of a Connection Agreement by creating mailbox-enabled users, mail-enabled groups, and contacts; then using the ADC to replicate them to the legacy Exchange directory service.

At this point, you've finished the ADC installation and you're ready to proceed with installing the first Exchange 2003 server. Ordinarily, at a major milestone such as this, you would want to do some verification testing. But you can't do a thorough test of the ADC until you have all the Connection Agreements, and this won't happen until you install the first Exchange 2003 server. For that reason, you'll find a section on verifying CA operation in the next section.

# Connection Agreement Properties

Although the Connection Agreement Wizard does a lot to simplify the creation of CAs, you'll find it useful to get familiar with the properties of the various types of CAs. You might need to modify the settings of a CA created by the CA Wizard. Or you might need to create a custom CA without the help of the wizard. You might also need to troubleshoot the operation of a CA, and that can get very tedious if you don't know how they operate with various settings.

## Recipient Connection Agreements

Open the Properties window for one of the User CAs created by the wizard. Figure 12.30 shows the General tab.

The wizard creates two-way connection agreements, meaning that changes made to either directory service replicate to the other service. This ensures that you have full synchronization throughout the migration.

These settings are stored in Active Directory, so if you want another ADC server to take over the replication duties, you can select a different server using the **Select a Server to Run** option.

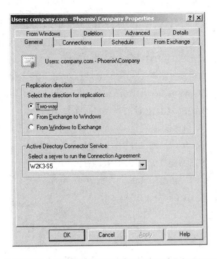

**Figure 12.30** Connection Agreement properties showing the agreement type and the name of the ADC server.

### Connection Settings

Select the Connections tab, shown in Figure 12.31. This tab allows you to select the endpoint server for each side of the Connection Agreement and the credentials used to access the directory service on that server.

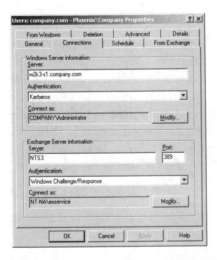

**Figure 12.31** Connections tab showing the two-endpoint servers in the Connection Agreement and the credentials used to make the connection.

If you decommission the legacy Exchange server acting as the endpoint to the Connection Agreement, use this tab to specify another legacy server. As you'll see in the next section, Exchange 2003 has a service called the Site Replication Service that maintains a replica of the legacy Exchange directory service on an Exchange 2003 server. You can point a CA at this SRS service rather than at a legacy Exchange server. The only caveat is that SRS listens at TCP port 379 rather than TCP port 389, the standard LDAP port.

If you change the password on either of the accounts used to access Active Directory or legacy Exchange, use this tab to change the passwords stored in the Connection Agreement. Failure to do so will be reported to the Application event log.

### Schedule Settings

Select the Schedule tab, shown in Figure 12.32. The default setting for CA replication is **Always**. This replicates a change as it occurs.

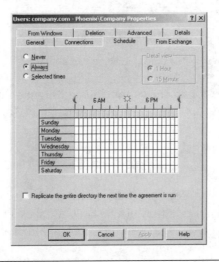

**Figure 12.32**    Schedule tab permits throttling back on replication to accommodate network restrictions, if any.

If immediate replication overloads a slow connection, you can elect to replicate periodically, such as hourly or every 15 minutes throughout a given window. Under general circumstances, you won't change the default setting.

### *"From Exchange" Settings*

Select the From Exchange tab, shown in Figure 12.33. Note that the CA replicates all changes from a given legacy site into the staging area OU you created in Active Directory. You should only see Universal Distribution Groups, contacts, and disabled user accounts for resource mailboxes in this OU. The ADC locates a user object in the OU where it resides.

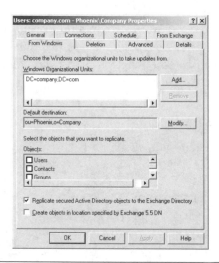

**Figure 12.33**   From Exchange shows the source, target containers, and the object types that will be copied from legacy Exchange to Active Directory.

### *"From Windows" Settings*

Select the From Windows tab, shown in Figure 12.34. This side of the CA works a little differently. The CA takes changes made to mail-enabled objects anywhere in the domain and replicates them to objects in the legacy site container.

If you think about it for a moment, this configuration might cause a problem. After all, the CA wizard creates several CAs, one for each legacy site. Each of these CAs pulls changes from the entire domain. This could lead to a situation where you mail-enabled an object in Active Directory, and the overlapping CAs each created a corresponding object in its own legacy site OU.

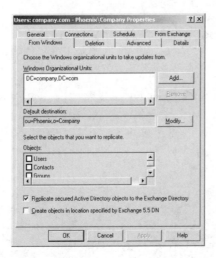

**Figure 12.34**   From Windows specifies the source and target containers for the Connection Agreement, but does not indicate the type of objects. This is determined by a custom filter that cannot be seen in the user interface.

To avoid this, Microsoft does a little magic trick. In the From Windows tab, take a look at the Objects field. The ADC uses this field to configure a filter in the Connection Agreement to search only for objects of the specified class. If you were to configure a CA manually and check each of the object types, the ADC would create a filter to search for all objects of the User, Group, and Contact class.

Notice in the Connection Agreement created by the CA Wizard that the Objects field contains a gray background, and none of the checkboxes have checks. Instead of using a standard filter, the CA Wizard inserts a custom filter into the CA that limits the search to objects in the same site as the Exchange server that forms the endpoint of the Connection Agreement. This search restriction prevents overlapping CAs from creating multiple objects in their own site OU based on a single mail-enabled Active Directory object.

Just in case you're interested in the full details, here's how the custom filter created by the CA Wizard works. It's good to know this information if you ever want to create a CA without the aid of the CA Wizard.

*continues*

Each mail-enabled object in Active Directory has an attribute called LegacyExchangeDN. As you might expect, this attribute corresponds to the Distinguished Name of the object in the legacy Exchange directory service.

The syntax of the LegacyExchangeDN attribute uses X.821 format rather than X.500 format, so an example would look like this: `/o=Company/ou=Phoenix/cn=phoenixuser100`.

When a user gets a mailbox, the Exchange Task Wizard determines the site of the user's home server and constructs a LegacyExchangeDN entry that corresponds to that site. For example, if you were to take a user with the logon name sydneyuser50 and give that user a mailbox on an Exchange server in Sydney, the LegacyExchangeDN attribute would look like this: `/o=Company/ou=Sydney/cn=sydneyuser50`.

When the CA Wizard creates a Connection Agreement, the wizard modifies the Active Directory search filter in the CA to look only for objects with a legacyExchangeDN that specifies the same site as the Exchange server acting as the endpoint of the CA. For example, if the Exchange server resides in the Phoenix site, then the CA search filter would look for LegacyExchangeDN entries equal to `/o=Company/ou=Phoenix/cn=*`.

### Advanced Settings

Select the Advanced tab, shown in Figure 12.35. The wizard configured the CA as a Primary CA for the Windows domain but not for the Exchange organization. Only a Primary CA can create new objects or delete existing objects. By preventing the CA from creating new objects in the legacy Exchange directory service, you avoid potential update loops in which changes to the same object would replicate back and forth between multiple sites.

The Advanced properties also tell the CA to create a disabled user account in Active Directory if it cannot match a mailbox owner to an Active Directory user. The other options include creating a *new* user object or a new *contact* object. These options have only limited utility, and you should not select them unless instructed by Microsoft Product Support Services in the event that you require their help to resolve a problem.

The Paged Results entry defines how many items the ADC will obtain in a single LDAP query. In Exchange 2003, Microsoft recommends leaving this setting at the default of 20 unless specifically instructed to use a higher number by a support technician or Microsoft consulting engineer. (The Exchange 2000 ADC Deployment Guide recommends raising this value to 99, but that does not apply to Exchange 2003.)

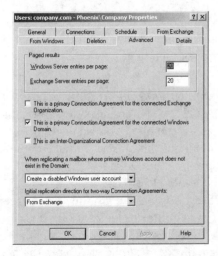

**Figure 12.35** Advanced tab shows that each CA is a Primary only on the Windows side and that an unmatched mailbox in legacy Exchange will create a disabled user account.

### Deletion Settings

Select the Deletion tab, shown in Figure 12.36. The default configuration deletes objects in one directory service when the corresponding object gets deleted from the other directory service.

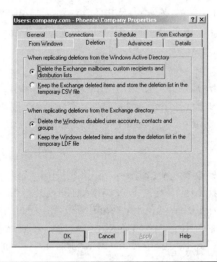

**Figure 12.36** Deletion tab shows that deleted objects in each directory service will cause action on the part of the other directory service, by default. The alternative is to save the action in a flat file for later application.

Replicating object deletions between the two directory services can get a little complex, depending upon the object type and directory service from where you delete it.

### Object Deletions Originating in Active Directory

If you delete a mailbox-enabled user, a mail-enabled group, or a contact in Active Directory, the object doesn't actually get deleted. Instead, the system strips off all but the most essential attributes, moves the object to a hidden container called Deleted Objects, and sets an attribute on the object called IsDeleted to TRUE.

The search criteria on the Connection Agreements created by the CA Wizard include a filter to look for objects with the IsDeleted attribute set to TRUE. When the ADC finds such an object, it instructs the legacy Exchange directory service to delete the corresponding object.

### Mail Attribute Deletions Originating in Active Directory

If you use the Exchange Task Wizard in Active Directory Users and Computers to revert a mailbox-enabled user, a mail-enabled group, or a contact back to a standard object (the task name is **Remove Exchange Attributes**), the wizard strips most of the e-mail attributes from the object and then sets the value for the LegacyExchangeDN attribute to ADCDisabledMail.

The search criteria on the Connection Agreements created by the CA Wizard include a filter to look for objects that have the LegacyExchangeDN attribute set to ADCDisabledMail. When the ADC finds such an object, it instructs the legacy Exchange directory service to delete the corresponding object.

### Object Deletions Originating in Legacy Exchange

On the legacy Exchange side, the action varies depending on whether the mailbox belongs to a real user or a disabled user linked to a resource mailbox.

- If you delete a resource mailbox, the ADC deletes the corresponding disabled user object in Active Directory.
- If you delete a standard mailbox, the ADC strips the e-mail attributes from the corresponding Active Directory object and sets the LegacyExchangeDN attribute to ADCDisabledMailByADC.

The search criteria on Connection Agreements created by the CA Wizard include a filter to look for objects that have the LegacyExchangeDN attribute set to ADCDisabledMailByADC. When the ADC finds such an object, it turns right around and attempts to delete the corresponding object from legacy Exchange, even though the object is already gone. This might seem redundant, but that's what happens.

*Points to Remember about Object Deletions and the ADC*
Here's a quick synopsis of the way the ADC handles object and attribute deletions:

- If you delete a mailbox-enabled user in Active Directory, the ADC deletes the corresponding mailbox in legacy Exchange.
- If you delete a mail-enabled group or contact in Active Directory, the ADC deletes the corresponding distribution list or custom recipient in legacy Exchange.
- If you remove the e-mail attributes from users, groups, or contacts in Active Directory, the ADC deletes the corresponding mailbox, distribution list, or custom recipient in legacy Exchange.
- If you delete a mailbox in legacy Exchange, the ADC strips the e-mail attributes from the corresponding user object in Active Directory.
- If you delete a distribution list or custom recipient in legacy Exchange, the ADC strips the e-mail attributes from the corresponding group or contact in Active Directory.

## Configuration Connection Agreements

Consider the legacy Exchange directory service replication topology diagrammed in Figure 12.37. Within each site, the Exchange servers send directory service updates directly to each other using Remote Procedure Calls (RPCs). Between sites, the bridgehead servers convert the directory service updates into messages that they send to other bridgeheads. When you start the migration to Exchange 2003, you introduce a new actor: the ADC server. You've already seen how the Connection Agreements created by the ADC keep recipients and public folders in sync between legacy Exchange and Active Directory. But that's not the whole story.

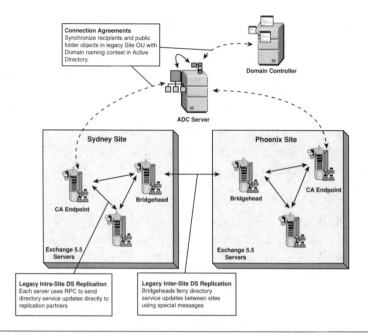

**Figure 12.37** Configuration Connection Agreement connects the legacy Configuration containers in each site with the Exchange Organization container in Active Directory.

Exchange 5.x stores server information in a Configuration container in the legacy Exchange directory service. Each Exchange server in a site knows about the other servers in the site by looking in this Configuration container. The legacy servers in a site won't know that you installed an Exchange 2003 server until they see the server's information in the legacy Configuration container. That's the job of the Configuration Connection Agreement, which is created automatically when you install the first Exchange 2003 server in the site.

### Configuration CA Function

When you install an Exchange 2003 server, Setup creates objects under the Exchange organization container in Active Directory that represent the following functions:

- Exchange server itself, including its operational settings
- Site addressing
- Connectors
- MTA and transport protocols

- Private and public mailbox storage parameters
- Recipient Policies
- Site (Administrative Group) configuration parameters
- Encryption and secure messaging parameters

The ADC synchronizes these objects with the legacy Exchange Configuration container using a Configuration Connection Agreement. The Configuration CA also connects the legacy Configuration container to the Recipient Policies container in Active Directory so that the ADC can update addressing policies. This is how Exchange 2003 finds out about the SMTP, X.400, and other proxy addresses currently used by legacy Exchange.

### Configuration CA Endpoints

During your migration from legacy Exchange to Exchange 2003, you'll be decommissioning legacy servers. At some point, a given site might not have any remaining legacy servers, but the Exchange 5.x servers in other sites must still replicate the legacy Configuration partition so they can calculate message routing.

You could leave a legacy server in each site until you're just about ready to finish your migration, but to help smooth the transition, an Exchange 2003 server pretends to be a legacy Exchange server so it can replicate the Configuration container to the other legacy servers. That's the job of the SRS. An upcoming section in this chapter titled "Site Replication Service Configuration" details the operation of the SRS.

## Public Folder Connection Agreements

Legacy Exchange public folders also act like standard recipients in that they can receive mail and belong to distribution lists. Active Directory represents mail-enabled public folders with a special object called Public Folder.

A Public Folder Connection Agreement in the ADC populates Active Directory with one Public Folder object for each public folder in the Public Folder Hierarchy. If you have 10,000 public folders in legacy Exchange, you'll end up with 10,000 Public Folder objects in Active Directory.

Public Folder CAs created by the Connection Agreement Wizard resemble Recipient CAs. Here are the differences:

- Both CA types define a two-way connection agreement with an Exchange server as the endpoint on one side of the CA and Active Directory on the other side.
- Both CA types limit the CA so that only the Windows side acts as a Primary CA.
- Both CA types have a default schedule of Always.

Their primary difference lies in the type of object included in the search criteria. A Public Folder CA searches only for objects of the Public Folder class in Active Directory and for public folders in legacy Exchange.

The target container in Active Directory is also different. A Public Folder CA points at the Microsoft Exchange System Objects container, as shown in Figure 12.38.

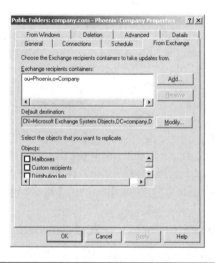

**Figure 12.38** Public Folder Connection Agreement properties showing that the destination is the Microsoft Exchange System Objects container so that Public Folder objects can be created to correspond with mail-enabled MAPI public folders.

When the ADC runs the Public Folder CA for the first time, the Microsoft Exchange System Objects container fills with objects representing public folders. Figure 12.39 shows the Microsoft Exchange System Objects container after the initial replication. (Select View | Advanced view in the console to see the container.)

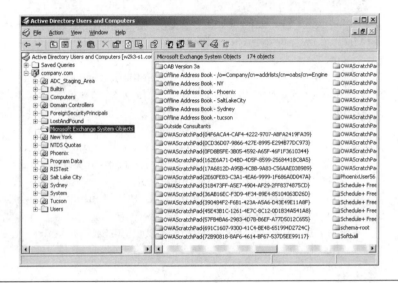

**Figure 12.39** Active Directory Users and Computers console showing Public Folder objects created by Public Folder CA.

# Initial Exchange 2003 Server Installation

You can't directly upgrade an existing Exchange 5.5 server to Exchange 2003. Once you've installed the ADC, select a site and install an Exchange 2003 server in that site. For best results, select the site that acts as the hub of your current organization.

The steps to install the first Exchange 2003 server in an existing legacy Exchange organization do not differ much from those that install an Exchange 2003 server in a pristine organization. Refer to Chapter 1, "Installing an Exchange 2003 Server," for the detailed installation steps.

The Exchange 2003 prescriptive checklist includes provisions for installing the first Exchange 2003 server in an existing legacy Exchange organization. Don't forget the prerequisite services on the server:

- NNTP (Nntpsvc)
- SMTP (Smtpsvc)
- WWW (W3svc)
- IIS Admin (Iisadmin)

Once you've installed the Exchange 2003 server, you should do some provisional testing to ensure that your migration infrastructure operates satisfactorily.

The primary differences in the installation of an Exchange 2003 server in a legacy organization occur in the background. Setup does the following:

- Replaces the placeholder name on the Organization object in Active Directory with the name of the legacy Exchange organization.
- Installs a Configuration Connection Agreement in the ADC that links the legacy Configuration container to the Organization container in Active Directory.
- Enables and starts the Site Replication Service (covered later in this chapter).

A short time after Setup completes, the Recipient Update Service places the newly installed Exchange server into the Exchange Domain Servers group.

Drum roll. Cymbals clash. You did it. You installed the first Exchange 2003 server in the legacy organization. You have a lot of work ahead of you, but for right now, you should test the system to make sure everything works right so far.

## Connection Agreement Testing

Now that you have a live Exchange 2003 server, you can test the Connection Agreements created by the ADC. Here's a list of experiments you should perform to familiarize yourself with the ADC operation. For the sake of getting the most experience possible from the experiments, check the Application Log on the ADC server during each experiment to see the events that occur as objects replicate back and forth between legacy Exchange and Active Directory.

- **Create a new mailbox-enabled user** and verify that the ADC creates a mailbox in legacy Exchange with an owner whose name matches the new user. You might want to use the LDAP Browser (LDP) to see how the ADC-Global-Names attribute gets fleshed out as the attributes replicate back and forth between Active Directory and the legacy Exchange directory service.

- **Create a new mail-enabled group** and verify that the ADC creates a distribution list in legacy Exchange.
- **Add members to a mail-enabled group** in Active Directory and then see if they appear in the legacy distribution list.
- **Connect to a legacy mailbox with Outlook** to make sure you have access permission via SIDHistory (if applicable) and to make sure you can add members to distribution lists and send mail to the members. Verify that the members appear in the group in Active Directory.
- **Create a new mail-enabled contact** and verify that the ADC creates a custom recipient in legacy Exchange. Check the legacy attributes to verify that the e-mail address you gave the contact appears in the custom recipient.
- **Create a new mailbox in legacy Exchange** using Admin and give the mailbox an owner from Active Directory who does not already have a mailbox. Verify that the ADC populates the user account with e-mail attributes so that the account now shows as a mailbox-enabled user.
- **Delete a mailbox in legacy Exchange** and verify that the ADC removes the e-mail attributes from the corresponding user in Active Directory. Do this for a user with a mailbox on the legacy Exchange server and for a user with a mailbox on the Exchange 2003 server. Note that the Exchange 2003 mailbox does not actually get deleted when you delete the mailbox in legacy Exchange. Instead, run the Mailbox Cleanup Wizard to see that the mailbox gets a big red X and that you can link it to the same or another user. See Chapter 5, "Managing Recipients and Distribution Lists," for details.
- **Delete a distribution list and a contact in legacy Exchange** and verify that the ADC strips e-mail attributes from the corresponding objects in Active Directory. Note that the Active Directory objects themselves remain and that the membership of a group remains intact.
- **Place a Universal Distribution Group on a public folder permission list** and verify that it gets promoted to a Universal Security Group in a few minutes. The Exchange Information Store service performs this upgrade, so you might want to check the Event Log for MsExchangeIS events.

- **Create a new public folder** using Outlook or ESM, and verify that the ADC creates a corresponding Public Folder object in the Microsoft Exchange System Objects container in the domain.
- **Delete a public folder** and verify that the ADC removes the Public Folder object from the domain.
- **Replicate public folder content** by including the new Exchange server in the replication list for each public folder using the steps outlined in Chapter 10, "Managing Public Folders." You'll eventually decommission the legacy server so you want to move all public folders and system folders to Exchange 2003 servers.
- **Verify that Schedule + Free Busy replicates to the new server** by opening a new user and creating an appointment and then opening another user and verifying that the appointment appears in the availability columns.

The final set of ADC tests involve the Configuration Connection Agreement created when you installed the first Exchange 2003 server in the site.

- **Legacy Exchange.** Launch Admin at a legacy Exchange server in the same site as the new Exchange 2003 server and verify that the new server appears in the Configuration container.
- **Active Directory.** Launch ESM and drill down to the Administrative Group representing the legacy site and verify that you have black-and-white icons representing the legacy Exchange servers.

If you don't see this information, force the CA to replicate by right-clicking the CA object and selecting Replicate Now from the flyout menu. Check the Event Log to make sure there aren't any errors. If you experience any issues, you can use the Diagnostics Logging tab in the properties window for a server in ESM to assist in troubleshooting (or to overwhelm you with information).

## Site Replication Service Configuration

When you install the first Exchange 2003 server in a site, the Exchange Setup program initializes the SRS. This service maintains a copy of the legacy Exchange directory service that it can replicate with legacy servers in the site, as shown in Figure 12.40.

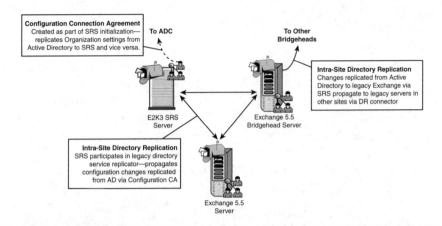

**Figure 12.40** Site Replication Service allows Exchange 2003 server to participate in legacy Exchange directory service replication to simplify Connection Agreement connections.

SRS acts as an endpoint for the Configuration Connection Agreement created in the ADC by Exchange Setup. This allows SRS to funnel organizational changes made in Active Directory into the legacy Exchange directory service, where they propagate to the legacy servers via standard directory service replication.

It's important to keep in mind that the SRS **does not** replicate directly to Active Directory. You still need the ADC to move data to and from Active Directory and the legacy Exchange directory service. The SRS simply makes it possible to home the Exchange side of a Connection Agreement to an Exchange 2003 server.

You should manually change the endpoints of Recipient and Public Folder CAs to point at SRS rather than a legacy Exchange server. In this way, you can decommission your legacy servers without losing synchronization with Active Directory.

SRS does not run as a clustered resource. Because the first Exchange 2003 server in a site must run SRS, you cannot install the first Exchange 2003 server in a site on a cluster. Install at least one standalone Exchange 2003 server to act as SRS and then install Exchange on the cluster. (This was also true for Exchange 2000.)

## Managing the SRS Directory

You cannot manage the content of the SRS directory directly from Exchange System Manager. It's a legacy directory service, so you need a copy of Admin, the legacy Exchange administration utility.

You can use Admin from another Exchange server or you can install it on your Exchange 2003 server (or management workstation) using an Exchange Setup option. Figure 12.41 shows the option.

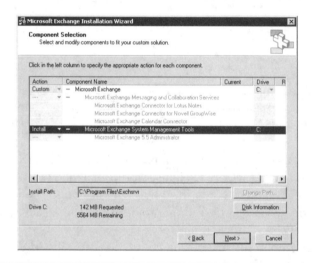

**Figure 12.41**    Installing the legacy Admin tool on an Exchange 2003 server allows you to manage an SRS databases and legacy Exchange servers.

Installing the legacy Admin tool also comes in handy because you can manage other legacy servers in addition to the SRS server. You do not need to run SRS to load the Admin tool.

## Configuring New SRS Servers

Exchange Setup installs SRS on every Exchange 2003 server, but only initializes the service on the first Exchange 2003 server in a legacy site. You can see the servers running SRS in ESM by drilling down to Tools | Site Replication Services. Figure 12.42 shows an example.

You can use ESM to start SRS on additional servers if you want to transfer Connection Agreement endpoints to another Exchange 2003 server. You must run ESM on the console of the server where you want to initialize SRS (or in a remote desktop session connected to the server).

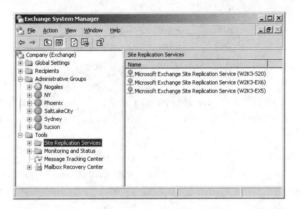

**Figure 12.42**   ESM showing SRS servers. Each site with a legacy Exchange server and an Exchange 2003 server must have an SRS server.

1. Right-click the **Site Replication Services** icon and select **New | Site Replication Service** from the flyout menu.
2. A popup window asks if you are sure you want to start the service. Click **Yes** to acknowledge.
3. The Initial SRS Replication window opens, offering you a choice of which legacy server or SRS server to replicate from during the initial population of the local directory service database. Figure 12.43 shows an example. Select a server and click **OK**. The Site Replication Service logon window opens, as shown in Figure 12.44.

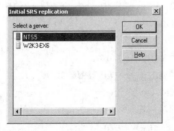

**Figure 12.43**   When creating a new SRS server, you can select the legacy server or the SRS server from which to pull initial replication.

4. Enter the password for the Exchange service account used by the SRS.

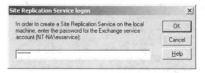

**Figure 12.44**   SRS logon window allows you to enter the credentials of the legacy Exchange service account.

Exchange now starts SRS on the server, initializes the legacy directory service database, and joins the replication topology of the site. You can now rehome Connection Agreements to the server as described in the next section.

## Changing Connection Agreement Endpoints

When the CA Wizard first creates the Recipient and Public Folder Connection Agreements, it selects a legacy Exchange server in each site to act as the endpoint for the CA. To keep from changing the CA endpoints from one legacy server to the next as you decommission them, rehome the CA endpoints to an SRS server and be done with it.

Change the endpoint of a CA using the Properties window for the Connection Agreement in the ADC Services console.

1. Select the Connections tab.
2. Change the server name in the **Exchange Server Information** field from the legacy Exchange server to the Fully Qualified Domain Name (FQDN) of the SRS server in that site.
3. **Important.** Change the port number from **389** to **379**. The SRS service listens for LDAP queries on port 379. This permits SRS to coexist with Active Directory if you run Exchange 2003 on a domain controller.
4. When prompted that the change requires a full replication, click **OK** to acknowledge.
5. Verify that the Connection Agreement operates correctly by making a small change in Active Directory and then manually running the CA to see if the change replicates to legacy Exchange.

# Completing the Migration

At this point, you've installed the ADC and your first Exchange 2003 server. You've replicated the public and system folders to the new server and verified that each of the Connection Agreements works.

You can now install additional Exchange 2003 servers in this and other sites and start laying out your new messaging infrastructure. This involves creating new Routing groups, moving mailboxes, moving connectors, decommissioning legacy servers, and shifting to Exchange Native mode.

## Create Routing Groups

Each legacy site forms a separate Routing group in Exchange 2003, so as soon as you install an Exchange 2003 server in a second site, you should create a Routing Group connector between them and remove the legacy Site connector. This has several benefits.

- You stop routing messages through the slow, cumbersome MTA on the legacy Exchange bridgeheads.
- You reduce your reliance on the error-prone Gateway Address Routing Table (GWART) and move toward using the Link State Table exclusively for message routing.
- Once you get multiple Exchange 2003 servers in each site, you can take advantage of fault tolerant message routing and reduce your reliance on a single bridgehead.

To replace the legacy Site connectors, just install a Routing Group connector between sites, select the Exchange 2003 as the bridgeheads, verify that messages flow between those two bridgeheads, and then remove the Site connectors using legacy Exchange Admin.

Do a final verification that mail sent from a user with a legacy Exchange home server in one site arrives in the mailbox of a user with a legacy Exchange mailbox in another site. This assures you that the legacy servers and the new servers all understand the new topology.

For safety's sake, once you have replaced sufficient Site connectors so that you don't need to worry about routing loops, you should start putting multiple routes between Routing groups to assure fault tolerance in case one network connection should go down.

For details on creating Routing Group connectors, and for details on SMTP routing and the operation of Link State tables, see Chapter 8.

## Identify Legacy Exchange Services

It's important to map out the legacy services so you have a good idea how to transfer their functionality to Exchange 2003 as you migrate. Be on the lookout for servers hosting the following features:

- **Internet Mail Service (IMS).** To retain access to Internet e-mail, make it a top priority to transfer your Internet mail from any legacy Exchange IMS servers to Exchange 2003 servers acting as bridgeheads for an SMTP connector. To assure continuity of service, leave the existing IMS connection in place with a high cost until you verify that the new SMTP connector works in all situations. See Chapter 8, "Message Routing," for details.
- **SNADS, PROFS, and ccMail connectors.** Exchange 2003 does not support these connectors. Leave a legacy Exchange server in place to host the connectors while you find some other method to connect to these services or convince users to abandon them.
- **Third-party fax connectors.** Verify that the vendor of the fax connector supplies an Exchange 2003 version and test it in your lab.
- **Routing Calculation Server.** While you retain legacy Exchange servers in an organization, you need to provide them with routing information via the GWART. Only one legacy server in a site calculates the GWART. You can select the calculation server using the legacy Admin utility. Drill down to the Configuration container for the site and open the Properties window for the Site Addressing object. Figure 12.45 shows an example. Select an Exchange 2003 server from the dropdown list. Any Exchange 2003 server can perform this function. It does not need to run SRS.

Before using an Exchange 2003 server to calculate the GWART, transfer all Internet mail routing to Exchange 2003 servers. When Exchange 2003 calculates the GWART, it removes the @ sign from the address scope. Legacy Exchange IMS requires this @ sign to work properly.

**Figure 12.45**   You can use legacy Admin to select a different routing calculation server when the time comes to decommission the server.

- **Bridgehead servers.** Before decommissioning a legacy server that acts as a bridgehead for a Site connector or a Directory Service connector, evaluate whether you still need the connector. In most circumstances, once you have Exchange 2003 servers in all sites, you do not want legacy Exchange servers to act as bridgeheads.
- **Address Book Views.** You cannot migrate legacy Address Book Views to Active Directory. Create custom address lists with LDAP queries that mimic the selection criteria used for a particular Address Book View.
- **Key Management Server (KMS).** If you have deployed secure messaging in your legacy Exchange organization, you'll have at least one legacy Exchange server acting as the KMS. Exchange 2003 does not have a KMS function. That's because Windows Server 2003 Certification Authorities can store private keys, so you do not need a KMS. See the Microsoft white paper titled, "Key Archival and Management in Windows Server 2003" (download from `http://snipurl.com/5z3s`) for instructions on transferring the KMS database to a Windows Server 2003 CA.

## Complete Mailbox Moves

During the initial testing of your first Exchange 2003 server, you moved a few user mailboxes from the legacy servers to the new server. Now that you have installed sufficient Exchange 2003 servers to handle your user population, continue moving mailboxes until all users have their mailboxes on new Exchange 2003 servers.

ESM can move four mailboxes at a time, so this portion of the migration should not take long unless you have users with extremely large mailboxes. See Chapter 7, "Managing Storage and Mailboxes," for details.

## Shift to Exchange Native Mode

Once you have decommissioned all your legacy servers, you can shift the Exchange organization to Native mode. This exposes the following additional features:

- **Move mailboxes between Administrative Groups**. In Native mode, you can move a user's mailbox from an Exchange server in one AG to an Exchange server in another AG, so long as you have Exchange Administrator permissions on both AGs.
- **Consolidate Administrative Groups**. Once you're in Native mode, you can create Administrative Groups that make sense from an IT operational perspective instead of the site-centric model in legacy Exchange. The only drawback is that you cannot move servers from one Administrative Group to another. You'll have to install a server in the new Administrative Group, move mailboxes and connectors to this server, and then decommission and reuse the old server. This is called a "swing" transfer. Native mode also allows you to have Routing Group boundaries that do not follow the boundaries of Administrative Groups.
- **Create Query-Based Distribution Groups**. The Native mode organization permits you to mail-enable a QDG so you can take advantage of the dynamic group membership features inherent in QDG operation.
- **8BITMIME on Exchange 2003 Bridgehead Servers**. If two bridgehead servers in a Native mode organization run Exchange 2003, then they use 8BITMIME for data transfers. This improves bandwidth utilization by nearly 15 percent, all other things being equal.
- **Automatic Zombie removal**. When Exchange 2003 evaluates trustees in an Access Control List, if it finds an entry referring to

an account that no longer exists, it removes the entry from the ACL. This eventually eliminates any performance issues arising from zombie entries on public folder permissions.

- **Mailbox-enable InetOrgPerson objects**. If you need to create instances of the InetOrgPerson class to use as User objects for compatibility with NDS or PeopleSoft or iPlanet, you can mail-enable and mailbox-enable those objects once the organization is in Native mode.

**You cannot reverse the shift to Exchange Native mode.** Once you save the configuration change, you can no longer introduce legacy Exchange servers into your organization.

Shifting to Native mode toggles the *msExchMixedMode* attribute in the Organization object to FALSE. Don't try using a utility to toggle it back to TRUE because other configuration changes are made in the background once an Exchange server sees the Native mode flag.

## Native Mode Prerequisites

You must decommission all legacy Exchange servers in the organization before shifting to Native mode. This involves removing (de-installing) Exchange from the servers. If you have servers that no longer function, you can delete the associated objects from Active Directory using Exchange System Manager. (You might need to remove the objects from the SRS using Admin, as well.)

You must also remove Site Replication Service from your organization by shutting down the service using ESM at each SRS server. SRS maintains a copy of the legacy Directory Service, so from the perspective of Exchange, an Exchange 2003 server running SRS represents a legacy server.

## Performing the Shift

When you're ready to do the shift, launch ESM and open the Properties window for the Organization object at the top of the tree. Figure 12.46 shows an example.

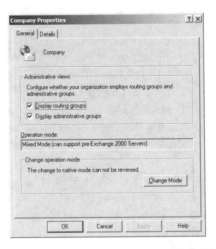

**Figure 12.46** The Organization properties window showing the Change Mode button, which will be available only if all prerequisites are met to shift to Exchange Native mode.

If you have done all the necessary prerequisites to make the change to Native mode, the Change Mode button will be available. Click the button, acknowledge the warning, click OK and you're done.

Yes, it's true.

You're done.

At least for now.

## Looking Forward

No doubt about it, this chapter contains the hardest work you'll probably ever do as an Exchange administrator. Completing the migration to Exchange 2003 makes you feel like you're soaring at 30,000 feet with nothing around you but blue sky, blue horizons, and, if you're an *X-Files* fan, a blue space alien who wants to take snapshots of your eyeballs. If it makes you feel any better, the steps you followed in this chapter are much simpler than an upgrade from Exchange 5.5 to Exchange 2000.

Still, you have earned the right to relax a while, but don't rest on your laurels quite yet. You need to make sure that your system doesn't become a nest for viruses and spam, and you need to make sure you have a good backup process in place so you can soar up there above the clouds without worrying that a simple deleted mailbox item will send you plummeting back to Earth.

# CHAPTER 13

# Service Continuity

Computers are not infallible. They merely impose a layer of orderliness over an underlying chaos so as to give the appearance of infallibility.

You know this to be truth, right? If you've been in this business for longer than…say… 48 hours, you've watched perfectly normal data systems succumb to forces that sabotage every safeguard you've put in place to protect them.

RAID arrays? Forget it. Can you say, "Multiple simultaneous drive crashes caused by a production line defect"? Dual power supplies? Somebody plugged them into the same circuit on the UPS. Dual network cards? Both share the same PCI bus so that when one faults, it takes out the other one. ECC memory? Bad DIMM controller. Clustered servers? Loss of shared Fibre Channel fabric. So on and so on.

In spite of your best efforts to protect the data on a server and provide 100 percent continuity of service to your users, Murphy's Law rules the universe and you just can't escape from it.

> Murphy's Law states the following: "If something can go wrong, it will go wrong, and it will go wrong at the worst possible time." The law has many corollaries. Visit `www.murphys-laws.com` for a compilation.

As far as Exchange is concerned, your ultimate safety net is a complete backup of the server and of the Exchange data stores on the server, but even then you aren't fully protected. When was the last time you tried to do a full restore of an e-mail server using the last full backup tape? And I don't mean as part of a planned event, staged to prove disaster preparedness to the CIO in advance of next year's budget negotiations. I mean a random drill titled, "This is Tuesday at 3pm and I'm turning off this Exchange server right now and you have two hours to get the users' e-mail back."

To be honest, I think disaster preparedness isn't so much about process and technology as it is about attitude. Exchange 2003 comes with a suite of data-protection features unprecedented in the history of Microsoft products, but if your management won't give you the infrastructure to implement them or the time to test them, then hey...you have nothing left but to keep the right attitude and do what you can.

This chapter primarily covers four areas:

- Antispam and antivirus
- Backup and restore
- Volume shadow copy services
- Clustering

I consider antispam and antivirus products to be different aspects of the same challenge, to deliver a quality stream of information to the users. The operational challenges encountered when deploying antivirus and antispam solutions follow parallel paths. Because just about every organization has an antivirus solution in place, I'll spend most of the section discussing antispam solutions.

In the backup and restore area, Exchange 2003 exposes an Application Programming Interface (API) for backups that nearly all vendors use, so I'm not going to bore you with a feature comparison. Most backup products differentiate themselves with management interfaces and centralized control features. A few strive to stand out for their Exchange support, and I'll give them a mention. For the most part, though, you can taste the essential ingredients of backup and restore in Exchange 2003 using the Ntbackup program that comes with Windows Server 2003.

The real news in Exchange 2003, when it comes to recoverability, is the support for snapshot backups and restores using the Volume Shadow Copy service in Windows Server 2003. Although Ntbackup doesn't take advantage of this technology, every third-party product that claims full support for Exchange 2003 gives you some capability for doing snapshot backups. This chapter describes how the technology works and what to expect from your vendor when it comes time to evaluate their offering.

Clustering isn't new in Exchange, but I think you'll find the cluster support for Exchange 2003 running on Windows Server 2003 to be both simpler than you might expect and more powerful than it first appears. Besides, I think you'll enjoy the experience of capping off your work with Exchange by building a full-fledged cluster.

# Antispam and Antivirus

Unsolicited e-mail and mail-borne viruses have grown from a minor nuisance into a pernicious waste of time and system resources as an unrelenting flood of worms and offers for pills, porn, and personal enhancement products pour through the Internet into your Exchange servers. You can't assure your users of high-quality service if your service insists on piling mountains of garbage, dangerous garbage, into their inboxes.

Just about every organization has put an antivirus solution in place. I'm sure your organization is no exception. You probably have also either deployed an antispam solution or are evaluating a few. The operational challenges in putting both types of tools in place follow parallel paths, so I'll discuss them in the same section. Let's start, though, with a look at spam.

## How Spammers Find You

Spammers harvest e-mail addresses from a variety of places, and one of their favorite places are Usenet newsgroups and your organization's Web sites. Educate your users and web developers to always obfuscate their e-mail addresses. For Usenet groups, a simple technique is to leave an e-mail address such as `user@REMOVE_THIS_company.com`. A human would know to remove the inserted text. A spambot would not, although more sophisticated e-mail harvesters are getting good at getting around this technique.

On public-facing Web sites, construct the e-mail hyperlinks with ASCII equivalents for the characters. For example, here is a clear-text address in a "mailto:" entry in a Web page:

```
<a href="mailto:Sales@Company.com">Click here to contact
➥sales.</a>
```

Visit `www.wbwip.com/wbw/emailencoder.html` for a quick ASCII encoder. Here is a preferred entry that uses ASCII numbers corresponding to the letters in the e-mail address:

```
<a href="mailto:&#115;&#097;&#108;&#101;&#115;&#064;&#099;
➥&#111;&#109;&#112;&#097;&#110;&#121;&#046;&#099;&#111;
➥&#109;">
```

Validated addresses have more value than unvalidated addresses, so spammers often include hyperlinks to graphics files in an HTML e-mail message. Here's an example:

```
<img alt="Wild Times" src="http://wildwildwild.biz/images/
➥wildtimes27.gif">
```

When the user opens the message, the e-mail application downloads the gif image from the spammer's Web sites, which gives user information to the spammer. These hyperlinks are called *beacons* because they notify the spammer that a live user has been contacted.

Outlook 2003, Outlook Express with XP SP2, and Outlook Web Access 2003 do not automatically download embedded graphics. Figure 13.1 shows the result.

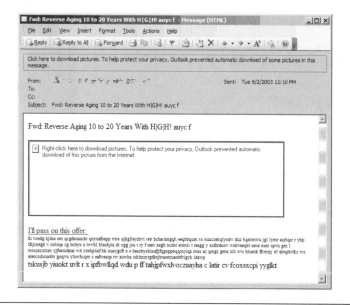

**Figure 13.1** Example Outlook 2003 message showing placeholder for blocked graphics link caused by beacon-blocking feature.

Beacon blocking has its disadvantages. Some popular message-tracking systems embed graphics hyperlinks in outbound messages. When the recipient opens the message, the e-mail client connects to the linked graphic and this sends a notification to the sender. Such a tracking system would not work if the client blocks access to the hyperlink target. The recipient could choose to add the sender to a whitelist—a list of acceptable senders.

## Open SMTP Relays

Once a spammer has a few hundred thousand e-mail addresses, he needs a way to send messages to those addresses without interference. If an SMTP server accepts incoming messages and forwards them regardless of the ultimate destination, it becomes an *open relay*. Figure 13.2 shows how an open relay works.

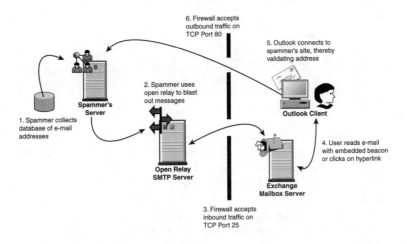

**Figure 13.2**    Flow of illicit spam through an open relay.

The SMTP service in Windows does not permit an anonymous entity from relaying. Only entities with domain credentials can relay, essentially blocking SMTP servers outside the organization.

Open SMTP relays have actually gotten fairly rare nowadays. Open proxy servers have become the exploit of choice for spammers. Many worms and viruses include a proxy service in their payload, permitting spammers and virus writers to gain access to a system and use it for a launching pad.

Spammers find open relays and proxies by scanning for machines that respond to common ports and then testing those ports using SMTP relay requests and proxy HTTP CONNECT requests. You can do these same kinds of tests yourself on the public interface of your servers. *Note:* Always get written permission from management before doing security probes.

From the public side of your network, connect to your public Exchange server using telnet with the following syntax:

```
telnet <exchange_server_name> 25
```

The server should respond with an SMTP banner, something like this:

```
220 EX1 Microsoft ESMTP MAIL Service, Version:
➥6.0.3790.0 ready at Wed, 4 Feb 2004 14:32:31 -0700
```

Now get a list of SMTP capabilities by entering EHLO (Extended Hello). When the server replies, use three SMTP commands to send a message—MAIL FROM, RCPT TO, and DATA—with the following syntax:

```
mail from: totallybogus@fabricatedaddress.biz
250 2.1.0 totallybogus@fabricatedaddress.biz....Sender OK
rcpt to: someusername@yahoo.com
250 2.1.5 someusername@yahoo.com
data
354 Start mail input; end with <CRLF>.<CRLF>
Subject: Your assistance most graciously and desperately
needed
Let me introduce myself. I am the grandson of the Duke of
Earl ➥and I need your help.
.
250 2.6.0 <EX-S1HM3SOlbpH71y00000008@ex1.actualsmptdomain.com>
➥Queued mail for delivery
quit
221 2.0.0 ex1.actualsmptdomain.com Service closing transmission
➥channel
Connection to host lost.
```

If a server accepts a RCPT TO address outside of its SMTP domain, you have found an open relay.

Testing for an open proxy is a little more difficult and requires special tools. One such tool is Proxy Analyzer from G-Lock Software, www.glocksoft.com. Point Proxy Analyzer at a machine and tell it which port or ports might be compromised. Then, let it see if it can connect to the port as a proxy. The tool has a scoring system to determine how ripe a machine is for exploits.

## Blocking Known Spammers

Use information from Spamhaus, www.spamhaus.org, and the Spamhaus Register of Known Spam Operations (ROSKO) at www.spamhaus.org/rokso/index.lasso, to identify spam culprits. You can also get a text-based list of SMTP domains and countries that host spammers at www.spamsites.org/live_sites.html. You can then import these lists into Exchange using the Message Delivery options, as follows.

Exchange has ways to filter incoming messages based on the sender's SMTP domain, the sender's IP address, or a lookup to a spam identification service provider. Use the Global Settings | Message Delivery object in ESM to configure filtering. Figure 13.3 shows the properties window.

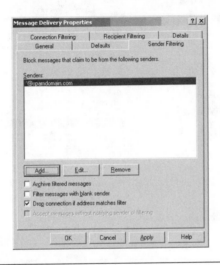

**Figure 13.3** SMTP properties showing Sender Filtering tab with an example SMTP domain specified for filtering.

To block every sender in a particular SMTP domain, use the syntax *@spamdomain.com, where spamdomain.com is the name of the SMTP domain you want to block. You can add as many SMTP domains as you like to the filter. The **Filter Messages With Blank Sender** option eliminates e-mail without return addresses.

The **Drop Connection If Address Matches Filter** option prevents the Exchange server from returning a Non-Delivery Report (NDR) to the spammer, an action that would validate the address and invite more spam.

Filters configured in the Message Delivery object do not take effect automatically. Instead, you must configure each SMTP virtual server to use the filter as follows:

1. Launch ESM and drill down to the **Protocols | SMTP** container under a server container.
2. Open the properties window for the Default SMTP Virtual Server.
3. In the **General** tab, click **Advanced**. This opens the Advanced window that lists the various IP addresses and ports assigned to the virtual server, as shown in Figure 13.4.

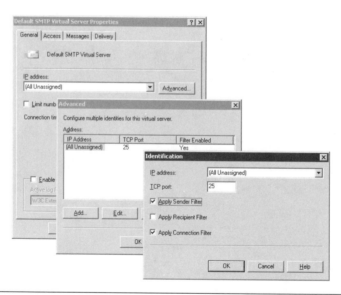

**Figure 13.4**   Applying a connection filter to an SMTP virtual server.

4. Click **Edit**. This opens the Identification window.
5. Check **Apply Sender Filter** and click **OK**.
6. Click **OK** again to close the **Advanced** window and then click OK one more time to save the configuration.
7. Repeat these steps for each SMTP virtual server for which you want to use the filter.

Now test to make sure the filter operates correctly. Use telnet to attempt a connection to the server as if it came from a blocked SMTP domain.

## Real-Time Block Lists

The problem with loading tons of SMTP domains into a Sender Filter is that you must constantly babysit the list. It's much simpler to use the services of one or more organizations that keep tabs on the invalid use of SMTP servers. These organizations go by the name of RBLs. The acronym expansion varies. Microsoft uses Real-Rime Block List. Other expansions include Real-Time Blackhole List and Real-Time Boycott List.

Despite the differences in names, all RBL providers have a similar intent when it comes to inappropriate SMTP use: Search it out, identify the source, and inform the public. They do not "block spam" in the traditional sense of providing an active filter. This would open them up to litigation. Instead, they compile passive lists and then offer the content of the lists to you for you to do the filtering. Neither you nor the RBL provider takes overt action against the spammer's servers.

The Mail Abuse Prevention System (MAPS) at www.mail-abuse.org is the most widely known fee-based provider. Examples of free providers include

- Distributed Server Boycott List (DSBL), www.dsbl.org
- Open Relay Database (ORDB), www.ordb.org
- SpamCop, www.spamcop.net
- Not Just Another Bogus List (NJABL), www.njabl.org.

For a complete list of RBL providers, visit the Declude Web site at www.declude.com/junkmail/support/ip4r.htm. The list includes a brief assessment of each RBL's strengths and weaknesses.

Many RBL providers have a lookup page at their Web site, where you can enter the SMTP domain or IP address of a suspected spammer. The Open Relay Database lookup page at www.ordb.org/lookup submits an entry to a variety of sites to get a comprehensive report, shown in Figure 13.5.

Some RBL providers give their clients a text file of identified spam sites. This text file can be loaded into a filter at the client's local e-mail servers. These block lists can get very long, and you must keep them updated regularly, but local filtering provides fastest performance, all other things being equal. Along with the list, the RBL provider includes instructions for loading the list into major e-mail servers, including Exchange.

Most RBL providers want you to sign a fair use agreement stating that their list is for your exclusive use and you will not advertise its contents. This protects both you and the RBL provider from litigation.

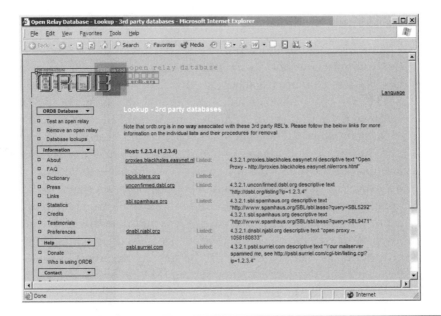

**Figure 13.5** Open Relay Database showing result of a comprehensive search for a suspected spammer's IP address.

## Reverse DNS RBL Services

Most RBL providers host an online lookup service that you access via a reverse DNS (RDNS), query so you do not need any special clients. To use an RDNS service, send the RBL provider a DNS request that contains the reverse IP address of the suspected server followed by the RDNS domain name of the RBL service provider. For example, the RDNS domain name for ORDB is `relays.ordb.org`.

The RDNS service returns an A record with a 127.0.x IP address, where the final x indicates a banned behavior type. Each provider uses slightly different codes. Here are the NJABL RDNS codes:

- 127.0.0.2 - Open relays
- 127.0.0.3 - Dial-up/dynamic IP ranges
- 127.0.0.4 - Spam sources
- 127.0.0.5 - Multi-stage open relays
- 127.0.0.8 - Systems with insecure CGI scripts that turn them into open relays
- 127.0.0.9 - Open proxy servers

Let's say you get a message you suspect to be spam. You can determine the IP address of the sender by viewing the message headers. In Outlook, right-click the message and select Options from the flyout menu. This opens the Message Options window, as shown in Figure 13.6. The Internet Headers field contains the information about the sending SMTP server. Just about the only header information you can trust is the Received From field. All the others could be, and probably are, forged by the sender.

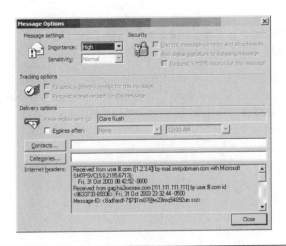

**Figure 13.6**    SMTP information gleaned from Options window for a message in Outlook.

In the example, the IP address of the sender's SMTP server is 1.2.3.4. To check this address using RDNS, submit a DNS query using Nslookup. I'll use the NJABL provider for an example. Here's the syntax of the RDNS lookup request:

```
C:\>nslookup 4.3.2.1.dnsbl.njabl.org

Non-authoritative answer:
Name:     4.3.2.1.dnsbl.njabl.org
Address:  127.0.0.9
```

A return code of `127.0.0.9` would indicate that the sending server is an open proxy, meaning that the owner might not even know the server is being used to send spam.

If you don't want to memorize return codes, use Nslookup in interactive mode to get a TXT record corresponding to the A record, if one is available. Here's the syntax:

```
C:\>nslookup
> set type=txt
> 4.3.2.1.dnsbl.njabl.org

Non-authoritative answer:
4.3.2.1.dnsbl.njabl.org text =

    "open proxy — 1058170803"
```

## Configuring a Connection Filter to Use an RDNS RBL Provider

It only takes a few minutes to configure Exchange 2003 to use an RDNS service. Open ESM and drill down to **Global Settings**. Open the properties window for the **Message Delivery** object. Select the **Connection Filtering** tab, shown in Figure 13.7.

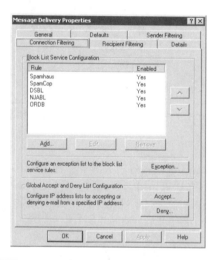

**Figure 13.7**    Connection filtering list showing Reverse DNS RBL providers.

Click **Add** to insert a new filtering rule, shown in Figure 13.8. Give the rule a **Display Name** and then specify the RDNS suffix for the provider. Obtain this information from the provider's Web site. Leave the error message at the defaults.

If a particular piece of unsolicited e-mail arrives from an SMTP server that has not yet been identified as a source of spam, you can add the IP address to the connection filter using the **Global Accept and**

**Deny List Configuration** option. Click **Deny** to open the Deny List window and then click **Add** to specify either a specific IP address or a range of addresses. Figure 13.9 shows an example.

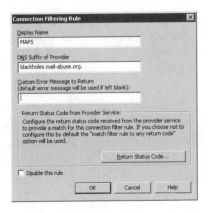

**Figure 13.8** Connection filtering rule showing selection of a Reverse DNS RBL provider.

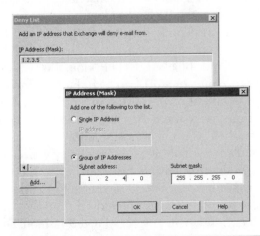

**Figure 13.9** Adding IP addresses to a set of blacklisted address ranges.

### *Apply the Connection Filter to SMTP Virtual Servers*

Now that you've defined a set of RDNS providers in a Connection Filter, apply the filter to the SMTP virtual servers as follows:

1. Launch ESM and drill down to the **Protocols | SMTP** container under a server container.
2. Open the properties window for the Default SMTP Virtual Server.
3. In the **General** tab, click **Advanced**. This opens the Advanced window that lists the various IP addresses and ports assigned to the virtual server.
4. Click **Edit**. This opens the Identification window.
5. Check **Apply Connection Filter**, click **OK**, and then keep clicking OK to save the configuration.
6. Repeat the steps for each SMTP virtual server for which you want to use the filter.

### RBL Limitations

RBL filtering, in and of itself, can't protect you completely from spam. First off, not all spam comes from open relay and proxies. Second, spammers have sophisticated ways to skip around from one exploited machine to another so that no one machine sends sufficient junk mail to get the attention of the RBL providers.

The major problem with using RBL filtering, though, is the large number of false positives you could experience. Desirable messages often come from blocked SMTP domains where a spammer has exploited a machine, or an IP can be unfairly or incorrectly listed.

If your organization gets listed on an RBL, subscribers will bounce messages from you to the RBL service. Depending on the sender's filtering configuration, you might not be informed of the block. This avoids large-scale disruption of the Internet during worm attacks. It also leaves your users wondering why no one is answering their e-mails.

Once you correct the condition that got you listed on an RBL, contact the provider to get your system removed from the list. RBL providers do not talk to each other in any coordinated fashion, so you might have to communicate with more than one of them. It can take as long as a week, maybe even longer, to clear your name from an RBL database. Don't bother trying to muscle the RBL provider into working faster. They deal with hard-core spammers every hour of every day, something that takes a Jabba the Hutt mentality. They aren't afraid of threats from you or your CEO or your lawyer. If you comply with standard SMTP practices, you will eventually get removed from their system.

## Challenge-Response Blocking

One way to block 100 percent of all spam is to force all unrecognized senders to identify themselves. This approach uses a service provider who does inbound filtering on incoming mail. If the service sees an inbound message from a sender who has not been sent a message previously, it escrows the message and returns a challenge to a sender asking for the sender to take an action.

The nature of the action depends on the vendor. For example, SpamLion (`www.spamlion.com`) asks the sender to click a hyperlink, similar to the registration verifications done by Internet mailing list managers such as Majordomo. SpamArrest (`www.spamarrest.com`) requires the sender to read a bitmap containing a word and to type that word into a reply.

Challenge-response systems have enviable filter performance characteristics, but they aren't always the perfect solution, especially in situations where a non-human sends a desirable message. Opt-in mailing lists are a prime example, as are vendor bulletins sent to inform customers of vital product information. Very few list managers take the trouble to reply to challenge-response messages, with the result that potentially useful information never makes it to the recipient. If the recipient isn't willing to take the time to preapprove a mailing list by domain name, then the list's mailings go right to the junk pile.

Another problem with the challenge-response approach is that the customers who use these systems depend on the quality of the vendor's messaging infrastructure. If the vendor's system should go down, or undergo an unforeseen load that makes it unreachable, or get brought down by a globally-based Distributed-Denial-of-Service (DDoS) attack, then all mail to and from the customer grinds to a halt.

## Signature-Based Filtering

Another type of spam and virus filtering examines message content and then uses a combination of keywords, rules, and content analysis to determine their "spamminess" or their capabilities for carrying a virus.

If the vendor updates the rulesets often, this approach can be tremendously effective. However, rules-based filtering can suffer due to the highly variable nature of nefarious content. A rules-based antispam engine might filter out a message with the subject "You Can Last Twice as Long" but pass over "You, Can La$t Twice /As Long mxplxct." Or a virus that would be trapped if it contained a .vbs file might get through if it is a .zip file.

Nearly all antivirus solutions use signatures of one form or another. The examples are too numerous to mention. Signature-based solutions often compete based on how quickly the signatures can be deployed, how soon a new outbreak can be fingerprinted and included in a signature file, and how convenient it is to distribute the signatures within an enterprise.

Several antispam vendors also use signatures because they have a predictable result and a known distribution mechanism. Examples of popular rules-based antispam products include

- iHateSpam from Sunbelt Software, `www.sunbeltsoftware.com`
- MailMarshal from NetIQ, `www.netiq.com`
- SurfControl from SurfControl, `www.surfcontrol.com`

## Hash-Based Filtering

Signature-based antivirus and antispam solutions have the potential for blocking valid messages that look suspicious to the filter mechanism. Hash-based filters aim to eliminate false positives by trapping instances of improper messages and reducing them to a digital fingerprint called a hash. In cryptography terminology, a hash is constructed from a one-way function whose output is a fixed length that is highly sensitive to the input. A good hashing function could modify 50 percent of the content of the hash in response to the change of a single byte in the input.

The vendor of a hash-based solution works hard to attract spam and viruses. When it validates the improper content, it produces a hash and sends out an update. The clients receive the hash and use it to evaluate incoming messages.

Hash-based filters have certain distinct advantages compared to signature solutions. They're very fast, because hashing algorithms have been optimized for top performance, and virtually infallible because the chances of two messages in the wild having the same hash is staggeringly improbable. The hash is also very compact, making it simpler to send a stream of updates to clients for rapid updates.

However, the laser-like focus of hash-based filters also becomes one of their primary disadvantages. Until the leading edge of a virus storm or initial release of a spam message intersects with a vendor's listening post, the clients will be wide open to the improper message.

An example of a hash-based solution is Brightmail Anti-Spam from Brightmail, www.brightmail.com.

## Bayesian Filters

To find a way to counter the slippery content of spam messages, many antispam vendors employ a decision process based on the work of an 18th century mathematician and minister named Thomas Bayes. In a document titled "Essay Towards Solving a Problem in the Doctrine of Chances," Reverend Bayes proposed that it's possible to infer the probability that an event will occur based on the number of times it has occurred in the past.

Bayesian logic defines a process by which a naïve learner gains knowledge about a subject, so a spam filter that uses Bayesian decision processes must be taught the difference between good e-mail and spam. This takes a little time. Most Bayesian filters break the contents of a message into tokens and then analyze the frequency of token usage compared to known spam examples. Figure 13.10 shows the result of a Bayesian analysis on a spam message done by a product called InBoxer, an Outlook plug-in from Audiotrieve (www.audiotrieve.com). As you can see, because 11 unwanted messages contained the word Viagra, the filter decides that the message has a 98.03 percent probability of being spam. Combine this with a blank subject line (also nearly always spam) and the filter decides to block the message.

The token-based analysis done by Bayesian filters makes them particularly adept at identifying messages containing word games. A sentence such as "Kure baldne$$ with hare im-plant$" might fool a rules-based filter but a Bayesian filter would know that tokens with odd characters nearly always indicate spam and rate the message accordingly. Carefully crafted messages, though, won't trigger a Bayesian filter. Also, many spammers avoid words entirely, choosing instead to embed graphics that can't be subjected to Bayesian analysis. These are blocked by Outlook Web Access and Outlook 2003.

Other antispam products with Bayesian filters include

- MailEssentials for Exchange/SMTP from GFI Software (www.gfi.com)
- OutlookSpamFilter from Novosoft (www.novosoft.com) that works as an Outlook plug-in
- SpamKiller from McAfee (based on legendary SpamAssassin technology (www.mcafee.com)

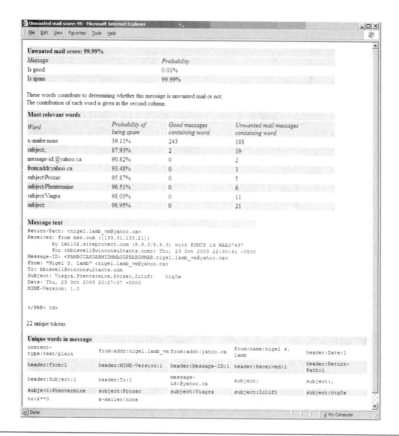

**Figure 13.10**    Mail score from Inboxer, a Bayesian filtering application.

## Edge Filters

You can install an antispam filter on a front-end server running SMTP. This would monitor SMTP traffic to and from your organization and either divert or tag suspicious messages. This keeps the spam from accumulating on your servers, which saves storage— because the edge filter sees all traffic—if it uses Bayesian filtering, it learns about spam patterns more quickly.

You can set up a smart host (a front-end SMTP server) with an antispam solution to block messages or tag them with a spam score and let the Exchange servers or Outlook clients filter for the scoring attribute. Exchange 2003 comes with a set of custom event sinks that antispam products can use for tag filtering. The upcoming Intelligent Message

Filter (IMF) from Microsoft will use these event sinks in conjunction with rules-based scanning and a decision-making matrix to tag and handle spam. Examples of Windows-based SMTP edge filters include

- OrangeBox Mail from Cobion, www.cobion.com
- MailSweeper SMTP Edition from Clearswift, www.clearswift.com
- Trend InterScan Message Security Suite, www.trendmicro.com

A service bureau also acts as an edge filter that routes all incoming and outgoing mail through their system to check for spam and viruses. Because a service bureau deals with millions of e-mails, their filters get to know spam signatures very quickly, making them efficient and effective at filtering spam and viruses. Example service bureaus include

- MessageLabs, www.messagelabs.com
- Postini, www.postini.com

Whether you have security concerns, privacy concerns, or reliability concerns, you should consult closely with the service bureau sales representatives prior to signing a contract and ensure that you have sufficiently stringent service level agreements so that you can terminate your service if you find it not to your liking.

## Store Filters

If your budget doesn't have room for additional servers/appliances, tiered firewalls, or service bureaus, and your public-facing Exchange server sits behind a moderately priced firewall that does port forwarding for incoming SMTP traffic, you can use store-based antispam and antivirus solutions. Since most major antivirus vendors also have an antispam product, you might want to take advantage of the guaranteed compatibility and possible price break in using both solutions. You stand the best chance of combining stability and performance by using products from the same vendor.

If you combine store-based antivirus and antispam solutions from different vendors, test thoroughly for compatibility. Pay particular attention to the quarantine strategies used by the two applications. You don't want a tussle over a message that looks like spam but has a virus payload to cause the server to get unstable.

## Client Filters

Even if you decide to implement edge and store filters for spam and viruses, you should always deploy client filters, as well. Users often supplement their corporate e-mail with POP mail obtained from outside mail servers. By deploying client-based filters, you provide a service to these users.

When evaluating client-side filters, check to see where blocked mail gets stored. If a client-side filter simply moves messages from the user's inbox to another server-side folder, then you've done a service to your users but not to yourself. If possible, find a client-side filter that will either do a hard delete on the junk mail after a short period of time or will shunt the junk mail into an alternate repository that resides on the local desktop.

Small shops with no Exchange servers can use the junk mail filtering capabilities of Outlook. Outlook 2000 and later have canned rules for recognizing junk mail and pornography. Outlook 2003 simplifies configuration with a Junk Mail button in the e-mail configuration tab in the Option menu. You can pre-populate the filter with lists obtained from the Internet. For example, the GazNET site (www.gaznet.com) has a downloadable list that can be placed directly in an Outlook profile. Also, Outlook 2003 has a smart filter that gets updated via Office Update.

# Backup and Restore Operations

As you read in Chapter 7, "Managing Storage and Mailboxes," the accidental deletion of a single item in a mailbox or the accidental deletion of a user account from Active Directory should not force you to do a tape restore. The Information Store retains deleted items for 7 days and deleted mailboxes for 30 days, by default, and you can easily bump those numbers higher without incurring too much additional storage overhead.

In this section, I'm going to use examples based on tape-based backups. I do this because it's the simplest solution to deploy in a lab. However, quite a few organizations have changed over to disk-based backup, either as part of a blended solution with disks in front of the tape drives or as part of an overall change in strategy away from tape-based backup. Before purchasing tape hardware for your production environment, I encourage you to investigate disk-based solutions. You'll find them surprisingly affordable.

Here are situations where you might find yourself queuing a backup tape:

- **Individual mailbox restores.** You might need to go to tape if a user scrambles the contents of a mailbox or a public folder so badly that you can't get it straightened out with individual item restores, or you have a user who tells you that he needs to get back a vitally important message he deleted exactly eight days ago.

- **Corrupted store.** It sometimes happens that one of the database files in the store becomes corrupt. You should monitor the event logs on your Exchange servers and take immediate action if you see any errors associated with database corruption. As an example, a -1018 error indicates that a hardware problem has caused the Cyclic Redundancy Check (CRC) for a page in the database to fail to match the CRC stored on tape. If you let errors such as this go uncorrected, the store might cease functioning, forcing you to restore uncorrupted copies of the database files, if you're lucky enough to have them.

- **Loss of a RAID array.** A corollary of Murphy's Law states, "If several things *could* go wrong, the one that *does* go wrong will cause the most damage." For example, a very expensive SAN could have one interface board on which a failure could disable an entire set of disks. If you use Exchange 2003 Enterprise Edition, you can mitigate against these types of failures by dividing your storage groups onto separate arrays so the loss of a single array would only impact the mailbox and public folder stores in that storage group.

- **Restoring an entire server.** Unless you spend a bit of a premium to get a highly available machine from Stratus (NEC) or IBM or HP, a typical Exchange server has a plethora of failure points. Right this second, perhaps, a little 23-cent capacitor on the motherboard of your Exchange server is about to explode because the supplier used a bootleg formula for the electrolyte. If this happens, and the call to your server vendor goes unanswered because the company has evaporated from the face of the planet, then you need a way to restore the data to a new machine.

In addition to events that impact Exchange servers directly, keep in mind that Exchange relies on a variety of services on other servers:

- **Active Directory.** If Exchange can't locate a domain controller, it can't read Organizational parameters and will refuse to operate.
- **Global Catalog.** An Exchange server must be able to query a Global Catalog server to get mailbox information for routing and to expand group membership.
- **Site Replication Service (SRS).** If your Exchange organization operates in Mixed mode, then you need SRS to act as a Connection Agreement endpoint so that changes made to the two directory services, Active Directory and legacy Exchange, can replicate back and forth.
- **IIS Metabase.** All configuration information for the critical transport protocols used by Exchange is stored in the IIS Metabase. If the Metabase becomes corrupt on an Exchange server, it's every bit as disastrous, operationally, as a failure of the Information Store or System Attendant.
- **Certification Authority (CA).** If you deploy secure messaging, the CA holds copies of the user's public encryption and digital signing keys, and possibly their private encryption keys as well. If this server goes down or becomes compromised, you need a way to restore the database so that you can regain access to the certificates that it issued.

Any recovery strategy for Exchange must include a fail-safe processes for backing up and restoring any or all of these services, either via tape or with redundant servers.

One final thought before we move on. At the risk of getting a little preachy, I just want to remind you (or remind you to remind your boss) that you don't want the first test of your recovery procedures to be a response to an emergency scenario. Plan out your responses and then practice them in your lab. I used to be a reactor operator on nuclear submarines, and believe me, I used to grouse as much as anyone else about endless drills and tedious operational reports. But when the "rods go down and the water comes in and the lights go out," as they say, it's comforting to know that you have recovery procedures that work if you know how to apply them correctly.

## Consistency Checking

The Information Store service exposes a Backup API that has functions for accessing mailbox and public folder stores while they're mounted and available for access by users. The Ntbackup utility in Windows Server 2003 and nearly all third-party backup applications make use of this Backup API. This does not mean that all Exchange backup applications operate the same. The Backup API simply provides a tool kit. Each vendor uses these tools in different ways.

Keeping the Information Store online during backups also permits the Backup API to manipulate the transaction logs to ensure that all items get committed to the main database files and to truncate (remove) any unneeded log files after the backups have been completed. You also get the advantage of a check of the database consistency as the pages stream out to the tape device.

### Online Analysis of Database Integrity

The EDB database in the Exchange store holds data in the form of pages, each page being 4K in size. When the Information Store service commits a page to the database, it calculates a checksum of the page contents and stores the checksum along with the page. When the Backup API accesses a page, the Information Store performs a checksum on the page and compares the result to the stored checksum. If the results do not match, the store pulls the page from disk again and repeats the checksum calculation. If the results still don't match, the Information Store service terminates the backup operation by sending the Backup API a special error code. It records the source of the error in the Event Log. The backup log might also list this information.

Typical causes of checksum errors during backup and restore include poor SCSI connectors or terminators; failing SCSI drives; failing tape devices; improperly written or incompatible SCSI, RAID, or tape device drivers; or timing errors. If you see checksum or -1018 errors in the Event Log, always deal with them immediately. And remember, they're caused by hardware, not by application compatibility.

Because of the additional processing performed by the Backup API, you'll typically see much longer backup and restore times for Exchange database files than you would see for data file backups of comparable size. If your organization finds this additional restore time unacceptable, you can elect to do your backups in two stages:

- First, do an API-based backup of the store to check for database errors and to truncate the transaction logs.
- Second, stop the Information Store service, do a regular file-based backup of the database files, and then start the store again.

If the store files should become corrupt, you can hurriedly copy the offline backup files in place of the current database files and mount the database.

E-mail is unavailable to users during offline backups, and restoring an offline backup does not include the ability to catch up the content with transaction logs, but you have the advantage of a very fast restore. If this is your ultimate goal, however, you should evaluate Exchange 2003 recovery solutions that make use of the snapshot backup features covered later in the chapter.

### Offline Integrity Analysis Using Isinteg

If you get a consistency error, you can use the Isinteg utility to get a more complete analysis of the problem. **Always run Isinteg tests in read-only mode.** If you decide that you need to do a repair to correct an error, I recommend that you get some guidance from Microsoft Product Support Services. The call costs very little compared to the value of the advice you'll get from a professional who does this sort of thing every day and will spend as much time as necessary to help you through the steps.

The following listing shows a sample Isinteg test. The database must be dismounted before running the test. The first two lines represent a single command string.

```
D:\Program Files\Exchsrvr\MDBDATA>isinteg -s server1 -verbose -l log.txt -
➥test folder,message,aclitem,mailbox,dumpsterprops
Databases for server server1:
Only databases marked as Offline can be checked
Index   Status        Database-Name
Storage Group Name: First Storage Group
   1    Offline       Mailbox Store (SERVER1)
   2    Online        MS2 - SG1
   3    Online        Public Folder Store (SERVER1)
Enter a number to select a database or press Return to exit.
1
You have selected First Storage Group / Mailbox Store (SERVER1).
Continue?(Y/N)y
Test reference table construction result: 0 error(s); 0 warning(s); 0
➥fix(es); 0 row(s); time: 0h:0m:0s
Test Folder result: 0 error(s); 0 warning(s); 0 fix(es); 183 row(s); time:
➥0h:0m:0s
```

```
Test Deleted Messages result: 0 error(s); 0 warning(s); 0 fix(es); 0
➡row(s); time: 0h:0m:0s
Test Message result: 0 error(s); 0 warning(s); 0 fix(es); 445 row(s); time:
➡0h:0m:0s
Test Attachment result: 0 error(s); 0 warning(s); 0 fix(es); 448 row(s);
➡time: 0h:0m:0s
Test Mailbox result: 0 error(s); 0 warning(s); 0 fix(es); 9 row(s); time:
➡0h:0m:0s
Test reference count verification result: 0 error(s); 0 warning(s); 0
➡fix(es); 0 row(s); time: 0h:0m:0s
Now in test   8(Row Count/Dumpster Count) of total   8 tests; 100%
➡complete.
```

## Backups and Transaction Logs

There are some fundamental differences in the way the Backup API works depending on the type of backup you perform.

### Full Backups

At the end of a full backup, the Backup API deletes the transaction logs, leaving only the main E00.log file and the highest numbered log file to act as a placeholder.

> The Ntbackup backup type called "Normal" does a full backup.

Full backups can take a long time to run. If you have a several 40GB mailbox stores and a 30GB public folder store in a storage group, it could take several hours to get a full backup of the entire storage group contents. (Exchange Standard Edition is limited to a single 16GB mailbox store and a single 16GB public folder store, so you have an outside limit on the backup window that depends only on the speed of your tape device and network.)

### Incremental and Differential Backups

An incremental backup saves only the transaction logs, not the main database files. This completes the nightly backups very quickly.

Figure 13.11 shows the Ntbackup management window with three sets of backup files. The first set represents a full (normal) backup that captured the mailbox store, the public folder store and the transaction logs for a storage group called EX1-SG1. The next two incremental backup sets captured just the transaction logs for the target storage group.

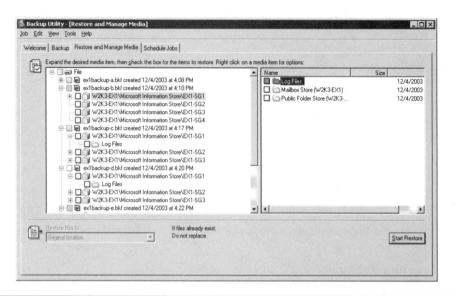

**Figure 13.11**    Backup catalog showing full backup on 12/4/2003 4:10 P.M. and incremental backups (log files only) at 4:17 P.M. and 4:20 P.M.

At the end of an incremental backup, the Backup API truncates the transaction logs, leaving only E00.log and the highest-numbered log as a placeholder. This means that to do a restore, you need the last full backup tape plus each night's incremental tape. This makes for a complex restore and increases the odds that a tape failure could abort the restore. (Not everyone backs up to tape, of course, but even if you do spindle-based backups of one form or another, there's a possibility of a media failure that would cause a more complex restoration scenario.)

In contrast, a differential backup also captures just the transaction logs, but it does not delete the historical logs. This means that each successive differential backup takes longer than the previous one, but if you ever need to restore, you need only the last full backup tape and the latest differential backup tape.

### Choosing Backup Types

From the point of view of fastest and simplest recovery, performing a full backup each night wins the contest hands down. However, this speed and simplicity comes at some expense:

- **Longer backups.** You'll have a much longer backup window, which can upset users who try to read their e-mail during the backups and get frustrated by the poor performance.
- **More tape drive time.** The backup server probably has other chores to do in addition to handling Exchange backups, so unless you can convince the backup operator to commit two or three drive heads to Exchange for a few hours, you might not have a sufficiently long backup window.
- **Possible maintenance conflicts.** Each night, the Information Store performs online maintenance to keep the databases compact and error-free. When backup starts for any store in a storage group, online maintenance stops for all stores in that storage group. Watch your event logs for maintenance errors and adjust your backup window accordingly.

If you can't support a full backup every night, fall back to differential backups. If your Exchange server gets so much traffic that a week's buildup of transaction logs would choke the drive holding the log files, then do incremental backups and remember to keep the nightly backup tapes on hand for a quick recovery, if one is required.

## Backup and Restore Process Overview

Before looking at the step-by-step procedures for backing up and restoring an Exchange server, it's helpful to understand some of the processes involved. This helps you visualize what's going on in the background when you run your nightly backup jobs and keeps you from making your recovery strategies too complex.

Let's start with a look at the various Exchange files involved in backups. Refer to Figure 13.12. The diagram shows example file locations for an Exchange server running Enterprise Edition. The server has a single storage group that contains two mailbox stores and the default public folder store.

E2K3
Mailbox Server

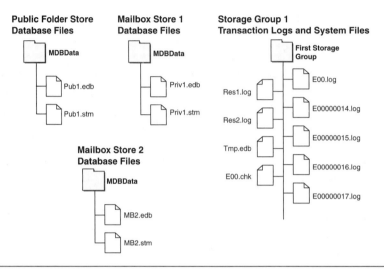

**Figure 13.12**   Diagram of typical configuration for mailbox stores in a single storage group with accumulated transaction logs.

### Fault Tolerance and File Locations

The main database files for each store, the EDB and STM files, are located on their own RAID array. File location makes no difference to the operation of the backup program, but it does play a role in controlling the extent of your recovery operations should an array fail.

If your service level agreements with your management and users (either formal or informal) have flexibility, you can save costs by putting multiple mailbox stores on the same RAID array. Just don't mix stores from different storage groups on the same array because this complicates the recovery.

All changes to the stores in a storage group first get saved to a set of transaction logs. The main transaction log for this storage group is E00.log. When this log gets full, the Information Store service changes the file name to the next sequential number and creates a new E00.log file.

The transaction logs reside on a separate RAID array to improve performance and enhance recoverability. It would take several simultaneous failures to bring down the both arrays holding the data files and the transaction logs at the same time. I'm not saying that couldn't happen, but disaster planning is like blackjack; they both rely on odds, and you improve your odds by putting the data files and the transaction logs on separate arrays.

Avoid single points of failure when possible. For example, you tempt Murphy by using separate RAID arrays but also by putting them all on the same RAID controller.

If you have a multithreaded backup application feeding a multidrive tape device, you can back up only one store at a time in a storage group. Furthermore, you have no control over the order of the backup. You can't say, "Back up these two stores first because they're most important." If you want to fine-tune the timing of your backups, create additional storage groups and put the stores in those storage groups.

If you are a VAR with small business clients who scream about the cost of every single component you install, then you aren't likely to have Exchange Enterprise Edition, so you can't spread your risk across multiple storage groups. You should still insist on using different arrays for the logs and data files, even if the arrays are on mirrored ATA drives, to get the benefits of recovery and improved performance.

### Backup Sequences

Let's say that it's a Sunday afternoon and you're about to do a full backup on the Exchange server files shown back in Figure 13.12. This backup captures the main database files and transaction logs E00000014.log through E00000017.log. Because you did a full backup, the Backup API truncated the logs, leaving just E00.log and E00000017.log.

The server now operates for a day, accepting new mail and sending mail and generally being a good Exchange server. On Monday evening, just before the backup job starts, the folder containing the transaction logs looks like the diagram in Figure 13.13.

The Information Store created several new transaction logs throughout the day as it added new items to the database. All of the items in these transaction logs have long ago been committed into the main database files. Just in case, though, the checkpoint file, E00.chk, has a pointer that indicates the location of any uncommitted items.

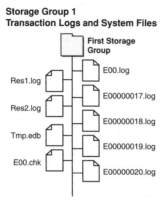

**Figure 13.13** Transaction logs after a full backup and a day's operation.

At this point, you perform an incremental backup. This commits any pending items into the main database files and removes all historical transaction logs except for E00000020.log.

The next night, Tuesday, you perform another incremental backup and capture that day's transaction logs, E00000020.log through E00000023.log. Wednesday night's backup captures E00000023.log through E00000026.log.

Use caution not to send the daily incremental Exchange backup tapes to offsite storage. It is embarrassing to delay a restoration while you wait for a representative from the storage company to find your tapes in its vault and dispatch a courier to put them back in your hands.

We now arrive at the fifth day following the full backup. A user reports to the Help Desk that she is unable to read any new mail and that when she presses the Send/Receive button, she gets the window shown in Figure 13.14, indicating that the server is not available. "It says to call my administrator, so I guess that's you, huh?" she tells the Help Desk technician. (Hopefully, in your production environment, you'll deploy a monitoring solution that would tell you of a problem before you hear it from your users.)

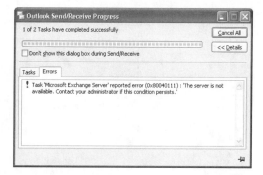

**Figure 13.14** Error message that makes administrator realize that store has dismounted.

The technician opens a trouble ticket and puts in a hurried call into your desk. You open ESM and discover that the mailbox store has dismounted and the Application log has filled with messages from MSExchangeIS telling a tale of woe about bad messages and inability to read the information store and other miserable news.

You make the determination that you have a corrupt mailbox store. You decide to restore the mailbox store from the last good backup. You retrieve the tapes and get ready to start restoring the store using the procedures covered later this chapter.

### Performing the Tape Restores

Before starting a restore, you should get copies of the database files to another location. This ensures that you have "saved state" on your server in the event that your backups fail and you need to start performing surgery on your database.

Here's where life gets interesting for you. You've been performing incremental backups each night, so you'll need lots of tapes: Sunday's full backup and each incremental nightly backup tape from Monday through Wednesday.

You'll also need the transaction logs currently on disk. These logs contain the items committed to the stores in the storage group starting at the end of Wednesday's incremental backup. Figure 13.15 shows the files.

You dismount the mailbox store and then, one by one, you restore the files from tape. Because the store has been corrupted, you configure the backup program to replace the existing mailbox store database files, priv1.edb and pub1.edb.

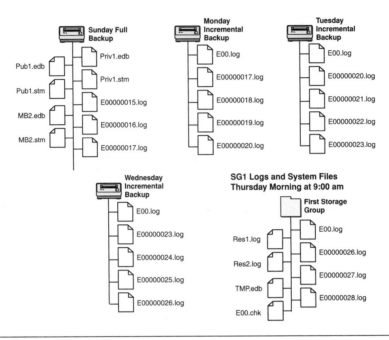

**Figure 13.15**   Full restore from tape required last full backup tape plus each incremental tapes to get the nightly transaction logs.

When you restore Sunday's full backup, the backup program overwrites the files on disk with the files from tape. The backup program then creates a little temp folder and stores the transaction logs from tape to the temp folder. The Backup API then creates a file called Restore.env that keeps track of the files that you restore from tape.

Now you restore the Monday incremental tape. The only items on that tape are the transaction logs, and you configure the backup program to save the logs into the same temp folder used to hold the log files from the Sunday full restore. You do the same for Tuesday's incremental tape. The final Wednesday tape, though, requires a slightly different process.

### Performing the Final "Hard Restore"

When you restore Wednesday's tape, you need to set a flag in the backup program to indicate that this is the last tape in the backup set. As you'll see when you get to the step-by-step procedure, this flag is displayed in ESM as one of the properties of the mailbox store.

1. When Ntbackup finishes restoring the final set of log files from this tape, it tells the Backup API to perform what's called a *hard restore*. During the hard restore, the Backup API uses the contents of Restore.env as a reference and then replays the contents of the transaction logs stored in the temp folder into the main database files.

2. Once the items in the historical transaction logs have been committed, the Backup API then commits the items in the current day's transaction logs. In the example, this would be E00000026.log through E00000029.log. This brings the main database files up-to-date with the last message received before dismounting the mailbox store.

3. The backup program then tells the Information Store to mount the mailbox store, or you can mount it manually. At that point, any inbound messages for recipients that have queued up in SMTP get delivered.

4. The end result? Users get all their mail back and their only discomfort was the loss of access to their e-mail during the interval when the mailbox store was dismounted. The other stores in the storage group were not disturbed.

You can minimize the duration of the mailbox store outage by keeping the mailbox store files as small as possible and by using differential backups, which retain all transaction logs since the last full backup.

### Operational Summary

Here are the high points to remember about online backup and restore operations:

- Full and incremental backups remove all unused transaction logs.
- Differential backups leave the transaction logs so that each night's backup includes all logs since the last full backup.
- Restoring a mailbox store does not impact other stores in the same storage group. The backup program selectively replays items from the transaction logs so that only the mailbox store being restored gets updated.
- When restoring incremental backups, put all transaction logs in the same temporary folder. A single Restore.env file controls the hard restore.

- If you choose to overwrite the existing mailbox store files, you could, if you desired, restore mailbox stores from different storage groups at the same time. This is useful when recovering an entire server.

## Brick-Level Backups

Backup and restore operations that use the Backup API swallow a store in one big gulp, like a snake swallowing an elephant. Users don't experience a mailbox store as a stream of pages, though, they experience it as a set of mailboxes, more specifically their *particular* mailbox, which is of course the most important mailbox on the server.

Restoring an individual mailbox from a tape obtained via the Backup API is somewhat more complicated than you might like. You must first restore the entire mailbox store into a temporary location called the Recovery Storage Group, then use Exmerge to dump the contents of the mailbox to a .pst file, then import the .pst file into the user's mailbox and merge the contents so that you don't overwrite any messages that arrived after he submitted the trouble ticket.

You cannot use Exmerge to save mailboxes larger than 2GB.

Although Microsoft does not directly support any other mailbox restore methods, many backup vendors provide a way to backup and restore individual mailboxes via a MAPI connection. This is called a *brick-level backup*, or often just called *brick backup*.

With a brick backup, you can restore an individual mailbox directly from tape without going through the hassle of restoring the entire mailbox store to the Recovery Storage Group.

The universe has an immutable law that says, "Convenience comes at a cost, with the amount of the cost inverse to the amount of convenience." Based on this law, brick backups are *very* convenient, so you shouldn't be surprised that they are *very* costly, at least in terms of processing load, disk I/O, network bandwidth, and miles of tape they consume.

In effect, a brick-level backup is no different than telling every user in the message store to open their mailboxes and read every single message and calendar item in every folder. Not only is the process extraordinarily intensive, it is also slow. *Very* slow. If a typical full backup of a mailbox store using the Backup API takes three hours, a brick backup might take nine hours or more depending on the size of the mailboxes.

Still, it's good to know that this option exists. Some organizations use brick backups for their most important mailboxes, defined as "mailboxes for users who control the IT budget." Some organizations have an approval process where users can submit requests that prove they have a need for a brick backup of their mailbox.

The situation vis-à-vis brick backups improves somewhat with Exchange 2003 running on Windows Server 2003. If you use backup software that supports the Volume Shadow Copy service, described later in the chapter, you can take real-time snapshots of the Information Store and use those to construct a brick-level image of a user's mailbox from which you can restore any or all items. Or you can do a regular backup, not a brick-level backup, and then take advantage of a third-party utility such as Ontrack PowerControls that can pull individual objects from an unmounted Exchange database. See www.ontrack.com/powercontrols.

## Performing Full Exchange Backups

You must have the Information Store running on the machine where you run Ntbackup. Proceed as follows:

1. Launch Ntbackup either from the Run window or from the Start menu using the path **Start | All Programs | Accessories | System Tools | Backup**.
2. The default configuration of Ntbackup uses a wizard. You can avoid the wizard in future launches by unchecking the **Always Start in Wizard Mode** option and then clicking Cancel and relaunching Ntbackup or by launching Ntbackup from the command line.
3. Select the Backup tab and then drill down to the Microsoft Exchange Server icon (Figure 13.16).
4. Expand the tree under the icon for the Exchange server and check the **Microsoft Information Store** icon. This selects all the storage groups under the icon and all the mailbox and public folder stores in each storage group.
5. Under **Backup Destination**, either select a local tape device or **File**.

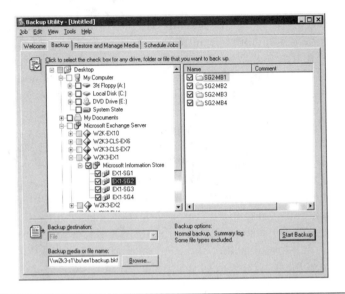

**Figure 13.16** Ntbackup window showing selection of all storage groups and mailbox stores on an Exchange server.

6. Under **Backup Media or File Name**, if you selected **File** as a destination, enter a path to the backup file. You can specify a local drive or a UNC path to a shared folder on another server.

7. Click **Start Backup**. A Backup Job Information window opens, as shown in Figure 13.17. Select the radio button labeled **Replace the Data on the Media with This Backup**.

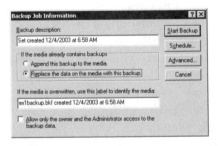

**Figure 13.17** Backup Job Information window with option to replace existing data on tape and to give tape a new name.

8. Click **Start Backup**. A Backup Progress window opens that displays the current status of the backup job. Figure 13.18 shows an example.

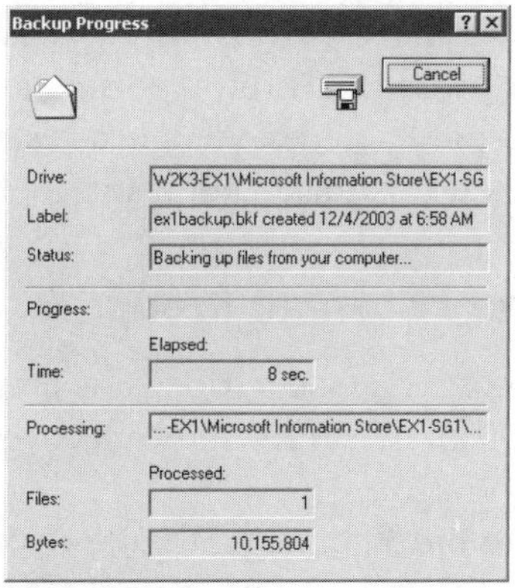

**Figure 13.18**     Backup Progress window showing Exchange backup in operation.

   **9.** When the backup completes, click the **Report** button and verify
   that all storage groups backed up successfully.
   **10.** Close the Backup Progress window and close Ntbackup.

At this point, you have a full backup of the storage group. Open
Explorer and navigate to the location of the transaction logs for each
storage group and verify that only two logs remain.

You're now ready to go through a recovery operation. Open Outlook
for a few test users and send messages back and forth and make changes
to one or two mailboxes in the store then proceed to the next section.

# Recovering Individual Mailboxes

You can recover a mailbox store while the production store remains
online and accessible by users. Exchange 2003 provides a separate storage group called the Recovery Storage Group where you can temporarily park the recovered mailbox store while you extract the user's mailbox
using Exmerge. The overall steps are as follows:

   **1.** Create a Recovery Storage Group.
   **2.** Link the Recovery Storage Group to the mailbox store containing the mailbox you want to recover.
   **3.** Recover the mailbox store to the Recovery Storage Group.
   **4.** Dump the user's mailbox contents to a .pst file using Exmerge.
   **5.** Import the .pst file into the user's currently active mailbox.

You cannot use the Recovery Storage Group to recover a public folder store. If a user with Editor permissions accidentally deletes a posting from a the public folder, you must restore the public folder store database files to their existing location and replay the transaction logs.

## Create Recovery Storage Group

To conserve memory, Exchange does not create the Recovery Storage Group by default. You must create the Recovery Storage Group prior to recovering a mailbox store.

You can create the Recovery Storage Group even if you have a full complement of regular storage groups. Create the recovery storage group as follows:

1. Launch ESM and drill down to the server where you want to do the recovery.
2. Right-click the server icon and select **New | Recovery Storage Group** from the flyout menu, as shown in Figure 13.19.

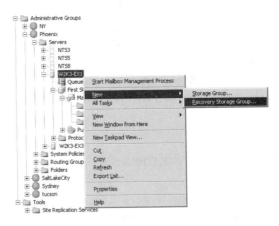

**Figure 13.19**    ESM showing Exchange server property menu with the New Recovery Storage Group option selected.

3. The Recovery Storage Group Properties window shows the location of the recovery storage group files. The default location is **Exchsrvr\Recovery Storage Group**, as shown in Figure 13.20. Select a location that has sufficient storage to hold your largest mailbox store.

**Figure 13.20** Recovery Storage Group Properties window showing default file locations.

4. Click **OK** to create the storage group. The name now appears in the list of storage groups. Leave ESM open and proceed to the next section.

## Recovering a Mailbox Store to the Recovery Storage Group

Now that you have a Recovery Storage Group, you can designate one or more mailbox stores for restoration into the storage group, and then restore the mailbox stores from tape or backup file.

You can restore multiple mailbox stores at the same time, but they must originate from the same storage group. The Recovery Storage Group has only one set of transaction logs. If you need to recover mailbox stores from different storage groups, do so in separate procedures and delete the restored files between procedures. Once the mailbox store has been restored, you can dump a user's mailbox to a .pst file using the Exmerge program. The detailed steps for this are listed in Chapter 7.

To recover a mailbox store to the Recovery Storage Group, proceed as follows:

1. In ESM, right-click the **Recovery Storage Group** icon and select the **Select Database to Recover** option from the flyout menu. This opens the Select Database to Recover window, as shown in Figure 13.21.

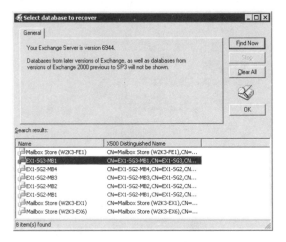

**Figure 13.21** Select the Database to Recover window showing a list of available mailbox and public folder stores that can be linked to the Recovery Storage Group.

2. Select the mailbox store you want to recover and click **OK**. The Mailbox Store Properties window opens so you can verify the name.

3. Click **OK** to add the mailbox store to the Recovery Storage Group.

4. Launch Ntbackup and select the **Restore and Manage Media** tab. Figure 13.22 shows an example.

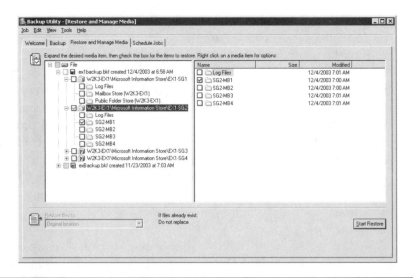

**Figure 13.22** Ntbackup window showing option to restore only a single mailbox store from a storage group.

5. Drill down through the backup file to the mailbox store you want to recover. You might see some delay as the system reads the catalog in the file. You don't need to check the transaction logs. Ntbackup decides on its own whether or not to use the transaction logs.

6. Click **Start Restore**. The Restoring Database Store window opens (Figure 13.23).

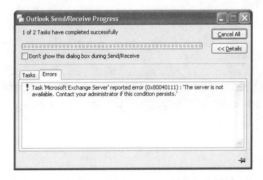

**Figure 13.23** Restoring Database Store window with entries for Exchange server and temporary location for log and Restore.env file.

7. Enter a local path for the log and patch files. If you have a large mailbox store, set aside sufficient space to hold the store.

8. Check the **Last Restore Set** option. This adds the content of the transaction logs to the main database.

9. Check the **Mount Database after Restore** option. This simplifies getting access to the mailboxes with Exmerge once the restoration has finished.

10. Click **OK** to start the restore. When it has finished, check the Recovery Storage Group folder on the server to see that a copy of the mailbox store files now reside in that storage group. You can also verify in ESM that the mailbox store is mounted, and you can see the mailboxes in it.

Refer to Chapter 7 for detailed steps in order to use Exmerge to recover an individual user's mailbox out of the recovery storage group. Point Exmerge at the Recovery Storage Group, as shown in Figure 13.24.

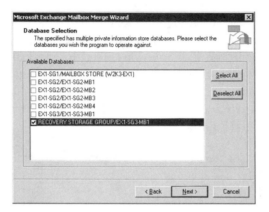

**Figure 13.24** Exmerge Database Selection window showing additional option to dump mailboxes from the Recovery Storage Group.

## Recovering a Mailbox Store

You might encounter situations where you want to restore an entire mailbox store and overwrite the existing store. For example, the store database might be corrupt.

When you restore an entire mailbox store, you cannot simply copy it from the Recovery Storage Group to the original location. You must restore it to its original location using the Backup API. This means that you need to overwrite the existing database files and then replay the transaction logs. Exchange databases are protected from accidental overwrites, so before you can do a full mailbox restore, you much check the option **This Database Can be Overwritten by a Restore** in the database properties for the mailbox store. Figure 13.25 shows an example.

### Direct Restore to Original Location

You must also dismount the database prior to restoring it. Once the database has been dismounted, proceed as follows

1. Launch Ntbackup.
2. Select the Restore and Manage Media tab.

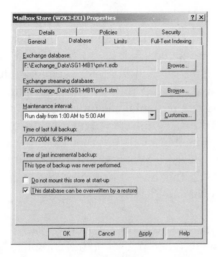

**Figure 13.25** Mailbox Store Database Properties window showing option to allow database to be overwritten by a tape restore.

3. Drill down to the backup job containing the mailbox store you want to recover. You do not need to select the transaction logs. The Backup API determines how to handle transaction log replays.

4. Click **Start Restore**.

5. When the Restoring Database Store window opens (Figure 13.26), enter the following information:

   ■ **Restore To.** Leave the name as the flat name of the Exchange server.

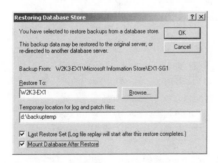

**Figure 13.26** Restoring Database Store window showing option to do a hard restore (Log File Replay) and to mount the store after replay.

- **Temporary Location for Log and Patch Files.** Enter a path to hold the log files and the Restore.env file. If you have incremental backups to restore following the full backup, use the same location for each incremental restore.
- **Last Backup Set.** Leave this option unchecked until the final incremental backup.
- **Mount Database after Restore.** This option remains dimmed as long as the Last Backup Set option is left unchecked. When you check the Last Backup Set option, check this one, too, unless you do not want to mount the store immediately.

6. Perform the restore, recovering each incremental backup in sequence. When Ntbackup has completed, close the application.

Checking the Last Backup Set option for the final incremental backup set tells Ntbackup to perform a hard restore, which replays the restored transaction logs and the current transaction logs. If you selected the Mount Database after Restore for the final backup set, verify that the store has remounted. Check the Event Log for any errors.

## Manual Hard Restore

Exchange 2003 stores hard recovery information in Restore.env. This file contains the instructions for replaying the transaction log copies from their restore location and then replaying the current transaction logs.

Restore.env is a binary file, but you can view the contents using the Eseutil command-line utility. Change to the folder holding the Restore.env file and then run Eseutil with the following syntax:

```
\program files\exchsrvr\bin\eseutil -cm
```

Here is a sample listing:

```
D:\temp2\First Storage Group>eseutil -cm
Microsoft(R) Exchange Server(TM) Database Utilities
Version 6.5
Copyright (C) Microsoft Corporation 1991-2000.  All Rights
➡Reserved.
            Restore log file: D:\temp2\First Storage Group
```

```
            Restore Path: D:\temp2\First Storage Group
              Annotation: Microsoft Information Store
         Backup Instance: First Storage Group
         Target Instance:
Restore Instance System Path:
   Restore Instance Log Path:
               Databases: 1 database(s)
           Database Name: Mailbox Store (SERVER1)
                    GUID: 969BDD66-C569-49D5-CA8F49D5BE04F2AC
            Source Files: D:\Exchsrvr\mdbdata\priv1.edb
D:\Exchsrvr\mdbdata\priv1.stm
       Destination Files: D:\Exchsrvr\mdbdata\priv1.edb
D:\Exchsrvr\mdbdata\priv1.stm
         Log files range: E0000007.log - E0000009.log
       Last Restore Time: Wed Dec 31 17:00:00 2003

          Recover Status: recoverNotStarted
           Recover Error: 0x00000000
            Recover Time: Mon Feb 26 11:29:26 2004
Operation completed successfully in 0.101 seconds.
```

If you forget to check the Last Backup Set option when restoring the final backup set, you can manually perform the final hard restore using Eseutil as follows:

```
eseutil /cc "d:\temp\first storage group" /t
```

The /cc option points to the temp files and /t tells eseutil to replay the portion of the transaction log affecting the selected storage group.

Mount the database and verify that the contents are correct by logging in as a user with a mailbox in that database.

# Recovering an Exchange Server

Instead of losing a RAID array or dealing with a corrupted mailbox store, you could lose an entire Exchange server. This could happen in a variety of ways. You might build your servers in a central location and then ship them out to the branch offices, and the shipper decided to test your packaging by dropping the box from the loading bay of a 747. Or a UPS power surge might turn your Exchange server into a fairly expensive rack spacer.

These types of circumstances don't occur very often, so the complete loss of a server doesn't appear to be likely. However, human error can figure into the cause of an outage, making the loss of a server somewhat more likely than you might think, based solely on mean-time-between-failure numbers on the components.

## Replace the Hardware and Operating System

When an Exchange server becomes unavailable, your first job is to get a new machine. You might have a spare, or your hardware vendor might be able to get you a replacement quickly. In the case of a lost operating system partition, you can replace the RAID controller and the boot drives.

You must then reinstall the operating system so you can install the backup agent and therefore do a tape restore of the operating system partition. You can use any computer name you like for this temporary installation.

If you have a locally attached tape device and you use Ntbackup for your backup application, you can recover the operating system partition using the Automated System Recovery (ASR) feature in Windows Server 2003. ASR allows you to boot from the Windows Server 2003 CD and connect to the tape device using information stored on a floppy and then commence a hands-off recovery. All enterprise-class third-party backup applications have a similar feature.

To take advantage of ASR, though, you must first have a useful backup of the operating system partition. But what if you don't have such a backup?

Then you perform a fresh installation of the operating system using the same name as the original Exchange server. Be sure to install all the service packs and hotfixes that were on the original machine.

You'll encounter a problem when you try to join the newly installed server into the domain because the computer account already exists in Active Directory. To work around this issue, right-click the computer's account in Active Directory Users and Computers and select Reset Account from the flyout menu. Then join the computer to the domain.

## Install Exchange with `/disasterrecovery` Switch

You now have a newly installed server with the same name as the original Exchange server but no Exchange services, so you can't mount the mailbox or public folder stores. You can't simply install Exchange because the server already exists in the organization. To work around this issue, run the Exchange setup program with the `/disasterrecovery` switch. This tells Setup to pull the configuration information from Active Directory.

This seems simple enough, and it is, but there's a caveat regarding storage location. Exchange stores the paths to the mailbox and public folder store databases, as well as the transaction logs, in the Registry. During Setup, you need to be careful to stipulate the correct path for these files.

### Restore Database Files

If the disaster that consumed the server also took the Exchange database files, your next step is to recover those files. The `/disasterrecovery` switch assumes that you'll be carrying on with this next step, so it flags each store in Active Directory with the Do Not Mount the Store at Next Startup option. This is an important step. The other Exchange servers have SMTP messages queued for delivery. The newly created mailbox stores must not be allowed to accept those incoming messages until the original store contents have been recovered.

Once you've recovered the mailbox stores, you'll need to clear the Do Not Mount option from each mailbox and public folder store. If the recovered Exchange server had its mailbox stores intact, you can clear the Do Not Mount option as soon as you have completed installing Exchange using the `/disasterrecovery` switch.

# Volume Shadow Copy

One of the important new features in Windows Server 2003 is its ability to accurately capture the point-in-time content of a data volume or volumes, and then make that content available to applications such as backup programs and file recovery utilities.

Point-in-time technologies have been around for awhile. Many storage vendors include point-in-time features in their hardware. These features use either of two methods to capture the state of files: split-mirror and copy-on-write.

- Split-mirror solutions first create a full block-by-block copy of a volume and then, when the mirrored volumes have synchronized, the mirror is broken to produce a faithful point-in-time replica.

■ Copy-on-write solutions avoid the large storage requirements of split-mirror by simply mapping out the data blocks on a volume and then saving the original content of a block as it changes. The file system presents an historical copy of a file by aggregating the unchanged blocks in the main volume with the saved blocks in the copy-on-write repository.

Regardless of the underlying technology used to make a point-in-time replica, a major challenge involves data consistency. You can appreciate this challenge if you have ever gotten together with your family for a holiday. Your uncle waves you and your cousins into position and fusses with a camera for a while. You know from experience that if you move or blink during the taking of the photograph, your smeared features and closed eyes will be prominently featured in the next family newsletter, so you are careful to stand still until you hear the shutter snap.

In the same way, a point-in-time service needs a way to communicate with applications so it can tell them to suspend operations and flush their buffers to avoid "blurred" data; that is, inconsistent content between database files, transaction logs, checkpoint files, and other support files.

The Volume Shadow Copy Service (VSS) acts as this communications middle man. It works with the file system to flush and hold cached data across multiple volumes and coordinates point-in-time operations with three groups of players: providers, requestors, and writers. Figure 13.27 shows how these elements fit together.

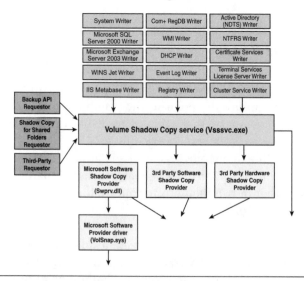

**Figure 13.27** Diagram showing connections between VSS Writers, Providers, and Requestors.

- **Providers** communicate more or less directly to the hardware, making device calls that initiate the split-mirror or copy-on-write transactions. VSS can work with both types of point-in-time copy solutions—split-mirror and copy-on-write—so long as the hardware vendor has written VSS support into the provider.
- **Requestors** need point-in-time services. Examples include backup applications, real-time file recovery utilities, and off-site storage solutions, among others.
- **Writers** are applications that store data on the volumes that VSS manages. VSS communicates to the Writers, telling them to flush buffers and do other data prep necessary to support a point-in-time operation. VSS obtains details on the operation of a particular Writer by reading an XML document that accompanies the application. To see the Writers installed on a server, use the Vssadmin tool with the syntax `vssadmin list writers`.

VSS can't do its job unless it can communicate with every application that stores data on a volume. If you run a third-party database or an application that relies on real-time data storage, and you want to perform point-in-time operations on the data volumes holding the application's data, you need to make sure the application includes VSS support. This won't happen overnight, but be sure to add VSS support on your specification list when you go out for bids.

Microsoft recognizes that many of its customers don't have the budget for high-end arrays with point-in-time capabilities, so they included a software-based VSS provider in Windows Server 2003. This provider runs as a service called the Microsoft Software Shadow Copy Provider, Swprv. The driver for this provider is Volsnap.sys.

The Microsoft software shadow copy provider can perform copy-on-write operations using directly attached drives and block-based storage area networks like Fibre Channel and iSCSI. Network Attached Storage devices based on Windows Storage Server 2003 also have VSS support.

## Shadow Copies of Shared Folders

The Exchange Backup API in Exchange Server 2003 includes a VSS requestor. This gives backup applications that support the API the ability to make a consistent, point-in-time shadow copy of stores both during a backup and when recovering individual mailboxes within the backup. VSS can use the Microsoft software provider if a hardware provider is not available, so you do not need to purchase additional hardware to support this feature.

The Ntbackup utility that ships with Windows Server 2003 does not take advantage of the point-in-time capability in the Exchange Backup API, but nearly all third-party backup solutions have an Exchange agent capable of requesting a point-in-time shadow copy.

You can see how VSS operates by looking at the volume shadow copy of shared folders feature. When you use the volume shadow copy feature, either for shared folders or backups, the Microsoft shadow copy provider uses files located in a super-hidden folder (marked with Hidden and System attributes) called System Volume Information at the root of the volume that you select to hold the block copies. Figure 13.28 shows an example.

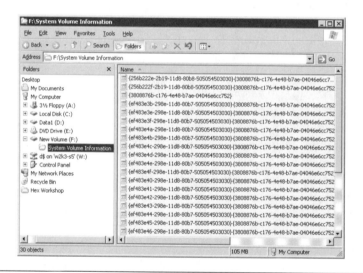

**Figure 13.28**    Diff area in hidden folder on volume. This is where VSS will put Exchange data blocks for backup applications that support shadow copies using Microsoft VSS provider.

The shorthand term for this folder is the "diff area," and the files inside are called the "diff files." In the figure, the files in the diff area represent shadow copies of a data volume taken by the shadow copies for shared folders feature. A backup program that makes a shadow copy using the Backup API places its diff file in the same folder.

The Windows Server 2003 Resource Kit has a set of shadow copy performance counters that you can install by running Volperf. The counters include the percent of overall disk space used by the diff area on a volume, the number of shadow copies in the diff area, the size of the diff area, and the space allocated to the diff area. You can configure alerts to warn of an approach to a limit. By default, the system allocates a maximum of 10 percent of the overall volume capacity to the diff area. You can increase this maximum size or define "no limit," if you use a dedicated drive to hold the volume of shadow copy tfiles.

## Backup Snapshot Operation

When you initiate a backup of a storage group using the Volume Shadow Copy Service, VSS creates a diff file and a map of the blocks used by the EDB and STM files, and the transaction logs. The service uses 16K blocks regardless of the underlying cluster size.

From that point forward, if the Information Store has a pending change to a block, the VSS service first copies the contents of the existing block to the diff area. The original blocks get added to the diff file in sequential order. When the Backup API reaches a block in the Information Store that has been changed, it backs up the block in the diff area, instead.

Microsoft Knowledge-Base article 820852 documents a backup problem that can occur as a result of the Volume Shadow Copy service if you perform a backup of System State and the Exchange Information Store in the same backup operation. The VSS provider locks all writers when Ntbackup initiates, and this prevents the Exchange Backup API from accessing the Exchange database files. The workaround is to backup System State in a separate job from the Information Store backups.

## Third-Party Backup Product and Shadow Copies

All the major backup vendors have agents that work with the Exchange 2003 Backup API, and they all have features that leverage shadow copies in one way or another.

When evaluating an Exchange backup solution, you should look first at compatibility with your existing backup hardware, the reliability of their restore processes, the availability of technical support, speed of the agents, and proven interoperability with your store-based antivirus and antispam applications.

But you should also include an analysis of their shadow copy features. And look for the collaborative relationships they form with storage vendors. Microsoft is working feverishly to leverage Windows storage capabilities into every conceivable niche in the industry, so backup vendors are trying to provide more powerful feature sets by joining forces with storage vendors.

For the most part, if you have already settled on one of the top-tier backup solutions, you'll probably be happy enough with their Exchange 2003 backup features. Here's a quick list in no particular order:

- **CommVault Systems Galaxy.** The Galaxy backup for Exchange has always boasted the fastest brick-level backups and now, with some newly integrated features from their Shadow Explorer product, they do a great job of leveraging Volume Shadow Copy services.

- **Veritas Backup Exec and NetBackup.** The commercial version of Backup Exec (in contrast to the free version in Windows) has won many awards and garnered much praise, but even people who love it admit that the interface is a bit quirky. In my experience, the quality of tech support at Veritas rises a notch above some of the other vendors, which certainly helps in a disaster situation.

- **Computer Associates ARCserve.** The latest ARCserve version, marketed as part of their BrightStor suite of products, continues the Computer Associates tradition of brilliant engineering combined with mind-numbing complexity. If you are already a seasoned user of Arcserve, you'll like the way they integrated Exchange 2003 backup features into the product.

- **Legato NetWorker.** Legato was purchased by EMC in October 2003, so you would not expect their NetWorker backup product to be either the least expensive or the simplest to operate. *But*, if you want speed and a wealth of features and tight integration with EMC's line of SAN equipment, you should at least arrange for a test drive.

- **Tivoli Storage Manager.** If you're an IBM shop and you can afford the support costs, then TSM is a no-brainer. Centralized management with lots of bells and whistles.

A couple of vendors sell Exchange solutions that go a step beyond backup and restore capabilities.

- **Storactive LiveServe.** LiveServe makes a real-time backup to disk that can then be backed up to tape at night.
- **Educom Exchange Archive Solution.** The EAS product isn't so much a backup and restore option as it is a way to do hierarchical storage management for your Exchange store. It allows you to move old, unused items into a central repository in a way that's transparent to the user.

You might also want to investigate online vaulting services, such as LiveVault, www.livevault.com.

Finally, look for hardware SAN and NAS vendors to start stepping up to the plate with an assortment of storage options at attractive prices that can do snapshot backups and restores of Exchange. (Exchange supports only the use of a NAS unit based on Windows Storage Server 2003—see Knowledge-Base article 839687.)

- **Network Appliance SnapManager.** When you combine Network Appliance's reputation for affordable storage products with its new Single Mailbox Recovery feature in SnapManager 3.0, you get a compelling package. (This product uses iSCSI, which is a block-based protocol and therefore is compatible with Exchange 2000 as well as Exchange 2003.)
- **HP StorageWorks Fast Recovery Solutions.** HP has done a great job of integrating Exchange support into its XP line of storage appliances.
- **IBM FAStT with Flashcopy.** It's a strange-looking name for a solid, high performance solution.

# Exchange Clusters

Every Exchange administrator, at one time or another, has played with the idea of building a cluster to hold the Exchange servers. After all, clusters appear to add incredible value to a messaging infrastructure because they increase availability. Windows Server 2003 Enterprise Edition comes with the capability of creating up to eight-node clusters without buying any additional licenses.

Even though you get clustering in shrink wrap for Windows Server 2003, the capability doesn't come for free. To build an eight-node cluster, you have to purchase eight licenses of Windows Server 2003 Enterprise Edition, which has a list price of $3,999. The street prices hover at just over half that amount, but that's still a considerable premium over Standard Edition, which lists for $999 (with a street price of around $700). You'll also need eight copies of Exchange Server 2003, which list for $3,999 (with a street price of $2,500 or so). Fortunately, the cost of the Client Access License (CAL) remains the same, whether the user connects to a cluster or a single server.

The increased availability offered by a cluster is a very real advantage, but only up to a point. Don't confuse *increased* availability with *high* availability. A two-node, shared-disk cluster has too many common points of failure to be considered a high-availability solution. And any clustered Exchange solution involves a brief period during a node failover when the mailbox stores are not available. This does not meet typical definitions for high availability, which require continuous service in the face of a wide variety of faults.

Here's where clusters help. If you have a single Exchange server and you want to install a service pack or a security patch on the operating system or on Exchange—or you want to upgrade the antivirus or the antispam applications, or install a new device driver or any other operation that requires restarting—you have to schedule downtime for the server. Because messaging is a mission-critical operation, you have to schedule that downtime in the off-peak hours, which means you're coming in on the weekend instead of playing with your kids or riding your dirt bike.

But with a cluster, you can fail over a node, install the patch or service pack or whatever, and then fail over to the next node and do the same until you've patched all the nodes on the cluster.

Each time you do a failover, you break connection to the shared Exchange resources, but only briefly, and if you deploy a modern Outlook client, the users might not even know anything happened.

This is not high availability, not by any stretch of the definition, but it does make scheduling maintenance much more convenient. And hey, if the cluster just happens to protect you when the motherboard fails on one of the cluster nodes, then you got an added benefit.

Availability is often measured in percent, such as 99.9 percent availability. This corresponds to 52 minutes of downtime a year, which might or might not include scheduled maintenance. An availability of 99.99 percent corresponds to 5 minutes per year.

This section of the book is not designed to make you an Exchange cluster expert. You should not deploy a production cluster without detailed, hands-on training using the specific hardware and software you select for your cluster. Rather, it's intended to show you how to get familiar with a cluster in a lab environment using virtual machines.

## Cluster Prerequisites

Clusters go down for two major reasons: hardware incompatibilities and boneheaded mistakes. So, when preparing to deploy a clustered Exchange solution, you have two important things to remember:

- Only use approved, tested, and certified hardware.
- Get detailed, extensive, hands-on training from the vendor that supplies you the hardware.

If you decide that you want to deploy a cluster, here are a few items to put on your checklist.

### Hardware Compatibility

If you want to build a server cluster, the first site you should visit is the Windows Server Catalog site at `www.microsoft.com/windows/catalog/server`.

The Windows Server Catalog replaces the Hardware Compatibility List.

The Windows Server Catalog lists the systems and components that have undergone hardware compatibility testing and received the Designed for Windows Server 2003 logo. Select the Hardware tab and click the Clustered Solutions hyperlink. This takes you to a list of the hardware that has been specifically tested to work in a clustered environment.

If your current server hardware does not appear in the Clustered Solutions section of the Windows Server Catalog, don't use it for clustering. Yes, I know you buy only high-quality machines from reputable suppliers and that they're fully compatible with Windows Server 2003 and you've never had a problem. But unless every component and subsystem has been certified as compatible with cluster operations, you're taking a chance that some little doohickey doesn't meet a timing specification or a buffer size or misses some other subtle requirement required for fault-free operation in a cluster, and boom, you're explaining why your fancy new equipment didn't protect the boss's mail.

You're going to spend thousands of dollars in software to put together a cluster. Don't try to save a few bucks with noncertified hardware. It's not worth the headaches later on.

### *Domain members*

When you configure a server to run the Cluster service, you either create a new cluster or join the server to an existing cluster. In either case, the server becomes a *node* in the cluster.

All cluster nodes must be members of the same domain. The nodes communicate with each other so they must authenticate. Windows Server 2003 uses Kerberos for inter-node authentication.

### *Hardware Requirements*

You'll need at least two servers to act as cluster nodes. Each server must have boot drives or a Host Bus Adapter (HBA) that allows it to boot from a SAN. Each server must have sufficient memory to run the Exchange resources assigned to it. Start with 2GB of RAM as a minimum and consider using the full 4GB, if you have sufficient DIMM slots.

Each server must have at least two network adapters. One of these adapters acts as the public interface for the node. The other adapter communicates solely with the other nodes.

You should not connect the cluster adapters on the main network. They produce considerable traffic and you do not want them to lose contact with each other. Ideally, you would connect all the cluster adapters to their own switch with a separate IP subnet. You can also use a VLAN if you're confident that your main network switch won't cause a communication interruption in the cluster. (The hardware might handle it, but can you trust every technician operating the switch to not cause a hiccup?)

The test configuration covered in this chapter uses a shared-disk cluster, meaning that the SCSI interfaces of the two cluster nodes connect to a single SCSI bus that has several drives acting as shared resources. You can also create clusters that use arbitrated-loop Fibre channel or iSCSI controllers.

In a production environment, you would want two Host Bus Adapters (HBAs) connected to the Fibre channel fabric or iSCSI controllers to get fault tolerance. Most hardware packages include a multipath solution so that a failure of a single component in the storage topology does not cause a loss of connection to the storage devices.

If this sounds like an expensive proposition, it all depends on your point of view. It's true that the cost of high-end storage and storage area interconnects can make your skin crawl, but the price of the middle tier products has dropped considerably in recent years and is still going down.

Just for an example (I chose HP, but every first tier vendor has a similar configuration), the ProLiant DL580 F200 nonintegrated cluster solution has two servers with dual Fibre-channel HBAs, dual Fibre-channel arbitrated loop controllers, and a storage area network array that uses SCSI 320 disks. The current street price for the package hovers in the neighborhood of $70,000 if you pack the array with 14 drives, include enough memory to handle Exchange, and include the street prices for the Enterprise Editions of Windows Server 2003 and Exchange Server 2003. If you have 2000 mailbox users, that's $350 per mailbox, not bad considering a good-quality PBX telephone on a user's desk has about the same end-to-end cost.

### Drive Configuration

You'll need to decide how the cluster nodes will access storage. All cluster nodes must have access to any drives that form a cluster resource.

A two-node cluster can share a drive via a shared SCSI cable. To use more than two nodes in a cluster, you'll need either arbitrated-loop Fibre Channel or iSCSI.

For shared storage, you'll need at least one shared drive to act as the quorum drive. All nodes in the cluster must be able to read and write to the quorum drive. In a two-node shared SCSI configuration, the quorum drive can be on the same SCSI bus as the drives you'll use for storage in the cluster. In an arbitrated loop Fibre channel or iSCSI configuration, assign a small LUN (1GB is more than sufficient) to act as the quorum drive.

### Active/Passive Versus Active/Active Clusters

Until you actually install a cluster the first time, probably the most difficult concept to understand is the separation between the nodes that run the cluster service and the resources that run within the cluster.

A cluster hosts one or more virtual servers. Each virtual server has the same kind of resources you would expect to find in a regular server—such as a network name and an IP address—and drives and application services and so forth.

The servers that run the cluster service are called *nodes*. Each node hosts a virtual server and its resources.

In a two-node cluster, if you create a single Exchange virtual server and assign it to one of the nodes, the other node does nothing until the first node fails. This is an *active/passive* cluster, the digital equivalent of Penn and Teller.

If you create two or more Exchange virtual servers and host one on each of the nodes, then you have an *active/active* cluster.

In an active/active cluster, if one of the underlying servers goes down—a *node failure*—the virtual Exchange server hosted by that node rolls over to the good node. Now that node hosts two virtual Exchange servers. This is certainly supported, but it presents a challenge to the Exchange designers.

You see, the good node already hosts an Exchange virtual server and it has assigned considerable memory to that server. Now you're asking the node to make room for yet another Exchange virtual server that has already allocated quite a bit of memory on its own node, and it expects the new host to respect those memory allocations. This is the digital equivalent of the Sopranos.

Not only does this memory apportionment slow down the failover, it raises the possibility that the active node just can't find sufficient contiguous memory to accommodate the second virtual server and rejects the failover.

Microsoft did extensive improvements in the memory handling of both Windows Server 2003 and Exchange Server 2003 to improve cluster operations, but it's still possible to make too many demands on system memory to get a clean failover. In Exchange 2000, Microsoft recommended a maximum of 1900 concurrent connections when using active/active clustering, and it has not revised that number upward for Exchange 2003. In fact, its emphatic recommendation, and mine as well, is to avoid active/active clustering completely.

### Storage Group Limits

If it bothers you (or your boss) to have the second server sit idle 95 percent of the time, you can use active/active clusters, but if you do, here's a limitation to keep in mind.

Each server node in a cluster can host a maximum of four storage groups. If a node goes offline and its virtual server fails over to an active node, the sum of the storage groups cannot exceed four. If it does, one or more storage groups will not be remounted. Apportion your storage groups so that no node hosts more than two storage groups.

### Mount Points for Cluster Drives

An 8-node cluster with 2 passive nodes and 2 storage groups per active node can host 12 storage groups and up to 60 stores (59 mailbox stores and one MAPI public folder store). That's a lot of storage, I think you'll agree.

If you put the transaction logs for each storage group on their own drive, and you put the mailbox stores for each storage group on their own drives, and you decide to give a few of the mailbox stores their own drive to improve recoverability, you're going to run out of drive letters on the underlying shared storage. Exchange 2003, running on Windows Server 2003, permits using mount points rather than drive letters for the shared drives.

A mount point represents the file system on a disk as a folder in the file system on another disk. Use these steps to create a mount point for demonstration purposes:

1. Open the Disk Management console (Diskmgmt.msc).
2. Right-click one of the drives on your test server and select **Change Drive Letters and Path.** This opens a Change Drive Letters and Path window.
3. Click **Add** to open an Add Drive Letter or Path window.
4. Click **Browse**, navigate to the C: drive on the server, and then click New Folder and give it a name such as Mount1.
5. Now go to the C: drive icon and open the **Mount1** folder. You'll be taken directly to the drive you mounted.

By using mount points rather than drive letters, you are not constrained by the limitations of the Western alphabet when creating shared disk resources.

### *Non-Clusterable Exchange Services*

The following Exchange services do not have cluster resources and therefore cannot run in a clustered environment:

- Active Directory Connector
- Connectors for Lotus Notes, and Groupwise
- Exchange Event service
- Site Replication Service
- Network News Transfer Protocol (NNTP): The NNTP service must be installed on each node of the cluster to run Exchange Setup, but the NNTP service itself does not have a clustered resource.

## Create Virtual Servers as Cluster Nodes

With the preliminaries out of the way, you're ready to create a virtual cluster. This consists of the following steps:

- Create the first virtual machine.
- Create the virtual disks for use by the cluster.
- Create the second virtual machine.
- Configure the cluster service on the two virtual machines and join them to the same cluster.

For this demonstration, I'm going to use VMWare 4.2 virtual machine technology. You could also use Microsoft Virtual PC or Microsoft Virtual Server.

You'll need 1GB of RAM on the host machine running VMWare. This permits you to assign 256MB of RAM to both virtual machines in the cluster and still have lots of memory left over for the operating system. If you have only 512MB of RAM available on the host machine, you can reduce the memory settings for the virtual machines to 192MB apiece.

You won't install Exchange on the virtual machines until you get the clustering service initialized and configured. Exchange Setup looks for the cluster service in memory and installs itself as a set of clusterable resources.

### Create First Virtual Machine

Use the vendor's instructions for creating a virtual machine. Specify an operating system of Windows Server 2003 Enterprise Edition, but don't install the operating system yet. Use the default settings that VMWare offers for the virtual machine: single CPU, 256MB of RAM, and a 4GB IDE boot drive.

### Configure an Additional Virtual Adapter

Cluster nodes require two network adapters, one to connect to the main network and one for use by the cluster nodes. Use the Add Hardware wizard in the Virtual Machine Control Panel to install a second network adapter in the virtual machine. Configure the virtual adapter to use Bridged Networking. This means that the network interface within the virtual machine can talk to the network using its own IP address and MAC address.

### Create Plain Disks

Storage in a virtual machine is simply a file on the host's hard drive. The virtual machine pretends that the file is a drive and mounts it using a hardware interface.

The virtual machine can use either a simulated IDE or SCSI drive as a boot drive, but the shared disks in the simulated cluster must use SCSI.

VMWare typically creates virtual disks that are owned by the virtual machine that creates them. The virtual SCSI disks used as shared cluster resources cannot be owned by a virtual machine because two virtual machines share access.

To avoid this problem, you'll be creating a few disk files that represent standalone SCSI drives that you'll configure to use a virtual SCSI channel shared by the two virtual machines. VMWare calls these *plain disks*.

Put the plain disk files in separate folder to keep them separate from the virtual machine you use to create them. This avoids confusion later when you have two virtual machines accessing the same files.

Use the following table for configuration settings when creating the plain disks:

**Table 14.1**    Plain Disk Configuration

| Function | Description | Size | Name | SCSI Channel |
|---|---|---|---|---|
| Quorum drive | Holds shared data for the cluster | 1GB | QuorumDisk.pln | channel 0:0 |
| Transaction log drive | Holds transaction logs for a storage group in the cluster | 4GB | TransLogs.pln | channel 0:1 |
| Exchange Database drive | Holds Exchange mailbox and public folder stores | 8GB | ExData1.pln | channel 0:2 |

You can use any name you like for the plain disk files, but be sure to give them a .pln extension so the virtual machine knows you're offering it a plain disk. Create a plain disk as follows:

1. Open the **Virtual Machine Settings** for the new virtual machine.
2. Click **Edit Virtual Machine Settings** to open the Virtual Machine Control Panel window.
3. Click **Add** to launch the Add Hardware Wizard (Figure 13.29).

**Figure 13.29**    VMWare Add Hardware Wizard with selection to add new hard disk.

4. Highlight the Hard Disk icon and click **Next** to open the Select a Disk window (Figure 13.30).

**Figure 13.30**    Select a Disk window showing option to create a new virtual disk.

5. Select **Create a New Virtual Disk**.
6. Click **Next**. This opens the Specify Disk Capacity window (Figure 13.31). Enter a capacity. See the list at the start of this procedure for the disks you'll create and their capacities.

**Figure 13.31**    Specify Disk Capacity window with option to create a fixed-length disk of a specified size.

7. Select the **Allocate All Disk Space Now** option. This creates a full disk rather than letting VMWare dynamically resize the disk. A fixed disk size is required for plain disks.
8. Click **Next**. An information window opens informing you that this operation might take a while.
9. Click **OK** to acknowledge the information message. The Specify Disk File window opens.

10. Navigate to an empty folder to hold the plain disk files. Assign the name based on the table at the start of the procedure.

11. Click **Advanced**. The Specify Advanced Features window opens (Figure 13.32),

12. Under **Virtual Device Node**, select the **SCSI** radio button and then select the SCSI channel from the table at the start of the procedure.

**Figure 13.32**    Specify Advanced Options window showing mandatory selection of SCSI device type and channel. Shared cluster disks must be SCSI.

13. Click **Finish**. VMWare creates the disk.

When you're all finished, the Virtual Machine Control Panel should show the boot disk, the additional SCSI disks, and the remaining hardware, as shown in Figure 13.33.

### Configure Plain Disks for Shared Use

From the perspective of the virtual machine, you now have a server with a single CPU, 256MB of RAM, a 4GB-IDE boot drive, and three attached SCSI drives. The cluster nodes share the SCSI drives, so you need to configure the virtual machine to not lock the drives for exclusive use. Do the following:

1. Find the .vmx file associated with the virtual machine. You'll find it in the folder where you created the machine, not the folder where you created the plain disks. You can locate the folder holding the .vmx file in the Virtual Machine Control Panel in the VMWare Workstation console.

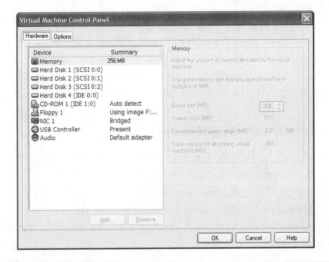

**Figure 13.33** Virtual Machine Control Panel showing hard disk configuration following creation of plain disks.

> If you see an .lck file in the same folder as the .vmx file, **do not edit** the .vmx file. The .lck file indicates that VMWare has locked the virtual machine. Close the Virtual Machine Control Panel to unlock the file.

2. Edit the .vmx file with Notepad. Don't double-click the file. That will start the Virtual Machine Control Panel and lock the file.

3. Add the following line anywhere in the file:

```
disk.locking = "FALSE"
```

4. Save the file and close Notepad.

### Install Operating System in Virtual Machine

Install Windows Server 2003 Enterprise Edition into the virtual machine. You can use any convenient method, including booting the virtual machine from the Setup CD or using a bootable network CD, and then connecting to a distribution point to access the installation files.

Before starting the Setup, decide on an IP configuration for the cluster. You'll need a public subnet and a private subnet.

Download the VMWare SCSI drivers from its Web site. The drivers come in the form of a virtual floppy, a file with an .flp.

During the installation, configure the server with a name and then accept the defaults for the remaining settings, including DHCP. You'll configure fixed IP addresses later.

After you've installed the operating system, you'll need to make a few changes to the system configuration of the virtual machine.

### Install VMWare SCSI Drivers

Install the VMWare drivers for the virtual SCSI device. The simplest way to do this is to use the Virtual Machine Workstation console to point the floppy at the .flp file you downloaded from VMWare.

Then, within the virtual machine, use the Device Manager console to update the SCSI device driver, just as you would for a standard piece of hardware.

Once the SCSI controller reflects normal operation in Device Manager, the Disk Management console will show the disks. (See Figure 13.34.)

Partition and format the virtual SCSCI drives. Give them a volume name that matches the file name you used for the plain disk file. This helps you remember how you configured the virtual disks.

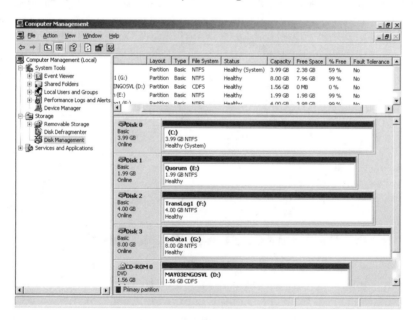

**Figure 13.34**    Disk Management console showing formatted virtual SCSI drives following installation of VMWare SCSI driver from the .flp file.

### *Statically Configure TCP/IP Parameters*

Configure the first network adapter with IP settings that put the adapter in the same network as the rest of the machines in your lab.

Configure the second adapter with a separate subnet shared only by the two cluster nodes. If this were a physical cluster, you would connect the Ethernet cables from the two interfaces to their own switch.

The cluster service does not like an adapter intended for private use to be listed in DNS or WINS, so for the private interface:

- Don't enter any DNS servers.
- Deselect the Register This Connection's Address in DNS.
- Disable NetBIOS over TCP/IP.

If you do not make these changes, you'll get a warning during the cluster configuration.

### *Install VMWare Tools*

VMWare, like the other virtual machine technologies, requires a special set of video and mouse drivers for the virtual machines. These drivers enable you to resize the screen and to move the mouse in and out of the virtual machine session without clicking Ctrl+Ins.

Install the VMWare tools into the virtual machine by selecting File | Install VMWare Tools from the main menu. Accept all the defaults at each screen. Acknowledge when warned about unsigned drivers, and click Continue Anyway for each one.

Restart the virtual machine when prompted.

## Duplicate the Virtual Machine

Now shut down the virtual machine and close the VMWare Workstation window. You're about to do the virtual machine equivalent of cloning a server with an imaging program. Create a second virtual server as follows:

1. Copy the virtual machine files to another folder.
2. Change the file names to match a new server name. I'll use W2K3-S201 in the examples.
3. Load the copy of virtual machine into VMWare.
4. Use the Virtual Machine Control Panel to change the path of the IDE virtual hard drive to the folder and VMX file of the copied virtual machine. (You'll get an error initially because the existing path is incorrect.)

5. Launch the second virtual machine and verify that you see all the drives.

6. Change the SID of the machine. My favorite tool for this is the NewSID utility from SysInternals, www.sysinternals.com. (See Figure 13.35 for a sample of the interface.) The NewSID utility changes the SID to a random value and prompts you for a new server name, then applies the change and restarts the machine. Very neat and fast.

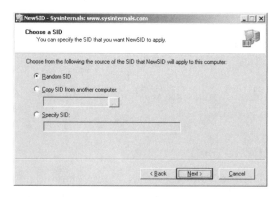

**Figure 13.35** SysInternals NewSID utility.

7. Once the server restarts, reconfigure the TCP/IP settings to use a different IP address in the public subnet and a different IP address in the private subnet.

8. Start the first virtual machine and verify that you do not get an "insufficient memory" error. You should have at least 1GB of RAM on the VMWare host.

Verify that you can see all four disks in both virtual machines. If the drives do not have drive letters on one of the virtual machines, use the Disk Management console to assign drive letters. You should use the same drive letters on both nodes to avoid confusion.

### Join Both Virtual Machines to Domain

Now join both machines to the domain. This requires another restart.

You might want to shut down both virtual machines at this point, close VMWare Workstation, and copy the two virtual machine folders, and the folder containing the shared SCSI drives, to a safe location. You can use these as backup images in case you want to do multiple configurations.

As an alternative, you can use a VMWare feature that saves changes in a Redo location and prompts you to apply them when you exit the virtual machine. This option can significantly reduce virtual machine performance, and I don't recommend it.

## Configure the Cluster

You're now ready to configure the cluster itself. This is considerably easier in Windows Server 2003 than in previous versions of Windows because the cluster service is already installed and ready to initialize.

First, create a user account in the domain to use as the Cluster Service account. The Cluster Administration console adds this account to the local Administrators Group on the server hosting the node.

Use the Exchange Administration Delegation Wizard in ESM to delegate the Exchange Full Administrator role to the Cluster Service account. This permits the cluster to make changes to Organization objects in Active Directory during failovers.

### Initialize Cluster

With the preliminaries out of the way, initialize the cluster as follows:

1. From Administrative Tools, launch the Cluster Administrator console.
2. In the Open Connection to Cluster window, select an **Action** of **Create New Cluster** and click OK. This starts the New Server Cluster Wizard.
3. Click **Next**. The Cluster Name and Domain window opens (Figure 13.36). The **Domain** field should reflect the membership of the node. Enter a name for the cluster itself. For example, enter **ExCluster1**.
4. Click **Next**. The Select Computer window opens. The **Computer Name** field should show the name of the local server. The Advanced button has an option to customize the cluster parameters. No customization is required at this point.
5. Click **Next**. The Analyzing Configuration window opens and the wizard analyzes the node's settings for anything that might not support a cluster, as shown in Figure 13.37.

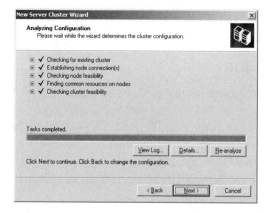

**Figure 13.36**    Cluster Name and Domain window showing entries for Cluster Name, which must be different than names of server nodes.

**Figure 13.37**    Analyzing Configuration window showing successful completion of prerequisite verification.

If the wizard doesn't like a configuration parameter, it will scold you about it and refuse to go forward. Common errors flagged by the wizard include forgetting to install dual network adapters, not configuring the adapters for different subnets, not providing a suitable quorum drive, or forgetting to remove DNS and WINS from the private network interface. The **Task Details** button displays a log entry that tells you the error. Correct any warnings or errors before proceeding. You can come back to this portion of the wizard as many times as you wish.

If you've seen *The Matrix*, you're probably familiar with the scene where Morpheus gives Neo his first taste of unreality by having him jump from one simulated skyscraper to another. Neo can't get it right and does a Wiley Coyote onto the street below. "Nobody does it the first time," say the other characters, "Nobody." That's the way you'll feel the first time you run the Cluster Configuration Wizard. Don't worry if you have to work for a while to get all the issues resolved. Nobody gets it right the first time.

6. Click **Next**. The IP Address window opens (Figure 13.38). Assign an IP address to the cluster. This is the IP address you will use to connect to the cluster, not to the individual nodes.

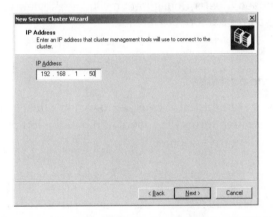

**Figure 13.38** IP Address window for entering the IP address for the cluster. This should be an address accessible from the general network.

7. Click **Next**. The Cluster Service Account window opens. Enter the credentials of the Cluster Service account you created in the domain. Unfortunately, this option does not have a browse window, so you have to remember the name exactly.

8. Click **Next**. The Proposed Cluster Configuration window opens, as shown in Figure 13.39. If the configuration looks right, click **Next** to begin the configuration.

9. When the cluster has been configured, click **Next,** and then **Finish** to exit the wizard.

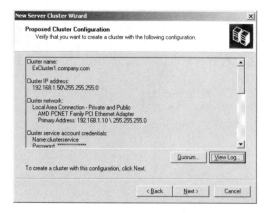

**Figure 13.39**    Proposed Cluster Configuration window. Review carefully to make sure all settings are correct before proceeding.

### Review the Settings

The Cluster Administrator console now shows the cluster configuration. The cluster name forms the root of a tree in the left pane of the window, as shown in Figure 13.40.

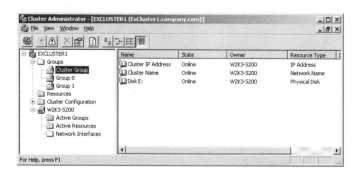

**Figure 13.40**    Cluster Administrator console showing the standard Cluster Group resources: IP Address, Name, and quorum disk.

The Groups folder contains the default Cluster Group configured by the New Cluster wizard. This group contains three resources: a Cluster IP Address, Cluster Name, and disk resource for the quorum disk. You'll find other groups that contain the disk resources assigned to the SCSI disks.

The Resources folder shows the available resources for the cluster, as shown in Figure 13.41. You should see resources assigned to the Cluster Group and to the various disk groups. Note that the two shared SCSI disks have been assigned resource names based on their drive letters. Note the letters. Later, you'll need to assign these resources to Exchange.

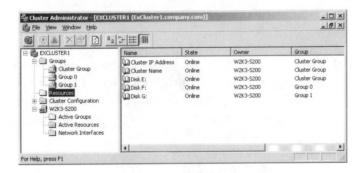

**Figure 13.41**    Resources folder showing all available resources in cluster, including the shared SCSI drives.

Under the Cluster Configuration folder, you'll find a Resource Types folder that shows you the available resources on the cluster node, as shown in Figure 13.42. Note that a cluster comes preconfigured with many network services that can be assigned to a cluster. The list does not contain Exchange resources because you haven't installed Exchange yet.

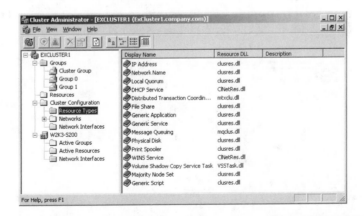

**Figure 13.42**    Resource Types folder showing the clusterable resources available on the cluster. Exchange resources do not appear because Exchange has not yet been installed on the nodes.

The node labeled with the server name lists the cluster groups and resources assigned to that node. If the node becomes inoperative, this icon gets a big red X.

### Add Second Cluster Node

At this point, you have a one-node cluster. Add the second server as a cluster node as follows:

1. From the main Cluster Administrator menu, select **File | Open Connection**. Select **Add Nodes to a Cluster** and verify that the Cluster Name field lists the correct cluster name. The Add Nodes Wizard starts. The first option is to select an operation (Figure 13.43.)

**Figure 13.43** Open Connection to Cluster window with option to add second node to cluster.

2. Click **Next**. The Select Computer window opens (Figure 13.44). Browse for the second node in the cluster and then click **Add** to put the name on the Selected Computer list.

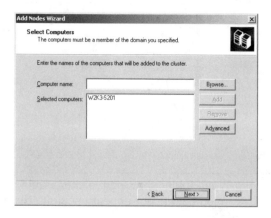

**Figure 13.44** Select Computers window with option to select the server to add to the cluster.

3. Click **Next**. The Analyzing Configuration window opens. Correct any errors or warnings before proceeding.

4. Click **Next**. The Cluster Service Account window opens. Enter the password of the Cluster Service account. This must be the same account used by the other node in the cluster.

5. Click **Next**. The Proposed Cluster Configuration window opens. If the configuration looks right, click **Next** to begin the configuration. When the cluster has been configured, click **Next** then **Finish** to exit the wizard.

Following the addition of the second node, scan through the Cluster Administrator folders to ensure that the resources look right. You should see both nodes with all resources assigned to the first node, as shown in Figure 13.45. The second node will have Network Interfaces but no cluster resources.

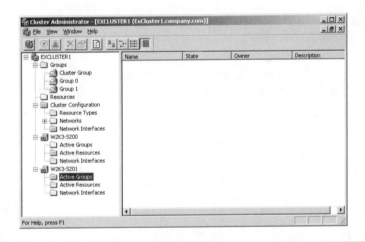

**Figure 13.45**    Cluster Administrator console following addition of second node. No resources assigned to node, but can act as failover for Cluster Group.

### Install Distributed Transaction Processing Resource

The cluster version of Exchange requires a Distributed Transaction Processing resource. Install this resource as follows:

1. Right-click the Cluster Group icon and select **New | Resource** from the flyout menu.

2. Select a **Resource Type** of **Distributed Transaction Coordinator** and give the resource a name of **MSDTC**, as shown in Figure 13.46.

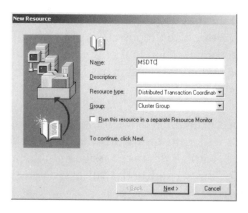

**Figure 13.46**    New Resource window showing addition of MSDTC resource, required for Exchange operation.

3. Click **Next**. Assign the resource to both nodes.
4. Click **Next**. Assign dependencies of **Cluster IP Address**, **Cluster Name**, and the disk resource, as shown in Figure 13.47.

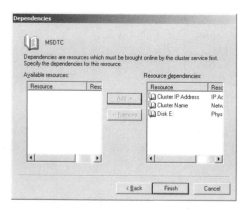

**Figure 13.47**    Resource Dependencies window showing that all Cluster Group resources are required by MSDTC.

5. Click **Finish**.
6. When the Cluster Manager adds the MSDTC resource to the Cluster Group folder, right-click the **Resource** icon and select **Bring Online** from the flyout menu.

## Install Exchange on Each Node

It's now time to install Exchange on the two virtual machines that are acting as cluster nodes. When you run Exchange Setup, it notices that you're installing onto a cluster node and it modifies the installation so as to create clusterable resources rather than executables that run on the machine itself.

An executable called Exres.dll acts as the interface between the cluster and Exchange. Setup initializes this interface so that you can create an Exchange virtual server in Cluster Administrator.

To install Exchange on a cluster node, make sure you meet the pre-requisites for a regular installation. Verify that IIS is running on each node. You'll need to install ASP.NET, SMTP, and NNTP.

Use a standard set of steps to install Exchange on the node. In your virtual machine, put the Exchange executables on the C: drive. You won't be prompted to select an Administrative Group. This is done as part of the virtual server configuration in the cluster.

**Install Exchange one node at a time.** This is very important. You can encounter race conditions and unresolved dependencies by installing Exchange simultaneously on multiple nodes in a cluster. If your patience wears thin quickly, bring along a Game Boy.

## Create Exchange Cluster Group

Once you have installed Exchange on both nodes of the cluster, you're ready to assign Exchange resources to the cluster. This involves creating quite a few resources and giving them names and selecting dependencies. You don't have to use the names I assign in the examples, but be sure that you make the names clear enough so that you can recognize the purpose of each resource as it's listed in Cluster Administrator.

### Create an Exchange Cluster Group

Leave the Default Cluster group alone. It owns the quorum drive and that's it. You'll create additional cluster groups for the Exchange virtual servers.

1. Open the Cluster Administrator console.
2. Right-click the **Groups** icon and select **New | Group** from the flyout menu (or press **Ctrl+G**).

3. Give the group a name, such as **Exchange Cluster** (Figure 13.48).
4. Add both nodes of the cluster as potential owners (Figure 13.49).
5. Click **Finish** to save the group.

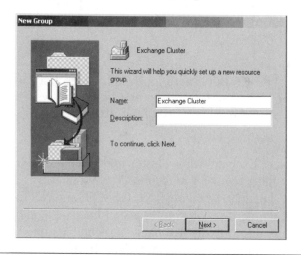

**Figure 13.48** New Group window showing name of new Exchange Cluster group.

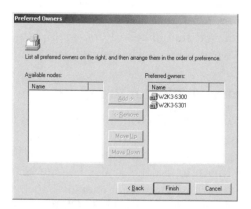

**Figure 13.49** Preferred Owners window showing both nodes as owners of Exchange resources.

Cluster Administrator now shows the Exchange Cluster group in the tree. The next steps create an IP address for the virtual Exchange server, give the server a name, and assign it shared disk resources.

### Add an IP Address Resource

1. Highlight the new group and press **Ctrl+N** to open the New Resource window.
2. Select a **Resource Type** of **IP Address** and give the resource a name such as **Exchange Server IP Address**, as shown in Figure 13.50. Other administrators will see this name, so use a consistent naming strategy or you'll drive your colleagues wacky trying to figure out what the resources do.

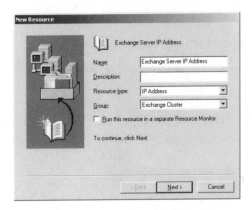

**Figure 13.50**    New Resource window showing new Exchange Server IP Address resource.

3. Click **Next**. In the Possible Owners window, assign both nodes as possible owners.
4. Click **Next**. The resource has no dependencies.
5. In the Exchange Server IP Address window, assign a static IP address to the virtual server along with a subnet mask, and select the public interface to use for publishing the service (see Figure 13.51). Assign the address to the public network interface.
6. Select **Enable NetBIOS for This Interface** so that downlevel Outlook clients can locate the service.
7. Click **Finish** to save the resource.

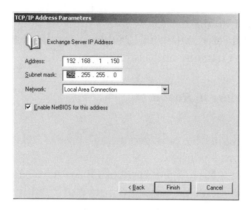

**Figure 13.51**    TCP/IP Address Parameters window showing IP address assigned to Exchange Cluster. Must be different than IP resource assigned to cluster.

### Add a Network Name Resource

One of the most confusing parts of creating clustered resources is getting all the names straight. The virtual Exchange server gets a different name than the cluster, which gets a different name than the underlying server nodes. This makes sense, when you think about it, because the same cluster can host multiple instances of an Exchange virtual server. Scrawl the names on a sticky note that you can put on your monitor to remind you of the names you assign.

1. Create a Network Name resource for the Exchange virtual server. The Name field does not contain the network name. It contains the resource name, which does not appear on the network. Give it a name such as **Exchange Virtual Server Network Name**, as shown in Figure 13.52.
2. Click **Next**. In the Possible Owners window, select both nodes.
3. Click **Next**. In the Dependencies window, add the **Exchange Server IP Address** resource to the dependencies list.
4. Click **Next**. In the Network Name Parameters window (Figure 13.53), enter the name for the Exchange virtual server. This is the name that will appear in ESM, so use a name that follows your Exchange server naming strategy, such as **W2K3-S20** or **W2K3-EXCLSTR-1**.
5. Enable the **DNS Registration Must Succeed** option to ensure that the cluster will not come online unless DNS is available.

**Figure 13.52**    New Resource window showing new Exchange Virtual Server
Network Name resource.

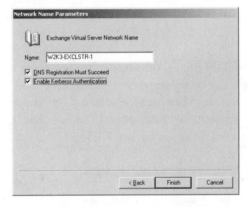

**Figure 13.53**    Network Name Parameters window showing selected name for
Exchange Virtual Server. This name appears in ESM.

6. Enable the **Kerberos Authentication** option to support Outlook 2003 clients, which use Kerberos for authentication to
   Exchange.
7. Make both nodes potential owners and assign the IP Address
   resource as a dependency.

### Add Disk Resources

The virtual Exchange server now needs disk resources so it can store
data files and transaction logs. The two shared SCSI drives you created
have been assigned to other groups. Assign these disk resources to the
Exchange Cluster group by dragging and dropping the icons.

Acknowledge all warning and information windows. When you're finished, the two disk icons reside in the Exchange Cluster folder.

### Bring Resources Online

Bring the IP Address and Network Name resources for the Exchange Cluster online. You have a couple of ways to do this. You can right-click the resources and select Bring Online from the flyout menu, or you can highlight the resource and press Ctrl+B. When this succeeds, the status of the icons changes to Online, and the icon loses the big red X.

## Create Exchange Virtual Server

With a name, IP address, and disk resources assigned to the Exchange Cluster, you're now ready to create the Exchange virtual server. This requires creating only a single resource, the System Attendant. The Cluster Administrator creates all the other resources automatically.

1. Highlight the **Exchange Cluster** icon and press **Ctrl+N** to open the New Resource window.
2. Select the **Microsoft Exchange System Attendant** resource and give the resource a name such as **Exchange System Attendant**, as shown in Figure 13.54.

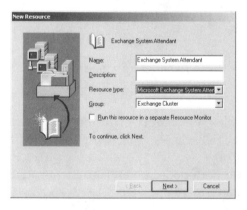

**Figure 13.54**   New Resource window showing new Exchange System Attendant resource. Exchange installs all other resources automatically.

3. Click **Next**. In the Possible Owners window, make both nodes potential owners.

4. Click **Next**. In the Dependencies window, assign dependencies of **Exchange Server IP Address**, **Exchange Virtual Server Network Name**, and both disk resources.

5. Click **Next**. In the Exchange Administrative Group window (Figure 13.55), assign the virtual server to an Administrative Group.

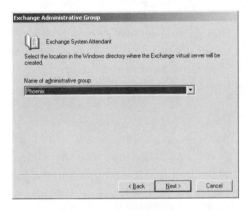

**Figure 13.55**    Exchange Administrative Group window showing option to add Exchange virtual machine to an existing Administrative Group. A cluster cannot be the first Exchange 2003 server in a legacy site because it cannot run SRS.

6. Click **Next**. In the Exchange Routing Group window, assign the virtual server to a Routing Group.

7. Click **Next**. In the Account and Password window (Figure 13.56), enter the password for the Exchange service, if you are still running in Exchange Mixed mode.

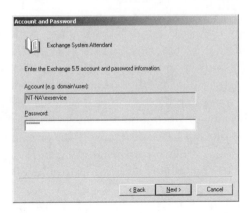

**Figure 13.56**    Account and Password window showing service account required to access legacy Exchange in Mixed mode organization.

8. Click **Next**. In the Data Directory window, make sure the disk and path information points at the 8GB shared data drive. If not, change the drive letter. **The target folder must be entirely empty or the virtual server creation will fail.**

9. Click **Next** to get a summary window, and then **Finish** to accept the settings and to create the virtual server. The system becomes unresponsive for a while as it creates the necessary resources. Once the resources have been created in Cluster Administrator, you'll see lots of red down arrows in the right pane of the console.

10. Highlight the **Exchange Cluster** icon and press **Ctrl+B** to bring the virtual server online.

When the last red arrow disappears and the State of each resource shows Online, you can give yourself a round of applause for successfully bringing a clustered Exchange server online. But you're not quite done.

By default, the System Attendant resource puts the transaction logs and the Exchange data files on the same volume. You need to move the transaction logs to a separate drive.

### Move Transaction Logs

Use Exchange System Manager to move the transaction logs to the shared disk you created to hold them. This process dismounts the stores in the storage group.

1. In ESM, open the Properties window for the Storage Group on the newly created Exchange server.

2. Click the **Browse** button next to the file location for the transaction logs.

3. Select the drive letter corresponding to the TransLogs disk and create a new folder to hold the logs for this storage group. You might want to create more storage groups, so give the folder a name that indicates the virtual server and storage group name.

   The system notifies you that the stores will be dismounted and the virtual server temporarily taken offline during the operation.

4. Once the logs have been moved, the information store remounts the storage group. Verify that you can access the storage group's mailbox and public folder stores from ESM.

You're still not quite done. Remember that the purpose of the cluster is to react well in times of peril. You need to provide a few perils.

## Test the Cluster

You should now test the reaction of the clustered Exchange resource to controlled failovers and failovers caused by node failures.

As a preliminary, use ESM to move a few mailboxes to the clustered server and then log on at a workstation and use Outlook to connect to of those mailboxes.

### *Move Exchange Cluster Group*

When you move a resource group from one node to the other, this initiates a controlled failover. Right-click the Exchange Cluster object and select Move Group. This takes the resources offline for a half-minute or so (Figure 13.57) while the system moves the resources to the other node. The resources then start automatically and the Exchange service comes back online. The Cluster Administrator window displays the name of the node that owns the resource group.

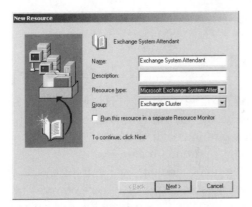

**Figure 13.57**    Exchange resources show as Offline, and the Exchange Cluster shows a big red exclamation point during the short time a node takes to go through failover to the other node.

### *Simulate Failure*

Simulate a failure in the operational node using the Move Group option from the flyout menu. Once again, the failover should take only a half-minute or so.

### Initiate Actual Failure

Simulate a crash of a server node by turning off the virtual machine in VMWare. Watch as the other server node reacts by failing the group to the active node.

### From Lab to Production

As I said at the start of this section, creating and working with a virtual cluster is not a substitute for actual hands-on training from a skilled clustering professional using the exact hardware you'll be using in production. When you set up a budget to purchase cluster hardware, be sure to include the cost of this training on the clustered hardware and the clustering software, as well as any applications such as Exchange that you plan on running on the cluster. Don't try to fly by the seat of your pants. Management generally has high expectations for the improved uptime that clusters are supposed to provide, and you don't want to be the administrator who crashes the cluster and disabuses them of these expectations.

# Looking Forward

That's it. You're done. Completed. Concluded. The job's finished. It's a wrap. You've accomplished your goal, concluded your business, and satisfied your aspirations. All that's left now is to put up your feet and browse through vacation brochures.

Enjoy the good feeling while it lasts...maybe as much as an hour...because you're still an e-mail administrator. Pretty soon the phone will ring and you'll be back in the real world again.

Still, you have a right to enjoy what you've accomplished. The good news is, the next version of Exchange won't be coming your way for quite a while.

Have fun.

# Building a Stable Exchange 2003 Deployment Infrastructure

The ultimate goal of an Exchange 2003 deployment is to get a stable and reliable messaging infrastructure. Before you can do that, you need a fairly extensive set of support services, including DNS servers, Active Directory domain controllers, and Global Catalog servers. The details for installing and configuring those support services fall outside the scope of this book, but without a good working knowledge of their operation, many of the design, configuration, and security requirements of Exchange 2003 won't make sense to you. For that reason, although it might seem a little off topic for a book on Exchange, this appendix contains a fairly detailed look at three critical areas of Windows operation:

- DNS design and operation
- Authentication and authorization mechanisms
- Active Directory design and operation

This may seem like a dreary slab of information to gnaw through, but these three topics cover nearly 80 percent of the problems commonly encountered by Exchange administrators.

# DNS Design and Operation

This section contains operational and configuration guidelines for DNS, only as they affect an Exchange 2003 deployment. It does not contain a comprehensive DNS deployment guide. For information about enterprise-wide deployment of Windows DNS, take a look at Microsoft's "Windows Server 2003 Deployment Kit", a free download from `www.microsoft.com/downloads/details.aspx?familyid=D91065EE-E618-4810-A036-DE633F79872E&displaylang=en`.

For a more comprehensive look at DNS operation and management, take a look at *DNS on Windows Server 2003* by Matt Larson, Cricket Liu, and Robbie Allen (O'Reilly, 2003) and my book *Inside Windows Server 2003* (Addison-Wesley, 2003).

## Name Formats

Windows networking entities, such as Exchange servers and Active Directory domain controllers, have a variety of name formats:

- **Flat names (also called NetBIOS names or friendly names).** Every Windows networking entity (servers, desktops, domains, workgroups, and users) have a name. For example, the ASGARD domain could have a server named LOKI and a user named THOR. Two Windows entities cannot have the same flat name in the same domain. In other words, the ASGARD domain can't have a user named THOR and a desktop named THOR.

I prefer the term "flat name" rather than "NetBIOS name" to avoid giving the impression that Windows entities use NetBIOS to communicate with each other. Use of the true NetBIOS interface has just about evaporated. When you read the phrase, "Windows machines communicate using NetBIOS," you can interpret that to mean, "Windows machines have a service called *NetBIOS-over-TCP/IP* that resolves a flat NetBIOS name into an IP address.

- **DNS names.** In contrast to flat NetBIOS names, Windows entities also have a *host name* used by the Domain Name System (DNS). All modern Windows platforms (Windows 2000 and higher) use their flat name as a host name. The combination of a Windows entity's host name with the full path to the root of the DNS namespace forms a unique name called the Fully Qualified Domain Name, or FQDN. Examples include W2K3-EX1.Company.Com and SMTP1.Northamerica.Company.Com.

- **User Principal Name (UPN).** A standard Internet name format that specifies the user's name and domain in the format `user@domain_name.root`. Examples include `jgarcia@deadhead.com` and `dick.cavett@wherearetheynow.org`. The domain name after the @ sign usually corresponds to a DNS domain.

- **Service Principal Name (SPN).** Each Windows service that uses Kerberos as an authentication protocol gets an SPN. The SPN contains the service name and the host where the service runs. A typical SPN format shows the service name followed by a forward slash, followed by the host's flat name or FQDN. For example, ldap/w2k3-s1 and ldap/w2k3-s1.company.com. If more than one server runs the same service, the SPN might have a third element for the domain name. Examples include `ldap/w2k3-s1.company.com/COMPANY`, and `ldap/w2k3-s1.company.com/company.com`.

## Windows Name Resolution Mechanisms

A Windows network client must have a way to resolve any and all name formats into an IP address. Figure A.1 shows the two mechanisms employed by Windows to resolve friendly names into IP addresses: NetBIOS name resolution and DNS name resolution.

The Windows service responsible for performing name resolution is called the TCP/IP Resolver, or simply the Resolver. The Resolver in modern Windows platforms uses DNS as its primary name resolution mechanism. When resolving names on behalf of certain Windows services, the Resolver can call upon help from a driver called NetBIOS-over-TCPIP, or NBT.

The two mechanisms used by the Resolver for handling lookups—DNS name resolution and NetBIOS name resolution—have quite a bit in common.

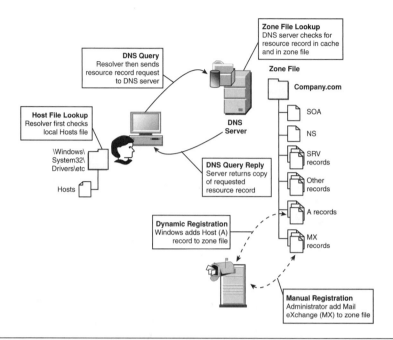

**Figure A.1** Diagram of Windows name resolution mechanisms.

- **Local lookup files.** Both resolution mechanisms consult a local file that stores machine names and IP addresses. The DNS resolution mechanism uses a Hosts file. The NetBIOS mechanism uses an LMHosts file. Both files reside in %windir%\ system32\drivers\etc\hosts. (The %windir% environment variable expands to show the full path to the system folder.) The major difference in the two mechanisms lies in when the Resolver consults the local file. DNS resolution consults the Hosts file first. NetBIOS resolution consults the LMHosts file last.

- **Local name caches.** Both resolution mechanisms store their lookup results in memory to speed up subsequent lookups of the same name. You can view the DNS Resolver cache by typing ipconfig /displaydns at a command prompt. To view the NBT Resolver cache, type nbtstat -c.

- **Central databases.** Both resolution mechanisms can consult a server that holds a database of *resource records* containing machine names and their IP addresses (among other items). The DNS mechanism consults a DNS server, whose database typically resides in a text file called a *zone file*. The NetBIOS mechanism consults a WINS server, which stores records in a Microsoft Jet (Joint Engine Technology) database.

Modern Windows platforms dynamically register their A (Host) and PTR (reverse lookup pointer) records in their DNS zone, and they register Host records along with a variety of NetBIOS services in WINS. Domain controllers register a variety of NetBIOS service records in WINS, used for features such as network browsing.

Active Directory domain controllers dynamically register SRV (Service Locator) records in DNS (not WINS.) These SRV records advertise services provided by the domain controllers, such as LDAP, Kerberos, and the Global Catalog.

If the DNS administrator disables the dynamic resource record registration for a DNS zone, you can enter these resource records manually into the DNS zone file.

Exchange 2003 and Active Directory domain controllers, and their clients, rely on DNS records to locate each other and to locate essential domain services. In addition, Internet DNS clients and e-mail servers rely on MX (Mail eXchange) records in DNS to locate the e-mail servers in a particular DNS domain. You must enter these MX records manually if an Exchange server supports access by Internet clients.

## Detailed DNS Transaction

When called upon to find the IP address associated with a name, the Resolver decides which mechanism to use based upon the nature of the application submitting the request.

- **DNS name resolution.** After checking the local DNS name cache, the Resolver consults the local Hosts file. If it does not find a listing for the requested name, it sends a resource record lookup query containing the FQDN of the host to DNS and waits for a reply.
- **NetBIOS name resolution.** After checking the local NBT name cache, the Resolver sends a resource record lookup request to WINS. If it does not get a response, or if the WINS server replies with a No ACK (no record in the database), the Resolver broadcasts the host name and waits for a reply from the target machine. If this fails, the Resolver checks the contents of the Lmhosts file.

You can remember the sequence of operations in Windows name resolution by learning the phrase Can We Buy Large Capacity Hard Drives. This mnemonic yields the initials CWBLCHD, which converts to Cache, WINS, Broadcast, Lmhosts, Cache, Hosts, and DNS. The first Cache refers to the NetBIOS name cache, and the second refers to the DNS name cache.

Because DNS lookups play such an important role to the operation of Exchange, let's take a closer look at the details of a typical DNS lookup, diagrammed in Figure A.2.

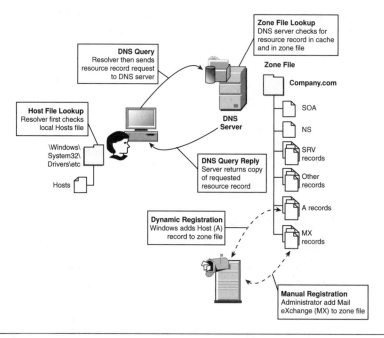

**Figure A.2**    DNS lookup transaction.

The process begins when a client tries to locate a server, in this case to send an e-mail. The transaction goes something like this:

1. The Resolver at the client sends a resource record request to the IP address of the DNS server identified in the local network adapter's TCP/IP settings (or obtained from DHCP).
2. The DNS server looks in its zone file, finds the requested record, caches a copy in memory and then returns a copy to the Resolver at the client.

3. The Resolver caches a copy of the resource record in memory and passes the content to the TCP/IP driver, which uses the IP address to build a packet containing the e-mail message.

If the DNS server has a copy of the zone file corresponding to the DNS domain in the record request, but does not have the requested resource record, it returns a negative response, called a No ACK or NAK. A modern Windows client caches NAK responses for 5 minutes (300 seconds). You can disable negative caching using this Registry entry:

```
Key: HKLM | System | CurrentControlSet | Services | DNSCache |
➥Parameters
Value: NegativeCacheTime
Data: 0 (REG_DWORD)
```

If name resolution requests need to transit one or more firewalls, here some port numbers to keep in mind:

- NetBIOS name registration and resolution broadcasts do not transit a router.
- NBT sends NetBIOS name registration requests to a WINS server using TCP port 137.
- NBT sends NetBIOS resource record requests to a WINS server using UDP port 137.
- The Resolver sends DNS resource record requests to a DNS server using UDP port 53, except when the requesting application wants more records than will fit in a 512-byte UDP datagram, in which case the Requestor uses TCP port 53 or negotiates a larger UDP datagram size using EDNS0.

## DNS Resolver Cache Content

DNS servers and clients cache the results of resource record requests. This speeds up subsequent lookups at the client and reduces load on the DNS servers. Servers and clients purge cached resource records based on a Time to Live (TTL) value in the record itself. You can view the content of a client's DNS Resolver cache using `ipconfig /displaydns`. This listing shows an example:

```
Windows IP Configuration


w2k3-ex2.company.com
────────────────────────

Record Name . . . . . : w2k3-ex2.company.com
Record Type . . . . . : 1
Time To Live  . . . . : 598926
Data Length . . . . . : 4
Section . . . . . . . : Answer
A (Host) Record . . . : 222.22.22.2


localhost
────────────────────────

Record Name . . . . . : localhost
Record Type . . . . . : 1
Time To Live  . . . . : 598926
Data Length . . . . . : 4
Section . . . . . . . : Answer
A (Host) Record . . . : 127.0.0.1
```

Whenever you troubleshoot DNS lookup problems, don't forget to clear out the local cache regularly. Do this using `ipconfig /flushdns`. This is especially important if you are adding new records into DNS and you want to get rid of cached NAK entries.

## DNS Suffixes and Suffix Search Order

DNS requires a Fully Qualified Domain Name (FQDN) in a resource record request. It isn't always convenient to type in a FQDN, especially for users, so Windows has several mechanisms for converting a flat host name into a FQDN.

For example, let's say you configure an Outlook client to connect to an Exchange server using the flat name W2K3-EX1. The TCP/IP Resolver must convert the flat name to a FQDN before it can query DNS, so it tacks on the DNS suffix of the client's Active Directory domain. This yields `w2k3-ex1.company.com`. If the client's DNS server holds the `Company.com` zone file, or if it can contact a DNS server in `Company.com`, then the client will get the A record corresponding to that FQDN.

If you have a single Active Directory domain in your organization, adding that domain's DNS suffix to every flat name lookup request works just fine. But if your organization has multiple Active Directory domains with Exchange servers in one domain and clients in another domain, then Outlook might have a problem.

For example, what if an Outlook user in `west.northamerica.company.com` tries to connect to an Exchange server in `company.com`? The Resolver first appends the DNS suffix `west.northamerica.company.com` to the flat name and queries DNS. The DNS server returns a NAK if it does not have a zone file for `west.northamerica.company.com` and it cannot locate a DNS server in `west.northamerica.company.com`.

Windows handles this dilemma by a process called *suffix devolution*. The Resolver strips off the leftmost element of the FQDN and tries again, repeating the process until it gets to the root of the namespace. This results in the following DNS queries:

- Host record for `w2k3-ex1.west.northamerica.company.com`
- Host record for `w2k3-ex1.northamerica.company.com`
- Host record for `w2k3-ex1.company.com`

In this example, the final query succeeds, but only after repeated queries down the tree. If you choose to rely on suffix devolution, keep in mind that it will not work if you have multiple trees in your DNS hierarchy or a discontiguous DNS namespace in your Active Directory forest. For example, if the Exchange server W2K3-EX1 were in `east.northamerica.com` and the Outlook client were in `west.northamerica.com`, suffix devolution would walk up the tree to `company.com`, but not down the tree to find the resource record.

To resolve flat names in a multi-tiered DNS namespace, you can configure the DNS clients with the DNS suffix of every domain in the forest. This cannot be done in DHCP. You can deploy the settings manually or use a central Registry management program to deploy the changes. This can cause complications in name lookups, so be sure you walk through all the resolution scenarios in your environment.

You can view and modify DNS suffix settings in the DNS tab of the Advanced TCP/IP Settings window of an interface. Figure A.3 shows an example. Select the Append DNS Suffixes in This Order radio button and then add the suffixes in your organization.

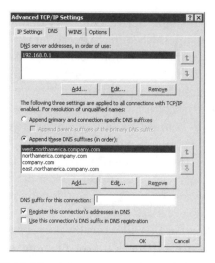

**Figure A.3**   Advanced TCP/IP Settings showing suffix search order.

## Zone Delegation

You can use a multilevel hierarchy in your DNS namespace, such as that shown in Figure A.4, but you'll need to configure delegation records in the parent domain that point to DNS servers in the child domain. For example, if an Exchange server in company.com needs to route an e-mail to an Exchange server in na.company.com, it sends a resource record request to the DNS server in company.com. If that DNS server doesn't have a way to locate a DNS server in na.company.com, it cannot fulfill the request and the e-mail doesn't get routed.

It doesn't take much work to delegate a zone in Windows Server 2003 DNS. Here's how it works:

1. Right-click the domain icon in the DNS management console and select **New Delegation** from the flyout menu. This starts the New Delegation Wizard.
2. Click **Next**. The Delegated Domain Name window opens, as shown in Figure A.5.
3. Enter the name of the child domain under **Delegated Domain**. The wizard fills out the FQDN for you.

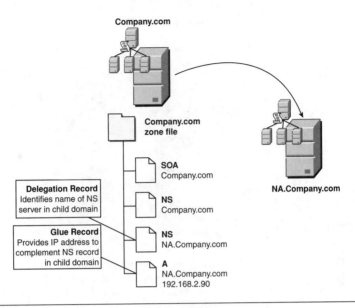

**Figure A.4** Diagram of DNS delegation showing NS and glue record for delegated zone.

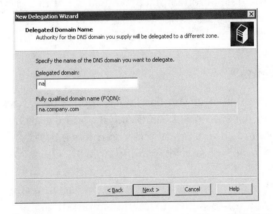

**Figure A.5** New Delegation Wizard showing Delegated Domain Name window.

4. Click **Next**. The Name Servers window opens.
5. Click **Add**. The New Resource Record window opens, as shown in Figure A.6. Enter the FQDN of the DNS server in the child domain and its IP address. Click **OK** to save the change and return to the Name Servers window.

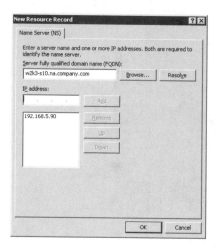

**Figure A.6**   New Resource Record window with name and IP address of DNS server in delegated zone.

6.  Click **Next** and **Finish** to save the change and close the wizard.

With the delegation in place, when a client in `company.com` asks for a resource record in `na.company.com`, the DNS server can use the NS and glue records to send a query to the DNS server in the child domain.

## Stub Zones

There's a problem with standard delegation. The DNS servers in the parent domain have no way of knowing if you take a DNS server down for maintenance. You must remember to remove the delegation record from the parent zone; otherwise, you end up with a *lame delegation*. Windows Server 2003 helps resolve this problem with a feature called *stub zones*.

A stub zone acts a little like a sneaky kid in a candy store. It knows that you want up-to-date information about the name servers in the child domain, but it doesn't have sufficient permissions to directly request a zone transfer. So it periodically asks an innocent question of the child DNS server, "Please give me all the NS records you currently have for this zone." The DNS server gets queries like this all day long and is happy to answer.

The parent DNS server then tucks these NS records into a separate zone file and refers to them when it is asked for a resource record in the child domain. It periodically refreshes the list, so there is very little chance of getting a lame delegation.

Creating a stub zone requires no special privileges in the child domain. Simply create a new forward look zone using the DNS Management console and select the Stub Zone option in the New Zone Wizard, as shown in Figure A.7.

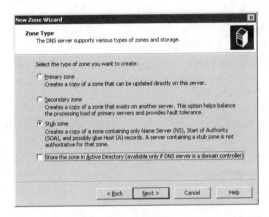

**Figure A. 7** New Zone Wizard showing Zone Type window with Stub Zone selection.

## Troubleshooting DNS Lookup Errors

Many apparent Outlook failures actually have a root cause in the configuration of the desktop's DNS settings. You can usually isolate DNS configuration errors using these utilities (along with ping, of course): Ipconfig, Nslookup, and Netdiag.

### Ipconfig

This utility tells you the TCP/IP settings for a machine. Run `Ipconfig /all` to list the DNS configuration settings. Here is an example:

```
C:\>ipconfig /all
Windows IP Configuration

        Host Name . . . . . . . . . . . . : xp-pro1
        Primary Dns Suffix  . . . . . . . : company.com
        Node Type . . . . . . . . . . . . : Hybrid
        IP Routing Enabled. . . . . . . . : No
        WINS Proxy Enabled. . . . . . . . : No
```

```
          DNS Suffix Search List. . . . . . . : company.com

Ethernet adapter Local Area Connection:

          Connection-specific DNS Suffix  .   : company.com
          Description . . . . . . . . . . . : Intel Ethernet
          ➥Adapter
          Physical Address. . . . . . . . . : 00-03-FF-DE-24-F2
          Dhcp Enabled. . . . . . . . . . . : Yes
          Autoconfiguration Enabled . . . . : Yes
          IP Address. . . . . . . . . . . . : 192.168.0.131
          Subnet Mask . . . . . . . . . . . : 255.255.255.0
          Default Gateway . . . . . . . . . : 192.168.0.100
          DHCP Server . . . . . . . . . . . : 192.168.0.2
          DNS Servers . . . . . . . . . . . : 192.168.0.1
          Primary WINS Server . . . . . . . : 192.168.0.1
```

### Nslookup

Once you know the identity of the DNS server used by the client, use the Nslookup utility to query the DNS server in interactive mode. Do this by typing **Nslookup** at the command prompt. This takes you to an interactive logon prompt. You want to know if the client can obtain two important items: the A record for the Exchange server and the SRV record for a Global Catalog server. Start by entering the FQDN of the Exchange server and verifying that you get back an authoritative reply, as shown in this listing:

```
C:\>nslookup
Default Server:  w2k3-s1.company.com
Address:  192.168.0.1

> w2k3-ex1.company.com.
Server:  w2k3-s1.company.com
Address:  192.168.0.1

Name:    w2k3-ex1.company.com
Address:  192.168.0.6
```

You have to do some nimble typing at this point. You want to query the DNS server for SRV records corresponding to Global Catalog

servers. First set the record filter to show SRV records and then request
Global Catalog SRV records. Follow the syntax in the example, but use
your own domain name:

```
> set type=srv
> _ldap._tcp.gc._msdcs.company.com.
Server:  w2k3-s1.company.com
Address:  192.168.0.1


_ldap._tcp.gc._msdcs.company.com          SRV service location:
          priority        = 0
          weight          = 100
          port            = 3268
          svr hostname    = w2k3-s1.company.com
_ldap._tcp.gc._msdcs.company.com          SRV service location:
          priority        = 0
          weight          = 100
          port            = 3268
          svr hostname    = w2k3-s4.company.com
w2k3-s1.company.com        internet address = 192.168.0.1
w2k3-s4.company.com        internet address = 192.168.1.4
```

Now that you know the name of each Global Catalog server, either
ping them to verify that the client can see them on the network or telnet
to TCP port 3268. If this succeeds, proceed.

### DNSLint

This tool comes in the Windows Server 2003 Support Tools, or you can
download it directly from the Microsoft Web site. It's a great tool that
can quickly ferret out potential DNS configuration errors and lame delegations that can cause failures in Active Directory and other applications
that rely on DNS.

As input, DNSLint takes the name of an Active Directory domain,
or the IP address of a domain controller and a DNS server that hosts the
forest root zone. The output is an HTML page containing details on the
DNS configuration and highlighting any errors. You can provide a list of
servers from a text file, useful for running periodic diagnostic tests from
a script. Here is an example listing from a DNSLint report:

```
Command run: dnslint /d company.com /v /s 192.168.0.2 /test_tcp
Domain name tested:    company.com
The following 1 DNS servers were identified as authoritative for the
➡domain:
DNS server: w2k3-s1.company.com
IP Address: 192.168.0.1
UDP port 53 responding to queries: YES
TCP port 53 responding to queries: YES
Answering authoritatively for domain: YES

SOA record data from server:
Authoritative name server: w2k3-s1.company.com
Hostmaster: hostmaster.company.com
Zone serial number: 238
Zone expires in: 1.00 day(s)
Refresh period: 900 seconds
Retry delay: 600 seconds
Default (minimum) TTL: 3600 seconds
Additional authoritative (NS) records from server:
w2k3-s2.company.com 192.168.0.2

Host (A) records for domain from server:
192.168.0.2
Mail Exchange (MX) records from server (preference/name/IP address):
None found
```

If DNSLint finds trouble spots, it highlights the entries in red in the HTML report. You can't get much more convenient than that.

### Netdiag

This general-purpose utility, part of the Windows Server 2003 Support Tools, runs a suite of tests designed to find network configuration errors. Three of the tests—DNS, DsGetDC, and DcList—have special significance when installing Exchange servers. Run the tests individually with a verbose switch (`netdiag /v`) to get detailed results. Here is an example listing:

```
DNS test . . . . . . . . . . . . . : Passed
Interface {24ED69E6-B47D-4B6F-98F2-61C189BACEB3}
   DNS Domain:
   DNS Servers: 192.168.0.1
```

```
    IP Address: 192.168.0.92
    Expected registration with PDN (primary DNS domain name):
      Hostname: W2K3-EX2.company.com.
      Authoritative zone: company.com.
      Primary DNS server: w2k3-s1.company.com 192.168.0.1
      Authoritative NS:192.168.2.10 192.168.1.4 192.168.2.9 192.168.0.1
                       192.168.0.3 192.168.0.103 192.168.0.2
Verify DNS registration:
  Name: W2K3-EX2.company.com
  Expected IP: 192.168.0.92
    Server 192.168.2.10: NO_ERROR
    Server 192.168.1.4: NO_ERROR
    Server 192.168.2.9: NO_ERROR
    Server 192.168.0.1: NO_ERROR
    Server 192.168.0.3: NO_ERROR
    Server 192.168.0.103: Error 9501 DNS_INFO_NO_RECORDS
    Server 192.168.0.2: NO_ERROR
  [WARNING]: The DNS registration for 'W2K3-EX2.company.com' is
             ➡correct only on some DNS servers. Please wait 15 min
             ➡for replication and run the test again.
```

As you can see, when you run Netdiag, you learn the server's name, its domain affiliation, its IP address, and the IP address of its DNS server. Fine, you could have gotten that from Ipconfig. But you also know the IP addresses of every authoritative DNS server for the company.com zone and you know that one of those servers, 192.168.0.103, has not replicated an up-to-date resource record for the host where you ran the test. Now run the DsGetDC test. Here's an example listing:

```
DC discovery test. . . . . . . . . : Passed

  Find DC in domain 'COMPANY':
  Found this DC in domain 'COMPANY':
    DC. . . . . . . . . . . : \\W2K3-S2.company.com
    Address . . . . . . . . : \\192.168.0.2
    Domain Guid . . . . . . : {01012378-A008-409D-9696-3C7F16BFBB62}
    Domain Name . . . . . . : company.com
    Forest Name . . . . . . : company.com
    DC Site Name. . . . . . : Phoenix
    Our Site Name . . . . . : Phoenix
    Flags . . . . . . . . . : DS KDC TIMESERV WRITABLE DNS_DC DNS_DOMAIN
                              DNS_FOREST CLOSE_SITE 0x8
```

```
Find PDC emulator in domain 'COMPANY':
Found this PDC emulator in domain 'COMPANY':
   DC. . . . . . . . . . . : \\W2K3-S3.company.com
   Address . . . . . . . . : \\192.168.0.3
   Domain Guid . . . . . . : {01012378-A008-409D-9696-3C7F16BFBB62}
   Domain Name . . . . . . : company.com
   Forest Name . . . . . . : company.com
   DC Site Name. . . . . . : Phoenix
   Our Site Name . . . . . : Phoenix
   Flags . . . . . . . . . : PDC emulator DS KDC TIMESERV GTIMESERV
➥WRITABLE

                            DNS_DC DNS_DOMAIN DNS_FOREST CLOSE_SITE 0x8

Find Windows 2000 DC in domain 'COMPANY':
Found this Windows 2000 DC in domain 'COMPANY':
   DC. . . . . . . . . . . : \\W2K3-S2.company.com
   Address . . . . . . . . : \\192.168.0.2
   Domain Guid . . . . . . : {01012378-A008-409D-9696-3C7F16BFBB62}
   Domain Name . . . . . . : company.com
   Forest Name . . . . . . : company.com
   DC Site Name. . . . . . : Phoenix
   Our Site Name . . . . . : Phoenix
   Flags . . . . . . . . . : DS KDC TIMESERV WRITABLE DNS_DC DNS_DOMAIN
                            DNS_FOREST CLOSE_SITE 0x8

DC list test . . . . . . . . . . . : Passed
```

This test tells you that the server where you ran Netdiag was able to find at least one domain controller that answers a standard domain controller lookup attempt. This could be an Active Directory domain controller or an NT domain controller. The test could also find the PDC Emulator in the domain and at least one Active Directory domain controller. Now run the DCList test to see how many domain controllers are available. Here's a sample listing:

```
Find DC in domain 'COMPANY':
Found this DC in domain 'COMPANY':
   DC. . . . . . . . . . . : \\W2K3-S2.company.com
   Address . . . . . . . . : \\192.168.0.2
   Domain Guid . . . . . . : {01012378-A008-409D-9696-3C7F16BFBB62}
   Domain Name . . . . . . : company.com
```

```
Forest Name . . . . . . : company.com
DC Site Name. . . . . . : Phoenix
Our Site Name . . . . . : Phoenix
Flags . . . . . . . . . : DS KDC TIMESERV WRITABLE DNS_DC DNS_DOMAIN
                          DNS_FOREST CLOSE_SITE 0x8
List of DCs in Domain 'COMPANY':
  W2K3-S2.company.com
  w2k3-s1.company.com
  W2K3-S3.company.com
```

This test tells you that the server where you ran the test was able to find details about at least one domain controller in its site and can find others in the same site, in case the first domain controller goes down. Don't even think about installing Exchange 2003 on a server until you resolve all Netdiag errors.

## Points to Remember about DNS Name Resolution

As you deploy Exchange and troubleshoot errors as they arise, keep these general rules about DNS in mind:

- Modern Windows platforms use DNS name resolution to find IP addresses both for fully qualified names and for flat names.
- Members of Active Directory domains rely on DNS to find domain controllers and Global Catalog servers. Without DNS, users cannot get authenticated, and therefore, they cannot access their Exchange mailboxes.
- DNS servers in a hierarchy should forward out-of-zone lookup requests to a DNS server in the top-level domain.
- In a DNS hierarchy, the DNS servers in each tier should have delegation records for the next tier down, along with a stub zone for that tier.
- Clients and DNS servers cache resource record query results for a period of time to save bandwidth. Make sure you clear the cache often when troubleshooting.
- A DNS server used as a forwarder needs sufficient horsepower to handle recursive lookup queries on behalf of the clients of all DNS servers who forward to that server.
- Windows Server 2003 has a conditional forwarding feature that enables you to define a specific set of forwarders for a given DNS domain.

# Windows Authentication and Authorization

When a user attempts to access a secured object, the operating system validates the user's identity and then determines if the user has sufficient access rights to open the item. Validating a user's identity is called *authentication*. Validating a user's access permissions is called *authorization*.

- To authenticate, a user must provide a unique set of *credentials*. In the vast majority of cases, these credentials take the form of a name and a password. Thanks to the increased awareness of security, some organizations have deployed *two-factor* authentication mechanisms that use a smart card or smart token along with a password. Details on these specialized authentication mechanisms fall outside the scope of this book, but the underlying identity verification systems are the same as those used to handle password credentials.

- For authorization, Windows assigned each user (and computer and group) a Security ID, or SID. Security objects such as NTFS files and Exchange mailboxes have an *Access Control List* that lists the SID of those users and groups that have access permission, and the type of access (read, write, modify, and so forth) they can exercise. Figure A.8 shows an example of an SID and its component parts.

### Security ID (SID)

Here's a quick breakdown of the SID elements:

- **Revision.** The first two characters, S-1, indicate that this is a revision 1 SID. All modern Windows platforms use an S-1 SID.
- **Issuing Authority.** The next number identifies the Issuing Authority for the SID. The SIDs representing users, computers and any groups created after initial Setup have a 5 for the Issuing Authority. Other issuing authorities include 0 for Null (null session connections), 1 for the World (Everyone group), 2 for Local (represents local terminal logons), and 3 for Creator (creator-owner and the creator-owner group).

- **Sub-Authority.** The number after S-1-5 is the Sub-Authority designator. When you see a 21 for Sub-Authority, you know that the SID belongs to a domain because the 21 designates a non-unique SID.

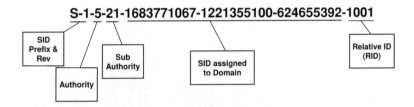

**Figure A.8**   Breakdown of SID elements.

- **Domain SID.** The next number is the unique SID assigned to the domain.
- **RID.** The number after the final dash is the Relative ID, or RID. Each security principal gets a unique RID assigned sequentially from a pool of RIDs. A domain controller called the RID Master apportions unique RIDs to the other domain controllers so they can create new security principals.

By appending the unique RID to the domain SID, the operating system ends up with a unique SID for each security principal, an SID that can be traced right back to the issuing domain. Each security principal must get a unique SID because Windows uses the SID on Access Control Lists (ACLs) for security objects such as NTFS files and Registry keys.

## Security Descriptor

Security objects, such as Exchange mailboxes, public folders, and Active Directory objects, each has a special data structure called a *security descriptor* that contains a permission list called an ACL. (Actually, a security descriptor has two ACLs: a *Discretionary ACL* (DACL) that controls access to the object itself and a *Security ACL* (SACL) that controls who can audit access to the object. Figure A.9 shows the content of a typical security descriptor.

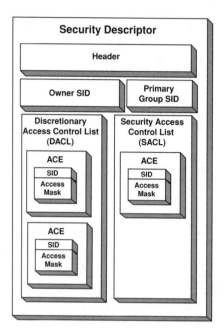

**Figure A. 9**    Content of security descriptor.

An ACL contains one or more *Access Control Entries* (ACEs). Each ACE has two parts:

- The SID of a security principal
- An access mask defining the permissions assigned to that security principal

An access mask is simply a 32-bit number where each bit has a meaning. For example, one bit controls READ access and another bit controls WRITE access, and there's a bit to control the ability to change the security descriptor and so forth.

## Access Tokens

Once a user gets authenticated, he begins to launch executable programs. Each program consists of a process with one or more threads. Each thread has code capable of accessing security objects such as mailboxes and public folders, so the operating system needs a way to link the thread with the user who launched the process. It does this using an access token.

An access token works something like the chain of command on a Navy ship. Once a ship is under way, the captain turns the helm over to a subordinate officer who assumes a role called the Conning Officer. "Take the conn, Mr. Sullivan," says the captain, to which Mr. Sullivan replies, "Aye, aye, Captain. This is Mr. Sullivan. I have the conn."

As long as the subordinate has the role of Conning Officer, the ship's crew must obey his orders as if they came directly from the captain. The Conning Officer often carries some sort of indicator that he has been granted this authority. The indicator might be a special cap or a uniform device, or just an especially grumpy look. In any case, that indicator acts as the subordinate's "token" that he is executing the captain's orders.

In Windows, a user's access token not only contains the user's SID, it also contains a significant amount of information about the user, including the following:

- The SID of each group to which the user belongs.
- The SID of each group to which any of those groups belong.
- A set of privileges assigned to the user, such as the ability to change the system time, to perform a back, to do a local logon, and so forth.
- A flag called *impersonation level* that indicates whether the token can be copied to other processes. Windows has four impersonation levels: Anonymous, Identification, Impersonation, and Delegation. Anonymous means that the user who initiated the process supplied no credentials whatsoever. The Identification flag says that the token cannot be copied. The Impersonation flag says that the token can be copied, but only to processes running on the same machine. The Delegation flag says that the token can be copied to processes on other machines.
- A user must have a local access token on any server where the user requires network access. For example, if an Outlook user tries to open a public folder on an Exchange server, then Outlook must initiate a series of transactions that results in the user having an access token on that Exchange server.

## Authentication Types

When an e-mail application such as Outlook connects to an Exchange server on behalf of a user, Exchange authenticates the user before granting access to the requested mailbox. Exchange supports these authentication options:

- **Plain text (Basic).** As the name implies, plain text authentication simply hands the user's password in clear text to the Exchange server. A packet sniffer can see the transaction and capture the password. Basic authentication works in a similar fashion, except that it obfuscates the password by encoding it using Base64. Microsoft provides a Base64 encoder/decoder as a free download. Look for B64_samp.exe in Knowledge Base article 191239. The code is not compiled. Compile it using Visual Studio.

- **Windows Challenge-Response.** This mechanism protects the user's password by not exposing it on the wire. The authentication server sends a random number—the challenge—to the client. The client manipulates the challenge using a derivative of the user's password and returns the result as a response. Win9x platforms use a challenge-response mechanism called LanMan (LM). NT-based platforms use a method called NT LanMan version 2 (NTLMv2) or an older version called simply NTLM. (Sometimes an option in the user interface says NTLM when it means NTLMv2, which is confusing, but not uncommon.)

- **Kerberos.** This mechanism uses a secret session key embedded inside a *ticket* issued by a trusted third party, a Key Distribution Center (KDC). All modern Windows platforms (Windows 2000, XP, and Windows Server 2003) use Kerberos when a member of an Active Directory domain.

You'll face many situations where a solid knowledge of the inputs and outputs of each Windows authentication mechanism comes in handy for troubleshooting, so let's review their operation, starting with the NTLMv2 challenge-response mechanism.

## NTLMv2 Challenge Response Authentication

When a user initiates a domain logon by pressing Ctrl+Alt+Del and entering a name and password, the Winlogon process takes these credentials and passes them to the Local Security Authority for processing.

The Local Security Authority starts by creating a *hash* of the user's password. A hash uses an algorithm that scrambles the input so thoroughly that the original contents cannot be derived directly from the hash.

Password-cracking programs such as l0phtcrack and Jack the Ripper don't analyze a password hash; they simply try one hash after another until they come up with the same combination of letters contained in the original password.

Windows 9x uses the DES hashing algorithm. Platforms derived from Windows NT use the RSA MD4 algorithm. ("MD" stands for Message Digest, a more formal term for a hash.)

The local security authority then calls upon the Netlogon service to handle the NTLMv2 transaction. Figure A.10 shows a diagram of the initial domain logon, during which a user gets a local access token on the desktop. Here are the details.

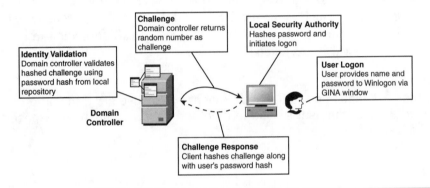

**Figure A.10**     Initial NTLMv2 domain logon challenge-response transaction.

  1. The user first logs onto the domain by pressing Ctrl+Alt+Del and entering a name and password. The local security authority hashes the password and notifies the domain controller of the logon request.

2. The domain controller responds with a 16-byte random number called a *challenge*. (NTLM uses an 8-byte challenge.) The challenge is sent in clear text. (In other words, you can see it using a packet sniffer.)

3. The desktop combines the challenge with the user's MD4 password hash and produces a new MD4 hash that it sends to the domain controller. NTLMv2 includes an 8-byte random number called *salt* to help deter dictionary attacks against the challenge-response transaction.

4. The domain controller obtains a copy of the user's password hash and validates the challenge response by performing the same hash as that used by the client. If the two results match, the user gets validated.

5. The domain controller returns a block of information about the user, such as the user's SID and the SID of any groups to which the user belongs. The desktop uses this information to build a local access token for the user.

Only the challenge and the hashed challenge response are transmitted on the wire. Neither the user's password nor the password hash are exposed to a packet sniffer.

At this point, the user is logged on only to the domain and the local desktop. Figure A.11 shows what happens when the user touches a member server.

6. The user launches an application that connects to a member server. Examples include Outlook connecting to Exchange or a network connection to a share point.

7. The member server opens a secure channel to its domain controller, which might not be the same domain controller as that used by the desktop.

8. The member server then acts as a conduit for a challenge-response transaction between the client and the domain controller. This transaction is called a *pass-through* authentication.

9. The domain controller validates the user's credentials and returns user information to the member server, which creates a local access token for the user.

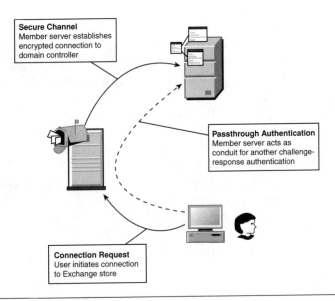

**Figure A.11**  NTLMv2 passthrough authentication.

As intricate as these transactions may seem, they happen so quickly that you don't realize anything is going on in the background. You see the internals of the authentication transactions only when they break. Typical problems include an inability of the member server to find a domain controller, or a breakdown in synchronization between the PDC—where the user's master account resides—and the BDC—where the member server authenticated and created its secure channel.

## Limitations of Windows Challenge-Response Authentication

The NTLMv2 authentication method has stood the test of time, and it is still used even in domains that have Active Directory for downlevel clients and processes that have not been redesigned to work with Kerberos. NTLMv2 has its problems, though. Here are some examples:

- **One-way authentication.** A domain member cannot verify the identity of a domain controller or member server performing pass-through authentication. This raises the possibility of man-in-the-middle attacks.

- **Limitless logon time.** Once a user has negotiated domain access via NTLM/NTLMv2, the user can stay on the domain forever unless an administrator has imposed a specific logoff time. A bad guy who manages to hijack a set of credentials can use them indefinitely.
- **No support for transitive trusts.** In a classic NT multi-master domain architecture, users from one domain can access resources only in a domain that directly trusts their domain.
- **No support for delegation.** If a service initiates a local process on behalf of a user, it *impersonates* the user by making a copy of the user's access token. Access tokens, like political bribes, only work locally. A server cannot take a user's local credentials and use them to log on to another server. This limits support for multi-tiered network applications.

## Kerberos Authentication

Modern Windows serves and desktops rely on Kerberos rather than NTLMv2 for authentication. Outlook 2003 takes advantage of Kerberos, so does Outlook Web Access running on Exchange 2003. Earlier versions of Outlook and OWA use NTLMv2.

Kerberos emerged from MIT's Project Athena with documentation in RFC 1510, "The Kerberos Network Authentication Service V5." Kerberos takes its name from the mythological three-headed hound that guarded the gates of the underworld. If you're interested about the spelling of the name Kerberos and details about the mythological origins of the name, take a look at the "Moron's Guide to Kerberos," www.isi.edu/~brian/security/kerberos.html.

### Kerberos Elements

Kerberos operates under the principle that two entities that have never met each other can still trust each other if they know a trusted third party, from which they get a secret number called a *session key*. A Kerberos transaction involves these parties (refer to Figure A.12):

- A client, called a *security principal*
- A target server, called a *validating server*
- A central credentials repository, called a *Key Distribution Center*, or KDC

The contents of the Kerberos database on the KDC determines the scope, or realm, of the KDC.

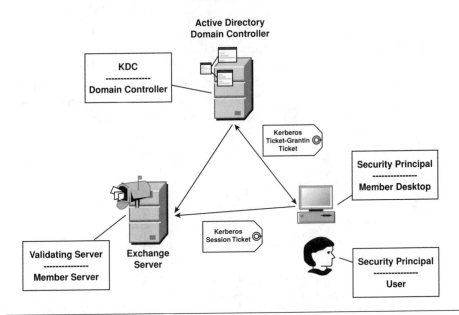

**Figure A.12** Correlation of Kerberos terms and Active Directory terms.

An Active Directory domain is also a Kerberos realm. All Active Directory domain controllers are Kerberos KDCs. Modern Windows servers (Windows 2000 and higher) take the role of Validating Servers. Security principals consist of users and member computers.

Windows domains that share a Kerberos trust belong to the same Active Directory *forest*. A user in one domain within a forest can access Kerberized resources on servers in any other domain. The Kerberos client on the desktop works in the background to obtain a Ticket-Granting Ticket for the target domain and uses that TGT to get a session ticket to the target server.

If you configure firewalls, or communicate with those who do, you'll need to know the ports used by Kerberos. A Windows KDC listens on TCP and UDP port 88. Unix Kerberos also uses TCP and UDP port 464 for the kpasswd (password reset) protocol. Windows does not use kpasswd.

### Kerberos Tickets

Kerberos transactions involve an item called a *ticket*. When a security principal (user or computer) tries to access a Kerberized service, such as the Exchange Information Store, the principal must submit a Kerberos ticket along with the first access request. It obtains this ticket from the KDC.

Figure A.13 shows the contents of a Kerberos ticket. The *session key* is the most critical element. When the security principal receives the ticket, it gets a copy of the session key encrypted with its password hash. The ticket itself is encrypted with the password hash of the target servers.

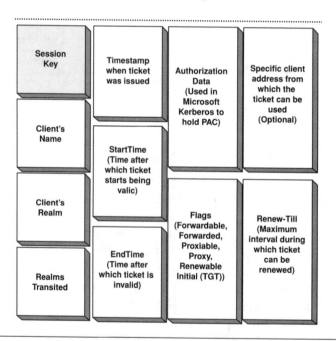

**Figure A.13**   Content of Kerberos ticket.

Along with the Kerberos ticket, the security principal sends a timestamp called an *authenticator* to the validating server. It encrypts this timestamp with the session key. Understanding the role of this session key is the secret to understanding a Kerberos transaction.

The validating server must first decrypt the Kerberos ticket to get a copy of the session key and then it uses the session key to decrypt the authenticator. If the server can't decrypt the ticket using its password hash, (indicating that the ticket was issued by an entity other than a KDC in its own realm), or if the insides of the ticket are garbled (indicating that someone fiddled with the contents), or if the session key inside the ticket won't decrypt the authenticator (indicating that someone is trying to fool the server), or if the timestamp inside the authenticator is more than five minutes off from the local time at the server (indicating that someone is replaying a previously issued ticket), then the server will refuse to permit access.

### Kerberos Ticket Types

Kerberos uses two types of tickets, one to control initial access to the realm and one to get access to a particular validating server. The ticket types are as follows:

- **TGTs.** The KDC issues these tickets to indicate that the security principal's credentials were valid at the time of initial network logon. A TGT acts as a kind of "pass" to get future tickets.
- **Session tickets.** The KDC issues session tickets to grant access to Kerberized services on member servers. For example, Outlook 2003 presents a Kerberos session ticket to an Exchange server when connecting to the Information Store service.

Kerberos avoids a man-in-the-middle exploit by permitting a Kerberos client to request *mutual authentication*. This operates as a mirror image of the initial connection transaction. The validating server creates an authenticator by encrypting a timestamp with the session key it obtained from the Kerberos ticket. It returns this authenticator to the client. The client decrypts the authenticator with its copy of the session key and checks the timestamp to verify that someone isn't replaying an earlier transaction.

### Authorization Data

When you present your pass at the gate of your employer, the gate guard validates your identity and lets you into the facility. You do not have leave to wander at will, poking your head through any open door or rummaging around in drawers. You can go only where you have *authorization* to go.

Kerberos does not, in and of itself, determine the privileges and permissions assigned to a security principal. When Microsoft decided to use Kerberos, it chose to include authorization information inside the Kerberos tickets using the *authorization data* field. You can download

PAC documentation from `www.microsoft.com/Downloads/Release .asp?ReleaseID=20597`.

When a Windows KDC builds a Ticket-Granting-Ticket, it populates the authorization data field with a data structure called a *Privilege Access Certificate*, or PAC. The PAC contains the user's SID, the SID of any groups to which the user belongs, and any domain-level privileges granted or denied to the user.

When the security principal submits the TGT and asks for a session ticket to a particular member server, the KDC copies the PAC from the TGT to the session ticket. The member server uses information in the PAC to build a local access token for the security principal.

### Points to Remember about Kerberos

If trying to follow the details of these Kerberos transactions makes your eyes cross, keep these main points in mind.

- All parties in a Kerberos-based transaction—the Exchange server, the desktop running Outlook, and the user—must belong to the same Active Directory forest so their Kerberos tickets can be issued by trusted KDCs.
- Only modern Windows platforms—Windows 2000, XP, and Windows Server 2003—use Kerberos for authentication. All other platforms use challenge-response authentication.
- Only services specifically coded to use Kerberos can take advantage of Kerberos session tickets. These are called Kerberized services. Examples include Windows file and print services, LDAP, and several Exchange 2003 services.
- A user obtains a Ticket-Granting-Ticket when first logging on to a domain then obtains session tickets when connecting to Kerberized services on member servers.
- A Kerberos-based client uses mutual authentication to validate the identity of a target server to prevent a man-in-the-middle exploit.
- Outlook 2003 uses Kerberos to authenticate to an Exchange 2003 server. All other Outlook clients use NTLMv2, even when running on a modern Windows platform.
- An Outlook 2003 client must first contact a domain controller to obtain a Kerberos ticket before it can touch a user's mailbox for the first time.

This completes the preliminary information about Windows authentication that you need to know to evaluate Exchange messaging transactions. Now let's get to know the components of Active Directory that Exchange uses to store information about servers and e-mail recipients.

# Active Directory Essentials

Every enterprise-class messaging system needs a directory service where it can store information about recipients, messaging servers, connectors, and so forth. Exchange 2003 does not have its own directory service. Instead, it uses Active Directory. This means that you must run either a Windows 2000 or Windows Server 2003 with at least one domain controller before you can deploy Exchange 2003. In production, you would need a more extensive directory service infrastructure so that you have fault tolerance and suitable performance.

Many weighty tomes have been written on Active Directory, and I don't intend on repeating them here. If you have no experience at all with Active Directory operations, then you should first install a domain in your lab and get familiar with creating new objects, replicating objects, and connecting to the domain from various clients.

Thankfully, only a few elements of Active Directory are absolutely essential to understand before installing Exchange 2003. These are

- Basic operation of an LDAP directory service
- Active Directory architecture, including object-oriented namespace structures and the Active Directory schema
- Domain architecture, including forests and trees and trust relationships
- Naming contexts and naming context replication
- Global Catalog services, including how to control GC contents and managing GC advertisement
- Flexible Single Master Operations (FSMOs)

## Active Directory Uses LDAP

In the mid-1980s, a set of standard bodies jointly proposed the architecture for a general purpose directory service that became known as

X.500. The hallmark of the X.500 directory service architecture was its innovative (at least for its time) object-oriented database structure and its nearly infinite scalability thanks to a provision that allowed dividing the directory information database into partitions that could be hosted by many different servers. Unfortunately, supporting this partitioning involved a complex set of protocols and an even more complex replication scheme.

In the early 1990s, network architects at the University of Michigan tired of the complexity of X.500 and pared it back a bit, retaining the underlying database structure but implementing a streamlined access protocol based on TCP/IP. They also did away with the complex referral protocols in X.500 and put the client in charge of following up on queries, similar to the way a DNS server chases down a recursive lookup query.

The wildly successful result of their work is called the Lightweight Directory Access Protocol, or LDAP. The current LDAP standard is documented in RFC 2251, "Lightweight Directory Access Protocol v3." A long list of other RFCs extend and enhance various LDAP features. When you deploy a Windows 2000 or Windows Server 2003 Active Directory domain, you're deploying a fully RFC-compliant LDAP directory service, similar in operation to iPlanet from Sun and the open-source OpenLDAP.

## LDAP Directory Elements

A directory service needs a way to identify entities in the real world. It does this by defining an *object* that represents the real-world entity, and then populates that object with *attributes* that describe the real-world entity. For example, the User objects in Active Directory have a variety of attributes that make them different from, say, the Group objects or the DNS Resource Record objects.

If you picture a spreadsheet where each row represents a real-world entity and each column represents an attribute that could have a value assigned to that entity, you have a pretty good picture of how Active Directory stores information. Table 1.1 shows an example.

Each object in the directory service gets a name. Most objects get a *Common Name*, or CN. For example, the Common Name of a user named Phoenix User60 would be `cn=phoenix user60`. (Windows does differentiate betweens names that use different cases; that is, `cn=Phoenix User60` and `cn=pHOENIX uSER60` represent the same object.)

**Table 1.1**   Tabular representation of objects in Active Directory

| Surname | Name | SAMAccount-Name | objectSid | userPrincipalName |
|---------|------|-----------------|-----------|-------------------|
| User60 | Phoenix User60 | phoenixuser60 | S-1-5-21-2705897113-3534554689-3977090560-1480 | phoenixuser60@company.com |
| User61 | Phoenix User61 | phoenixuser61 | S-1-5-21-2705897113-3534554689-3977090560-1481 | phoenixuser61@company.com |
| User62 | Phoenix User62 | phoenixuser62 | S-1-5-21-2705897113-3534554689-3977090560-1482 | phoenixuser62@company.com |
| User63 | Phoenix User63 | phoenixuser63 | S-1-5-21-2705897113-3534554689-3977090560-1483 | phoenixuser63@company.com |

Some objects hold other objects in the LDAP tree, similar to the way file system folders hold files and other folders. These objects are called *containers*. In LDAP, just about any object can be a container. Microsoft designed Active Directory so that an administrator can create only one type of general purpose container object. Its designator is *Organizational Unit*, or OU. Some objects rely on DNS entries for their name. They get a designator called *Domain Component*, or DC.

An object-oriented database uses a structure in which some container objects hold other container objects to form a hierarchy called a *tree*, as shown in Figure A.14. Each object in the tree has a unique identifier formed by combining its common name with the common names of all the containers between the object and the root of the tree. This unique identifier is called a *Distinguished Name*, or DN.

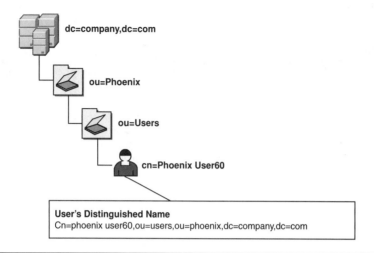

**Figure A.14**   Distinguished name describes the object location in directory tree.


## LDAP Searches

A directory service really has only two fundamental functions. It stores information and replies to search requests for that information. You can do a rudimentary search of Active Directory simply by launching the Windows Address Book via **Start | All Programs | Accessories | Address Book**.

If you click the Find People icon in the address book, you'll get a Find People window, as shown in Figure A.15. Use the Look in dropdown box to select Active Directory and then type a letter in the Name field. Then click the Find Now button.

The Address Book applet now submits an LDAP search request to an Active Directory domain controller asking for every User, Computer, and Group object in the directory service whose common name starts with the letter you selected.

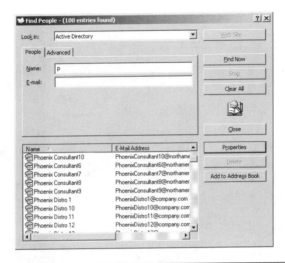

**Figure A.15**   Result of Windows Address Book search of Active Directory.

## Naming Contexts and LDAP Searches

The LDAP (and X.500) term for the directory service database is a *Directory Information Base*, or DIB. A DIB can have separate portions, each hosted by one or more servers called *Directory Service Agents*, or DSAs.

> An Active Directory domain controller is also an LDAP DSA. You'll see the initials DSA in many of the error messages left by Active Directory components and in special tools used to interact with Active Directory.

X.500 uses the term *partition* to describe the portion of the DIB hosted by a DSA. In LDAP terminology, a partition in the DIB is called a *naming context*. You'll see these two terms, partition and naming context, used interchangeably in Microsoft documentation. But naming context is more correct, and I use that term throughout this book.

Consider the Active Directory diagram in Figure A.16. This represents an Active Directory *forest*, a forest comprised of two domains. The domain names occupy a contiguous DNS namespace, so this is also an Active Directory *tree*, but from an Exchange perspective, the only thing that matters is that the domains belong to the same forest.

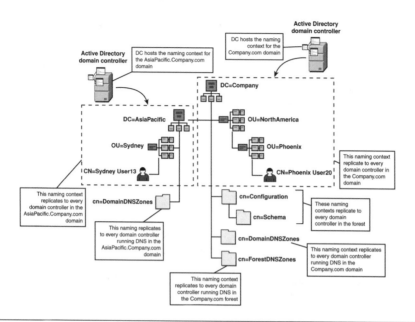

**Figure A.16**    Naming contexts in an Active Directory forest.

The two domains share a two-way, transitive Kerberos trust relationship. The term "two-way" refers to the fact that the two domains trust each other, so security principals in each domain can access resources in the other domain once they have been granted access. The term "transitive" refers to the fact that the trust flows between all domains in the forest regardless of how many other intervening domains there might be.

Each domain in the forest forms a separate naming context. In addition, Active Directory uses other naming contexts to hold objects that support special features. Each domain controller in the forest hosts the following naming contexts:

- Read-write replica of its own domain naming context
- Read-write replica of the Configuration naming context
- Read-only replica of the Schema naming context
- Read-write replica of the DomainDNSZones naming context for its domain (Windows Server 2003 only)
- Read-write replica of the ForestDNSZones naming context for the forest (Windows Server 2003 only)

## Naming Contexts and Exchange

Exchange uses the domain naming context to store objects that represent public folders and special accounts for Exchange system mailboxes (as shown in Figure A.17), along with the users, groups, and contacts it uses to determine who gets mail and where the mailboxes reside.

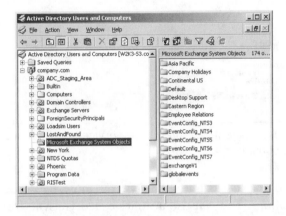

**Figure A.17**   Exchange system objects stored in Domain naming context.

Exchange stores objects that represent servers and protocols and other Organization components inside the Configuration naming context under the Services container. After you install the first Exchange 2003 server, you can view the contents using Active Directory Sites and Services after enabling the Show Services Node option in the View menu. Figure A.18 shows an example. In production, you would manage these objects using the Exchange System Manager console.

Every domain controller in the forest has a replica of the Configuration naming context; an Exchange server can use any domain controller to get up-to-date configuration information about the Exchange organization. The Configuration naming context can hold only one Exchange organization container, so a forest can host one and only one Exchange organization.

Windows Server 2003 has a feature called a Forest Root trust that makes it possible to create a two-way, transitive trust between the root domains of two forests. This is so users in any domain, in either forest, can access resources in the domains within the other forest. This simplifies access to resources such as files and printers, but it does not simplify Exchange.

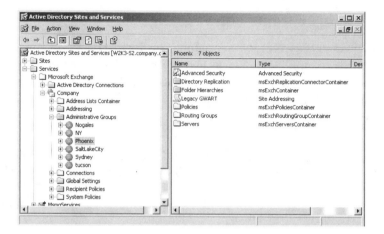

**Figure A.18** Exchange objects as seen from Services node in Active Directory Sites and Services console.

If you have separate forests, you must have separate Exchange organizations. You can use a utility called Galsync from the Microsoft Identity Integration Server feature pack to replicate objects back and forth between two forests, but this falls outside the scope of this book. Even with Galsync in place, maintaining separate Exchange organizations imposes several operational limitations:

- **No inter-forest access to public folders.** Users in remote forests do not have SIDs in the domain hosting the Exchange servers, so they cannot access public folders using standard Messaging function calls.

- **No inter-forest access to user's calendars and appointment information.** Users from remote forests do not have access to other users' calendar information in the Exchange Store because they lack security credentials.

- **Routing cannot span forests.** Exchange defines an area of high-speed, reliable data communications between Exchange servers as a *Routing group*. A Routing group is a logical collection of servers used to control mail flow and public folder referrals. Servers within a Routing group communicate in a point-to-point manner. Routing groups communicate with each other over special connectors. These connectors cannot bridge Routing groups in separate organizations because they rely on objects in the Configuration naming context.

- **Administration cannot span forests.** Exchange allows you to collect Exchange servers together under administrative containers in the organization called *Administrative Groups*. Administrators in an Administrative Group within one organization cannot be given rights in an Administrative Group within another organization.

## Global Catalog

As you can imagine, having multiple Domain naming contexts complicates LDAP searches in a forest. After all, if you submit a search request asking for all users whose common name starts with *D*, you expect to get a reply that encompasses all naming contexts, not just the naming context hosted by that particular Active Directory domain controller. In other words, an LDAP directory service must be capable of performing a *deep search*.

Ordinarily, to fulfill a deep search, the client must submit the search request to a domain controller in each domain. This is called *chasing referrals*. The chase might include domain controllers in widely separated geographic regions, which takes time and requires wide area network traffic. Also, the client needs to know where to find a domain controller for each domain. That's where DNS comes into the picture. The client uses the Service Locator (SRV) records in DNS to find domain controllers.

Active Directory avoids the performance penalties inherent in a deep LDAP search by providing *Global Catalog*, which contains a partial replica of every object in every Domain naming context in the forest. By querying a Global Catalog server rather than a standard domain controller, an Active Directory client can get an authoritative response to a deep LDAP search without chasing referrals.

## Partial Attribute Set

The Global Catalog contains a replica of every object in every Domain naming context in a forest, but only a few of the available attributes. It does this to reduce database size and to limit replication traffic.

A flag called IsMemberOfPartialAttributeSet, in the Schema object for an attribute, determines whether or not the attribute gets included in the Global Catalog. You can see the flag using the ADSI Editor (Adsiedit.msc) that comes in the Windows Server 2003 Support Tools. Figure A.19 shows an example.

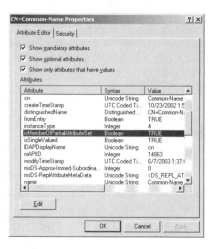

**Figure A.19** ADSI Editor view of attributes for a schema object that shows the IsMemberOfPartialAttributeSet attribute, which controls inclusion in the Global Catalog.

Setting the IsMemberOfPartialAttributeSet flag to TRUE for an attribute in Windows Server 2003 has a minimal impact. However, in Windows 2000, adding even one item to the Partial Attribute Set requires a complete rebuild of the Global Catalog. This can have a severe impact on operations if you have a large number of Global Catalog servers scattered around the globe in locations with poor wide area network connections.

## Global Catalogs Listen on TCP Port 3268

A Global Catalog server listens for LDAP queries on TCP port 3268 in addition to standard LDAP port 389. This allows clients to differentiate between standard domain controllers and Global Catalog servers. You can check for a listen at TCP port 3268 by running `Netstat -an` at the console of a Global Catalog server.

When a Global Catalog server receives an LDAP search request on port 3268, it has three possible ways it can handle the request:

- If the search request involves an attribute or attributes in the Partial Attribute Set (PAS), the server responds with a dataset containing the requested objects and attributes.
- If the search request involves an attribute or attributes not in the PAS, but the objects reside in the Global Catalog server's own

domain, the server responds to the request with a dataset containing the requested objects and attributes. It obtains this information from the full replica of the local Domain naming context hosted by every domain controller in that domain.

- If the search request involves an attribute or attributes not in the PAS—and the objects reside in another domain—the server responds with a referral to the other domain, forcing the client to chase the referral to complete the search.

## Designating a Global Catalog Server

You can designate just about any domain controller in a forest as a Global Catalog server. The Active Directory Sites and Services console displays an icon under each domain controller called NTDS Settings. The Properties window for this icon has a checkbox called Global Catalog. Figure A.20 shows an example.

**Figure A.20**   NTDS Settings for a domain controller that has been configured to be a Global Catalog server.

Check the box and click OK and that's that. In a few minutes, the server starts replicating the other Domain naming contexts, and as soon as it gets all the domains, it puts an SRV record in DNS that tells the world that it now accepts Global Catalog queries. Figure A.21 shows the Global Catalog records in DNS.

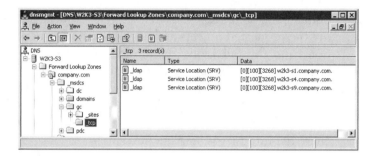

**Figure A.21**     SRV records in DNS that advertise Global Catalog servers.

If you have a single domain in your forest, you should designate every domain controller as a GC server. This ensures that you have sufficient GC servers to handle Exchange 2003 services. This change incurs no performance penalty, no increased storage requirements, and no increased replication. If you have multiple domains, select your GC servers with an eye toward maximizing their effectiveness while limiting the underlying replication traffic. At least one domain controller in each domain must remain a standard domain controller so that it can host the Infrastructure Flexible Single Master Operations role.

## Global Catalog and Universal Groups

Exchange 2003 uses Active Directory groups as distribution lists. It prefers to use Universal groups so that the groups can have members from any domain in the forest, as shown in Figure A.22.

Windows supports creating Universal groups exclusively for use as distribution lists, but Exchange and Windows also need the ability to control access to resources, something that requires a Security group, not a Distribution group. A Windows Server 2003 domain must run at a functional level of Windows 2000 Native or higher to support the creation of Universal Security Groups.

Universal groups also differ from Global and Domain Local groups because the Global Catalog contains their membership list. That's because a user in one domain might belong to a Universal group in another domain. So without a Global Catalog, each domain controller would need to chase referrals to get the membership from individual domain controllers in each domain, when every user logged on.

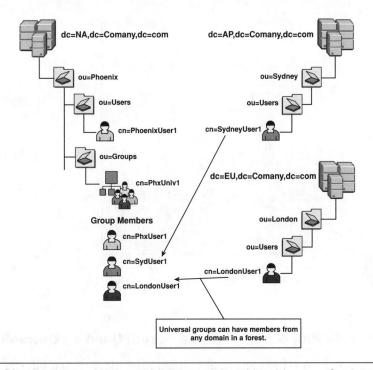

**Figure A.22**   Diagram of Universal group membership with users from any domain.

Let me stress that any distribution lists in a multi-domain environment absolutely should use Universal groups. For more information, read Microsoft Knowledge Base articles 318074 and 281489 about permission errors and inability to fully expand group membership when using Global groups for e-mail distribution.

## Global Catalog Servers and Exchange Address Lists

When you start a new message in Outlook and click the To button, you get a Select Names window that shows names from the Global Address List, or GAL. Figure A.23 shows an example.

The GAL represents one of the most valuable assets in Exchange, so you want an accurate, up-to-date list each time a user clicks the To button.

To achieve timeliness and accuracy, Outlook requests a copy of the GAL from a Global Catalog server, which responds to the request by performing a forest-wide LDAP search for all users, groups, and contacts that have e-mail attributes.

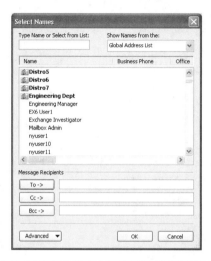

**Figure A.23**    Global Address List (GAL) displayed in Outlook.

## Identifying Global Catalog Server Used by Outlook

Outlook selects a Global Catalog server based on a referral from an Exchange server. Outlook 2003 makes it simple to identify which Global Catalog server the Outlook client uses. With Outlook open, hold down the Ctrl key, right-click the Outlook icon in the Notification Area, and select Connection Status from the flyout menu, as shown in Figure A.24.

**Figure A.24**    Outlook icon in Notification Area showing the Connection Status option.

This opens a Connection Status window, as shown in Figure A.25. This window shows the connections made for Directory services and to the user's Exchange server. It may also list one or more Public Folder connections if the user has touched the public folder hierarchy in Outlook.

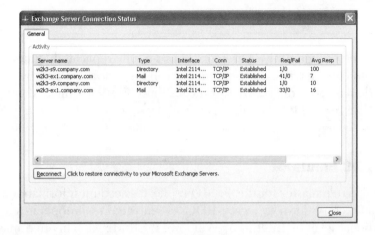

**Figure A.25** Outlook 2003 Connection Status window showing current connections to Exchange and Global Catalog servers.

Earlier versions of Outlook require a bit more gymnastics to determine the Global Catalog server's identity. Open Outlook and then use the menu selections to navigate as follows: **Tools | Address Book | Tools | Options | Global Address List | Properties**. This opens a Properties window, as shown in Figure A.26 that lists the current GC.

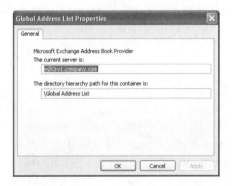

**Figure A.26** Outlook 2000 view of GAL properties showing provider name. Provider is a Global Catalog server.

# Flexible Single Master Operations

Even though Active Directory boasts a fully replicated, multiple master directory service, a few operations can be performed only by designated domain controllers. Microsoft calls these Flexible Single Master Operations, or FSMOs. A domain controller responsible for a certain FSMO is called a role master. Active Directory defines five FSMOs.

## PDC Emulator

The role master for this FSMO replicates account information in Active Directory down to legacy BDCs when the domain operates at a functional level of Interim or Windows 2000 Mixed. This role master also acts as a final arbiter of bad passwords, provides a Simple Network Time Protocol (SNTP) secondary time standard, and is the preferred domain controller for making group policy modifications.

If the PDC Emulator goes down, users who have the Help Desk change their passwords and then immediately try to log on with their new password might get locked out if the local domain controller does not have a copy of the new password hash. This lockout can affect older versions of Outlook if passthrough authentication at the Exchange server connects to a different domain controller than the user's logon server.

Also, Exchange users who access their e-mail via Outlook Web Access, or from a remote location, might have a password change request refused if they inadvertently lock themselves out of the domain.

## RID Master

The role master for this FSMO maintains a pool of Relative IDs (RIDs). All Windows security principals (users, Security groups, computers, and Inetorgperson objects) have a RID that, coupled with the domain SID, forms a unique security identification within a forest.

A loss of the RID Master does not have a direct impact on Exchange, but eventually you won't be able to create new user or group accounts.

## Infrastructure Master

The domain controller holding this role maintains consistent names for security principals from one domain that have been placed in groups in another domain.

The Infrastructure Master is important for Exchange because it ensures that changes to security principal names get distributed to other domains that might have that security principal in a Distribution or Security group. If you open the Properties window for a Universal group and select the Members tab and see icons with gray hair in the list of group members, you know that the source object's name change has not yet been updated by the Infrastructure Master.

## Domain Naming Master

This role master is the only domain controller capable of creating new entries in the Partition container for a forest. A domain is also an LDAP naming context, making the Domain Naming Master the only machine capable of authorizing the creation of a new domain.

This role has no direct impact on Exchange operation.

## Schema Master

The role master for this FSMO is the only domain controller that can modify the contents of the Schema naming context.

You must have the Schema Master online and available when installing the Active Directory Connector (ADC) or when running Exchange /Forestprep. Either of these operations modify the schema.

## Determining Role Master Identities

There are several ways to find the identities of the FSMO role masters. The hard way is to use the AD management consoles. For the domain-based FSMOs (PDC Emulator, Infrastructure Master, and RID Master), open AD Users and Computers, right-click the domain name, and select Operations Masters from the flyout menu, as shown in Figure A.27.

For the Domain Naming master, open the Active Directory Domains and Trusts console, right-click the Active Directory Domains and Trusts icon at the top of the tree, and select Operations Master from the flyout menu.

For the Schema master, you must first register the Schema management snap-in by opening a console prompt, navigating to the %windir%\System32 folder, and entering:

```
regsvr32 schmmgmt.dll
```

**Figure A.27**    Domain object flyout menu showing the option to look at the
Operations Masters (FSMOs) for the domain.

Now open an empty MMC console and add the Active Directory
Schema snap-in. Then right-click the Schema icon at the top of the tree
and select Operations Masters from the flyout menu.

In each case, you'll get a window that shows the name of the operations master and the name of the domain controller that has the focus of
the tool, as shown in Figure A.28.

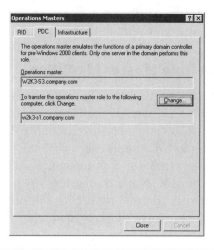

**Figure A.28**    Operations Masters window showing preparations for transferring
PDC Emulator role to another domain controller.

You can transfer a FSMO role to the server identified in the second
field of the Operations Master window by clicking Change. Do not perform this operation until you have evaluated all the ramifications. Refer
to Microsoft documentation.

# Legacy Exchange Operation

If you plan on upgrading an Exchange 5.x organization to Exchange Server 2003, you will encounter certain restrictions based on the design and operation of the legacy Exchange directory service. If you are not already familiar with legacy Exchange operations, this appendix contains an overview of the architecture of a legacy Exchange organization and points out the reasons for many of the operational restrictions imposed on Exchange Server 2003.

## Legacy Exchange Directory Service Structure

If you are already familiar with the structure and operation of the legacy Exchange directory service, feel free to skip this section. If you have only just recently started working with legacy Exchange, it's worth your time to understand some of its inner workings so you can manage the transition with as few problems as possible.

### Legacy Directory Partitions

If you launch the Admin.exe utility in legacy Exchange using the -r switch (r stands for "raw"), you get a more-or-less direct view of the contents of the legacy directory service database, Dir.edb. Figure B.1 shows an example.

The directory service contains objects that represent the servers, recipients, distribution lists, custom recipients, protocols, and processes used by legacy Exchange to control storage and message routing.

The icon at the top of the tree in the left pane represents the Exchange organization. Each of the icons just under the organization represents partitions in the directory service database. If you're familiar with LDAP lingo, a partition is also called a "naming context."

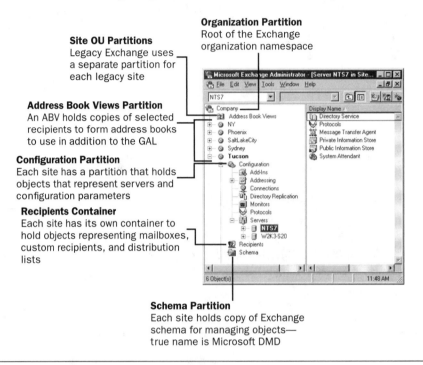

**Organization Partition**
Root of the Exchange organization namespace

**Site OU Partitions**
Legacy Exchange uses a separate partition for each legacy site

**Address Book Views Partition**
An ABV holds copies of selected recipients to form address books to use in addition to the GAL

**Configuration Partition**
Each site has a partition that holds objects that represent servers and configuration parameters

**Recipients Container**
Each site has its own container to hold objects representing mailboxes, custom recipients, and distribution lists

**Schema Partition**
Each site holds copy of Exchange schema for managing objects—true name is Microsoft DMD

**Figure B.1**    Legacy Exchange directory service structure as seen using Admin -r (raw).

### Sites

In legacy Exchange, servers that communicate with each other using a reliable, high-speed connection form a *site*. Because Wide Area Network (WAN) connections between sites generally use slow, expensive communication technologies, legacy Exchange uses two different message routing techniques, one for routing messages between servers in the same site and one for routing messages between sites.

- Within a site, legacy Exchange servers use Remote Procedure Calls (RPCs) to transfer messages.
- Between sites, designated servers called *bridgeheads* use X.400 to route messages to and from each other.

The legacy Exchange directory service represents a site as a container object called an Organizational Unit, or OU. Unlike OUs in Active

Directory, each Site OU in legacy Exchange also represents a partition in the directory service database.

Bridgehead servers replicate read-only copies of their Site OU to bridgehead servers in other sites via a pathway called a Directory Replication Connector. Other Exchange servers within a site obtain a copy of these read-only OU containers from the bridgeheads.

Using the information in these read-only containers, an Exchange server accumulates knowledge about the recipients in the other sites. It uses this knowledge to compile the Global Address List (GAL) and to find a recipient's home Exchange server for message routing.

### Recipients Container

Each site has its own Recipients container that holds objects representing mailboxes, distribution lists, and custom recipients.

Because the Recipients container for each site resides in the Sites OU's partition, you cannot move legacy Exchange servers and mailboxes between sites via a simple drag and drop. Microsoft provides special utilities that essentially dump the directory service information into a set of files that can be imported into another site to facilitate server moves and mailbox transfers.

### Configuration Partition

Each site has its own Configuration partition where it stores objects that define the operational parameters for the Exchange servers in that site and the connectors that represent pathways to other sites.

Read-only copies of the configuration partitions replicate between sites. Servers use the information in those read-only containers to calculate messages and to do other chores.

### Address Book Views

Legacy Exchange permits creating special address books that hold a subset of the GALs. For example, an administrator can create an address book that contains just the recipients in North America. These special address books are called *Address Book Views*.

An Address Book View in legacy Exchange contains a full copy of the objects representing the recipients that meet the selection criteria for the View. Changes made to a recipient object in the Recipient container also change the copy residing in the Address Book View container, and these changes replicate separately because the Address Book View is a separate container.

To avoid all this copying and duplicate replication, Exchange 2003 does not import legacy Address Book Views into Active Directory. It also does not automatically convert the selection criteria for an Address Book View into a custom address list. If you use Address Book Views, you must manually create custom address lists with LDAP queries that correspond to the criteria you used to create the original Address Book Views.

## Graphical View of the Legacy Container Structure

Figure B.2 shows the structure of the legacy Exchange directory service. Each folder labeled "NC" represents a separate naming context (partition).

If you examine this structure closely, you'll see many similarities with the arrangement of Exchange 2003 objects in Active Directory. This is not a coincidence. Microsoft retained many of the Exchange design elements both for backward compatibility and for simplicity of use.

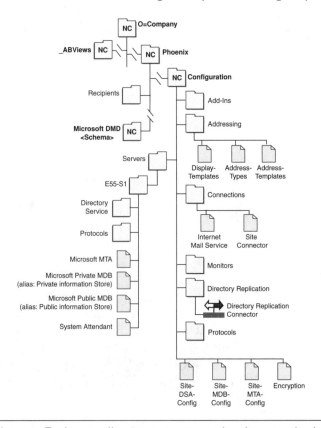

**Figure B.2**    Legacy Exchange directory structure showing standard partitions for the Organization, Site, Configuration, Schema, and Address Book Views.

# Exchange 5.5 and Windows NT 4.0

The legacy Exchange directory service contains information about e-mail recipients, but it does not store passwords or other domain information. That's the job of a domain controller. Instead, legacy Exchange associates each mailbox with an NT account, as shown in Figure B.3.

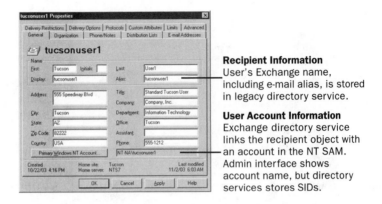

**Recipient Information**
User's Exchange name, including e-mail alias, is stored in legacy directory service.

**User Account Information**
Exchange directory service links the recipient object with an account in the NT SAM. Admin interface shows account name, but directory services stores SIDs.

**Figure B.3**   Legacy recipient showing alias corresponding to mailbox name and NT account name.

## Security Account Manager Database

An NT domain controller stores user credentials in a special Registry hive called the Security Account Manager database, or SAM. You can view the contents of the SAM by changing the permissions on the hive to give read-only access to your account or to local administrators. Figure B.4 shows an example. (Never do this on a production domain controller because you might accidentally do something to corrupt the contents of the SAM.)

Each user account is represented in the SAM by a key with a number called a Relative ID, or RID. Inside this key sit two binary values that contain the user's password hash along with the configuration information you see when you run User Manager for Domains. (Computers also get entries in the SAM, and you see the content of their RID keys when you run Server Manager.)

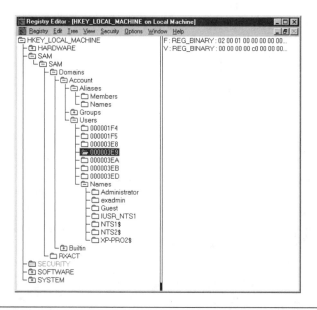

**Figure B.4** NT SAM showing user accounts represented by RIDs with an index under Names.

The combination of the RID with the Security ID (SID) of the domain forms a unique SID for each user, computer, and group. Windows uses this SID like a social security number. When you want to give access to a security object, you make an entry on an Access Control List that identifies the user by the user's SID.

The SAM indexes the RID keys by linking them to friendly names listed under the Names key. That's why NetBIOS names have to be unique within a domain. You can't have two identical entries in the Names index.

When a user logs on, the NT domain controller scans the Names index to find the logon name, and then it accesses the associated RID key to get the user's password hash so it can perform a challenge-response authentication to validate the user's identity.

Each user and computer account in the SAM contains two binary values with contents such as the user's password hash, allowable logon times, and so forth. When a user authenticates in the domain, the domain controller obtains the user's password hash from the SAM and uses it to verify the user's logon credentials.

## SIDs and Mailbox Recipients

Legacy Exchange links a mailbox with an owner using the user's SID. You can see this link by looking at the raw directory information for a mailbox. Do this by launching Admin with the -r (raw) switch, and then highlighting a recipient and pressing Shift+Enter. Figure B.5 shows an example.

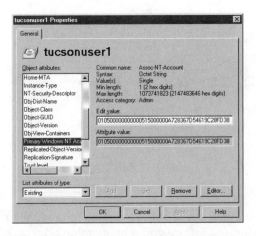

**Figure B.5**    Raw attributes of legacy Exchange recipient showing Assoc-NT-Account attribute containing NT domain SID.

The Primary Windows NT Account attribute (common name Assoc-NT-Account) contains the user's SID in Octet String syntax. (You're probably more familiar with the S-1-5-###-### format, but as Gertrude Stein would say, a SID is a SID is a SID, regardless of the syntax.)

## SID and Mailbox Access

The link between a user's domain SID and a recipient object in the Exchange directory service is a crucial part of controlling access to a legacy mailbox. Here's a brief description of a typical mailbox access transaction to give you a sense of how legacy Exchange relies on the user's domain account information. See Figure B.6.

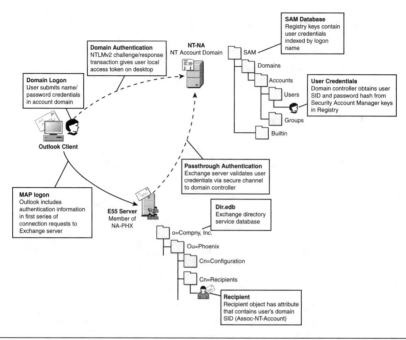

**Figure B.6** Legacy Outlook client obtains domain credentials and then connects to Exchange server using passthrough authentication.

- The user authenticates in the NT domain using the NTLMv2 authentication described in Chapter 1, "Installing an Exchange 2003 Server." This transaction validates the user's identity, and then transfers the user's SID to the local operating system to store an access token along with the SID of any groups to which the user belongs.

- When the user launches Outlook to connect to the Exchange server and opens the user's mailbox, the initial connection contains the user's logon name. The Exchange server establishes a secure channel to a domain controller and initiates a passthrough authentication to validate the user's identity. Exchange then grants access to the user's mailbox and any public folders to which the user has access.

This process changes a bit only if the user logs on to an Active Directory domain but still accesses an Exchange 5.5 mailbox. The user authenticates in the domain using Kerberos, but Outlook cannot use Kerberos to connect to Exchange 5.5 so it falls back on NTLMv2 and passthrough authentication.

## Unique SIDs and Exchange 2003 Migration

Unfortunately, legacy Exchange does not absolutely *require* that a mailbox be linked to a valid NT account. A mailbox remains intact even if the associated user account is deleted from the SAM.

Furthermore, it's quite common to link more than one Exchange mailbox to the same NT account. For example, conference rooms commonly get *resource mailboxes* so users can view free/busy information when scheduling times. The admin assistant responsible for the conference rooms typically owns the resource mailboxes.

Active Directory and Exchange 2003 do not share this ownership flexibility. A user account in Active Directory can own one and only one mailbox in Exchange 2003. If you have 10 conference rooms, you must have 10 user objects in Active Directory, one for each conference room.

When the time comes to migrate to Exchange 2003, you must have one-to-one mapping between legacy Exchange recipients and Active Directory user objects. Microsoft provides tools that make it simple to identify resource mailboxes and to automate the process of creating new user accounts that represent those mailboxes.

## Viewing Dir.edb with the LDAP Browser (Ldp)

You can use the Ldp utility from the Windows Server 2003 Support Tools to view the contents of the legacy Exchange directory service. Figure B.7 shows an example. Use the Connection menu in Ldp to select the name of an Exchange 5.5 server. Bind to the server using credentials that have administrator privileges in the Exchange organization. Select **View | Tree** from the main menu and enter the organization name using the prefix o=; for example, o=company.

The resultant tree in the left pane of the Ldp window shows the structure of the legacy Exchange directory service, but the attribute list in the right pane might seem a bit short, especially if you've seen the full attribute list using the Raw mode of Admin. Legacy Exchange hides many attributes from LDAP browsers to prevent inadvertent manipulation.

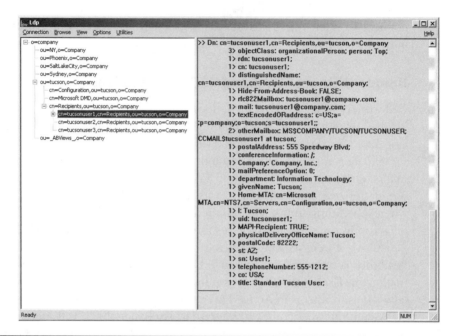

**Figure B.7**   LDAP Browser (Ldp) window showing legacy attributes from Exchange 5.5 directory service.

Just for testing, you can change the way a legacy Exchange attribute behaves when touched by an LDAP client. The Exchange schema has a setting called Heuristics for each attribute. The Heuristic value uses bit flags to control the following settings:

- Bit 0. Inter-site replication (1 means replicate)
- Bit 1. LDAP flag (1 means display to LDAP clients)
- Bit 2. Authentication level (1 means block anonymous access)
- Bit 3. Operational flag (1 means not accessible via ADSI)
- Bit 4. Admin UI flag (1 means show to Admin tool)

So, a Heuristics value of 21 would correspond to a binary value of 10101, meaning that the attribute would display in the Admin tool, would not display to anonymous users, and would replicate between sites.

If you want to see an attribute ordinarily hidden from LDAP, use the Raw mode of Admin to expose the Heuristics attribute and then add 2 to the current value. Use caution. If you make a mistake, you could stop inter-site replication and might interfere with other production activities. Do this only in a lab environment.

## File Dump of Legacy Exchange Attributes

The raw view of Admin provides a convenient way to view legacy Exchange attributes, but if you want a text file of an object's attributes to use for later reference, you can take advantage of a little-known Admin feature. While in Raw mode, hold down the Ctrl key as you open the raw properties of an object. This writes the object's attributes to a file called Admindmp.txt in Exchsrvr\Bin. Here is an example listing for an account called Exadmin:

```
Mailbox     9/4/03  3:07 PM
Obj-View-Containers: values: 1
    [1]   '/o=Company/ou=Phoenix/cn=Recipients'
Object-Class:    values: 3
    [1]   '2A864886F714010316'
    [2]   '2A864886F71401032E'
    [3]   '550600'
Directory Name:    'exadmin'
Instance-Type:     '5'
When-Created:      '030603015218Z'
When-Changed:      '030604220719Z'
Display Name:      'exadmin'
USN-Created:       '1751'
Obj-Dist-Name:     '/o=Company/ou=Phoenix/cn=Recipients/cn=exadmin'
DSA-Signature:     'E0D00D7B6095D711BCCB0003FFDD251B'
Object-Version:    '2'
USN-Changed:       '1857'
E-mail Addresses: values: 2
    [1]   'SMTP:exadmin@Company.com'
    [2]   'X400:c=US;a= ;p=Company;o=Phoenix;s=exadmin;'
NT-Security-Descriptor:       '010004807800000094000000000000001400000020
➡064000100000000000024001A0000000105000000000000515000000F371DA36C56A410DDD
➡20C333EB030000610064006D0069006E006900730074006500720020006400F006D0061
➡0069006E00200007300065007200760065007200730000000000000000010500000000000515
➡000000F371DA36C56A410DDD20C333F40100000105000000000000515000000F371DA36C5
➡6A410DDD20C333F4010000'
USN-Source:    '1751'
Primary Windows NT Account:   '0105000000000000515000000F371DA36C56A410DDD20
➡C333EB030000'
Deliv-Ext-Cont-Types:    values: 1
    [1]   '2A864886F7140501'
Delivery-Mechanism:       '0'
Home-MTA:    '/o=Company/ou=Phoenix/cn=Configuration/cn=Servers
➡/cn=NTS2/cn=Microsoft MTA'
```

```
Alias Name: 'exadmin'
Allow rich text:   '1'
Use IS defaults:   '1'
Trust level:       '20'
Title:             'Service Account'
Home-MDB:      '/o=Company/ou=Phoenix/cn=Configuration/cn=Servers
➥/cn=NTS2/cn=Microsoft Private MDB'
```

If you're wondering what on Earth would ever motivate you to want this kind of information, here's an example situation where you might find it useful. It sometimes happens that the connection between Active Directory and the legacy Exchange directory service fails for some reason during the migration. It might be a bug or a configuration error or just a celestial anomaly.

As part of your recovery, you might be called upon by Microsoft Product Support Services to make direct changes to the legacy Exchange directory service or to Active Directory using tools such as Ldp or the ADSI Editor (Adsiedit.msc) or others. By first harvesting the current mailbox settings using a raw attribute dump, you can get familiar with the operation of the tool prior to using it in production.

Not to mention that this is your chance to become the alpha geek among your Exchange colleagues. This might get you a better position at the softball games, such as beer coach.

# Legacy Exchange Replication Limitations

Legacy Exchange defines the word *site* as an area of low-latency, reliable network connections. As shown in Figure B.8, each site constitutes a separate partition in the legacy Exchange information base to reduce inter-site replication and to eliminate the possibility that administrators in separate sites might change the same object during the same replication interval, necessitating the intervention of complex conflict resolution mechanisms.

Directory service updates propagate to all Exchange servers within a site using a fully meshed topology. Intra-site directory replication uses Remote Procedure Calls (RPCs), a protocol that demands fast response and tolerates few timeouts.

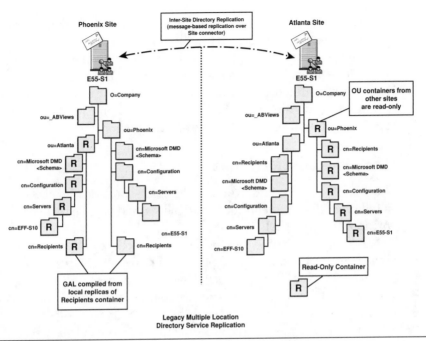

**Figure B.8**   Diagram of legacy Exchange inter-site replication showing that partitions replicate as partial, read-only containers to other sites.

Directory replication between sites takes the form of X.400 messages sent between bridgehead servers. Converting directory service updates to mail messages requires the intervention of the Message Transfer Agent (MTA), which creates a processing bottleneck at the bridgeheads. Also, directory service updates vie with standard messages for transport, which increases latency.

## Sites as Management Boundaries

Balkanizing the legacy Exchange directory service into separate site partitions might provide greater control over replication, but it imposes an administrative penalty. The site structure required for controlling replication often does not reflect the administrative structure of the Exchange team.

Permissions configured for one partition do not get inherited by other partitions, so administrators in a centrally-managed Exchange organization must put themselves on the permission list of the Site, Configuration, and Organization containers in each site. This hodge-podge of security permissions makes management more difficult and produces problems that can get nasty to troubleshoot.

Exchange 2003, by dint of its marriage to Active Directory, does not need these inter-site management boundaries. Once the Exchange organization has shifted to Native mode, all servers can reside in a single Administrative group regardless of their geographic location. Exchange 2003 uses Routing Groups to control message transfer.

## Lack of Global Referrals

Each legacy Exchange server must be able to provide e-mail clients with a full list of the recipients, distribution lists, and custom recipients in the organization, the GAL.

A directory service can search for objects stored in partitions on other servers, but this exacts a performance penalty. Instead, each legacy Exchange server hosts a replica of every other site partition. This allows any Exchange server in the organization to respond authoritatively to GAL requests.

If a server does not receive directory service updates because of a replication failure, then users in one site will see a different GAL than users in other sites. Also, because the directory service uses information in the site containers to expand the membership of distribution lists, a replication failure can cause a breakdown of mail distribution.

Active Directory uses a similar workaround to avoid expensive deep directory searches. A Global Catalog server aggregates the various Domain naming contexts in a forest. This enables a Global Catalog server to authoritatively respond to LDAP queries whose scope includes objects in other domains.

# Detailed Deployment Log Contents

This appendix contains a description of the tests performed by DSScopeScan and a sample log file listing for each test. The DSScopeScan tests create the following log files. The content of these files is described in this appendix:

- Exdeploy-Progress.log
- Dsconfigsum.log
- Exdeploy.log
- Gcvercheck.log
- Orgnamecheck.log
- Usercount.log
- Vercheck.log

## DSConfigSum

This utility reports the total number of sites and the number of servers in each site. Here's an example listing:

```
- Exchange 5.5 Directory Configuration Summary (DSConfigSum)
DSConfigSum provides summary information about your current
➥topology. Details are logged to dsconfigsum.log.

    - Total number of servers: 4
    - Total number of sites: 2
```

Make sure the total server count matches your records. If the utility does not see a server, you can experience replication issues, public folder access issues, and potential migration problems. Here's an example detailed listing:

```
Site: Phoenix
Number of servers: 2
  Server: NTS3  Version 5.5 (Build 2653.23: Service Pack 4).
  The public folder store for server 'NTS3' is 'NTS3'.
  The server 'NTS3' has the Internet Message Service
➥installed.
  Server 'NTS3' is the directory replication bridgehead for
➥the inbound Exchange 5.5 sites 'ou=Sydney,o=Company'.
  Server 'NTS3' is the directory replication bridgehead for
➥the outbound Exchange 5.5 sites 'ou=Phoenix,o=Company'.
  Server: NTS5  Version 5.5 (Build 2653.23: Service Pack 4).
  The public folder store for server 'NTS5' is 'NTS5'.

Site: Sydney
Number of servers: 2
  Server: NTS4  Version 5.5 (Build 2653.23: Service Pack 4).
  The public folder store for server 'NTS4' is 'NTS4'.
  Server 'NTS4' is the directory replication bridgehead for
➥the inbound Exchange 5.5 sites 'ou=Phoenix,o=Company'.
  Server 'NTS4' is the directory replication bridgehead for
➥the outbound Exchange 5.5 sites 'ou=Sydney,o=Company'.
  Server: NTS6  Version 5.5 (Build 2653.23: Service Pack 4).
  The public folder store for server 'NTS6' is 'NTS6'.

- Total number of servers: 4
- Total number of sites: 2
```

# DSObjectSum

This utility reports the total number of public folders, distribution lists, distribution lists with hidden membership, and custom recipients. Here's an example listing:

```
- Exchange 5.5 Directory Object Summary (DSObjectSum)

DSObjectSum provides summary information about the objects
➥available in your Exchange 5.5 organization.

    - Number of Exchange 5.5 public folders: 16
    - Number of Exchange 5.5 distribution lists: 100
    - Number of Exchange 5.5 distribution lists with
    ➥hidden membership: 12
    - Number of Exchange 5.5 custom recipients: 20
```

You may get entries in the test log indicating that you do not have sufficient permission to view hidden folders or permission to access other Exchange information. If this is the case, the ADC server may not belong to the same domain as the Exchange server. Verify that you have a functioning trust relationship between the two domains and that the account you're using to install the ADC has Service Account Admin permissions for the Exchange organization, site, and configuration container.

## UserCount

This test reports the total number of recipients (users) in the organization and is broken down by site. Here's an example listing:

```
- Exchange 5.5 Directory User Count (UserCount)
UserCount reports the total number of users in each site and the
➥total number of users in the Exchange 5.5 directory. Details
➥are logged to usercount.log.

    - Total number of users: 201
```

The detailed listing in the UserCount.log file breaks down the count by site. Here's an example:

```
#*** Exchange 5.5 DS User Count finished: 01/09/2004
➥06:07:28 ***#
#*** Exchange 5.5 DS User Count began: 06/09/2003
➥06:18:25 ***#
Site: Phoenix
Number of mailboxes: 102
```

*continues*

```
Site: Sydney
Number of mailboxes: 99


- Total number of users: 201
#*** Exchange 5.5 DS User Count finished: 06/09/2003 06:18:26
➡***#
```

If the counts don't match your expectations, verify that the legacy Exchange server has fully replicated the content of its site container and that the site bridgeheads have replicated with all other sites.

If replication appears up-to-date, and UserCount still returns an incorrect number, point DsScopeScan at another Exchange server to see if you get a different result. Murphy's Law says that you will initially select the one server in your entire organization that has a replication or a permission error.

## Vercheck

This test verifies that you have the right Exchange version and service pack level on your Exchange servers. You must have at least one server in each site running Exchange 5.5 SP3 or higher. Here is a detailed listing:

```
Site 'Phoenix' has an Exchange 5.5 server SP3 or later
installed.
Server: NTS3  Version 5.5 (Build 2653.23: Service Pack 4).
Server: NTS5  Version 5.5 (Build 2653.23: Service Pack 4).

Site 'Sydney' has an Exchange 5.5 server SP3 or later installed.
Server: NTS4  Version 5.5 (Build 2653.23: Service Pack 4).
Server: NTS6  Version 5.5 (Build 2653.23: Service Pack 4).
```

If you are not running Exchange 5.5 SP4 on all your Exchange servers, and if you do not want to take the trouble to upgrade service packs at the outset of the transition to Exchange 2003, be sure to use an Exchange 5.5 SP3 or higher server as the endpoint of any ADC Connection Agreement.

# Index